Key to Regional and Road Maps

MANITOBA (MB) Pg.181
48
ONTARIO (ON) Pg.182
QUÉBEC (PQ) Pg.184
NEWFOUNDLAND (NF) Pg.187
PRINCE EDWARD ISLAND (PE) Pg.186
NEW BRUNSWICK (NB) Pg.186
NOVA SCOTIA (NS) Pg.186
28
MINNESOTA (MN) Pg.116
MAINE (ME) Pg.104
VERMONT (VT) Pg.166
NEW HAMPSHIRE (NH) Pg.127
46
MASSACHUSETTS (MA) Pg.110
RHODE ISLAND (RI) Pg.155
WISCONSIN (WI) Pg.174
42
NEW YORK (NY) Pg.132
44
CONNECTICUT (CT) Pg.78
MICHIGAN (MI) Pg.112
IOWA (IA) Pg.96
30
PENNSYLVANIA (PA) Pg.150
NEW JERSEY (NJ) Pg.128
DELAWARE (DE) Pg.80
MARYLAND (MD) Pg.106
WASHINGTON (DC) Pg.172
ILLINOIS (IL) Pg.90
INDIANA (IN) Pg.94
OHIO (OH) Pg.142
WEST VIRGINIA (WV) Pg.173
VIRGINIA (VA) Pg.168
40
MISSOURI (MO) Pg.120
32
KENTUCKY (KY) Pg.100
NORTH CAROLINA (NC) Pg.138
TENNESSEE (TN) Pg.158
OKLAHOMA (OK) Pg.146
ARKANSAS (AR) Pg.66
SOUTH CAROLINA (SC) Pg.156
ALABAMA (AL) Pg.60
GEORGIA (GA) Pg.86
34
MISSISSIPPI (MS) Pg.118
38
36
LOUISIANA (LA) Pg.102
FLORIDA (FL) Pg.82
18
55
PUERTO RICO (PR) Pg.190
VIRGIN ISLANDS (VI) Pg.190

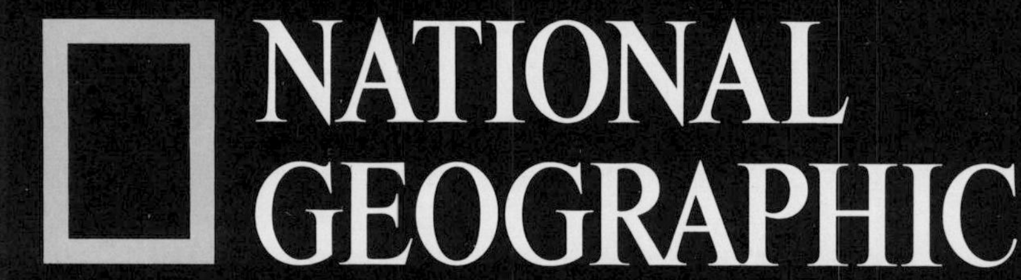

The American Road

Atlas & Travel Planner

United States
Canada
Mexico

Published by GeoSystems Global Corporation
in Association with National Geographic Maps
and Melcher Media, Inc.

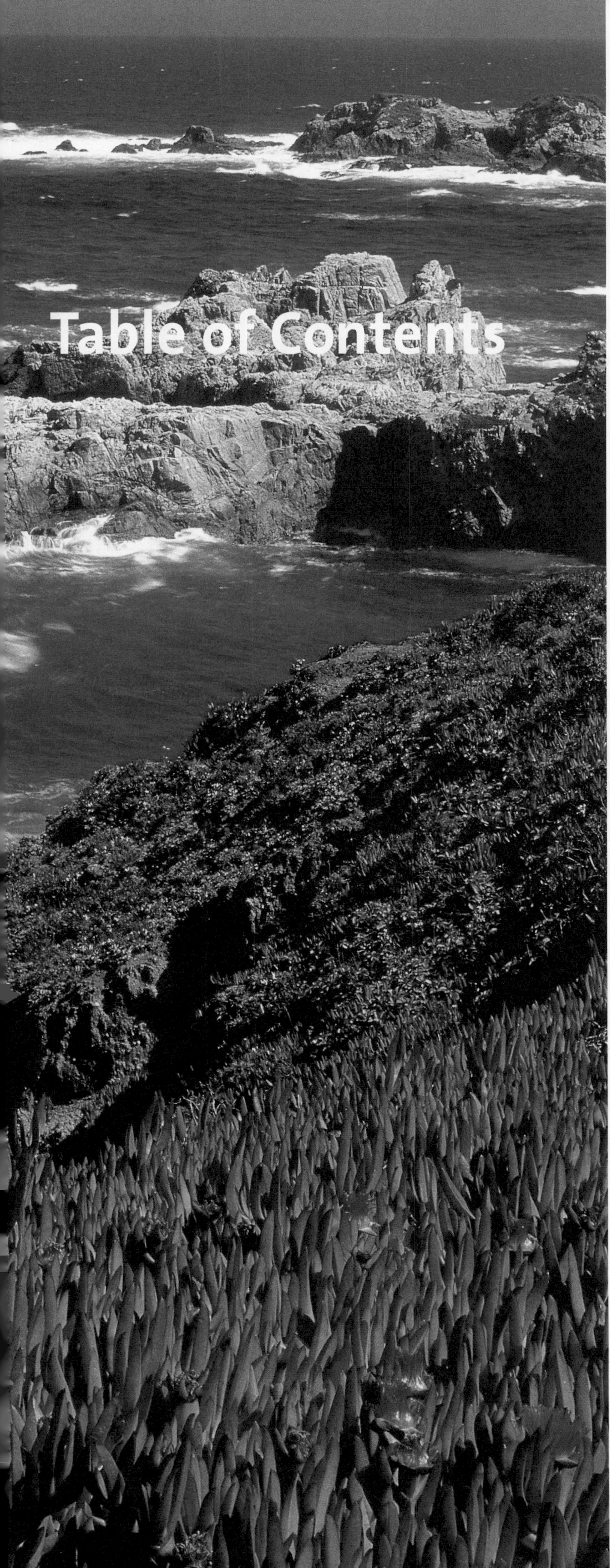

Table of Contents

Foreword

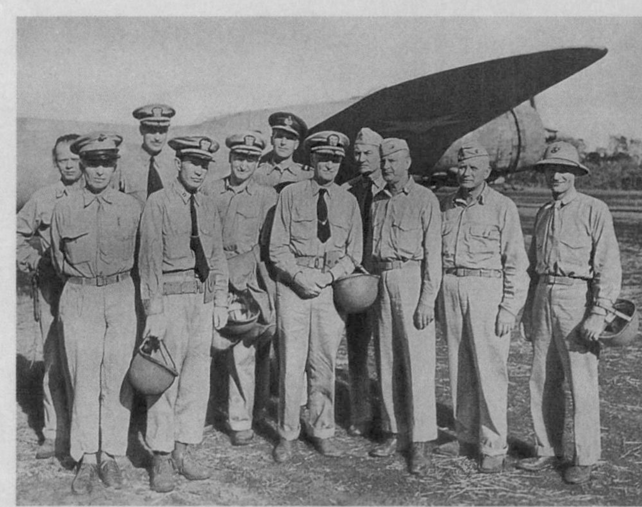

Thanks to the "unexpected but most welcome helping hand" of a National Geographic map, Admiral Nimitz (fifth from right) arrived safely at embattled Guadalcanal in September 1942.

It was September 1942, and Fleet Adm. Chester Nimitz, charged with command of the Navy's Pacific forces in the aftermath of Pearl Harbor, was aboard a B-17 bomber over the Coral Sea. The pilot became lost just as a heavy rainstorm hit, and the crew's map showed only a few of the many islands in the area. Fortunately, a Marine officer aboard the plane was carrying a National Geographic map of the Pacific Ocean. The map included an inset of the Solomon Islands that showed the chain in detail. With it, the crew was able to deduce its position and fly to a safe landing.

Even fifty years ago National Geographic's maps represented a venerable tradition and a reputation for accuracy and quality. In fact, the Society's first map dates to the magazine's June 1899 issue and was inauspiciously titled "Theater of Military Operations in Luzon." Since then, the Society has published thousands of maps, chronicling the shifting boundaries of politics and science, depicting in its signature style the structure of the universe, the mountains and chasms of the ocean floor, the lifting of the Iron Curtain, and the icy heights of Mount Everest.

Where it once took three months' work to draw the mountains on this "Map of Reaches of the Nation's Capital," topographical relief on the road maps (pages 56–191) in this book is rendered in a matter of minutes by custom, state-of-the-art computer software.

National Geographic's maps and globes, its *Atlas of the World* (now in its sixth edition), and – most recently – a host of electronic maps on the Internet and on CD-ROM all support the Society's mission to increase and diffuse geographic knowledge. Throughout its 110-year history the Society has sought innovative ways to bring geography alive.

The American Road is the latest in our recent efforts to serve the traveling public with great maps. We at National Geographic feel that a map is intrinsically educational and endlessly fascinating – whether it's a reference map of the world or a road map of your state. What better way to learn about geography than to travel, map in hand, down our own highways and byways? Professional explorers are often featured on the pages of the Society's publications. But exploration and adventure are, after all, personal pursuits as well. We hope that this book will be your companion on your own voyages of exploration – both real and imagined – across our wondrous continent. And we hope, as well, that our maps will guide you safely to your destination, just as they did for Admiral Nimitz a half century ago.

– ALLEN CARROLL, *MANAGING DIRECTOR, NATIONAL GEOGRAPHIC MAPS*

Nothing reveals America as vividly as the open road. Of the millions of miles of pavement lacing the continent, certain highways never fail to take drivers outside themselves. Traveling across the bright, scrub-strewn Mojave Desert on an empty highway, it's easy to understand how mysterious yet liberating the West must have seemed to pioneers. Likewise, an afternoon ramble through Connecticut's Litchfield County can yield insight into the way the green, pastoral hills of New England shaped a young nation's consciousness. Ironically, in today's world of digital information and instant gratification, one of the tried-and-true ways to de-accelerate is to get in a car and hit the highway.

In the summer of 1913, a motor caravan traveled from Indianapolis to San Francisco to promote the proposed Lincoln Highway. The motorcade confirmed the value of paved roads.

Since the days of the Model T Ford, cars have fueled the frontier imagination of Americans. The excitement of travel inspired the nation's first coast-to-coast highway as much as the practical considerations of commerce, defense, or the wish, as Theodore Roosevelt put it, to "tighten the nation." Known today as U. S. 30 over much of its path, the Lincoln Highway followed the most direct route possible from New York City's Times Square to San Francisco's Lincoln Park. In 1913, "direct" meant a stitched-together, 3,389-mile hodgepodge of bumpy roads, including sections of the Pony Express route and roads traveled by the Overland Stages. The Lincoln Highway promised inconveniences ranging from mud to floods and washed-out roads. A guidebook of the time promoting the highway called it "something of a sporting proposition." Despite all the humps and gullies, one impressed early traveler exclaimed that "you will never be bored!"

During the tour, the Lincoln Highway caravan enjoyed some of America's most scenic corners, including Lake Tahoe's Emerald Bay.

If nothing else, the Lincoln Highway confirmed the American passion for roaming under big skies. This book serves as your ultimate field guide for driving vacations to all corners of the continent. Within these pages you'll find the most advanced maps of North America's highways to date. The atlas also offers travel-planning guidance to fascinating stops along the way – giving drivers both the inspiration and the means to make any road trip a memorable one. In **The American Road**, we hope to bring to life the spirit of the old Lincoln Highway, where road trips were as much about the journey as the destination.

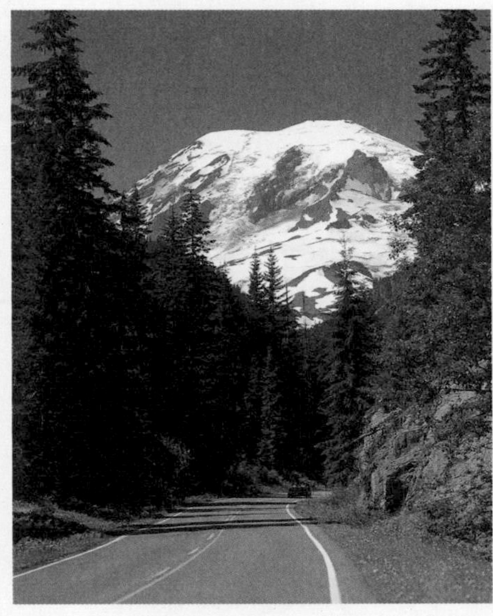

The modern highways that crisscross America often lead to unexpected, inspiring views, such as the one of Mount Rainier above.

– THE EDITORS

How to Use This Book

The American Road Atlas & Travel Planner has been designed as the complete all-in-one tool for driving vacations. To get the most out of the book, remember that, unlike a reference atlas or travel guide, it serves several purposes at once: To inspire road vacations, to help choose specific travel destinations, to help plan the most scenic routes along the way, and–as a road atlas–to let you navigate confidently once you are on the road.

Four main chapters–Regional Guides, Road Maps, National Parks, and Scenic Drives–plus the Index cover the most salient aspects of road travel. Recognizing that travelers often use car trips to take in more than one state at a time, **The American Road** looks at North America region by region, picking out the most distinctive and popular attractions in each of 24 geographical areas, from the Pacific Northwest to Northern New England. The regions include all 50 states and all 10 Canadian provinces, plus Mexico, Puerto Rico, and the U.S. Virgin Islands. Each of the book's sections has its own color code, which is used throughout the volume to help in easy cross-referencing.

For example, start by looking at the Far West pages from the Regional Guides chapter, shown below. The topographical map can be used as a starting place. Page numbers on the boxed insets lead you to in-depth descriptions about national parks and scenic drives in their respective chapters. For road networks, the yellow circular tabs on the right side of the page direct you to specific state-by-state mapping in the Road Maps chapter. Finally, red tabs direct you to specific pages in the Index, where extensive listings of place-names and points of interest help you find unfamiliar destinations on the road maps quickly.

Regional Guides Pages 8–55

These guides serve as excellent starting places for planning any vacation, offering an overview of what each of 24 regions offers in terms of outdoor activities, cultural landmarks, special events, and scenery. A hand-painted topographical map shows the lay of the land, detailing the mountain ranges, plains, deserts, river valleys, and other features that make each region distinct.

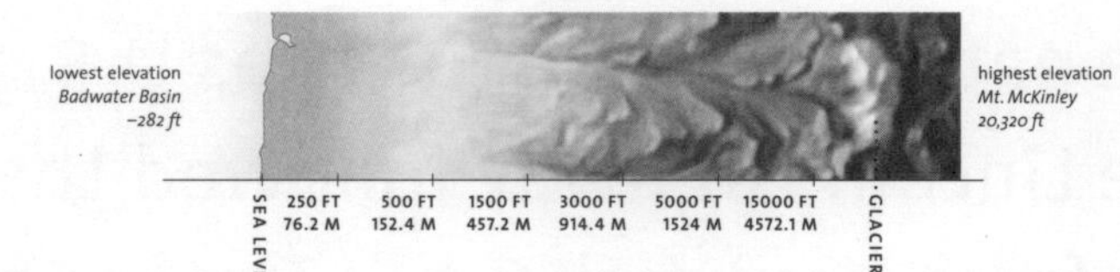

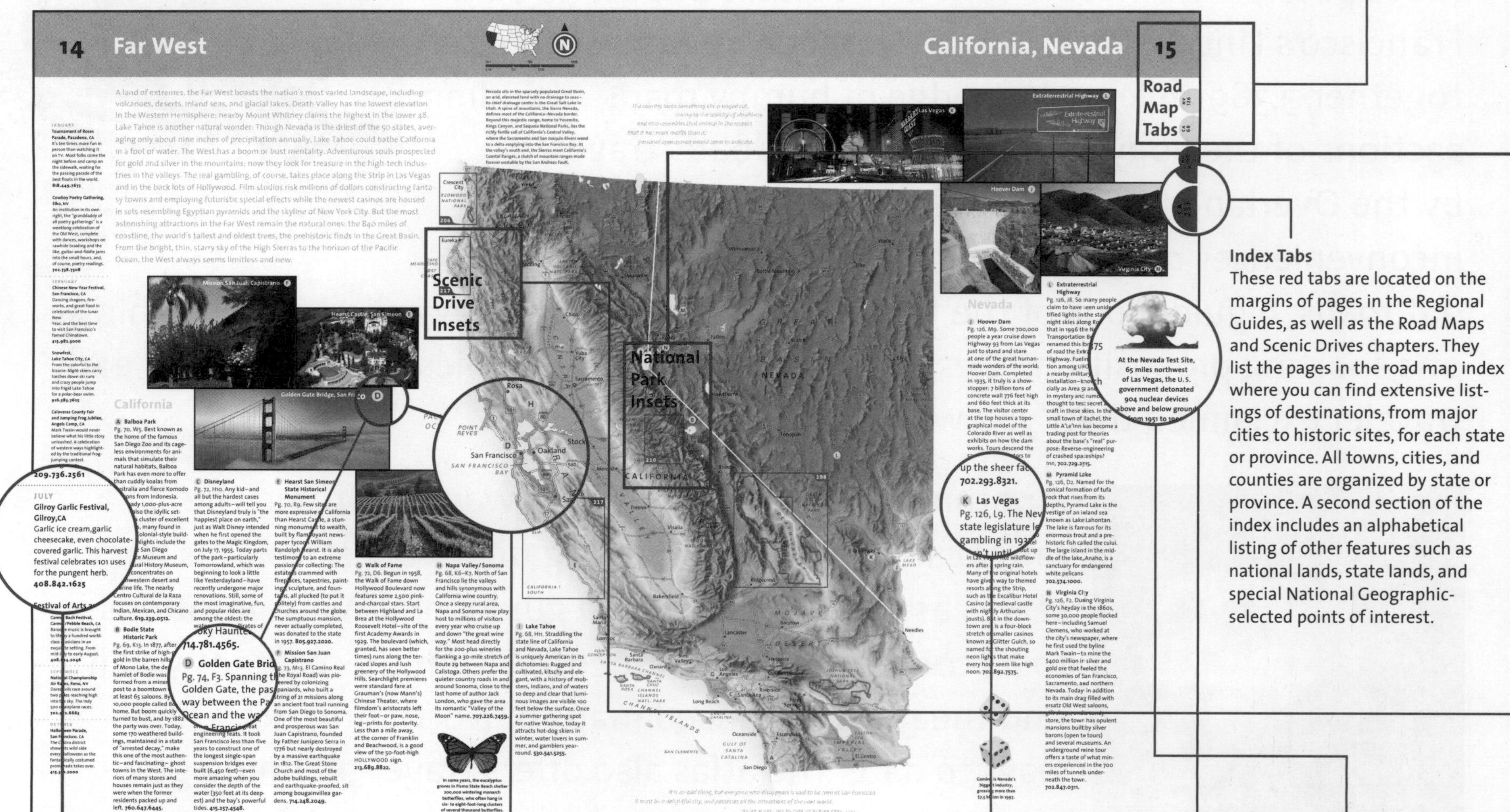

Index Tabs

These red tabs are located on the margins of pages in the Regional Guides, as well as the Road Maps and Scenic Drives chapters. They list the pages in the road map index where you can find extensive listings of destinations, from major cities to historic sites, for each state or province. All towns, cities, and counties are organized by state or province. A second section of the index includes an alphabetical listing of other features such as national lands, state lands, and special National Geographic-selected points of interest.

Calendar of Regional Events

An at-a-glance calendar of top regional events includes everything from big festivals to small-town fairs. Look here for listings of major sports attractions; theater, art, and film festivals; parades; and colorful celebrations of local culture. Be sure to call ahead as dates are subject to change.

Each Region's Top Attractions

A selection of the most distinctive and characteristic landmarks are described in each region by state. Succinct profiles offer travelers a window on what makes each region special and what type of recreational and cultural activities are available. Possible destinations include state parks, wildlife refuges, historic sites, museums, and urban attractions. Contact telephone numbers aid travel planning. When it is not possible to list the phone number for a specific site–for example, when the attraction is an area in a state rather than a single place–the appropriate local or regional travel office or chamber of commerce has been substituted.

Map Coordinates

Coordinates for each landmark tell you where to easily locate the attraction on indicated maps in the Road Map chapter. Coordinates refer to the map grid quadrant as marked along the margins of each road map.

Indigenous Wildlife, Special Harvests, Major Industry

Fascinating facts about native plants and animals, the biggest local crops, and each region's greatest achievements in industry and engineering add to the rich tapestry of the area's character.

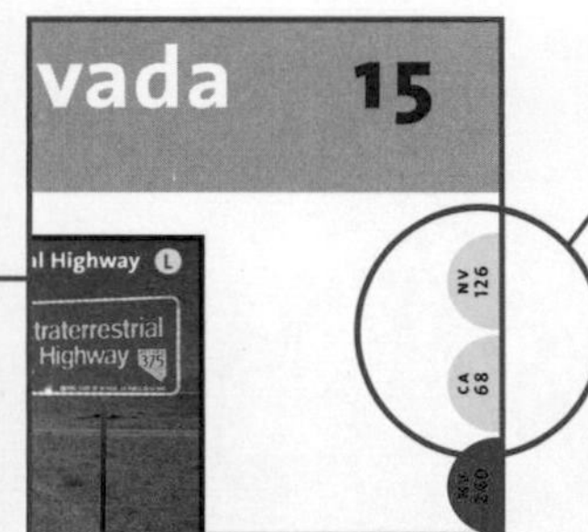

Road Map Tabs
Yellow tabs for each state in the region list the pages in the Road Maps chapter where you'll find state, territorial, and provincial road maps.

Road Maps Pages 56–191

Road maps for all 50 states appear alphabetically, followed by Canadian provinces, organized from west to east. Also included are Mexico, Puerto Rico, and the U. S. Virgin Islands.

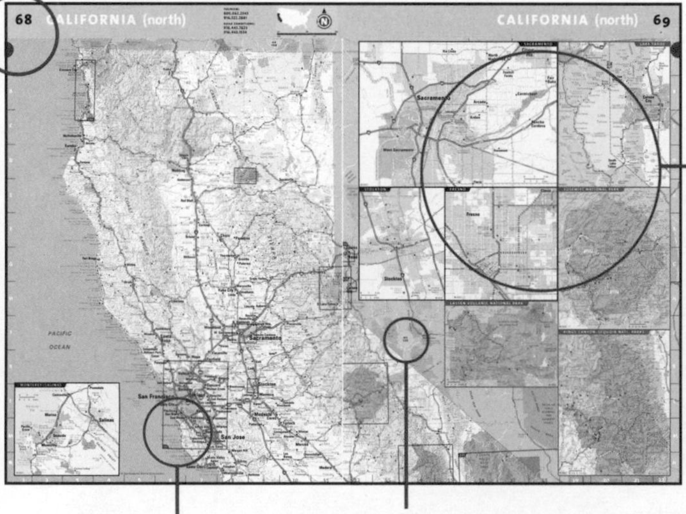

Inset Map Boxes
Red boxes outline areas featured in larger scale, including greater metropolitan regions, city downtowns, national parks, and major recreation areas. When a detail map does not appear on the same page as its home map, a page number in white type points you to the correct page.

Quick Map-to-Map Navigation
Handy yellow buttons indicate adjacent states and their page numbers, making it easier to navigate from state to state.

Detail Maps
Larger-scale city and downtown maps show the level of detail you need to navigate in a new city. Select national parks and major recreational areas are also highlighted.

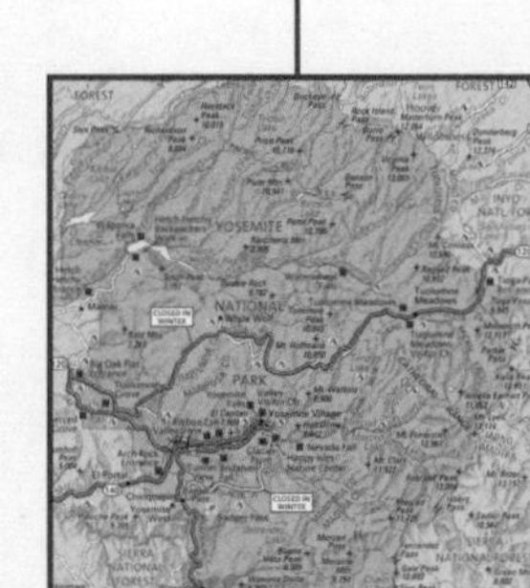

National Parks Pages 192–213

A selection of 28 top national parks—primarily in the United States, with two in Canada—are described in detail. Profiles reveal the natural and human histories that make each of these wonders like no other place in the world. To help plan visits, specific hikes and other activities for outdoors enthusiasts, from easy to strenuous, are highlighted.

National Park Insets
Inset boxes on the regional maps outline those parks which are featured in the National Parks chapter. Page numbers direct you to the appropriate page.

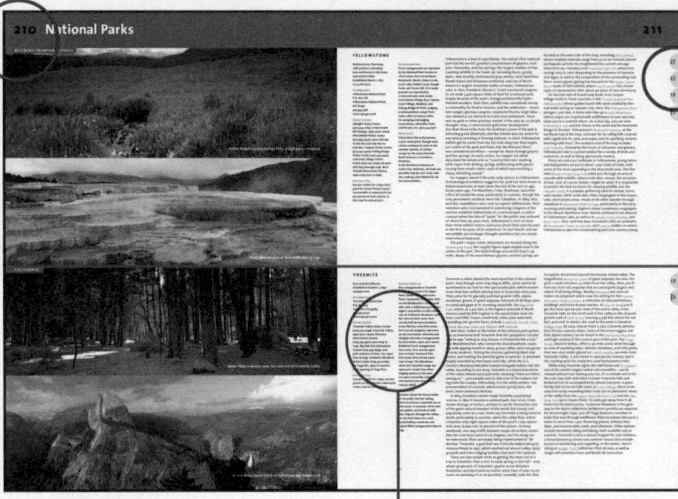

Easy Cross-Reference to Park Maps
Each park features at least two yellow road-map tabs. The top tabs direct you to the states in which the parks appear. Tabs labeled "Park" indicate the specific page on which each individual park detail map appears.

How to Get There, When to Go
Learn how to get away from the crowds, where to camp, and whom to contact for reservations.

Scenic Drives Pages 214–227

Detailed route descriptions of 36 of America's most memorable highways and byways help you get off the beaten path and journey into landscapes alive with the presence of history and wildlife.

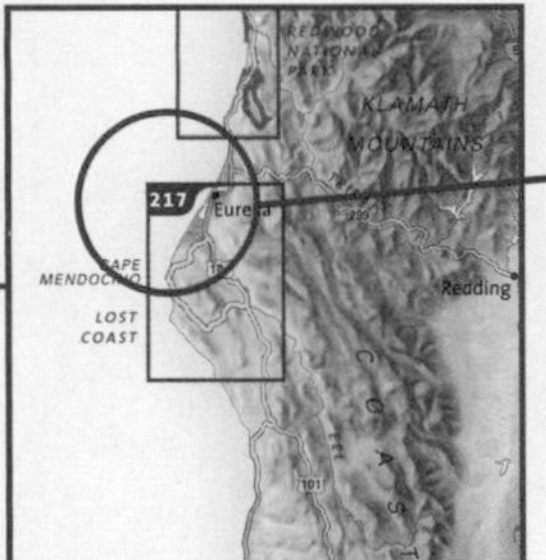

Scenic Drive Insets
Inset boxes pick out National Geographic-selected scenic routes in each region. Page numbers indicate where in the Scenic Drives chapter to find a trip itinerary and detail map.

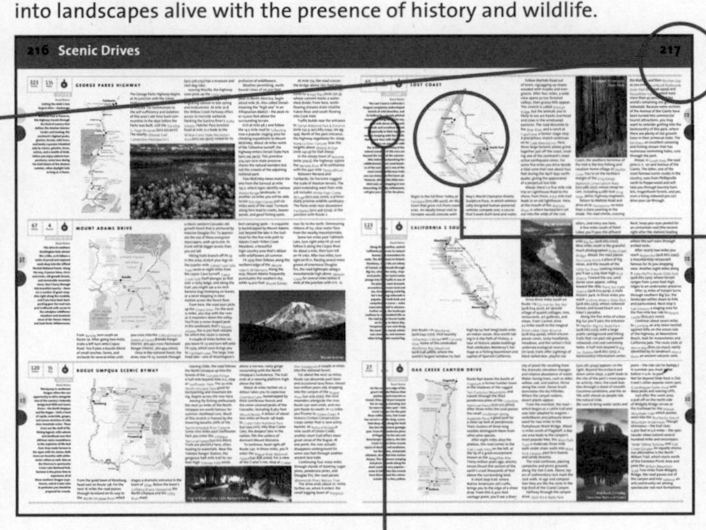

Detailed Route Maps
With specific roadside landmarks spotted, these maps show each drive in detail, aiding point-to-point navigation.

Tips on the Road Ahead
Special "Road Notes" tell you what kind of terrain to expect—for example, mountainous ridges and passes, dense forest, rolling plains, or flat marshland. The notes also give advisories on seasonal road conditions and the advantages of traveling at specific times of year.

Road Map Legend

TRANSPORTATION

CONTROLLED ACCESS HIGHWAYS
- Free
- Toll; Toll Booth
- Under Construction
- Interchange and Exit Number
- Ramp (Downtown maps only)
- Rest Area; Service Area (Yellow with facilities)

OTHER HIGHWAYS
- Primary Highway
- Secondary Highway
- Multi-lane Divided Highway (Primary and secondary highways only)
- Other Paved Road
- Unpaved Road (Check conditions locally)

HIGHWAY MARKERS
- Interstate Route
- U.S. Route
- State or Provincial Route
- County or Other Route
- Business Route
- Trans-Canada Highway
- Canadian Provincial Autoroute
- Mexican Federal Route

OTHER SYMBOLS
- Distances along Major Highways (Miles in U.S.; kilometers in Canada and Mexico)
- Tunnel; Pass
- Scenic Route
- Wayside Stop
- One-way Street
- Port of Entry
- Airport
- Railroad (Downtown maps only)
- Auto Ferry; Passenger Ferry

RECREATION AND FEATURES OF INTEREST

- National Park
- National Forest; National Grassland
- Other Large Park or Recreation Area
- Small State Park with and without Camping
- Public Campsite
- Trail
- Point of Interest
- Visitor Information Center
- Public Golf Course; Private Golf Course (Professional tournament location)
- Hospital (City maps only)
- Ski Area

CITIES AND TOWNS

- National Capital; State or Provincial Capital
- County Seat (State maps only)
- Cities, Towns, and Populated Places (Type size indicates relative importance)
- Urban Area (State and province maps only)
- Large Incorporated Cities (City maps only)

OTHER MAP FEATURES

- JEFFERSON — County Boundary and Name
- Time Zone Boundary
- Mt. Olympus 7,965 — Mountain Peak; Elevation (Feet in U.S.; meters in Canada and Mexico)
- Perennial; Intermittent River
- Perennial; Intermittent; Dry Water Body
- Dam
- Swamp
- Glacier

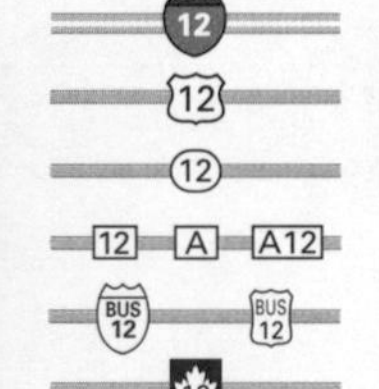

Regional Guides

10 Alaska

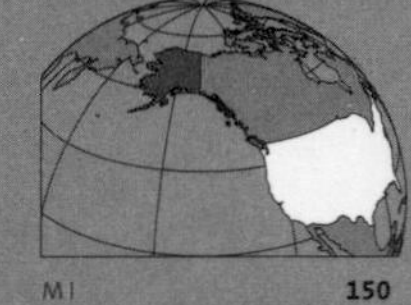

For more than a century, Alaska has been America's last frontier, a raw edge of the world that has drawn Jack London in search of adventure, John Muir to seek new natural wonders, and prospectors bound for Klondike gold. Today the frontier spirit lives on in Alaska, however improbable that may seem in an era of global economies and high technology. Roads have been paved and land developed around Anchorage and other cities; riches have been extracted from the state's fisheries, forests, and oil fields—and yet people have done little more than establish a beachhead. Alaska is so big it could be cut in half and Texas would become the nation's third largest state. Less than one percent of Alaska's 365 million acres bear any sign of human habitation. It still harbors true wilderness in many varieties, from the riotously productive rain forests of the panhandle, to the vast tundras of the Arctic, to the hulking, glaciated massifs of the Alaska Range and the Chugach and Wrangell Mountains. All of the big wildlife that the state is known for—humpback whales and orcas; half-ton brown bears; caribou, moose, and wolves—are still present in good numbers. And there are still families homesteading in the bush, wresting a living from country hundreds of miles away from anything like a road—though they may have a satellite hookup to cable TV and the Internet.

The great Yukon River cuts the Alaskan interior almost in half, carving tremendous valleys along the way, as it makes its 1,265-mile journey from the state border to the Bering Sea. The mazelike convergence of land and water in the famed Inside Passage of the panhandle was sculpted into its present form by thousands of years of glacial ice scoring its way toward the sea, and eventually melting.

In God's wildness lies the hope of the world – the great fresh, unblighted, unredeemed wilderness.

– JOHN MUIR, NOTE FROM ALASKA, 1890

JANUARY

Russian Christmas, Kodiak
A colorful event celebrating the city's pioneer ties to Russia. Orthodox parishioners follow a twirling star through the streets and sing traditional songs at Kodiak homes.
907.486.3854

MARCH

Iditarod Trail Sled Dog Race, Anchorage to Nome
The world's longest dogsled race heads through the streets of Anchorage, mushes through mountains and ice-locked seas, and ends 9 to 13 days later in Nome.
907.376.5155

Bering Sea Ice Golf Classic, Nome
Don't expect to find Tiger Woods at this six-hole tournament played on the frozen Bering Sea. Astroturf greens are laid on the ice, and competitors have at it. No drops!
907.443.5535

APRIL

World Extreme Skiing Championship, Valdez
Held in the extreme terrain of the Chugach Mountains, this event attracts competitors from around the world. Skiers swoosh down slopes of 35 to 55 degrees and descents of 800 to 2,000 vertical feet.
907.835.2108

MAY

Polar Bear Swim, Nome
You've got to get your entire body wet, in water that is 35 degrees or less, if you want one of the much-valued certificates proving you've swum the Bering Sea.
907.443.5535

JUNE

Midnight Sun Festival, Fairbanks
What do you do on the summer solstice with more than 22 hours of direct sunlight? Celebrate with sporting events, a parade, lots of street activities, and baseball played under the midnight sun.
907.452.8671

JULY

Moose-Dropping Festival, Talkeetna
It shouldn't be surprising that a town whose only paved road is lined with log cabins and clapboard houses would put on a summer festival whose biggest event is a moose-nugget toss.
907.733.2487

AUGUST

Seward Silver Salmon Derby, Seward
This thriving port town draws a lot of anglers hoping to hook one of the specially tagged salmon worth $10,000 to $100,000.
907.224.8051

NOVEMBER

Alaska Bald Eagle Festival, Haines
This month the winter population of American bald eagles reaches its peak as some 3,000 eagles congregate around the banks of the Chilkat River, feeding on late-running salmon. This three-day event includes nature tours and educational seminars about the great birds.
907.766.2202

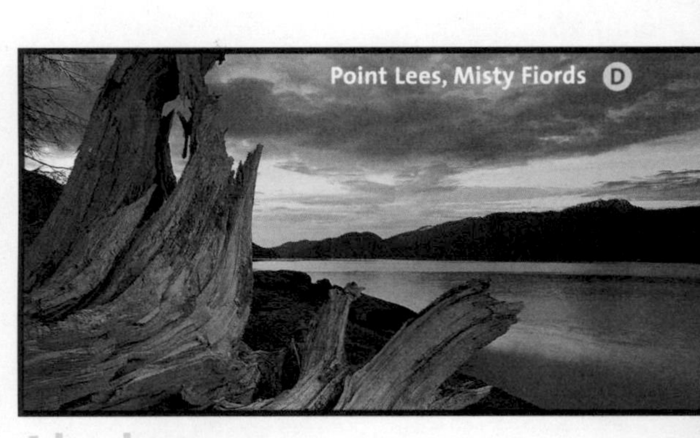
Point Lees, Misty Fiords D

Mount McKinley H

Kenai River, Kenai National Wildlife Refuge G

BERING STRAIT

ST. LAWRENCE ISLAND

ST. MATTHEW ISLAND

NUNIVAK ISLAND

BERING SEA

PRIBILOF ISLANDS

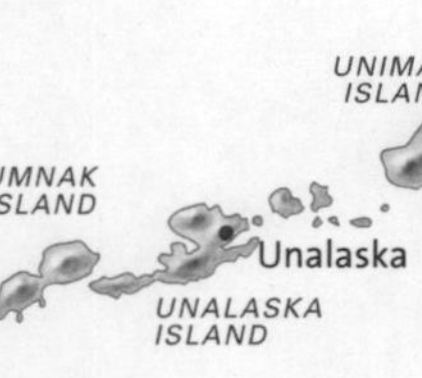

Alaska

A Alaska Highway

Pg. 62, D8. Only the bold used to take on the 1,519-mile Alaska Highway from Dawson Creek, British Columbia, to Fairbanks. Hazardously narrow and rough surfaced, with gaps of 200 miles or so between the roadhouses that served as outposts of civilization, the Alaska Highway became the stage for a kind of ongoing road epic peopled by an odd mix of soldiers, long-haul truckers, Airstream-trailer vacationers, and nomadic bikers. With improvements to road and services, it's not the wilderness expedition it used to be, but driving the Alaska Highway is still a unique way to experience the northern vastness. Fishing and wildlife-watching are outstanding along the entire route. **250.785.2544.**

B Mendenhall Glacier

Pg. 62, F10. A popular day trip from Juneau, the Mendenhall Glacier is just 13 miles from downtown. Built up during the mini ice age some 3,000 years ago, the glacier is a 12-mile-long river of ice whose face above water averages 80 feet high and nearly 1.5 miles wide. Near the visitor center is Steep Creek, where in early summer you can get a close-up view of red salmon spawning. **907.586.7955.**

C Aleutian Islands

Pg. 62, H1. The Bering Sea and North Pacific are separated by this 1,700-mile-long archipelago, a place of ferocious storms, earthquakes, and volcanoes. But however inhospitable these islands may seem, they are worth visiting to fish for 100-pound halibut, to hike the heather-covered hills of the islands, and to learn firsthand about the native Aleut people and their sad interactions with outsiders, enslaved by Russians in the 18th century and occupied by the Japanese during World War II. **907.581.2612.**

D Misty Fiords National Monument

Pg. 62, H12. About ten miles east of Ketchikan are over two million acres of some of Alaska's most spectacular water country. Misty Fiords is accessible only by boat or plane but is well worth the journey. A land of glacial lakes and stunning waterfalls, the area is home to large populations of bears, moose, bald eagles, and even wolves. It's also one of the world's premier sea kayaking grounds, with several United States Forest Service backcountry cabins beckoning amid the sheer granite cliffs and rain forest giants. **907.228.6214.**

E Dalton Highway

Pg. 62, B7. The long trip up the 414-mile Dalton Highway is a driving adventure like no other in North America, crossing the expanse of the Alaskan interior, climbing up and over the Brooks Range, and stopping at the end of the earth—literally as far north as you can drive on this continent. The demands of driving the "Haul Road," built to service the trans-Alaska pipeline, should not be underestimated: Lay in supplies like a CB radio, extra gasoline, and several spare tires. Along the way are caribou, wolves, grizzlies, and big mosquitoes—pack bug repellent. The pipeline parallels the road all the way to invitingly named Deadhorse, on the edge of Prudhoe Bay oil fields; from here you can arrange tours through the high-tech machinery of the oil complex and to the shores of the Arctic Ocean. **907.456.0527.**

F Earthquake Park

Pg. 62, K5. On Good Friday in 1964 a magnitude 8.4 earthquake, the strongest ever recorded in North America, rocked Anchorage, sending big chunks of land—along with houses and buildings—into Cook Inlet. The cost in human life was worse in communities located on Prince William Sound, where tsunamis swept away scores of people. The five-minute quake killed some 130 in all. Earthquake Park, at the northwest end of the city, marks the event with an interpretive trail describing the earthquake, the damage done, and subsequent changes to the area. **907.343.4474.**

G Kenai National Wildlife Refuge

Pg. 62, F7. Caribou, mountain goats, Dall sheep, brown and black bears—they're all home in this two-million-acre refuge, but the extensive wetlands here are especially attractive to moose. These shaggy beasts can be spotted on the Kenai Canoe Trails, two waterways linking more than 140 miles of lakes and rivers in the northern part of the refuge. The majority of visitors come to fish the Kenai River for king salmon that run up to 90 pounds. These monsters are so compelling to anglers that the shoulder-to-shoulder, fiercely competitive fishing conditions in July have gained a name—combat fishing. **907.262.7021.**

H Mount McKinley

Pg. 62, E6. At 20,320 feet, Mount McKinley is North America's highest peak, the rooftop of the continent. It's also what visitors to Denali National Park are most interested in seeing, but long-hanging clouds often obscure its fabled summit. The top 7,000 feet are capped in snow and ice year round, and McKinley remains one of the world's toughest mountaineering challenges – dozens of climbers have died on McKinley, and only about half who make the attempt actually reach the summit. **907.683.2294.**

AK 62
AK 232

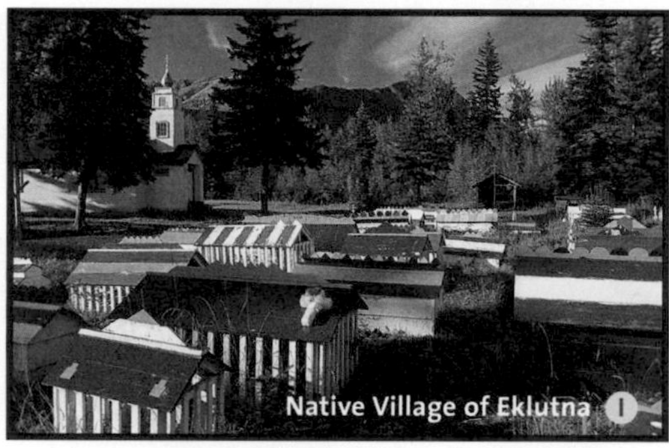
Native Village of Eklutna I

I Native Village of Eklutna

Pg. 62, F7. Reminiscent of brightly painted playhouses with banana yellow walls and vibrant blue roofs, the peculiar little huts at the Eklutna village, near Anchorage, are actually native spirit houses, meant to protect the treasured possessions of the recently departed. **907.688.6020.**

J Ketchikan

Pg. 62, H11. Rain-soaked Ketchikan has long been the southern panhandle's bustling hub. Originally a Tlingit fishing village, it was a rowdy timber and cannery town through the first half of this century, and it is still a center of the area's native cultures–more Haida, Tsimshian, and Tlingit live in its environs than anywhere else in Alaska. Several galleries purvey serious native art, and the Totem Heritage Center holds a large collection of vintage 19th-century totems and other artifacts. North and south of town are two totem parks, where you can see the brooding forms in their intended setting–amid the mist and giant trees of southeast Alaska's rain forest. **907.228.6214.**

K Kodiak Island

Pg. 62, H6. Alaska's largest island sits in the Gulf of Alaska, 90 miles south of the Kenai Peninsula. Although its largest community, Kodiak, is the oldest permanent European settlement in the state, the island still feels very much like the frontier. Commercial fishing owns the waters–Kodiak is among the most productive fishing ports in the U.S.–but the resident half-ton brown bears own the island itself. Given a diet that includes a bounty of salmon, it's no surprise that Kodiak bears have developed into the largest of their species in the world. **907.486.4782.**

L Haines

Pg. 62, F10. An offbeat, artsy town with an end-of-the-road feel, Haines is graced each fall by up to 3,000 bald eagles who arrive to feed on a late salmon run. It's also center of a Chilkat and Chilkoot Tlingit cultural renaissance, most visibly in the Chilkat Dancers, who perform traditional ceremonial dances in full costume from May through September. High-quality Tlingit carvings and crafts are displayed at several galleries in town. **800.458.3579.**

Totems are still made by the Tlingit, Haida, and Tsimshian tribes. Totem poles tell stories using symbolic animals, and they can be seen near Ketchikan at the world's largest standing collection of totem poles, Saxman Totem Park.

Kodiak Island K

In spite of the perception that Alaska is the cold, harsh north, more than 450 species of birds reside there. Alaska's state bird, the ptarmigan, is notorious for its mysterious population fluctuations.

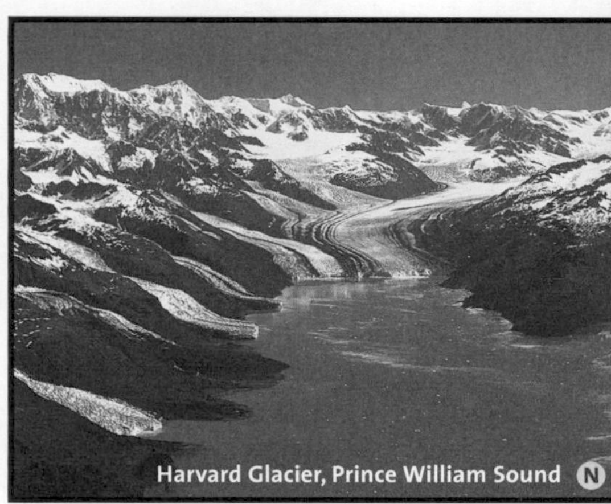
Harvard Glacier, Prince William Sound N

Prince of Wales Island M

M Prince of Wales Island

Pg. 62, H11. The commercial fishing grounds around Ketchikan are so productive that the town has labeled itself the "salmon capital of the world." But recreational anglers can head for nearby Prince of Wales Island, where luxurious fishing lodges provide guide service. About 2,000 miles of public gravel roads allow car access into the wild interior. In addition to the salmon streams, there's an abundance of other wildlife, including mink, Sitka deer, and brown bears. **907.228.6214.**

N Prince William Sound

Pg. 62, F7. The essence of marine Alaska, Prince William is an island and ice-berg-choked sound whose usually glass-smooth waters harbor an amazing array of life: humpback whales, orcas, seals and sea lions, millions of migratory birds. Damaged by the 1989 Exxon Valdez oil spill, the sound is returning to near-pristine condition. It's also the site of a number of dramatic fjords. From tour boats out of Whittier or Valdez you can watch as glaciers crackle, pop, and finally calve building-size slabs of ice into the sound with tremendous force. **907.465.2010.**

O Sitka National Historical Park

Pg. 62, G10. By the late 18th century, Russian fur traders had advanced into the panhandle. Here they found a formidable opponent in the Tlingit, a rich and sophisticated trading culture already equipped with European flintlock rifles. In 1802 the Tlingit stormed the Russian-American Company fort, killing most of its defenders. Two years later, after withstanding a barrage from a Russian gunship, the Tlingit left during the night–never submitting to Russian rule. The park preserves the battleground, features a number of impressive totem poles amid giant spruce trees, and has a cultural center where Tlingit artisans produce carvings, costumes, drums, and other traditional items. **907.747.6281.**

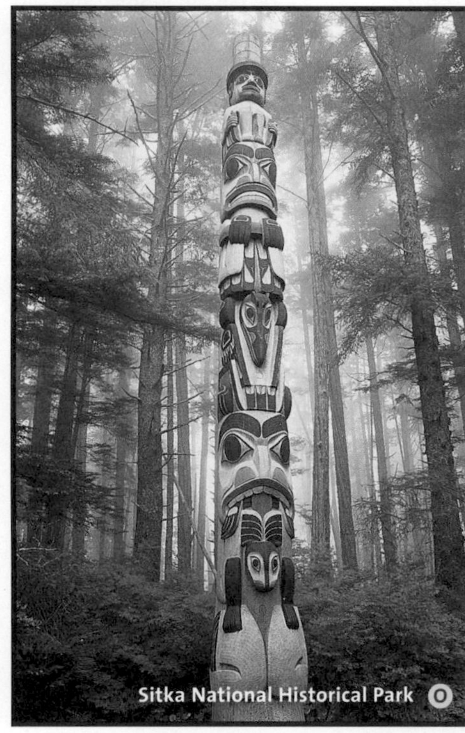
Sitka National Historical Park O

Bristol Bay is the red salmon capital of the world, and the Kenai River is famous for record-size king salmon, including the largest king salmon caught in the world on rod and reel, at 97 pounds.

Pacific Northwest

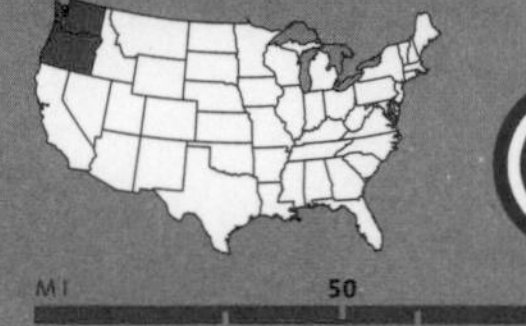

One of the last parts of the lower 48 to be fully explored and settled, the Pacific Northwest has shed its provincial reputation in recent years and is now hailed as an innovator: In the arts, from world-class theater to grunge music; in cuisine, with award-winning microbrews, wine, and coffee; and in its commitment to balancing environmental concerns with development. Such successes, coupled with spectacular natural beauty, have resulted in high media profiles for cities like Seattle and Portland, both of which have topped national urban livability lists. In Western Washington, the Olympic Peninsula offers the sublime contrast of temperate rain forests against glaciered mountain peaks. With nearby waters patrolled by playful and crafty orcas, Puget Sound and its hundreds of islands and peninsulas provide a marine retreat where evergreen forests surround pastoral hamlets and tranquil coves. Just across the volcanic Cascade Range lies a desert basin brought into agricultural production by irrigation. With help from dams on the Columbia River, the region is now noted for the state's beloved apples as well as cherries, wheat, pears, and wine grapes. In Oregon, the same pattern repeats: The west is characterized by a dramatic, rocky coastline; inland lies the verdant Willamette Valley and, across the Cascades, the sagebrush flats and ranches of eastern Oregon's high desert.

The Cascade Range cuts across both Washington and Oregon, acting as a barrier for coastal weather systems and keeping things wet and mild in the west and more arid in the east. The mighty Columbia River flows along the Washington–Oregon border.

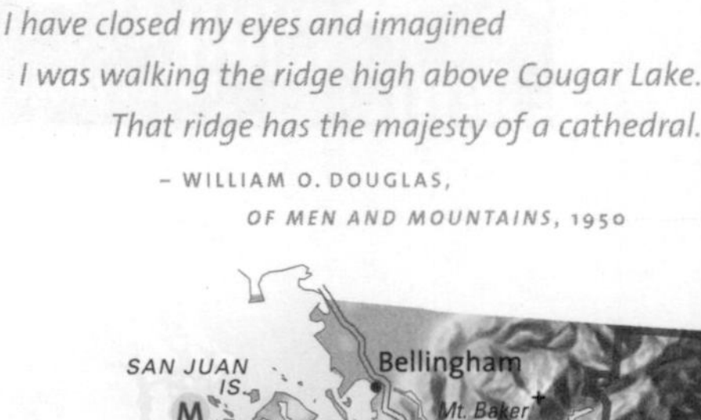

Packed tight in a New York City subway,
I have closed my eyes and imagined
I was walking the ridge high above Cougar Lake.
That ridge has the majesty of a cathedral.

— WILLIAM O. DOUGLAS, *OF MEN AND MOUNTAINS*, 1950

APRIL
Washington State Apple Blossom Festival, Wenatchee, WA
Here in the fruit basket of the Northwest, a vast array of produce thrives—but the apple is still king. Wenatchee becomes a wonderland of blossoms in late April and early May, and dozens of events celebrate the flowering of commercial orchards.
509.662.3616

MAY
Northwest Folklife Festival, Seattle, WA
Billed as the largest festival of its kind in the U.S., Folklife is an ethnic extravaganza celebrating traditional arts, with participatory dancing (square, swing), jam sessions, craft demonstrations, and music workshops.
206.684.7300

JUNE
Portland Rose Festival, Portland, OR
The Grand Floral Parade is the second largest in the country. Eighty events in 25 days, including parties, music, and celebration, with a special welcome mat laid out for the Navy crews docked downtown.
503.227.2681

Oregon Shakespeare Festival, Ashland, OR
It's definitely worth the trip to this eclectic town of Victorian homes and galleries to catch its Tony Award-winning festival of the Bard's best. Productions run February through October, but the Elizabethan outdoor stage opens in June.
541.482.4331

JULY
World Championship Timber Carnival, Albany, OR
TIIIIM-BERRRR! At this popular event, people throw on their red plaid shirts, suspenders, and heavy boots to celebrate the industry with logging contests—rolling, climbing, chopping—and showmanship galore. Bring your own ax.
800.526.2256

Oregon Brewers Festival, Portland, OR
Long famous for wonderful beers, Oregon is home to over 75 small breweries, and Portland is the place to quaff the best microbrews in the business. This outdoor spectacle is held at the river's edge at Waterfront Park, with many of the nation's finest microbreweries in attendance. Cheers!
503.778.5917

AUGUST
Washington State International Kite Festival, Long Beach, WA
This seemingly endless stretch of sand on Washington's windy southern coast is the ideal locale for kite flying, and every August the sky fills with kites manned by both amateurs and the pros. The festival includes competitions, night flying, and fireworks.
800.451.2542

SEPTEMBER
Bumbershoot, Seattle, WA
An old English term for umbrella, this Bumbershoot is a mammoth annual music festival that draws big names of all genres. In spite of its name, sunny skies often bless the festival over Labor Day weekend. Food, crafts, film screenings, and dance performances round out the offerings.
206.281.7788

Phantom Ship Island, Crater Lake C

Columbia River Gorge F

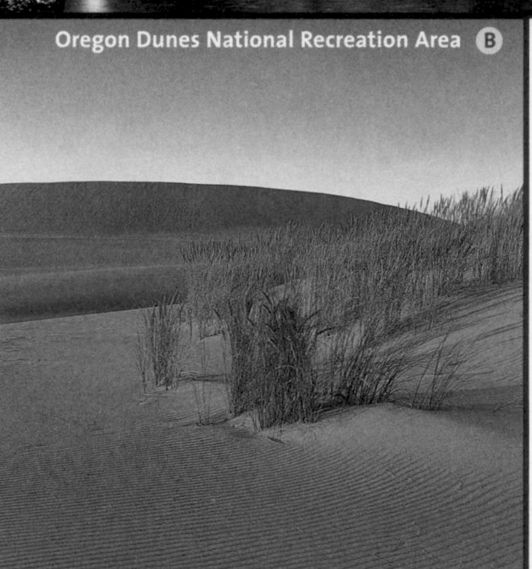

Oregon Dunes National Recreation Area B

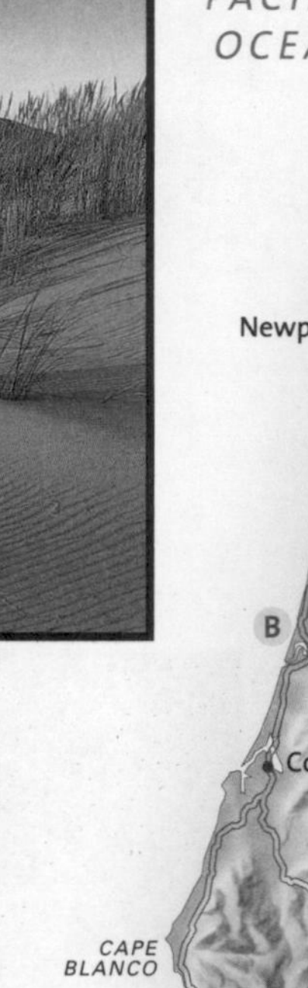

Timberline Lodge H

Oregon

A The American Advertising Museum
Pg. 148, C5. Dedicated to the art and science of promotion, Portland's American Advertising Museum is a shameless—and amusing—look at the history of an industry that some say is the second oldest profession. Permanent exhibits include classic '50s television ads, and print ads from 1700 to the present. But the most interesting display showcases the all-time-best ad campaigns, like "I Heard It Through the Grapevine" (California Raisin Council) and "Does She or Doesn't She?" (Clairol). **503.226.0000.**

B Oregon Dunes National Recreation Area
Pg. 148, H1. So steep and rugged is the southern Oregon coastline that there is little room for sand to accumulate. Pacific Ocean currents carry this burden of sand north to the central Oregon coast, where a 50-mile beach allows the sand to wash ashore. The result, Oregon Dunes, is 50 square miles of sand towering as high as 400 feet above sea level. Hiking and bridle trails have been established, and the area is noted for its uniquely contrasting ecosystems, which include wetlands, tree islands, and estuaries. **541.271.3611.**

C Crater Lake
Pg. 148, K6. The deepest lake in the U.S. (1,932 feet at its bottom), Crater Lake is a round, uncannily sapphire blue body of water trapped in a caldera. After Mount Mazama erupted nearly 7,000 years ago, rain and snowmelt gradually filled the crater with water. Half a million people visit annually to boat, hike, ski, and fish. **541.594.2211.**

D End of the Oregon Trail Interpretive Center
Pg. 148, D5. Oregon City was the official terminus of the Oregon Trail, and therefore the ultimate destination of many of the estimated 300,000 pioneers who made the cross-country trek to the Northwest in the mid-1800s. Shaped like an enormous covered wagon, this new museum commemorates the pioneers' struggles and successes—as well as the hardships of the Native Americans displaced by them. **503.657.9336.**

E Hells Canyon National Recreation Area
Pg. 149, B17. A chasm almost 8,000 feet deep, forged by the Snake River, Hells Canyon is North America's deepest river gorge. Bighorn sheep and mountain lions populate the high canyon walls, while blue herons dot the river's edge and bald eagles soar overhead. Rugged and difficult to explore, Hells Canyon's rewards are plentiful, including the awe-inspiring view from the lookout near Hat Point. **541.426.5546.**

F Columbia River Gorge National Scenic Area
Pg. 148, B7. This precipitous chasm, stretching 70 miles along the Columbia River from just east of Portland, is fed by more than 70 waterfalls that thunder from steep basalt cliffs. The tallest, Multnomah Falls, at 620 feet, is Oregon's highest. Ranging in width from one-half to three-quarters of a mile, the gorge is a natural wind tunnel, and has become a prime spot for windsurfing, especially near Hood River. **541.386.2333.**

G International Rose Test Gardens
Pg. 149, C18. Here, roses are tested for durability and disease, and earn their pedigrees. Spread across 4.5 acres of hillside in Portland's Washington Park in sight of Mount Hood, the gardens boast over 550 varieties of roses, including old and rare types. In summer, the terraces are filled with delirious color and heady scent. **503.823.2223.**

H Timberline Lodge
Pg. 148, D7. Perched at an altitude of 6,000 feet on the southern flank of Mount Hood, Timberline Lodge is one of the greatest architectural achievements of President Franklin Delano Roosevelt's Works Progress Administration. Completed in 1937, this vast stone-and-log showplace was crafted to blend with its surroundings. A six-sided central tower emulates Mount Hood's peak, and even the exterior paint was custom-mixed to complement mountain frost. Details were handcrafted by WPA carpenters and blacksmiths, and the stone fireplace soars three stories in the open lobby. Today, the lodge is the centerpiece of a skier's paradise renowned for 30 runs, a 2,660-foot vertical drop, and year-round snow. **503.272.3311.**

WA 170
OR 148
VA 247
OR 244

Nicknamed the Rose City, Portland boasts rose gardens that are among the most renowned in the world, with over 550 varieties and more than 21,200 roses.

Washington

I Grand Coulee Dam
Pg. 171, E16. A hydroelectric marvel that's been called the eighth wonder of the world, the Grand Coulee Dam in north-central Washington is the biggest producer of hydroelectric power in North America. When completed in 1941, it was the largest human-made structure ever built. The visitor center provides information on the geologic history of the Columbia River and its hydropower, and elevators take visitors as far as 320 feet into the mammoth structure. **509.633.9265.**

J Lake Chelan
Pg. 171, D13. Fifty-five miles long and 1,500 feet at its deepest points, Lake Chelan's cold, pristine waters are fed by both glacial meltwater and mountain streams. Central Washington's favorite playground offers canoeing, swimming, fishing, water-skiing, camping, biking, and hiking. The northwest end of the lake, the Stehekin area, is more rustic and wild than the south, and is flanked by the wilderness peaks of the mighty North Cascades. **509.682.3503.**

K Mount St. Helens National Volcanic Monument
Pg. 170, J9. Before May 18, 1980, Mount St. Helens was just another comely, snow-clad Cascade peak. But on that day, the volcano erupted, taking 57 lives and pushing a mushroom cloud of ash 15 miles skyward. Two decades later, the volcano still rumbles and spits steam, just enough of a performance to entertain the thousands of visitors to Mount St. Helens National Volcanic Monument. Established in 1982, the 110,000-acre site includes a wasteland of blasted trees, as well as the buried Spirit Lake Lodge and the Harmony Falls Lodge. Trails lead into the blast zone. **360.247.3900.**

L Port Townsend
Pg. 170, D8. Nestled in the Olympic Peninsula's northeast corner, this turn-of-the-century seaport boomed when speculators wagered that it, not Seattle, would be a West Coast transcontinental-rail terminus. A handsome stone-and-brick business district sprang up along the harbor, and extravagant homes graced the bluffs above the city. When the terminus went to Seattle, the town died and for many years was all but deserted. Now a showplace of period architecture, some of the elegantly restored Victorian homes are B&Bs, and the old storefronts reveal antiques stores, fancy boutiques, and art galleries. **360.385.2722.**

M San Juan Islands
Pg. 170, C7. Located where Puget Sound and the straits of Georgia and Juan de Fuca meet, the islands number 743 at low tide and 428 at high tide. Only four–San Juan, Orcas, Lopez, and Shaw–welcome visitors, with regular ferry service from Anacortes on the mainland, and each offers spectacular natural beauty and an easygoing pace. Half the fun is getting there–with luck you'll see orcas, bald eagles, or other wildlife on the crossing. Bicycles are the preferred means of transport across the islands; quiet, winding country roads thread through sheep-filled meadows and evergreen forests. **360.468.3663.**

N Space Needle
Pg. 170, B1. A kitschy, pseudo-space-age vestige of the 1962 World's Fair, Seattle's Space Needle is the city's most famous landmark and, more than 30 years later, remains its most popular tourist attraction. Once a towering skyscraper, the Needle is dwarfed by today's soaring city skyline. No matter. Visitors still clamor to ride the glass elevator up 520 feet to the circular observation deck, or to eat and drink at the revolving restaurants. **206.443.2100.**

Seattle is home to Boeing, the world's biggest aerospace manufacturer. The company is so large that if all the roofed floor space where Boeing employees work were housed in office buildings, it would take up more than 30 skyscrapers the size of New York's Empire State Building.

O Yakima Valley
Pg. 171, J13. The roadside sign that proclaims it "the Palm Springs of Washington" may be a bit tongue-in-cheek, but Yakima's sun-drenched climate does make this area the country's leading producer of apples, winter pears, and hops. Today, however, wine is the new star in central Washington. Some 27 wineries dot the Yakima River valley, in towns such as Zillah, Prosser, Sunnyside, and Wapato, where grapes flourish thanks to loamy soil and more sunshine than California. Modest family wineries plus granddaddy Chateau Ste. Michelle welcome visitors for tastings. **509.248.2021.**

San Juan Islands M

Mount St. Helens National Volcanic Monument K

Ann Starrett House, Port Townsend L

Space Needle, Seattle N

Rainier, from Puget Sound, is a sight for the gods, and when one looks upon him he feels that he is in the presence of the gods.

– PAUL FOUNTAIN, *THE ELEVEN EAGLETS OF THE WEST*, 1905

Oregon is the Beaver State, and desire for beaver pelts inspired initial exploration of the Pacific Northwest in the late 1700s, primarily by British fur companies.

Far West

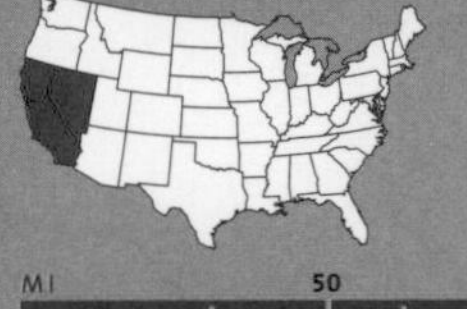

A land of extremes, the Far West boasts the nation's most varied landscape, including volcanoes, deserts, inland seas, and glacial lakes. Death Valley has the lowest elevation in the Western Hemisphere; nearby Mount Whitney claims the highest in the lower 48. Lake Tahoe is another natural wonder: Though Nevada is the driest of the 50 states, averaging only about nine inches of precipitation annually, Lake Tahoe could bathe California in a foot of water. The West has a boom or bust mentality. Adventurous souls prospected for gold and silver in the mountains; now they look for treasure in the high-tech industries in the valleys. The real gambling, of course, takes place along the Strip in Las Vegas and in the back lots of Hollywood. Film studios risk millions of dollars constructing fantasy towns and employing futuristic special effects while the newest casinos are housed in sets resembling Egyptian pyramids and the skyline of New York City. But the most astonishing attractions in the Far West remain the natural ones: the 840 miles of coastline, the world's tallest and oldest trees, the prehistoric finds in the Great Basin. From the bright, thin, starry sky of the High Sierras to the horizon of the Pacific Ocean, the West always seems limitless and new.

Nevada sits in the sparsely populated Great Basin, an arid, elevated land with no drainage to seas—its chief drainage center is the Great Salt Lake in Utah. A spine of mountains, the Sierra Nevada, defines most of the California–Nevada border. Beyond this majestic range, home to Yosemite, Kings Canyon, and Sequoia National Parks, lies the richly fertile soil of California's Central Valley, where the Sacramento and San Joaquin Rivers wend to a delta emptying into the San Francisco Bay. At the valley's south end, the Sierras meet California's Coastal Ranges, a clutch of mountain ranges made forever unstable by the San Andreas Fault.

JANUARY

Tournament of Roses Parade, Pasadena, CA
It's ten times more fun in person than watching it on TV. Most folks come the night before and camp on the sidewalk, waiting for the passing parade of the best floats in the world. **818.449.7673**

Cowboy Poetry Gathering, Elko, NV
An institution in its own right, the "granddaddy of all poetry gatherings" is a weeklong celebration of the Old West, complete with dances, workshops on rawhide braiding and the like, guitar-and-fiddle jams into the small hours, and, of course, poetry readings. **702.738.7508**

FEBRUARY

Chinese New Year Festival, San Francisco, CA
Dancing dragons, fireworks, and great food in celebration of the lunar New Year, and the best time to visit San Francisco's famed Chinatown. **415.982.3000**

Snowfest, Lake Tahoe City, CA
From the colorful to the bizarre: Night skiers carry torches down ski runs and crazy people jump into frigid Lake Tahoe for a polar-bear swim. **916.583.7625**

Calaveras County Fair and Jumping Frog Jubilee, Angels Camp, CA
Mark Twain would never believe what his little story unleashed. A celebration of western ways highlighted by the traditional frog-jumping contest. **209.736.2561**

JULY

Gilroy Garlic Festival, Gilroy, CA
Garlic ice cream, garlic cheesecake, even chocolate-covered garlic. This harvest festival celebrates 101 uses for the pungent herb. **408.842.1625**

Festival of Arts and Pageant of the Masters, Laguna Beach, CA
Degas's dancers and Norman Rockwell's home scenes are re-created by live models on an indoor stage. Also one of the largest arts-and-crafts fairs in the state. **714.494.1145**

Carmel Bach Festival, Carmel/Pebble Beach, CA
Baroque music is brought to life by a hundred world-class musicians in an exquisite setting. From mid-July to early August. **408.624.2046**

SEPTEMBER

National Championship Air Races, Reno, NV
Daredevils race around two poles reaching high into the sky. The Indy 500 of airplane races. **702.972.6663**

OCTOBER

Halloween Parade, San Francisco, CA
The Castro district shows its wild side every Halloween as the fantastically costumed promenade takes over. **415.391.2000**

Golden Gate Bridge, San Francisco D

Napa Valley H

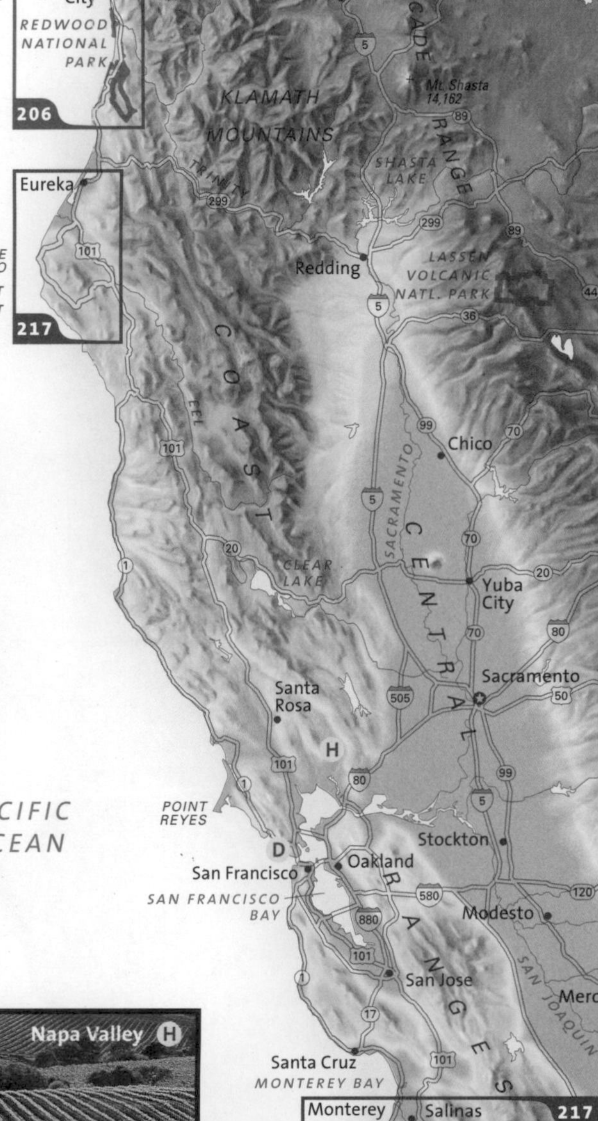

California

A Balboa Park
Pg. 70, W5. Best known as the home of the famous San Diego Zoo and its cageless environments for animals that simulate their natural habitats, Balboa Park has even more to offer than cuddly koalas from Australia and fierce Komodo dragons from Indonesia. The shady 1,000-plus-acre park is also the idyllic setting for a cluster of excellent museums, many found in Spanish Colonial-style buildings. Highlights include the extensive San Diego Aerospace Museum and the Natural History Museum, which concentrates on southwestern desert and marine life. The nearby Centro Cultural de la Raza focuses on contemporary Indian, Mexican, and Chicano culture. **619.239.0512.**

B Bodie State Historic Park
Pg. 69, K13. In 1877, after the first strike of high-grade gold in the barren hills north of Mono Lake, the desolate hamlet of Bodie was transformed from a miners' outpost to a boomtown with at least 65 saloons. By 1879, 10,000 people called Bodie home. But boom quickly turned to bust, and by 1882 the party was over. Today, some 170 weathered buildings, maintained in a state of "arrested decay," make this one of the most authentic–and fascinating– ghost towns in the West. The interiors of many stores and houses remain just as they were when the former residents packed up and left. **760.647.6445.**

C Disneyland
Pg. 72, H10. Any kid–and all but the hardest cases among adults–will tell you that Disneyland truly is "the happiest place on earth," just as Walt Disney intended when he first opened the gates to the Magic Kingdom, on July 17, 1955. Today parts of the park–particularly Tomorrowland, which was beginning to look a little like Yesterdayland–have recently undergone major renovations. Still, some of the most imaginative, fun, and popular rides are among the oldest: the watery, raucous Pirates of the Caribbean and the spooky Haunted Mansion. **714.781.4565.**

D Golden Gate Bridge
Pg. 74, F3. Spanning the Golden Gate, the passageway between the Pacific Ocean and the waters of San Francisco Bay, the Golden Gate Bridge rises up out of the fog, eerily beautiful and impossible, one of the world's great engineering feats. It took San Francisco less than five years to construct one of the longest single-span suspension bridges ever built (6,450 feet)–even more amazing when you consider the depth of the water (350 feet at its deepest) and the bay's powerful tides. **415.257.4548.**

E Hearst San Simeon State Historical Monument
Pg. 70, R9. Few sites are more expressive of California than Hearst Castle, a stunning monument to wealth, built by flamboyant newspaper tycoon William Randolph Hearst. It is also testimony to an extreme passion for collecting: The estate is crammed with fireplaces, tapestries, paintings, sculpture, and fountains, all plucked (to put it politely) from castles and churches around the globe. The sumptuous mansion, never actually completed, was donated to the state in 1957. **805.927.2020.**

F Mission San Juan Capistrano
Pg. 73, M13. El Camino Real (the Royal Road) was pioneered by colonizing Spaniards, who built a string of 21 missions along an ancient foot trail running from San Diego to Sonoma. One of the most beautiful and prosperous was San Juan Capistrano, founded by Father Junípero Serra in 1776 but nearly destroyed by a massive earthquake in 1812. The Great Stone Church and most of the adobe buildings, rebuilt and earthquake-proofed, sit among bougainvillea gardens. **714.248.2049.**

G Walk of Fame
Pg. 72, D6. Begun in 1958, the Walk of Fame down Hollywood Boulevard now features some 2,500 pink-and-charcoal stars. Start between Highland and La Brea at the Hollywood Roosevelt Hotel–site of the first Academy Awards in 1929. The boulevard (which, granted, has seen better times) runs along the terraced slopes and lush greenery of the Hollywood Hills. Searchlight premieres were standard fare at Grauman's (now Mann's) Chinese Theater, where filmdom's aristocrats left their foot–or paw, nose, leg–prints for posterity. Less than a mile away, at the corner of Franklin and Beachwood, is a good view of the 50-foot-high HOLLYWOOD sign. **213.689.8822.**

H Napa Valley/Sonoma
Pg. 68, K6–K7. North of San Francisco lie the valleys and hills synonymous with California wine country. Once a sleepy rural area, Napa and Sonoma now play host to millions of visitors every year who cruise up and down "the great wine way." Most head directly for the 200-plus wineries flanking a 30-mile stretch of Route 29 between Napa and Calistoga. Others prefer the quieter country roads in and around Sonoma, close to the last home of author Jack London, who gave the area its romantic "Valley of the Moon" name. **707.226.7459.**

In some years, the eucalyptus groves in Pismo State Beach shelter 200,000 wintering monarch butterflies, who often hang in six- to eight-foot-long clusters of several thousand butterflies.

I Lake Tahoe
Pg. 68, H11. Straddling the state line of California and Nevada, Lake Tahoe is uniquely American in its dichotomies: Rugged and cultivated, kitschy and elegant, with a history of mobsters, Indians, and of waters so deep and clear that luminous images are visible 100 feet below the surface. Once a summer gathering spot for native Washoe, today it attracts hot-dog skiers in winter, water lovers in summer, and gamblers year-round. **530.541.5255.**

NV 126
CA 68
NV 240
CA 233

The country looks something like a singed cat, owing to the scarcity of shrubbery, and also resembles that animal in the respect that it has more merits than its personal appearance would seem to indicate.

—MARK TWAIN, c. 1864

Las Vegas K

Extraterrestrial Highway L

Hoover Dam J

Virginia City N

Nevada

J Hoover Dam
Pg. 126, M9. Some 700,000 people a year cruise down Highway 93 from Las Vegas just to stand and stare at one of the great human-made wonders of the world: Hoover Dam. Completed in 1935, it truly is a show-stopper: 7 billion tons of concrete wall 776 feet high and 660 feet thick at its base. The visitor center at the top houses a topographical model of the Colorado River as well as exhibits on how the dam works. Tours descend the 53 stories in elevators to view turbines and look up the sheer face. **702.293.8321.**

K Las Vegas
Pg. 126, L9. The Nevada state legislature legalized gambling in 1931, but it wasn't until 1946, when gangster Bugsy Siegel opened the lavish Flamingo on today's Strip, that hotel casinos began to sprout up in Las Vegas like wildflowers after a spring rain. Many of the original hotels have given way to themed resorts along the Strip, such as the Excalibur Hotel Casino (a medieval castle with nightly Arthurian jousts). But in the downtown area is a four-block stretch of smaller casinos known as Glitter Gulch, so named for the shouting neon lights that make every hour seem like high noon. **702.892.7575.**

L Extraterrestrial Highway
Pg. 126, J8. So many people claim to have seen unidentified lights in the stark night skies along Route 375 that in 1996 the Nevada Transportation Board renamed this lonely stretch of road the Extraterrestrial Highway. Fueling speculation among UFO believers, a nearby military installation—known unofficially as Area 51 and cloaked in mystery and rumor—is thought to test secret aircraft in these skies. In the small town of Rachel, the Little A'Le'Inn has become a trading post for theories about the base's "real" purpose: Reverse-engineering of crashed spaceships? Inn, **702.729.2515.**

M Pyramid Lake
Pg. 126, D2. Named for the conical formation of tufa rock that rises from its depths, Pyramid Lake is the vestige of an inland sea known as Lake Lahontan. The lake is famous for its enormous trout and a prehistoric fish called the cuiui. The large island in the middle of the lake, Anaho, is a sanctuary for endangered white pelicans. **702.574.1000.**

N Virginia City
Pg. 126, F2. During Virginia City's heyday in the 1860s, some 30,000 people flocked here—including Samuel Clemens, who worked at the city's newspaper, where he first used the byline Mark Twain—to mine the $400 million in silver and gold ore that fueled the economies of San Francisco, Sacramento, and northern Nevada. Today, in addition to its main drag filled with ersatz Old West saloons, gift shops, and a candy store, the town has opulent mansions built by silver barons (open to tours) and several museums. An underground mine tour offers a taste of what miners experienced in the 700 miles of tunnels underneath the town. **702.847.0311.**

At the Nevada Test Site, 65 miles northwest of Las Vegas, the U.S. government detonated 904 nuclear devices above and below ground from 1951 to 1992.

Gaming is Nevada's biggest industry, grossing more than $7.5 billion in 1997.

It is an odd thing, but everyone who disappears is said to be seen at San Francisco. It must be a delightful city, and possesses all the attractions of the next world.

—OSCAR WILDE, *THE PICTURE OF DORIAN GRAY*, 1891

16 Southwest

The power of the Southwest's timeless landscape resides in the vivid light and broad canvas of sky. Red rock buttes and painted deserts are only part of this startling terrain. The Rocky Mountains and Great Plains venture into New Mexico, and if you grabbed Arizona by two corners and shook it, its mountain ranges and canyons would unfurl into a state larger than Texas. The Grand Canyon is only the most overwhelming of the region's stunning sculptured flourishes, and each of three deserts that help make the Southwest the land of the sun has a distinct face—the massive saguaros of the Sonoran, the barren expanses of the Mojave, and the scrub brush of the Chihuahuan Desert. Perhaps nowhere else in North America are the lives of ancient peoples so palpable as in the Southwest, where pre-Columbian pueblos still stand beside flowing water, and the ruins of cliff-side communities perch high above lonely canyons, once homes of the mysterious Old Ones—ancestors of modern Hopi, Zuni, and Pueblo Indians. Nearer history draws in the era of Spanish colonization and some of the oldest European settlements on the continent, and the Wild West spirit of the 19th century rounds out a past that still shapes and enriches a unique regional culture.

The Sonoran Desert reaches up from Mexico to cover most of southern Arizona, and the Chihuahuan Desert blankets much of southern New Mexico. The northern sections of the Southwest are dominated by the 5,000-foot-high Colorado Plateau and its deep canyons, including one of the world's greatest natural wonders, the Grand Canyon.

JANUARY
Barrett-Jackson World's Greatest Classic Car Auction, Scottsdale, AZ
In search of the ultimate set of wheels? Here's where to find one-of-a-kind classics and supercharged muscle cars alike. America's largest and most prestigious antique-car auction draws enthusiasts from around the world.
602.273.0791

MARCH
Scottsdale Arts Festival, Scottsdale, AZ
Arts and crafts from across the nation abound at this annual event in an upscale Phoenix suburb that has become a major center for Western, Native American, and contemporary art.
602.994.2787

MAY
Santa Fe Trail Heritage Days, Las Vegas, NM
Once a convenient overnight stop on the Santa Fe Trail, New Mexico's Las Vegas celebrates its trade-route heyday amid the city's rich mix of well-preserved Victorian, adobe, and territorial architecture.
800.832.5947

JULY
Prescott Frontier Days, Prescott, AZ
This former gold- and copper-mining town has plenty of history to celebrate, including its reign as capital of the Arizona Territory and its claim to the oldest rodeo in America, which is the centerpiece of this event.
520.445.3103

AUGUST
Carlsbad Caverns Bat Flight Breakfast, Carlsbad Caverns National Park, NM
No doubt, Alfred Hitchcock would have been inspired by this annual dawn breakfast picnic, where visitors gather to watch up to 500,000 Mexican free-tailed bats return to roost in the caves of Carlsbad. While the breakfast only happens once a year, people can see the bats any morning from March to October.
505.785.2232

SEPTEMBER
Jazz on the Rocks, Sedona, AZ
There's something very relaxing about listening to music outdoors in Sedona's red rock canyons, which may explain why so many big-name musicians perform here.
520.282.1985

OCTOBER
Taos Mountain Balloon Rally, Taos, NM
Just before sunset in the cold mountain air, over 60 balloonists fire up their propane tanks, unfurling a towering garden of hot-air balloons. Free tethered rides are offered to the public.
800.732.8267

DECEMBER
Old Town Luminaria Festival, Albuquerque, NM
An old New Mexican holiday tradition is to set lit candles in paper bags along walkways and rooflines. The illuminated neighborhoods can be admired on foot or from specially provided buses.
505.764.3700

Parade of Lights, Page, AZ
Dozens of boats elaborately decorated with holiday lights slowly cruise along Lake Powell. Watch from shore or take a boat ride on the lake for a different view.
800.528.6154

Arizona produces 65 percent of the nation's copper, utilized mostly by the construction and electrical industries. Since 1982, pennies have contained only 2.5 percent copper.

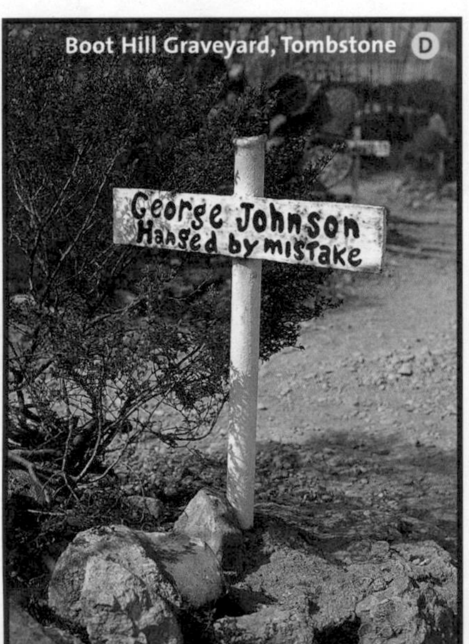

Boot Hill Graveyard, Tombstone D

Monument Valley G

The glories and the beauties of form, color, and sound unite in the Grand Canyon—forms unrivaled even by the mountains, colors that vie with sunsets, and sounds that span the diapason from tempest to tinkling raindrop, from cataract to bubbling fountain.

—J.W. POWELL, CANYONS OF THE COLORADO, 1895

Arizona

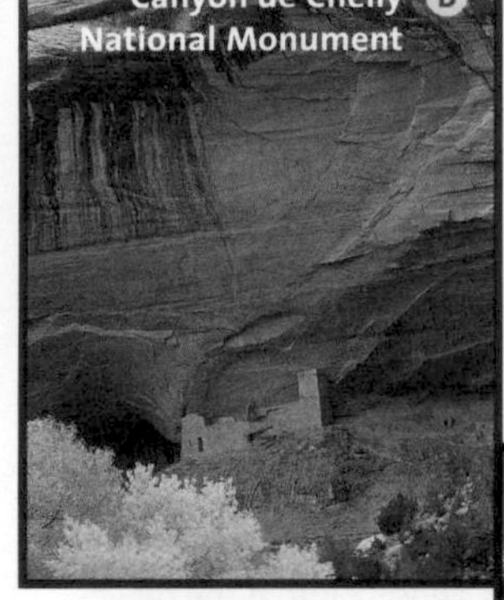

Canyon de Chelly National Monument B

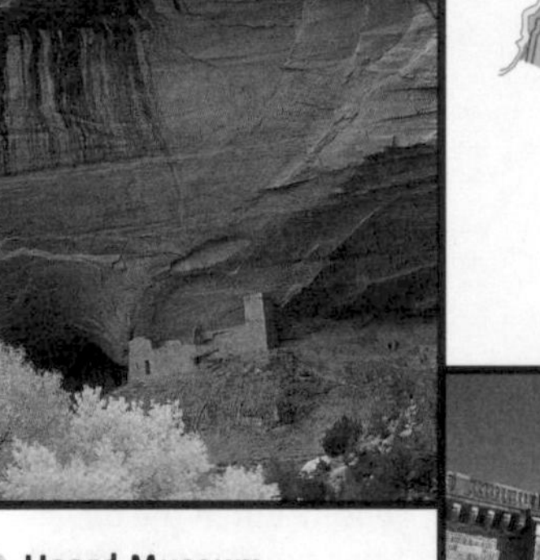

London Bridge E

A Arizona-Sonora Desert Museum
Pg. 65, N9. More a zoo than a museum, this innovative 20-acre complex in Tucson Mountain Park offers a rare chance to see myriad desert creatures—javelinas, scorpions, coyotes, bighorn sheep, bald eagles—in the wild or in admirable re-creations of their habitats. The museum is also a spectacular botanical garden, displaying more than 1,300 species of plants indigenous to the Sonoran Desert, including the giant saguaro and over 200 other cacti. **520.883.2702.**

B Canyon de Chelly National Monument
Pg. 64, C12. Deep in the heart of Arizona's Indian country are the spectacular sheer, red-hued cliffs of Canyon de Chelly (pronounced de-SHAY), which shelter more than 100 prehistoric sites, including the ruins of some beautiful Puebloan cliff dwellings that date back at least seven centuries. Exhibits at a visitor center near the mouth of the canyon offer an introduction to the area and its peoples. **520.674.5500.**

C Heard Museum
Pg. 63, D6. The best thing about Phoenix's museum dedicated to the native peoples of the Southwest may be the "Old Ways, New Ways" interactive exhibit, where you can step into an authentic Navajo hogan, Apache wickiup, or Hopi corn-grinding room. The museum also boasts an extensive collection of Hopi kachina dolls, 400 of which are on display, and artists are frequently on hand to demonstrate beadworking, weaving, or carving. **602.252.8840.**

D Tombstone
Pg. 65, P11. The history of the West could be distilled from the events that occurred in Tombstone, a brawling, lawless boomtown that was the site of an infamous shoot-out near, but not quite at, the O. K. Corral. Gunfights—now staged—are still a big attraction here, as is the Boot Hill Graveyard, where the three losers of the O. K. shoot-out are buried: Billy Clanton and brothers Tom and Frank McLaury. **520.457.2211.**

E London Bridge
Pg. 64, G2. In 1968, a real estate developer bought London Bridge from the British government, shipped all 33,000 tons of granite across the Atlantic in 10,276 slabs, and reassembled the 1831 span at Lake Havasu City in the Arizona desert. What seemed like a crazy scheme has become a brilliant marketing ploy—only the Grand Canyon draws more tourists to the state. **800.242.8278.**

F Meteor Crater Natural Landmark
Pg. 64, F9. Most meteoroids that make it through the earth's atmosphere are about the size of a charcoal briquette. But the meteor that slammed into central Arizona about 49,000 years ago must have been huge, judging by the mile-wide, 60-story-deep dent it created. Though the crater bowl is off-limits, guided tours visit the rim and a museum sheds light on meteors. **520.289.5898.**

G Monument Valley
Pg. 64, A11. Like the Eiffel Tower or Big Ben, Monument Valley appears familiar to even first-time visitors, probably because its lonely buttes, rising heroically out of the desert floor, have been film and television stars since director John Ford found roles for them in some of his Westerns. A 17-mile loop drive takes you past most of the more familiar landmarks. **801.727.3287.**

NM 130
AZ 64
NM 241
AZ 232

Quarai, Salinas Pueblo Missions (L)

Adobe home, Santa Fe (N)

Taos Pueblo (O)

The moment I saw the brilliant, proud morning shine high up over the deserts of Santa Fe, something stood still in my soul . . . For a greatness of beauty I have never experienced anything like New Mexico. . . . Just day itself is tremendous there.

– D. H. LAWRENCE, "NEW MEXICO," c. 1936

New Mexico

More different types of hummingbirds–some 15 species–can be sighted in southeastern Arizona than anywhere else in the U.S. The tiny, colorful creatures (the largest is a mere five inches) are the only species of bird known to fly backward.

(H) Chaco Culture National Historical Park

Pg. 130, D3. Some 16 miles from the nearest paved highway lies one of the most important archaeological centers in North America. Located throughout the 17-mile canyon are the remains of 12 major Chacoan "great house" structures and more than 3,400 smaller archaeological sites dating from pre-Columbian and later periods. The largest, Pueblo Bonito, stood five stories tall in places and once had 600 to 800 rooms and 37 kivas, large circular structures used for important religious and social ceremonies. **505.786.7014.**

(I) El Morro National Monument

Pg. 130, F3. Popularly known as Inscription Rock, this 200-foot-high sandstone outcropping is covered with names etched by explorers, pioneers, and soldiers over the centuries. The first European to do so was a Spaniard, Don Juan De Onate, who wrote his name near some ancient petroglyphs in 1605. About 2,000 more did the same until the practice was outlawed in 1906. Inscription Loop Trail, a half-mile walk along the base of the formation, permits a close-up view of the inscriptions, while Mesa Top Loop Trail, a two-mile switchback hike, takes visitors to the A'ts'ina Pueblo on top, which dates from the 1200s. **505.783.4226.**

(J) International UFO Museum and Research Center at Roswell, New Mexico

Pg. 131, T4. Although the U.S. Air Force has released films and documents supporting its claims to the contrary, many are convinced a UFO crashed near here one night in July 1947. But even skeptics will enjoy Roswell's homage to close encounters. Read witness accounts of the 1947 incident, ponder conspiracy theories, or visit the world's only art gallery exclusively featuring UFO, alien, and outer-space art. **505.625.9495.**

(K) Los Alamos

Pg. 130, D7. Here at the birthplace of the atomic bomb, the Bradbury Science Museum chronicles the history of nuclear technology and the $2 billion Manhattan Project, which developed the bombs dropped on Hiroshima and Nagasaki in 1945. The Los Alamos Historical Museum, housed in a rustic log building that was once the dining hall for the Manhattan Project community, details life in Los Alamos when it was a government-created secret city. **505.662.8105.**

(L) Salinas Pueblo Missions National Monument

Pg. 130, G7, H7, G6. Situated near several salt lakes an hour south of Albuquerque, the Salinas Pueblo missions were established by Franciscans, beginning in the 1620s, to Christianize the native population. The three modest missions, constructed of limestone and sandstone inside three separate Indian pueblos, were abandoned by the 1670s. Ruins of both the missions and the pueblos–Quarai, Gran Quivira, and Abo–still stand. **505.847.2585.**

(M) Sandia Peak

Pg. 131, R13. It takes about 20 minutes for the Sandia Peak Aerial Tramway to travel its 2.7-mile arc of cable, but it's a beautiful ride to the summit, one that takes you from the Sonoran Desert through forests of piñon and ponderosa pines and junipers. Go at sunset, when a golden blanket seems to drop slowly across the scrubland surrounding Albuquerque. There's an observation deck at the 10,378-foot summit, and trails on the back side for hiking, mountain biking, and skiing. **505.856.7325.**

With their unusual humanlike forms, the giant saguaro cacti are a striking sight in the Sonoran Desert of Arizona and New Mexico. The saguaro are one of only two groups of cacti that are large enough to be considered trees.

(N) Santa Fe Plaza

Pg. 131, T8. The Santa Fe Trail opened in 1822, linking Santa Fe to Independence, Missouri, and the city's plaza has been a major hub of trade ever since. You'll find dozens of Native Americans and others selling jewelry, pottery, and other handcrafted items within the shadow of the modest but elegant Palace of the Governors, the oldest continuously used public building in the country. The 1610 adobe structure now houses an outstanding collection of artifacts spanning New Mexico's rich history. **800.777.2489.**

New Mexico grows the vast majority of U.S. chile peppers. Besides adding heat and flavor to food, chiles are used in pharmaceuticals and cosmetic dyes – in fact, zoo-kept flamingos stay pink thanks to chile in their food.

(O) Taos Pueblo

Pg. 130, C8. For perhaps a thousand years, Tewa-speaking Taos Pueblo Indians have lived astride a river in two sprawling, multistory adobe structures. If you visit the pueblo–northernmost of 19 Native American pueblos in New Mexico and the only one where the original structures are inhabited–remember that this is neither a museum nor abandoned ruins. The pueblo is closed to visitors for a month or longer every spring. **505.758.1028.**

(P) White Sands National Monument

Pg. 131, L6. Pristine 20- to 60-foot mounds of pale gypsum migrate across the floor of the Tularosa Basin at a rate of 6 to 20 feet a year. The 16-mile Dunes Drive, which changes periodically with the gypsum's movement, loops through the heart of the dune field; hikers can enjoy 6.2 miles of marked trails. Located 15 miles west of Alamogordo, White Sands is the world's largest gypsum dune field, covering 275 square miles. **505.679.2599.**

Longhorn Country

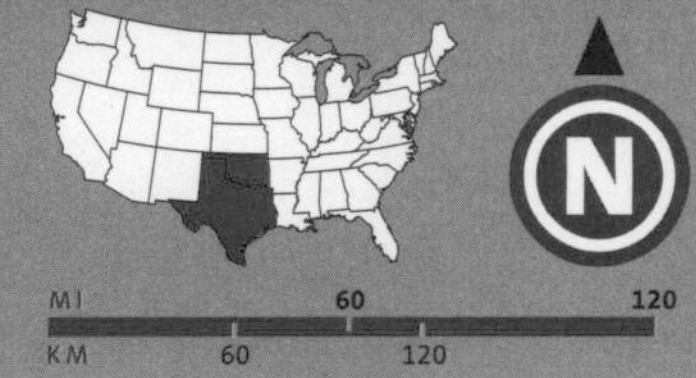

Texas has Spanish roots that reach back to late 18th-century settlements and missions, the first of which was Mission Ysleta in today's El Paso. Texan settlers won independence from Mexico in 1836, and before statehood in 1845, Texas reigned as an independent republic. During this time, country to the north served as the last stop on the Trail of Tears–the land of "removal" where displaced Native Americans tried to create a separate homeland in what became Oklahoma. Both Texas and the Sooner State were born of strong farm and ranch stock, growing up along the Chisholm Trail, which ran north from near San Antonio through cow towns like Fort Worth and the Indian Territory to railheads in Kansas. The great cattle drives of the 1860s and 1870s were followed by the discovery of oil, first at Bartlesville, Oklahoma, in 1897, and then near Beaumont, Texas, a few years later. By the start of the Roaring Twenties, more than half of America's oil was produced in Longhorn Country, just in time to fuel the country's greatest migration along the Mother Road, Route 66, during the Great Depression.

A vast plateau, the High Plains of the Texas Panhandle and western Oklahoma are the southern extreme of the Great Plains. Many major rivers traverse these states: The Red River forms much of the Oklahoma–Texas border as it drains into the Mississippi; and the Rio Grande, one of the longest and most historic rivers in North America, forms about 1,250 miles of the U. S.–Mexico border.

FEBRUARY

Charro Days Fiesta, Brownsville, TX
Starting with the traditional *grito* yell and a blast of mariachi music, this southernmost Texas city celebrates the *charro*–skilled horseman, hero of neighboring Mexico's folklore–with parades, street dances, and carnivals . . . not to mention great food. Begins last Thursday of the month.
956.542.4245

APRIL

World Championship Hog Calling Competition, Weatherford, OK
What do you call a 300-pound sow? Whatever you want, so long as it will get her to come to feed. Just don't try the same thing with your date at the Hog Call Ball that follows.
405.772.3301

Fiesta San Antonio, San Antonio, TX
The city's Hispanic roots come out in full force during this boisterous, exuberant, citywide party that includes parades, costume balls with revelers in historical outfits, and great Tex-Mex food.
210.227.5191

Buccaneer Days, Corpus Christi, TX
The Spanish established a trading post here in 1839, an event that is celebrated in this Gulf town with activities on land and sea. Watch or participate in the sailing regattas around the harbor; creatively designed floats are on display in parades throughout the historic district.
512.882.3242

JUNE

Santa Fe Trail Daze, Boise City, OK
Bus tours take you around the country to explore historical reminders of this epic trail. There's also a championship posthole-digging contest.
580.544.3344

Red Earth Festival, Oklahoma City, OK
Representatives from a hundred tribes in Oklahoma and throughout the U. S. and Canada gather for a competitions, displays of traditional crafts and fine arts, and dancing contests.
405.427.5228

SEPTEMBER

State Fair of Oklahoma, Oklahoma City, OK
Check out the two-headed chickens and the giant bulls, and don't miss the professional championship rodeo either.
405.948.6700

NOVEMBER

Beavers Bend Folk Festival, Broken Bow, OK
It's worth a visit just to see the area's spectacular fall foliage, which acts as a backdrop to this annual festival of local arts, music, and regional food.
405.494.6497

International Championship Chili Cookoff, Terlingua, TX
How do you like your chili? Beans or no beans, hotter than a pistol or mildly seasoned? Find out at the granddaddy of chili cook-offs.
806.352.8783

Enchanted Rock State Natural Area C

Padre Island National Seashore D

San Antonio Missions National Historic Park H

Texas

A The Alamo
Pg. 163, S24. Although little remains of the state's most visited landmark, the Alamo is still a symbol of Texas and the independent spirit that founded it. All 189 fighters who held the Alamo for 13 days in 1836 died but were not forgotten: Their deaths became a rallying cry for Gen. Sam Houston as he and his troops soon defeated the Mexican army at the Battle of San Jacinto. Visitors can tour the old mission church and view artifacts pertaining to the Alamo's heroes, including Jim Bowie and Davy Crockett. **210.225.1391.**

B Big Thicket National Preserve
Pg. 162, N23. This 86,000-acre preserve was established in 1974 to protect the unique biological crossroads where swamp, forest, plains, and desert converge. The diversity of flora and fauna is dramatic: 300 species of birds, 50 different reptiles (including a small population of alligators), and nearly 1,000 types of flowering plants. **409.246.2337.**

C Hill Country
Pg. 163, N14. Some visit Hill Country because of its climate, said to be one of the most moderate in the nation. But most come for attractions like Enchanted Rock State Natural Area, site of a massive dome of pink granite towering 425 feet that is shrouded in Native American legends of ghost fires and human sacrifices. Nearby Kerrville is home to the Hill Country Museum, a Romanesque stone building filled with local memorabilia. Billing itself as "cowboy capital of the world," Bandera is surrounded by working and guest ranches. Concan's Garner State Recreation Park offers family-oriented activities along the Frío River. And Ingram's Stonehenge in the Hills replicates not only the English megaliths but also Easter Island-type monuments. **830.792.3535.**

King Ranch in Texas is the largest ranch in the United States, covering more area than all of Rhode Island.

D Padre Island National Seashore
Pg. 163, U17. This barrier island's early claim to fame was based on legends of galleon treasure shipwrecked offshore. Today it's noted for wide sandy beaches, excellent fishing, and abundant bird and marine life. Largely uninhabited, Padre Island stretches along the Gulf Coast for more than 113 miles, with 45-foot-high sand dunes and warm offshore water. Camping is permitted in designated areas, but a ban on treasure hunting and metal detectors is strictly enforced. **512.937.2621.**

E Panhandle-Plains Historical Museum
Pg. 160, E10. Housed in the restored T-Anchor Ranch in Canyon, Panhandle-Plains Historical Museum is dedicated to the preservation of northwest Texas heritage. The Petroleum Wing displays an authentic wooden cable-tool drilling rig, along with exhibits on the boom years of the 1920s and '30s. A rancher's home, saloon, blacksmith shop, and school are featured in Pioneer Town, and exhibits on ranching include saddles, guns, and a chuck wagon. At Palo Duro Canyon State Park, a short drive to the east, brilliant multicolored rock walls rise 800 feet above a seemingly humble fork of the Red River. Museum, **806.656.2244.** Park, **806.488.2227.**

When oil drillers struck the Lucas Gusher in Beaumont in 1901, the piping was blown straight out of the ground. The site produced 75,000 barrels of oil a day in its first year of production.

F Space Center Houston
Pg. 164, K7. The past, present, and future of space flight are revealed on a grand scale at Space Center Houston, located in the NASA Lyndon B. Johnson Space Center. Interactive exhibits, films, and tours are dedicated to the adventures and accomplishments of NASA's manned spaceflight programs, and visitors can simulate landing the space shuttle, touch a moon rock, and experience a simulated flight in the Manned Maneuvering Unit. **800.972.0369.**

G The Sixth Floor Museum at Dealey Plaza
Pg. 164, H8. There once was a land called Camelot, but it came to a violent end on November 22, 1963, when Lee Harvey Oswald allegedly shot John F. Kennedy from a sniper's nest on the sixth floor of the Texas Book Depository. Many Texans, embarrassed by the stigma, tried to have the dowdy red-brick building torn down, but instead the sixth floor was turned into a thought-provoking museum exploring the life, times, death, and legacy of JFK. On view are films (including portions of the always freshly horrifying home movie by Abraham Zapruder), historic photographs, and artifacts relating to Oswald and other, unwilling participants in the shocking event, including Lyndon Johnson and J.D. Tippit, a Dallas policeman who was murdered while trying to question Oswald. **214.747.6660.**

H San Antonio Missions National Historical Park
Pg. 163, W21. Besides the Alamo, four other missions were founded by Franciscans in the early 18th century, intended as bases for converting the local Coahuiltecan. Mission Concepción looks much as it did when completed in 1755, with fragments of frescoes decorating the interior. Mission San Francisco de la Espada is, like the others, an active parish and has been restored several times. With its carved stone ornamentation, Mission San José is the most beautiful and offers a complete portrait of daily mission life. Mission San Juan Capistrano's charming little chapel with a bell tower creates a unique spiritual ambience. **210.534.8833.**

OK 146
TX 160
OK 243
TX 246

Oklahoma is part of the High Plains, wide and flat.
If you raise your arms, they touch the sky,
and if you spread them, they reach the end of the earth.

—DOUGLAS REED, *FAR AND WIDE*, 1951

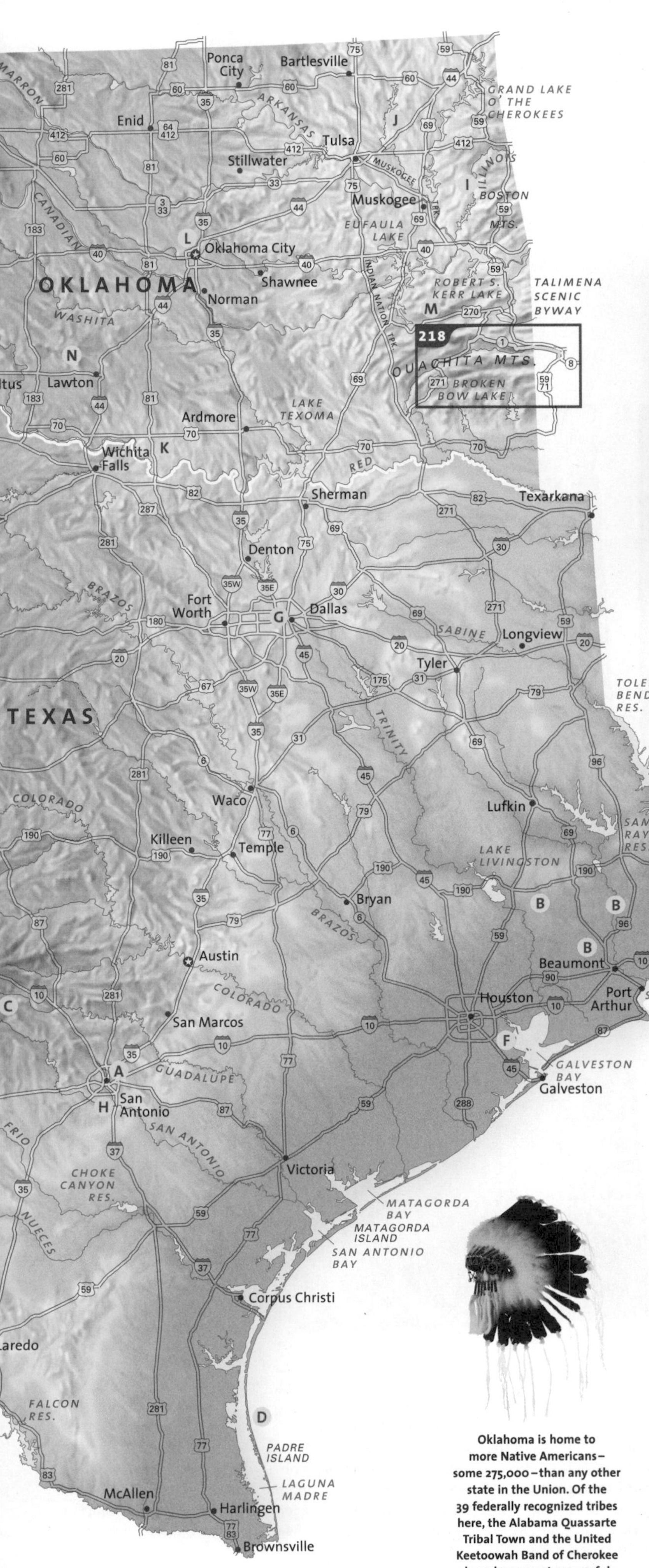

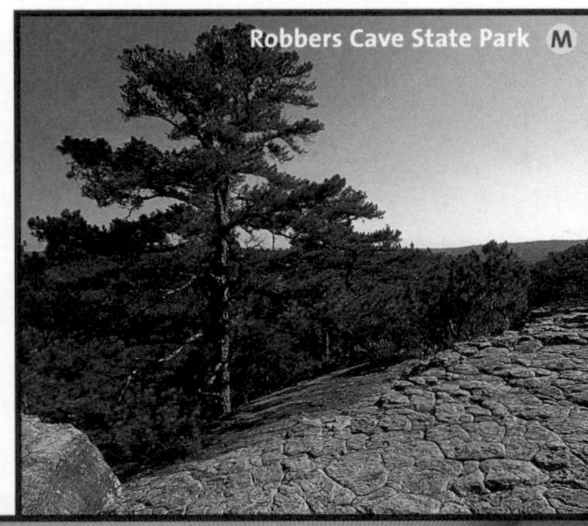
Robbers Cave State Park (M)

National Cowboy Hall of Fame & Western Heritage Center (L)

Cherokee Heritage Center (I)

Wichita Mountains Wildlife Refuge (N)

Oklahoma

(I) Cherokee Heritage Center
Pg. 147, E19. Tahlequah—the termination point of the Trail of Tears—became the Cherokee Nation's capital in 1841. Today, Cherokee customs are re-created in the Cherokee Heritage Center, which includes the Tsa-La-Gi Ancient Village, illustrating daily life before European contact, and the Cherokee National Museum, which presents exhibits on Cherokee history. The Trail of Tears Drama, held July to mid-August, reenacts the Cherokee saga from forced exile to Oklahoma statehood in 1907. **918.456.6007.**

(J) Will Rogers Memorial
Pg. 147, C17. Upon entering this museum in Claremore dedicated to America's unofficial ambassador, visitors are greeted by a large statue of Rogers, the base engraved with his most famous statement, "I never met a man I didn't like." Placed regally on a 20-acre hilltop, the memorial contains photographs, films, radio broadcasts, and hundreds of personal mementos. Rogers's collection of rare saddles and cowboy items is also on view. **918.341.0719.**

(K) Chisholm Trail
Pg. 146, K12. Created to herd the millions of cattle roaming Texas after the Civil War, the Chisholm Trail stretched from Texas to Kansas railheads, where the cattle were shipped east. Visitors to the Chisholm Trail Museum in Kingfisher are treated to a firsthand experience of living conditions in the late 1800s. Exhibits chronicle the business of Westerners, respectable and otherwise, from trail blazer Jesse Chisholm to outlaws Dick Yeager and the Dalton Gang. **405.375.5176.**

(L) National Cowboy Hall of Fame & Western Heritage Center
Pg. 146, J4. One of the world's largest collections of Western lore, the National Cowboy Hall of Fame, in Oklahoma City, is an affectionate tribute to the men and women who pioneered the West. Paintings by Frederic Remington and Charles Russell are found here alongside pop-cult items like the John Wayne collection. The Rodeo Hall of Fame preserves the culture created by cowboys and cowgirls, whose trophies, saddles, and lassos are on exhibit. **405.478.2250.**

(M) Robbers Cave State Park
Pg. 147, G18. The main passageways (once leading to a 20-by-20-foot room) have caved in since outlaws like Jesse James and Belle Starr used this area to escape federal authorities, but the legends have been kept alive by the more recent discovery of a stash of gold rings. Located outside Wilburton, the park is popular among rappelers, equestrians, and cave explorers. Lookout Point, at the summit, provides a panoramic view of the Fourche Maline River Valley. **918.465.2565.**

(N) Wichita Mountains Wildlife Refuge
Pg. 146, H10. Designated a reserve in 1901, the Wichita Mountains Wildlife Refuge (near Lawton) is home to bison, elk, deer, and Texas longhorn cattle. Its 60,000 acres are maintained in a wild state, but a paved scenic highway allows glimpses of wildlife from a car. Observe the annual roundup of the big animals when helicopters and four-wheel-drive vehicles are used to herd them into an elaborate corral. **405.429.3222.**

Oklahoma is home to more Native Americans—some 275,000—than any other state in the Union. Of the 39 federally recognized tribes here, the Alabama Quassarte Tribal Town and the United Keetoowah Band of Cherokee have been most successful in retaining their languages and cultures.

Texas is a state of mind. Texas is an obsession.
Above all, Texas is a nation in every sense of the word.

—JOHN STEINBECK, *TRAVELS WITH CHARLEY*, 1962

20 Southern Rockies

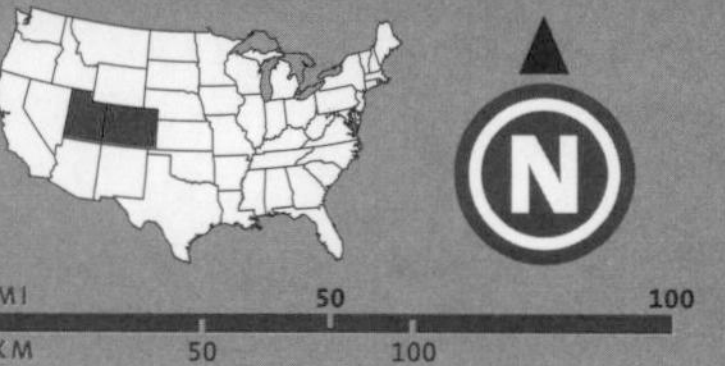

For pathfinder John C. Fremont, crossing the southern Rockies in the 1840s must have seemed a fool's errand. After trekking for weeks across the prairie, he and his men were forced to scale snowcapped peaks, making their way down the western slope through dense forests. They had mighty rivers to cross and maze-like canyons to navigate before coming to the arid land of the Great Basin. The extreme terrain of the southern Rockies shaped the early crossings as well as the temperaments of the settlers who followed, from the industrious Mormons to the dreamers and schemers digging for gold and silver. That resourceful spirit is still evident today in old mining towns like Park City and Telluride, which have preserved their rich histories while reinventing themselves as major ski resorts. The cities have erected an array of cultural attractions, yet most visitors to the region are still drawn by Utah's great national parks and Colorado's stunning mountains. In its beauty and remoteness, the land that rose up to test Fremont's will continues to challenge the human imagination.

The Wasatch Range and Rocky Mountains run like twin spines down the centers of neighboring Utah and Colorado, separated by the Colorado Plateau. To the west of the peaks is the vast expanse known as the Great Basin; to the east, the Great Plains.

A weird, lovely, fantastic object out of nature like Delicate Arch has the curious ability to remind us – like rock and sunlight and wind and wilderness – that out there is a different world, older and greater and deeper by far than ours, a world which surrounds and sustains the little world of men as sea and sky surround and sustain a ship.

–EDWARD ABBEY, *DESERT SOLITAIRE*, 1968

JANUARY

National Western Stock Show and Rodeo, Denver, CO
What do ranchers do in the middle of winter? They go to Denver to exhibit–and buy–horses and cattle. Sheep, hogs, llamas, and a vast array of farm machinery are also on display. This is the largest livestock show in the world.
800.336.6977

Sundance Film Festival, Park City, UT
Hollywood pulls on its snow pants to find the next big thing at Robert Redford's annual showcase of independent film.
801.322.1700

FEBRUARY

Steamboat Springs Winter Carnival, Steamboat Springs, CO
Almost like a rodeo on ice, with strange events like snow-shovel racing, broomball, and a parade on skis.
800.922.2722

JUNE

Mountain Man Rendezvous, Kit Carson, CO
Modern mountain men–and women–gather to celebrate the fur-trapping days of yore with fancy costumes, Dutch-oven cookery, 19th-century craft-making sessions, and black-powder shooting contests.
719.962.3532

Telluride Bluegrass Festival, Telluride, CO
Some of the best bluegrass, folk, and country musicians get together for outdoor shows in Town Park, with its breathtaking views.
800.624.2422

Utah Shakespearean Festival, Cedar City, UT
The setting is stunning and so are most of the productions of the Bard's work. Modern plays also share the festival's calendar, which runs through early September.
435.586.7878

JULY

Crested Butte Wildflower Festival, Crested Butte, CO
The "wildflower capital of Colorado" celebrates its natural resource with tours, exhibits, art workshops, and a sale of antique botanical prints.
800.545.4505

AUGUST

Festival of the American West, Wellsville, UT
Beware of the guys trying to sell you snake oil at the medicine show, part of a celebration of the people and events that created the West.
800.225.3378

SEPTEMBER

Oktoberfest Vail, Vail, CO
Events include a reenactment of the 1810 wedding of King Ludwig I of Bavaria to Princess Therese, celebration of which, the story goes, was the first Oktoberfest.
970.476.9090

Temple Square District, Salt Lake City (F)

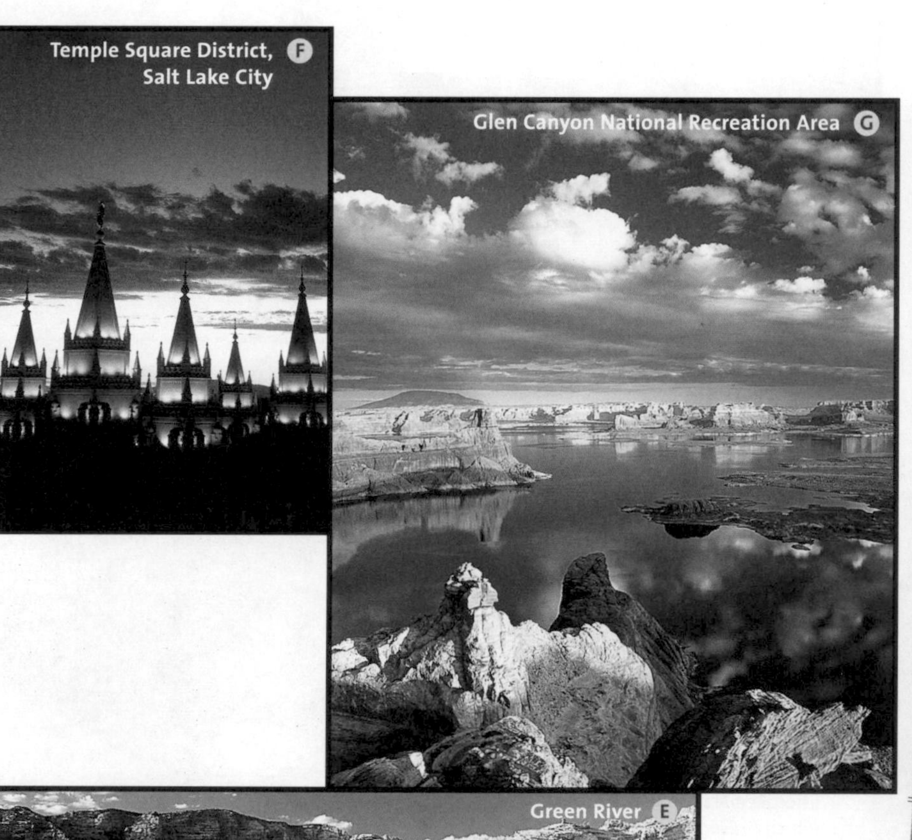

Glen Canyon National Recreation Area (G)

Green River (E)

Great Salt Lake (C)

Utah

(A) Coral Pink Sand Dunes State Park
Pg. 165, N3. Sand buggies and four-wheelers race gleefully up and down wind-ribbed pink hills in a section of this 3,700-acre park. Quieter moments among the 200-foot-tall dunes await those who venture in on the hiking trails, where mule deer, coyote, eagle, and jackrabbit sightings are common. But watch out for rattlesnakes. **435.648.2800.**

(B) Moab
Pg. 165, K8. Moab today is the capital of extreme sports–mountain biking, rock climbing, river rafting, you name it. Many residents have launched businesses–from outdoor guide companies to chic bed-and-breakfasts–to facilitate the thrill seekers. **800.635.6622.**

(C) Great Salt Lake
Pg. 165, E3. The story goes that Brigham Young chose to end the Mormons' cross-country odyssey at the barren Salt Lake Basin because he figured no one else would want the place. Though as much as eight times saltier than the ocean, the West's largest lake is an appealing enough environment for tens of thousands of gulls and waterfowl who nest or pass through. It's also a dynamic natural wonder: In just the past century, it has varied in size from about 1,000 square miles to nearly 2,500. **801.250.1898.**

(D) Natural Bridges National Monument
Pg. 165, M7. A nine-mile scenic loop takes you through this compact park, best known for its three pink-and-white sandstone natural bridges–Sipapu, Kachina, and Owachomo–all carved by tributaries of the Colorado River following the last ice age. The park is also noted for its early Puebloan ruins and artifacts. **435.692.1234.**

(E) Green River
Pg. 165, J7. This riverside burg of 866 has become a popular launching site for hikers, bikers, and ATVers who want to explore the desert, and for rafting businesses that guide small groups on expeditions through canyon land. Trips range from excursions over relatively calm waters to adventures down whitewater rapids and include inexpensive day trips or multiday floats. **435.564.3526.**

(F) Temple Square District, Salt Lake City
Pg. 165, B8. At the heart of Utah's meticulously planned capital, a 15-foot-tall stone wall encloses historic Temple Square, world headquarters of the Mormon Church. The square's centerpiece is the Salt Lake Temple, whose soaring east spire is crowned with a golden statue of the angel Moroni. Just to the west stretches the oblong dome of the Tabernacle, home of the world-famous Mormon Tabernacle Choir. The public is welcome to visit the Tabernacle on tours or for concerts. **800.537.9703.**

(G) Glen Canyon National Recreation Area
Pg. 165, M6. From above, Lake Powell's former life as several rivers is evident. Created by the 1966 completion of Arizona's Glen Canyon Dam on the Colorado River, the lake backed up into some 90 once-dry side canyons, creating a shoreline more than 1,900 miles long. The nation's second largest artificial lake now serves as a popular play pool for water-skiers, houseboaters, and fishermen. Bullfrog Marina is a good jumping-off point for waterborne excursions to the world's largest natural stone bridge, at Rainbow Bridge National Monument. **520.608.6404.**

CO 76
UT 165
CO 233
UT 247

Aspen N

Dinosaur National Monument J

Durango & Silverton Narrow Gauge Railroad I

Great Sand Dunes National Monument K

Colorado

H Black Canyon of the Gunnison National Monument
Pg. 76, H8. Upon viewing the chasm guarding the Gunnison River, some feel awe, others vertigo, and more than a few sense something ominous about the sunless canyon that cuts a gash in the Colorado Plateau. South Rim Road takes you to eleven overlooks, including Narrows View, where the canyon slims to a 1,150-foot gap and plunges 1,725 feet from rim to floor. **800.873.0244.**

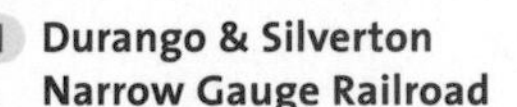

I Durango & Silverton Narrow Gauge Railroad
Pg. 76, M7. The Denver & Rio Grande Western Railroad once carried freight and passengers throughout the Colorado mountains, but all that remains is one dazzling 45-mile run, from Durango to Silverton. One to four times a day, a coal-fired steam locomotive chugs out of Durango's 1882 depot and pulls a string of period coaches through the San Juan National Forest. You can hop off for an afternoon of fishing or get to Silverton by lunchtime; the ride's leisurely pace means a round-trip and the stopover will fill a day. **888.872.4607.**

Palisade, Colorado, is famous for its fruit orchards, which produce 300,000 bushels of peaches each year.

J Dinosaur Valley
Pg. 76, G6. The Cretaceous and Jurassic periods come back to life in this esteemed Grand Junction museum. In one room, menacing dinosaur robots swing their tails and roar as you walk by. Also interesting is an active paleontology laboratory. In Dinosaur National Monument, 100 miles north, bones of giants such as the stegosaurus can be seen. **970.243.3466.**

K Great Sand Dunes National Monument
Pg. 77, K12. Hard against the Sangre de Cristo Mountains, far from any sea or desert, lounge the tallest sand dunes in North America. It's a lot of work to reach the top of the tallest dune, piled some 700 feet high, but the views of the valley—and the sliding, bouncing descent—make it worth the effort. **719.378.2312.**

L Telluride
Pg. 76, K7. This famed ski town has so many summer festivals that a do-nothing weekend might be the best hope its 1,500 residents have of catching a breather. The big events include the Bluegrass Festival in June, a jazz celebration in August, and a noted film festival over Labor Day weekend. Come winter, skiers flood challenging slopes that overlook Telluride's box canyon. **800.525.3455.**

Colorado is a grand seat to see the world from.
—WILL ROGERS, 1933

A member of the squirrel family, the yellow-bellied marmot is known in the high country of Utah as a "whistle pig" because of its unusual warning shriek.

M United States Air Force Academy
Pg. 77, G14. Even doves are likely to be intrigued by this officer-training campus, which sits appropriately in the sky-high community of Colorado Springs. Founded in 1954, the 18,000-acre campus is well known for its unusual architecture, particularly the chapel spires, made of tubular aluminum in the shape of tetrahedrons. A visitor center has exhibits on academy history and cadet life. **719.333.7742.**

N Aspen
Pg. 76, F9. Aspen began with a boom. In the 1880s it grew from ragtag mining camp to one of the world's top silver producers. Now famed for its daunting slopes, glamorous denizens, and après-ski nightlife, Aspen is still dotted with large Victorian houses and grand public structures like the 1889 Wheeler Opera House. **970.925.1940.**

O Black American West Museum & Heritage Center
Pg. 77, E14. You'd never know it from early Hollywood Westerns, but perhaps a third of the cowhands who worked in the Old West were African Americans. This fine Denver museum chronicles the lives and contributions of black cowboys, soldiers, homesteaders, and pioneers in the crossing and taming of the Western frontier. **303.292.2566.**

The place names of the northern Rockies speak of earlier times and legendary characters. Cody, Cheyenne, and Custer evoke the spirit of a rugged land and a turbulent history: Native American tribes, prospectors, cowboys, soldiers, settlers, and mountain men have all left their mark here. After Lewis and Clark traveled through Montana and Idaho in 1805–6, fur trappers followed, hunting beaver into the 1840s and later guiding pioneers along the Oregon Trail. Today, Butte and ghost towns like Bannack are reminders of the great mountain gold rush of the 1860s that lured settlers and, in turn, inflamed conflict with the Sioux. The northern Rocky Mountains are the spine of Wyoming and Montana, separating east from west in the continental United States. To the east are wide expanses of open country, large-scale farms and ranches, and isolated pockets of civilization. To the west are forests, logging towns, and, increasingly, resorts and trophy homes belonging to the sports and entertainment elite.

Two great landforms meet in this rugged country of sky-high mountains and open prairies: the Rocky Mountains and the Great Plains. From the long ridge of the Continental Divide, great rivers like the Snake, Columbia, and Missouri start their journeys either west, toward the Pacific Ocean, or east, toward the Gulf of Mexico.

I glance higher for some hint of the weather, and the square of air broadens to become the blue expanse over the Montana rangeland, so vast and vaulting that it rears, from the foundation of the plains horizon, to form the walls and roof of all life's experience that my younger self could imagine, a single great house of sky.

—IVAN DOIG, *THIS HOUSE OF SKY*, 1978

JANUARY

Winter Carnival, McCall, ID
When the snow flies around this unspoiled resort community, the townsfolk get ready for spirited contests in ice-sculpting, dogsledding, and cross-country skiing.
208.634.7631

FEBRUARY

Race to the Sky Sled Dog Race, Helena, MT
If you don't have time to travel to Alaska, try out this dogsled race. Mushers take on the Montana wilderness for days at a time in this 350-mile contest.
406.442.4008

MAY

Cowboy Poetry & Music Festival, Rock Springs, WY
Cowboy poets from across the West gather in Rock Springs to recite their rhymes in one of the oldest gatherings of this new literary genre.
307.362.6212

JULY

Sun Valley Ice Shows, Sun Valley, ID
At dusk on Saturdays throughout the summer, Olympic champion figure skaters like Oksana Baiul and Scott Hamilton perform in an outdoor rink at historic Sun Valley Resort.
800.635.8261

Salmon River Days, Salmon, ID
The little town at the heart of one of the great white-water rafting runs in the West closes one of its streets for three days to celebrate the Fourth of July in the way only a little town could.
208.756.2100

Cheyenne Frontier Days, Cheyenne, WY
A hefty prize purse – the largest for any outdoor rodeo in the world – draws the best to this celebration, which also includes country-western entertainment and parades.
307.778.7200

AUGUST

Running of the Sheep, Reedpoint, MT
Oh, sure, it's easy to outrace a hefty bull, but try and outrun a few thousand sheep. One of the oddest small-town festivals in Montana, this event harkens back to the days when shepherds brought their flocks down through the town's streets after a summer in mountain meadows.
406.326.9911

NOVEMBER

Bobcat-Griz Football Game, Missoula or Bozeman, MT
You can divide the state's population between those who favor the University of Montana and those who root for Montana State. Everybody shows up for this game.
406.243.4051

Coeur d'Alene Lake D

Sun Valley C

Sawtooth National Recreation Area B

Idaho

A Craters of the Moon National Monument
Pg. 89, L6. The charred volcanic landscape of this preserve in south-central Idaho invites comparison to the moon, with its desolate lava plains and cauldron of craters. This 83-square-mile showcase of volcanism – part of a vast lava flow that oozed out of the earth's crust – supports a surprising variety of life, including 150 bird species and more than 200 plant types. A seven-mile loop road, open from late April to mid-November, offers an easy way to see most of the highlights. **208.527.3257.**

B Sawtooth National Recreation Area
Pg. 89, J4. The Sawtooth Mountains slash across one side of this sprawling recreation area, which embraces three other mountain ranges, several large lakes, rolling meadows, dozens of hot springs, and the headwaters of the Salmon River. The most popular section is along the east slope of the Sawtooth Range, where there's easy access to several hundred miles of trails. Another way to see the wilderness is on a white-water trip down the Salmon; outfitters offer half-day and one-day trips. **208.727.5013.**

C Sun Valley
Pg. 89, K5. Looking for a way to increase travel aboard the Union Pacific Railroad, W. Averell Harriman created a European-style ski resort near the old mining town of Ketchum in 1936. He then hired a publicist to lure stars like Gary Cooper and Lucille Ball, and the rich and famous have been coming ever since. Skiing is the main attraction, but in summer Sun Valley is a great base for hiking, fishing, and rafting down the Salmon River. **800.634.3347.**

D Coeur d'Alene Lake
Pg. 89, C1. The Idaho Panhandle is known for thick forests and scores of beautiful deep-blue lakes. One of these jewels, Coeur d'Alene, has been a popular tourist destination since the 1910s, when the preferred way to cruise its 20-mile expanse was to hop on a paddle-wheel steamboat. Lake cruises are still popular; some take you up the St. Joe River, where waters can buoy daylong rafting trips. **208.765.4000.**

E Shoshone Falls/ Shoshone Ice Caves
Pg. 89, M5, L5. Shoshone Falls is known as the Niagara Falls of the West, though at 212 feet it's about 50 feet higher than Niagara. Forty-five miles north of the falls are the Shoshone Ice Caves, home to a three-block-long underground lava cave chilled to about 30°F. Falls, **208.736.2265.** Caves, **208.886.2058.**

F Nez Perce National Historical Park
Pg. 89, E2. A collection of 38 sites spread across four states, this unique park focuses on the Nez Perce's early encounters with European Americans – at missions, gold camps, and on battlefields. The visitor center, in Spalding, overlooks the Clearwater River where Presbyterian missionaries settled in 1838, and uses artifacts and a film to introduce the tribe's history and culture. **208.843.2261.**

I asked an Idaho patriot why potatoes were so big. Answer: "We fertiliz'em with cornmeal and irrigate them with milk."

—JOHN GUNTHER, *INSIDE U.S.A.*, 1947

Idaho is the land of Famous Potatoes, a nickname that started in 1927 as a motto on the state license plate.

WY 176
MT 122
ID 89
WY 248
MT 240
ID 234

Montana

G Bighorn Canyon National Recreation Area
Pg. 123, J14. The Yellowtail Dam on the Bighorn River creates a 71-mile-long reservoir that snakes through high limestone cliffs on the Montana–Wyoming border. The main access point in Montana is at Fort Smith, though many water sports enthusiasts float in from the marina at Lovell, Wyoming. Tour-boat excursions are available, as are boat rentals and campgrounds. **406.666.2412.**

H Flathead Valley
Pg. 122, C4. Crystal blue Flathead Lake is the center of Flathead Valley, the resort and recreational hub of western Montana. Trout are plentiful here and landlocked salmon can be caught in spring and fall. Nearby is the Pablo National Wildlife Refuge, where some 80,000 mallards, Canada geese, coots, and other waterfowl stop over during their migrations. At the northern end of the valley is Big Mountain, one of Montana's largest ski resorts. **406.752.5501.**

I Little Bighorn Battlefield National Monument
Pg. 123, J15. On June 25, 1876, Lt. Col. George Armstrong Custer and all of the men in his immediate command–more than 250 members of the Seventh Cavalry–died here in battle with 2,000 warriors from the Sioux and Cheyenne nations. A 4.5-mile car tour of the battlefield chronologically recounts the day's grisly events, but it's better to walk the land, listening to the prairie winds in the dry grass and imagining the ghastly sounds of battle. **406.638.2621.**

J Virginia City/Nevada City
Pg. 122, J7. In 1863 a small group of prospectors struck gold off the Yellowstone River. Within a year, up sprang Nevada City and its sister, Virginia City–the Montana gold rush was on. Today Virginia City is a popular historical site, with two small museums and a boothill cemetery (a graveyard of people who died violently, or "with their boots on"). Just a mile west is Nevada City, a ghost town of weathered shops and houses filled with antiques and mementos. The Alder Gulch Work Train makes the half-hour trip between the two cities. **406.843.5377.**

One of the nation's largest remaining prairie elk populations, at about 5,500 head, is located in the Missouri River Breaks in Montana.

Flathead Valley H

K Museum of the Rockies
Pg. 122, J9. Known for its dinosaur collection, planetarium, early Native American artifacts, and frontier curiosities like buggies, wagons, and early automobiles, this Bozeman museum takes you from the birth of the Rockies to the dawning of the 20th century. The planetarium includes a tour of the night sky, using Native American legends about the creation of the universe. **406.994.2251.**

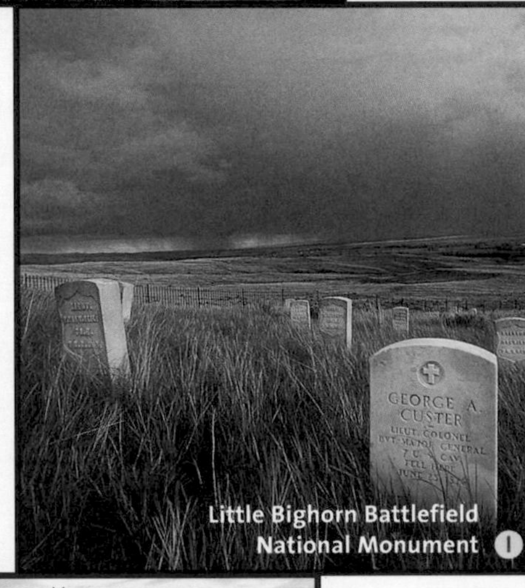
Little Bighorn Battlefield National Monument I

Virginia City J

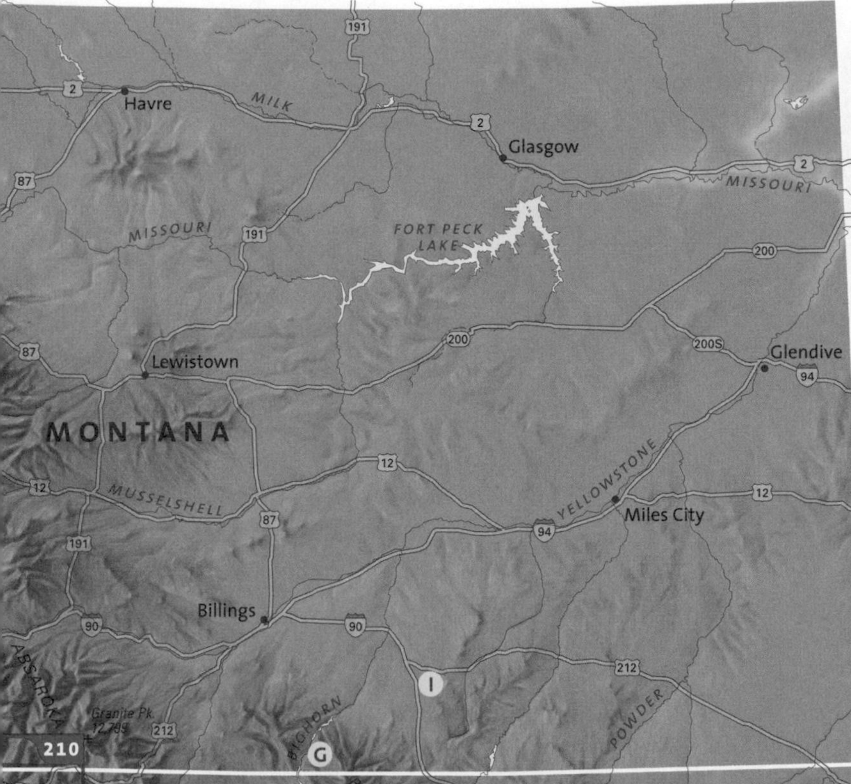

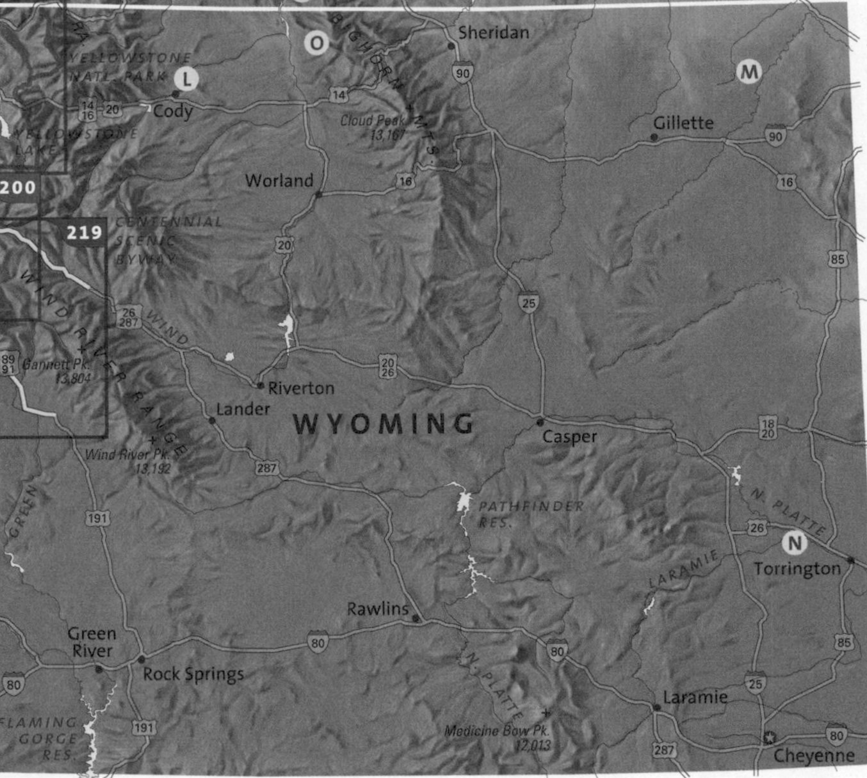

Wyoming

L Buffalo Bill Historical Center
Pg. 176, B6. In the town Buffalo Bill Cody named for himself, the biggest draw is a complex of four museums holding an unparalleled collection of Western art and Americana. One is devoted to firearms, another to the Plains Indians, and another to the work of artists like Charles M. Russell and Frederic Remington. Of course, Cody needs a museum of his own, because the world's most famous cowboy fit into one adventurous lifetime the Pony Express, the Civil War, the Indian Wars, and his world-traveling Wild West Show. **307.587.4771.**

Devils Tower National Monument M

M Devils Tower National Monument
Pg. 176, A12. In 1906 Teddy Roosevelt made this geological wonder the nation's first designated monument. A sacred site to Native Americans, this lonely cluster of rock columns (one reaching 865 feet) was also an important landmark to westward-bound pioneers, who could spot it rising above the plains from a hundred miles away. Its sheer, striated face makes it a popular challenge for climbers. **307.467.5283.**

Fort Laramie National Historic Site N

N Fort Laramie National Historic Site
Pg. 176, F12. Don't look for this former fur-trading post in Laramie: Despite the name, it's nearer the Nebraska border. Acquired by the United States Army in 1849, the site became a major military post and an important stopping point for pioneers traveling the Oregon Trail. With painstaking care, about a dozen historic structures have been restored and refurnished, including the cavalry barracks, officers' quarters, and post trader's store. **307.837.2221.**

O Medicine Wheel Natural Historic Landmark
Pg. 176, A8. As at Stonehenge, mystery shrouds the meaning of the 28 limestone spokes that comprise the ancient Medicine Wheel. But there is little doubt that this site atop Medicine Mountain was and still is sacred to Native Americans. Constructed between A.D. 1200 and 1700, the landmark – 80 yards around and now protected behind a wire fence – is still used by the Arapaho, Sioux, Shoshone, Crow, Cheyenne, and other tribes during the ceremonial season, June through October. **307.548.6541.**

Rodeo was originally a way for cowboys to showcase their riding skills, but it has grown into an immensely popular entertainment. Cody, Wyoming, the "rodeo capital of the world," has held close to 90 rodeos each summer since 1938, drawing 100,000 spectators annually.

I looked into a gulf 1,700 feet deep with eagles and fish hawks circling far below.
And the sides of that gulf were one wild welter of color –
crimson, emerald, cobalt, ochre, amber, honey splashed with port wine,
snow white, vermilion, lemon, and silver gray, in wide washes. . . .
So far below that no sound of its strife could reach us, the Yellowstone River ran –
a finger-wide strip of jade green.

– RUDYARD KIPLING, *AMERICAN NOTES*, 1891

Northern Great Plains

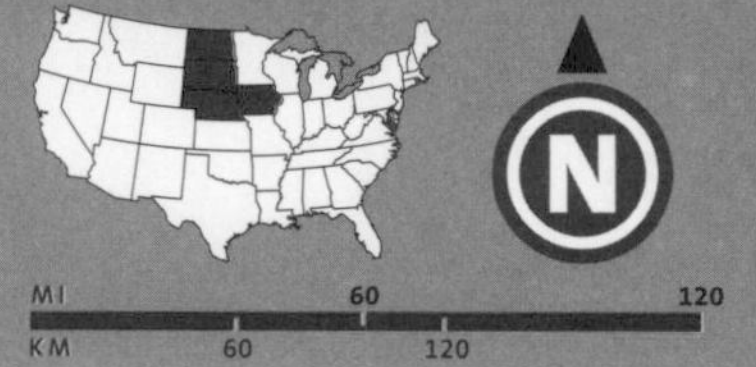

Far from a flat, monotonous sea of grass, the northern reaches of the Great Plains are a gently sloping highland accented by buttes, sandhills, badlands, rolling farmlands and grasslands, and beautiful valleys. Formed by glaciers 20,000 years ago, this land was once roamed by camels and three-toed horses. The Great Plains begin just east of the Missouri River where the drift prairie gives way to the mineral-rich Missouri Plateau. For 500 miles the land rises, at an average rate of ten feet a mile, across the Dakotas and Nebraska, until it bumps into the Rocky Mountains. The northern Great Plains were the setting for the West's expansion, and the land is crisscrossed by historic byways such as the Oregon and Mormon Trails. Many of its cities began as frontier outposts for supplying the 350,000-plus pioneers who waited for spring to begin traveling in the deep, muddy ruts left by prairie schooners headed for the Far West. It's also rich in Western legend: Early explorers Lewis and Clark came this way, as did Colonel Custer, Wild Bill Hickok, and Calamity Jane. For the most part, it's still a land of wide-open spaces with a large rural population and a strong agrarian economy.

Iowa's relatively flat land of gently rolling prairies is filled with deep, black soil, some of the most fertile farm country in the world. To the west, a gradual increase in elevation leads to the hills and highlands of the Great Plains, which extend on the east side of the Rockies from Texas north into Canada.

I would never have been president if it had not been for my experiences in North Dakota.

– THEODORE ROOSEVELT

MARCH

North Dakota Winter Show, Valley City, ND
The end of winter is celebrated in a state-fair atmosphere that includes steer roping, bull riding, and other traditional rodeo events. There's also livestock contests and pioneer dancing.
800.437.0218

Crane Watch, Platte, NE
One of the most magnificent sights anywhere in the Great Plains is watching half a million sandhill cranes swoop over the Platte River as they return to the adjoining wetlands in spring. Special sunrise and sunset crane tours are organized by a volunteer group, Wings Over the Platte.
800.658.3178

JUNE

NCAA College World Series, Omaha, NE
Omaha's Rosenblatt Stadium is host to one of the best collegiate sports playoffs in the nation. Teams play baseball for weeks in an effort to make the finals.
800.332.1819

Laura Ingalls Wilder Pageant, De Smet, SD
The Little House on the Prairie comes to life for three weekends beginning in June as South Dakota celebrates this famous author with an outdoor play based on her stories. There are also tours of the Ingalls' family home.
605.692.2108

Iowa Games Regional Qualifying Festival, Waterloo and Cedar Falls, IA
Men and women from all over Iowa compete in track and field, swimming, and other Olympic sports at this festival, which is open to people of all ages and abilities.
319.233.3531

JULY

Northern Plains Indian Culture Fest, Knife River Indian Villages National Historic Site, ND
The earth-lodge-dwelling Mandan, Hidatsa, Arikara, and other Northern Plains tribes show off their art, dancing, and crafts at this annual event.
701.745.3300

SEPTEMBER

Great Plains Old Time Fiddling Contest, Vermillion, SD
You couldn't have a square dance without a fiddle player, which is why a musician who could really play that instrument was an asset to any rural community. Dueling fiddlers compete to see who's the best of the best.
605.677.5306

Ghost Baseball Players, Dyersville, IA
Actors and ball players dress up as Shoeless Joe Jackson and other immortals of the game, coming out of the cornfields of the *Field of Dreams* movie site. Last Sunday of each month from June to September.
800.443.8981

DECEMBER

Victorian Christmas, Deadwood, SD
Wild Bill Hickok and Calamity Jane might be a little surprised at how the town fathers dress up this once wild town in Victorian finery every year for a turn-of-the-century Yuletide celebration.
605.578.1876

Harold Warp Pioneer Village E

Carhenge B

Chimney Rock National Historic Site C

Nebraska

A Ashfall Fossil Beds State Historical Park
Pg. 125, F14. Some of the best-preserved fossils of prehistoric rhinos, horses, camels, saber-toothed deer, and birds have been discovered beneath the farmlands near Royal. Because of a quick burial in a volcanic eruption, the fossils here are virtually intact and remarkably lifelike. A visitor center features a fossil preparation lab, and walkways provide close-up views of paleontologists at work. **402.893.2000.**

B Carhenge
Pg. 124, F4. Stonehenge was built around 2000 B.C. by Stone Age Britons as a ceremonial ground. Jim Reinders conceived Carhenge 4,000 years later. Composed entirely of aging automobiles, Carhenge replicates Stonehenge in shape and orientation, as each of the 33 cars is similar in size to a slab from the original mysterious landmark.
308.762.4954.

C Chimney Rock National Historic Site
Pg. 124, H3. The frontier superhighway known as the Great Platte River Road was followed by 350,000 settlers and gold diggers from the early 1840s to 1866. Many landmarks along the way, like the hair-raising descent down Windlass Hill, were dreaded. But most everyone was happy to spot the spires of Chimney Rock, rising 500 feet above the Platte River Valley, as it was considered a halfway mark on the great migration to the West.
308.586.2581.

D Nine-Mile Prairie
Pg. 125, K17. These 230 acres of unsullied prairie, located nine miles from downtown Lincoln, give the visitor an idea of what early pioneers saw on their arduous journey west. Enjoy a peaceful setting as you walk among the more than 300 species of swaying grasses and wildflowers. **402.472.1546.**

E Harold Warp Pioneer Village
Pg. 125, L12. Mr. Warp intended that Pioneer Village serve as a monument to the frontier spirit of his parents, who homesteaded near the site in the 1870s. It does this and much more. America's development from the 1830s to modern times is illustrated with seven generations of kitchens, bedrooms, cars, tractors, airplanes, bicycles—you name it—housed in 26 buildings located in Minden.
308.832.1181.

In Nebraska, cows outnumber humans by more than four to one. The state is home to 28,000 beef cattle producers and had a cattle population of 6.65 million by the early months of 1998.

We were at sea – there is no other adequate expression – on the plains of Nebraska.

– ROBERT LOUIS STEVENSON, *ACROSS THE PLAINS WITH OTHER MEMORIES AND ESSAYS*, 1892

SD 157
ND 141
NE 124
IA 96
SD 245
ND 242
NE 240
IA 236

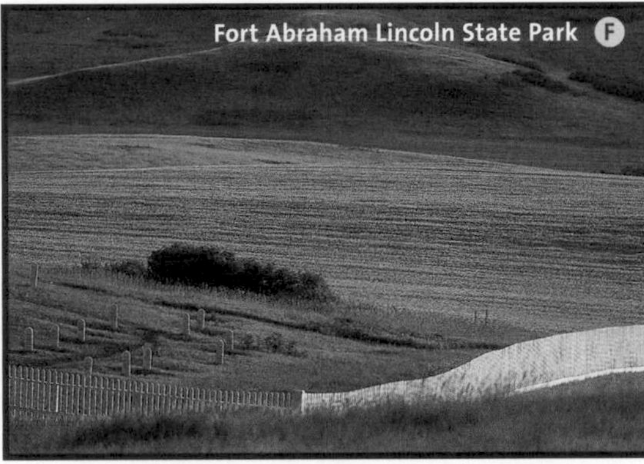

Fort Abraham Lincoln State Park F

North Dakota produces almost 80 percent of the nation's supply of durum wheat, and total wheat production in North Dakota averages 300 million bushels a year.

North Dakota

F Fort Abraham Lincoln State Park
Pg. 141, F6. This military fort was established in 1872 to protect frontier settlers and railroad surveyors. Within the 1,000-acre park, south of Mandan, are reconstructions of military buildings and the four earth lodges of On-a-Slant Indian Village, occupied by the peaceful Mandan Indians between 1650 and 1750 and reconstructed by the Civilian Conservation Corps in the 1930s. The commanding officer's quarters were Colonel Custer's home before his ill-fated campaign at Little Bighorn. **701.663.9571.**

G Fort Mandan
Pg. 141, E5. The Lewis and Clark expedition spent more time in North Dakota than any other state, largely because they camped during the winter of 1804–5 at Fort Mandan (north of Washburn). Here, they trained their Corps of Discovery into a polished team while learning about the yet-to-be-explored country from their Native American hosts, the Mandan and Hidatsa tribes. **701.462.8535.**

H J. Clark Salyer National Wildlife Refuge
Pg. 141, B6. North Dakota's largest refuge consists of nearly 60,000 acres of marshland, meadows, river-bottom hardwoods, and sandhills. White-tailed deer, mink, muskrat, red fox, and coyote are often spotted from the road. A visitor station, observation tower, and bird-watching platforms are located near headquarters in Upham. **701.768.2548.**

South Dakota

I Crazy Horse Memorial/ Indian Museum of North America
Pg. 157, E2, J4. Destined to be the world's largest sculpture, the Crazy Horse mountain carving will eventually be over 560 feet high, 640 feet long, and the centerpiece of a cultural memorial to the man who routed Custer at Little Bighorn. Commissioned in 1947 by the Lakota chiefs, the work-in-progress can be viewed from a visitor complex, which houses the splendid Indian Museum of North America. **605.673.4681.**

J Wall Drug
Pg. 157, E4. In 1931, Ted Hustead opened a tiny drugstore in Wall. He discovered, in 1936, how effective roadside advertising could be and blanketed the region's highways with billboards offering free ice water to travelers. Now the largest drugstore in the world (about three-quarters of a block), the giant shopping emporium displays more than 5,000 pairs of cowboy boots and includes the 530-seat Western Art Gallery Restaurant, where you can still get five-cent coffee. **605.279.2175.**

K Mitchell Corn Palace
Pg. 157, F10. Every fall since 1892, Mitchellians have plastered the walls of their downtown auditorium with part of the local corn harvest, creating elaborate murals. One year's work featured leaping antelope, clashing bison, and roving coyote. The turreted and domed Corn Palace, originally built to encourage settlement following the construction of the railroads, today is an homage to South Dakota's agrarian character. **800.257.2676.**

L Jewel Cave National Monument
Pg. 157, F2. Within this 110-mile underground labyrinth are rooms as large as 150 by 200 feet and passageways as long as 3,200 feet. The Formation Room is one highlight of a 90-minute scenic tour through chambers decorated with calcite crystals, stalactites, and stalagmites. For the adventurous, a spelunking tour offers a four-hour journey through undeveloped portions of the cave. **605.673.2288.**

Mitchell Corn Palace K

M Mount Rushmore National Memorial
Pg. 157, E2. The 60-foot visages of George Washington, Thomas Jefferson, Abraham Lincoln, and Theodore Roosevelt comprise one of America's most recognizable landmarks, a "shrine to democracy." Three miles south of Keystone, in the Black Hills, Mount Rushmore's setting and scale (each eye alone is 11 feet across) are an expression of creator Gutzon Borglum's desire that the presidents be placed "as close to heaven as we can . . . to show posterity what manner of men they were." **605.574.2523.**

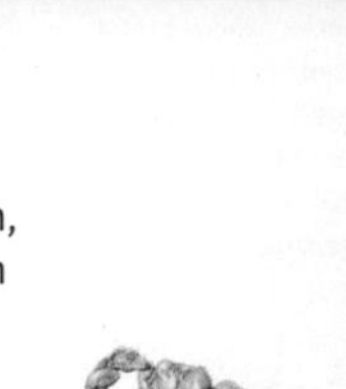

Discovered in the Black Hills gold rush of 1876, South Dakota's Homestake Goldmine is the world's largest continuously operating gold mine. To date, 38 million ounces of gold have been recovered from Homestake.

Field of Dreams, Dyersville P

Iowa is the nation's leading producer of pork, and about a quarter of U.S. pigs and hogs are found on Iowa farms.

Iowa

N Amana Colonies
Pg. 97, H15. In 1842 the Community of True Inspiration, a German religious group, left Buffalo, New York, for this placid valley in Iowa, where they built seven villages called the Amana Colonies. Each village was laid out on a traditional 18th-century German plan with a single long main street. All property except personal items like clothing was owned collectively. Amana is no longer a religious commune, but many of the Colonies' original products–crafts, wine, breads, cheese–are sold at Old World-style shops. **800.245.5465.**

O Effigy Mounds National Monument
Pg. 97, C16. Although different groups of Native Americans constructed burial mounds all over the country, only in a small area including northeastern Iowa were they built in the shapes of animals. A total of 191 mounds have been discovered north of Marquette, at Effigy Mounds National Monument, atop 400-foot limestone bluffs. Dating from 500 B.C. to A.D. 1300, 29 of them are bear and bird effigies. **319.873.3491.**

P Field of Dreams
Pg. 97, E17. The people of Dyersville appreciate the value of play. The town is home to three farm-toy companies, manufacturers of many of the items found in the local National Farm Toy Museum. So when the *Field of Dreams* film crew left behind a baseball diamond carved out of a cornfield on the edge of town, Dyersvillians knew how to make the most of it. From April to November, visitors are welcome to play ball or pose for photos on the old movie set. **319.875.2311.**

Imes Covered Bridge Q

Q Madison County Covered Bridges
Pg. 96, K8. Madison County's six covered bridges have always had a romantic aura, even before novelist Robert James Waller and Hollywood immortalized them. Most are within a five-mile radius of Winterset, which has acquired a bit of aura itself as the birthplace of John Wayne. His family's modest 1880s house is open for tours. **515.462.1185.**

R Maquoketa Caves State Park
Pg. 97, F18. Rugged bluffs, limestone formations, and, of course, caves are the highlights of this park just northwest of Maquoketa. From the 1,100-foot-long Dancehall–equipped with walkways and a lighting system–to the tiny Dugout, the caves transport visitors back to a primeval geological age. Pottery, arrowheads, spears, and other relics of Native American habitation have been found here. **319.652.5833.**

Viewed at a distance, these lands exhibit the appearance of extensive villages and ancient castles, but under forms so extraordinary, and so capricious a style of architecture, that we might consider them as appertaining to some new world, or ages far remote.

–FRENCH MISSIONARY PIERRE-JEAN DE SMET, 1848

The fields have turned, yellow and light brown;
central Iowa gets most of its autumn from the fields.
Trees and brush trim the roadsides and fence rows vividly,
but the great reaching planes of quiet colors are the fields.

–HAMLIN GARLAND, *A SON OF THE MIDDLE BORDER*, 1917

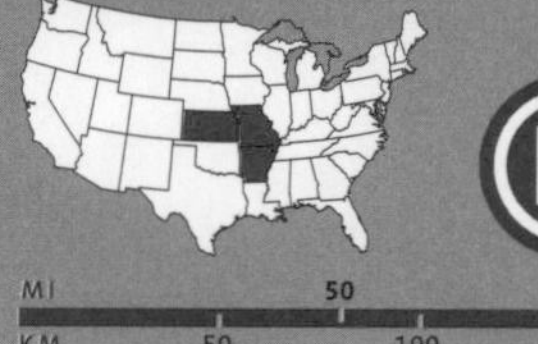

Once the ancestral hunting grounds of nomadic Osage, the sprawling prairies of the southern Great Plains cover a prehistoric inland sea that left a wealth of intriguing fossils behind, as well as valuable mineral deposits of coal and gypsum. The region's predominant geographic feature is the picturesque Ozark Plateau, extending north from the Arkansas River and across southern Missouri. Thousands of years of erosion have left a landscape of ragged ridges and deep valleys with unusual limestone outcroppings. Because the area was all but isolated from the rest of the country for decades, it was often described as a foreboding, mountainous terrain with sleepy hollows that were home to a strange rural culture. These days the Ozark heritage is more likely to be celebrated than shunned, and a combination of great natural beauty and an expanded economy make this the fastest growing rural area in the country. The southern Great Plains also boast cosmopolitan cities like Kansas City and St. Louis, former frontier towns where Conestoga wagons gathered before beginning the long trek west. Today they're major hubs for air, rail, and water transport, as well as centers of Western heritage.

The Missouri and Mississippi Rivers flow across the central plains, draining much of the land that stretches between the Rocky and Appalachian Mountains. The two great rivers come together near St. Louis and flow south to the Gulf of Mexico.

Kansas, in sum, is one of our finest states and lives a sane, peaceful, and prosperous life.

—PEARL S. BUCK, *AMERICA*, 1971

APRIL
Lake of the Ozarks Dogwood Music Festival, Camdenton, MO
Blooming dogwood trees are the perfect excuse for a combination music festival and arts-and-crafts show. There's also plenty of good barbecue.
800.769.1004

MAY
Picklefest, Atkins, AR
Pickle enthusiasts have their day with eating and juice-drinking contests, a tasting booth, and tours of the Atkins pickle plant.
501.641.1147

JUNE
Beef Empire Days, Garden City, KS
Hamburgers, tri-tip, kabobs—there are about a hundred different ways to prepare beef, as evidenced at this cook-off that also includes a Western-art show and a cowboy-poetry contest.
316.275.6807

JULY
Tom Sawyer Days, Hannibal, MO
The childhood home of Mark Twain—known then as Samuel Clemens—celebrates with a mighty frog-jumping contest and a just-for-fun fence-painting championship. Take a look at the author's boyhood home while you're there.
573.221.2477

SEPTEMBER
Walnut Valley Festival, Winfield, KS
Some of the best guitar pickers in the country get together every fall for this acoustic music festival.
316.221.3250

18th & Vine Heritage Festival, Kansas City, MO
An important center of traditional American blues and jazz celebrates its history with a downtown party that rocks all night.
816.474.8463

OCTOBER
Apple Days, Topeka, KS
Sample cider and taste some apple pie at this festival celebrating the fall apple harvest. Events are held on the grounds of a turn-of-the-century mansion.
785.295.3888

King Biscuit Blues Festival, Helena, AR
Some say this Mississippi River town is the birthplace of the blues. They make a strong case by hosting one of the largest blues festivals in the nation every year.
501.338.9144

NOVEMBER
World's Championship Duck Calling Contest and Wings Over the Prairie Festival, Stuttgart, AR
Festivities for the world and state duck calling championships include a duck gumbo cook-off and the Queen Mallard pageant.
870.673.1602

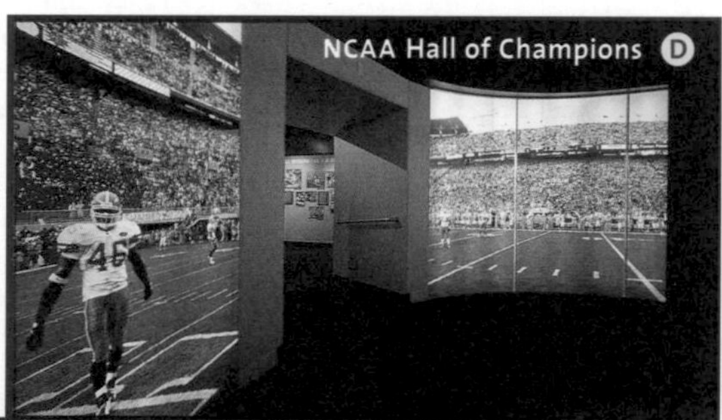
NCAA Hall of Champions D

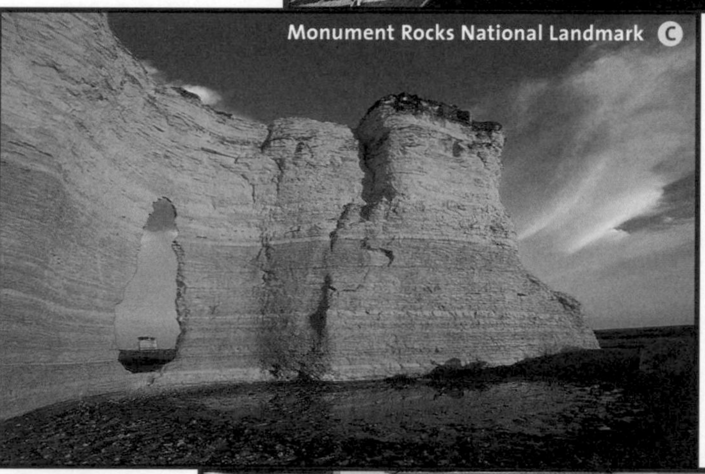
Monument Rocks National Landmark C

Colby
Hays
Salina
Great Bend
KANSAS
McPherson
Garden City
Dodge City
Hutchinson
Liberal
SMOKY HILL
ARKANSAS
CIMARRON

Kansas

Officer's parlor, Fort Scott B

A Big Basin Prairie Preserve
Pg. 98, J6. It appears to be a small valley, but Big Basin, west of Ashland, is actually an enormous sinkhole created when underground salt and gypsum deposits were dissolved over time by water. Empty spaces formed underground between the rocks, and the land collapsed – leaving a sinkhole a mile across where herds of buffalo now range freely. **316.227.8609.**

B Fort Scott National Historic Site
Pg. 99, G18. Established in 1842 to police the Indian frontier as settlers moved west, Fort Smith housed dragoon soldiers who escorted parties along the Oregon and Santa Fe Trails, maintained contact with Plains Indians, and explored unmapped territory. The restored site consists of 20 buildings, a parade ground, and five acres of tallgrass prairie. **316.223.0310.**

C Monument Rocks National Landmark
Pg. 98, E4. Often called the Chalk Pyramids, Monument Rocks (in Oakley) is the state's first national landmark. Rising majestically out of flat prairie, these chalk monoliths were deposited under a sea 200 million years ago, then carved into their current shape by water and ice erosion. The remains of ancient marine life can be found throughout the area. **785.672.4862.**

D NCAA Hall of Champions
Pg. 119, H3. A unique tribute to college athletics past and present, the Hall of Champions in Overland Park covers all 22 sports governed by the NCAA, with video presentations, some 900 photographs, and special exhibits. Two 360-degree photomurals give you a chance to imagine what it's like to be on the field for the kickoff of a college football game or to stand at center court during the Final Four. **800.735.6222.**

E Garden of Eden
Pg. 98, D9. On a quiet street in the small prairie town of Lucas lies the Garden of Eden, a concrete and limestone sculpture garden built by Samuel Dinsmoor between 1905 and his death in 1933. Dinsmoor, a Civil War veteran, turned 113 tons of concrete into biblical statuary surrounding his house, itself made out of limestone carved to look like logs. Political messages crop up around the grounds, subtle and not-so-subtle shots at big business and the affluent. On his death, Dinsmoor himself became part of the garden. His embalmed remains rest in a glass coffin in a 40-foot limestone mausoleum. **785.525.6395.**

Missouri

F Branson
Pg. 120, M6. Nestled in the hills of the Ozarks, this once quiet lakeside resort is now giving Nashville a run for its money as the capital of country music. Branson's music tradition began in the early 1960s, with the Baldknobbers, a troupe of country entertainers; continued with the establishment of Presley's Mountain Music Jubilee in 1967; and today is celebrated nightly in nearly 40 theaters along the Strip. Small-town charm is one attraction for entertainers like Andy Williams, Mickey Gilley, and Tony Orlando, who have theaters here, and provides an equally welcoming environment for the more than five million visitors who flock here yearly. **417.334.4136.**

G Pony Express Museum
Pg. 119, F9. The Pony Express Museum, located at the site of the historic stables in St. Joseph, illustrates the brief history of the mail service and its daredevil riders. Formed in 1860, the Pony Express operated as a vital postal connection from St. Joseph to Sacramento, California. The riders would cover almost 2,000 miles in less than ten days, stopping at about 190 stations, but still couldn't compete with the telegraph. **816.279.5059.**

Arrow Rock State Historic Site H

H Arrow Rock State Historic Site
Pg. 120, E6. The spirit of Missouri's frontier years lingers in this historic village where the Santa Fe Trail crossed the Missouri River. The canopied boardwalk shades the entrances to white-framed, redbrick buildings, all of which look about as they did when wagon trains passed through or stopped for a rest. Historic buildings include the church, a jail, the old courthouse, the home of artist George Caleb Bingham, and the 1834 Old Tavern, where visitors can dine in a frontier atmosphere. **816.837.3330.**

I Lake of the Ozarks State Park
Pg. 120, H7. Considered Missouri's most scenic area, the Lake of the Ozarks State Park features 89 miles of shoreline, with boat launching facilities and two public beaches. In the park's southeast corner is a picturesque one-lane suspension bridge. In the Ozark Caverns, which can be explored with handheld lanterns, the spectacular Angel's Shower is a ceaseless flow of water that seems to fall from a rock ceiling. **573.348.2694.**

AR 66
MO 120
KS 98
AR 232
MO 239
KS 236

As an agricultural region,
Missouri is not surpassed by
any state in the Union.
It is indeed the farmers' kingdom.

–ANONYMOUS,
THE HISTORY OF JACKSON COUNTY, 1881

Ozark National Forest (N)

Buffalo National River (K)

Ozark Folk Center (M)

Arkansas

(K) Buffalo National River
Pg. 66, C8. This magnificent free-flowing stream is somewhat difficult to access by car; so the best way to see this magnificent free-flowing stream and its surrounding park is by canoe or trail. Visitors can enjoy the water's tranquillity as they float past spectacular 440-foot limestone bluffs and hillsides packed with trees and wildflowers. White-water rafting is available in the upper district. **870.741.5443.**

(L) Arkansas & Missouri Railroad
Pg. 66, A2. Passengers ride in restored vintage 19th-century cars on a scenic excursion through the southern edge of the Ozarks from Van Buren to Springdale and back. The railroad crosses trestles 250 feet above the floor of wooded valleys in the Boston Mountains and passes through the 1882 Winslow Tunnel. Back in Van Buren, a visit to Old Main Street might evoke cinematic memories: Its stretch of 70 restored buildings has been used as a set in many Westerns. **800.687.8600.**

Five species of bats live in Lake of the Ozarks State Park, including the red bat, which camouflages itself by hanging from trees by one foot to masquerade as a leaf, and the gray bat, which can eat nearly 3,000 mosquitoes in one night.

(M) Ozark Folk Center
Pg. 66, C10. Sample the Ozarks' rich heritage through music, dance, and crafts in the Ozark Folk Center, a living-history museum located north of Mountain View. The season runs from mid-April to early November, during which visitors can take in homemade craft demonstrations and live entertainment. Musical performances are acoustic only, turn-of-the-century style. **501.269.3851.**

(N) Ozark National Forest
Pg. 66, D7. The million acres of the Ozark National Forest offer a complete recreational experience. Although hardwood trees make up 65 percent of the forest, the flora is indeed diverse, including more than 500 species of trees and woody plants. Hiking trails crisscross the forest; among the most popular is the Ozark Highlands Trail, which winds through 160 miles of wooded terrain. **501.968.2354.**

(O) Toltec Mounds Archaeological State Park
Pg. 66, G10. Outside of Little Rock are the remains of a group of ancient earthworks known as Toltec Mounds, which have attracted national attention for a century. Their name is misleading, as the mounds were not built by the Toltecs of Mexico but rather by Native Americans from further north. Though some of the mounds were once inhabited, they may have been used for religious and burial purposes and as celestial navigation markers. **501.961.9442.**

Branson (F)

Gateway Arch, St. Louis (J)

(J) Gateway Arch
Pg. 121, J19. Designed by Eero Saarinen in 1947 and completed in 1965, the 630-foot stainless-steel arch is almost double the height of the Statue of Liberty, making it the tallest man-made monument in the U.S. Visitors can ride a tram to the top, where park rangers are happy to explain that the arch was built as a memorial to Thomas Jefferson, the early pioneers, and national expansion. The site includes the Museum of Westward Expansion. **314.425.4465.**

Home of the famous tornado rider, Dorothy of *The Wizard of Oz*, Kansas averages 47 tornado touchdowns every year.

The world's largest brewer, with annual beer sales in recent years approaching 100 million barrels, St. Louis's Anheuser-Busch is also the country's biggest buyer of rice and the world's largest recycler of aluminum cans.

If I could rest anywhere, it would be in Arkansaw,
where the men are of the real half-horse, half-alligator breed
such as grows nowhere else on the face of the earth.

– DAVID CROCKETT, 1834

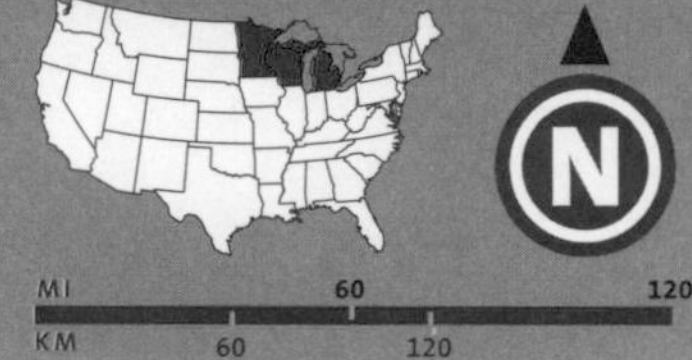

All the Great Lakes combined make up the largest freshwater grouping in the world, and they are epic not only in scale but in natural riches. From the dairy lands of Wisconsin to the great auto plants of Michigan, this region has been one of the country's biggest producers. Since European explorers first arrived in the 1600s, the land has been exploited for fur, lumber, iron, and copper ore. Where once Native American guides helped trappers navigate complicated waterways in canoes, today there are vast shipping lanes, with seagoing freighters traveling via the St. Lawrence Seaway to ports like Green Bay and Duluth. Despite the presence of open-pit mines, the area's North Woods offer glimpses of an untamed world where the northern lights brighten the night sky, and where Ernest Hemingway's "Big Two-Hearted River" is in reality the Fox River of Michigan's Upper Peninsula. Even if Paul Bunyan and his blue ox did not create Minnesota's 10,000-plus lakes, there is no shortage of adventure and natural splendor here, from wintry cross-country skiing trails to spring cherry blossoms on Grand Traverse Bay.

Forming a watery staircase that spans 750 miles, the Great Lakes drop 24 feet from Superior to Michigan and Huron. Another 8 feet separates that pair from shallow Erie. Ontario, the smallest, lies 326 feet lower – a descent that includes the 167-foot plunge of the Niagara Falls.

Minnesotans are different from the rest of us. . . . Minnesotans fasten their seat belts. Minnesotans hold the door for you. Minnesota men don't leave the toilet seat up. Minnesotans do not blow their horn behind you when the light turns green; they wait for you to notice. Minnesotans are nicer than other people.

– CHARLES KURALT, *CHARLES KURALT'S AMERICA*, 1995

JANUARY

The Plymouth International Ice Sculpture Spectacular, Plymouth, MI
Amateur and professional ice carvers from around the world carve more than 200 magnificent ice sculptures.
313.459.6969

Saint Paul Winter Carnival, St. Paul, MN
In North America's oldest and largest winter carnival, the frigid depths of a Twin Cities winter come to life for a week with antique sleigh and cutter parades, fireworks, car races on ice, and ice-carving and snow-sculpting competitions.
612.223.4700, 800.488.4023

FEBRUARY

North American Snowmobile Festival, Cadillac, MI
Lake Cadillac hosts the state's biggest snowmobile event when 10,000 snowmobilers and spectators gather for forest rides and games such as snowmobile poker and ice volleyball.
616.775.0657

Dyno American Birkebeiner, Cable to Hayward, WI
The nation's largest and most prestigious cross-country ski marathon – 52 kilometers – draws thousands of skiers from around the world.
715-634-5025, 800.872.2753

JUNE

The Frankenmuth Bavarian Festival, Frankenmuth, MI
Michigan's "Little Bavaria" rolls out the *willkommen* mat for its annual multi-day heritage celebration, hosting some of the nation's best polka bands and serving up locally brewed ale, homemade bratwurst, and pretzels.
517.652.8155

JULY

National Cherry Festival, Traverse City, MI
In the Grand Traverse region, known for the world's greatest concentration of tart cherries, this summer resort town hosts a multiday celebration that includes parades, fireworks, big-name entertainers, and tasty cherry pies.
616.947.4230, 800.968.3380

AUGUST

The Great Circus Parade, Milwaukee, WI
Antique circus wagons make their annual pilgrimage from Baraboo to re-create an authentic 19th-century parade and circus.
608.356.8341, 608.356.0800

World Lumberjack Championships, Hayward, WI
Pro lumberjacks from around the world test their mettle in such classic events as speed sawing, pole climbing, and birling.
715.634.2484

SEPTEMBER

Mackinac Bridge Labor Day Bridge Walk, Mackinaw City and St. Ignace, MI
The traditional once-a-year walk across Big Mac, the soaring five-mile span that connects the Upper Peninsula and Lower Michigan, attracts politicians and proletariat alike – on foot, in wheelchairs, and in baby strollers.
906.643.7600

Ladies and gentleman, I was warned to be out of here in plenty of time to permit those who are going to the Green Bay Packers game to leave. I don't mind running against Mr. Nixon, but I have the good sense not to run against the Green Bay Packers.

– JOHN F. KENNEDY, AT A 1960 CAMPAIGN APPEARANCE IN GREEN BAY

Split Rock Lighthouse F

Great Hall, Grand Portage National Monument E

Mall of America A

Minnesota

A Mall of America

Pg. 115, H4. Die-hard shoppers may have finally met their match in the Mall of America. The greatest (or, at least, biggest) mall in the U. S., this four-story shopping complex-cum-entertainment emporium is the Lourdes of consumerism. Containing nearly twice the amount of steel as the Eiffel Tower and large enough to accommodate a week's worth of NFL football games side by side, the Mall of America boasts not only upwards of 520 stores but also movies, comedy, dancing, down-home theater – and, as if that weren't enough, its own roller coaster and Ferris wheel. **612.883.8800.**

B Boundary Waters Canoe Area Wilderness

Pg. 116, F13. Deep in the Superior National Forest, northern lights glow over stands of pine, spruce, fir, alder, and birch, while loons bob on the more than 1,000 portage-linked lakes of the famous Boundary Waters Canoe Area Wilderness. No motorized boats are allowed in most parts of this watery boreal retreat, which adjoins Canada's Quetico Provincial Park. Laid-back Ely serves as a gateway to the wilderness, complete with canoe rentals and guide services, and is also home to the popular International Wolf Center, where a resident pack can be heard howling at night. Boundary Waters Reservation Center, **800.745.3399.** Superior National Forest, **218.626.4300.**

C Itasca State Park

Pg. 116, J5. At serene Lake Itasca, the headwaters of the Mississippi emerge from a forest of stately red and white pines. An ankle-deep brook here, the Mississippi seemingly flows in the wrong direction, northeast to Lake Bemidji, before getting on with its 2,348-mile run to New Orleans. **218.266.2100.**

D Pipestone National Monument

Pg. 117, T2. Native Americans still quarry pipestone (a special type of clay stone) here to carve ceremonial pipes and other sacred objects. Artisans demonstrate their craft at a visitor center from April to October, and a quarter-mile trail traverses the quarry and surrounding prairie. **507.825.5464.**

E Grand Portage National Monument

Pg. 116, B12. In the late 18th century, this remote outpost was a fur-trading hub for the North West Company. The partially reconstructed depot commemorates the French-Canadian voyageurs and Native Americans who spent their lives paddling between the Northwest and Montréal with furs and trade goods. In the summer, company employees collected wages and met with Native Americans to transfer their goods over land in a traditional celebration known as a rendezvous. At nearby Grand Portage, or "great carrying place," participants circumvented the unnavigable rapids of the Pigeon River by carrying their canoes on an 8.5-mile trail. Today the trail is popular with hikers and cross-country skiers. **218.387.2788.**

F Split Rock Lighthouse

Pg. 116, J12. Sitting atop a 130-foot headland over rocky shoals, this lighthouse was completed in 1910 after 215 sailors drowned during a disastrous shipping season. A history center at the restored lighthouse offers exhibits on lake navigation, shipwrecks, and the U. S. Lighthouse Service. **218.226.6377.**

Minnesota's North Woods are home to more wolves – some 2,000 total – than live in all of the rest of the lower 48 states combined.

MI 112
WI 174
MN 116
MI 236
WI 248
MN 239

Miner Castle, Pictured Rocks National Lakeshore I

Henry Ford Museum H

Porch at Grand Hotel, Mackinac Island J

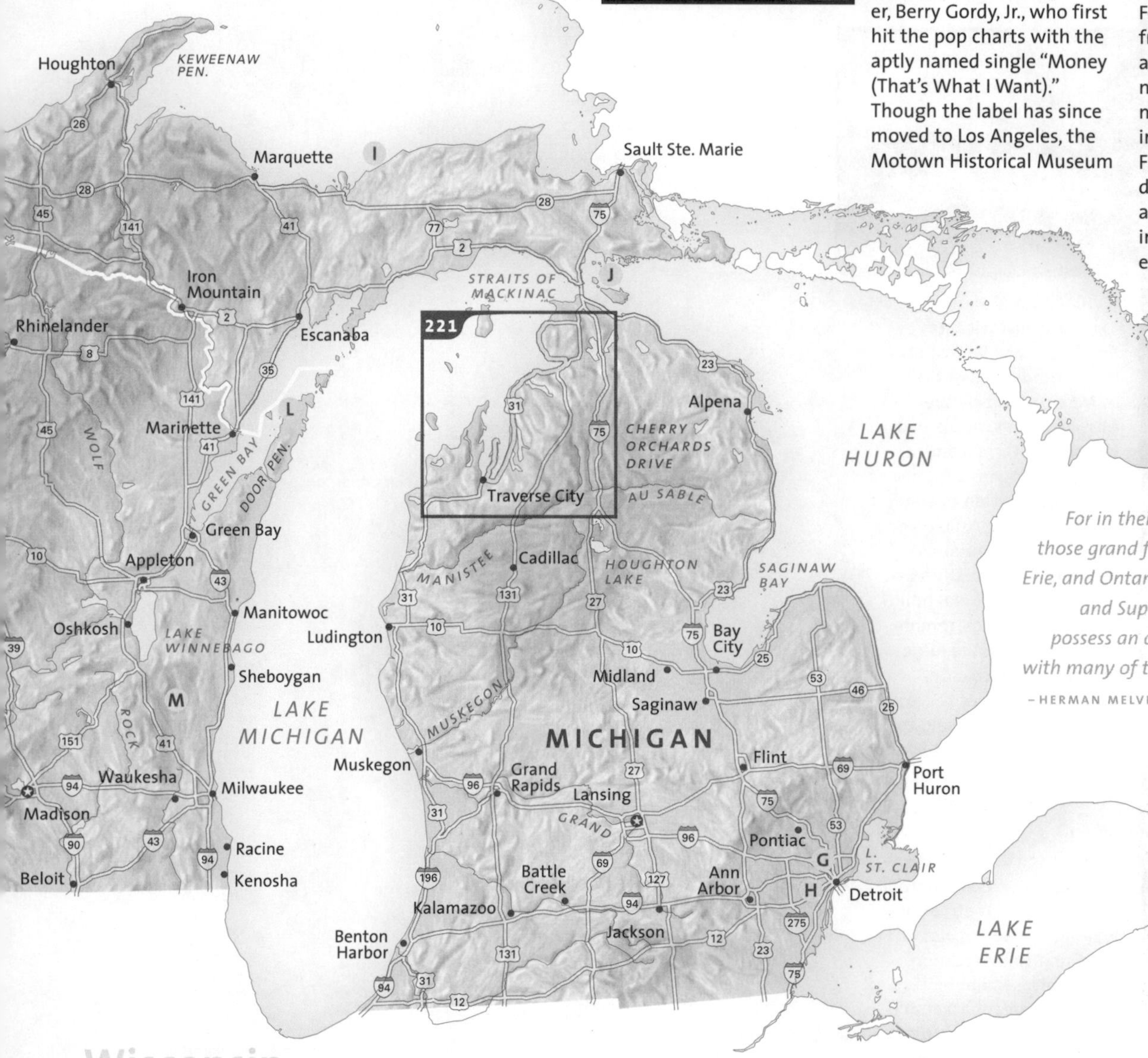

Michigan

G Motown Historical Museum
Pg. 114, K8. Though best known for its automobiles, the town called Motor City is also the birthplace of another distinctly American product: the Motown sound. Motown was founded in 1959 by a Ford factory worker, Berry Gordy, Jr., who first hit the pop charts with the aptly named single "Money (That's What I Want)." Though the label has since moved to Los Angeles, the Motown Historical Museum preserves Gordy's small white-and-blue house, where artists like the Supremes, Marvin Gaye, and Stevie Wonder revolutionized pop music in the '60s. Wedding gospel and rhythm and blues with a trademark pop beat, the sound perfected by Gordy lives on here in the bare-bones "Studio A" and in memorabilia such as Michael Jackson's glove. **313.875.2264.**

H Henry Ford Museum & Greenfield Village
Pg. 114, K6. Just outside Detroit, in Dearborn, such gems of Americana as George Washington's travel chest and Edison's laboratory are on view here, along with the entire Wright Cycle Shop (which Ford bought and moved from Ohio). Ford's remarkable tribute to Yankee ingenuity includes, naturally, much on his own proudest invention, the modern car. From Model Ts to roadside diners, the glories of U.S. auto culture are captured in a loving multimedia extravaganza. **800.835.5237.**

I Pictured Rocks National Lakeshore
Pg. 112, C4. One of the most attractive stretches of the rugged Upper Peninsula coast, Pictured Rocks is a 15-mile strip of multicolored sandstone cliffs, eroded by wind and water into palisades, arches, and castle-like formations. Cruises from Munising offer spectacular views. Further along stretch 12 miles of sand and pebble beaches and the Grand Sable Banks, topped by dunes. With nearby camping, the area attracts hikers, photographers, sunbathers, and the hardiest of swimmers. Superior, coldest and deepest of the Great Lakes, seldom warms to more than 60°F. **906.387.3700.**

J Mackinac Island State Park
Pg. 112, F8. With horse-drawn carriages and bicycles (no cars allowed) Mackinac Island is an outpost of a simpler, uncluttered life – you have to take a ferry to get there. Named after a Chippewa word for "great turtle," the island's roots as a posh summer resort date to the Gilded Age, when the famous Grand Hotel was built. Featuring the longest porch in the world, the Grand–the largest of many fine hostelries on the island–offers tranquil views of Lake Huron. Once a base for John Jacob Astor's American Fur Company, Mackinac Island still maintains its 18th-century British fort, complete with costumed rifle drills. **800.454.5227.**

Michigan's Traverse City, home of the annual National Cherry Festival, is surrounded by 6,380 acres of sweet cherry and 14,900 acres of tart cherry orchards.

For in their interflowing aggregate, those grand fresh-water seas of ours, – Erie, and Ontario, and Huron, and Superior, and Michigan, – possess an ocean-like expansiveness, with many of the ocean's noblest traits . . .

– HERMAN MELVILLE, *MOBY DICK*, 1851

About one-third of the cheese produced in the U.S. comes from the dairy lands of Wisconsin.

Wisconsin

K Apostle Islands
Pg. 174, C5. As they retreated nearly 10,000 years ago, Ice Age glaciers left behind the 22 Apostle Islands, where wind and water have sculpted fantastic bays, red cliffs, and pristine sand beaches. Once inhabited by prehistoric Indians, the Apostles were visited in colonial times by fur traders, followed in the 19th century by loggers, fishermen, and then quarriers, who cut brownstone for tony town houses as far away as New York. In addition to swimming, fishing, boating, and camping, visitors can see remains of the islands' past in scenic lighthouses, an abandoned quarry, and an old commercial fishing camp. **715.779.3397.**

L Door County
Pg. 174, H13. One of Wisconsin's leading vacation spots, Door County, on a 70-mile-long finger of land that separates Lake Michigan and Green Bay, offers low-key resorts, shining weather, and cherry and apple orchards. The county's name came from French explorers who labeled the treacherous straits at its head Porte des Morts – "door of the dead." The waters around the peninsula are a scuba diver's paradise, with more than 200 charted shipwrecks just offshore. With ten lighthouses and a dozen fishing villages, Door County deserves its title as the "Cape Cod of the Midwest." **920.743.4456, 800.527.3529.**

M Ice Age National Reserve
Pg. 175, N11. In the northern portion of the Kettle Moraine State Forest, a scenic drive winds through wooded hills, ridges, and valleys that reveal a wild glacial landscape. Kames (conical hills), kettles (depressions), eskers (ridges or mounds), and other landforms along the drive testify to the collision of two wedges of ice during the Wisconsin period of the Pleistocene epoch. Off the main road, the Long Lake Recreation Area offers swimming, boating, camping, and woodsy trails. Kettle Moraine State Forest, Northern Unit, **414.626.2116.** Ice Age Visitor Center, **920.533.8322.**

Wisconsin Dells N

N Wisconsin Dells
Pg. 175, N7. At Wisconsin Dells, the Wisconsin River cuts through a spectacular seven-mile gorge. By tour boat or canoe, you can glide past fantastic stone formations in the sheer cliffs. **608.254.8088, 800.223.3557.**

Circus World Museum O

O Circus World Museum
Pg. 175, N7. Birthplace, in 1884, of the Ringling Brothers Circus, Baraboo is now home to a museum showcasing the history of the American circus, with live big top shows during the summer and the world's largest collection of circus wagons. **608.356.8341, 608.356.0800.**

Apostle Islands K

Heartland

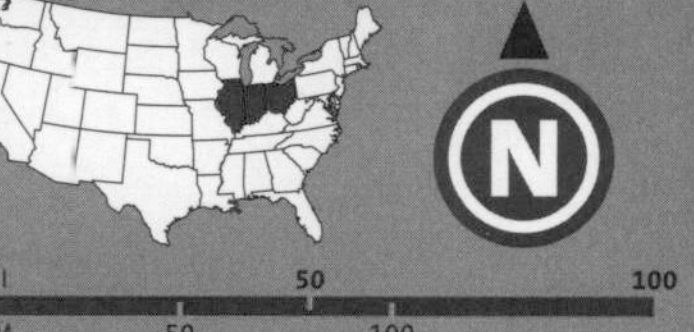

Heavily industrialized along their northern tier on Lake Erie and Lake Michigan, the Heartland states are nonetheless agricultural outriders of the rich prairielands to the west. The Ohio River, long a highway of settlement and commerce between East and West, forms the region's southern border.

Calling the states of Ohio, Indiana, and Illinois the "Heartland" is a practice that came only with the perspective offered by westward expansion – well into the 19th century, these future states were part of a wild frontier known as the Northwest Territory. But as the western reaches of the continent were settled, the lands immediately south of the Great Lakes did begin to seem like the heart of the country. This wasn't just a matter of geography: Picture a small town where people wave at neighbors from big front porches, or any scenario that embodies America's sense of itself at its simple best, and the setting might as well be here. The Heartland is the threshold of the prairies. This is farm country, no question. But the notion that turning the old "Northwest" into farmland merely involved busting prairie sod to reveal the rich soil beneath overlooks the fact that the region's early settlers also cut thousands of square miles of forest. The Heartland's other great reputation as the nation's industrial dynamo has been diminished by the rise of a service economy. But much of this region's character was forged by and continues to reflect the muscular industrial cities that gird the southern shores of the Great Lakes from Cleveland to Chicago. The Heartland was once unequaled in the business of making things. It still makes plenty of things, and grows an awful lot of corn in the bargain.

Chicago will give you a chance.
The sporting spirit is the spirit of Chicago.

– LINCOLN STEFFENS IN HIS AUTOBIOGRAPHY, 1931

MAY
Indianapolis 500 Festival, Indianapolis, IN
Before the phrase "Gentlemen, start your engines" launches what has been called the "greatest spectacle in racing," ticket holders are invited to join celebrities, drivers, and bands in the IPALCO Festival Parade.
800.638.4296

JUNE
Columbus Arts Festival, Columbus, OH
Hundreds of North America's best artists display their work at a juried festival along the Scioto River as top local performers entertain with rock, country, and bluegrass music.
614.224.2606

JULY
Indiana Black Expo, Indianapolis, IN
More than 30 events at this national showcase of African American culture and heritage focus on a multitude of subjects, from art to religion to politics.
800.323.4639

Dayton Air Show, Dayton, OH
The Wright brothers' hometown hosts one of the world's largest air shows, with precision jet teams, aerobatics, parachutists, and hot-air balloons.
937.898.5901

SEPTEMBER
Auburn Cord Duesenberg Festival, Auburn, IN
The festival features a classic car auction – where Greta Garbo's 1933 Duesenberg Victoria sold for $2.8 million in 1991 – and a Parade of Classics, as well as quilt, antique, and arts and crafts shows.
219.925.3600

OCTOBER
Pumpkin Show, Circleville, OH
The state's oldest festival displays more than 100,000 pounds of pumpkin-related products and features three stages of entertainment, contests, and rides.
614.474.7000

NOVEMBER
Magnificent Mile Lights Festival, Chicago, IL
Occurring each year on the Saturday before Thanksgiving, this holiday-season festival of ice-carving demonstrations, strolling carolers, traditional holiday foods, and the unveiling of commercial window displays culminates in a parade on Michigan Avenue and fireworks on the lake. Displays stay up through January.
312.642.3570

DECEMBER
Christmas in Old Nauvoo, Nauvoo, IL
Restored homes and shops, decorated 1840s-style with handmade period ornaments, are opened for tours.
217.453.2237, 800.453.0022

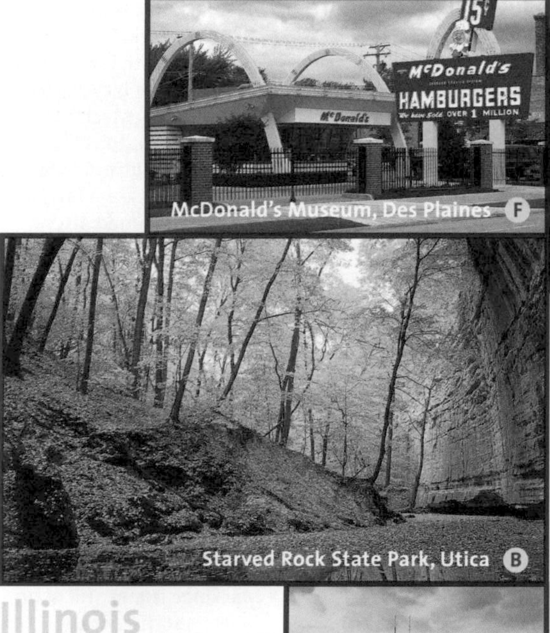

McDonald's Museum, Des Plaines (F)

Oak Park (A)

Starved Rock State Park, Utica (B)

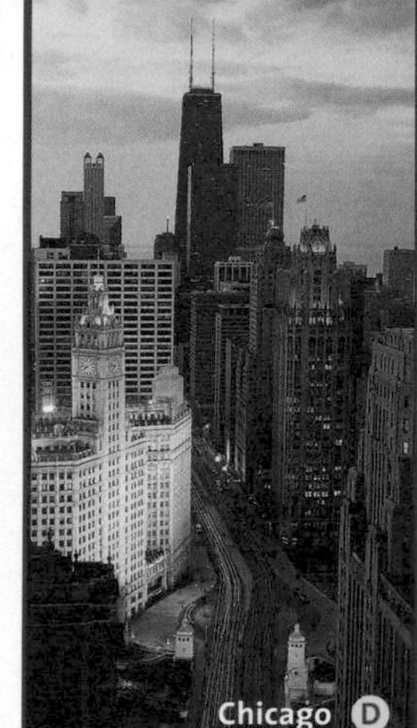
Chicago (D)

Illinois

(A) Oak Park
Pg. 90, C12. This leafy Chicago suburb figured prominently in the lives of two of America's greatest creative geniuses, men who transformed the techniques and vocabularies of their respective crafts. Oak Park was the boyhood home of Ernest Hemingway, a fact commemorated today at the North Oak Park Avenue home in which the writer was born in 1899, and at a museum a block and a half away. Beginning in 1889, Frank Lloyd Wright lived and worked in Oak Park. Local sites associated with Wright include his home and studio; the Frank Lloyd Wright Prairie School of Architecture Historic District, which includes 12 Wright buildings; and the Unity Temple, considered revolutionary for its pared-down ecclesiastical design. The Ernest Hemingway Foundation of Oak Park, **708.848.2222.** Frank Lloyd Wright Home and Studio, **708.848.1976.**

(B) Starved Rock State Park, Utica
Pg. 90, E9. The French explorer LaSalle once paddled beneath the majestic bluffs and through the shadowy canyons of the Illinois River here, in what is now state parkland. Today's visitors can enjoy hiking, camping, fishing, boating, and bridle trails, as well as the comforts of the handsome log-and-stone Starved Rock Lodge and Conference Center, with its 94 guest rooms, 16 cabins, and great hall dominated by a massive fireplace and decorated with Native American art. Starved Rock and Mathiessien State Park, **815.667.4726.** Starved Rock Lodge and Conference Center, **815.667.4211.**

(C) Cahokia Mounds State Historic Site
Pg. 121, E18. The largest prehistoric Indian city north of Mexico, built by the Mississippians, flourished between A.D. 700 and 1400, peaking in 1100 with a population of some 10,000 to 20,000. Sixty-eight of the original 120 mounds, used mostly as bases for ceremonial buildings or residences, remain. Monk's Mound, the largest on the 2,200-acre site, measures 100 feet tall, covers 14 acres, and is said to be the largest prehistoric earthen structure in the Americas. **618.346.5160.**

(D) Chicago
Pg. 90, C12. Like New York with its magnificent harbor, Chicago was a metropolis waiting to happen. Its central Great Lakes location, at the intersection of America's breadbasket and factory belt, assured that this little railroad junction would grow to greatness in the decades following the Civil War. What could not have been so easily predicted is that Chicago would give the world a new urban architecture, a style ironically at odds with the expansive horizontality of the Illinois prairie. Beginning in the 1880s, a school of architects that included Daniel Burnham and John Wellborn Root began to take Chicago skyward. Abandoning traditional all-masonry construction for the steel frame and the glass curtain wall, making full use of the elevator, the Chicago School invented the concept of vertical real estate. The Chicago Architecture Foundation offers walking tours covering the last 100 years in architecture. **312.922.3432.**

(E) Dixie Truckers Home / Route 66 Hall of Fame
Pg. 90, H8. Immortalized in song, on TV, and in American legend, shunpikers traveling between Chicago and Los Angeles still get their "kicks on Route 66." The two-lane blacktop winds through tiny towns left behind when Interstates 55 and 40 were built, and past all-night truck stops, giant billboards, neon-lit motels, and peeling tourist courts. The road has been designated a historic state highway, and in McLean one of the oldest truck stop plazas, Dixie Truckers Home, built in 1928, includes a hall of fame packed with memorabilia guaranteed to assure that the highway John Steinbeck called the Mother Road lives on in America's memory. **309.874.2323.**

(F) McDonald's Museum
Pg. 92, F6. The 1955 red-and-white tiled McDonald's in Des Plaines where Ray Kroc flipped his first burger has been reconstructed. The museum is easy to find – there are four 1955 automobiles parked outside. Inside, exhibits highlight the restaurant chain's history and early equipment. Call in advance, as the museum closes during winter. **847.297.5022.**

Chicago became home of the electric blues soon after World War II, as Mississippi Delta blues musicians traveled north to find work and settled in the area.

OH 142
IN 94
IL 90
OH 243
IN 235
IL 235

Indiana

G Conner Prairie
Pg. 94, J9. This living-history museum in Fishers re-creates one year – 1836 – in the life of the Northwest Territory (today's Midwest). In Prairietown, a fictional settlement, costumed interpreters go about daily life, working at the blacksmith's forge, reciting lessons at the schoolhouse, and – because 1836 was an election year – staging the occasional political rally. The restored William Conner Estate, built in 1823 by a prominent fur trader and businessman, is open for tours and serves as the centerpiece of an indoor museum on early Indiana. **317.776.6000.**

H Indiana Dunes National Lakeshore
Pg. 94, B5. Remnants of continental glaciation on the southern shore of Lake Michigan have created an amorphous environment of dunes, marshes, swamps, bogs, and ponds that supports an unusually eclectic collection of plants and flowers, including cacti, arctic bearberries, and southern dogwoods. A state park, near Chesterton, encompasses three miles of the lakeshore's 22 and has some wonderful beaches as well as numerous hiking trails. A visitor center traces the development of the shorelines's plant and animal life. **219.926.7561, ext. 225.**

I Children's Museum of Indianapolis
Pg. 93, K17. "Where kids grow up and adults don't have to" is the motto of the world's largest children's museum and the nation's first CineDome, a five-story "put-you-in-the-action" film theater. The complex houses 110,000 artifacts (including a mummy), ten major galleries, and 356 square feet of hands-on activities. **317.924.5431.**

J Indianapolis Motor Speedway & Hall of Fame Museum
Pg. 93, L16. The great Indianapolis Speedway opened in 1909 as a test grounds for motor cars. In 1911, when it hosted the first Indianapolis 500, the official program announced the Speedway as "the greatest racecourse in the world." Today, it still holds the title – thanks largely to its one-million-dollar signature race. Held on the Sunday before Memorial Day, the 500 draws hundreds of thousands of Indy car aficionados, many of whom also enjoy the preceding time trials that narrow the field to the final 33 drivers. The "Wasp" that won that inaugural race in 1911, at an average speed of 74.6 mph, is on display at the adjacent Hall of Fame Museum, along with more than 75 other winning cars and examples of cars built in Indianapolis, including the Stutz, Marmon, and Duesenberg. **317.484.6747.**

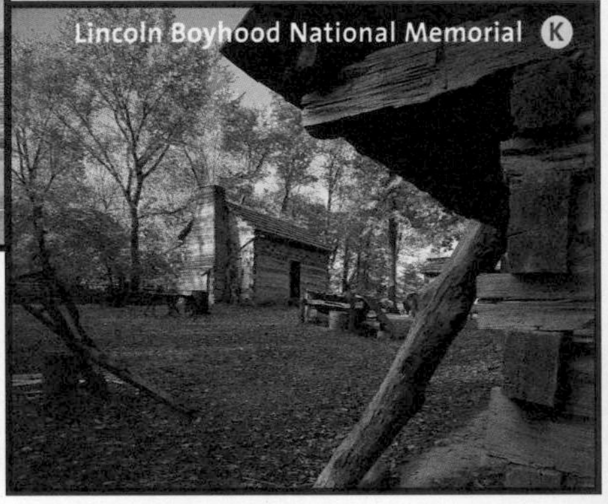

K Lincoln Boyhood National Memorial
Pg. 95, T5. The 16th president recalled his childhood home as a "wild region, with many bears and other wild animals still in the woods." Except for the bears, the 1820 farm painstakingly re-created here looks much as one did in Lincoln's day. The farm is the centerpiece of the 200-acre memorial in Lincoln City, which contains historic and interpretive exhibits and halls dedicated to Lincoln and his mother, who is buried on the grounds. **812.937.4541.**

In this country you can look farther and see less than any other place in the world.

– A 19TH-CENTURY SAYING ABOUT THE GREAT PLAINS, WHEN GRASSLANDS STRETCHED FROM INDIANA TO THE ROCKIES

In their heyday, Bedford's limestone quarries, in southern Indiana, supplied stone for New York's Empire State Building, Rockefeller Center, and Grand Central Station, as well as for the Indiana War Memorial and Chicago's Tribune Tower.

Columbus is a town in which almost anything is likely to happen and in which almost everything has.

– JAMES THURBER, "MORE ALARMS AT NIGHT" IN *MY LIFE AND HARD TIMES*, 1933

Ohio

L Cuyahoga Valley National Recreation Area
Pg. 143, E15. A river floodplain, streams, creeks, forested valleys, and plateaus characterize a 22-mile section of the Cuyahoga River, which flows between Cleveland and Akron. Historical structures and exhibits narrating the history of the valley and the Ohio & Erie Canal line the Erie Canal Towpath Trail, which parallels the remains of the canal and runs the entire length of the recreation area. **216.526.5256.**

M Amish Country
Pg. 143, K14. Ohio is home to the world's largest population of Amish, a religious sect whose members live and worship as their ancestors did, driving horse-drawn buggies, living in homes without electricity, and wearing the black clothing that identifies them as the "Plain People." Most live in a north-central part of the state known as Amish country. Visitors can tour Yoder's Amish Home, a working farm; buy Amish crafts; sample baked goods at roadside stands; and stop at the McDonald's in Millersburg, outfitted with a drive-through window at buggy height. The best place to begin is the Mennonite Information Center in Berlin. **330.893.3192.**

N United States Air Force Museum
Pg. 144, W9. Located near Dayton, the world's largest and oldest military-aviation museum, whose slogan is "Where Eagles Rest," exhibits more than 300 aircraft and missiles, from early biplanes to the advanced hardware used during the Persian Gulf war. The aircraft of several presidents are on display, as is the Apollo 15 command module and the B-29 that dropped the atom bomb on Nagasaki in 1945. **937.255.3286.**

O Pro Football Hall of Fame
Pg. 142, B9. It seems appropriate that a place dedicated to honoring pro-football greats should welcome visitors at the door with a seven-foot bronze statue of one of its best, the Native American who in 1912 ran two 90-yard kickoff-return touchdowns in a row: Jim Thorpe. It's also fitting that Canton, where the pro game was born, in 1920, should host such a shrine. Galleries honor Hall of Fame inductees, and the film *100-Yard Universe*, shown in Game Day Stadium on a 20-by-42-foot screen, is the first sports spectacle to be presented in Cinemascope. **330.456.8207.**

P Rock and Roll Hall of Fame and Museum
Pg. 143, B14. More than a collection of dubious memorabilia like Jim Morrison's Boy Scout uniform and one of Bob Marley's dreadlocks, Cleveland's homage to rock and roll features intelligent presentations on rockabilly, rhythm and blues, Motown, psychedelia, punk, hip-hop, and grunge, along with an extensive collection of artifacts charting the lives of legends like Elvis Presley, the Beatles, and Little Richard. Situated on the Lake Erie shoreline, in a building designed by I. M. Pei, this is the only institution in the world devoted to documenting the cultural form that has energized youth for almost half a century. **216.781.7625.**

Q Serpent Mound State Memorial
Pg. 144, S7. A serpent-shaped mound nearly a quarter-mile long and five feet high is one of the nation's largest and finest remaining prehistoric American effigy mounds. It is believed that the mound, perched on a bluff overlooking Ohio Brush Creek near Locust Grove, was profoundly significant in the religious mythology of its builders. **937.587.2796.**

Goodyear Tire and Rubber Company, the world's largest rubber manufacturer, in Akron, Ohio, is named after Charles Goodyear, who discovered how to vulcanize rubber, in his kitchen in 1839.

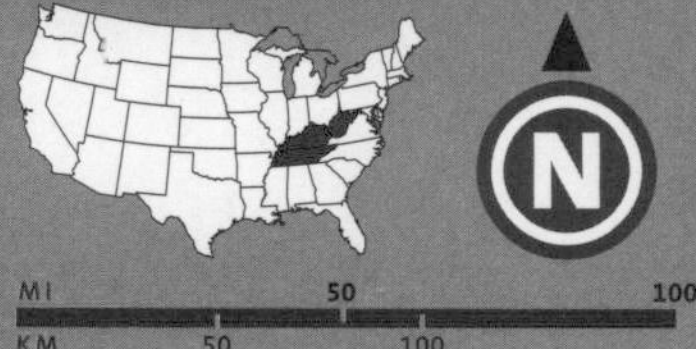

A formidable barrier to colonial Virginians desiring to break free of the coastal plain, the ancient escarpments of the Appalachians were breached by Daniel Boone in 1775 via the Wilderness Road through Cumberland Gap. Much of Tennessee, Kentucky, and West Virginia lies along the Allegheny region of the southern Appalachian Mountains. West Virginia's portion of the Appalachians begins in the Allegheny Mountains, rising from the Shenandoah Valley to the east. Farther south, along the Tennessee–North Carolina border, are the Great Smoky Mountains, which derive their name from the bluish haze of moisture that rises from the leaves of dense stands of hardwood trees. These mountains possess a human history as richly textured as their woodlands and ancient folds of granite, gneiss, and schist. Along the Alleghenys, backwoods farmers preserved remnants of colonial-era language, crafts, and culture well into the 20th century. Heading west, the terrain changes dramatically. The Ohio River drains a fertile region of hills and valleys in West Virginia and in Kentucky's Bluegrass country. Kentucky and Tennessee reach all the way to the Mississippi River, into rich bottomlands and an entirely different cultural sphere. It is in reference to a Memphis landmark, in fact, that the oft-repeated local maxim claims, "the Mississippi Delta begins in the lobby of the Peabody Hotel."

Straddling the Appalachians, West Virginia's terrain is a tortuous series of ridges and hollows. Kentucky and Tennessee share the heights of the Allegheny Mountains in the east, then descend westward to fertile lowlands along the Mississippi Valley.

Man has squatted here and there over the fair heritage, but his shabby improvements have the air of poachers' huts amidst this luxuriant beauty of nature. It is landscape gardening on the largest scale.

– FREDERICK LAW OLMSTED ON KENTUCKY, *A JOURNEY THROUGH TEXAS*, 1857

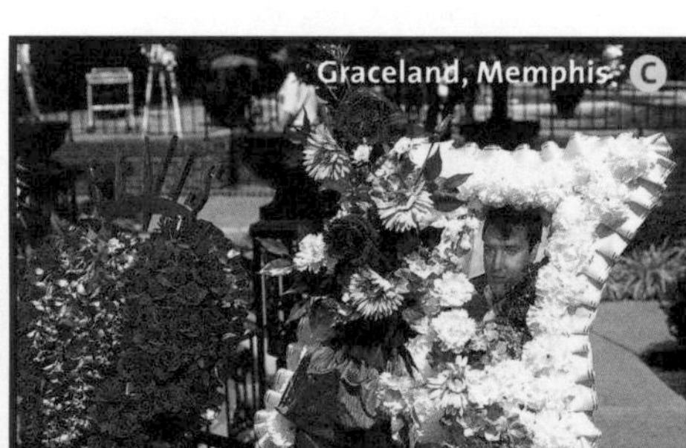
Graceland, Memphis C

Opryland USA, Nashville B

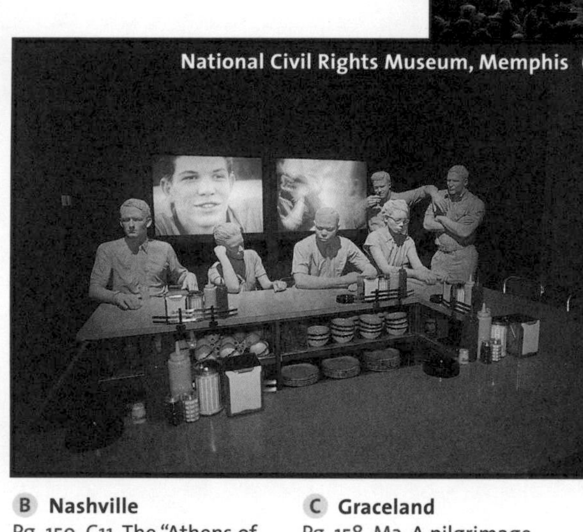
National Civil Rights Museum, Memphis F

Tennessee

A Museum of Appalachia
Pg. 159, C19. Beginning with a few farm implements purchased in 1962, local school superintendent John Rice Irwin snapped up thousands of artifacts at auctions and family-home sales across Appalachia. Irwin's treasures became the nucleus for a 70-acre complex outside Norris that now includes more than 30 authentic log cabins and buildings, and a huge barn housing a superlative collection of pioneer relics and memorabilia. Bluegrass jam sessions are usually in progress on the front porch of the 1840s Great House, and every day the harmonies of old-time religion resound from the museum's log chapel. **423.494.0514.**

B Nashville
Pg. 159, C11. The "Athens of the South" is a hub for banking, insurance, and publishing and home to several distinguished colleges and universities, as well as a training ground for preachers and missionaries, boasting more than 700 churches. But the majority of Nashville's tourist trade is centered on its status as the hallowed ground of country music, rooted in the culture of rural migrants who came to the city in the 1920s. The Grand Ole Opry, America's longest running radio program, was broadcast for 30 years from the Ryman Auditorium, a former revival house built in 1891 by a riverboat captain who got religion. Long a venue for launching or busting country and western music careers, the show is now headquartered in Opryland USA, a giant entertainment complex. **615.259.4700.**

C Graceland
Pg. 158, M3. A pilgrimage to The King's opulent Memphis mansion on Elvis Presley Boulevard begins outside with the stone wall covered with messages from adoring fans. Then on to the house itself, a combination of modest decor and '70s-style capriciousness (for example, the Jungle Den's shag-carpeted ceiling). Across the street, visitors can climb aboard Elvis's custom jets, the *Lisa Marie* and *Hound Dog II*, and see what may be the world's most famous pink Cadillac. The mansion is located ten miles from downtown Memphis and the Music Hall of Fame, where visitors can explore the roots of Presley's style, from the urban blues of 1920s Beale Street to Otis Redding. **901.332.3322.**

Sixty percent of cotton produced in the country and at least 25 percent of world cotton production is handled by members of the Memphis Cotton Exchange.

The great height of the trees, the quantity of pendant vine branches that hang amongst them, and the variety of gay plumaged birds, particularly the small green parrot, made us feel we were in a new world.

– FRANCES TROLLOPE ON MEMPHIS, *DOMESTIC MANNERS OF THE AMERICANS*, 1832

D Center for Southern Folklore
Pg. 158, F2. Located in Memphis, the center exhibits and sells locally crafted folk art by day. At night some of the region's best known performers–including Ruby Wilson, the "Queen of Beale Street," and venerable pianist Mose Vinson–hold forth in the downstairs coffee-and-beer bar. There's also lots of jazz and gospel. **901.525.3655.**

E The Hermitage
Pg. 158, K10. This Greek Revival mansion in Nashville, built for President Andrew Jackson and his wife in 1819, is filled with family furnishings and personal effects. The 625-acre estate includes the Jacksons' original 1804 log cabins, a working springhouse, slave quarters, a smokehouse, and a detached kitchen. A monument in a shaded corner of the garden marks the graves of the president and his wife. **615.889.2941.**

F National Civil Rights Museum
Pg. 158, K2. The Lorraine Motel in Memphis, site of Dr. Martin Luther King, Jr.'s assassination on April 4, 1968, is now a museum tracing the history of the American Civil Rights Movement, from union organizer A. Philip Randolph to the Black Panthers. **901.521.9699.**

APRIL

American Quilter's Society National Show and Contest, Paducah, KY
Quilters from around the country gather for one of the nation's largest shows of its kind.
502.898.7903

MAY

Webster County Woodchopping Festival, Webster Springs, WV
Lumberjacks from all over the world compete, accompanied by a championship turkey-calling contest, parades, and square dancing.
304.847.7666

Kentucky Derby and Derby Festival, Louisville, KY
Festivities leading up to the legendary horse race, which is held each year on the first Saturday in May, begin two weeks before the event.
800.928.3378

International Bar-B-Q Festival, Owensboro, KY
Devotees of the original "slow food" flock to the "barbecue capital of the world" for the riverfront festival, which features rides, crafts, entertainment and outstanding barbecue.
502.926.6938

JUNE

Great American Brass Band Festival, Danville, KY
Return to turn-of-the-century America as bands from across the country gather to play and compete.
800.755.0076

JULY

Old Time Fiddler's Jamboree and Crafts Festival, Smithville, TN
Twenty-eight categories of old-time music – including clogging, buck dancing, five-string banjo, and Dobro – are performed. Fiddlers compete for the title of Grand Champion.
615.464.6444

Jamboree in the Hills, St. Clairesville, WV
Country stars from radio station WWVA's Jamboree USA perform live outdoors at the "Super Bowl of country music."
800.624.5456

AUGUST

Elvis Week, Memphis, TN
Dozens of events throughout the city, including dances, a candlelight vigil, and a trivia contest, are devoted to celebrating the life of Memphis's most famous adopted son.
800.238.2000

Tennessee Walking Horse National Celebration, Shelbyville, TN
Ten days and nights of high-stepping excitement as more than 2,000 Tennessee Walking Horses and their riders compete for money, awards, and World Grand Champion titles.
615.684.5915

OCTOBER

IBMA Bluegrass Fan Fest, Louisville, KY
The world's best bluegrass musicians gather to play and compete.
502.684.9025, 888.438.4262

The Tennessee Fall Homecoming at the Museum of Appalachia, Norris, TN
More than 400 old-time musicians, singers, craftspeople, and artisans join together to demonstrate rural pioneer activities and celebrate the culture and heritage of Appalachia.
423.494.7680

Cumberland Gap National Historical Park H

Churchill Downs J

Kentucky

G Berea
Pg. 101, J13. This pretty little town in Kentucky's coal district is home to one of the country's most distinctive institutions of higher learning. Berea College was founded by abolitionists in 1855 to serve the young people of Appalachia—both white and black—at no cost. Today the majority of the school's students still come from the region, the college is still tuition-free, and part of the labor program, Student Craft Industries, ensures that Appalachian crafts and traditions will live on through the generations. Professional artisans have shops and studios around town, and the Appalachian Museum commemorates old-time crafts. **800.598.5263.**

H Cumberland Gap National Historical Park
Pg. 101, N16. Although it had been used by Native Americans for centuries, not until 1750 did Dr. Thomas Walker document the location of this natural passage through the Allegheny Mountains. A quarter century later, Daniel Boone and 30 axmen blazed what became the gap's Wilderness Road, and by 1800 between 200,000 and 300,000 settlers had trekked through to Kentucky. Today the gap is part of the country's largest National Historical Park—20,305 acres of forest and mountains, with magnificent overlooks, the remains of a Civil War fort, hiking trails, and Hensley Settlement, a restored Appalachian community. **606.248.2817.**

I Cumberland Falls State Resort Park
Pg. 101, M13. Set amid Daniel Boone National Forest's 687,000 acres is the largest waterfall east of the Rockies after Niagara Falls. Cascading over rocks in a 125-foot-wide curtain, the water drops 68 feet into the Cumberland River. This is one of the few places in the world where visitors can regularly expect to see a moonbow. The phenomenon is visible on clear nights during a full moon, when moonlight illuminates the perpetual mist created by water striking the bottom of the gorge. A convenient gateway to the park is near the town of Corbin. **800.325.0063.**

J Churchill Downs
Pg. 100, C7. The most exciting two minutes in sports occur each year on the first Saturday in May, when the world's best three-year-old horses come to the Downs in Louisville to vie for a chance at immortality in the first leg of the Triple Crown. And as sports crowds go, this one is noted for its sentimentality, giving way to mass emoting during renditions of "My Old Kentucky Home." The Kentucky Derby Museum presents a 360-degree multimedia show as well as race-related exhibits. **502.637.1111.**

K Land Between the Lakes
Pg. 100, M1. Between Barkley and Kentucky lakes in western Kentucky and Tennessee is a wooded peninsula managed by the Tennessee Valley Authority as a national demonstration area in recreation, environmental education, and resource management. Among the highlights on the peninsula: The Homeplace, a living-history farm that re-creates the life of a rural farm family before the Civil War; and the 700-acre elk and bison range, populated by the first elk to inhabit the area in more than 140 years and the largest publicly owned herd of buffalo east of the Mississippi River. **502.924.2000.**

Thoroughbred horse breeding farms in Kentucky are concentrated in the six-county area, in and around Lexington, known as the Bluegrass. Since 1936, 250 champion horses have been bred there, including Seattle Slew, Citation, and Count Fleet—all Triple Crown winners.

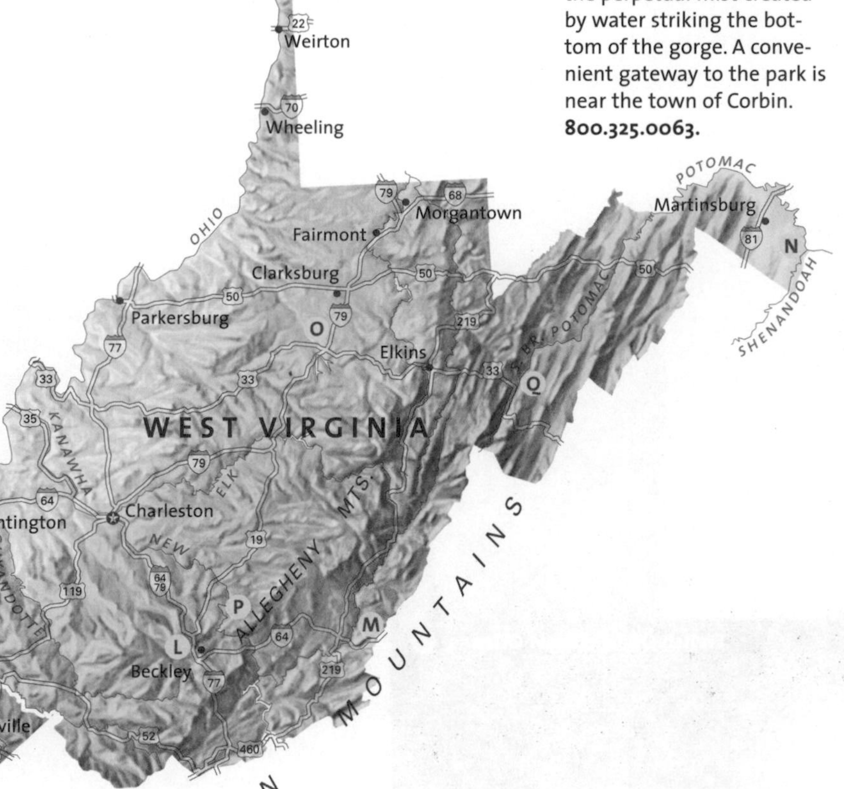

The views are magnificent, the valleys so beautiful, the scenery so peaceful. . . .

— ROBERT E. LEE, ON THE CHEAT MOUNTAIN REGION, WEST VIRGINIA, 1861

West Virginia

L Exhibition Coal Mine
Pg. 173, H4. The dangerous calling of those who descend deep into the earth for coal is brought home with visceral clarity in a tour of the Exhibition Coal Mine in Beckley, the industry's hub in southern West Virginia. A miner-guide accompanies visitors, who are transported into a gaping hole in a hillside via a mine trolley. Above ground are some traditional camp buildings brought from old mining camps and a small museum containing panoramic photos of coal camps, tools, equipment, and miners' clothing. **304.256.1747.**

M The Greenbrier
Pg. 173, H7. One of America's finest resorts, the 6,500-acre Greenbrier at White Sulphur Springs is built on the site of a mineral spring celebrated for its alleged curative powers as early as 1778. Today the mineral waters still flow beneath an 1830s springhouse at the 670-room hotel, and guests can still luxuriate in mineral baths—although the Greenbrier's modern focus is on golf, tennis, horseback riding, and fine cuisine. A museum is now housed in the President's Cottage, which was used as a retreat for five presidents in the early 19th century. **304.536.1110.**

A coal stratum underlies four-fifths of the counties in the southern and north-central sections of West Virginia; the state is the country's leading producer of bituminous (soft) coal.

N Harpers Ferry National Historical Park
Pg. 173, C13. Harpers Ferry was the site of a U.S. arsenal targeted by radical abolitionist John Brown and his 21-man "army of liberation" in 1859 as part of a plan to seize weapons with which to arm a slave revolt. The band of rebels (which included two of Brown's sons and five black men) was captured at the arsenal by federal troops commanded by future Confederate general Robert E. Lee. Brown was hanged for treason, insurrection, and murder. Today the 2,300-acre park at the confluence of the Shenandoah and Potomac Rivers encompasses several museums detailing the town's role in the Civil War and the early civil rights movement. **304.535.6298.**

O Jackson's Mill & Historic District
Pg. 173, D6. Located near Weston, this historic district complex includes the boyhood home of General Thomas "Stonewall" Jackson; the family gristmill, built circa 1837; the restored Blaker Mill, featuring an unusual horizontal waterwheel; and a reconstructed early 19th-century cabin. **304.269.5100.**

P New River Gorge National River
Pg. 173, H5. One of North America's oldest rivers has carved a spectacular gorge through the southeastern part of the state, and a 53-mile stretch of its lower end, designated a National River, has become perhaps the premier spot for white-water rafting in the East. The New River Gorge Bridge, the longest steel arch in the world, towers 876 feet above the river. The Canyon Rim Visitor Center in Lansing traces the area's natural and human history. At the gorge's southern end stands Hinton, a turn-of-the-century railroad town. Dozens of workers' houses, imposing civic buildings, and brick-paved streets are slowly crumbling but still intact. **304.465.0508.**

Q Seneca Rocks
Pg. 173, E9. The thousand-foot-tall strata of Tuscarora sandstone, which dates back to the Silurian Period, is among the most impressive rock formations in the East. Extremely popular with climbers, the rocks are part of the Monongahela National Forest, 909,084 acres of rugged mountains and woods. **304.567.2827.**

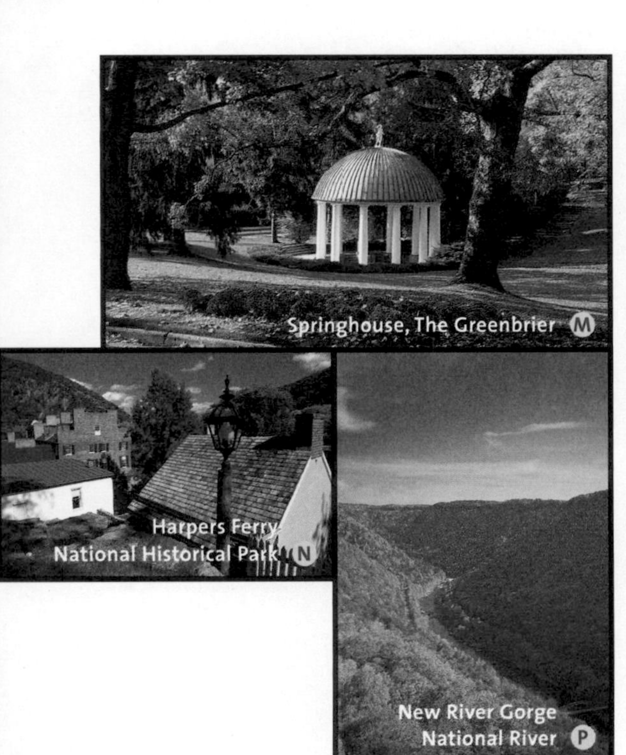

Springhouse, The Greenbrier M

Harpers Ferry National Historical Park N

New River Gorge National River P

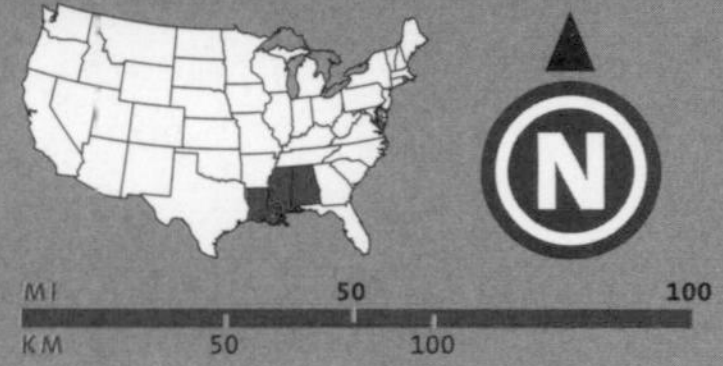

The heart of the American Deep South – Alabama, Mississippi, and Louisiana – lies largely along a coastal plain defined by two great bodies of water: the Mississippi River and the Gulf of Mexico. Snaking lazily along most of Mississippi's western border, Old Man River makes its way into Louisiana, arcs through New Orleans, and empties into the Gulf at the end of a delta that grows steadily with silt carried over half a continent. West of the river's last stretch lies the Louisiana bayou country, a half-submerged territory of swampland, shallow lakes, and forested islands. Further north, a floodplain between Memphis and Vicksburg, known as the Mississippi Delta, is the birthplace of the haunting American folk poetry called the Delta Blues. Not all of the Dixie heartland lies along bottomlands and coastal plains. The southern anchor of the Appalachian Mountains is in northeastern Alabama, a place of hills and valleys and deep woods where the plantations of the antebellum South were slow to take root. As late as the 1830s, when the planters' great houses had long flourished in Mississippi and Louisiana, much of Alabama's uplands were near wilderness, settled piecemeal by poor farmers whose homesteads fit no one's idea of a stately manor. More than a century later, the state became a flash point for the civil rights movement with historic confrontations in Montgomery, Birmingham, and Selma.

Alabama, with a heavily forested interior, came later to plantation agriculture than its neighbors – but enjoyed in its old port of Mobile a magnificent location for shipbuilding and commerce. Mississippi and Louisiana are creatures of the Mississippi River, which endowed both the famously fertile Delta and the busy port of New Orleans.

When you're in Mississippi, the rest of America doesn't seem real. And when you're in the rest of America, Mississippi doesn't seem real.

– BOB PARRIS MOSES, c. 1961

FEBRUARY

Mardi Gras, Mobile, AL
Two weeks of festivities lead up to the numerous parades of Fat Tuesday, featuring elaborate theme floats. It's all a bit less hectic, and more down-home, than in New Orleans.
334.434.7304

Mardi Gras, New Orleans, LA
Rollicking, raucous, and ritualistic, Mardi Gras is New Orleans's legendary carnival, featuring free-wheeling street celebrations, formal masquerade balls, and the famous parade in which the "Krewes" try to outdo each others' floats and costumes.
504.566.5003, 800.672.6124

MAY

Contraband Days Festival, Lake Charles, LA
During the first two weeks of May, the city honors Jean Lafitte, "the gentleman pirate," and the contraband treasures he is said to have cached on the shores of Lake Charles, with a mock pirate invasion, night boat parade, and other festivities.
318.436.5508

Indian Bayou Festival and B. B. King's Homecoming, Indianola, MS
Blues legend B. B. King returns to his hometown each year, bringing his legendary guitar Lucille. There's also a barbecue cook-off.
601.887.4454

JUNE

Steamboat Jubilee and Floozie Day, Natchez, MS
The famous 1870 steamboat race between the *Robert E. Lee* and the *Natchez* is reenacted amidst a carnival atmosphere.
800.647.6724

JULY

Choctaw Indian Fair, Philadelphia, MS
Celebrity entertainers, traditional Indian dancing, the World Series Stickball Games, and blowgun and drumbeat demonstrations are annual staples at this one-of-a-kind fair.
601.650.1685

SEPTEMBER

The Original Southwest Louisiana Zydeco Music Festival, Opelousas, LA
Performers play authentic Creole and Zydeco music in the rural setting where it was born.
318.942.2392

Mississippi Delta Blues and Heritage Festival, Greenville, MS
Nationally and internationally known artists perform at one of the South's largest music festivals, dedicated to the plaintive native sound of the Delta.
800.467.3582

OCTOBER

National Shrimp Festival, Gulf Shores, AL
Four days of beachfront festivities include a parade, music, arts and crafts, and a sumptuous abundance of seafood.
334.968.6904

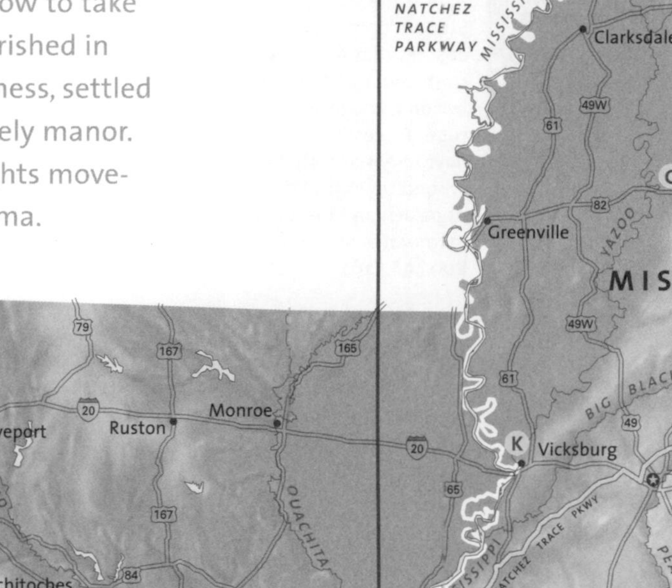

Louisiana heron, Creole Nature Trail (A)

French Quarter, New Orleans (D)

Oak Alley Plantation, Great River Road (E)

Louisiana

(A) Creole Nature Trail National Scenic Byway
Pg. 102, K5–K7, L5–L7. The only National Scenic Byway in the Gulf south, the 180-mile Creole Nature Trail in southwest Louisiana takes in four wildlife refuges and a bird and butterfly sanctuary. The Sabine National Wildlife Refuge is the largest waterfowl preserve on the Gulf Coast, with a walking trail that allows visitors to get up close and personal with resident alligators. Lacassine National Wildlife Refuge centers upon a freshwater marshland that attracts up to 800,000 ducks and geese. And the Peveto Woods Bird and Butterfly Sanctuary is a 41-acre island providing refuge for as many as two million migratory songbirds each spring. **800.456.7952.**

(B) Audubon Park & Zoological Gardens
Pg. 103, C17. More than 1,800 local and exotic animals – including white alligators and a white tiger – representing 415 species dwell in simulations of their natural habitats. New Orleans's marvelous zoo, one of the most highly rated in the country, is located in elegant Audubon Park along the river. Itself a natural habitat for recreationists, the park is shaded by palms and venerable oaks, dotted with fountains and lagoons. **800.774.7394.**

(C) Natchitoches
Pg. 102, E7. In 1714, a French trader built a small fort near a village of Natchitoches (pronounced NA-ki-tish) Indians. The outpost grew into the oldest permanent European settlement in the Louisiana Territory, and its 33-block historic district encompasses the largest assortment of French Creole architecture in the Mississippi Valley. **800.259.1714.**

(D) French Quarter
Pg. 103, E16. First settled by 18th-century French colonists and consisting of 66 full and 16 partial city blocks, the French Quarter is famous for its Creole architecture, good food, great music, and laissez-faire spirit. The best way to tour is on foot: Many sites are packed into a few blocks, and the streets tend to be narrow and congested, particularly during Mardi Gras. Any visit should include Jackson Square, with its colonial, religious, and historic commercial buildings facing the Mississippi; a stop at the Café du Monde for café au lait and beignets (powdered-sugar doughnuts); and a night of jazz at tiny, deliciously decrepit, magnificent Preservation Hall. Free walking tours begin at Jean Lafitte National Historical Park and Preserve's Visitor Center in the French Market. **504.589.2636.**

(E) Great River Road Plantations
Pg. 103, B15, K13, K12. For a glimpse of southern gentry life (and what slavery made possible), six of Louisiana's legendary 18th- and 19th-century oak-shaded antebellum plantations line a stretch of the Great River Road, which begins in New Orleans and continues north along the Mississippi River to Natchez. Among them are Destrehan, built in 1787 and the oldest intact plantation house in the lower Mississippi Valley; the magnificent Greek Revival Houmas House Plantation and Gardens, once Louisiana's largest sugar plantation; and Nottoway Plantation, also known as the White Castle of Louisiana, the largest plantation home in the South. Each is unique, and all are open for tours. **800.672.6124.**

In Louisiana, the live-oak is the king of the forest, and the magnolia is its queen.

– ACTOR JOSEPH JEFFERSON IN HIS AUTOBIOGRAPHY, 1917

Louisiana provides more than a quarter of all seafood caught in the United States – including jumbo Gulf shrimps, plump salty oysters, and swamp crawfish, all of which are used in spicy Cajun cuisine.

AL 60
MS 118
LA 102
AL 232
MS 239
LA 237

Illinois Memorial, Vicksburg National Military Park (K)

Gulf Islands National Seashore (H)

Melrose Plantation Home, Natchez (J)

Mississippi

(F) Beauvoir
Pg. 118, N2. This seaside home in Biloxi, completed around 1852 and once the retirement estate of Confederate president Jefferson Davis, served as the Mississippi Confederate soldiers' home from 1903 to 1957. Today the house and pavilions have been restored, and most of the furnishings are original. The museum in the Confederate Men's Hospital exhibits personal items and memorabilia of southern Civil War veterans. The cemetery contains more than 700 graves as well as the Tomb of the Unknown Soldier of the Confederate States of America. **601.388.9074.**

(G) Cotton Row
Pg. 118, E6. At Greenwood's cotton exchange, the second largest in the nation, factors still grade fibers by hand, using the same methods employed in antebellum Mississippi – a skill that will become obsolete within the next few years, when all classing will be handled by computer. Overlooking the Yazoo River, the 19th-century Cotton Row – now on the National Register of Historic Places – once housed 57 offices, and is still home to 24 of the original businesses as well as the infamous Ram Cat Alley and Front Street, which once boasted as many bars as cotton factors. **800.748.9064.**

(H) Gulf Islands National Seashore
Pg. 118, N9. The longest of the country's 11 national seashores is a fragile strand of barrier islands stretching about 150 miles, from Santa Rosa Island in Florida to Mississippi's West Ship Island off the Gulf Coast. Two of Mississippi's four barrier islands, Horn and Petit Bois, are the only federally designated wilderness areas on the Gulf Coast and harbor alligators, raccoons, snakes, migrating seabirds, and butterflies. Horn Island and Petit Bois are open to wilderness camping and accessible by private or charter boat. **228.875.9057.**

(I) Oxford
Pg. 118, C7. The town that William Faulkner called Jefferson in several of his novels is home to "Ole Miss," the state's university, chartered in 1844. General Ulysses S. Grant and his troops occupied the campus in 1862, and the original buildings survived the torching of the city in 1864. Nearly a century later, in 1962, James Meredith, the first African American to attend Ole Miss, was escorted through the hallowed halls by federal troops. **800.758.9177.**

(J) Natchez
Pg. 118, J3. When cotton was king, the port of Natchez grew to grandeur as wealthy planters erected neoclassical showplaces atop the bluffs above the Mississippi River. Today the town includes more than a hundred of these antebellum homes, 32 of which can be toured during the annual Natchez Spring Pilgrimage; additional houses are open during the Fall and Christmas Pilgrimages. No doubt, some of the wealth amassed by plantation owners made its way down to Natchez Under-the-Hill, a waterfront gambling and red-light district once referred to as "Sodom on the Mississippi" and now restored as an entertainment and shopping area. **800.647.6742.**

(K) Vicksburg National Military Park
Pg. 118, H2. The port of Vicksburg was the Confederacy's key bastion on the Mississippi River. President Lincoln appreciated the city's strategic significance, and in the late spring of 1863 sent General Ulysses S. Grant and 50,000 men to begin a siege of the "Gibraltar of the Confederacy." On July 4, after a campaign considered by many historians to be the most ingenious military action in American history, Vicksburg surrendered. The 1,700-acre park offers a 16-mile auto tour past monuments, markers, and re-created earthworks. **601.636.0583.**

Mississippi's largest longleaf pine forests extend approximately 150 miles inland from the coast, but only about 240,000 acres are left of this strong, clean, and straight pine, which is often used for telephone poles.

When I get to be a composer /
I'm gonna write me some music about Daybreak in Alabama. /
And I'm gonna put the purtiest songs in it
Rising out of the ground like a swamp mist /
And falling out of heaven like soft dew.

– LANGSTON HUGHES, "DAYBREAK IN ALABAMA," 1940

Each winter more than a hundred American bald eagles make their home at Lake Guntersville State Park in northern Alabama.

U.S.S. *Alabama* Battleship Memorial Park, Mobile (Q)

The Civil Rights Memorial (M)

Antebellum home, Mobile (N)

Alabama

(L) Bellingrath Gardens & Home
Pg. 61, S2. The former estate of Coca-Cola magnate Walter D. Bellingrath is one of North America's premier horticultural showplaces: 65 acres of meticulously landscaped formal gardens. The estate's centerpiece is Mirror Lake, a five-acre pool whose surface reflects the colors of the gardens. The main house, overlooking the sweeping Great Lawn, houses an extensive collection of 18th- and 19th-century furniture, porcelain, and glassware. **334.973.2217.**

(M) The Civil Rights Memorial
Pg. 60, K8. It will probably never be known with certainty just how many people died for the cause of civil rights. But the names of 40, killed by police and white supremacists, are etched on Maya Lin's black granite table, which stands in front of the Southern Poverty Law Center in Montgomery. Water flows continuously across the table's surface, a poignant reference to the quotation inscribed on the wall behind, taken from the Book of Amos, and so powerfully invoked by Dr. Martin Luther King, Jr., in his speeches: ". . . until justice rolls down like waters and righteousness like a mighty stream." **334.264.0286.**

(N) Mobile
Pg. 61, R3. Down on the Gulf Coast, tucked behind the barrier beaches that protect Mobile Bay from open water, Alabama's only seaport holds to one of the South's oldest traditions. Founded by the French in 1710, Mobile has celebrated Mardi Gras even longer than its slightly younger though more grandly fated neighbor, New Orleans. During the Civil War, Mobile was one of the Confederacy's most vital ports, and was home base for many blockade runners. Today downtown Mobile and its surrounding historic districts preserve a substantial number of houses such as Oakleigh, a Greek Revival gem that illustrates mid-19th-century life in upper-class Mobile. **334.434.7304.**

(O) Tuskegee Institute National Historic Site
Pg. 60, K9. Former slave Booker T. Washington arrived in Tuskegee in 1881 with the dream of founding a college for African Americans. With the help of his first class (30 students), Washington erected a small building and began offering secondary education and teacher training. Later the school developed a program of agricultural and industrial training, which garnered international recognition. Today 26 of more than 160 buildings on the 1,500-acre campus are included in the National Historic Site. **334.727.3200.**

(P) U.S. Space & Rocket Center
Pg. 60, B7. Blast into space at 4 g's of force on Space Shot, see movies filmed in space by astronauts on Spacedome Theater's 67-foot domed screen, check out America's only full-scale Space Shuttle exhibit, or rocket into the unknown on the Journey to Jupiter flight simulator. Dozens of hands-on displays and one of the world's largest collections of space and rocket hardware are available to help visitors explore space from the ground up. Bus tours of NASA's Marshall Space Flight Center leave from the Space & Rocket Center, which adjoins the U.S. Space Camp Training Center at Huntsville. **205.837.3400.**

(Q) U.S.S. *Alabama* Battleship Memorial Park
Pg. 61, T9. Dedicated to Alabama's war veterans, this 155-acre park in Mobile is home to several military artifacts, including the U.S.S. *Alabama*, which earned nine battle stars for service in the Pacific during World War II. Visitors can climb aboard the ship's decks, sit in the turrets, and check out the mess, captain's cabin, and crew areas. **334.433.2703.**

MI 50 100
KM 50 100

If the Gulf of Mexico and the Atlantic Ocean ever wanted to meet over land, their highest obstacle in Florida would be a scant 345 feet. Though relatively flat, the land of sunshine and coconut palms is certainly never dull. Florida's landscape is home to rich and diverse habitats – many of which were far from attractive to visitors before large-scale drainage, mosquito control, and air-conditioning. Known best for theme parks from Walt Disney World to Weeki Wachee Spring's City of Mermaids, and for top-shelf resort playgrounds like The Breakers in Palm Beach, the real Florida is in places still surprisingly wild. Stunning white sand beaches like the Panhandle's acclaimed St. Andrews gleam no less in the wake of Hurricane Opal. More than 2,500 sinkhole lakes dot the state's panhandle and northern region, a land where longleaf-pine forests sit astride black-water rivers and where the country's oldest city of European descent is found in St. Augustine. In the tropical south, shallow Lake Okeechobee feeds the Everglades. Called a "river of grass," this fragile saw-grass wetlands is a refuge for threatened creatures like the Florida panther and American crocodile. Just as it is sometimes hard to tell shore from sea in the saltwater marshes and barrier islands along its coasts, Florida is a shifting land of many faces – where strip mall and fecund mangrove swamp sit in awkward proximity.

Beneath the surface of the northern part of Florida, fissures and cracks in the limestone bedrock have left a landscape dotted with hundreds of freshwater springs and thousands of sinkholes. Near Gainesville, at Devils Millhopper State Geological Site, a sinkhole 120 feet deep and some 600 feet wide testifies to the porous nature of the state's underbelly. To the south, a giant ecosystem includes tropical forests, the Everglades, and coral reefs off the keys.

The state with the prettiest name,
the state that floats in brackish water,
held together by mangrove roots.

– ELIZABETH BISHOP, "FLORIDA," 1939

JANUARY
Annual Florida Citrus Festival and Polk County Fair, Winter Haven
An 11-day celebration of the citrus industry is set in a country-fair atmosphere, with livestock exhibits, quilt shows, and entertainment.
941.967.3175

FEBRUARY
Speed Weeks, Daytona
The world's best road racers and stock-car drivers converge on the Daytona International Speedway for some of motor sport's biggest events from the Rolex 24 through the Daytona 500.
904.254.2700

Silver Spurs Rodeo, Kissimmee
Professional bull and bronco riders, calf ropers, bareback riders, steer wrestlers, barrel racers, and all-around cowboys compete in the largest rodeo in the eastern United States. This twice-yearly event also occurs in October.
800.327.9159

APRIL
Florida Heritage Festival, Bradenton
A monthlong celebration commemorating the 1539 landing of Hernando de Soto near the mouth of the Manatee River and honoring the area's Spanish heritage.
941.747.1998

MAY
SunFest, West Palm Beach
The state's premier music, arts, and waterfront festival features national recording artists and showcases professional arts-and-crafts collectibles.
561.659.5992

AUGUST
Miami Reggae Festival
One of the country's largest reggae festivals features a full day of performances by international artists.
305.891.2944

OCTOBER
Fantasy Fest, Key West
The Southernmost City pulls out all the stops with Caribbean carnival revelry, Halloween parades, and a touch of wrong-time-of-the-year Mardi Gras.
305.296.1817

NOVEMBER
WJCT's Jacksonville Jazz Festival
This weeklong festival brings in nationally known artists and features the Great American Jazz Piano Competition.
904.353.7770

DECEMBER
Nights of Lights, St. Augustine
More than a million tiny white lights illuminate St. Augustine's bayfront and buildings in its historic downtown during December and January.
800.653.2489

Kennedy Space Center, Merritt Island C

LAKE SEMINOLE
223
Pensacola
CHOCTAWHATCHEE BAY
Fort Walton Beach
FLORIDA PANHANDLE SCENIC DRIVE
Panama City
APALACHICOLA
Tallahassee
G
APALACHEE BAY
CAPE SAN BLAS

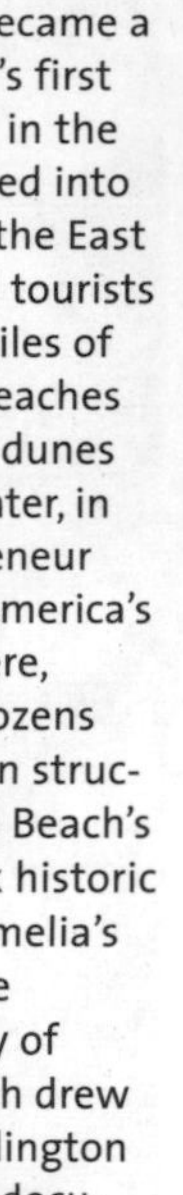

Spring break, Daytona Beach F

John Pennekamp Coral Reef State Park E

Amelia Island A

A Amelia Island

Pg. 83, E17. In its remarkably tangled history, Amelia Island has been governed by eight different nations or individuals, hence its nickname, the "Isle of Eight Flags." The island became a terminus of Florida's first cross-state railroad in the 1860s and burgeoned into a resort, but when the East Coast Railway lured tourists farther south, its miles of Allegheny quartz beaches and towering sand dunes were left behind. Later, in 1935, black entrepreneur A. L. Lewis created America's first black resort here, American Beach. Dozens of restored Victorian structures in Fernandina Beach's more than 50-block historic district testify to Amelia's golden age of white tourism; the heyday of black tourism, which drew the likes of Duke Ellington and Count Basie, is documented at the American Beach Museum, lovingly administered by Lewis's great-granddaughter. **800.226.3542.**

B Canaveral National Seashore

Pg. 83, J19. Just north of Kennedy Space Center is a 57,000-acre wilderness area that preserves the longest undeveloped beach on Florida's east coast. Favored by sea turtles, pelicans, alligators, and manatees, the seashore is an unspoiled realm of barrier beaches, lagoons, and dunes. Surfers congregate at the southern end of the shore. The Space Center's huge hangars and gantries loom to the south at the edge of the wilderness. **407.267.1110.**

C Kennedy Space Center

Pg. 83, K19. Every manned rocket since America's space age dawned in 1958 has been launched from this 140,000-acre site on Merritt Island. Two IMAX theaters in the Kennedy Space Center Visitor Complex show movies featuring awesome images of Earth shot from space (*The Dream Is Alive*) and footage of astronauts going about their daily chores on a space shuttle. Visitors have a choice of two bus tours: The Kennedy Space Center Tour, which includes a stop at the new Apollo/Saturn V Center; or the Cape Canaveral Tour, which takes in the Mercury facilities and other historical sites. **407.452.2121.**

D Homosassa Springs State Wildlife Park

Pg. 83, J14. Source of the Homosassa River, this freshwater spring spews millions of gallons of water per hour at a constant temperature of 72°F to 74°F. At the Fish Bowl underwater observatory, visitors can view thousands of native fish, as well as manatees that have been injured by boats and taken here for refuge and recuperation. Nature trails lead past protected habitats housing an orphaned bear, an endangered Key deer, bobcats, and other indigenous wildlife. **352.628.2311.**

E John Pennekamp Coral Reef State Park

Pg. 84, T20. More than 500 species of fish and approximately 40 kinds of coral enliven the waters of the country's first underwater park, in Key Largo. The park is named for the *Miami Herald* editor whose lengthy crusade rescued the reef here from commercial scavengers. More than 10,000 years in the making, a network of patch reefs extends four to five miles out from the shore. Concessionaires rent snorkel and diving equipment, and run glass-bottom and charter boats out to the reef. **305.451.1202.**

F Daytona Beach

Pg. 83, H18. Between 1902 and 1935, drivers such as Barney Oldfield and Major Henry Segrave set 13 speed records at Daytona Beach (the highest recorded speed on the beach was 276.82 mph, in 1935). Today race cars, motorcycles, and go-carts do the same at nearby Daytona International Speedway. But tradition continues: Cars and buggies can still drive along portions of the 23-mile beach, which is 500 feet wide at low tide. And during spring break, when thousands of college students flock to the beach, sunbathers might feel more relaxed in the middle of the speedway. **800.854.1234.**

G Wakulla Springs State Park

Pg. 82, F10. Juan Ponce de León believed the springs he found here in 1513 to be the "fountain of youth." Movie buffs may recognize the scenery from Tarzan films and *Creature from the Black Lagoon*, which were filmed here. Located 15 miles south of Tallahassee, Wakulla Springs, one of the world's deepest freshwater springs, continues to yield an average of 400,000 gallons of crystal-clear water per minute from a cavern thousands of feet deep, which has yet to be fully explored by divers to find the source. Glass-bottom-boat tours offer views of the 185-foot-deep basin when the springs are clear. **850.224.5950.**

Florida's citrus regions are in the central and southern parts of the state, with more than 14,000 citrus growers cultivating some 100 million trees on over 850,000 acres.

FL 82
FL 234

On the more than 1,100 golf courses in Florida–200 more than in any other state–an amazing 55 million rounds of golf are played each year.

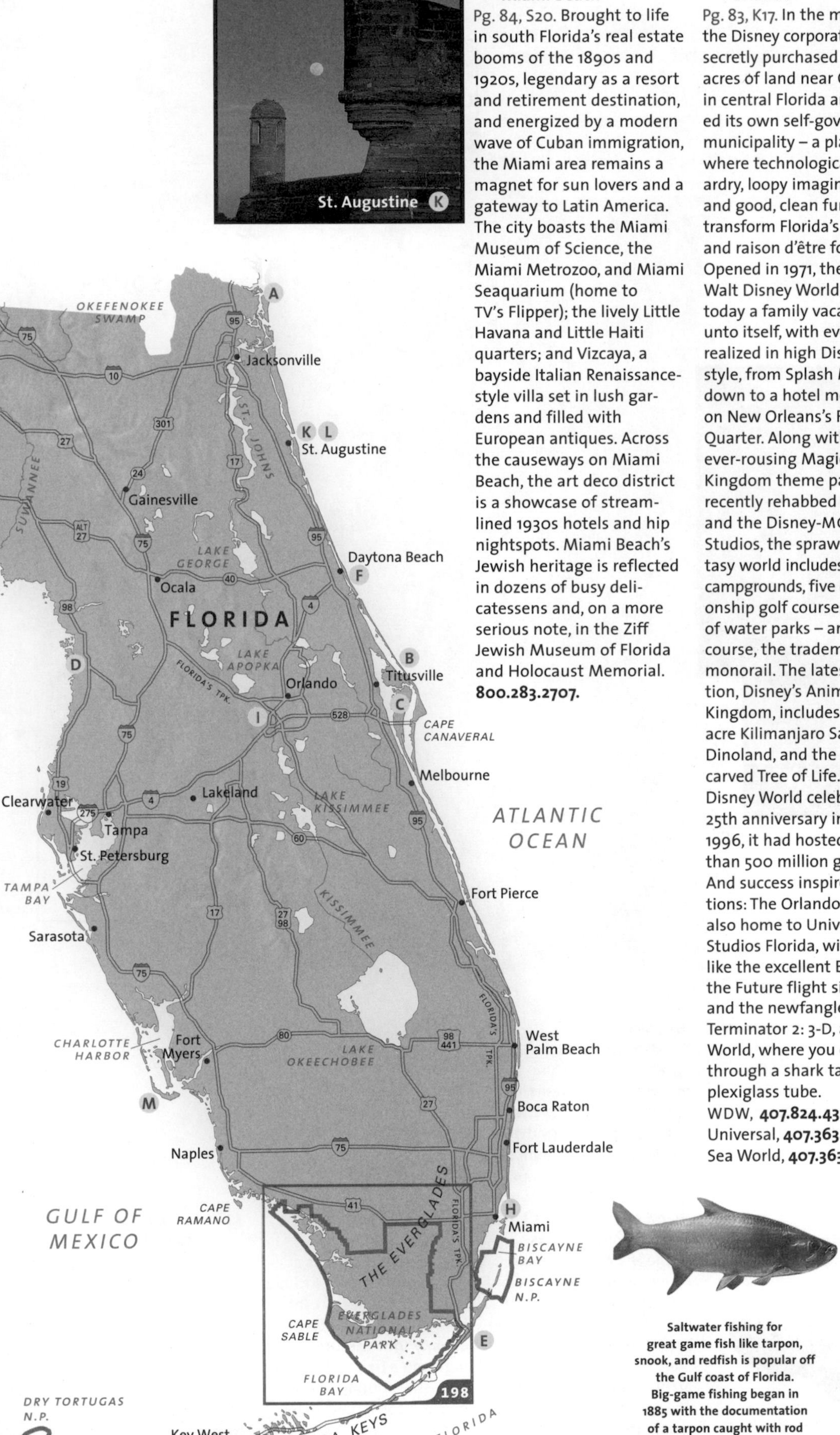

H Miami/ Miami Beach

Pg. 84, S20. Brought to life in south Florida's real estate booms of the 1890s and 1920s, legendary as a resort and retirement destination, and energized by a modern wave of Cuban immigration, the Miami area remains a magnet for sun lovers and a gateway to Latin America. The city boasts the Miami Museum of Science, the Miami Metrozoo, and Miami Seaquarium (home to TV's Flipper); the lively Little Havana and Little Haiti quarters; and Vizcaya, a bayside Italian Renaissance-style villa set in lush gardens and filled with European antiques. Across the causeways on Miami Beach, the art deco district is a showcase of streamlined 1930s hotels and hip nightspots. Miami Beach's Jewish heritage is reflected in dozens of busy delicatessens and, on a more serious note, in the Ziff Jewish Museum of Florida and Holocaust Memorial. **800.283.2707.**

I Walt Disney World/ Orlando

Pg. 83, K17. In the mid-1960s the Disney corporation secretly purchased 27,500 acres of land near Orlando in central Florida and created its own self-governed municipality – a place where technological wizardry, loopy imagination, and good, clean fun would transform Florida's economy and raison d'être forever. Opened in 1971, the greater Walt Disney World Resort is today a family vacation unto itself, with every detail realized in high Disney style, from Splash Mountain down to a hotel modeled on New Orleans's French Quarter. Along with the ever-rousing Magic Kingdom theme park, the recently rehabbed EPCOT, and the Disney-MGM Studios, the sprawling fantasy world includes its own campgrounds, five championship golf courses, a clutch of water parks – and, of course, the trademark monorail. The latest addition, Disney's Animal Kingdom, includes the 100-acre Kilimanjaro Safari, Dinoland, and the 14-story carved Tree of Life. When Disney World celebrated its 25th anniversary in October 1996, it had hosted more than 500 million guests. And success inspires imitations: The Orlando area is also home to Universal Studios Florida, with rides like the excellent Back to the Future flight simulator and the newfangled Terminator 2: 3-D, and Sea World, where you can ride through a shark tank in a plexiglass tube.
WDW, **407.824.4321.**
Universal, **407.363.8000.**
Sea World, **407.363.2613.**

Saltwater fishing for great game fish like tarpon, snook, and redfish is popular off the Gulf coast of Florida. Big-game fishing began in 1885 with the documentation of a tarpon caught with rod and reel off Sanibel Island.

J Key West

Pg. 84, V16. Outermost of the Florida Keys accessible by car, Key West has transformed itself from the sleepy haunt of anglers, smugglers, and lighthouse keepers into a quirky, festive destination where locals and visitors alike make a daily celebration of watching the sunset. The one-man legend who did the most to feed Key West's mystique was Ernest Hemingway, who wrote, fished, and caroused here in the 1930s. Hemingway's big Spanish Colonial house is a major attraction; nearby is the Little White House of President Harry Truman. John James Audubon recorded the Key's birdlife in 1832, and some of his original engravings are on view at the Audubon House, set in a tropical garden. **800.527.8539.**

K St. Augustine

Pg. 83, F17. This graceful city of Spanish Colonial buildings made of coquina (a natural, cementlike, petrified seashell and sand material) is the oldest in the United States, settled by the Spanish in 1565. The Spanish Quarter Village includes half a dozen restored homes and lovely gardens as well as artisans who demonstrate Spanish Colonial skills like candle-making and blacksmithing. The early days of Florida tourism are recalled in the Spanish-Moorish architecture of the opulent Alcazar Hotel. **800.653.2489.**

L St. Augustine Alligator Farm Zoological Park

Pg. 83, F17. The world's only complete collection of all 22 living species of crocodilians resides in this park. In the Land of Crocodiles exhibit, visitors follow an elevated walkway winding through a rookery (roosting and nesting area) and across an alligator swamp. Among the more formidable past tenants: Gomek, a 17-foot crocodile from New Guinea, whose imposing frame is on display. **904.824.3337.**

M Sanibel & Captiva Islands

Pg. 84, Q15–Q16. Accessible by causeway from the Gulf Coast mainland in Fort Myers, Sanibel and Captiva are nonetheless worlds unto themselves. Searching for rare shells is the big local pastime–the "Sanibel stoop" is the hunched-over posture adopted by seekers of shells washed in by the unique pattern of currents and tides. Development of the two islands is concentrated along the coast; bayside, the J.N. "Ding" Darling National Wildlife Refuge is a primeval realm of mangrove swamps and brackish marshes, where egrets and alligators hold sway. **941.472.1080.**

Miami Beach is where neon goes to die.

– LENNY BRUCE, BEFORE 1966

Coastal South

The coastal South – North Carolina, South Carolina, and Georgia – is the South of the great antebellum plantations, of mysterious swamps and lonely outposts of windswept barrier beach, of tiny villages in mountain hollows. Like a boxer leading with his chin, the southern Atlantic seaboard presents a vulnerable face to the fierce ocean. All too often, North Carolina's Cape Hatteras and Outer Banks make the news as the landfall site of hurricanes. Usually, though, the Outer Banks are a peaceful realm of shorebirds and tumbling waves. Farther south, land and sea meet along marshy tidelands and island chains where rice and Sea Islands cotton plantations built great fortunes in antebellum days. The coastal region's twin belles, Charleston and Savannah, are two of America's most gracious and architecturally delightful cities. A vast, fertile swath of land separates the South's Atlantic shores from the Piedmont, and from where the Appalachians begin. From North Carolina's tobacco farms to Georgia's peach orchards and peanut fields, agriculture still reigns along the coastal plain. But the New South is also a realm of industry and trade, nowhere better exemplified than in Atlanta, Georgia's capital. The westernmost portions of this coastal region are anything but coastal: At 6,684 feet, North Carolina's Mount Mitchell is the highest point in the eastern U.S., part of the southern Appalachian chain that includes the Great Smokies and the Blue Ridge.

MARCH
Festival of Houses and Gardens, Charleston, SC
The historic neighborhoods and private gardens of one of America's most beautiful cities reveal themselves to visitors during this month-long event.
803.723.1623

APRIL
Vidalia Onion Festival, Vidalia, GA
The onion capital celebrates its namesake harvest with a street dance, rodeo, air show, road races, house tour, and cooking school.
912.538.8687

MAY
Ole Time Fiddler's and Bluegrass Festival, Union Grove, NC
The oldest festival of its kind in North America, this down-home, family-oriented get-together highlights traditional American music through fiddle contests, informal jam sessions, and workshops.
704.539.4417

MAY
Spoleto Festival U.S.A., Charleston, SC
Originally founded by composer Gian Carlo Menotti, this 17-day festival fills Charleston's historic churches and theaters with more than 120 performances of opera, dance, theater, jazz and classical music.
803.722.2764

JULY
Fantastic Fourth Celebration, Stone Mountain, GA
Stone Mountain Park explodes during a three-day celebration featuring a huge laser show and the South's most spectacular Fourth of July fireworks.
770.498.5702

AUGUST
Rock City's Annual Fairy Tale Festival, Lookout Mountain, GA
Fairy tales seem to come to life at this summer festival featuring magicians, clowns, storytellers, and a host of fairy-tale and storybook characters.
800.854.0675

SEPTEMBER
Mayberry Days, Mount Airy, NC
For three days each fall, residents of Andy Griffith's real-life hometown celebrate Mayberry, his TV hometown on *The Andy Griffith Show*. Thousands of fans march in the Mayberry Days parade and wait on block-long lines to order pork-chop sandwiches at the Snappy Lunch cafe.
800.286.6193

OCTOBER
Big Pig Jig, Vienna, GA
A parade, pageants, a 5-km Hog Jog, hog calling, and three nights of big stage shows accompany the Annual Georgia Barbecue Cooking Championship.
912.268.8275

Stone Mountain Highland Games and Scottish Festival, Stone Mountain, GA
The clans gather for this world-famous festival of all things Scottish – including such traditional Scottish athletic competitions as Tossing the Caber (best described as heaving a telephone pole), Celtic music and dancing, and hearty Highland food.
770.521.0228

Forming part of the border between South Carolina and Georgia, the formidable Chattooga River is one of hundreds – along with the Altamaha, Savannah, Chattahoochee, and Black Warrior – that originate in the sparsely populated Appalachian Mountains and gather force crossing the Piedmont, a broad swath of foothills that descend to the lowlands. Rich with fecund salt marshes on its shores, the southeast's coastal plain offered early settlers fertile plantation lands and secure harbors sheltered by barrier islands.

Georgia

A Atlanta
Pg. 86, F4. The capital of the New South, Atlanta rose like a phoenix from the ashes that William Tecumseh Sherman left behind on his march to the sea. Settled in 1837 as a railroad terminus, Atlanta today is a financial, industrial, and commercial titan with more than 4,700 manufacturing facilities, including Coca-Cola, whose World of Coca-Cola museum pays homage to the drink that was invented here. Underground Atlanta – a $142 million, three-level shopping mall and entertainment complex – has one story actually underground at the city's original downtown street level, which was covered over with railroad viaducts in the late 19th century. **404.521.6600.**

B Chickamauga & Chattanooga National Military Park
Pg. 86, B2. America's first and largest national military park commemorates Civil War battles fought in 1863 to control the strategic railway center of Chattanooga, Tennessee. The 8,000-acre site encompasses the battlefields of Chickamauga, Orchard Knob, Lookout Mountain, and Missionary Ridge. It was on the last site that Union troops under General Ulysses S. Grant finally gained control of the approaches to Atlanta. **706.866.9241.**

C Martin Luther King, Jr. National Historic Site
Pg. 85, G6. America's greatest civil rights leader was born and lived in a Queen Anne-style house in the Sweet Auburn district – the heart of black Atlanta for most of the 20th century. His home, the Ebenezer Baptist Church where he preached, and his grave site and memorial are all located within this two-square-block area, one of the most popular (and most revered) sites in the state of Georgia. **404.331.5190.**

D Okefenokee National Wildlife Refuge
Pg. 87, Q9. The alligator is king at Okefenokee, a Creek word meaning "land of trembling earth." It's estimated that 10,000 to 12,000 of the big reptiles call the refuge home, and given the terrain – 396,000 acres of dense swamp – it's doubtful that anyone will want to challenge their reign in the near future. The reedy marshes and heavy canopy of cypress trees dripping with Spanish moss are also a perfect environment for a wide variety of birds: Approximately 234 species thrive here. **912.496.3331.**

Georgia is the nation's leading producer of peanuts and pecans, harvesting close to 1.5 billion pounds of peanuts and an average of 100 million pounds of pecans each year.

E Savannah Historic District
Pg. 87, U12. The urban preservation movement scored a landmark victory when Savannah's grid of residential streets punctuated by tree-shaded public squares was saved. More than 1,500 structures have been restored, thanks to the Historic Savannah Foundation. Arrayed around the live oaks and Spanish moss of the "outdoor living rooms" is some of the South's finest antebellum architecture, a mélange of Regency, Georgian, Italianate, and neo-Gothic styles. Founded in 1733, Savannah was a port of entry for slaves, and their history is documented at the King-Tisdell Cottage in the Historic District, which is slowly undergoing restoration. **800.444.2427.**

I want to say to General Sherman . . .
that from the ashes he left us in 1864
we have raised a brave and beautiful city;
that somehow or other we have caught
the sunshine in the bricks and mortar of our homes.
– HENRY W. GRADY, *ATLANTA CONSTITUTION*, 1886

F Georgia's Stone Mountain Park
Pg. 85, E10. Attractions at this 3,200-acre park include a riverboat cruise, an antebellum plantation complex of early 19th-century buildings, and a free nightly laser light show during the summer. But the largest draw is the Confederate Memorial Carving, the largest bas-relief sculpture in the world. Images of three of the South's Civil War heroes – Jefferson Davis, Robert E. Lee, and Thomas J. "Stonewall" Jackson – consume three acres on the north face of 300-million-year-old Stone Mountain. **770.498.5702.**

G Tallulah Gorge State Park
Pg. 86, C6. Georgia's newest state park showcases one of the most spectacular gorges in the eastern United States – a chasm two miles long and nearly 1,000 feet deep. The park offers visitors the chance to learn about an underground hydroelectric system that carries water from Tallulah Lake to the power plant at the bottom of the gorge. **706.754.7970.**

NC 138
SC 156
GA 86
SC 245
NC 242
GA 234

There prevails here [Charleston] a finer manner of life, and on the whole, there are more evidences of courtesy than in the northern cities.

– JOHANN DAVID SCHOEPF, *TRAVELS IN THE CONFEDERATION 1783–1784*

Pinehurst K

Biltmore Estate, Asheville H

Outer Banks J

North Carolina is the nation's largest tobacco-growing state, producing two-thirds of the nation's bright-leaf tobacco, which is primarily used to make cigarettes.

Autumn on the Outer Banks is purely a sorcerer's spell: so clear you can see each grain of sand on the great dunes, and bathed in a light that is indescribable.

– ANNE RIVERS SIDDONS, *OUTER BANKS*, 1991

North Carolina

H Biltmore Estate
Pg. 139, M15. George Washington Vanderbilt–grandson of Cornelius Vanderbilt, the illustrious "Commodore" of New York Central Railroad fame–used his share of the family fortune to construct the largest private house America has ever seen. Biltmore, in Asheville, is a 250-room French Renaissance-style chateau framed by 8,000 acres–landscaped by Frederick Law Olmsted–on which Vanderbilt practiced advanced theories of forest cultivation. Completed in 1895, this Xanadu of the South includes an indoor palm court and a bowling alley. **800.543.2961.**

I Cherokee Indian Reservation
Pg. 138, L4. Long before European settlement in the New World, some 25,000 Cherokee inhabited an area spanning the Ohio River to Alabama. In 1837, President Andrew Jackson forced the Cherokee nation into exile in Oklahoma. More than 16,000 men, women, and children set out on a 1,200-mile migration that came to be known as the Trail of Tears – a quarter of them died along the way. A few hundred Cherokee eluded the march by disappearing into the Blue Ridge mountains. Today, their descendants live on in this reservation bordering Great Smoky Mountains National Park. A high point at the Museum of the Cherokee Indian is the syllabary invented by Sequoyah in 1821. At the Oconaluftee Indian Village, a re-created Cherokee village of the 1750s, dugout-canoe construction and other skills are demonstrated. **800.438.1601.**

J Outer Banks
Pg. 139, G19. Heralded by the beam of 208-foot black-and-white striped Cape Hatteras Lighthouse, this fragile arc of barrier islands resonates with the history of the Lost Colony of Roanoke Island and the Wright brothers' first flight, drowses in the quaint isolation of Ocracoke village, and trails off southward into the starkly beautiful wilderness of Cape Lookout National Seashore. **800.446.6262.**

K Pinehurst
Pg. 138, G8. Donald Ross began his fabled career as golf course architect when he built his first complete course here, Pinehurst No. 2. Nearby was the site of the first known miniature golf course, as well as one of the country's first driving ranges. And if this weren't enough to earn this shady Sandhills area its title "golf capital of the world," it also boasts 41 golf courses (and counting). **800.346.5362.**

L Wright Brothers National Memorial
Pg. 139, C19. On December 17, 1903, the bicycle manufacturers from Dayton, Ohio, Orville and Wilbur Wright, launched themselves into history when, after several autumns spent testing gliders and fighting mosquitoes on a lonely, windy stretch of sand called the Kill Devil Hills, they made the first powered-airplane flight. Reproductions of the Wrights' 1902 glider and 1903 flier, as well as their spartan living quarters, are on exhibit. **919.441.7430.**

Chattooga National Wild & Scenic River O

Middleton Place Gardens R

Charleston Historic District N

South Carolina

M Cape Romain National Wildlife Refuge
Pg. 156, H10. The state's greatest wilderness expanse – 64,000 acres of barrier islands, forests, and saltwater marshes–stretches for 22 miles along the Atlantic coast. The U.S. Fish and Wildlife Service has preserved the natural habitat, providing sanctuary for numerous species, including the threatened loggerhead turtle. The refuge is also a haven for naturalists, anglers, and hikers. A two-mile national recreation trail and the undeveloped "Boneyard Beach" are on Bull Island, three miles off the mainland. A ferry leaves from Moore's Landing at Awendaw. **803.928.3368.**

N Charleston Historic District
Pg. 156, H9. The concentration of elegant homes that line the streets of Charleston's old quarter near the Ashley River is a reminder that antebellum high life wasn't centered solely on the plantation. Architectural stars include the 1803 Joseph Manigault House; the 1808 home of trader Nathaniel Russell, notable for its flying staircase; and the prerevolutionary Heyward-Washington House, in which President Washington slept in 1791. **803.868.8118.**

O Chattooga National Wild & Scenic River
Pg. 156, B1. The river made famous in the film version of James Dickey's novel *Deliverance* begins in the North Carolina Appalachian mountains and drops an average of 49.3 feet per mile as it races through Sumter National Forest, making the upcountry a paradise for rafters, canoers, and kayakers. Beginners are advised to tackle the white-water rapids with an experienced guide. **864.638.9568.**

P Grand Strand/ Myrtle Beach
Pg. 156, E12. The Grand Strand is a 60-mile skein of ocean resorts reaching from the North Carolina border halfway to Charleston. Alternately bustling and bucolic, the Strand's centerpiece is the vacationers' mecca of Myrtle Beach, boasting warm-water ocean bathing, nightclubs and amusement parks, seafood restaurants, and nearly 100 golf courses. In the 1940s, the Grand Strand was a hotspot for rhythm-and-blues dances, where South Carolinians learned to do the shag. Shunned by the white establishment at the time, the shag is now the official state dance. **800.356.3016.**

Q Sea Islands
Pg. 156, K8. South Carolina's coastline is dotted with islands, many of which have grown from sleepy backwaters to major golfing resorts within the last 50 years. Kiawah Island has four championship courses; Isle of Palms has two. But the undisputed queen of resorts is 12-mile-long Hilton Head, bordered by one of the last major unpolluted marine estuaries on the East Coast. The site of prosperous Sea Islands cotton plantations until the Civil War, the island was later populated by a community of freed slaves. The modern era arrived in 1956 with completion of a bridge to the mainland, and today the megaresort island boasts 22 golf links, including Harbour Town Golf Links, site of the MCI Heritage of Golf tournament in the spring. Hilton Head Island, **800.523.3373.** Kiawah and Isle of Palms, **800.868.8118.**

R Middleton Place Gardens/Magnolia Plantation & Gardens/Audubon Swamp Garden
Pg. 156, H9. For more than 100 years before the Civil War, Charleston was surrounded by vast rice plantations, whose wealthy owners delighted in creating intricate gardens. In 1741, Henry Middleton began designing what is now the oldest surviving formally landscaped garden in North America. Today, Middleton Place, considered in its founder's day to be the premier garden of the 13 colonies, is a living museum of colonial plantation life and a model of garden restoration. The 50-acre garden at world-famous Magnolia Plantation, just a few minutes away, dates from the 1680s and is the country's oldest continually planted garden. On a less formal note, nearby Audubon Swamp encompasses 60 acres of unspoiled black-water cypress and tupelo swamp. **800.868.8118.**

South Carolina's shoreline includes the 24,000-acre Santee Coastal Reserve, a haven for deer, alligators, and waterfowl, as well as for the threatened sea turtles that come ashore to lay their eggs.

The Capital Area

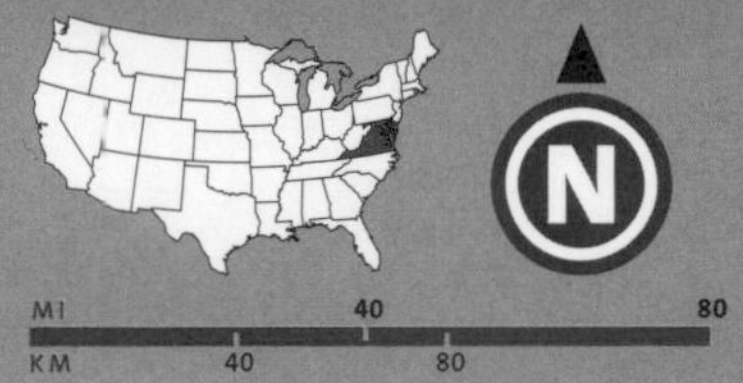

The fertile tidelands surrounding the Chesapeake Bay nurtured one of colonial America's most comfortably established societies – and, not coincidentally, provided a proving ground for some of the nation's most illustrious founding figures. After the Revolutionary War, this hinge region between North and South seemed the logical place to locate the new national capital. The District of Columbia, with its federal city of Washington, was carved from Maryland and Virginia territory. The topography of the states surrounding the capital is a progression from sea level to the Piedmont to the Appalachians. Much of Delaware's coastline, and significant portions of Maryland's and Virginia's as well, face the open Atlantic along a stretch that is sometimes heavily developed – as at Maryland's Ocean City – and sometimes remarkably pristine, as along wild Assateague and Chincoteague Islands. But the region's greatest saltwater presence is the Chesapeake Bay. Baltimore's H.L. Mencken called the bay an "immense protein factory," and so it is: The bay's warm waters, though degraded by pollution, have long been a shellfish cornucopia, producing a bounty of local favorites like blue crabs and oysters. Not far beyond Washington, the tidelands give way to the first foothills of the Appalachians. A drive through western Maryland and Virginia is a lesson in the obstacles faced by pioneers, and these regions remain rugged and picturesque today.

The fertile Delmarva Peninsula, which contains the entire state of Delaware as well as parts of Maryland and Virginia, lies east of the Chesapeake Bay, a flooded estuary of the Susquehanna River. West of the nation's capital, which sits on the banks of the Potomac river, the Maryland and Virginia hinterlands climb from tidewater to the mountains of the Appalachian range.

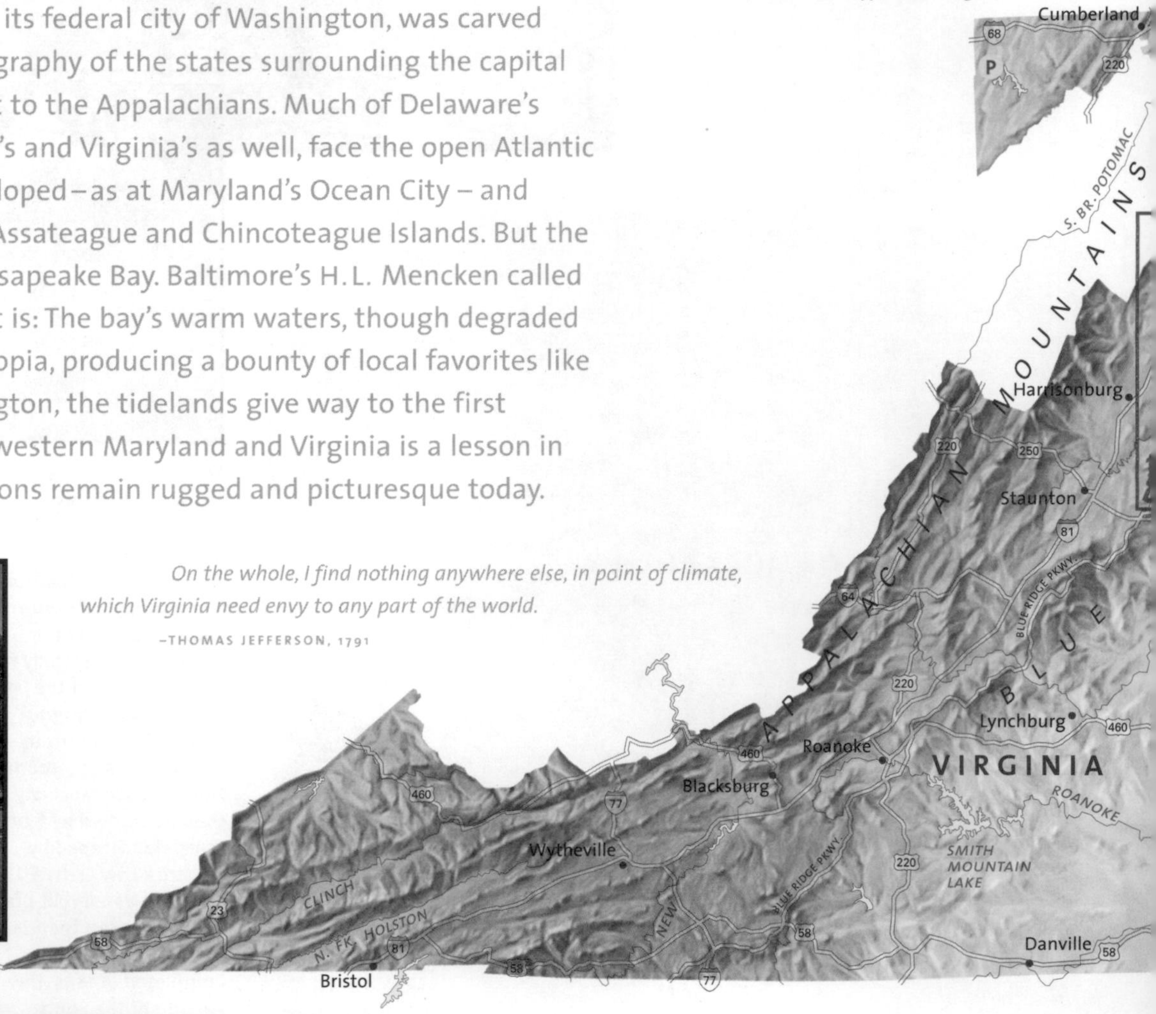

On the whole, I find nothing anywhere else, in point of climate, which Virginia need envy to any part of the world.

–THOMAS JEFFERSON, 1791

Washington is a city of Southern efficiency and Northern charm.

– JOHN F. KENNEDY, 1961

APRIL

National Cherry Blossom Festival, Washington, D.C.
Washingtonians celebrate the blossoming of more than 6,000 Japanese cherry trees with festivities that include the crowning of the Cherry Blossom Festival Queen and a parade.
202.547.1500

Historic Garden Week, statewide, VA
The gardens of more than 200 private and historic homes are open for tours during the state's peak blooming period.
804.643.7141

MAY

Preakness Celebration, Baltimore, MD
The city takes on a carnival air – with concerts, festivals, and a parade – in anticipation of the running of thoroughbred racing's Preakness Stakes at Pimlico Race Course.
800.282.6632

National Pike Festival, western MD
All of the modes of transportation used in the early 1800s, when the National Pike became the first federally funded inter state highway, return to the streets to celebrate the road's history.
301.791.3246

Virginia Gold Cup, The Plains, VA
The nation's premier steeplechase event is held in horse country.
540.347.2612, 800.697.2237

Winterthur Point-to-Point Races, Winterthur, DE
Exciting amateur competitions include steeplechase and flat races. The day includes a parade of antique horse-drawn carriages, canine demonstrations, and pony races, as well as a tailgate-picnic competition.
302.888.4600, 800.448.3883

JULY

Independence Day Celebration, Washington, D.C.
Activities include colonial military maneuvers, a parade down Constitution Avenue, free entertainment, and a concert by the National Symphony Orchestra followed by fireworks over the Washington Monument.
202.619.7222

AUGUST

Old Fiddlers' Convention, Galax, VA
Musicians from around the world gather to jam and compete in the largest musical convention of its kind in the country.
540.236.8541

DECEMBER

National Christmas Tree Lighting Pageant of Peace, Washington, D.C.
Accompanied by seasonal music and caroling, the president lights the National Christmas Tree.
202.619.7222

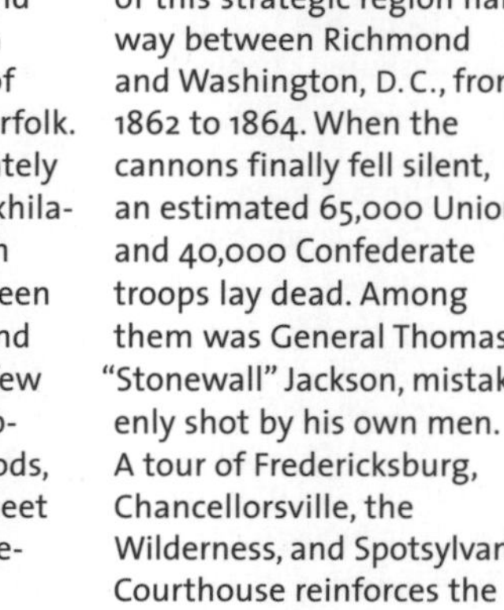

Fifty years ago, hogs were fed peanuts to help achieve the unique flavor of Smithfield's famous hams; today the prized taste is entirely due to a special curing method.

Arlington National Cemetery D

Colonial Williamsburg Historic Area E

Monticello, Charlottesville C

Virginia

A Chesapeake Bay Bridge-Tunnel

Pg. 169, L18. Phrases such as "one of the wonders of the modern world" and "stretches as far as the eye can see" are apt for this $200 million engineering masterpiece, which crosses 17 miles of open sea and links Virginia's Eastern Shore with the cities of Virginia Beach and Norfolk. But they don't adequately evoke the feeling of exhilaration that comes with driving for miles between the Chesapeake Bay and the Atlantic Ocean, a few yards above water, submerging for brief periods, then rising again to meet the gulls and sky, sometimes eye-to-eye with passing ships.

B Fredericksburg & Spotsylvania National Military Park

Pg. 169, G13, F13. Four of the bloodiest battles of the Civil War were fought within a 17-mile radius of Fredericksburg, as each side struggled for control of this strategic region halfway between Richmond and Washington, D.C., from 1862 to 1864. When the cannons finally fell silent, an estimated 65,000 Union and 40,000 Confederate troops lay dead. Among them was General Thomas "Stonewall" Jackson, mistakenly shot by his own men. A tour of Fredericksburg, Chancellorsville, the Wilderness, and Spotsylvania Courthouse reinforces the words Lee spoke near here in 1862: "It is well that war is so terrible – we should grow too fond of it." **540.373.6122.**

C Charlottesville

Pg. 169, G11. Many illustrious citizens have hailed from this town nestled in the foothills of the Blue Ridge Mountains. But none left so lasting an impression as Thomas Jefferson, president, statesman, and architect. Founder of the University of Virginia, Jefferson planned both its curriculum (secular, which was unusual at the time) and every detail of its noble design – the lovely serpentine garden wall and the Rotunda's neoclassic dome. Equally impressive is Jefferson's nearby home, the memorably whimsical Monticello, considered by many to be the finest private residence ever built in America. Beginning with an early version of automatic doors, the interior is filled with innovative gadgets and appliances created by Jefferson. An underground passage leads to the slave quarters, and beyond is a hardwood grove in which Jefferson is buried. Monticello, **804.984.9800.**

D Arlington National Cemetery

Pg. 172, E5. The cemetery is the great equalizer of patriots, the place where some of America's greatest leaders and thousands of its unsung heroes rest side by side. The 612-acre grounds, built on land confiscated from Robert E. Lee at the outbreak of the Civil War, is the burial site of such famous sons as John and Robert Kennedy, Joe Louis, and Oliver Wendell Holmes, Jr. The 1818 Arlington House, Lee's home, is now restored and open to the public. **703.607.8052.**

E Colonial Williamsburg Historic Area

Pg. 167, G7. Virginia's 18th-century capital was a bustling center of government, commerce, artisanship, and society. By the 1920s, when local priest Dr. William A.R. Goodwin – convinced that automobiles were destroying America's small towns – launched a campaign to restore it, Williamsburg was in serious decline. In 1934, Colonial Williamsburg opened as a theme park. Today the 173-acre living-history museum of 88 original buildings and hundreds of replicated structures is one of the world's most meticulously researched historic sites. **800.447.8679.**

C&O Canal, Georgetown F

District of Columbia

F Georgetown

Pg. 172, H1. Already a busy Potomac port 50 years before work began on the federal city of Washington, Georgetown has since become the capital's elite address. The neighborhood's handsome row-house architecture is epitomized along the portions of N Street known as Smith's Row (circa 1815) and Cox's Row (circa 1790s), while the bistro-and-boutique scene is liveliest around Wisconsin Avenue and M Street. Skirting Georgetown, a portion of the Chesapeake & Ohio Canal is now a national historical park. During the mid 1800s, the canal linked the coast and the Appalachian frontier. Today its towpath is treasured by strollers, bicyclists, in-line skaters, and joggers. Visitor Center, **301.767.3714.**

G National Mall

Pg. 172, E6. Stretching two miles, from the Capitol to the Lincoln Memorial, the Mall reconciles grandeur and democracy. Its vast open space of promenades, manicured lawns, reflecting pools, and cherry trees is lined with stately architecture. Exclamation point to a life of greatness, the Washington Monument, a 555-foot marble obelisk towers over the Mall at its center. Overlooking the Tidal Basin to the south, the Jefferson Memorial, modeled on Rome's Pantheon, stands in tribute to the third president. West of the Washington Monument stands the Wall – the somber black granite Vietnam Veterans Memorial, inscribed with the names of 58,209 dead or missing. The imposing figure of Abraham Lincoln looks on from a Doric temple directly west of the beautiful Reflecting Pool. **202.485.9880.**

Delaware is like a diamond,
diminutive, but having within it inherent value.

– JOHN LOFLAND, 1847, QUOTED IN THE FEDERAL WRITERS' PROJECT, *DELAWARE: A GUIDE TO THE FIRST STATE*, 1938

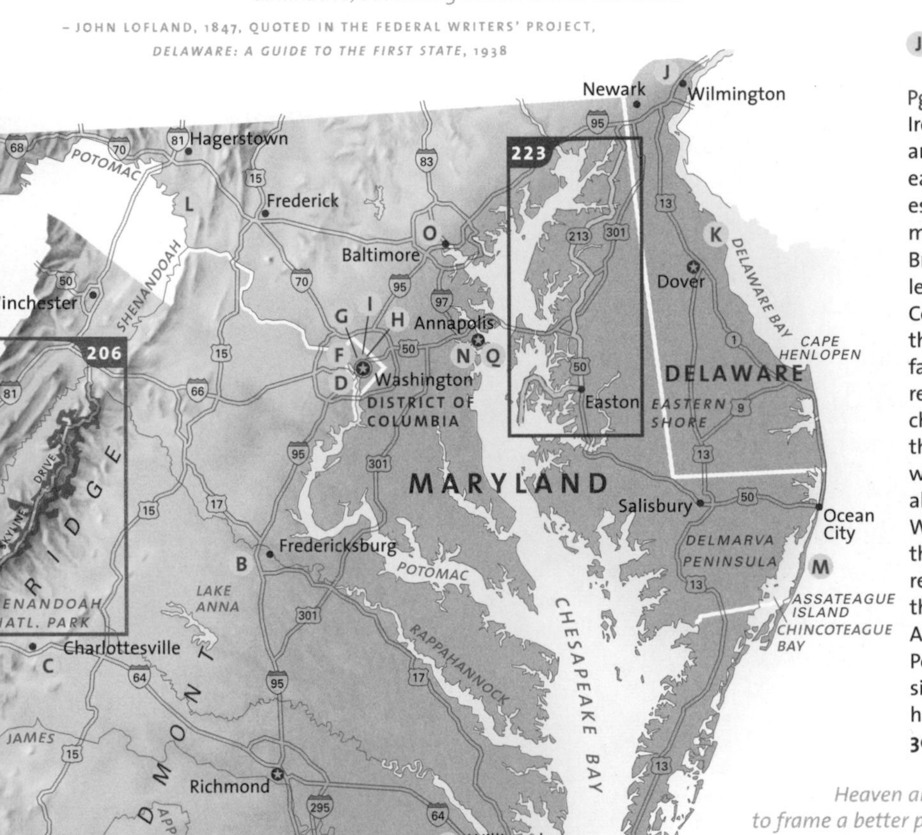

Heaven and earth never agreed
to frame a better place
for man's habitation.

– JOHN SMITH, ON CHESAPEAKE BAY, 1606

Delaware

J Hagley Museum & Library
Pg. 80, B8. When Éleuthère Irénée du Pont and his sons arrived from France in the early 19th century, they established a black-powder mill on the banks of the Brandywine River. Their legacy is the Du Pont Company, which became the world's largest manufacturer of gunpowder and remains a giant in the chemical industry. Many of the original mill buildings, which stretch for two miles along the Brandywine near Wilmington, are part of this 235-acre museum that reveals a great deal about the birth and growth of American industrialism. Du Pont's Georgian-style mansion, Eleutherian Mills, also has a tour schedule. **302.658.2400.**

Hagley Museum & Library, Wilmington J

K Bombay Hook National Wildlife Refuge
Pg. 80, F3. Each spring and fall, tens of thousands of ducks and geese migrating along the Atlantic flyway land at this nearly 16,000-acre tract of protected tidal salt marsh and wooded swampland to refuel. Thousands of shorebirds arrive in May and June, ready to gorge on the freshly laid eggs of horseshoe crabs along the bay shore and in the mudflats. Thus replenished, they depart for their subarctic breeding grounds. **302.653.6872.**

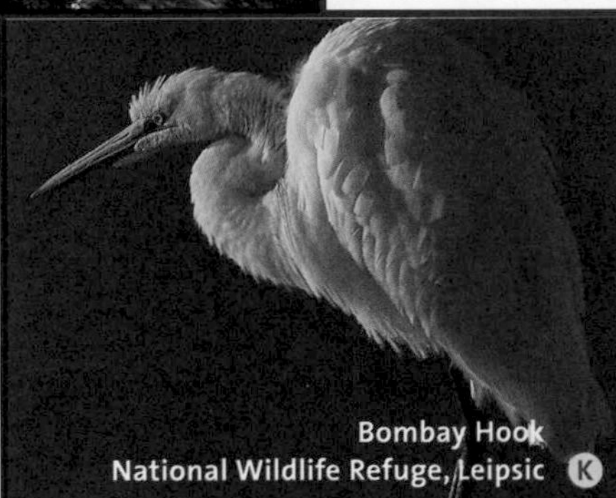
Bombay Hook National Wildlife Refuge, Leipsic K

Assateague Island M

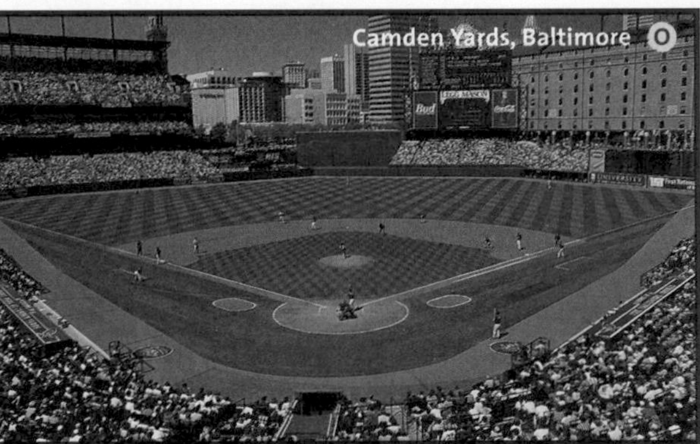
Camden Yards, Baltimore O

White House I

Maryland boasts the biggest blue crab catch in the nation, with an average of 44.4 million commercial pounds pulled from Chesapeake Bay each year. The seasonal favorite is savored from April through November with famously delicious crab cakes, crab soup, and spicy steamed whole crabs that diners "pick" at tables covered in brown paper.

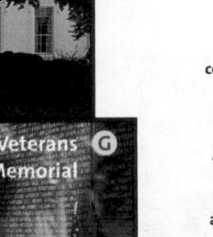

Vietnam Veterans Memorial G

H U.S. Capitol
Pg. 172, E6. "A pedestal waiting for a monument" is how French architect Pierre L'Enfant characterized the land known as Jenkins Hill when, in 1791, he was looking for a place to erect the "Congress House." Today the gleaming white marble building, set in 227 acres of lush greenery, is one of the country's best recognized landmarks. Here, lawmakers gather under a massive 180-foot-high cast-iron dome to shape the country's legislative policies. **202.225.6827.**

The 14 Smithsonian museums contain 140 million items; fewer than one percent of them are on display at any single time.

I White House
Pg. 172, E5. Designed by Irish immigrant James Hoban in 1792, furnished with toilets by Thomas Jefferson, burned by the British during the War of 1812, structurally restored during the Truman Administration, and redecorated by Jacqueline Kennedy, the Executive Mansion offers one of Washington's most popular tours. Many presidents have left their mark, perhaps none more so than Richard Nixon, who turned the swimming pool installed by John F. Kennedy into today's press area. **202.456.7041.**

Maryland

L Antietam National Battlefield
Pg. 106, C8. On September 17, 1862, the forces of George McClellan met those of Robert E. Lee in an effort to stop Lee from invading northern territory for the first time in the Civil War. When the smoke cleared, 23,110 men were dead, wounded, or captured, and Antietam had earned the awful distinction of being the bloodiest single day of combat in American history. Exhibits at the site in Sharpsburg, with explanatory markers around the battlefield, recount the progress of the battle. On the first Saturday of each December, 23,110 candles are lit across the field at dusk to commemorate the dead. **301.432.5124.**

M Assateague Island National Seashore
Pg. 107, L20. Ocean City and Assateague Island were once a single landmass, until a hurricane ripped them apart in 1933. Now a narrow 37-mile-long barrier island that straddles the Maryland–Virginia border, Assateague's main attractions are its wild ponies, bird-watching (of more than 200 varieties), three educational nature trails illustrating the island's ecosystems (dune, forest, marshland), and unspoiled beaches. **410.641.1441.**

N Banneker-Douglass Museum of African-American Life and History
Pg. 107, N13. Named for abolitionist and former slave Frederick Douglass and the great black scientist Benjamin Banneker, this museum in Annapolis is the official repository of Maryland's African American heritage collections. Highlights include the Herbert M. Frisby Collection of papers, artifacts, and fossils relating to the explorer and science educator's 40-year career of Arctic research; and the Thomas Baden Collection of prints, papers, and equipment belonging to the Annapolis photographer. **410.974.2893.**

O Oriole Park at Camden Yards
Pg. 108, E6. Home of the Baltimore Orioles, Camden Yards pioneered the retro styling of the latest generation of ball fields. Nearby is the birthplace of the game's greatest player, Babe Ruth. His Baltimore home-turned-museum contains photographs, taped interviews, and Orioles memorabilia. Oriole Park, **410.685.9800.** Babe Ruth Birthplace and Museum, **410.727.1539.**

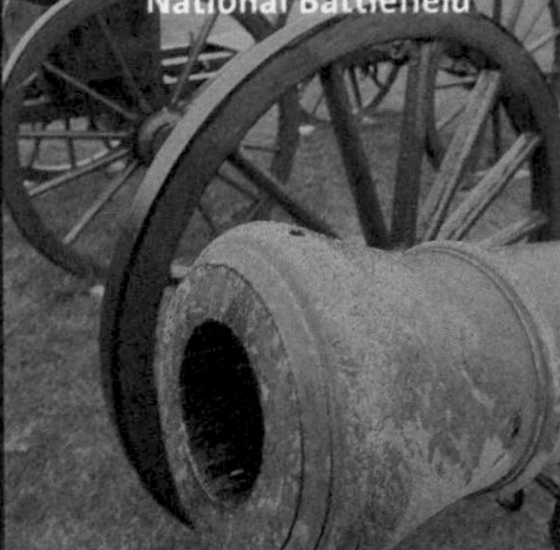
Antietam National Battlefield L

P Upper Youghiogheny River
Pg. 106, C1. For expert (Class IV and V) rafters, Maryland's "Upper Yough" is a legendary challenge—a ten-mile stretch of river that offers seven miles of continuous rapids, more white water in a shorter distance than any other river in the East. As the river flows north from West Virginia toward Pittsburgh, it cascades off the 4,100-foot Blackwater Escarpment, past Swallow Falls State Park, and then through the 800-foot Upper Yough gorge. Youghiogheny White Water Expeditions, **800.248.1893.**

Q U.S. Naval Academy
Pg. 108, M8. The undergraduate college of the U.S. Navy at Annapolis has been training officers since 1845 on its 338-acre riverfront campus. The sarcophagus of one of America's greatest naval figures—Revolutionary War hero John Paul Jones—lies in state in the college chapel's lower-level crypt. **410.293.3363.**

Middle Atlantic

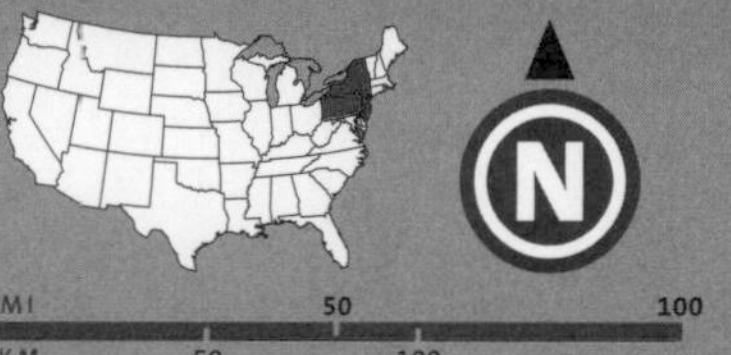

Success has brought a bewilderingly dense concentration of people to the cities of Pennsylvania, New Jersey, and New York – but the middle Atlantic hinterlands still boast some of the East's loveliest and most varied natural landscapes. The lordly Hudson River meets the Atlantic at the port of New York, a vast harbor seemingly made for international commerce, where New York and New Jersey have marshaled their greatest amalgam of industry and urban development. Travel a few-score miles, though, and the scene shifts remarkably. The New Jersey shore is a resort-dotted 120-mile expanse of white-sand beach; inland, the eerily silent Pine Barrens virtually defy human interference, and thousands of acres of vegetable and dairy farms earn New Jersey its nickname, "the Garden State." Northward past the beetling black cliffs called the Palisades, the Hudson leads to a New York that belies the Manhattan stereotype. The jumble of rounded hills and deep valleys called the Catskills, and farther north the sublime peaks of the Adirondacks, are still favored haunts of solitude seekers. Likewise, Pennsylvania isn't all Philadelphia. Pennsylvania Dutch Country is a preindustrial idyll, the Pocono Mountains a honeymooners' retreat. But where the Monongahela and Allegheny Rivers come together to form the Ohio, Pittsburgh and its 150-year reign as the capital of steel stand as a reminder that the middle Atlantic states are all about getting things done.

With its source in the Adirondack Mountains, the Hudson River empties into the Atlantic at New York Bay. The region's other great rivers are the Delaware and the Susquehanna, which drain New York, New Jersey, and Pennsylvania along their respective routes to the Delaware and Chesapeake Bays. In northeastern Pennsylvania, rugged folds of Appalachians bear rich seams of anthracite, historically important but today commercially slight.

On our left, the bold features of nature [the Palisades] rise as in the days of yore, unimpaired, unchangeable; grey cliffs, like aged battlements, tower perpendicularly from the water to their height of several hundred feet.

– FRANCIS HALL, *TRAVELS IN CANADA AND THE UNITED STATES IN 1816 AND 1817*, 1818

JANUARY
Mummers Parade, Philadelphia, PA
The world-famous New Year's Day parade features 30,000 spectacularly costumed mummers, including string bands and comics.
215.636.1666

FEBRUARY
New Jersey Flower and Patio Show, Somerset, NJ
Beautifully landscaped gardens and floral designs, covering 82,000 square feet, are on exhibit during this four-day event.
732.919.7660

MAY
Wildwood International Kite Festival, Wildwood, NJ
The country's oldest sport-kite festival includes the East Coast Buggy Blast, the East Coast Stunt Kite Championship, and an International Indoor Kite Championship.
215.736.3715

Original Philadelphia Antiquarian Book Fair, Fort Washington, PA
Vendors gather to sell out-of-print books, prints, maps, autographs, and ephemera.
215.757.1132

JUNE
Mermaid Parade, Coney Island, Brooklyn, NY
A true celebration of big-city diversity, this kitschy parade revels in glitter, feather boas, and fishnet stockings, drawing everyone from East Village drag queens to Coney Island's own Sideshows by the Seashore stars, like '97 parade queen Jennifer Miller, the bearded lady.
718.372.5159

JULY
The Original Pennsylvania Dutch Folk Festival, Summit Station, PA
Authentic Pennsylvania Dutch culture, food, pageantry, quilts, music, and historic reenactments are highlights of this annual celebration.
610.683.8707

SEPTEMBER
Miss America Pageant, Atlantic City, NJ
There she goes: The crowning of Miss America follows the Boardwalk parade and three nights of talent and beauty competition.
609.345.7571

OCTOBER
Oyster Festival, Oyster Bay, NY
One of Long Island's largest street fairs features oyster eating and shucking contests, paddleboat tours, a 5-km race, and a historical boat show.
516.922.6464

NOVEMBER
New York Marathon, New York, NY
Watched by the sports world's largest number of spectators, nearly 30,000 competitors – picked by lottery, with no qualifying requirements – make this annual run through the boroughs.
212.860.4455

On the whole, I'd rather be in Philadelphia.

– NATIVE SON W. C. FIELDS'S EPITAPH FOR HIMSELF, 1946

Pennsylvania

A Pittsburgh

Pg. 151, N3. Built at the dramatic confluence of the Allegheny, Monongahela, and Ohio Rivers, Pittsburgh has been designated one of the country's most livable cities, where postmodern architecture resides comfortably with artifacts of industrial wealth. Area attractions include the Carnegie Science Center, with more than 250 interactive exhibits and a planetarium, and the Andy Warhol Museum, which chronicles the Pittsburgh native's career. For splendid panoramas and a look at a fascinating 19th-century transportation technology, take the Duquesne or Monongahela Inclines, trams that ascend steep hills at dizzying angles. **800.359.0758.**

B Brandywine River Museum

Pg. 153, R21. Most people visit this fine museum in Chadds Ford for its Andrew Wyeth paintings, which depict the nearby countryside that Wyeth calls home. But just as captivating are the canvases of N.C. Wyeth, Andrew's father, the early 20th-century master whose illustrations for books such as *Treasure Island* and *The Yearling* once set young minds to dreaming. **610.388.2700.**

C Fallingwater

Pg. 151, R5. The critic Robert Hughes has said that after Thomas Jefferson's Monticello, Fallingwater is America's greatest work of residential architecture. Built in 1936, this is Frank Lloyd Wright's masterpiece: With a cocksureness that in a lesser talent would have been hubris, Wright improved upon a waterfall by cantilevering a house over the cascade. Nowhere is nature better served by steel, concrete, and glass. **412.329.8501.**

D Gettysburg National Military Park

Pg. 153, S14. "The world will little note, nor long remember what we say here, but it can never forget what they did here," President Lincoln prophesied in 1863 when he delivered his Gettysburg Address at the site of the bloodiest battle of the Civil War. Mute artillery pieces, the crumbling stone walls where sharpshooters crouched, legendary landmarks such as Little Round Top and Seminary Ridge, and more than 1,300 monuments recall the battle that left 51,000 men dead, wounded, or missing, and turned the tide of war. **717.334.1124.**

E Longwood Gardens

Pg. 153, R21. In the 1920s, chemical heir Pierre S. du Pont, an avid horticulturalist, decided to create a public park on the grounds of his estate. His 1,050-acre garden fantasy-world, ranked among the world's finest, includes flowers, ornamental shrubs, fountains, pools and lakes, and magnificent topiary. So that the fantasy wouldn't end with the first frost, he also built an enormous conservatory complex and filled it with flowering plants. **800.737.5500.**

One of the world's unique bird-watching spots is Presque Isle State Park, where one can see more than 320 different species native to an amazing diversity of environments – from shore-dwelling sandpipers and plovers to thrushes and blue jays of the forest.

Gettysburg National Military Park D

Philadelphia Museum of Art G

Lancaster County F

F Amish Country

Pg. 153, R19. Several groups, primarily of German and Swiss descent, came to the rich, rolling farmland of Lancaster County in the 18th century seeking religious freedom. Known collectively under the misnomer Pennsylvania Dutch (from *Deutsch*, German), the diverse sects still hold fast to the beliefs and customs of their ancestors. The Amish, who reject such modern innovations as telephones and automobiles, are perhaps the best known. Their distinctive foods – chicken-corn chowder, scrapple, shoofly pie – and handicrafts are staples of roadside stands and shops throughout the county. **800.723.8824.**

G Philadelphia

Pg. 153, R23. It is no idle claim that the United States was born in Philadelphia. The Independence National Historical Park is a clutch of colonial-era landmarks associated with the founding of the nation, including buildings where the Declaration of Independence was penned and signed, the Liberty Bell, and a tribute to that most mercurial of Founding Fathers, Ben Franklin. The excellent Philadelphia Museum of Art has the world's biggest Marcel Duchamp collection. Park, **215.597.8974.** Museum, **215.763.8100.**

Longwood Gardens E

NJ 128 | NY 132 | PA 150 | NJ 241 | NY 240 | PA 244

And New York is the most beautiful city in the world?
It is not far from it. No urban night is like the night there . . .
Squares after squares of flame, set up and cut into the aether.
Here is our poetry, for we have pulled down the stars to our will.

– EZRA POUND, *PATRIA MIA*, 1912

New York

H Catskill Mountains
Pg. 133, R20. They're far from the loftiest American mountains, but the Catskills can lay claim to inspiring America's first native movement in painting. The Hudson River School, personified in the romantic canvases of Thomas Cole and Frederick Church, awakened Americans to the glories of nature. Visitors flock to the Catskills to camp, hike, fish, and ski, and to revel in the wondrous kaleidoscope of color – shades of orange, ocher, and gold – created by fall foliage. The Catskills have another, vastly different claim to fame: Along the string of summer resorts called the Borscht Belt, the sardonic humor of New York City's Jews – Eddie Fisher, Mel Brooks, and Jackie Mason among others – became the signature style of American comedy. Sullivan County Visitors Association, **800.882.2287.** Ulster County Tourism, **800.342.5826.**

Chrysler Building, NYC N

Lake Placid, Adirondack Park I

Chinatown, NYC K

I Adirondack Park
Pg. 133, E21. The largest park in the lower 48 states is a six-million-acre swath of forest wilderness dotted with more than 2,300 mountain lakes and ponds (including the slender, winding 33-mile-long Lake George), 1,200 miles of rivers, and some of the East's finest trout streams, like the Ausable. Olympic hopefuls flock to Lake Placid to train at the vast Olympic Sports Complex, site of the 1932 and 1980 games. New York Visitor Center, **518.327.3000.** Newcomb Visitor Center, **518.582.2000.**

J U.S. Military Academy
Pg. 134, U22. Ever since 1802, when President Thomas Jefferson ordered the institution of a training school for United States Army officers, the U.S. Military Academy at West Point has minted leaders for war and peace. Aside from its military museum and the window on cadet life that it offers visitors, West Point occupies a staggeringly beautiful perch on the scenic Hudson. **914.938.2638.**

K Chinatown
Pg. 137, L16. Neon is no slave to the letters of the Roman alphabet in New York City's Chinatown. Enlivened and enlarged by a new era of Asian immigration, Mott Street and its environs bustle with seafood restaurants where fish are plucked live from saltwater tanks, markets that sell traditional Chinese medicines, and street vendors who sell homemade bean curd and wondrous harvests of Asian greens. **212.484.1222.**

L Statue of Liberty/ Ellis Island
Pg. 136, J6. It is estimated that one out of four Americans is descended from immigrants who arrived at Ellis Island. The main processing building has been meticulously restored and now presents a moving chronicle of the immigrants' often harrowing last lap before gaining access to the refuge promised by Lady Liberty. Ferry, **212.269.5755.** Parks, **212.363.7772.**

M National Baseball Hall of Fame
Pg. 133, M18. Baseball wasn't invented in Cooperstown but this is where the game's great talents and its long hold on America are most intensely revered. Ruth, Gehrig, DiMaggio, Mays, Robinson, Aaron, Clemente – the all-star team of the ages inhabits these plaques, these stats, these weathered bits of leather and wool. **607.547.7200.**

N Chrysler Building
Pg. 137, E19. Emblem of 1920s optimism and paean to the automobile age – its ornamentation suggests hubcaps and radiator gizmos – the Chrysler Building is perhaps New York's greatest art deco monument. The brainchild of auto magnate Walter Chrysler (who was eager to build the world's tallest structure), the flamboyant skyscraper was initially scorned by tastemakers. "Heaven help the person who looks at this building without the help of distance and heavy mists," Lewis Mumford sniffed. But over the years, the Chrysler Building's sheer exuberance has earned the genuine affection of New Yorkers and others of good sense. **212.682.3070.**

At the turn of the century, rivers like the Beaverkill and Willowemoc in the Catskill Mountains became famous as the cradle of American dry fly-fishing, and the nearby town of Roscoe has proclaimed itself "trout town USA."

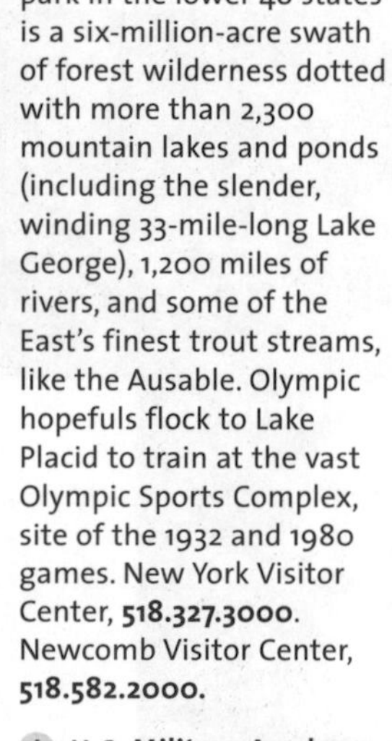

Pine Barrens R

Cape May P

New Jersey

O Atlantic City
Pg. 129, S9. Before the casinos opened, in 1978, public awareness of this once-popular resort had dwindled to recognition of street names in the game of Monopoly. (For a glimpse of the grand beachfront hotels long past their glory days, check out the early Jack Nicholson film *The King of Marvin Gardens*.) Now a bettor's mecca, Atlantic City's "renaissance" attracts a steady stream of gamblers and sightseers who parade up and down the four-mile boardwalk, taking a break from fortune's wheel or merely enjoying the passing show. **609.348.7100.**

P Cape May
Pg. 129, V6. This tiny town at the southernmost tip of the state found a commercial niche in tourism early in the game: It was advertising its pleasures in the Philadelphia press as early as 1745. Founded in 1620, Cape May is one of the Atlantic coast's oldest resorts, a delightfully old-fashioned confection of tidy tree-lined streets with unique boutiques and elegant, gingerbread-trimmed houses. The ornate Emlen Physick Estate, designed in 1879 by architect Frank Furness, is a fine example of the town's more than 600 pastel-painted Victorian abodes. The watch room of the lighthouse at Cape May Point State Park offers panoramic views of the ocean and bay. **609.884.9562.**

Q Edison National Historic Site
Pg. 136, F3. America's most acclaimed inventor worked at his "invention factory" in West Orange from 1887 to 1931, refining prototypes for devices such as the phonograph and the motion picture camera. Included in the tour are Edison's chemistry lab, a replica of the world's first motion picture studio, and a tinfoil recording of Edison reciting "Mary Had a Little Lamb." **973.736.0550.**

R Pine Barrens
Pg. 129, N8. This sparsely populated 2,000-square-mile oasis of pine forests and cedar swamps in southern New Jersey surprises visitors with its size as well as its proximity to Manhattan, a scant 60 miles to the north. The heart of the Barrens, a 336,000-acre area in the northern half of the 1.1-million-acre Pinelands National Reserve, is a designated Preservation Area District and a paradise for environmentalists and outdoor enthusiasts (the easy-going Mullica is a great canoeing river). **609.894.9342.**

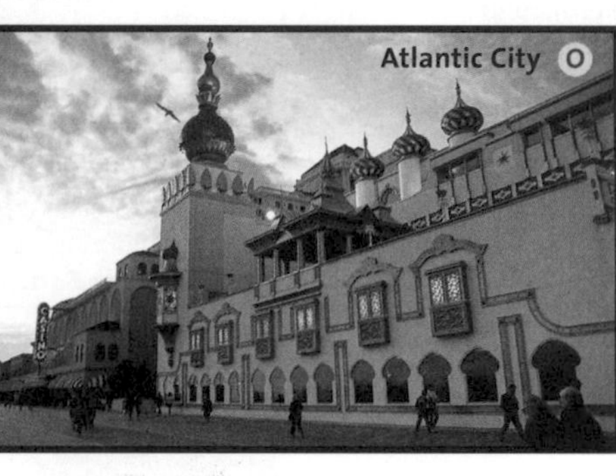

Atlantic City O

New Jersey's shoreline has long been popular with vacationers, but they might be surprised to find out that the state's large fishing industry harvests two of every three surf clams and ocean quahogs consumed in the world.

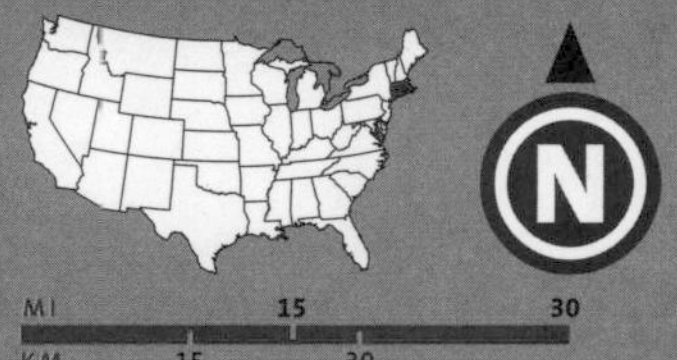

Southern New England

The terrain of southern New England is part of American myth. Here is where the Pilgrims landed, where the "shot heard round the world" echoed across an old wood bridge, where religious rebel Roger Williams named a city after God's Providence, and where secular rebel Paul Revere galloped into legend. New England's most populous region – Massachusetts, Connecticut, and Rhode Island – nevertheless offers plenty of unspoiled nature. From the sandy shores and saltbox houses of Cape Cod, the traveler can ferry north to Boston, the old City on a Hill. Out beyond Boston's shadow, the gentle hills of Massachusetts roll west to meet the broad valley of the Connecticut River, then rise to the Berkshires' serene heights. Aptly named the Ocean State, Rhode Island geared up around ragged Narragansett Bay and sent trading ships to earth's end; and later Newport's incomparable location at the bay's mouth made it the resort of choice for Gilded Age magnificoes. Connecticut's northeastern quiet corner is a surprisingly rural enclave within two hours of Hartford, Boston, and Providence. And the last few miles of the Connecticut River, before it empties into Long Island Sound, comprise a region where natural and human-made environments have drawn a rare and lovely truce.

Their coastlines raggedly cut like pieces of a jigsaw puzzle by Narragansett, Buzzards, and Cape Cod Bays, Massachusetts and Rhode Island favored early maritime ventures. Cape Cod itself, along with Martha's Vineyard and Nantucket, is largely a gift of Ice Age glaciers. The hilly central portions of Massachusetts and Connecticut are drained by the Connecticut River, New England's longest, which empties into Long Island Sound at Old Saybrook.

JANUARY
Warm Up to Winter, Farmington Valley, CT
Several towns in the area enliven winter with a program of Early American Hearth house tours, special events, and loads of tasty food (events last through March).
800.493.5266

APRIL
Boston Marathon, Boston, MA
The Patriot's Day 26.2-mile course starts in Hopkinton, winds through eight cities and towns, and finishes near Copley Square.
617.236.1652

MAY
Brimfield Antique Shows, Brimfield, MA
Bargain for tchotchkes and Chippendale alike at this incredible gathering of more than 4,000 antique dealers from all over North America, along a one-mile stretch of Route 20. Three six-day sessions, in May, July, and September.
413.283.6149, 413.283.2418

Lime Rock Grand Prix, Lakeville, CT
The largest road race in North America features top sports-car drivers who turn the quiet roads in and around Lakeville into a thrilling, high-octane derby site.
800.722.3577

JUNE
Festival of Historic Houses, Providence, RI
The houses of College Hill, with the largest concentration of colonial homes in America, are open for tours.
401.831.7440

Jacob's Pillow, Becket, MA
From late June through early August, the United States' oldest dance festival attracts dancers and troupes from around the world.
413.243.0745

JULY
Newport Regatta, Newport, RI
The East Coast's premier regatta in the United States' favorite yachting capital.
401.846.1983

AUGUST
Newport JVC Jazz Festival, Newport, RI
One of the most prestigious jazz events in the U.S. showcases legendary performers and rising stars.
401.847.3700

SEPTEMBER
Norwalk Seaport Association's Oyster Festival, East Norwalk, CT
This waterfront festival celebrates Long Island Sound's seafaring past with oyster shucking and oyster slurp-off contests, tall ships, harbor cruises, entertainment, and fireworks.
888.701.7785

DECEMBER
Anniversary Reenactment of the Boston Tea Party, Boston, MA
After gathering at Old South Meeting House to debate the tax levied by England, patriots march to the replica Tea Party Ship and dump tea in Boston Harbor. Held each year on the weekend nearest the Tea Party's actual anniversary, December 16th.
617.338.1773

We say the cows laid out Boston.
Well, there are worse surveyors.

– RALPH WALDO EMERSON, "WEALTH" IN *THE CONDUCT OF LIFE*, 1860

Litchfield Hills B

Housatonic Meadows State Park F

Mark Twain House, Hartford C

Connecticut

A Barnum Museum
Pg. 78, M9. Entrepreneur, writer, politician, and perhaps the greatest showman on earth, Phineas Taylor Barnum was an American phenomenon. He introduced to the world the three-ring circus, General Tom Thumb, and Jenny Lind, the Swedish Nightingale. Exhibits at the turreted Byzantine-Romanesque Revival Museum in Bridgeport highlight P.T.'s career as entertainment wizard and Bridgeport mayor, and include such crowd pleasers as a 4,000-piece miniature circus and Tom Thumb's tiny velvet suit. **203.331.9881.**

B Litchfield Hills
Pg. 78, D6. Often described as a Yankee Brigadoon, northwestern Connecticut's Litchfield Hills are quintessential New England – a land of gently rolling hills, narrow roads dotted with farms, chaste white churches with graceful steeples, and manicured villages. Elegant Litchfield, settled in 1719, has the feel of a thriving 18th-century town that has been preserved in time. Many of the sleepy hill towns played a significant role in Connecticut and United States history, documented in local museums. **860.567.4506.**

C Mark Twain House
Pg. 79, K18. The prowlike front and wraparound porches of Samuel Clemens's home in Hartford evoke the writer's beloved riverboats. Inside, the ornate dining room and whimsical library reveal a taste for Victorian opulence coupled with a humorist's love of quirks and ironies. The distinguished man of letters often played "jungle" with his daughters and butler in the plant-filled conservatory. But his favorite room was in the third-floor pinnacle of the house – a combination study, smoking room, and billiard parlor where Twain entertained guests and created his most enduring characters. **860.493.6411.**

Groton has been known as the submarine capital of the world since World War I, when it became the U.S. Navy's first submarine base. The city is home to the Navy-operated Submarine Force Museum, where the U.S.S. *Nautilus* – the world's first nuclear submarine – is on display.

D Mystic Seaport
Pg. 79, H15. The largest maritime museum in the U.S. summons up the flavor and sinew of life in a 19th-century New England seaport. Costumed interpreters at the 17-acre living-history museum practice traditional maritime crafts in more than 60 restored buildings. Try to appreciate the details of everyday life aboard the museum's premier attraction, the *Charles W. Morgan*, the country's last wooden whaler, with a visit to the blubber room, below deck. Here, huge slabs of pungent whale blubber were cut up before being tossed into iron pots on the main deck and boiled down to an oily sludge. **888.973.2767.**

E Foxwoods Resort Casino
Pg. 79, F15. Foxwoods, in Mashantucket near Ledyard, is the megamall of casinos. About 11,000 employees work to ensure that the 18 million people a year who travel to the world's largest gambling emporium enjoy themselves and if they lose, have a good time doing it. To date, the owners, the Mashantucket Pequot Tribal Nation, have contributed more than half a billion dollars to the state of Connecticut. **800.752.9244.**

F Housatonic Meadows State Park / Cornwall Bridge
Pg. 78, C5. On the banks of the Housatonic River, the park is a popular spot for fly-fishing, picnicking, and hiking. The summit of the 2.5-mile Pine Knob Loop Trail offers breathtaking vistas of the river and the Litchfield Hills. Just up the road in West Cornwall is the Cornwall Bridge, noted for its intricate latticework truss. **860.927.3238.**

There is a sumptuous variety about the New England weather that compels the stranger's admiration – and regret. . . . In the spring, I have counted 136 different kinds of weather inside of 24 hours.

– MARK TWAIN, 1876

MA 110
RI 155
CT 78
MA 238
RI 245
CT 233

Old Sturbridge Village (I)

Walden Pond State Reservation (K)

Nauset Beach Lighthouse, Cape Cod (L)

Massachusetts

(G) Adams National Historic Site
Pg. 111, E14. John Adams's career took him to the high councils of the American Revolution and ultimately the presidency. But he started life in a farmhouse in what is now suburban Quincy. The site includes his birthplace, built in 1681, as well as the home where Adams's son, sixth president John Quincy Adams, was born. **617.770.1175.**

(H) Boston / Cambridge
Pg. 111, E14. Nearly 150 years older than the republic it sparked to life, Boston has been many cities: 17th-century Puritan outpost; colonial capital of Revere, Hancock, and the Adamses; Victorian "hub of the universe" for Brahmins and literati; and player in modern trends ranging from gritty machine politics to the high-tech revolution. The evocative Freedom Trail links historic touchstones such as Paul Revere's House, the Boston Massacre Site, and the U.S.S. *Constitution*. Other attractions include the gaslit streets of Beacon Hill, the rich Victorian facades of Back Bay, and the world-class Museum of Fine Arts. Nearby Cambridge is a center of higher learning, with Harvard University, the Massachusetts Institute of Technology, and an international student population that supports a dense concentration of bookstores and lively cafés. Boston, **800.888.5515.** Cambridge, **617.441.2884.**

(I) Old Sturbridge Village
Pg. 110, G8. In a fastidious re-creation of a New England rural village of the 1830s, more than 40 superbly restored buildings have been moved from throughout the region to this 200-acre living-history museum. Costumed staff perform the routines of everyday life, and even the livestock and crops are bred to simulate old New England varieties. **800.733.1830, 508.347.3362.**

(J) Springfield
Pg. 110, G6. Established in 1636, Springfield has become the premier city of the Connecticut River valley. The Springfield Armory National Historic Site, which produced small arms for every United States conflict from the War of 1812 to Vietnam, is now a museum with exhibits on the history of firearms. As the birthplace of basketball, in 1891, Springfield was the logical choice for the game's Hall of Fame, which honors immortals from George Mikan to Michael Jordan. The downtown Quadrangle is lined with museums, including the Connecticut Valley Historical Museum and the Springfield Science Museum. Spacious Forest Park is home to an excellent small zoo which inspired native son Dr. Seuss, whose father was the superintendent. **800.723.1548.**

(K) Walden Pond State Reservation
Pg. 111, D13. In a cabin on the shores of this half-mile-long pond near Concord, Henry David Thoreau conducted the two-year experiment in solitude and self-sufficiency described in his book *Walden*. A cairn marks his cabin site, and a full-size model of the spartan structure stands near the visitor center. **978.369.3254.**

(L) Cape Cod / Nantucket Island / Martha's Vineyard
Pg. 111, G20, N19, M17. A spectacularly successful experiment in the preservation of unspoiled lands, the Cape Cod National Seashore features dunes, marshes, ponds, and lonely moors from the elbow to the fist of the cape's upturned arm. Elsewhere the cape is a study in human contrasts: the busy resort town of Hyannis, the shady lanes and sea captains' homes of the villages on the quiet bay side, and the quirkily vibrant hubbub of Provincetown, an 18th-century fishing port with a modern overlay of bohemian and gay culture. A ferry ride away from the cape lie the one-time whaling islands of Martha's Vineyard and Nantucket, chic summer retreats where solitude reigns in the off-season. **508.362.3225.**

(M) Plimoth Plantation
Pg. 111, H16. In 1627, daily life at Plimoth Plantation, the primitive first settlement of the Mayflower Pilgrims, who landed just north in 1620, showed few outward signs of thanksgiving: Plimoth residents lived in modest cottages, hunting, fishing, raising domesticated pigs, and sending back to England for spices. At this living-history museum, authentically costumed "Pilgrims" go about their daily chores, conversing only in the dialect of the day. The adjacent Hobbamock's Homesite, a typical single-family dwelling of the Wampanoag, showcases crafts, like canoe-making, basketry, and weaving, that settlers borrowed to survive. **508.746.1622.**

Nearly 40 percent of the nation's harvest of cranberries is grown in bogs on or near Cape Cod. Besides the 5 percent sold as fresh fruit, these tangy berries end up as ingredients in 700 to 800 products, from cereals to salsas.

Where bay and tranquil river blend,
And leafy hillsides rise,
The spires of Providence ascend
Against the ancient skies.

— H. P. LOVECRAFT, "PROVIDENCE," c. 1924–37

Rhode Island

(N) Block Island
Pg. 155, N3. Twelve miles off Little Rhody's southern shore lies a speck of land known for its windswept moors, sand cliffs, salt and freshwater ponds, and refreshing lack of cigarette boats. Block Island is legendary for shipwrecks – more than 200 in its history, one of which is commemorated at the Palatine Graves. A nightmare for early sailors, the island is a paradise for today's fishermen: Ocean waters teem with bluefish, flounder, striped bass, and tuna. **800.383.2474.**

(O) Providence
Pg. 155, E5. One of New England's oldest and largest cities, Providence was founded in 1636 by Roger Williams, an exile of Massachusetts who had quarreled with Puritans over religious freedom. The clergyman named the site at the northern reaches of Narragansett Bay in gratitude for God's Providence in helping him find refuge from persecution. Today, Rhode Island's capital city is home to a diverse ethnic population and numerous students passing through its institutions of higher learning. A down-and-out Edgar Allan Poe briefly courted a younger poet, Sarah Whitman, who lived on leafy, brick-lined Benefit Street on lovely College Hill. **800.233.1636.**

Salve Regina College, Newport (P)

Shore at Mohegan Bluffs, Block Island (N)

Providence (O)

(P) Newport
Pg. 155, J6. When Italian navigator Giovanni da Verrazano first saw this island in 1524, it was called Aquidneck – Isle of Peace – by native inhabitants. He christened it Refugio, and indeed Newport later provided refuge for Quakers and for Jews, who established the first synagogue in North America here in 1763. But it wasn't persecuted minorities or the huddled masses who changed the face of this fading seaport. The United States' wealthiest families – the Vanderbilts, Astors, Belmonts, and the like – arrived during the Gilded Age to build their seaside mansions of marble, crystal, and gold. For a taste of robber baron – style extravagance, visit The Breakers, built by Cornelius Vanderbilt II in 1895 as an Italian Renaissance palazzo, or Rosecliff, a New World version of Versailles's Petit Trianon designed by Stanford White in 1902. **401.845.9123.**

(Q) Slater Mill Historic Site
Pg. 155, B9. Native Americans called the spot on the Blackstone River where Pawtucket now stands "place of rushing waters." These waters gave birth to the American industrial revolution. In 1793, an English immigrant named Samuel Slater harnessed the river for the nation's first-ever waterwheel-powered textile machinery. Today, Slater Mill is a working museum. **401.725.8638.**

Mass production of jewelry in the States began in 1794, when Rhode Island inventor Nehemiah Dodge developed a process for gold-plating base metal. Providence is still the principal jewelry-making site in America, with more than 20,000 people employed in jewelry manufacturing.

Northern New England

In New England's northern tier, respect for a rich colonial heritage is tempered by the dry wit of its self-reliant, frugal, hardworking residents. The setting is spectacular, with wilderness hemming the old communities, from Down East coastline to wild, inland forests. Maine faces the Atlantic along a granite coast so fantastically convoluted that it would reach across the United States if stretched to a straight line, and even the most seasoned of the state's legendary schooner captains would be challenged to name all of her salt-sprayed islands. To the west the land rises, cresting in New Hampshire's Mount Washington and the lesser peaks of the White Mountains. Deep in the wilderness at New Hampshire's northern extreme, New England's longest river, the Connecticut, spills down from a series of cold blue lakes to begin its 407-mile journey to the sea. Between the Connecticut River and New England's "west coast" on Lake Champlain lies a state that has become as much an ideal of rural idyll as a geographical entity. Vermont is defined primarily by the small towns that dot its hills and valleys. The least urbanized state in the Union, this land of green mountains clings to its old self-image as a realm of yeoman farmers – in fact, it was once an independent republic.

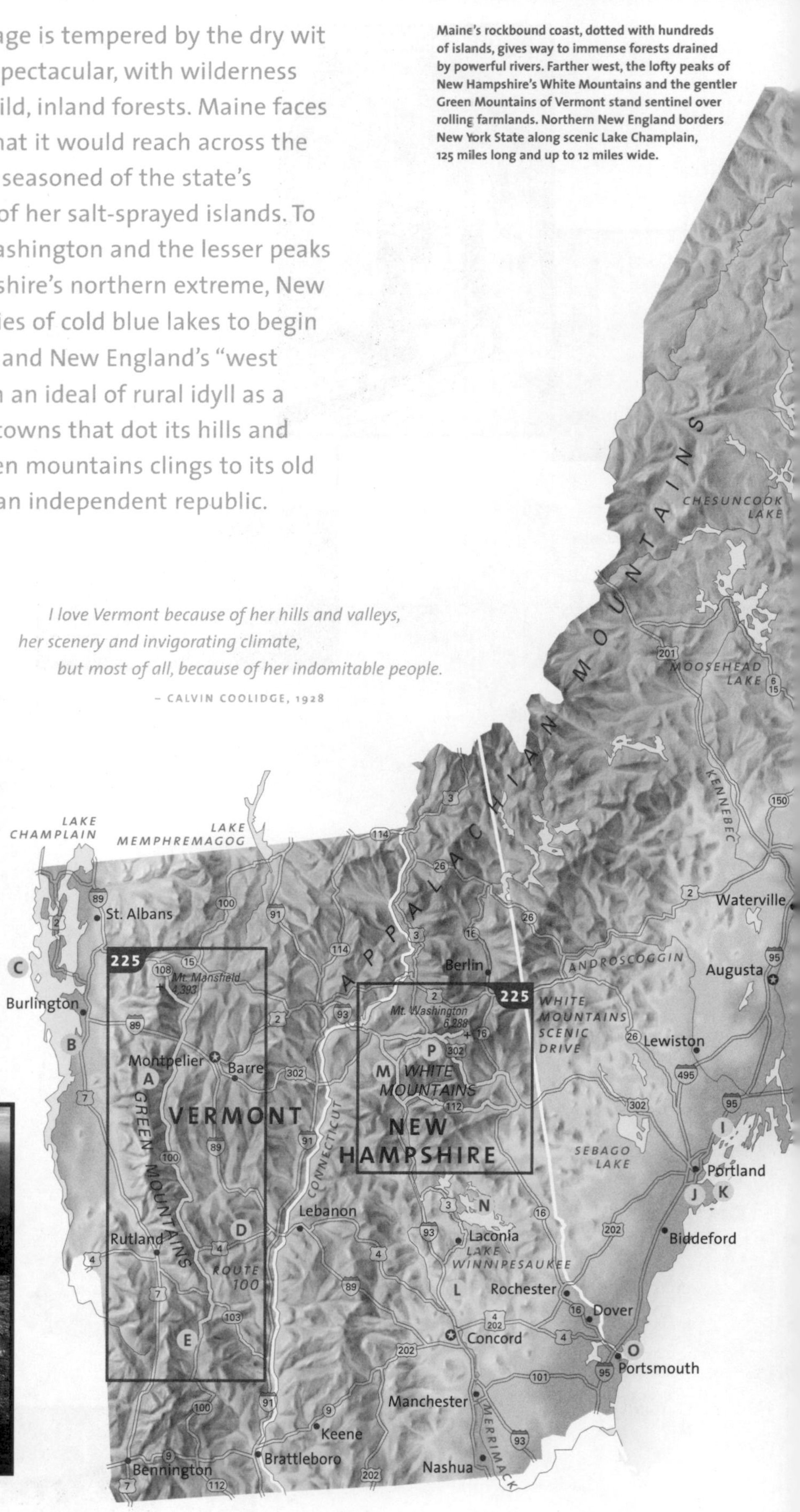

Maine's rockbound coast, dotted with hundreds of islands, gives way to immense forests drained by powerful rivers. Farther west, the lofty peaks of New Hampshire's White Mountains and the gentler Green Mountains of Vermont stand sentinel over rolling farmlands. Northern New England borders New York State along scenic Lake Champlain, 125 miles long and up to 12 miles wide.

MARCH

Maine Maple Sunday
The governor kicks off this statewide event with a proclamation, and several dozen maple-sugar producers open their doors for tours and sampling. Savor the traditional snack of "sugar on snow" (that's syrup poured on shaved ice, for out-of-towners) with plain doughnuts.
207.287.3491

MAY

MooseMainea Celebration, Greenville, ME
The state's favorite mammal is stalked by humans on guided moose-watching safaris in a monthlong celebration that includes mountain-bike and canoe races, fly-fishing contests, a rowing regatta, a craft fair, and, yes, moose stories.
207.695.2702

JUNE

Quechee Hot-Air Balloon Festival and Craft Fair, Quechee, VT
Twenty hot-air balloons float above the Village Green, while clowns, musicians, artisans, and cloggers entertain folks below. A balloon ride can be had for a fee.
802.295.7900

AUGUST

Maine Lobster Festival, Rockland, ME
This five-day event, held at Harbor Park overlooking Penobscot Bay, features all sorts of waterfront recreation, parades, marine exhibits, boat and helicopter rides – and, of course, steamed lobsters.
800.562.2529

Craftsmen's Fair, Newbury, NH
Shaker and folk arts are among the items on view at this annual hands-on craft fair held at Mount Sunapee State Park, with demonstrations and educational workshops.
603.224.3375

SEPTEMBER

Northeast Kingdom Fall Foliage Festival, Marshfield, Walden, Cabot, Plainfield, Peacham, Barnet, Groton, St. Johnsbury, VT
Towns throughout Vermont honor the fall foliage with village tours, bazaars, exhibits, and sumptuous church suppers.
802.563.2472

NOVEMBER

Traditionally Yours, Jackson, NH
Christmas is celebrated the traditional way in this three-week festival (weekends from Thanksgiving to mid-December) of gingerbread-house workshops, sleigh rides, tobogganing parties, a torchlight parade down Eagle Mountain, and a Victorian-style ice-skating party at Nestlenook Farm.
800.866.333

I love Vermont because of her hills and valleys,
her scenery and invigorating climate,
but most of all, because of her indomitable people.

– CALVIN COOLIDGE, 1928

Billings Farm and Museum D

Vermont Country Store E

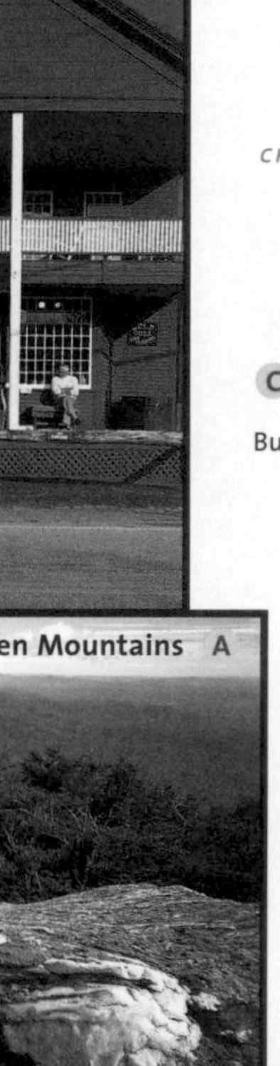

Green Mountains A

Vermont

A Green Mountains
Pg. 166, D5. A north-south ridge running the length of the state, the Green Mountains are the defining feature of Vermont, possessing an aura of remoteness and deep-woods mystery worthy of many a loftier range. An hour's drive from Burlington, their summit, 4,393-foot Mount Mansfield, is accessible both by tall road and gondola. Green Mountain National Forest covers two huge swaths of the central and southern ranges, totaling more than 350,000 acres, 60,000 of which are federally protected wilderness. In winter, the range's icy peaks become the East Coast's biggest ski destination, with resort towns ranging from charming Stowe (home of *The Sound of Music*'s Trapp Family Lodge) to the bustling Killington ski area. Outdoor adventures abound year-round, and some of the most scenic and challenging portions of the 265-mile Long Trail are within the forest's borders. **802.747.6700.**

B Shelburne Museum
Pg. 166, K8. Sugar heiress Electra Havemeyer Webb began collecting Americana in her youth. By the time she died in 1960, her sure eye and vast wealth had helped create New England's Smithsonian, the Shelburne Museum. Many of the 37 buildings that dot its 45 manicured acres, south of Burlington on Lake Champlain, were moved to the site and are themselves priceless American relics, including a 168-foot, three-lane covered bridge built in 1845 and an 1871 Lake Champlain lighthouse. Webb's collection of collections includes 80,000 pieces and boasts everything from fine art (paintings by Monet and Andrew Wyeth) to folk art (cigar store Indians and weather vanes). The trove of 1,000 antique dolls is world famous. **802.985.3346.**

C Lake Champlain
Pg. 166, D3. Shared by Vermont, New York State, and Québec, Lake Champlain is a 125-mile-long jewel often referred to as the "sixth Great Lake." Near Burlington, where the lake reaches its greatest width, at roughly 12 miles, New York's Adirondacks and Vermont's Green Mountains are visible to the west and east. The lake is easily accessible by private or excursion boat. The *Spirit of Ethan Allen* (named for the Revolutionary War hero) offers summer tours, and the Lake Champlain Ferry runs between Burlington and Port Kent, New York, from spring through fall. **802.863.3489.**

D Billings Farm & Museum
Pg. 166, H5. In 1871, railroad baron and returned native son Frederick Billings bought land in his hometown to found a scientifically run farm and progressive reforestation program. Billings Farm, operated continuously since then, has evolved into a working museum. Today, its pedigreed jerseys produce milk for a local dairy cooperative; a vast barn serves as a museum of farm life and implements; and the farm manager's house offers a rare glimpse of rural living that must have been the envy of 19th-century Woodstock. **802.457.2355.**

E Vermont Country Store
Pg. 166, J4. The utilitarian and the rustic meet at the Vermont Country Store, founded more than 50 years ago by Vrest Orton, a writer who sought to re-create the atmosphere of the small-town general stores of his youth. Starting with traditional items such as penny candy, big wheels of Vermont cheddar, calico yard goods, and old-time kitchenware, Orton built a nationwide mail-order business whose catalog, The Voice of the Mountains, reaches homes all over America. The original store, facing Weston's village green, has added room after rambling room over the years, but the potbellied stove still stands in its place of honor.
802.824.3184.

The biggest harvest of maple sap in the country is a welcome harbinger of spring in Vermont, where from late February to early April, approximately 395,000 gallons of syrup are produced from 40 times as much sap.

ME 104
NH 127
VT 166
ME 237
NH 240
VT 247

The rocky ledge runs far into the sea,
And on its outer point, some miles away,
The lighthouse lifts its massive masonry,
A pillar of fire by night, of cloud by day.

—HENRY WADSWORTH LONGFELLOW, "THE LIGHTHOUSE," 1846

ST. JOHN
Presque Isle
Houlton
Mt. Katahdin 5,267
ST. CROIX
Calais
PENOBSCOT
MAINE
Bangor
GRAND MANAN CHANNEL
MT. DESERT ISLAND
ACADIA NATIONAL PARK
ACADIA N.P. 194
PENOBSCOT BAY
GULF OF MAINE
ATLANTIC OCEAN

Castine H

Camden G

Portland Head Light K

Baxter State Park F

Maine

F Baxter State Park
Pg. 104, F7. Baxter State Park exists thanks to former governor Percival Baxter. In 1931, after unsuccessful attempts to persuade the state legislature to buy the land, Baxter began to purchase a wilderness tract of more than 200,000 acres in the Millinocket region, "to be forever left in its natural wild state." Several thousand acres have been added since, and the park remains as wild as ever. Its centerpiece, Mount Katahdin, is Maine's highest peak, at 5,267 feet; Katahdin's summit, Baxter Peak, marks the northern terminus of the Appalachian Trail. With 175 miles of trails – some quite rugged, like the four-mile Abol – the preserve is a paradise for backcountry enthusiasts. **207.723.5140.**

G Camden
Pg. 105, Q7. When Captain John Smith saw the future site of Camden on an exploratory voyage up the coast in 1614, he reportedly described it as "adjoining to the high mountains of Penobscot, against whose feet the sea doth beat." The town that sprung up around the natural harbor has been a summer resort since the mid-1800s, and wealthy vacationers began building their palatial summer homes here at the turn of the century. Norumbega (now a B&B) was one of the more extravagant. The streets are lined with 19th-century sea captains' homes, and a fleet of windjammers, available for coastline cruises, docks in the picturesque harbor. **207.236.4404.**

H Castine
Pg. 105, P8. Situated on a peninsula at the confluence of the Penobscot and Bagaduce Rivers, Castine's strategic placement, rather than its beauty, provoked a 200-year battle for possession among four countries. Today, markers around the town narrate that rich history. Castine's 19th-century heyday as a major shipbuilding center and its reign as one of the wealthiest towns per capita in the country are revealed in the elegant domestic architecture and handsome public buildings that line its quiet streets. **207.326.4502.**

I L.L. Bean
Pg. 105, R4. Leon Leonwood Bean opened a mail-order business in 1912, specializing in the now ubiquitous, rubber-below and leather-above Maine Hunting Shoe. Today, the four-floor L. L. Bean flagship store in Freeport is open 24-7, year-round, and attracts some 3.8 million shoppers annually, outfitting duck hunters, fly fishers, and soccer moms alike with everything from flannel sheets to ten variations on the original Hunting Shoe. Clustered around this retail goliath are more than 110 smaller chain stores, forming a vast outdoor mall. **207.865.1212.**

J Portland
Pg. 105, S3. Since its founding in 1632, Portland has burned and been rebuilt four times, and yet has prospered. Worldly from the start – home to a free black population who worked as longshoremen – the city evolved from a tiny village to lumber port and railroad terminus to shipbuilding center to regional business capital and major tourist destination. When Henry Wadsworth Longfellow christened his native town the "jewel by the sea," it hadn't yet become Maine's largest city, but Portland still retains much of the charm that captivated the poet. The Wadsworth-Longfellow House, where he grew up, is open for tours and contains family furnishings and mementos. Downtown and surrounding neighborhoods feature superb federal- and Victorian-era mansions and buildings. **207.772.4994.**

K Portland Head Light
Pg. 105, S3. Originally commissioned when Maine was a district of Massachusetts, the colony's first lighthouse began operation in 1791. Standing 101 feet above high tide on the lower jaw of Casco Bay near Cape Elizabeth, the lighthouse still warns ships away from this treacherous section of coastline, and has an excellent museum in the former keeper's quarters. **207.799.2661.**

Maine lobsters are prized by chefs and diners alike for their intense flavor. In annual harvests of recent years, more than 30 million pounds of lobsters have been landed to satisfy that market.

She's one of the two best states in the Union.
Vermont's the other.

– ROBERT FROST, *NEW HAMPSHIRE*, 1923

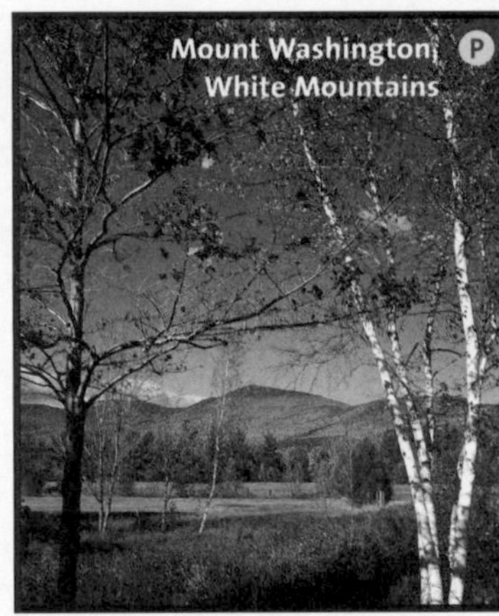
Mount Washington, White Mountains P

Franconia Notch State Park M

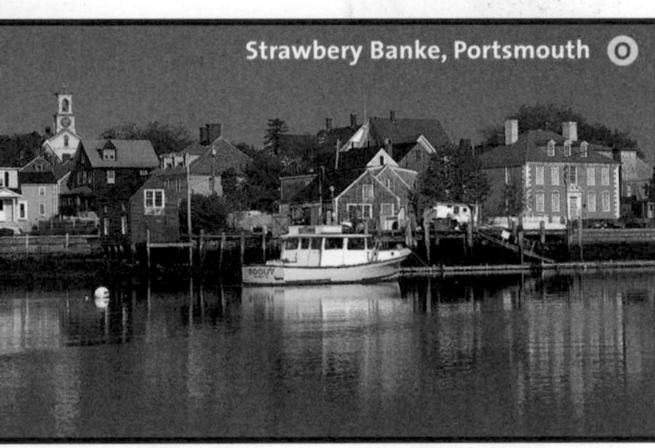
Strawbery Banke, Portsmouth O

New Hampshire

L Canterbury Shaker Village
Pg. 127, K7. By the 1850s, the Shaker compound at Canterbury housed more than 300 followers of the sect founded by Ann Lee in 1792. The grounds and 25 of the community's original 100 white-frame structures have been restored into a living museum. Legend has it that the radiant sugar maples that line Meeting House Lane were planted for orphans adopted by the celibate Shakers. **603.783.9511.**

It's always exciting to spot one of New Hampshire's burgeoning moose population – the resident number of 13 recorded in 1900 blossomed to 5,900 by 1996 – unless one of these 700- to 1,100-pound giants is standing in the middle of the road.

M Franconia Notch State Park
Pg. 127, F6. This 6,440-acre park of fir, spruce, and birch forest lies between the Franconia and Kinsman Mountains and covers some of the White Mountains' most spectacular natural attractions. Best known is the Granite State's signature profile (and official symbol), the Old Man of the Mountain, whose 40-foot, naturally sculpted visage juts out from Cannon Mountain above Profile Lake. Also within park boundaries is the 800-foot narrow gorge called the Flume – discovered by 93-year-old Aunt Jess Guernsey in 1808 during a fishing trip. **603.823.5563.**

N Lakes Region
Pg. 127, H8. This is the countryside made famous in the movie *On Golden Pond* – a land where cool, shady forests crowd the shores of glacial lakes, and centuries-old villages are aproned with tidy farms. One look at the view from industrialist Thomas Plant's stone Castle in the Clouds, high in the Ossipee Mountains near Moultonborough, and it's easy to see why the tycoon plunked down $7 million for this palatial aerie and its 5,200 surrounding acres in the early 1900s. **800.531.2347.**

O Portsmouth
Pg. 127, L10. A working port since colonial days, Portsmouth handily blends its workaday environment with its other big industry, tourism, to create a city where lobster boats, boutiques, and even a 200-year-old working navy yard all seem perfectly at home. Today, a ten-acre museum, named Strawbery Banke after the first permanent settlement, preserves 42 structures representing four centuries of the city's life, and Portsmouth Trail takes the visitor through exquisite examples of Georgian and federal architecture, including the 1758 John Paul Jones House. **603.436.1118.**

P White Mountain National Forest
Pg. 127, G7. Stretching across New Hampshire into Maine, the forest covers 774,085 acres of rugged mountain ranges, waterfalls, covered bridges, hiking trails, downhill and cross-country ski trails, and some of the most magnificent views in the East. Although the summit of the Northeast's highest peak, 6,288-foot Mount Washington, is in the clouds much of the time, and its weather can be ferocious (with winds at hurricane force), getting up there on the historic Cog Railway is half the fun. Less intrepid travelers can drive to the top via the eight-mile Mount Washington Auto Road, while the truly adventurous can reach the summit on a number of challenging trails. **603.528.9528.**

Eastern Canada

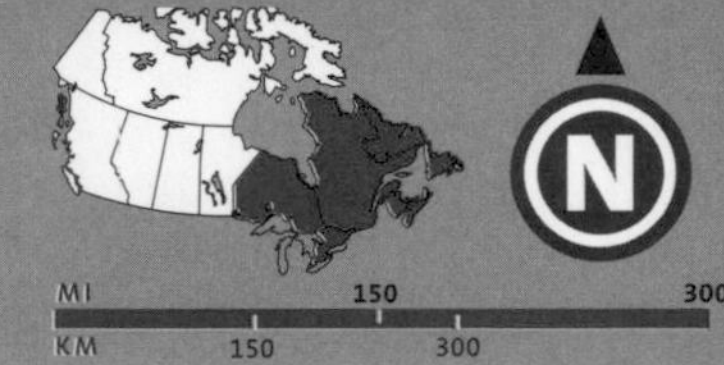

FEBRUARY

Charlottetown Winter Carnival, Charlottetown, PE
Parades, fireworks, and sporting events are highlights of Atlantic Canada's premier winter festival.
902.892.5708

Winter Carnival of Québec City, PQ
A citywide celebration of winter for the whole family, with art exhibits, sporting events such as the famed canoe race across the ice-choked St. Lawrence, ice sculptures (and an ice palace), and general bonhomie.
418.626.3716

APRIL

The Shaw Festival, Niagara-on-the-Lake, ON
From mid-April through October the works of George Bernard Shaw and his contemporaries come alive on three stages in the heart of Ontario's wine country.
800.511.7429

JULY

Signal Hill Tattoo, St. John's, NF
A "tattoo" is an extravaganza of military music and precision drills – this one features blazing cannons, musket firings, dress ceremonies, and a marching band in an authentic display of exercises originally performed by the Royal Newfoundland Companies.
709.772.5367

Montréal International Jazz Festival, Montréal, PQ
One of the world's leading jazz festivals, Montréal's big-name extravaganza is famous for its free outdoor concerts.
514.523.3378

AUGUST

Royal St. John's Regatta, Quidi Vidi Lake, St. John's, NF
The oldest continuous sporting event in North America features a day of fixed-seat rowing races and "the world's biggest garden party."
709.729.0862

SEPTEMBER

Toronto International Film Festival, Toronto, ON
Established directors and little-known independents alike present their latest dramas, comedies, documentaries, and animated films at one of the world's top-rated film festivals.
416.967.7371

OCTOBER

Celtic Colours, Cape Breton Island, NS
An international Celtic festival featuring the sounds of local artists together with the burgeoning talents of the global Celtic community. Concerts, dancing, theater, and Celtic-language events make this an exciting ten days.
902.539.8800

Kitchener-Waterloo Oktoberfest, ON
Canada's largest Bavarian festival – celebrated in an area settled by Germans in the early 19th century – is also the biggest Oktoberfest outside Germany.
519.570.4267

DECEMBER

Winter Festival of Lights, Niagara Falls, ON
The festival, which begins in late November and runs through early January, includes illumination of Horseshoe Falls and a spectacular fireworks show on New Year's Eve.
800.563.2557

The eastern portion of the world's second largest nation (after Russia) is founded upon two grand topographical features. The first is the Canadian Shield, a vast granite expanse that includes some of the oldest rocks on earth, reaching from the Arctic nearly as far as the St. Lawrence River Valley. This is the Canada of forbidding beauty and grim legend – explorer Jacques Cartier called Labrador's subarctic wilderness "the land God gave Cain." The second, far more welcoming feature is the St. Lawrence River itself. Gateway to the New World for adventurers like Cartier and Samuel de Champlain, the greater St. Lawrence runs from its headstream, Minnesota's St. Louis River, in the heart of North America, through the Great Lakes, and into the Atlantic Ocean. Valley farmlands of Québec sit within a few miles of the great river port Montréal, the vibrant city where European traditions mingle with commercial vitality. An economic seat of Canada, Toronto stands on Lake Ontario, the watery gateway from the Atlantic seaboard to the inland prairies. To the east, Canada's maritime provinces cluster around the Gulf of St. Lawrence on the Atlantic, where isolated, rocky Newfoundland is a great plateau bordered by coastal fishing villages. By contrast, graceful Prince Edward Island, with its distinctive red soil and bountiful potato fields, is called the "garden of the gulf." Peninsular Nova Scotia seems at first to be all rocky headlands and lobster boats, until a look into its interior reveals the gentle green contours of the Annapolis Valley. And New Brunswick, beyond its old coastal cities, is a pulpwood empire laced by rushing salmon streams.

Craggy Newfoundland and mainland Labrador are no strangers to offshore icebergs and Atlantic gales. Nova Scotia enjoys one of the world's finest natural harbors, at Halifax; its interior – and that of New Brunswick – is heavily forested, while Prince Edward Island is mostly cleared for farming. The St. Lawrence River drains much of Ontario and Québec, carrying the waters of the Great Lakes to the sea.

Some say that no one ever leaves Montréal, for that city, like Canada itself, is designed to preserve the past, a past that happened somewhere else.

–LEONARD COHEN, *THE FAVOURITE GAME*, 1963

Niagara Falls A

Toronto C

Ontario

A Niagara Falls
Pg. 132, C1. In 1901, Anna Taylor, a Michigan schoolteacher, was the first to ride over Niagara Falls in a barrel. Now, due to strict regulations, most people prefer to view the world-famous cataract from one of the *Maid of the Mist* boats, which sail tantalizingly close to the spray; from the numerous vantage points such as Queen Victoria Park; or from the Observation Deck atop Skylon Tower. For the frustrated, Ride Niagara offers a high-tech submersible simulation. **800.563.2557.**

B Thousand Islands Region
Pg. 183, G17. There are actually 1,865 officially recognized islands here, some just meeting the local qualifying standards – two trees and six square feet of ground. Others are large enough to have served as elaborate retreats for tycoons and celebrities such as John Jacob Astor and Irving Berlin. One of the most famous is Heart Island, site of turreted Boldt Castle, which was built by a turn-of-the-century hotel entrepreneur and is now open for tours. A good jumping-off point for island cruises is the town of Gananoque. **800.668.2746.**

C Toronto
Pg. 183, J11. Ontario's provincial capital and Canada's largest city, Toronto is a metropolis of contrasts: Glittering skyscrapers towering over lakefront parks, old-fashioned gardens, snug residential neighborhoods, and some of the safest and cleanest streets of any urban center. The cosmopolitan city's 2.3 million inhabitants represent most of the nationalities of the world, and they have created a cultural treasure-house: After New York and London, Toronto is the third most important theater city in the English-speaking world, and its Royal Ontario Museum is Canada's largest public museum. The CN Tower features the Space Deck – the world's highest public observation gallery (1,463 feet). **800.363.1990.**

New Brunswick

D Bay of Fundy
Pg. 186, K7. The Bay of Fundy is famous for its tides, the highest in the world. At some points along the shore the vertical difference in water level from high to low tide is nearly 50 feet – as tall as a four-story building. One of the most dramatic places to witness this phenomenon is at the Rocks Provincial Park on Hopewell Cape. **506.734.3429.**

E Kings Landing Historical Settlement
Pg. 186, H5. The sights, sounds, and society of a 19th-century New Brunswick rural village have been carefully re-created at this living museum in Fredericton, which displays its superb collection of provincial furnishings, tools, and fashions in context. Costumed docents demonstrate crafts and go about their daily chores in more than 70 buildings, including homes, a school, a store, several mills, and farms. **506.363.5090.**

F Roosevelt Campobello International Park
Pg. 186, K5. James and Sara Roosevelt brought their year-old son, Franklin, to Campobello Island in 1883. From the time their summer home was built three years later, Campobello was the future president's "beloved island." Today much of its southern tip is preserved as Roosevelt Campobello International Park. The Roosevelt "cottage" is a rambling red gambrel-roofed structure, built in 1897 and presented to Franklin and Eleanor by his mother as a belated wedding present in about 1909. The 34-room house, furnished with family possessions, is open for guided tours. **506.752.2922.**

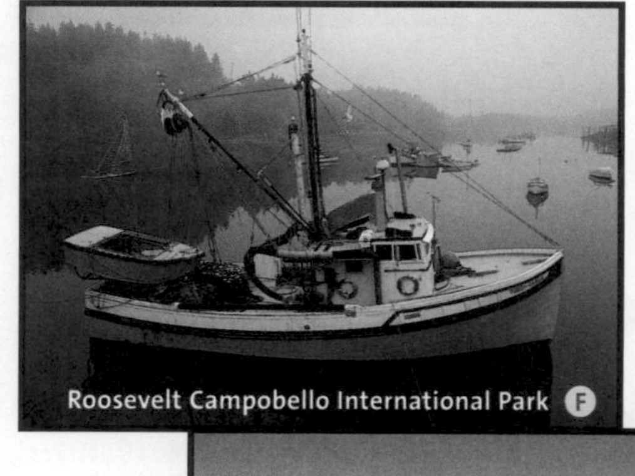

Roosevelt Campobello International Park F

Kings Landing Historical Settlement E

PE 186 · NF 187 · NS 186 · NB 186 · PQ 184 · ON 182 · PE 250 · NF 249 · NS 249 · NB 249 · PQ 250 · ON 249

Approximately 650,000 woodland caribou, primarily of the George River herd, make their semiannual migration through the northern Québec wilderness.

Gaspé Peninsula G

Québec City

Québec

G Gaspé Peninsula
Pg. 186, B6. Sparsely populated and starkly beautiful, the peninsula thrusts eastward for some 150 miles between the mouth of the St. Lawrence River and Chaleur Bay. At its heart, Gaspésie Provincial Park offers splendid opportunities for hiking and cross-country skiing in the Chic-Choc Mountains. The Gaspé also boasts fine salmon fishing and outfitters who specialize in dogsledding expeditions along remote wilderness trails. At the peninsula's eastern extreme, Percé Rock–pierced rock, named for its naturally formed arch–rises majestically from the Gulf near Bonaventure Island, a haven for thousands of gannets. **418.763.3301.**

H Montréal
Pg. 185, L12. Among French-speaking cities, only Paris is larger than Montréal. Founded in 1642 on the St. Lawrence River, the sprawling island metropolis was named Mount Royal after the rugged hilltop at its center, today a scenic park. The modern city, easily toured via a silent, rubber-wheeled subway, offers attractions such as the Museum of Fine Arts; the spacious Botanical Gardens; the Biodome, where world habitats are re-created indoors; and the vast network of underground walkways and shops at Plâce Ville-Marie. Aficionados of ethnic cuisines flock to the lively, polyglot Boulevard St.-Laurent neighborhood. **800.363.7777.**

I Québec City
Pg. 185, H17. Thanks to the only walled city in North America, in its Vieux-Québec section, Québec City retains much of the character it possessed as a mighty fortress-town, high on a rock above the St. Lawrence, founded by Samuel de Champlain and ruled by the governors of New France. Yet Québec is also one of the New World's most romantic cities, with its ancient narrow streets, stairway, and funicular linking the shops and squares of the Lower Town to the walled quarter above. At Québec's heart stands one of the continent's most photographed hotels, the turreted Château Frontenac. From the château, it's an easy walk to the Museum of Civilization; the Citadel, with its colorful changing-of-the-guard; the stately buildings of the National Assembly; and the Grand Allée's chic sidewalk cafés. **418.522.3511.**

L'Anse aux Meadows National Historic Site J

Gift of God I will make thee worthy.

—SAMUEL DE CHAMPLAIN, UPON LANDING IN 1608 AT WHAT IS NOW QUÉBEC CITY

Newfoundland

J L'Anse aux Meadows National Historic Site
Pg. 187, A18. A thousand years ago, Vikings reached Newfoundland from their settlements in Greenland, braving the Atlantic in their merchant ships called *knarrs*. Whether or not Newfoundland was the "Vinland" discovered by Leif Eriksson and immortalized in medieval Icelandic sagas, the foundations of eight turf and timber buildings found here, beside Epaves Bay on the northern tip of the island, remain the only authenticated Norse site in North America. The outlines of sod houses are still visible, and replicas of a longhouse, a forge, and an animal shed show how these intrepid adventurers lived. **709.623.2608.**

K Signal Hill National Historic Site
Pg. 187, H19. From this hill high above one of the oldest European settlements in North America, the arrival of ships was announced to the townspeople of St. John's by a series of flag signals. The British built the Queen's Battery here during the Napoleonic Wars, and after they withdrew in 1870, the buildings were used as a hospital. Just below Cabot Tower, begun in 1897 to commemorate the 400th anniversary of Newfoundland's discovery and the 60th year of Queen Victoria's reign, Guglielmo Marconi received the first transatlantic wireless signal, on December 12, 1901. **709.772.5367.**

The pristine Miramichi River in northern New Brunswick divides into 27 large and small salmon rivers, and is world famous for its sport salmon fishing. In 1995, 110 angler days brought in 25,000 Atlantic salmon.

Nova Scotia

L Halifax
Pg. 186, L10. Once known as the "Guardian of the North," Halifax was founded as a naval garrison to serve Britain's burgeoning 18th-century empire. Its massive citadel looms over the tidy port city like a North American Gibraltar. The city's working inner harbor is neatly divided from its glistening downtown waterfront, where the schooner *Bluenose* displays her brass and varnish amid wharves lined with shops, bistros, and the superb Maritime Museum of the Atlantic. A few blocks inland, the Public Gardens are an Edwardian confection of flower-lined pathways, swans in a meandering lagoon, and a perfect little bandstand that suggests imperial swagger. **800.565.0000.**

The waters of the Bay of Fundy are home to 7,200 of the world's second largest mammal – the finback whale – which can grow to a length of 80 feet and a weight of 100 tons.

Halifax L

M Fortress of Louisbourg National Historic Site
Pg. 187, H16. The largest historical reconstruction in North America is a faithful re-creation of a portion of a 250-year-old walled fortress built by the French. Costumed guides perform the everyday life of fortress residents, both ordinary folk and soldiers. Visitors eager for total immersion in the 18th century can dine at one of three period restaurants. Although the prices are 20th century, a dish such as *hachis de boeuf* (meat pie) along with a mug of hot buttered rum, will summon up the spirit of old French Canada. **902.733.2280.**

Prince Edward Island

N Green Gables
Pg. 191, E7. In 1908, Lucy Maud Montgomery published *Anne of Green Gables*, a novel about a winsome, red-haired orphan from Prince Edward Island who is adopted by an elderly brother and sister. Anne was destined to become the unofficial ambassador of Canada's smallest province: Tourists throughout the world make pilgrimages to the homes frequented – and immortalized – by Ms. Montgomery. The most famous is Green Gables, the farmhouse in Cavendish that inspired the setting for *Anne*. The 1880s house on the grounds of Prince Edward Island National Park has been refurbished to portray the Edwardian provincial background of the novels. **902.672.6350.**

O Charlottetown
Pg. 187, G11. Settled by the French and later ceded to the British, Charlottetown has been PEI's capital since 1765 and still retains much of the flavor of a colonial port. In 1864, representatives of Britain's colonies north of the U. S. border met here to create a unified Dominion of Canada. The Confederation Centre of the Arts, opened in 1967 as part of Canada's centennial celebration, houses a large collection of Canadian art, including works by portraitist Robert Harris and original manuscripts of Lucy Maud Montgomery. The provincial legislature still meets at Province House National Historic Site, where the 1864 confederation conference was held. **800.463.4734.**

Green Gables N

It's about a 2,400-kilometer drive along the Trans-Canada Highway, Canada's great Mother Road, from the Pacific coast of British Columbia to the Ontario border. If you just sat back and watched the scenery – like rail passengers did 50 years ago – you might think you were actually passing through several countries. From Vancouver, in the west, you'd leave behind a mountainous coastline dotted with thousands of islands in the ascent to the thickly forested western slopes of the Canadian Rockies. At Kicking Horse Pass, you'd cross the Continental Divide into Alberta, passing a glacial watershed that feeds three oceans: the Pacific, the Atlantic, and the Arctic. From the Rockies, the land steps down through treeless foothills and rolling pastureland before flattening into the endless miles of prairie that cover the central and southern sections of Saskatchewan and Manitoba. Once home to as many as 60 million buffalo, this glacier-smoothed farmland is now Canada's breadbasket. To the north, wheat and barley fields end where the vast subarctic forest begins, dotted with some 200,000 lakes. The people of western Canada are as varied as the terrain. Numerous native tribes continue to live on the land inhabited by their ancestors, and many communities have been shaped by religious pioneers – Mennonites, Hutterites, and Doukhobors – who fled Europe and Russia. Other settlers have come from the Far East: Vancouver has more citizens of Chinese descent than any city outside of Asia.

The Prairie Provinces include Manitoba, Saskatchewan, and Alberta. Near-level Manitoba has many lakes and rivers – including Lake Winnipeg (larger than Lake Ontario) – most of which drain into Hudson Bay. The Canadian Rockies rise from the prairies in southwestern Alberta, reaching to the north and west through Canada's most mountainous province, British Columbia, and into the Yukon Territory and Alaska. Components of the Rockies, such as the Monashee, Cariboo, and Selkirk Mountains in British Columbia are roughly paralleled, further west, by the Coast Mountains.

FEBRUARY
Le Festival du Voyageur, Winnipeg, MB
Manitoba commemorates its French-Canadian heritage, when fur traders were king, with this ten-day winter carnival that includes period costumes, arts and crafts, and a downtown street party.
204.237.7692

APRIL
Saskatchewan Indian Federated College Powwow, Regina, SK
One of the largest gatherings of Native Americans in Canada. Dancers from around North America perform, and there's plenty of native crafts and foods.
306.779.6111

JULY
Shakespeare on the Saskatchewan Festival, Saskatoon, SK
The players set up a tent by the river and perform two Shakespeare plays throughout the summer. Near the Mendel Art Gallery.
306.653.2300

Calgary Exhibition and Stampede, Calgary, AB
This wild celebration of the West has been held since 1912. Highlights include the chuck-wagon race at Stampede Park and one of the biggest rodeos in Canada.
800.661.1260

Klondike Days, Edmonton, AB
Just about the entire town celebrates the gold-rush days of 1898, when thousands of prospectors came through here on their way north.
403.479.3500

Kamloops Cattle Drive, Kamloops, BC
As many as 400 cowboys – some who do it for a living and some who've never been on a horse – go on a weeklong ride through the interior of British Columbia. Beginners are welcome, or you can rent space on a wagon.
800.288.5850

AUGUST
Peach Festival, Penticton, BC
The Okanagan Valley celebrates its biggest agriculture crop with a festival that is 50 years old. The weeklong event includes music, sporting events, and lots of peaches.
250.493.4055

First Peoples' Festival, Vancouver Island, BC
This three-day event is a tribute to those who were here first and includes ceremonial dances, a market of artists' work, and traditional storytelling.
250.384.3211

SEPTEMBER
The Fringe – Vancouver's Theatre Festival, Vancouver, BC
Vancouver hosts an eclectic group of theater, dance, and musical groups from around the world for this 11-day festival modeled after the popular event in Edinburgh, Scotland.
604.257.0350

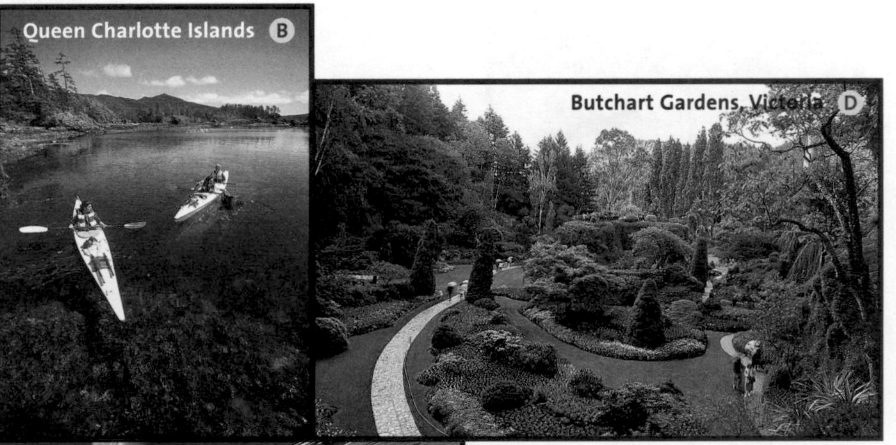
Queen Charlotte Islands B

Butchart Gardens, Victoria D

Chinese New Year parade, Vancouver C

British Columbia

A Okanagan Valley
Pg. 179, L11–M11. Lots of sun makes this valley inland from Vancouver a popular summer destination for those in search of rural pleasures. Irrigated by dams along the Okanagan River, the valley is the center of western Canada's fruit production. Apricot, plum, pear, and cherry orchards line the river, and vineyards clamber up the hillsides. Penticton, between lakes Okanagan and Skaha, is nicknamed Peach City, and Kelowna, the valley's largest town, grows a third of all Canada's apples. **250.860.5999.**

The northern Vancouver Island orca population, thought to be approximately 200, is one of the largest known single concentrations in the world.

B Queen Charlotte Islands
Pg. 177, E1. Eight hours by ferry from Prince Rupert, this verdant archipelago of 138 islands lies close to the Alaskan panhandle. Dense, dripping rain forest shelters abundant wildlife, and the rocky coastline, indented with fjords and straits, is habitat to sea mammals and birds. There is little human habitation – perhaps a thousand Haida still live here. Ninstints, an old Haida village on Anthony Island, is now a World Heritage Site. Sea kayakers, hikers, sailors, and scuba divers come to these primordial islands, delighting in real edge-of-the-world isolation. **250.559.8316.**

C Vancouver
Pg. 178, M7. Canada's most culturally diverse city, Vancouver is an important link between East and West, past and future. The East can be found in Vancouver's large Chinatown, with hundreds of exotic shops and markets. The Western past is in Gastown, the redbrick heart of Old Vancouver, built when lumber barons and railway magnates ruled. Look to the future across busy Burrard Inlet to the city's business district, dense with gleaming office towers. No part of Vancouver is far from nature. With the city situated on a series of peninsulas, the sea is a fundamental aspect of daily life. The bustling public market is located on Granville Island, and sharing the downtown peninsula is 1,000-acre Stanley Park, a preserve of forest and beach. **604.683.2000.**

D Victoria
Pg. 178, N7. Capital of British Columbia, Victoria is home to more British expatriates than any other city in Canada, and it shows. Double-decker buses, tea houses, lovely Victorian architecture, and spectacular gardens are hallmarks of the city. Butchart Gardens has more than a million blooming plants on a 55-acre private estate. Shopping is excellent along historic Government Street, and cutting-edge restaurants specialize in fresh Pacific fish and seafood. The downtown area overlooks a lovely harbor bustling with sailboats, ferries, and inquisitive seals. **250.953.2033.**

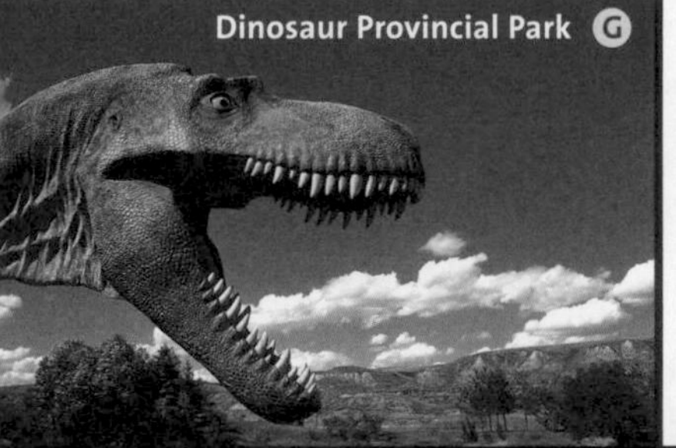
Dinosaur Provincial Park G

Columbia Icefield F

Canada produces more than a quarter of the world's newsprint, and British Columbia alone contributes about a fifth of that amount.

Alberta

E Bar U Ranch National Historic Site
Pg. 179, K16. Cattle drives brought steer north to the Alberta foothills beginning in the 1880s. Bar U Ranch, a well-preserved historical site located near Longview, celebrates the area's ranching traditions with tours of 35 original buildings and special events like brandings and roundups. At the very least, you'll get to see some horseplay. **800.568.4996.**

BC 178 | AB 178 | SK 180 | MB 181 | BC 249 | AB 249 | SK 250 | MB 249

Saskatchewan harvests, on average, 14.5 million metric tons of wheat a year and provides Canada with more than 50 percent of its spring wheat.

Big Muddy L

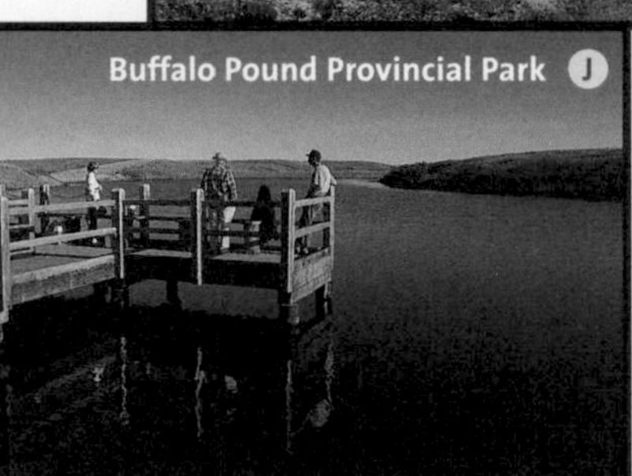

Buffalo Pound Provincial Park J

Saskatchewan

J Buffalo Pound Provincial Park
Pg. 180, K7. Back in the mid-1800s, the central prairies of Saskatchewan were home to so many plains bison that, according to one report, a single herd passing might take four days. Buffalo Pound is a fascinating relic of ancient times, before the advent of guns and horses, when nomadic hunters used natural prairie coulees – small ravines lower than the surrounding landscape – to corral buffalo into a "pound" where hunters could slay the animals with spears and lances. A small herd of plains bison has roamed the park since 1972. **306.694.3659.**

K Little Manitou Lake
Pg. 180, H7. Three times saltier than ocean water and denser than the Dead Sea, the waters of Little Manitou Lake, northeast of Watrous, have long been a mecca for the ailing. Manitou, an Indian word for the Great Spirit or protector, was a sacred spot for Plains Indians who ascribed healing powers to the briny water. Safe passage was assured across even hostile territory if the stricken's destination was Little Manitou Lake. Since the 1920s, visitors have come to bob in the lake or take therapeutic mineral baths and relax at the Manitou Springs Resort. **306.946.2831.**

L Big Muddy
Pg. 180, N7. It may sound like a mighty river, and it once was, but Big Muddy, a vast valley full of swirling sandstone sculptures, etched buttes, and cone-shaped hills, hasn't had a proper river run through it since the end of the ice ages. Around the turn of the century, Big Muddy country was the northern terminus of the Outlaw Trail, used by rustlers to herd stolen livestock, and its rugged terrain sheltered outlaws like Sam Kelly and Butch Cassidy. Tours of the dramatic landscape include landmarks from the region's outlaw and Indian past. **800.667.7191.**

Now I possess and am possessed of the land where I would be,
And the curve of half Earth's generous breast shall sooth and ravish me!

– RUDYARD KIPLING ON THE CANADIAN PRAIRIE, "THE PRAIRIE," 1908

F Columbia Icefield
Pg. 179, H13. The 143-mile Icefield Parkway connects Lake Louise and Jasper, winding beneath soaring glacier-notched peaks, traversing three deep river valleys, and passing turquoise-colored lakes. But no sight along the route is more dramatic than the vast Columbia Icefield. A remnant of the ice ages, the ice field is composed of six main glaciers, covering some 125 square miles near Mount Athabasca at depths up to 1,150 feet. **403.852.6550.**

G Dinosaur Provincial Park / Royal Tyrrell Museum of Paleontology
Pg. 179, K18. The Alberta Badlands, a region of eroded canyons and arid coulees, belie their ancient maritime past: 75 million years ago this area was a low-lying coastal plain. About a hundred years ago, a local rancher stumbled onto a trove of dinosaur bones jutting from a canyon wall. Thus began the fossil excavations that have unearthed some 300 skeletons of more than 35 different dinosaur species, including the gorgosaurus, a smaller cousin of the tyrannosaurus. The park offers five excellent self-guided trails and a paleontology lab. About two hours drive away, outside Drumheller, is probably the finest dinosaur museum in the world, the Royal Tyrrell Museum of Paleontology. Filled with engaging, imaginative exhibits, it has three dozen fully articulated dinosaur skeletons, including a complete Tyrannosaurus rex. Park, **403.378.4342.** Museum, **403.823.7707.**

H Elk Island National Park
Pg. 179, F17. A delightful gem of a national park, Elk Island is a half hour's drive from Edmonton. Founded as a sanctuary for elk, the park now shelters the endangered wood bison and protects a rapidly vanishing ecosystem, the aspen parkland. The wildlife – moose, deer, more than 200 bird species – is easy to spot from hiking trails. **403.992.2950.**

I West Edmonton Mall
Pg. 179, F16. There's nothing ordinary about Edmonton's gigantic shopping-amusement complex. You can find just about anything in its 800-plus stores, but most visitors come to sample the entertainment: The world's largest indoor amusement park, a miniature golf course, 19 cinemas, more than a hundred restaurants, a casino, a World Waterpark, and a full-size replica of Columbus's ship the *Santa Maria.* If that isn't enough, you can take in the dolphin show or catch a ride in a submarine. **403.444.5300.**

Spirit Sands, Spruce Woods Provincial Park N

Manitoba

M Manitoba Museum of Man and Nature
Pg. 181, E19. Part of Winnipeg's Centennial Centre, the Manitoba Museum of Man and Nature recounts the province's natural and human history. Exhibits include a dramatic diorama of native buffalo hunts, an authentic Assiniboin tepee, and a full-scale replica of the *Nonsuch*, a 17th-century ship whose 1668 voyage from England spurred the founding of the Hudson's Bay Company. **204.956.2830.**

N Spruce Woods Provincial Park
Pg. 181, M14. This ecologically significant preserve covers prairie grasslands, a forest of white spruce, the wide Assiniboine River, and a desertlike area called Spirit Sands. An extremely fragile terrain, these rolling sand dunes are not really arid since they receive twice as much rain as a true desert; carefully marked interpretive trails explain the area's religious significance to native peoples. A canoe route down the Assiniboine provides glimpses of the park's wildlife, prairie elk among them. **204.834.3223.**

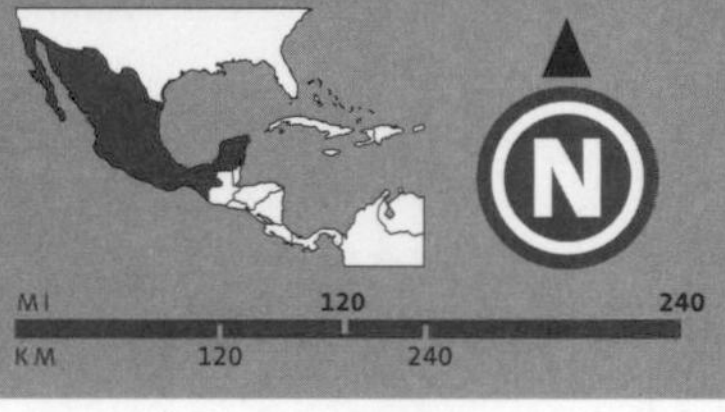

Mexico

Named for Méxitli, the Aztec god of war, Mexico often seems torn between its rich past and difficult future. For more than two thousand years, great Indian civilizations built majestic cities rivaling any other culture in the world at the time. Invaded and destroyed by conquistadors in the 16th century, Mexico was ruled by Spain until 1821, when it gained independence and established a republic. But the descendants of the early societies–Mayan, Aztecan, Olmec, Zapotec, among others–have maintained many indigenous traditions in spite of (often uncontrolled) modernization. Cultural variety is Mexico's hallmark, with more than 50 distinct peoples and languages. As diverse as its peoples, Mexico's topography is a study in extreme contrasts, from the arid lands of Baja and northern Mexico to the fertile, verdant hills and valleys of the central highlands and the Bajío above Mexico City, to the subtropical lowlands of the southern Yucatán Peninsula. The contrast between the hot, inhospitable northern regions of the country and the mild, lush south is also reflected in the disparity of wealth between rich and poor states. Mexico is a challenging, often violent, but rewarding country, both for Mexicans and travelers.

Like a glass slipper, with Baja as its heel, Mexico links the U.S. and Central America. Bordered by the Pacific Ocean, the Gulf of Mexico, and the Caribbean Sea, Mexico is dominated by two rugged north-south mountain ranges, the Sierra Madre Occidental and the Sierra Madre Oriental, which overlook arid coastal plains to the east and west, and the Sonoran and Chihuahuan desert regions in the north. A mild temperate central plateau reaches to Mexico City, beyond which the mountains achieve their greatest heights (18,855 feet) in the Cordillera Neo-Volcánica. To the east, the tropical rain forests of southern Chiapas give way to thorny forest in the upper Yucatán Peninsula.

JANUARY
Fiesta de Enero, Chiapa de Corzo, Chi. Actually a series of colorful festivals including parading dancers called *Las Chuntaes*, as well as processions of men wearing wooden masks with *ixtle* "hair," and musical and other celebrations.
961.24535

APRIL
Feria de San Marcos, Aguascalientes, Agu. One of Mexico's biggest fairs, this three-week event includes bullfights, rodeos, free concerts, and a magical parade on April 25, the saint's day.
49.15.8620

MAY
Fiesta de la Santa Cruz, San Miguel de Allende, Gua. This festival of the sacred cross includes food, music, and dancing.
415.20900

Cinco de Mayo, Puebla, Pue. The anniversary of Mexico's victory over France at the 1862 Battle of Puebla is celebrated grandly here with parades and music.
22.46.1285

JULY
Feria Nacional, Durango, Dgo. One of the best festivals in Mexico, held in honor of the town's founding. Events include a large arts-and-crafts fair plus entertainment by big-name Mexican musicians and dancers.
18.112139

OCTOBER
Festival Internacional Cervantino, Guanajuato, Gto. Students began performing the works of Miguel de Cervantes back in the 1950s. Since then, this event dedicated to the author of *Don Quixote* has become one of the largest arts festivals in the country.
5.5147365

Fiestas de Octubre, Guadalajara, Jal. Free entertainment all month long, plus cultural, sporting, and musical events.
3.660.3186

NOVEMBER
Día de los Muertos, Oax. Day of the Dead is celebrated throughout Mexico–particularly colorfully in the villages throughout the Oaxaca valley. On November 1st and 2nd families build elaborate altars and visit the graves of friends and relatives bearing gifts of garlands and favorite foods.
951.64828

Día de Jumil, Taxco, Méx. *Jumiles* are brown beetles that migrate to the hills behind Taxco to reproduce. On the first Monday after the Day of the Dead, the people of Taxco collect thousands of these insect delicacies, which are then mixed into salsas or eaten plain.
762.26616

DECEMBER
Las Posadas, Mexico City, D. F. Joseph and Mary's journey is reenacted in candlelight processions leading to nativity scenes around the Alameda.
5.250.8555

And there under an intense light sky lies a shining plain succulent with sugar-cane and corn among the cacti, a bright rich tropical country miraculously laved: green, green, green, the Valley of Mexico.
—SYBILLE BEDFORD, *A VISIT TO DON OCTAVIO*, 1953

Copper Canyon D

Cabo San Lucas C

Baja California and Northern States

A Tijuana's Avenida Revolución
Pg. 188, A1. More Americans tour Tijuana than perhaps any other city in the world, and most of them end up at Avenida Revolución. Once a mecca for gamblers and sex-show aficionados, "La Revo" is now a duty-free shopping zone and bazaar, offering high-quality Mexican handicrafts, leather goods, and name-brand European clothing at south-of-the-border prices (you're expected to bargain for most items). **66.881685.**

B Baja's Whale Lagoons
Pg. 188, F4. Whales can be spotted almost anywhere along Baja's Pacific coastline, but the protected lagoons offer the best vantage. Every fall, pods of gray whales leave their summer feeding grounds in Alaska and head south to Bahía Magdalena, Laguna Ojo de Liebre, and Laguna San Ignacio. During the mating season of December through March, visitors can watch the whales from designated observation points. **112.40100.**

Some of the best deep-sea fishing in the world can be found near Cabo San Lucas, at the tip of Baja California.

C Cabo San Lucas
Pg. 188, H5. At the southernmost tip of Baja, where the cool blue waters of the Pacific flow into the warm turquoise waters of the Gulf of California, sits Cabo San Lucas, a popular resort area known for its raucous nightlife and superb beaches. But the big draw is sport fishing. Blue marlin, weighing up to 1,500 pounds, and giant dorado, wahoo, sailfish, and grouper are common. Many of the 10,000 game fish caught off the coast every year are released to fight another day. **112.40100.**

D Copper Canyon
Pg. 188, D7. Barranca de Cobre is actually deeper and wider than the Grand Canyon, though it gets far fewer tourists. That's partly because of the difficulty in reaching these awesome canyons (seven, in fact) carved out of the Sierra Madre Occidental midway between Chihuahua and Mexico's west coast. The drive from Creel can be hair-raising. An alternative is the remarkable Chihuahua al Pacífico Railway from Creel to Los Mochis. In addition to zigzagging around Copper Canyon, the route covers 86 tunnels, 39 bridges, and several picturesque towns. Passengers are free to disembark and spend a day hiking or riding horses up the canyons. **14.101077.**

Pacific Coast and Highlands

E Acapulco
Pg. 189, M12. Miles of beaches are Acapulco's principal attraction, but it has its share of eccentricities, among them the famed *clavadistas*, who dive from the Quebrada's cliffs into a rock-enclosed sliver of ocean, and La Capella Submarina, a one-ton bronze statue of Our Lady of Guadalupe submerged underwater, reached by glass-bottomed boat. In the older section of town is the labyrinthine Mercado de Artesanías, where you can bargain over Mexican handicrafts. **74.844416.**

F San Miguel de Allende
Pg. 189, J11. Designated a national monument in 1926, San Miguel–renamed to honor native son and Independence hero Ignacio de Allende–is set in a ravishingly beautiful area of the Bajío. The hillside town was home to many Guanajuato silver barons, whose wealth is reflected in the stately mansions that crowd its narrow cobblestoned streets. Today San Miguel attracts American retirees and expatriate artists, charmed by its elegance, cheap lodging, and the Instituto Allende, an English-speaking arts and language school. San Miguel boasts 300 churches within a ten-mile radius, but the most extraordinary is La Parroquia, the parish church. Its soaring spires are the work of Zeferino Gutiérrez, an Indian mason inspired by Europe's Gothic edifices. **415.26565.**

G Guadalajara
Pg. 188, J9. Traditions die hard in Guadalajara. Consider that free concerts of Jaliscan music have been held every Thursday and Sunday in the Plaza de Armas since 1898. Tequila, the sombrero, the Mexican Hat Dance, and mariachi music all originated in Guadalajara, Mexico's second largest city and historic hub of revolutionary agitation. The great muralist Jose Clemente Orozco executed his most brilliant work here, in the Hospicio Cabañas. Nearby, the enclosed Mercado Libertad offers traditional food and handicrafts, and the Plaza Tapatia is lined with swank department stores and restaurants. Guadalajara's downtown, virtually unchanged since colonial days, centers on a cathedral surrounded by four verdant plazas. **3.658.2222.**

La Quebrada, Acapulco E

H El Fuego Volcano
Pg. 188, K9. The sulfurous smell that often wafts through Colima comes from the occasional burps of El Fuego, a 13,993-foot, officially active volcano looming over the otherwise serene state capital. A park rings the mountain, and a dirt road gets you close enough for a relatively easy hike to the summit. **331.24360.**

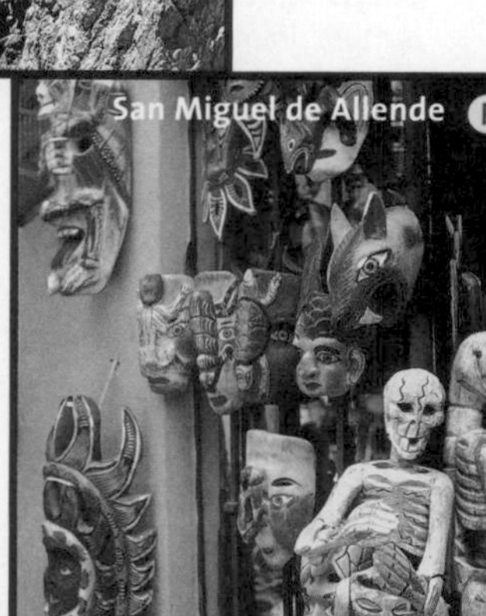
San Miguel de Allende F

MEX 188
MEX 251

Chapultepec Park, Mexico City (I)

Palacio de Cortés, Cuernavaca (K)

Gulf and Central Valley

(I) Mexico City
Pg. 189, K12. Sprawling, polluted, noisy, crime-ridden, marked by extremes of deep poverty and conspicuous wealth–in spite of all this, Mexico's capital exerts the seductive pull of all great cities. Its history as a vibrant metropolis began in 1345 with the Aztec, when it was called Tenochtitlán. Hernán Cortés captured the city in 1521, and the Spanish founded a colonial outpost on the wreckage of the Indian empire, paving the *zócalo* (central plaza) with stones from Aztec pyramids. Flanking an entire side of this vast square is the Palacio Nacional, containing Diego Rivera's stunning panorama of Mexican history. Just off the zócalo is the Templo Mayor, the Aztec ceremonial site excavated in 1978 after electrical workers stumbled upon a huge stone sculpture of the goddess Coyolxauhqui. West along elegant streets past the Alameda, a lush garden park, is Mexico City's premier boulevard, the ten-lane Paseo de la Reforma. Its southern terminus is the grand Bosque de Chapultepec, 1.5 square miles of woods, lakes, and cultural institutions. The highlight is the preeminent anthropological museum, a world-renowned collection covering almost every aspect of Mexican civilization from Mesoamerica to the Aztecs. **5.250.0123.**

(J) Frida Kahlo Museum
Pg. 189, K12. Confined to a wheelchair as a teenager after a gruesome road accident, artist Frida Kahlo reflected in her riveting canvases a life of tremendous psychological and physical pain, in spite of which she played a pivotal role in Mexico's dynamic post-Revolutionary intellectual scene. The house where she lived with Diego Rivera from 1929 to 1954, in the Coyoacán section of Mexico City, is now a museum containing fascinating mementos of the period. **5.554.5999.**

(K) Cuernavaca
Pg. 189, L12. One of Mexico's most cosmopolitan cities, Cuernavaca has long attracted an eclectic group of the well-heeled and indolent. Heiress Barbara Hutton built a fabulous Japanese-style home here and author Malcolm Lowry based his novel *Under the Volcano* on life in Cuernavaca. The conquistador Hernán Cortés, who torched the city in 1521, built a medieval palace with turrets and moats as his private asylum. The Palacio de Cortés now houses exhibits on archaeology, colonial history, and the Mexican Revolution, and includes a mural series by Diego Rivera. **73.143872.**

As Mexico's quintessential beast of burden, the burro is prized for its adaptiveness and its ability to work hard under adverse conditions.

Oaxaca (L)

Chichén Itzá (M)

Yucatán, Chiapas, and Oaxaca

(L) Oaxaca
Pg. 189, M14. For centuries, the fertile valley of Oaxaca has been home to the Mixtec and Zapotec Indians, and their ancient sites ring the state capital. Among the many attractions of this convivial, densely populated city on the eastern slopes of the Sierra Madre del Sur are superb crafts and perhaps the best markets in the country, where one can find handwoven rugs, black San Bartolo pottery, embroidery, and gold and jade jewelry. Oaxaca's colonial legacy is conspicuous as well in elaborately embellished baroque monuments such as the Church of Santo Domingo. **951.64828.**

(M) Chichén Itzá
Pg. 189, J19. Here at Chichén Itzá on the Yucatán Peninsula, where Mayan civilization flourished from A.D. 550 to 900, the Pyramid of Kukulcán is actually an architectonic rendition of the Mayan celestial calendar. During the spring and autumn equinoxes, the serpent's head and tail at the bottom and top of the main staircase are united by an undulating shadow cast by the setting sun. The restoration of Chichén Itzá includes El Caracol, a domed observatory with an interior spiral staircase; the Juego de Pelota, a ball court with wall reliefs depicting game scenes; and the Sacred Cenote, a huge well into which Mayans tossed offerings to the gods. **99.239568.**

(N) Cozumel
Pg. 189, J20. The western seaside of this small island south of Cancún boasts miles of spectacular coral reef that can be viewed by glass-bottomed boat–the water is crystal-clear straight to the bottom–or explored with scuba gear (guides are recommended). Palancar Reef, introduced to the world by Jacques Cousteau in 1961, is now a protected reserve where a diverse assortment of marine life–rainbow-hued parrot fish, yellow-tailed damselfish–swim among coral formations that include the exquisite, rare black variety. **800.446.3942.**

(O) Parque Nacional Palenque
Pg. 189, L17. The ruins of Palenque, among the most important Mayan archaeological finds in Mexico, sit amid the tropical jungle of the Chiapas Highlands. Abandoned for unknown reasons during the tenth century, the city was not discovered until the 1840s. Even today, only a fraction of the site has been excavated. El Palacio has a cloistered courtyard with exquisite relief carvings of giant figures, arched corridors, and a four-story stone tower. The Templo de las Inscripciones is a stepped pyramid decorated with seventh-century hieroglyphics. **961.24535.**

(P) Rain Forest
Pg. 189, M17. Less than a fifth of Mexico's rain forest remains today; perhaps the largest area is Selva Lacandona in eastern Chiapas. Heavy rain and steamy heat produce a complex ecosystem where blooming orchids (more than 50 species) take root beneath the dense canopy of mahogany and other hardwoods. Jungle fauna–howler monkeys, jaguars, ocelots, anteaters, macaws, toucans, boa constrictors–still own the terrain. Although Mexico's eco-tourism industry is in its infancy, a number of trips are offered. **800.446.3942.**

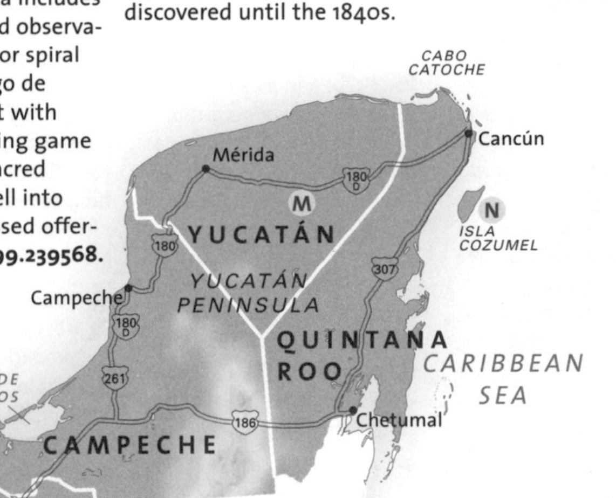

North America's only mainland flock of flamingos–population estimated at 25,000–can be seen living and breeding in the estuaries of the Yucatán Peninsula.

Some 40 years after statehood, Hawaii still retains the air of an exotic foreign port, a string of sunny, verdant peaks rising unexpectedly from the azure Pacific. This ethereal chain of islands is draped with green rain forests and silver waterfalls, circled by white- and black-sand beaches, and marked by the fiery presence of the earth's most persistently active volcano. While some may decry the tourist deluge accelerated by TV's *Hawaii Five-O* in the 1970s, Hawaii continues to offer stunning and diverse scenery, from striking plants to vividly alive coral reefs, as well as the famous, friendly "aloha spirit" of its *kamaaina* (locals). An archipelago stretching more than 1,500 miles, Hawaii is technically composed of 132 islands and atolls. Its six major ones—Kauai, Oahu, Molokai, Lanai, Maui, and the "Big Island" of Hawaii—sit at the southeastern end of the chain. Settled first by Polynesian mariners a thousand years before Captain James Cook anchored the HMS *Resolution* off Kauai in 1778, Hawaii is today a true melting pot of races and cultures, including Hawaiian natives, Filipinos, Chinese, and Japanese, with whites (or *haoles*) in the minority.

The Hawaiian Islands are crests of volcanic mountains built by magma welling up from beneath the ocean floor over millions of years. Measured from their bases at the bottom of the Pacific, these mountains are the tallest in the world. The youngest of the Hawaiian islands is also the largest: The Big Island of Hawaii is almost twice the size of the others combined and is still growing, thanks to its two active volcanoes, Kilaueu and Mauna Loa. Also on Hawaii is the chains' highest point, at 13,796 feet, dormant Mauna Kea. Southeast of Hawaii, a new island, called Loihi, is slowly growing toward the surface.

In what other land save this one is the commonest form of greeting not "Good day," nor "How d'ye do," but "love"? That greeting is Aloha—love, I love you, my love to you. . . . It is a positive affirmation of one's own heart-giving.

— JACK LONDON, *MY HAWAIIAN ALOHA*, 1916

FEBRUARY
Chinese New Year Celebration, Lahaina, Maui
Culturally diverse Hawaii pulls out all the stops for this holiday, as electrifying lion dances, traditional music, and fireworks liven the Wo Hing Temple on Front Street.
808.667.9175

MARCH
Dakine Hawaiian Pro-Am Windsurfing Challenge, Ho'okipa, Maui
Come to the most famous windsurfing spot on Maui to watch daredevils swarm on the churning waves like multicolored butterflies. Crowds gather on the lava-rock bluffs with binoculars and camcorders to witness this most unique spectator sport.
808.575.9264

APRIL
Merrie Monarch Festival, Hilo, Big Island
The premier hula competition and event of the year, this festival draws a multitude of hula *halau* (schools) to Hilo, where performers dance ancient and modern hula, perform traditional chanting, and play ancient Hawaiian instruments.
808.935.9168

MAY
Big Island Bounty, Mauna Lani, Big Island
This three-day festival on the grounds of the Orchid at Mauna Lani Resort is a nonstop immersion in the newest developments of Hawaiian Regional Cuisine, a cross-cultural culinary style that's gaining renown nationwide.
808.885.2000

JUNE
King Kamehameha Celebration Floral Parade, all islands
Watch this dazzling and fragrant parade on any of the main islands, and celebrate King Kamehameha Day (June 11) with a ceremony at his statue on the Big Island, where he met his untimely demise.
808.586.0333

SEPTEMBER
Aloha Festival, all islands
Throughout the Aloha State, September and October are the months to party—with the nebulous reason being the famous "aloha spirit" of the islanders. Enjoy floral parades, Hawaiian royal balls, steel-guitar festivals, storytelling, horse racing, fishing tournaments, ukulele performances, and fireworks.
808.545.1771

OCTOBER
Ironman World Championship, Kailua-Kona, Big Island
Go down to the Kailua-Kona Pier to witness the start or finish of what is considered one of the most extreme triathlons in the world, a course that includes fields of lava and Kailua Bay. Parties and a Parade of Countries are added bonuses; just follow the hard-bodies.
808.329.0063

DECEMBER
Gerry Lopez Pipe Masters, Ehukai Beach Park, Oahu
Held at the North Shore's famous Banzai Pipeline break, this annual showdown of the world's top surfers is the longest running pro surf competition in the U. S.
714.851.2774

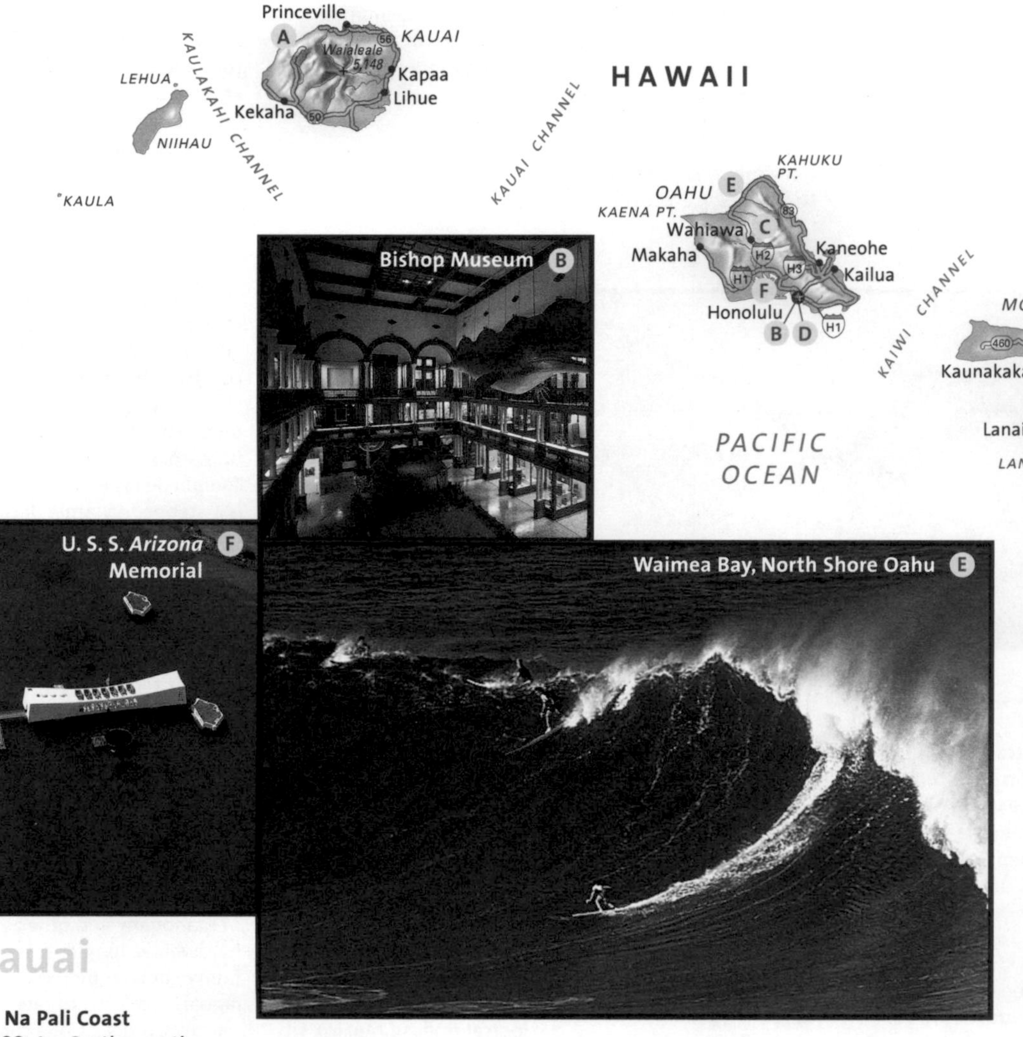

Kauai

A Na Pali Coast
Pg. 88, A2. On the northwest side of the Garden Isle, cliffsides drop like heavy green draperies to churning surf 2,700 feet below. This rugged and remote strip of land is only accessible to those willing to make an effort, but the rewards include staggering views of magical, velvet spires that the producers of *South Pacific* used to effectively evoke Bali Hai. No roads penetrate the Na Pali Coast, so options for exploration are limited to helicopter tours, boat excursions, or hikes.
808.245.3971.

The pineapple, which thrives in Hawaii's rich, well-drained, volcanic soil, has become a symbol of the tropics and especially of Hawaii. Nearly 95 percent of Hawaii's pineapple harvest is shipped to the mainland United States.

Oahu

B Bishop Museum
Pg. 88, K3. This world-famous museum, dedicated to the natural and social history of Polynesia and the Pacific, began as a repository for the royal collection of Princess Bernice Pauahi, last direct descendant of King Kamehameha the Great. The king's own war god is included among the museum's 3 million items, along with Melanesian masks, an authentic grass house, war clubs, and a full-size sperm whale, which hangs in the central hall. **808.847.3511.**

C Dole Pineapple Plantation
Pg. 88, F3. Driving from the populated southern side of the island to the north, high-rises fade into flat expanses of pineapple fields with velvety green mountains as a backdrop. It's here, just north of Wahiawa on the Kamehameha Highway, where you'll find the Dole Pineapple Plantation. Enjoy frozen drinks and freshly picked pineapple, displays on the history of the pineapple in Hawaii, and a garden growing 21 different varieties of pineapple. Just outside the visitor center, the world's largest and longest permanent garden maze—made of 11,400 different species of Hawaii plants, including varieties of the state flower, hibiscus—has a special pineapple garden in its elusive center. **808.621.8408.**

D Iolani Palace
Pg. 88, L3. Iolani was the royal residence until Queen Liliuokalani was overthrown in 1893. It served as the queen's prison (where she wrote several cherished songs, including "Aloha Oe"), and later became the capitol building for the Territory of Hawaii. The only royal residence in the United States, the Renaissance-style mansion is now entirely restored, and guided tours offer visitors a glimpse into its regal throne room, lavish entertaining spaces, and gleaming koa-wood floors, furniture, and staircases.
808.538.1471.

E North Shore
Pg. 88, D3, E3. The highlights of Oahu's northern coast are two of the most famous surfing spots in the world, Sunset Beach and Waimea Bay. Though calm and gentle in the summer months, winter weather systems create the world's highest surfable waves—up to 30 feet—and gawking at daring surfers becomes a spectator sport.
800.464.2924.

F U.S.S. *Arizona* Memorial
Pg. 88, G4. For a sobering glimpse of World War II's "day of infamy," visit the U.S.S. *Arizona* Memorial at Pearl Harbor. A tribute to 2,341 American servicemen killed during the surprise Japanese attack on December 7, 1941, the memorial lies atop the sunken battleship where more than 1,100 men were entombed. The Navy operates a free boat tour to the site, where Hawaiian leis, left in homage, often color the water.
808.422.2771.

More than 1,150 kinds of plants are unique to Hawaii, but most of the fragrant orchids used to make the traditional symbol of welcome, the lei, were brought to the island from other areas including Thailand, China, and Australia.

Maui

G Haleakala Crater
Pg. 88, E9. According to Polynesian legend, it was in this wondrous crater that the demigod Maui held the sun captive to give his people more daylight hours. Whatever time you arrive—watching sunrise here is popular—this dormant volcanic crater (really a valley formed by erosion) is stark and otherworldly. It's a 3,000-foot drop from the public observatory on the rim to the floor, which measures 19 square miles and is filled with volcanic rubble, cinder, and lava flow and is home to one of the world's rarest plants, the silversword. **808.572.9306.**

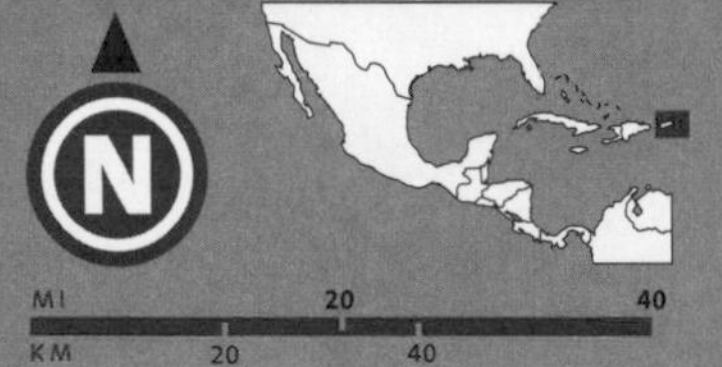

Puerto Rico and the Virgin Islands, America's footholds in the Caribbean Basin, are relative latecomers to U.S. sovereignty. Puerto Rico was a Spanish colony until 1898, when the U.S. gained possession at the close of the Spanish-American War. The U.S. Virgin Islands (part of the chain remains a British colony) were purchased from Denmark in 1917. Puerto Rico is ruggedly mountainous, with low-lying terrain largely confined to its coastal plains and inland valleys. During the age of exploration, Puerto Rico was the strategic gateway to the New World, and San Juan, the island's capital, was the "rich port" from which the island took its name. Moderating trade winds, along with superb beaches, have made the island a popular resort destination. Forty miles east, the U. S. Virgin Islands consist of St. Thomas, St. John, and St. Croix, along with 65 much smaller islets. The Francis Drake Channel divides the American and British islands, and is considered by yachting enthusiasts to be among the world's great cruising grounds. As any observer can tell from the deck of a boat sailing the channel, all of the Virgin Islands demonstrate the abrupt rise from the sea that indicates volcanic origin.

Volcanoes launched Puerto Rico and the Virgin Islands from the ocean floor. Today, their steep and rugged terrain typifies that of Caribbean islands formed in volcanic tumult. An east-west mountain chain sharply divides the northern and southern portions of Puerto Rico, with the north receiving considerably greater amounts of rainfall.

Very fair and full of promise
Lay the island of St Thomas:
Ocean o'er its reefs and bars
Hid its elemental scars;
Groves of cocoanut and guava
Grew above its fields of lava.

– BRET HARTE, "ST THOMAS," *A GEOGRAPHICAL SURVEY*, 1868

APRIL

Virgin Islands Carnival, Charlotte Amalie, St. Thomas
The world-famous celebration, with "mocko jumbies" (stilt dancers), dancing, music, a food fair, a carnival village, and a parade put on entirely by children.
340.776.3112

Mavi Carnival, Juana Diaz, PR
A traditional carnival in honor of *mavi*, a fermented drink made from the bark of the ironwood tree. Festivities include a parade, floats, music, and lots of mavi.
787.837.2185

MAY

Puerto Rico Heineken Jazz Fest, San Juan, PR
The celebrated Latin jazz festival features top international stars performing alongside local musicians.
787.277.9200

JUNE

Albonito Flower Festival, Albonito, PR
The annual festival features exhibits and sales of the most popular and newest varieties of tropical flowers and plants, as well as pottery, garden accessories, and food.
787.735.4070

JULY

Barranquitas Artisans' Fair, Barranquitas, PR
The island's oldest crafts fair, with carvings, basketry, musical instruments, pottery, folk music, and traditional foods.
787.857.2065

AUGUST

International Billfish Tournament, San Juan, PR
Anglers go after blue marlin weighing up to 900 pounds in one of the world's premier game-fishing tournaments.
787.722.0177

SEPTEMBER

Inter-American Festival of the Arts, San Juan, PR
The three-week series of musical performances includes classical, popular, and folk music, as well as modern-dance productions and musical theater.
787.721.7727

NOVEMBER

Jayuya Indian Festival, PR
The culture and traditions of the island's original natives, the Taino, are highlighted at a festival of arts and crafts, music, games, and the Miss Taino Indian Pageant.
787.828.1241

DECEMBER

Crucian Christmas Festival Three Kings Day Parade, Christiansted, St. Croix
A huge parade with floats, musicians, and marching bands highlights this festival. It continues into January; the host city changes each year.
340.773.0495

All the islands are beautiful, but this last appears to exceed all others in beauty.

– CHRISTOPHER COLUMBUS, ON SIGHTING PUERTO RICO, 1493

Puerto Rico

A Arecibo Observatory
Pg. 190, B2. A 20-acre dish, nestled in a huge sinkhole 568 feet below, gathers radio waves from space. Located in Arecibo and run by Cornell University, the observatory has made some formidable discoveries, including the first pulsars and quasars. A visitor center explains the workings of the observatory and the universe. **787.878.2612.**

B Caguana Indian Ceremonial Park
Pg. 190, B2. Approximately 800 years ago, the indigenous Taino people built ten *bateyes* (courts) for recreational and religious purposes. The Institute of Puerto Rican Culture maintains a small museum at the 13-acre landscaped park in Utuado. **787.894.7325.**

C Rio Camuy Cave Park
Pg. 190, B2. The Rio Camuy begins its subterranean journey near the town of Lares, coursing through one of the hemisphere's most massive cave networks. Trams spiral visitors 200 feet underground to the mouth of the massive Clara Cave. The subterranean footpath winds through a series of limestone caves and sinkholes. **787.898.3100.**

D San Juan National Historic Site
Pg. 190, A6, A7. The buildings and fortifications of Old San Juan are among the best preserved of Spain's colonial relics. The district is largely sandwiched between early military fortifications El Morro and San Cristóbal, both now National Historic Sites. Among the more than 400 restored buildings are La Fortaleza, the oldest governor's mansion still used for that purpose in the Western Hemisphere, and Iglesia de San José, the family church of Juan Ponce de León's descendants. **787.722.1709.**

E El Yunque (Caribbean National Forest)
Pg. 190, B5. The only tropical rain forest in the U. S. National Forest System is nicknamed for one of the twin peaks (in Spanish, the anvil) that tower over it. Cool temperatures, more than 100 billion gallons of annual rainfall, and 240 tree species–some unique to the area–characterize the 28,000-acre preserve. Nature trails provide opportunities for close inspection of 20 species of native orchids, more than 50 types of ferns, and some 50 bird species, including the endangered Puerto Rican parrot. **787.888.1810.**

Coffee, with it's high rate of return per acre farmed, is the most valuable crop in Puerto Rico, where almost half of the approximately 20,000 farms are less than ten acres in size.

The mongoose was originally imported from India to hunt rats and other pests. With its taste for bird and turtle eggs, this permanent resident of the Virgin Islands is today a pest in its own right.

U.S. Virgin Islands

F Charlotte Amalie
Pg. 190, D5. In the city's heyday, according to American observer Alexander Hamilton, "gold moved through the streets in wheelbarrows." Founded by the Danes, the islands' capital, located on St. Thomas, was once ringed by sugar plantations. In 1724 it became a free port, attracting infamous pirates like Blackbeard. Today, goods are still shipped from around the world, and the pretty town is popular with cruise-ship tourists looking for bargains. Most of the buildings in the Historic District were built after a series of devastating fires between 1804 and 1832. An exception is Fort Christian, completed in 1678, which stands on the waterfront overlooking the bay. Now a museum, it features exhibits on the native Arawak and the lavish life of planters and traders. **340.774.8784.**

G St. John
Pg. 190, D6. Just nine miles long and five miles wide, St. John is barely a speck in the northeastern Caribbean, but it boasts some of the region's finest beaches as well as Virgin Islands National Park, which covers nearly three-quarters of the island. The island's capital, Cruz Bay, is sedate by comparison to Charlotte Amalie, and the only other settlement, Coral Bay, consists of a few houses. Almost entirely green, St. John's atmosphere is more laid-back and the pace slower than on islands with a more developed tourist industry–although it can claim resort accommodations that equal the Caribbean's best. **809.776.6201, 340.774.8784.**

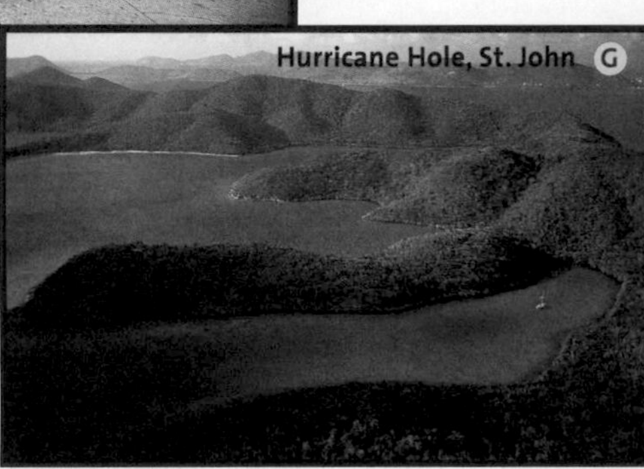

H Christiansted National Historic Site
Pg. 190, E6. In the late 18th and early 19th centuries, the sugar industry flourished on St. Croix, which became the capital of the "Danish Islands in America." Denmark's royal governors took up residence at Christiansted; the first of the line, Frederick Moth, designed the town to resemble Oslo, Norway, with boulevards, promenades, and handsome civic structures. When the sugar market crashed, Christiansted was left behind as a testament to a lost era. **340.774.8784.**

Road Maps

CANADIAN CITIES

MEXICAN CITIES

PUERTO RICAN CITY

NATIONAL PARKS & RECREATION AREAS

*Also has downtown city map.

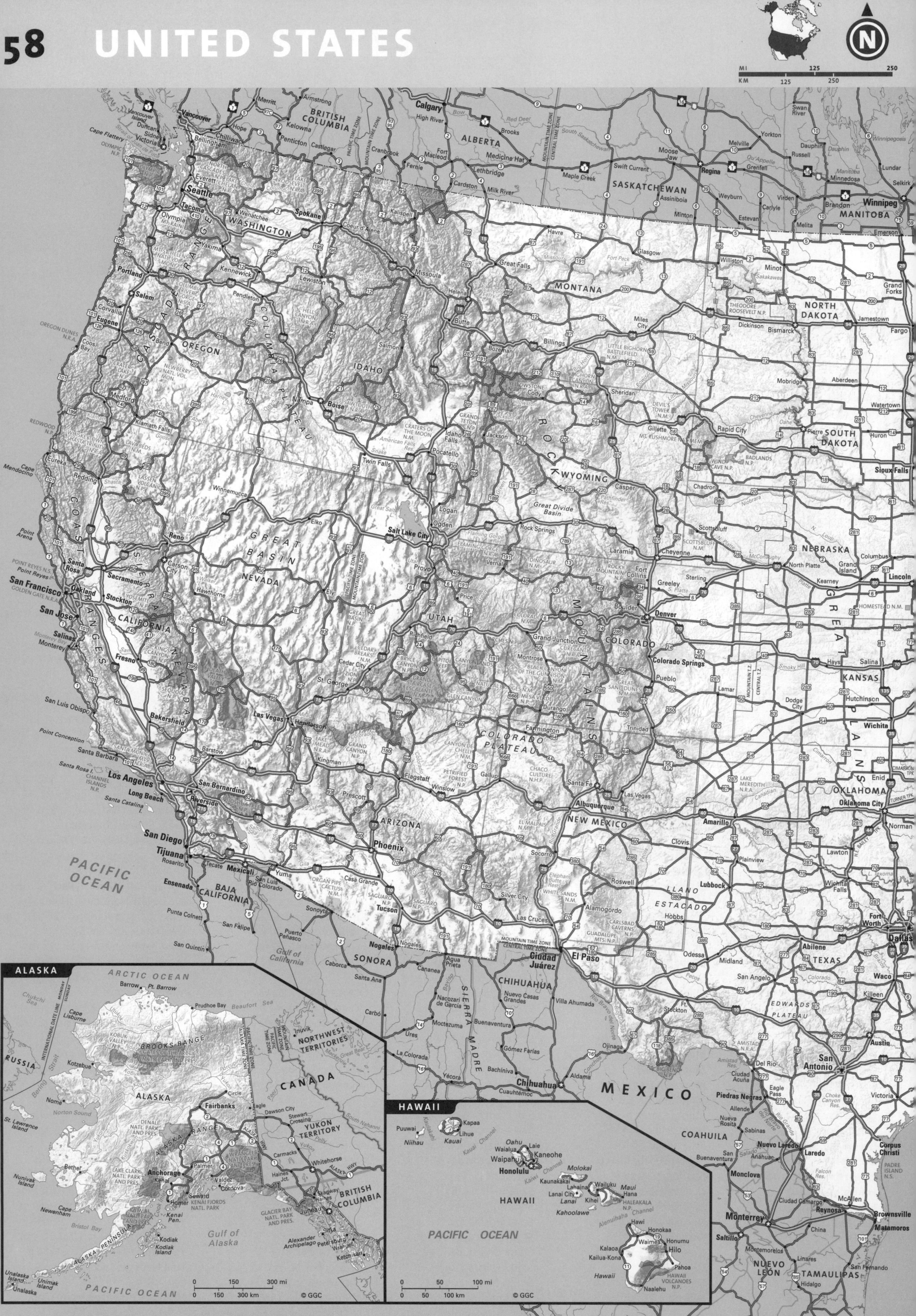
PACIFIC OCEAN
WASHINGTON
OREGON
CALIFORNIA
NEVADA
IDAHO
MONTANA
WYOMING
UTAH
COLORADO
ARIZONA
NEW MEXICO
NORTH DAKOTA
SOUTH DAKOTA
NEBRASKA
KANSAS
OKLAHOMA
TEXAS
BRITISH COLUMBIA
ALBERTA
SASKATCHEWAN
MANITOBA
MEXICO
BAJA CALIFORNIA
SONORA
CHIHUAHUA
COAHUILA
NUEVO LEÓN
TAMAULIPAS
GREAT BASIN
COLORADO PLATEAU
ROCKY MOUNTAINS
GREAT PLAINS
LLANO ESTACADO
EDWARDS PLATEAU
SIERRA NEVADA
CASCADE RANGE
COAST RANGES
COLUMBIA PLATEAU
SIERRA MADRE
Seattle
Portland
San Francisco
Los Angeles
San Diego
Las Vegas
Phoenix
Salt Lake City
Denver
Boise
Albuquerque
El Paso
Dallas
San Antonio
Oklahoma City
Calgary
Vancouver
Regina
Winnipeg
ALASKA
ARCTIC OCEAN
BROOKS RANGE
ALASKA RANGE
Anchorage
Fairbanks
Juneau
CANADA
YUKON TERRITORY
NORTHWEST TERRITORIES
RUSSIA
Gulf of Alaska
PACIFIC OCEAN
HAWAII
Honolulu
Hilo
Kauai
Oahu
Molokai
Maui
Hawaii
PACIFIC OCEAN
MI 125 250
KM 125 250
© GGC
© GGC

ALABAMA

TOURISM:
800.252.2262
334.242.4169

ROAD CONDITIONS:
334.242.4378

MI 10 20 30
KM 10 20 30

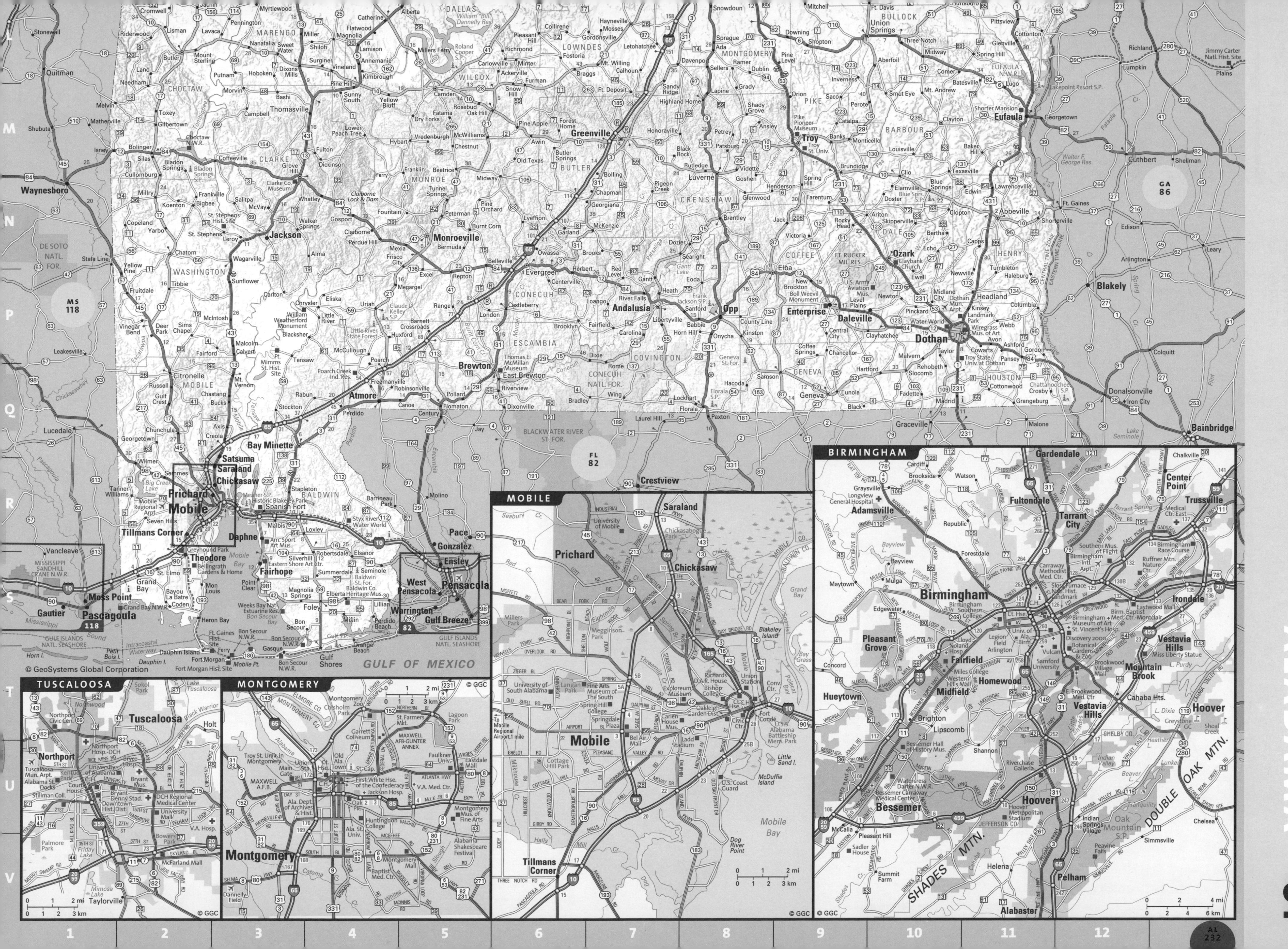
BIRMINGHAM
MOBILE
MONTGOMERY
TUSCALOOSA
GULF OF MEXICO
© GeoSystems Global Corporation

TOURISM:
907.465.2010

ROAD CONDITIONS:
907.273.6037

MI 125 250
KM 125 250

AK 232

FAIRBANKS

DENALI NATIONAL PARK

ANCHORAGE

JUNEAU

ALEUTIAN ISLANDS

Kenai Attractions
Fort Kenai
Russian Orthodox Church

Wasilla Attractions
Mus. of Alaska Trans & Industry
Page Museum

Kodiak Attractions
Alutiiq Museum
Baranov Museum
Russian Orthodox Church

Haines Attractions
Alaska Indian Arts Center
Fort Seward
Sheldon Museum
& Cultural Center

Skagway Attractions
Historic District
Klondike Gold Rush N.H.P.
Scenic Railroad
Trail of '98 Museum
Mendenhall Glacier

Sitka Attractions
Castle Hill S.H.S.
Isabel Miller Museum
Old Sitka S.H.P.
Russian Bishop's House
Sheldon Jackson College
Sheldon Jackson Museum
Sitka N.H.P.

Wrangell Attractions
Petroglyph Beach
Tlingit Tribal House
Wrangell Museum

Ketchikan Attractions
Totem Bight S.H.P.
Totem Heritage Center
Tongass Hist. Mus.

All distance calculations on this page are in miles.

PHOENIX
DOWNTOWN PHOENIX
FLAGSTAFF
TUCSON
Phoenix
Scottsdale
Glendale
Peoria
Mesa
Tempe
Chandler
Gilbert
Avondale
Goodyear
Buckeye
Apache Junction
Fountain Hills
Paradise Valley
Sun City
Sun City West
Surprise
Casa Grande
Coolidge
Flagstaff
Tucson
South Tucson
Tanque Verde
GILA RIVER INDIAN RES.
SALT RIVER INDIAN RESERVATION
TONTO NATL. FOREST
CORONADO NATIONAL FOREST
SAGUARO NATL. PARK (EAST)
© GeoSystems Global Corp.
© GGC

TOURISM:
800.842.8257
602.230.7733
ROAD CONDITIONS:
602.651.2400, EXT. 7623
ROAD CONSTRUCTION:
602.255.6588
MI 25 50
KM 25 50
NAVAJO INDIAN RESERVATION
HOPI IND. RES.
PAINTED DESERT
MOENKOPI PLATEAU
COCONINO PLATEAU
KAIBAB PLATEAU
GRAND CANYON
MOGOLLON PLATEAU
FORT APACHE IND. RES.
SAN CARLOS IND. RES.
TONTO NATL. FOR.
COCONINO NATL. FOR.
PRESCOTT NATL. FOR.
HUALAPAI IND. RES.
AQUARIUS MOUNTAINS
HUALAPAI MTS.
BLACK MTS.
SHIVWITS PLATEAU
UINKARET PLATEAU
VERMILION CLIFFS
HURRICANE CLIFFS
LAKE MEAD NATL. REC. AREA
MOJAVE NATIONAL PRESERVE
PACIFIC TIME ZONE
MOUNTAIN TIME ZONE
Page
Tuba City
Kayenta
Chinle
Window Rock
Gallup
Fort Defiance
St. Johns
Holbrook
Winslow
Snowflake
Show Low
Springerville
Eagar
Flagstaff
Williams
Sedona
Cottonwood
Camp Verde
Prescott
Prescott Valley
Chino Valley
Payson
Globe
San Carlos
Superior
Apache Junction
Mesa
Scottsdale
Phoenix
Glendale
Tempe
Chandler
Gilbert
Peoria
Surprise
Sun City
Avondale
Buckeye
Wickenburg
Kingman
Bullhead City
Laughlin
Lake Havasu City
Needles
Parker
Blythe
Quartzsite
Las Vegas
N. Las Vegas
Henderson
Boulder City
St. George
Washington
Hurricane
Kanab
Fredonia
Colorado City
Mesquite
Shiprock

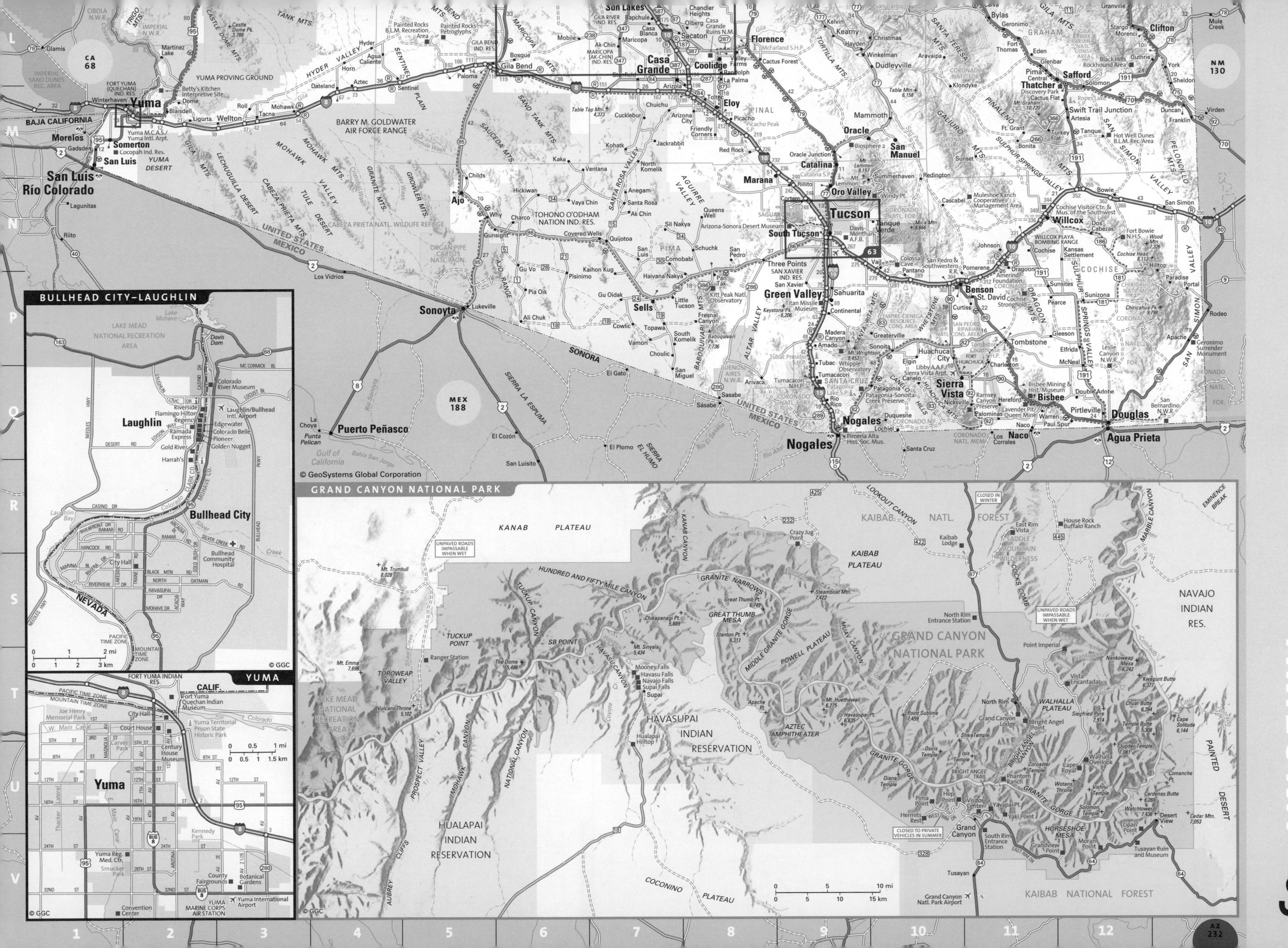
BULLHEAD CITY–LAUGHLIN
YUMA
GRAND CANYON NATIONAL PARK
© GeoSystems Global Corporation

TOURISM:
800.628.8725
501.682.7777

ROAD CONDITIONS:
501.569.2374

ROAD CONSTRUCTION:
501.569.2227

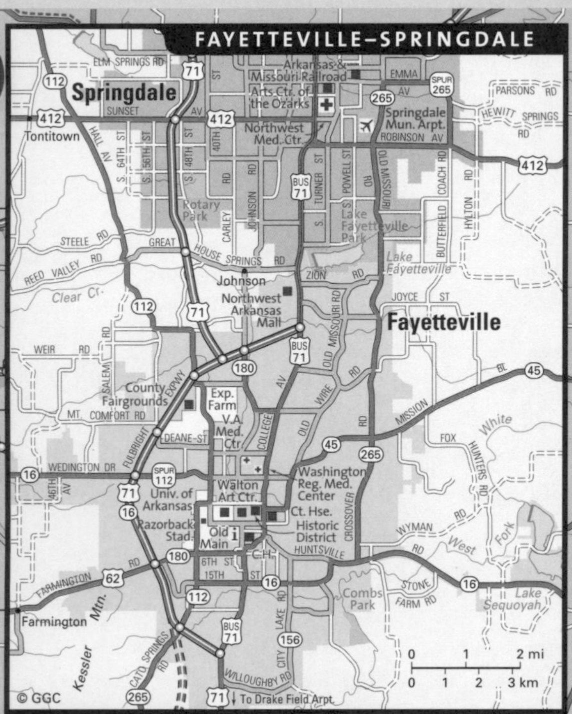

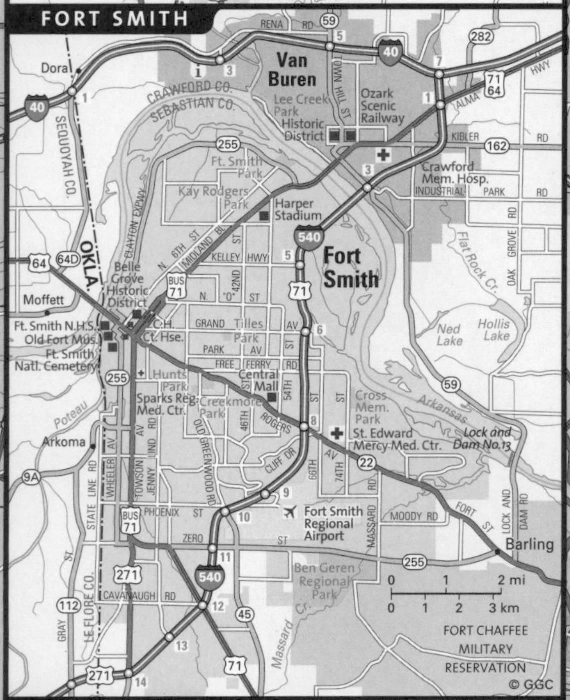

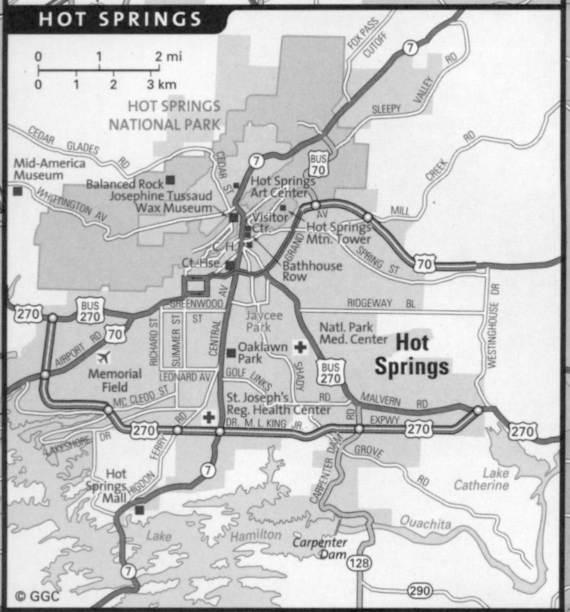

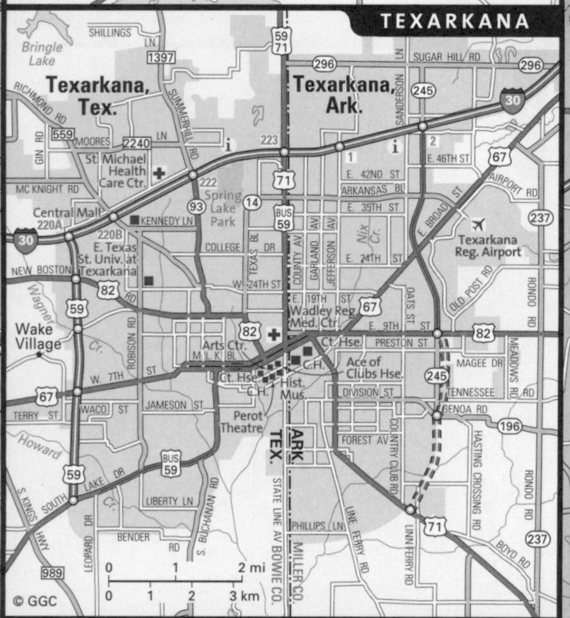

MI 20 40
KM 20 40

FAYETTEVILLE–SPRINGDALE

0 1 2 mi
0 1 2 3 km

© GGC

FORT SMITH

0 1 2 mi
0 1 2 3 km

© GGC

HOT SPRINGS

0 1 2 mi
0 1 2 3 km

© GGC

TEXARKANA

0 1 2 mi
0 1 2 3 km

© GGC

JONESBORO
PINE BLUFF
LITTLE ROCK
Memphis
Jonesboro
Pine Bluff
Little Rock
North Little Rock

TOURISM:
800.862.2543
916.322.2881

ROAD CONDITIONS:
916.445.7623
916.445.1534

MI 0 25 50
KM 0 25 50

PACIFIC OCEAN

MONTEREY–SALINAS

© GGC

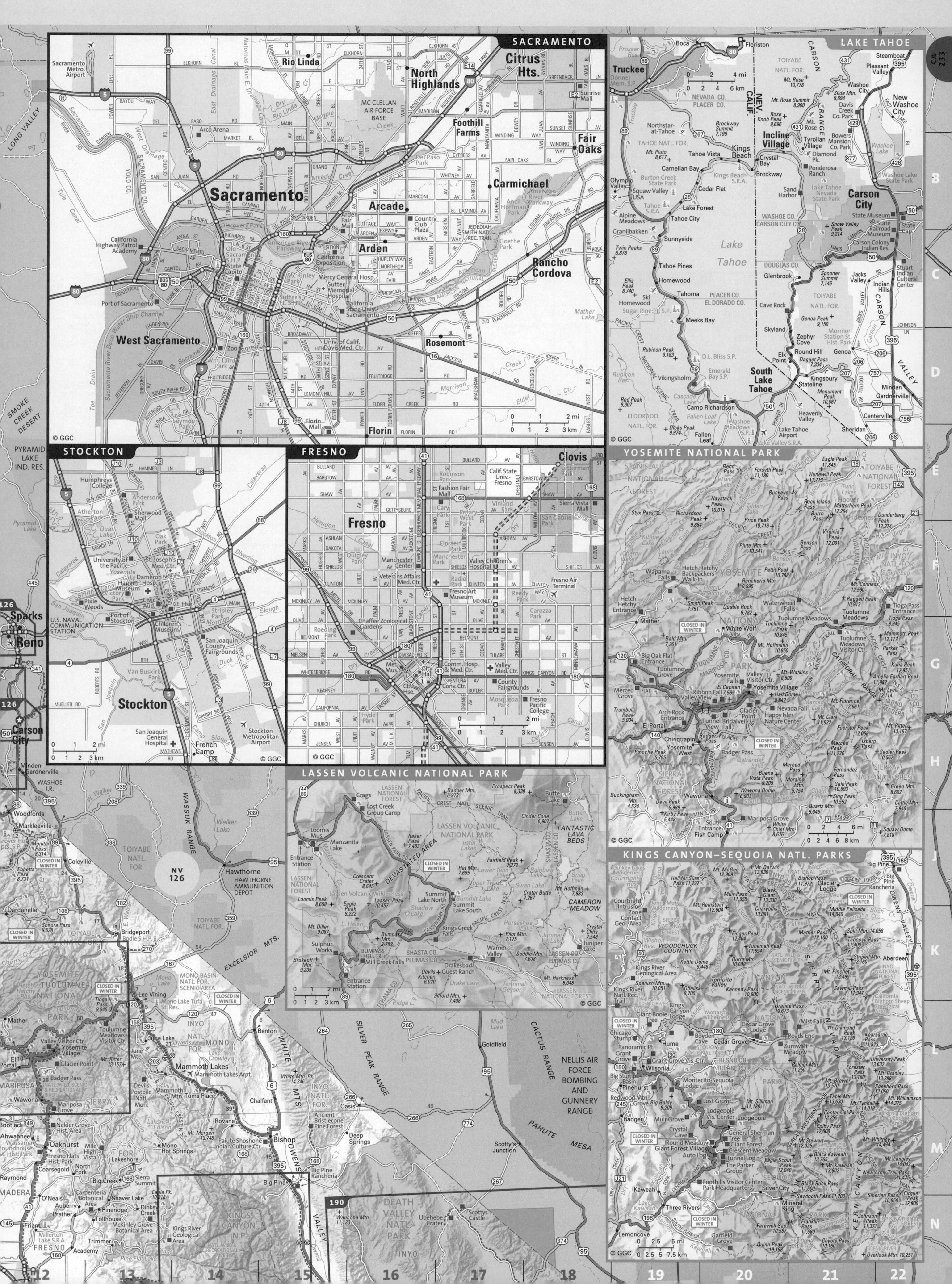
SACRAMENTO
Sacramento
Rio Linda
North Highlands
Citrus Hts.
Foothill Farms
Fair Oaks
Carmichael
Arcade
Arden
Rancho Cordova
West Sacramento
Rosemont
Florin
LAKE TAHOE
Truckee
Incline Village
Kings Beach
Carson City
Lake Tahoe
South Lake Tahoe
STOCKTON
Stockton
FRESNO
Fresno
Clovis
YOSEMITE NATIONAL PARK
LASSEN VOLCANIC NATIONAL PARK
KINGS CANYON–SEQUOIA NATL. PARKS
NELLIS AIR FORCE BOMBING AND GUNNERY RANGE
Reno
Sparks
Mammoth Lakes
Bishop
Hawthorne

TOURISM:
800.862.2543
916.322.2881

ROAD CONDITIONS:
916.445.7623
916.445.1534

MI 0 25 50
KM 0 25 50

BAKERSFIELD

SANTA BARBARA

OXNARD–VENTURA

SAN DIEGO

DOWNTOWN SAN DIEGO

PACIFIC OCEAN

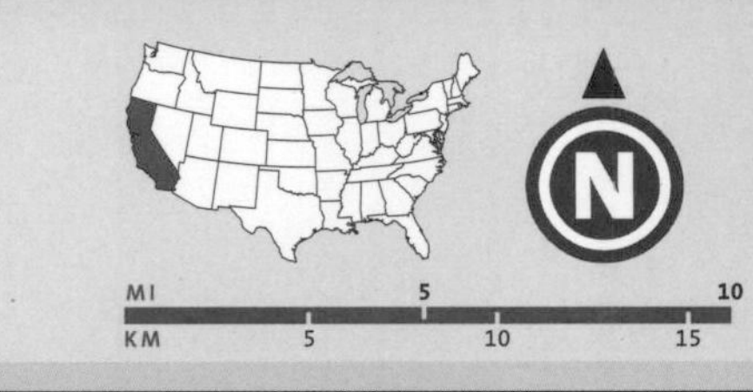

SAN GABRIEL MTS.
ANGELES NATIONAL FOREST
SANTA SUSANA MTS.
BIG MOUNTAIN
SIMI HILLS
SAN FERNANDO VALLEY
VERDUGO MTS.
SANTA MONICA MTS.
SANTA MONICA MOUNTAINS NAT'L REC. AREA
Santa Clarita
Moorpark
Simi Valley
Thousand Oaks
Oak Park
Agoura Hills
Westlake Village
Malibu
San Fernando
Burbank
Glendale
La Crescenta
La Canada Flintridge
Altadena
Pasadena
Sierra Madre
Monrovia
Azusa
Duarte
Arcadia
Los Angeles
West Hollywood
Beverly Hills
Santa Monica
Culver City
View Park
Windsor Hills
Ladera Hts.
Marina del Rey
Inglewood
Lennox
Hawthorne
El Segundo
Lawndale
Manhattan Beach
Hermosa Beach
Redondo Beach
Torrance
Gardena
Carson
Lomita
Palos Verdes Estates
Rolling Hills Estates
Rancho Palos Verdes
Athens
Huntington Park
Florence
Walnut Park
Maywood
Bell
Bell Gdns.
Cudahy
Vernon
Commerce
E. Los Angeles
Montebello
Monterey Park
Alhambra
San Marino
South Pasadena
Temple City
San Gabriel
Rosemead
El Monte
South El Monte
S. San Gabriel
Baldwin Park
West Covina
La Puente
Hacienda Heights
Pico Rivera
Whittier
Santa Fe Springs
Downey
South Gate
Lynwood
Willowbrook
Compton
Paramount
Bellflower
Norwalk
S. Whittier
La Mirada
La Habra Hts.
La Habra
Buena Park
Fullerton
Cerritos
Artesia
Lakewood
La Palma
Cypress
Hawaiian Gardens
Los Alamitos
Anaheim
Stanton
Garden Grove
Rossmoor
Signal Hill
Long Beach
Seal Beach
Westminster
Midway City
Fountain Valley
Huntington Beach
Costa Mesa
Newport Beach
Santa Monica Bay
PACIFIC OCEAN
San Pedro Bay
San Pedro Channel
SANTA CATALINA ISLAND
Avalon

DOWNTOWN LOS ANGELES
Dodger Stadium
CHINATOWN
Union Station
Little Tokyo
Convention Center
© GGC

Hesperia
Wrightwood
Cajon Junction
CAJON CANYON
SAN BERNARDINO NATIONAL FOREST
ANGELES NATIONAL FOREST
Crestline
Lake Arrowhead
Running Springs
San Bernardino
Rancho Cucamonga
Fontana
Rialto
Highland
Glendora
San Dimas
Claremont
Upland
La Verne
Covina
Pomona
Montclair
Ontario
Colton
Grand Terrace
Loma Linda
Redlands
Yucaipa
Calimesa
Walnut
Diamond Bar
Chino
Chino Hills
Rowland Heights
Riverside
Moreno Valley
Banning
Beaumont
Cherry Valley
Brea
Yorba Linda
Placentia
Norco
Corona
Home Gardens
Woodcrest
Perris
Orange
Villa Park
Tustin
Santa Ana
Irvine
Lake Forest
Mission Viejo
Laguna Hills
Aliso Viejo
Laguna Niguel
Laguna Beach
San Juan Capistrano
Dana Point
San Clemente
Rancho Santa Margarita
CLEVELAND NATIONAL FOREST
SANTA ANA MTS.
Lake Elsinore
Canyon Lake
Sun City
Menifee
Lakeland Village
Wildomar
Murrieta
Temecula
Hemet
San Jacinto
SAN JACINTO VALLEY
LAKEVIEW MTS.
ELSINORE MTS.
SANTA MARGARITA MTS.
SAN MATEO CANYON
CAMP PENDLETON MARINE CORPS BASE
Fallbrook
Rainbow
PECHANGA INDIAN RESERVATION
PALA INDIAN RESERVATION
© GeoSystems Global Corporation
11
12
13
14
15
16
17
18
19
20
B
C
D
E
F
G
H
J
K
L
M
N

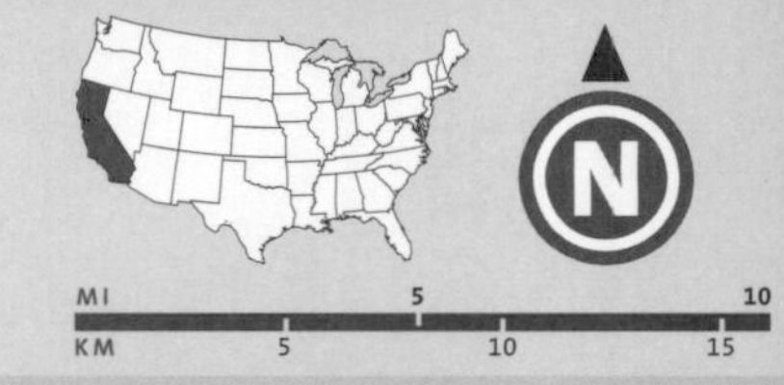

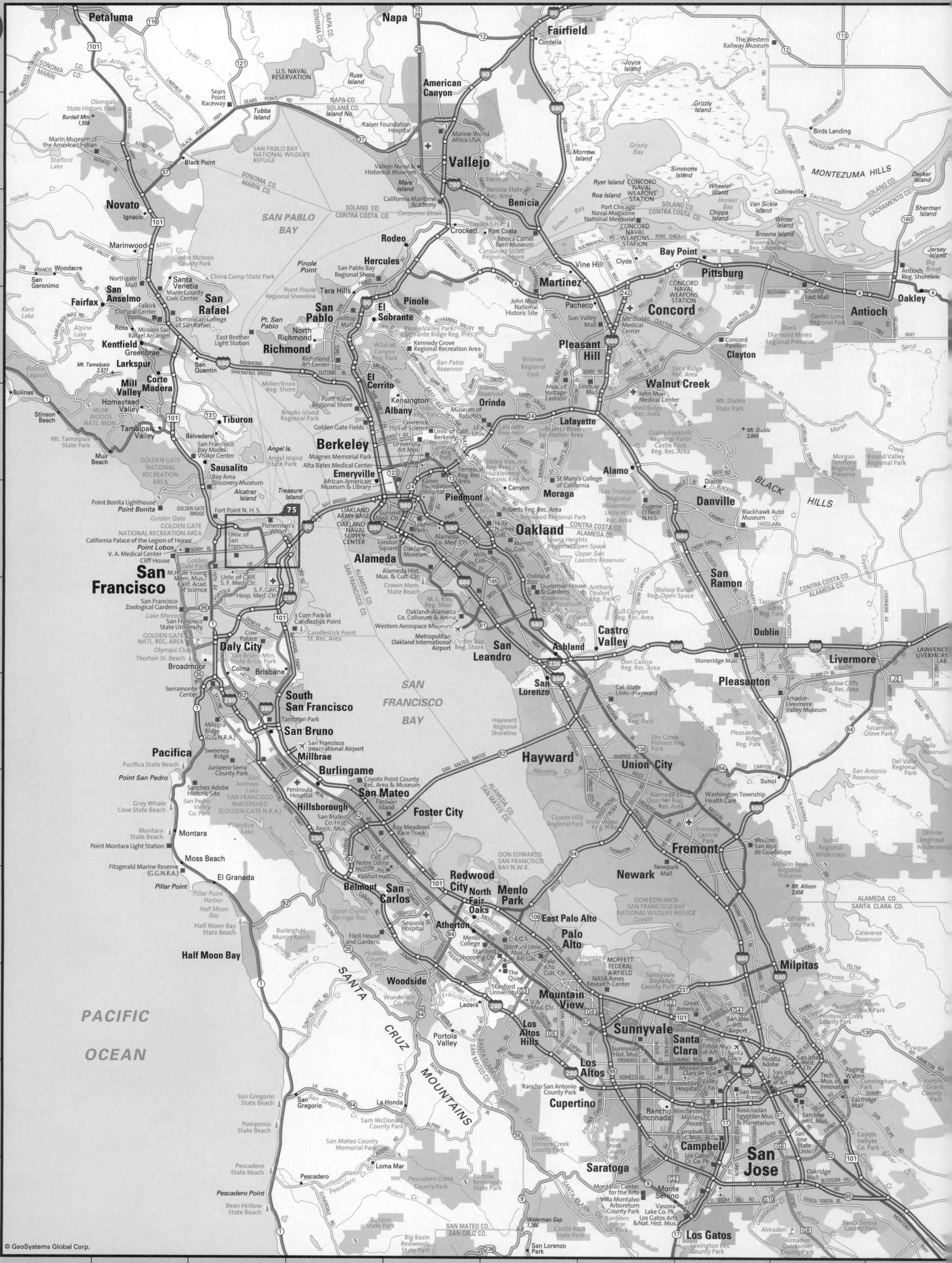

Petaluma
Napa
Fairfield
Novato
American Canyon
Vallejo
Benicia
San Rafael
San Pablo
Richmond
Pinole
Martinez
Concord
Pittsburg
Antioch
Oakley
Pleasant Hill
Walnut Creek
Berkeley
Emeryville
Oakland
Alameda
Piedmont
Orinda
Lafayette
Moraga
Danville
San Ramon
Dublin
Pleasanton
Livermore
Castro Valley
San Leandro
Hayward
Union City
Fremont
Newark
Sausalito
San Francisco
Daly City
South San Francisco
San Bruno
Pacifica
Millbrae
Burlingame
San Mateo
Foster City
Redwood City
Menlo Park
Palo Alto
Mountain View
Sunnyvale
Santa Clara
Milpitas
San Jose
Cupertino
Campbell
Saratoga
Los Gatos
Half Moon Bay

SAN PABLO BAY
SAN FRANCISCO BAY
PACIFIC OCEAN
SANTA CRUZ MOUNTAINS
MONTEZUMA HILLS
BLACK HILLS

© GeoSystems Global Corp.

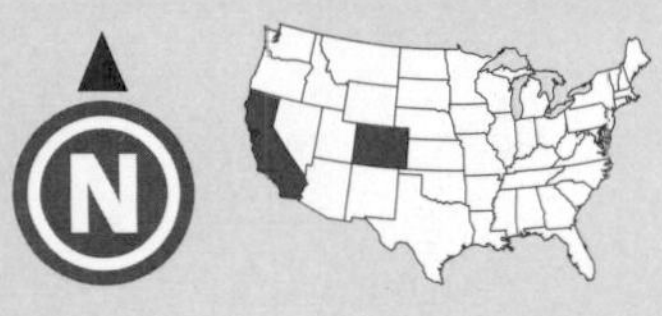

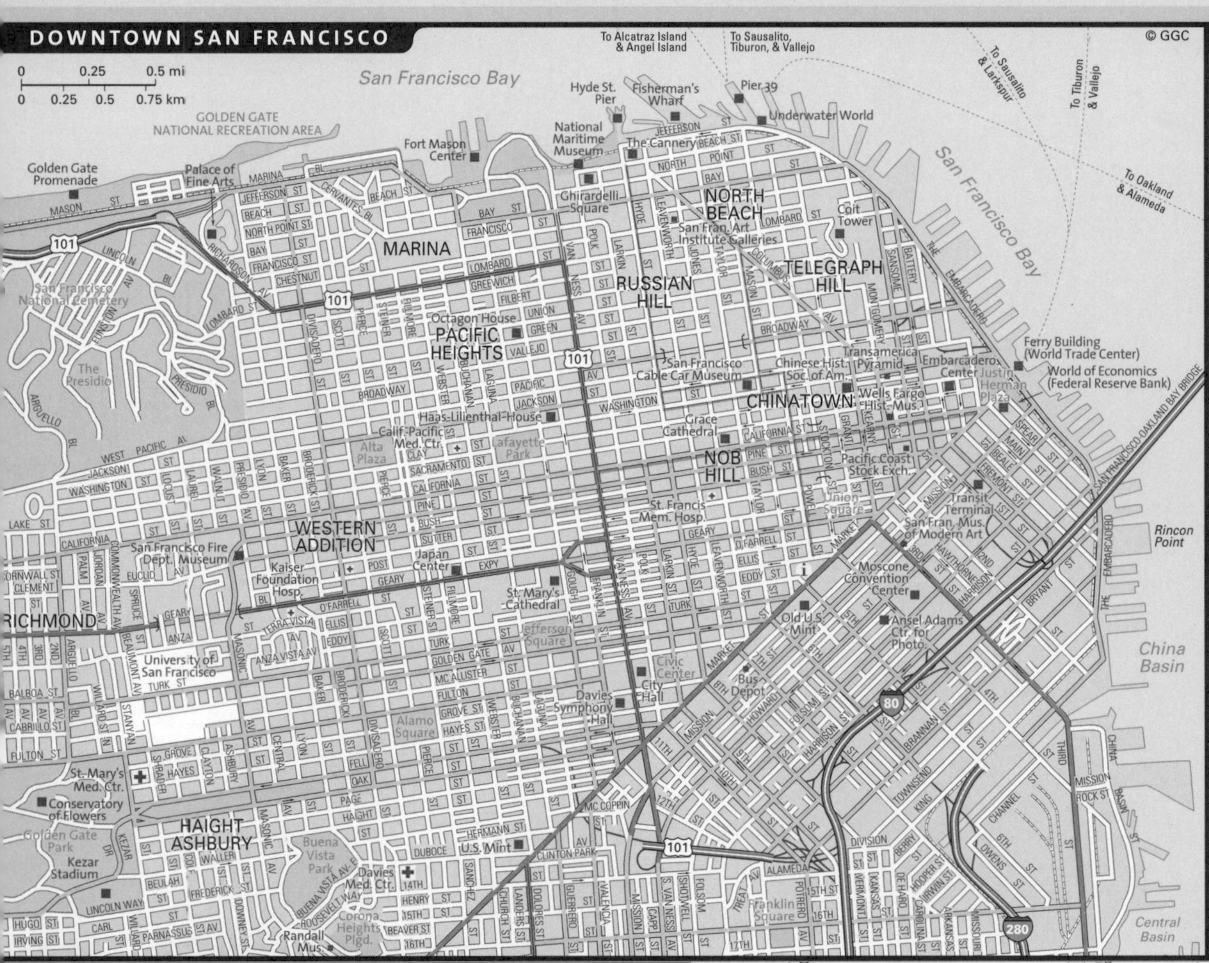

DOWNTOWN SAN FRANCISCO

0 0.25 0.5 mi
0 0.25 0.5 0.75 km

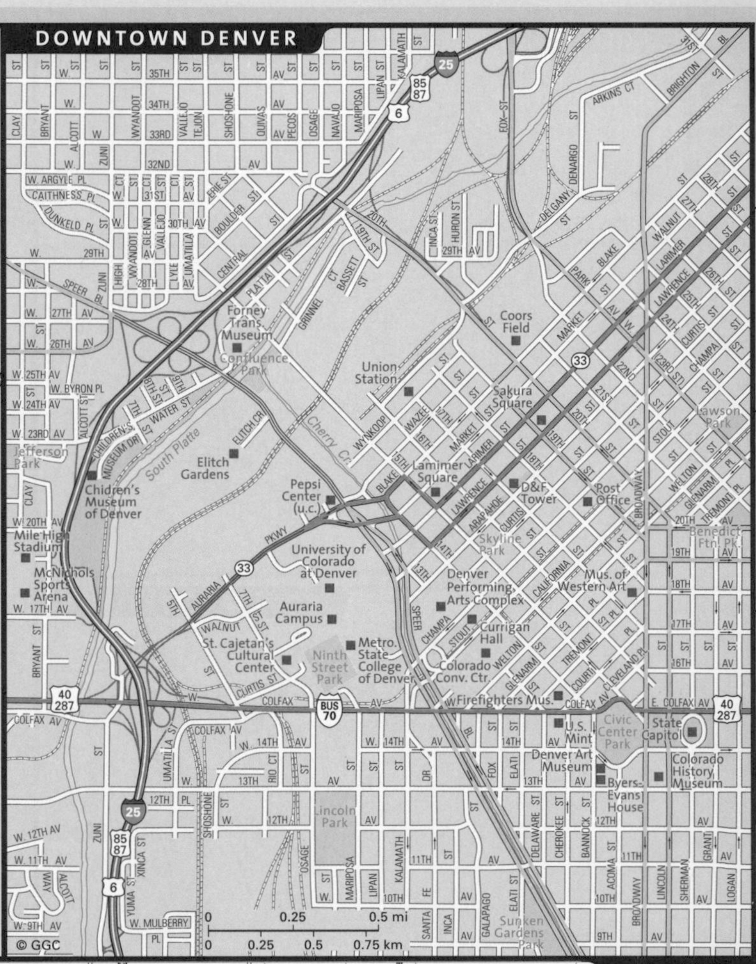

DOWNTOWN DENVER

0 0.25 0.5 mi
0 0.25 0.5 0.75 km

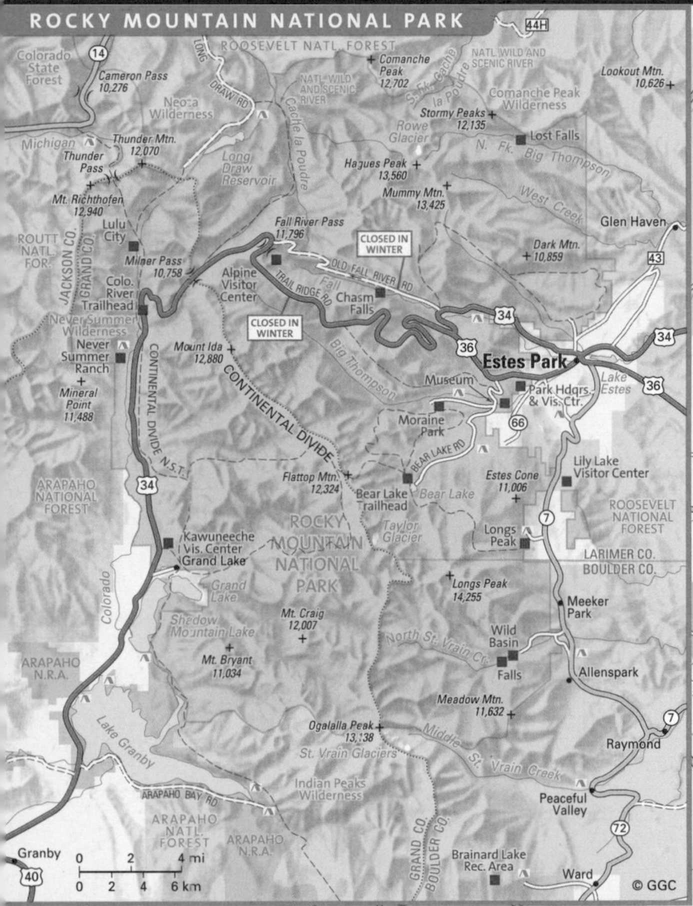

ROCKY MOUNTAIN NATIONAL PARK

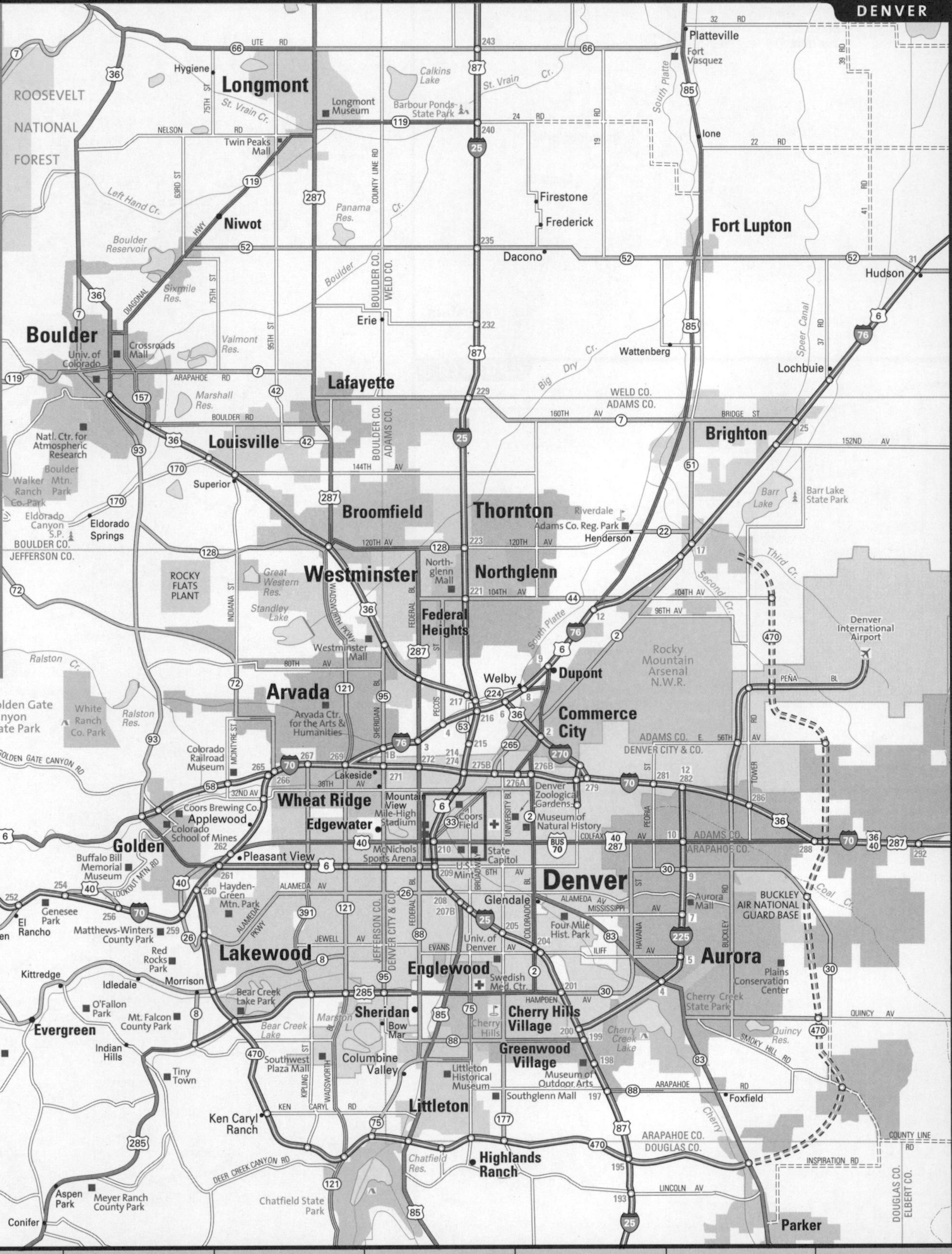

0 2 4 mi
0 2 4 6 km

DENVER

0 2 4 6 mi
0 2 4 6 8 km

TOURISM:
800.265.6723
303.892.1112

ROAD CONDITIONS:
303.639.1234

ROAD CONSTRUCTION:
303.573.7623

MI 20 40
KM 20 40

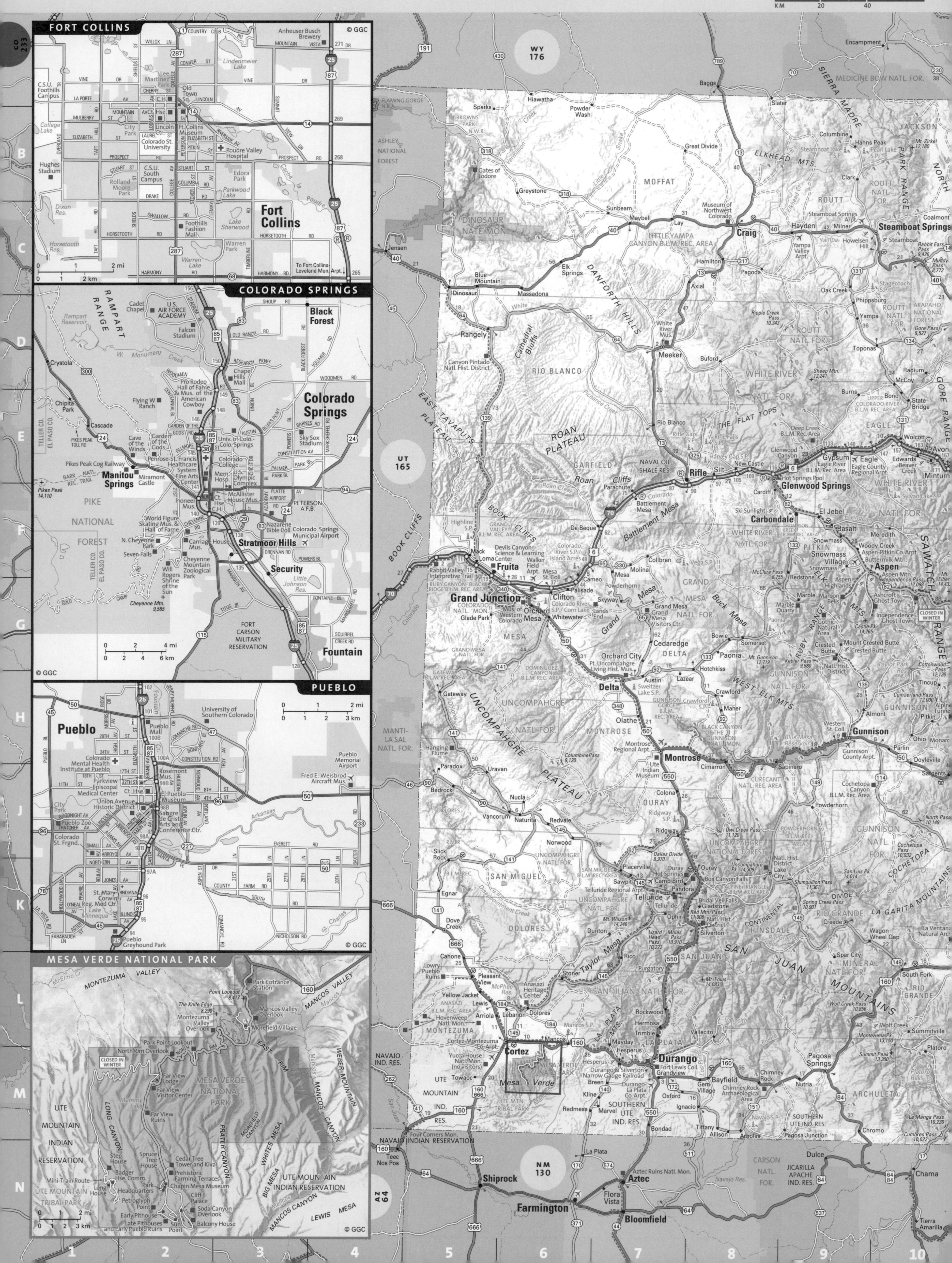

CO 233

FORT COLLINS

COLORADO SPRINGS

PUEBLO

MESA VERDE NATIONAL PARK

WY 176

UT 165

NM 130

AZ 64

© GGC

Laramie
Cheyenne
Kimball
Sidney
Ogallala
Pine Bluffs
Julesburg
Fort Collins
Greeley
Windsor
Loveland
Estes Park
Longmont
Boulder
Sterling
Fort Morgan
Brush
Akron
Yuma
Wray
Holyoke
Westminster
Arvada
Golden
Thornton
Broomfield
Lafayette
Louisville
Brighton
Fort Lupton
Denver
Aurora
Lakewood
Littleton
Englewood
Evergreen
Parker
Castle Rock
Limon
Burlington
Vail
Leadville
Breckenridge
Colorado Springs
Manitou Springs
Woodland Park
Security
Fountain
Black Forest
Cañon City
Salida
Florence
Pueblo
Pueblo West
Rocky Ford
La Junta
Las Animas
Lamar
Eads
Cheyenne Wells
Kit Carson
Walsenburg
Trinidad
Alamosa
Monte Vista
Springfield
Raton
Boise City
PAWNEE NATIONAL GRASSLAND
COMANCHE NATL. GRASSLAND
ROCKY MOUNTAINS
SANGRE DE CRISTO MTS.
WET MOUNTAINS
CULEBRA RANGE
SAN LUIS VALLEY
SOUTH PARK
WELD
LOGAN
SEDGWICK
PHILLIPS
MORGAN
WASHINGTON
YUMA
ADAMS
ARAPAHOE
ELBERT
KIT CARSON
LINCOLN
CHEYENNE
EL PASO
CROWLEY
KIOWA
PUEBLO
OTERO
BENT
PROWERS
LAS ANIMAS
BACA
HUERFANO
CUSTER
FREMONT
COSTILLA
CONEJOS
WY 176
NE 124
KS 98
OK 146
NM 130
CENTRAL TIME ZONE
MOUNTAIN TIME ZONE
© GeoSystems Global Corporation

TOURISM:
800.282.6863

ROAD CONDITIONS:
860.594.2650

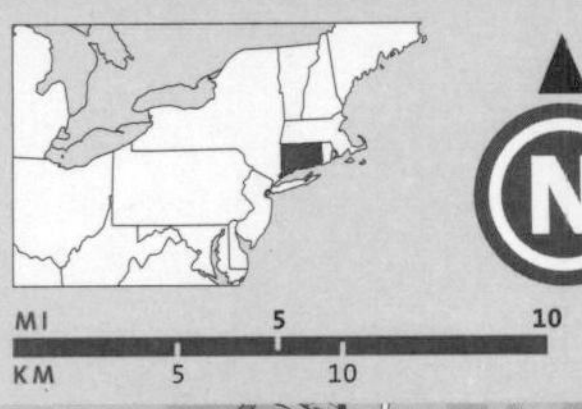

MI 0 5 10
KM 5 10

N

WATERBURY

Waterbury

NEW HAVEN–BRIDGEPORT

STAMFORD

Long Island Sound

MA 110

NY 132

NJ 128

CT 233

MA 110
RI 155
CT 233
NEW LONDON
HARTFORD
155
110
East Longmeadow
Southbridge
Webster
Oxford
Whitinsville
Franklin
Bellingham
Foxboro
Mansfield
Woonsocket
Cumberland Hill
Plainville
North Attleboro
Attleboro
Pascoag
Valley Falls
Central Falls
Pawtucket
Greenville
North Providence
Providence
East Providence
Cranston
Somerset
Barrington
Warwick
West Warwick
Fall River
Bristol
East Greenwich
Putnam
Danielson
Stafford Springs
Storrs
Vernon
Windsor
Manchester
Willimantic
Coventry
Plainfield
Moosup
Jewett City
Colchester
Norwich
New London
Groton
Mystic
Pawcatuck
Westerly
Niantic
Essex
Deep River
Old Saybrook
Block Island Sound
Long Island Sound
Fishers I.
Plum I.
Gardiners I.
Rocky Pt.
Orient Pt.
Waterford
Ansonia
Woodbridge
Hamden
North Haven
Shelton
Derby
Orange
West Haven
New Haven
East Haven
Branford
Milford
Bloomfield
Blue Hills
Hartford
Wilson
South Windsor
West Hartford
East Hartford
Elmwood
Wethersfield
Glastonbury
Newington
New Britain
Rocky Hill
South Glastonbury
Kensington
© GGC
11
12
13
14
15
16
17
18
19
20
B
C
D
E
F
G
H
J
K
L
M
N

TOURISM:
800.441.8846
302.739.4271

ROAD CONSTRUCTION:
800.652.5600 (DE)
302.739.4313

MI 5 10 15
KM 5 10 15

WILMINGTON

DOVER

DELAWARE

ATLANTIC OCEAN

Delaware Bay

© GeoSystems Global Corporation

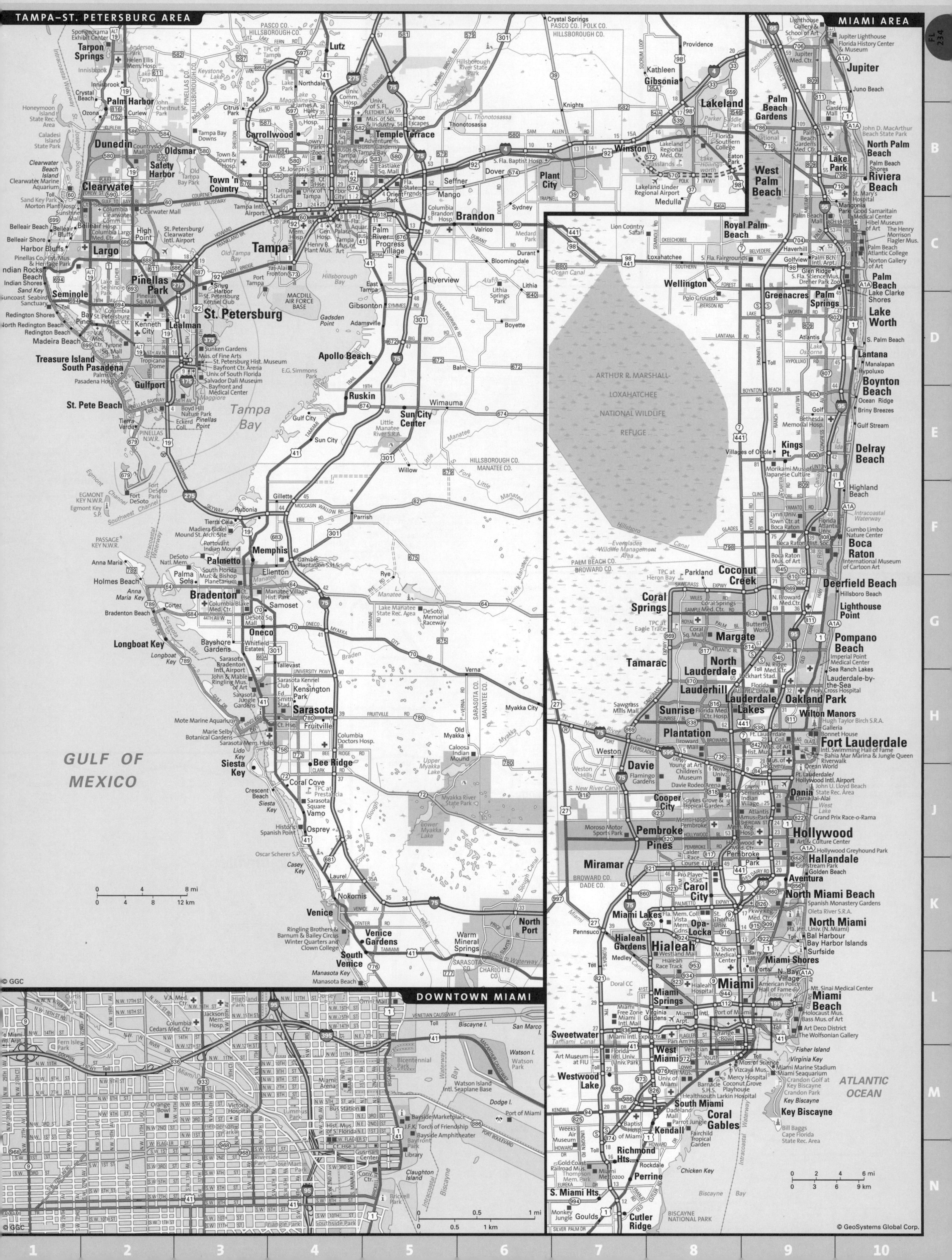

TAMPA–ST. PETERSBURG AREA

GULF OF MEXICO

Tampa Bay

MIAMI AREA

ARTHUR R. MARSHALL-LOXAHATCHEE NATIONAL WILDLIFE REFUGE

ATLANTIC OCEAN

DOWNTOWN MIAMI

TOURISM:
888.735.2872

ROAD CONDITIONS:
800.475.0044 (I-10 AND I-75)
800.749.7453 (FL TURNPIKE)

MI 20 40
KM 20 40

PENSACOLA

PANAMA CITY

TALLAHASSEE

GULF OF MEXICO

ORLANDO

JACKSONVILLE

ATLANTIC OCEAN

© GGC

GAINESVILLE
DAYTONA BEACH
MELBOURNE–KENNEDY SPACE CENTER
Gainesville
Ormond Beach
Holly Hill
Daytona Beach
South Daytona
Port Orange
Titusville
Cocoa
Merritt Island
Cape Canaveral
Cocoa Beach
Melbourne
ATLANTIC OCEAN
GULF OF MEXICO
Thomasville
Valdosta
Quitman
Jacksonville
Lake City
Live Oak
Perry
Starke
Palatka
St. Augustine
Ocala
Silver Sprs.
Ormond-by-the-Sea
New Smyrna Beach
Deltona
Sanford
Orlando
Kissimmee
Leesburg
Brooksville
Spring Hill
Tampa
Clearwater
St. Petersburg
Lakeland
Winter Haven
Palm Bay
Vero Bch.
© GeoSystems Global Corporation

TOURISM:
888.735.2872

ROAD CONDITIONS:
800.475.0044 (I-10 AND I-75)
800.749.7453 (FL TURNPIKE)

GA 234

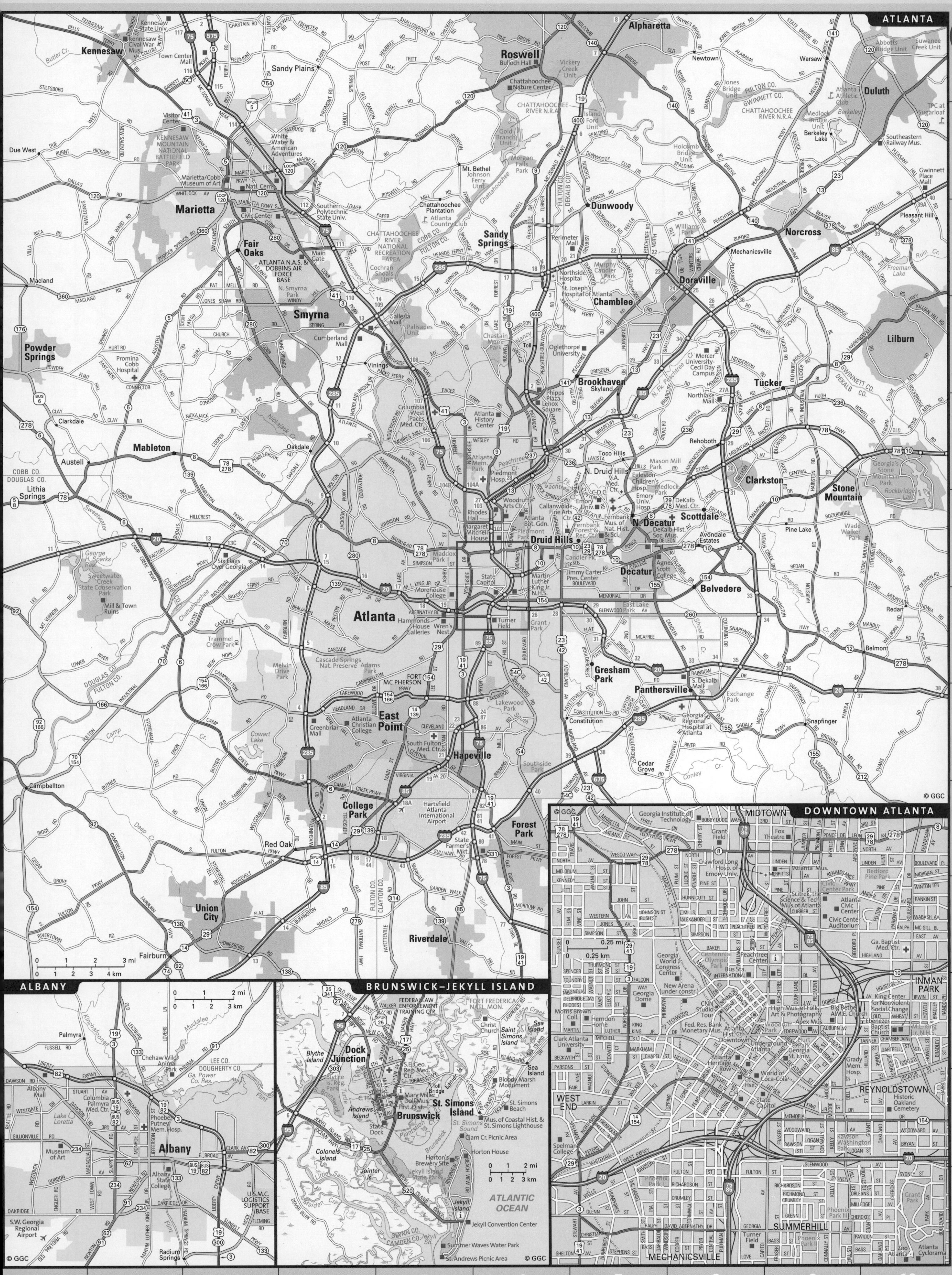

ATLANTA

DOWNTOWN ATLANTA

ALBANY

BRUNSWICK–JEKYLL ISLAND

TOURISM:
800.847.4842
404.656.3590

ROAD CONDITIONS:
404.656.5267

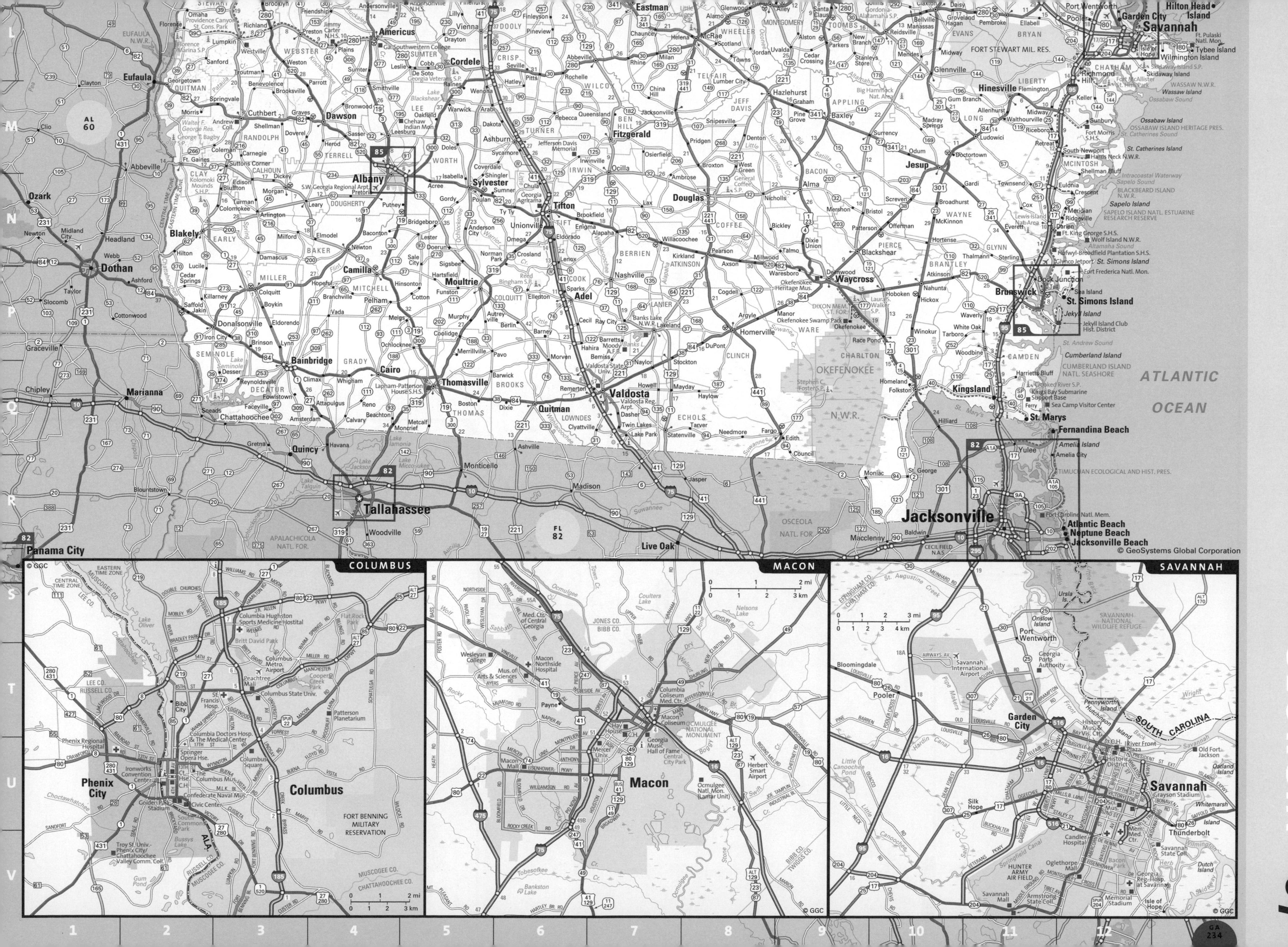
ATLANTIC OCEAN
COLUMBUS
MACON
SAVANNAH
Savannah
Hilton Head Island
Tybee Island
Hinesville
Brunswick
St. Simons Island
Jekyll Island
St. Marys
Kingsland
Fernandina Beach
Jacksonville
Atlantic Beach
Neptune Beach
Jacksonville Beach
Waycross
Valdosta
Douglas
Tifton
Fitzgerald
Cordele
Americus
Albany
Moultrie
Thomasville
Bainbridge
Tallahassee
Dothan
Eufaula
Panama City
Marianna
Columbus
Phenix City
Macon
Garden City
Pooler
FORT BENNING MILITARY RESERVATION
OKEFENOKEE N.W.R.
APALACHICOLA NATL. FOR.
OSCEOLA NATL. FOR.
© GeoSystems Global Corporation

TOURISM:
800.464.2924
808.923.1811
ROAD CONSTRUCTION:
808.536.6566

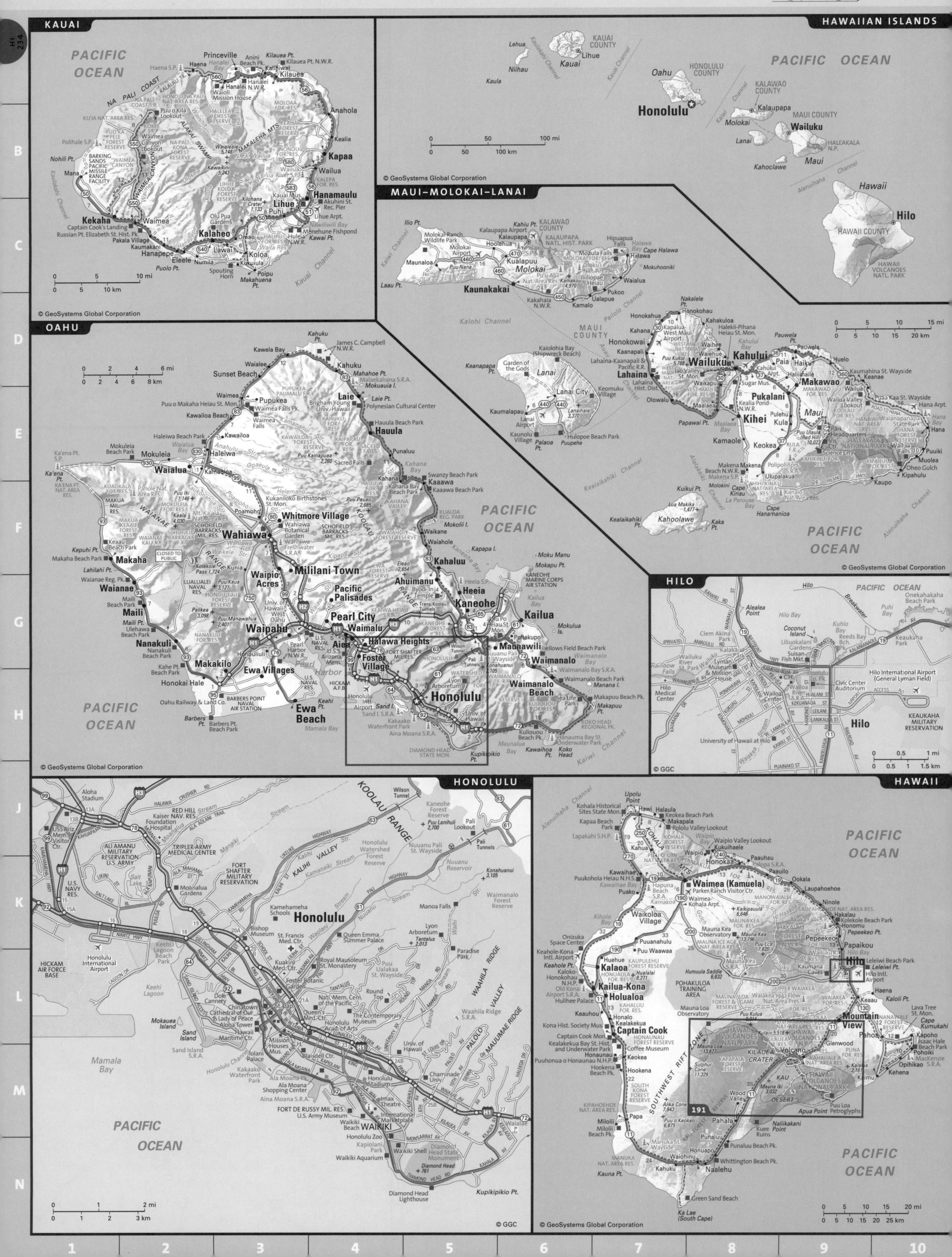

KAUAI

PACIFIC OCEAN

Princeville, Haena, Hanalei, Kilauea, Anahola, Kealia, Kapaa, Wailua, Hanamaulu, Lihue, Puhi, Kalaheo, Lawai, Koloa, Poipu, Eleele, Hanapepe, Waimea, Kekaha, Mana, Numila, Omao

NA PALI COAST, WAIMEA CANYON, ALAKAI SWAMP, MAKALEHA MTS.

Waialeale 5,148, Kawaikini 5,243

Kauai Channel, Kaulakahi Channel

Nohili Pt., Kilauea Pt., Makahuena Pt., Puolo Pt., Kawai Pt.

0 5 10 mi
0 5 10 km

HAWAIIAN ISLANDS

PACIFIC OCEAN

Lehua, Niihau, Kaula, Kauai, KAUAI COUNTY, Lihue, Oahu, HONOLULU COUNTY, Honolulu, KALAWAO COUNTY, Kalaupapa, Molokai, Lanai, MAUI COUNTY, Wailuku, Maui, HALEAKALA N.P., Kahoolawe, Hawaii, Hilo, HAWAII COUNTY, HAWAII VOLCANOES NATL. PARK

Kaulakahi Channel, Kauai Channel, Kaiwi Channel, Alenuihaha Channel

0 50 100 mi
0 50 100 km

MAUI-MOLOKAI-LANAI

Ilio Pt., Kalaupapa, Kaunakakai, Maunaloa, Kualapuu, Hoolehua, Halawa, Pukoo, Kamalo, Ualapue, Laau Pt.

Molokai, Lanai, Lanai City, Kahoolawe, Maui

Kapalua, Honokowai, Kaanapali, Lahaina, Olowalu, Wailuku, Kahului, Paia, Haiku, Pukalani, Makawao, Kula, Kihei, Kamaole, Keokea, Makena, Hana, Kipahulu, Kaupo, Huelo, Keanae

MAUI COUNTY, PACIFIC OCEAN

Kalohi Channel, Pailolo Channel, Auau Channel, Kealaikahiki Channel, Alalakeiki Channel, Alenuihaha Channel

0 5 10 15 mi
0 5 10 15 20 km

OAHU

Kahuku Pt., Kahuku, Laie, Hauula, Punaluu, Kaaawa, Kahana, Waiahole, Kahaluu, Heeia, Kaneohe, Kailua, Maunawili, Waimanalo, Waimanalo Beach, Honolulu, Hawaii Kai

Sunset Beach, Waimea, Pupukea, Haleiwa, Waialua, Mokuleia, Kaena Pt., Makaha, Waianae, Maili, Nanakuli, Makakilo, Ewa Villages, Ewa Beach, Barbers Pt., Honokai Hale

Wahiawa, Whitmore Village, Mililani Town, Waipio Acres, Waipahu, Pearl City, Waimalu, Aiea, Halawa Heights, Foster Village, Pacific Palisades, Ahuimanu

KOOLAU RANGE, WAIANAE RANGE

PACIFIC OCEAN

Kaiwi Channel

0 2 4 6 mi
0 2 4 6 8 km

HILO

PACIFIC OCEAN, Hilo Bay, Breakwater, Hilo, Hilo International Airport (General Lyman Field), KEAUKAHA MILITARY RESERVATION, University of Hawaii at Hilo, Coconut Island, Liliuokalani Gardens, Wailuku River St. Park, Rainbow Falls, Hilo Medical Center

0 0.5 1 mi
0 0.5 1 1.5 km

HONOLULU

Honolulu, KOOLAU RANGE, KALIHI VALLEY, Aloha Stadium, Red Hill, Fort Shafter Military Reservation, Moanalua Gardens, Hickam Air Force Base, Honolulu International Airport, Keehi Lagoon, Sand Island, Bishop Museum, Chinatown, Aloha Tower, Hawaii Maritime Ctr., Iolani Palace, Ala Moana Shopping Center, Waikiki, Honolulu Zoo, Kapiolani Park, Waikiki Aquarium, Diamond Head 761, Diamond Head Lighthouse, Kupikipikio Pt., Manoa Falls, Lyon Arboretum, Univ. of Hawaii, Waahila Ridge, Palolo Valley, Maunumae Ridge

Mamala Bay, PACIFIC OCEAN

0 1 2 mi
0 1 2 3 km

HAWAII

Upolu Point, Hawi, Halaula, Kapaau, Waipio, Honokaa, Paauilo, Waimea (Kamuela), Kawaihae, Waikoloa Village, Puuanahulu, Kalaoa, Kailua-Kona, Holualoa, Keauhou, Captain Cook, Honaunau, Hookena, Papa, Milolii, Pahala, Punaluu, Naalehu, Waiohinu, Ka Lae (South Cape), Volcano, Glenwood, Mountain View, Keaau, Pahoa, Kapoho, Kalapana, Hilo, Papaikou, Pepeekeo, Honomu, Laupahoehoe

Mauna Kea 13,796, Mauna Loa 13,677, Hualalai 8,271, KILAUEA CRATER, HAWAII VOLCANOES NATL. PARK, SOUTHWEST RIFT ZONE, KAU DESERT, KOHALA MTS.

Alenuihaha Channel, PACIFIC OCEAN

0 5 10 15 20 mi
0 5 10 15 20 25 km

TOURISM:
800.847.4843
208.772.1200 (COEUR D'ALENE)
208.233.6724 (POCATELLO)

ROAD CONDITIONS:
208.336.6600 (WINTER)
208.376.8028 (BOISE)

ROAD CONSTRUCTION:
208.334.8888

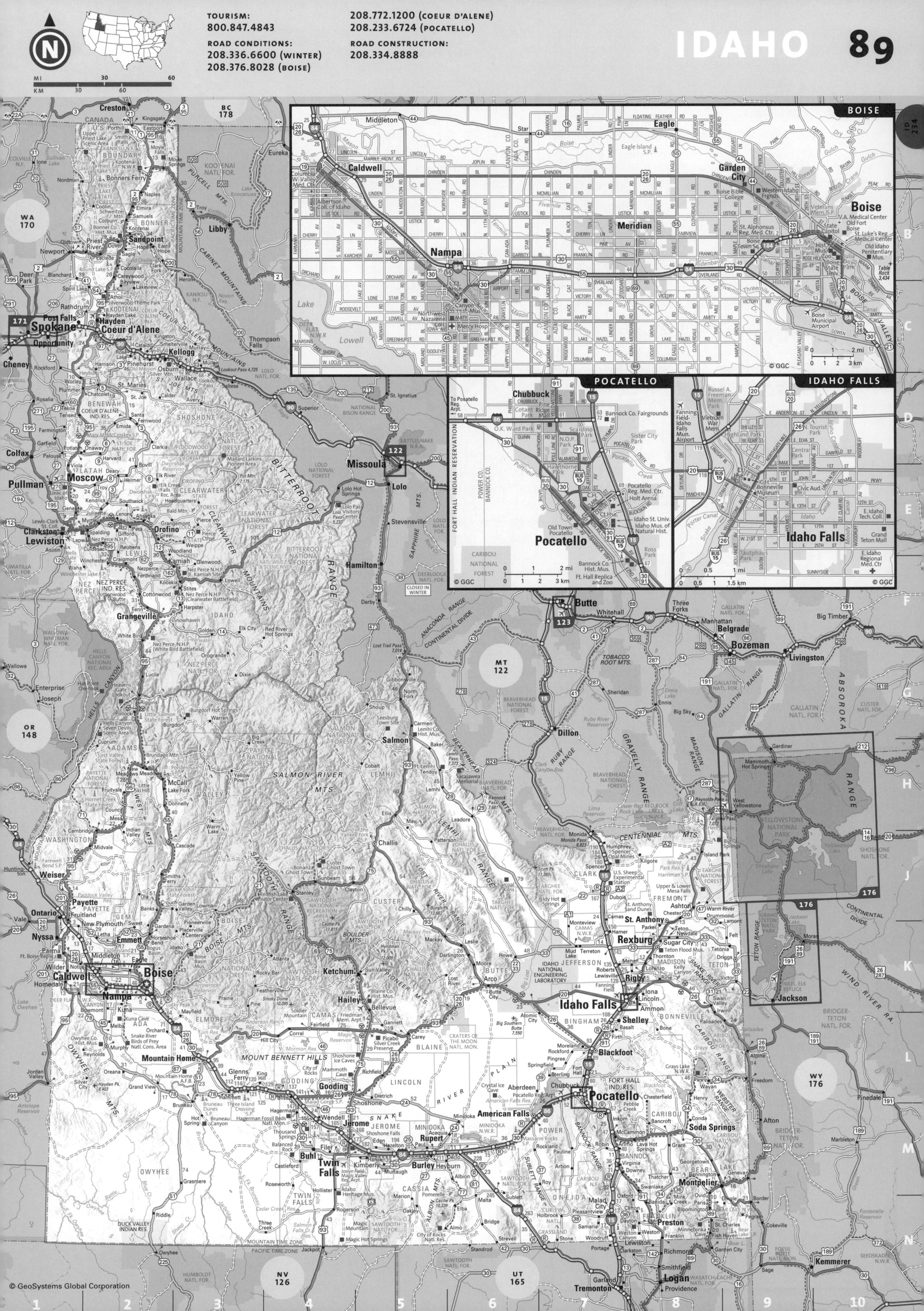

TOURISM:
800.226.6632
312.814.4732
ROAD CONDITIONS:
800.452.4368
(EXCEPT TOLL ROADS)
312.368.4636
N
MI 10 20 30
KM 10 20 30 40
EASTERN TIME ZONE
CENTRAL TIME ZONE
LAKE MICHIGAN
IN 94
WI 174
IA 96
MO 120
IL 235
Chicago
Rockford
Peoria
Springfield
Champaign
Urbana
Danville
Decatur
Bloomington
Normal
Kankakee
Joliet
Aurora
Elgin
Waukegan
Evanston
De Kalb
Rock Island
Moline
Davenport
Bettendorf
Dubuque
Galesburg
Quincy
Macomb
Burlington
Keokuk
Muscatine
Freeport
Sterling
Dixon
Ottawa
La Salle
Pontiac
Streator
Kewanee
Pekin
Lincoln
Clinton
Rantoul
Watseka
Gary
Hammond
ROCKFORD
Loves Park
Machesney Park
© GGC

CHAMPAIGN–URBANA
SPRINGFIELD
QUAD CITIES
IN 94
KY 100
MO 120
IL 235
St. Louis
Springfield
Champaign
Urbana
Davenport
Rock Island
Moline
Bettendorf
East Moline
Evansville
Terre Haute
Paducah
Carbondale
Cape Girardeau
Mt. Vernon
Effingham
Vandalia
Alton
© GeoSystems Global Corporation

N
MI 4 8
KM 4 8

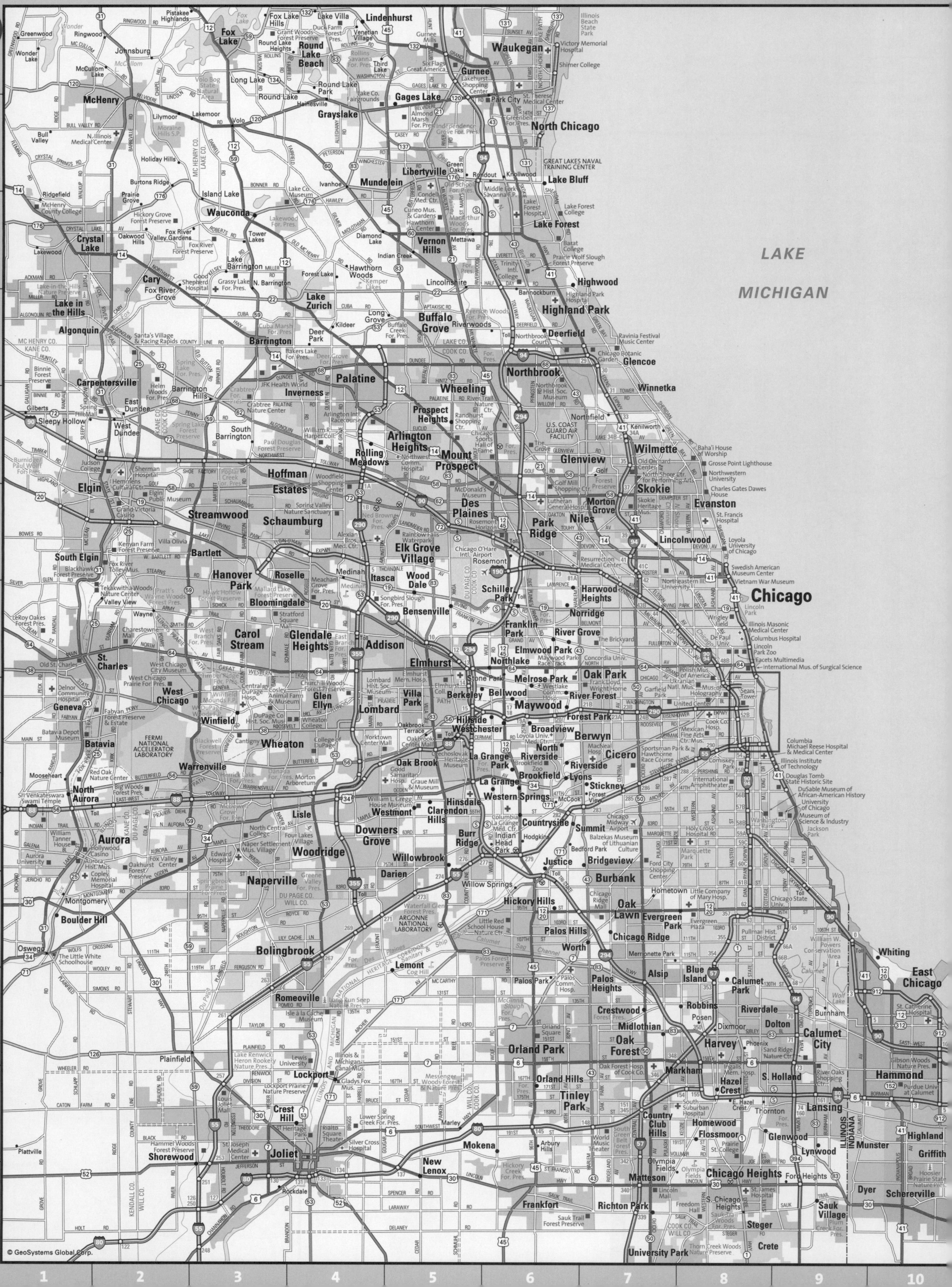

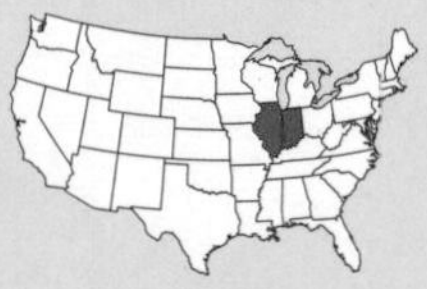

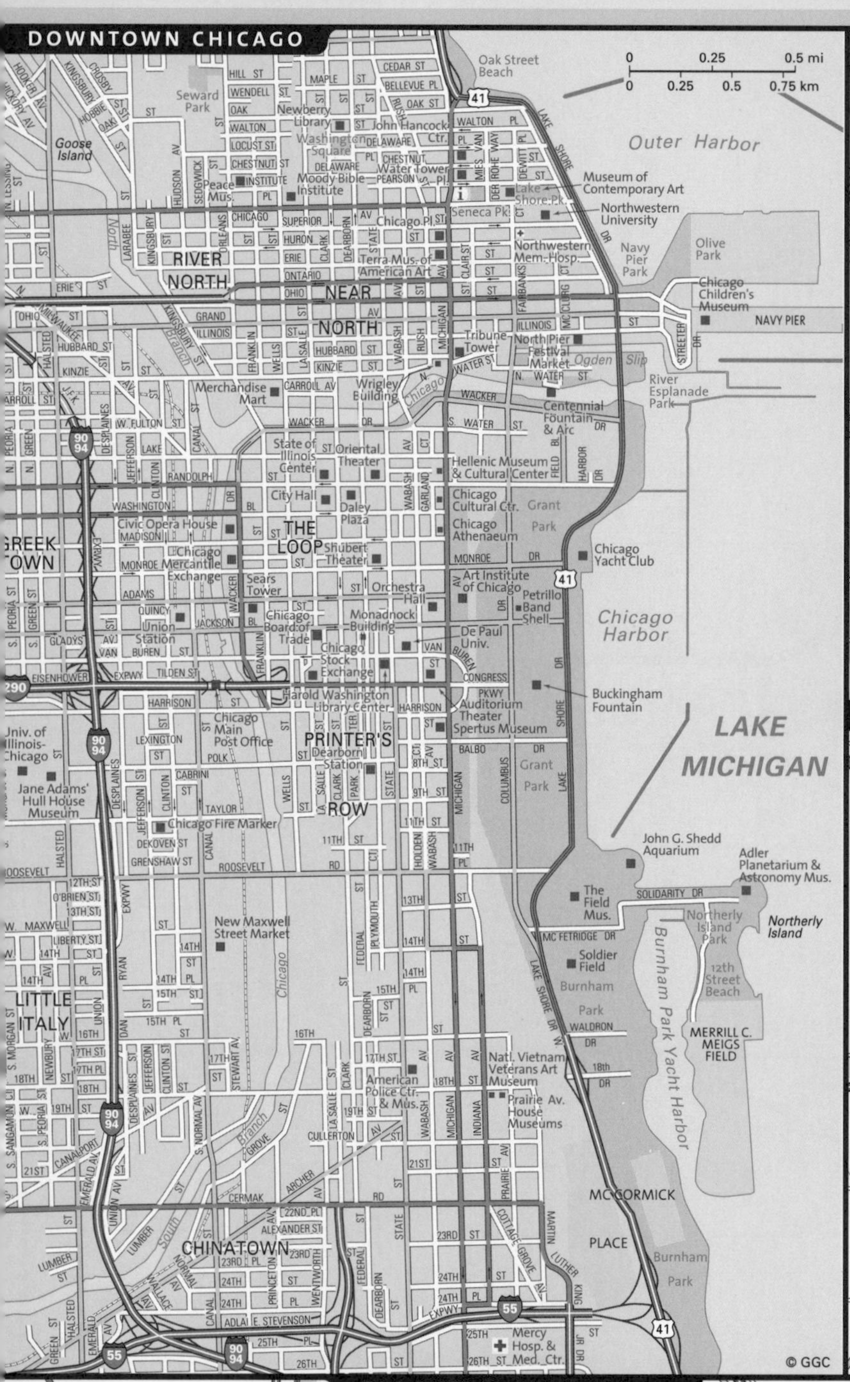
DOWNTOWN CHICAGO
RIVER NORTH
NEAR NORTH
THE LOOP
PRINTER'S ROW
CHINATOWN
LITTLE ITALY
LAKE MICHIGAN
Outer Harbor
Chicago Harbor
Navy Pier Park
© GGC

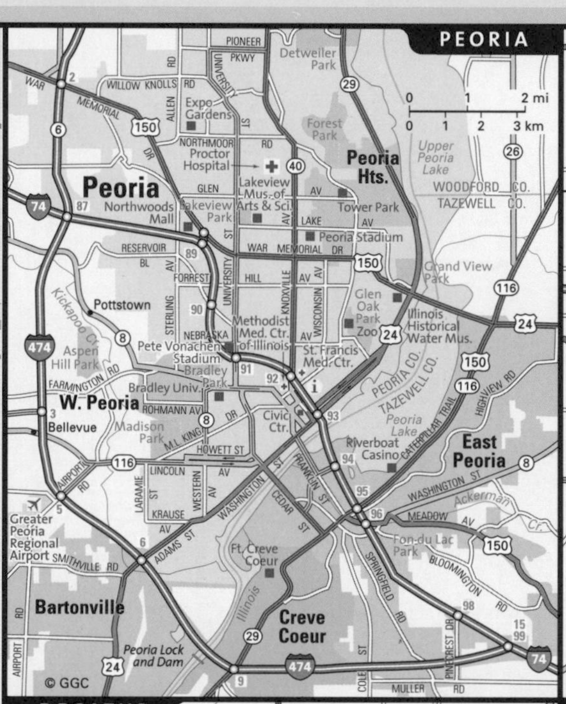
PEORIA
Peoria
Peoria Hts.
W. Peoria
East Peoria
Bartonville
Creve Coeur
© GGC

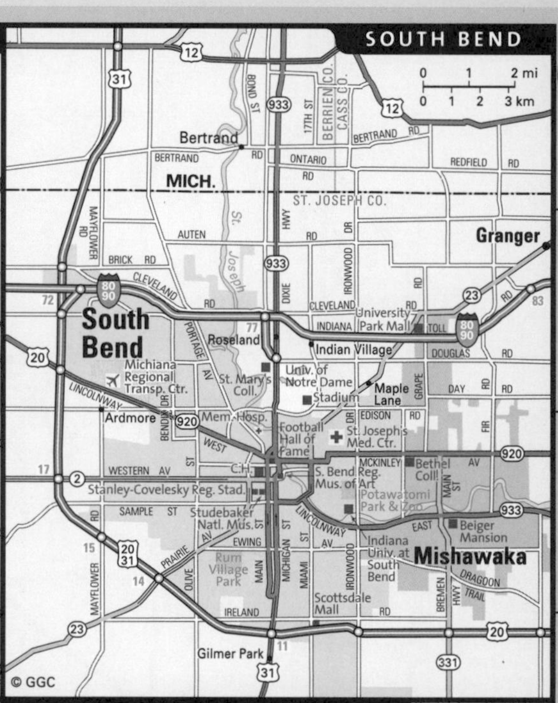
SOUTH BEND
South Bend
Mishawaka
Granger
Bertrand
MICH.
© GGC

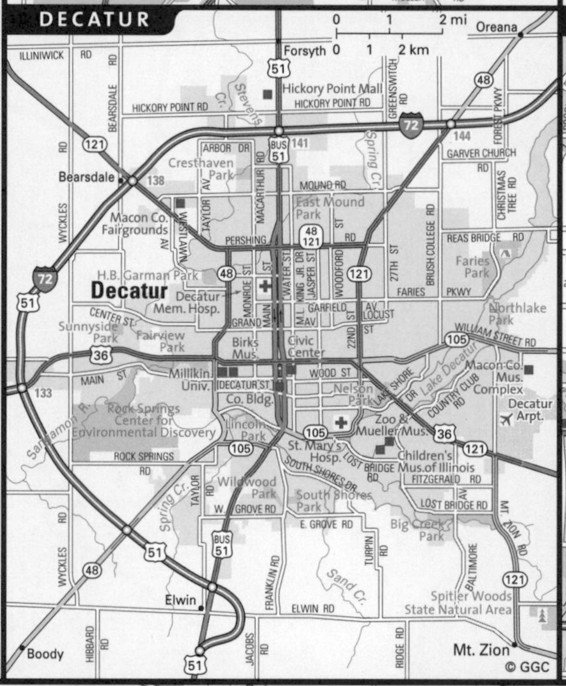
DECATUR
Decatur
Forsyth
Oreana
Mt. Zion
Elwin
Boody
Beardsdale
© GGC

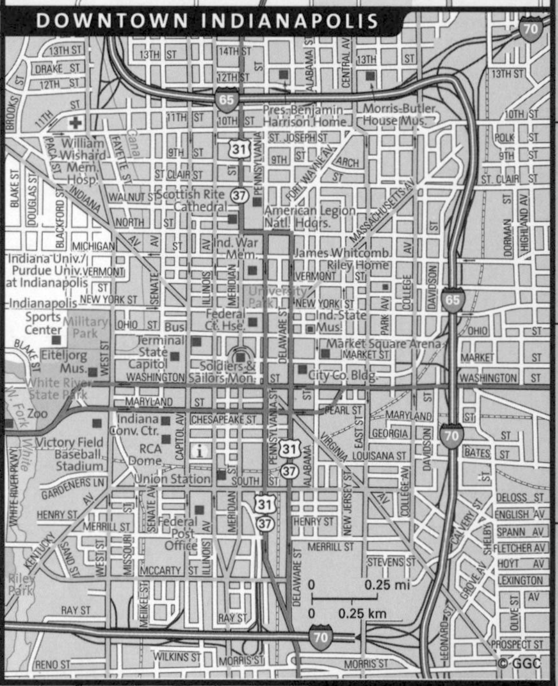
DOWNTOWN INDIANAPOLIS
© GGC

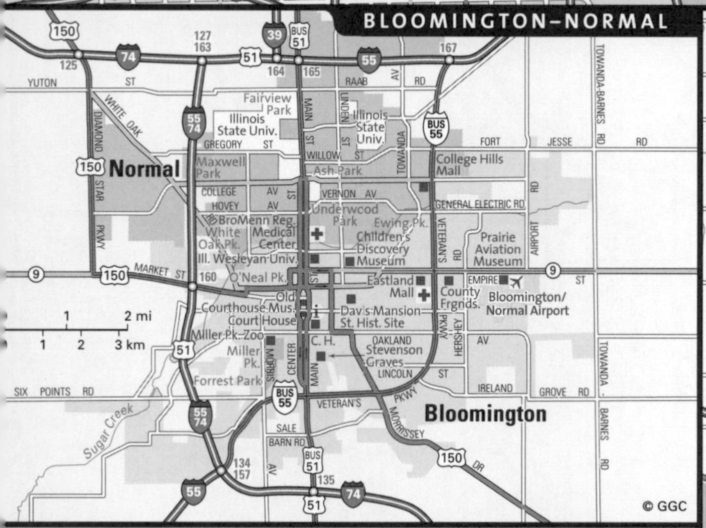
BLOOMINGTON–NORMAL
Normal
Bloomington
© GGC

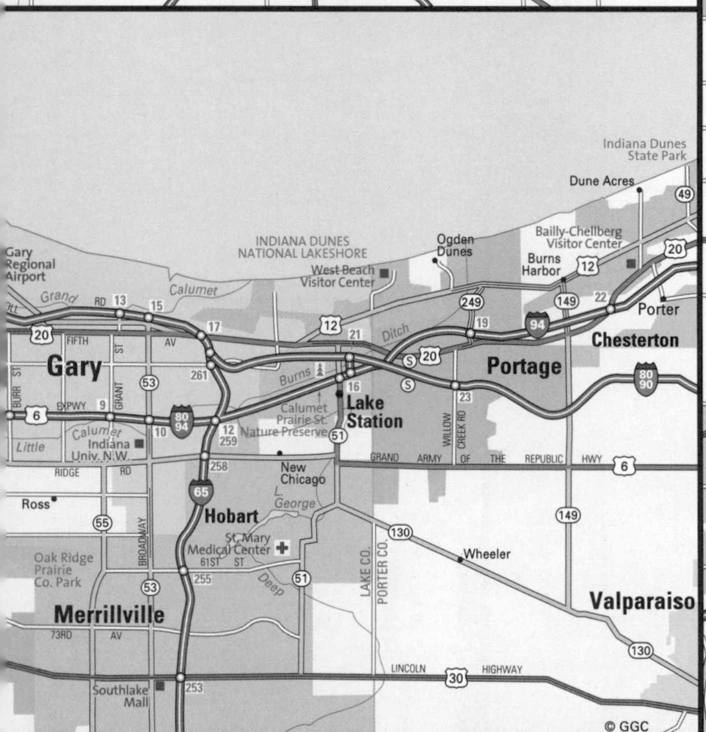
Gary
Portage
Chesterton
Lake Station
Hobart
Merrillville
Valparaiso
INDIANA DUNES NATIONAL LAKESHORE
© GGC

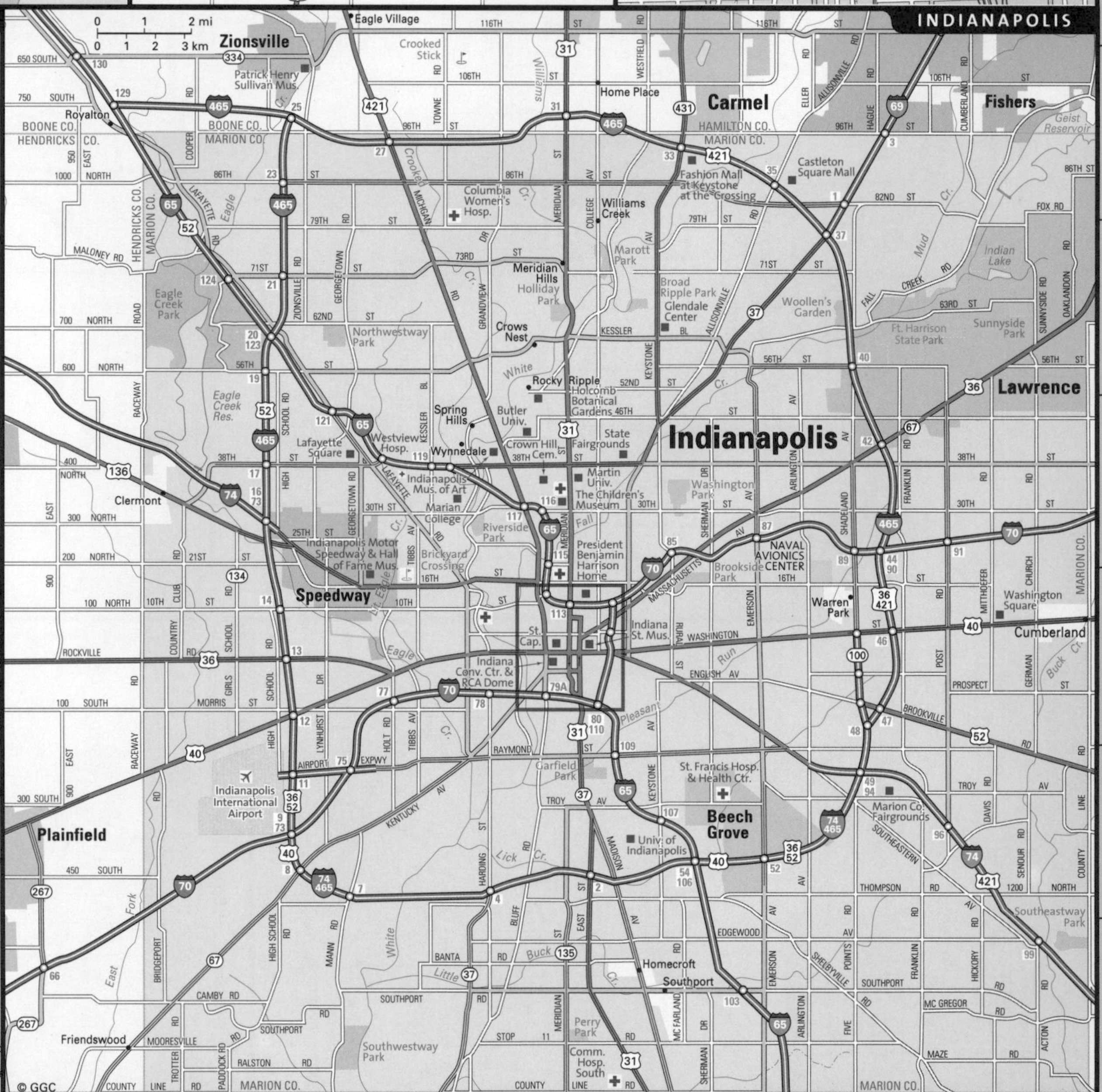
INDIANAPOLIS
Indianapolis
Zionsville
Carmel
Fishers
Lawrence
Speedway
Plainfield
Beech Grove
Cumberland
© GGC

TOURISM:
800.759.9191
ROAD CONDITIONS:
317.232.8300 (NOV–APR)
N
MI 10 20
KM 10 20
FORT WAYNE
ELKHART
LAFAYETTE

TERRE HAUTE
BLOOMINGTON
MUNCIE
EVANSVILLE
© GeoSystems Global Corporation

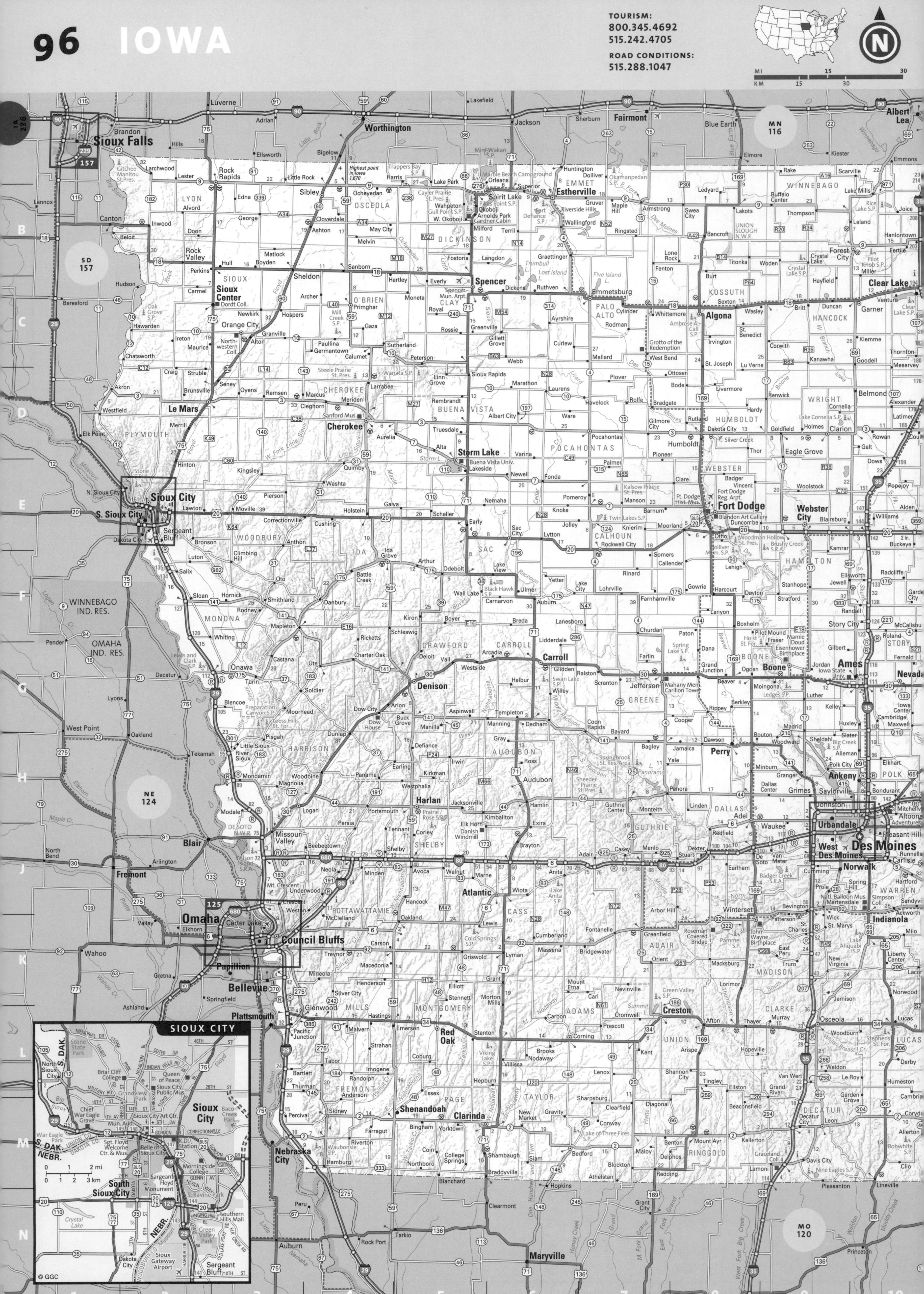
TOURISM:
800.345.4692
515.242.4705
ROAD CONDITIONS:
515.288.1047
MI 15 30
KM 15 30
SIOUX CITY
© GGC
SD 157
MN 116
NE 124
MO 120
Des Moines
Sioux City
Council Bluffs
Omaha
Sioux Falls
Ames
Fort Dodge
Mason City
Highest point in Iowa 1,670

DES MOINES
CEDAR RAPIDS
Cedar Rapids
Davenport
Des Moines
Dubuque
Waterloo
Iowa City
Burlington
Keokuk
© GeoSystems Global Corporation

TOURISM:
800.252.6727
785.296.2009

ROAD CONDITIONS:
800.585.7623 (KS)
785.291.3000

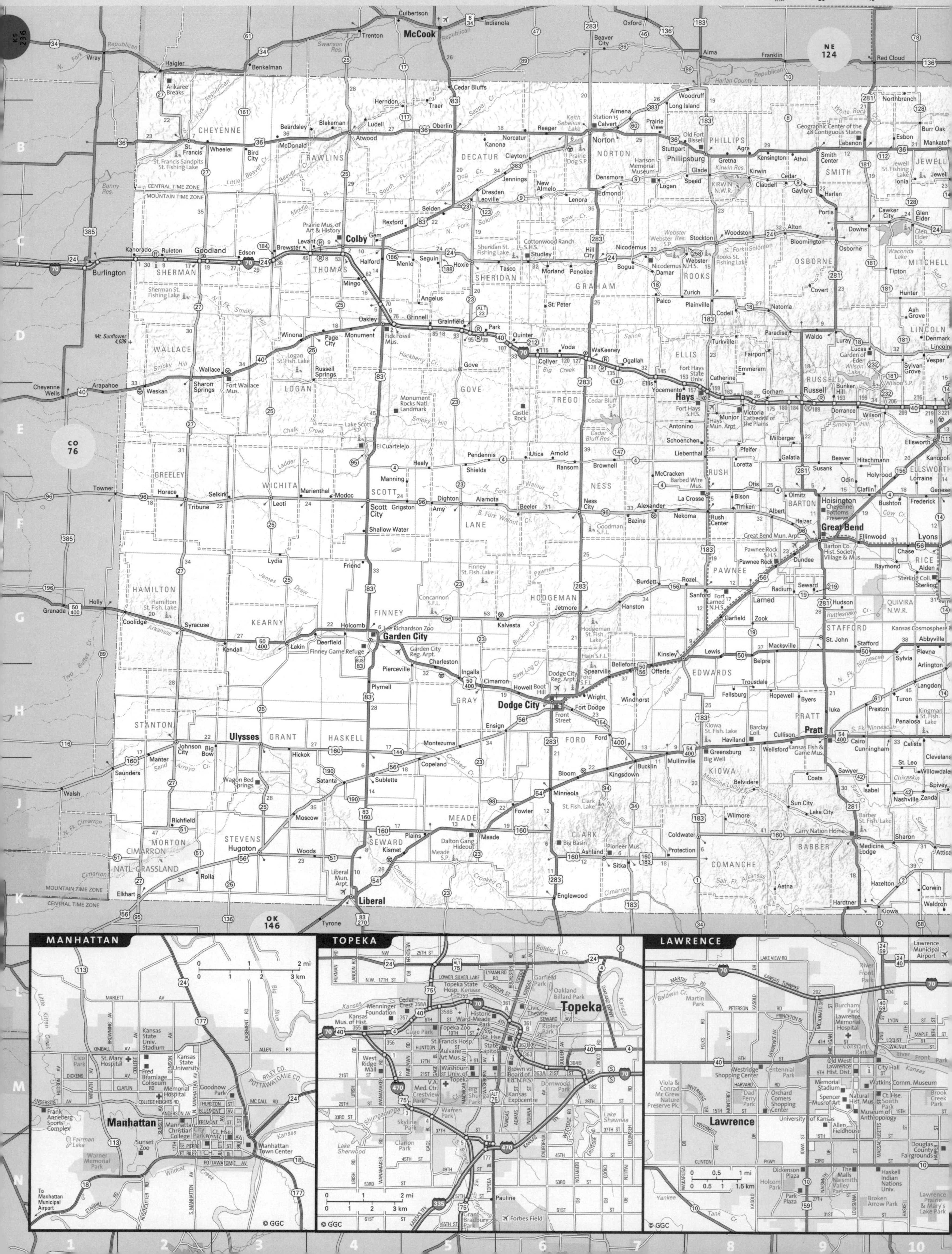
MI 20 40
KM 20 40
CHEYENNE
RAWLINS
DECATUR
NORTON
PHILLIPS
SMITH
JEWELL
SHERMAN
THOMAS
SHERIDAN
GRAHAM
ROOKS
OSBORNE
MITCHELL
WALLACE
LOGAN
GOVE
TREGO
ELLIS
RUSSELL
LINCOLN
ELLSWORTH
GREELEY
WICHITA
SCOTT
LANE
NESS
RUSH
BARTON
RICE
HAMILTON
KEARNY
FINNEY
HODGEMAN
PAWNEE
STAFFORD
EDWARDS
STANTON
GRANT
HASKELL
GRAY
FORD
KIOWA
PRATT
MORTON
STEVENS
SEWARD
MEADE
CLARK
COMANCHE
BARBER
Goodland
Colby
Oakley
Hays
Great Bend
Garden City
Dodge City
Liberal
Ulysses
Pratt
Hugoton
Phillipsburg
Norton
McCook
NE 124
CO 76
OK 146
KS 236
CENTRAL TIME ZONE
MOUNTAIN TIME ZONE
CIMARRON NATL. GRASSLAND
MANHATTAN
Manhattan
TOPEKA
Topeka
LAWRENCE
Lawrence
© GGC

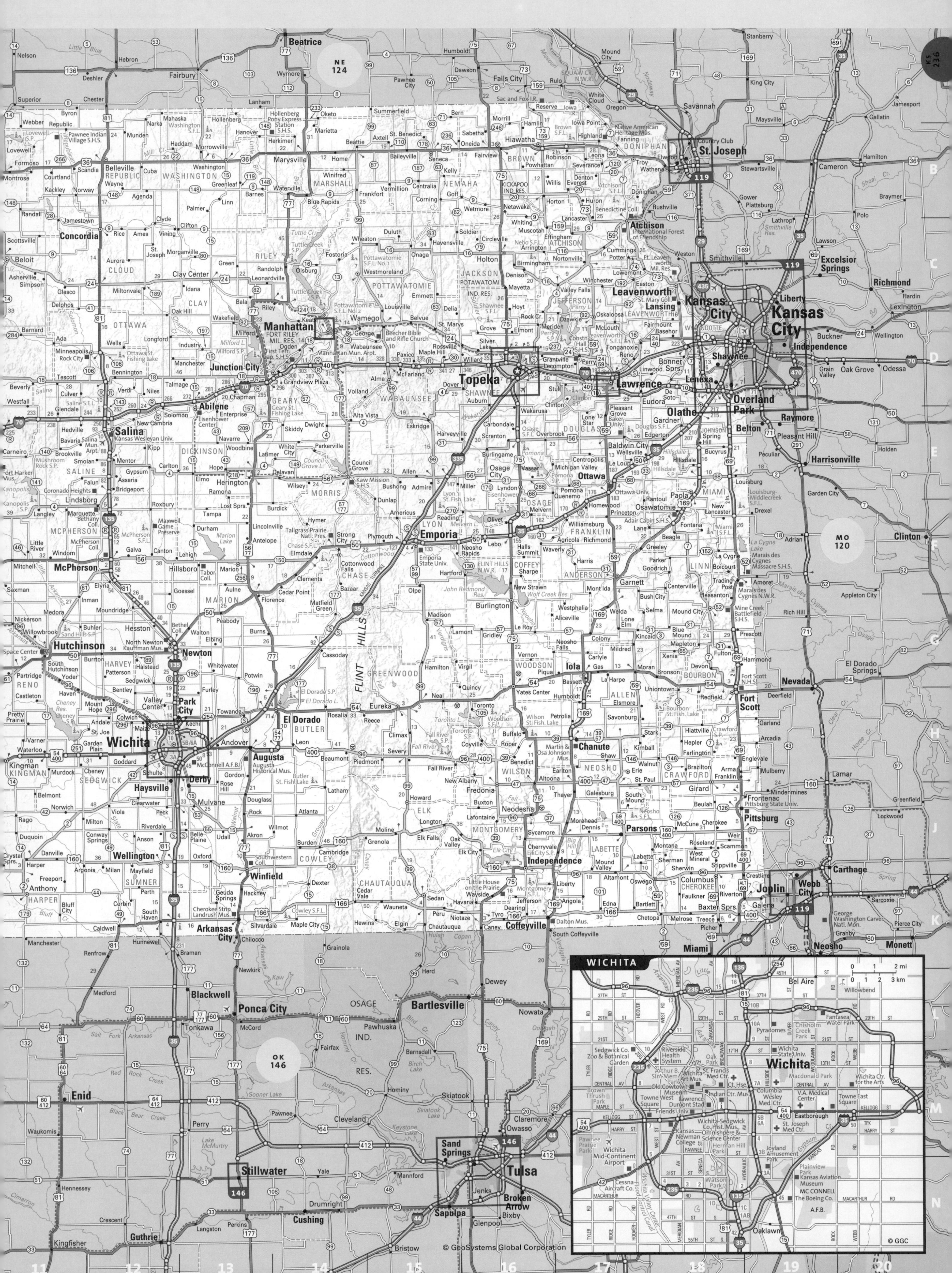

TOURISM:
800.225.8747

ROAD CONDITIONS:
800.459.7623

MI 0 10 20 30
KM 0 10 20 30

OWENSBORO

BOWLING GREEN

LOUISVILLE

WESTERN KENTUCKY

MAMMOTH CAVE NATL. PARK

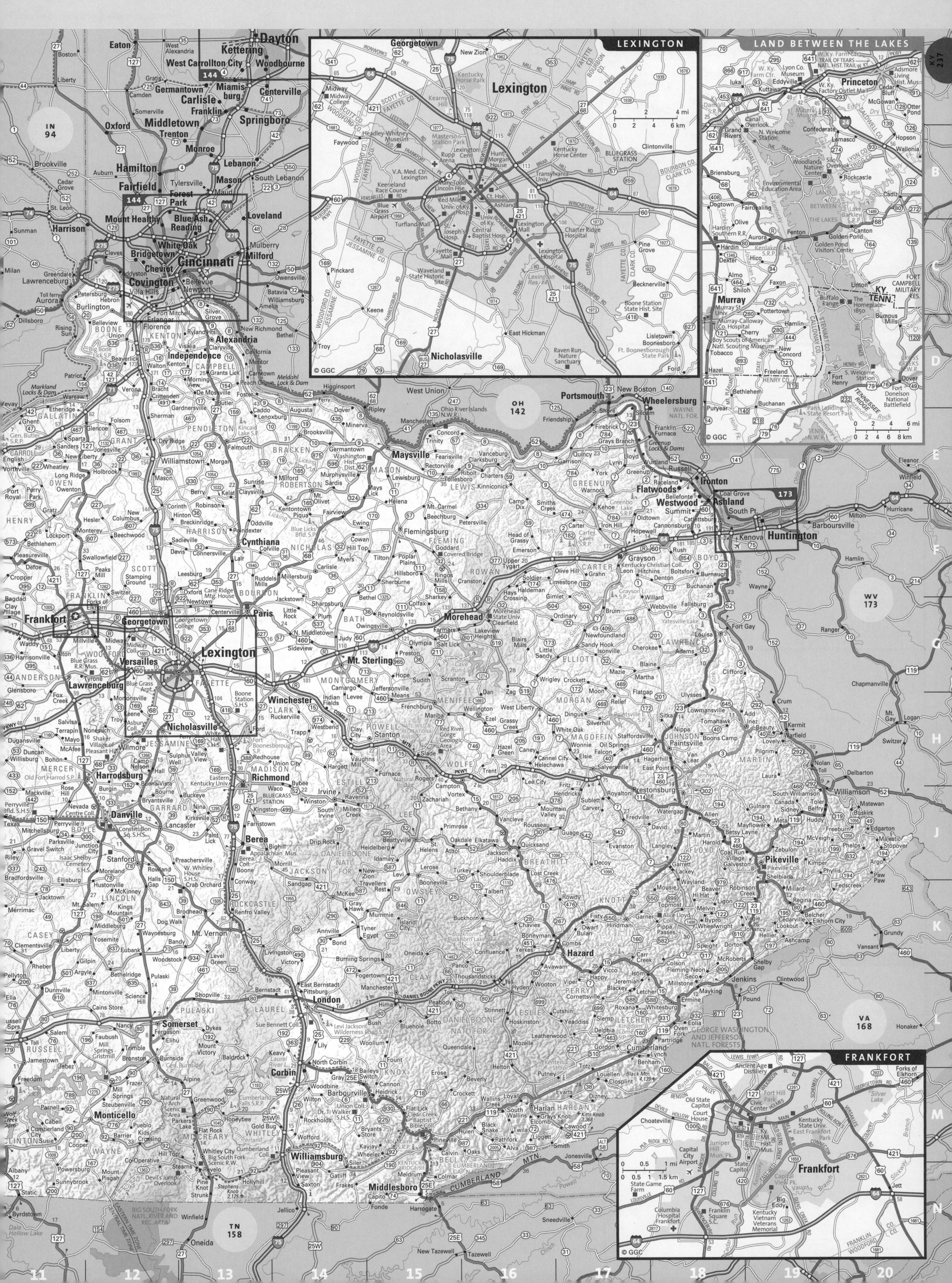
LEXINGTON
LAND BETWEEN THE LAKES
FRANKFORT
Lexington
Frankfort
Louisville
Cincinnati
Covington
Dayton
Kettering
Hamilton
Middletown
Georgetown
Versailles
Nicholasville
Richmond
Winchester
Paris
Maysville
Ashland
Huntington
Portsmouth
Morehead
Mt. Sterling
Danville
Harrodsburg
Lawrenceburg
Berea
London
Corbin
Somerset
Hazard
Pikeville
Middlesboro
Williamsburg
Monticello
Murray
Princeton
IN 94
OH 142
WV 173
VA 168
TN 158
© GGC

TOURISM:
800.695.4064
504.342.8100

ROAD CONDITIONS:
504.379.1541

MI 0 20 40
KM 0 20 40

SHREVEPORT

MONROE

LAKE CHARLES

LAFAYETTE

GULF OF MEXICO

© GGC

NEW ORLEANS
DOWNTOWN NEW ORLEANS
BATON ROUGE
New Orleans
Metairie
Kenner
Chalmette
Baton Rouge
Port Allen
Lafourche
Houma
Thibodaux
Morgan City
Franklin
Jeanerette
Donaldsonville
Gonzales
Plaquemine
Zachary
Baker
Denham Sprs.
Hammond
Ponchatoula
Covington
Mandeville
Slidell
Bogalusa
Picayune
Gulfport
Biloxi
D'Iberville
Ocean Springs
Gautier
Pascagoula
Long Beach
Pass Christian
Bay St. Louis
Waveland
Mobile
Prichard
Saraland
Natchez
Vicksburg
Tallulah
Lake Providence
Winnsboro
Vidalia
Ferriday
New Roads
Raceland
Larose
Cut Off
Lake Pontchartrain
Lake Borgne
Chandeleur Sound
Breton Sound
GULF OF MEXICO
HOMOCHITTO NATL. FOR.
DELTA NATL. FOR.
DE SOTO NATL. FOR.
GULF ISLAND NATL. SEASHORE
BRETON N.W.R.
DELTA N.W.R.
FRENCH QUARTER (VIEUX CARRE)
Louisiana Superdome
Baton Rouge Metropolitan Airport
AR 66
MS 118
AL 60
LA 237
11
12
13
14
15
16
17
18
19
20
B
C
D
E
F
G
H
J
K
L
M
N

TOURISM:
800.533.9595
207.623.0363

ROAD CONDITIONS:
207.287.3427

ACADIA NATIONAL PARK
PORTLAND
LEWISTON–AUBURN
ATLANTIC OCEAN
MOUNT DESERT ISLAND
© GeoSystems Global Corporation

TOURISM:
800.445.4558
410.767.3400

ROAD CONDITIONS:
800.749.0737
301.513.9639

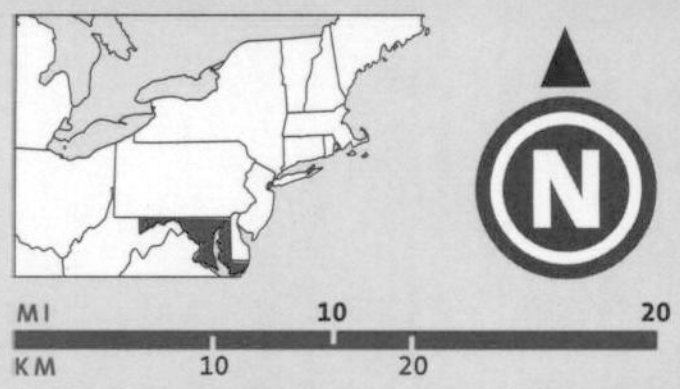

MI 10 20
KM 10 20

WASHINGTON, DC AREA

HAGERSTOWN

FREDERICK

© GGC

Philadelphia
Baltimore
Washington
Annapolis
Dover
Wilmington
CHESAPEAKE BAY
ATLANTIC OCEAN
Delaware Bay
ANNAPOLIS
© GeoSystems Global Corporation

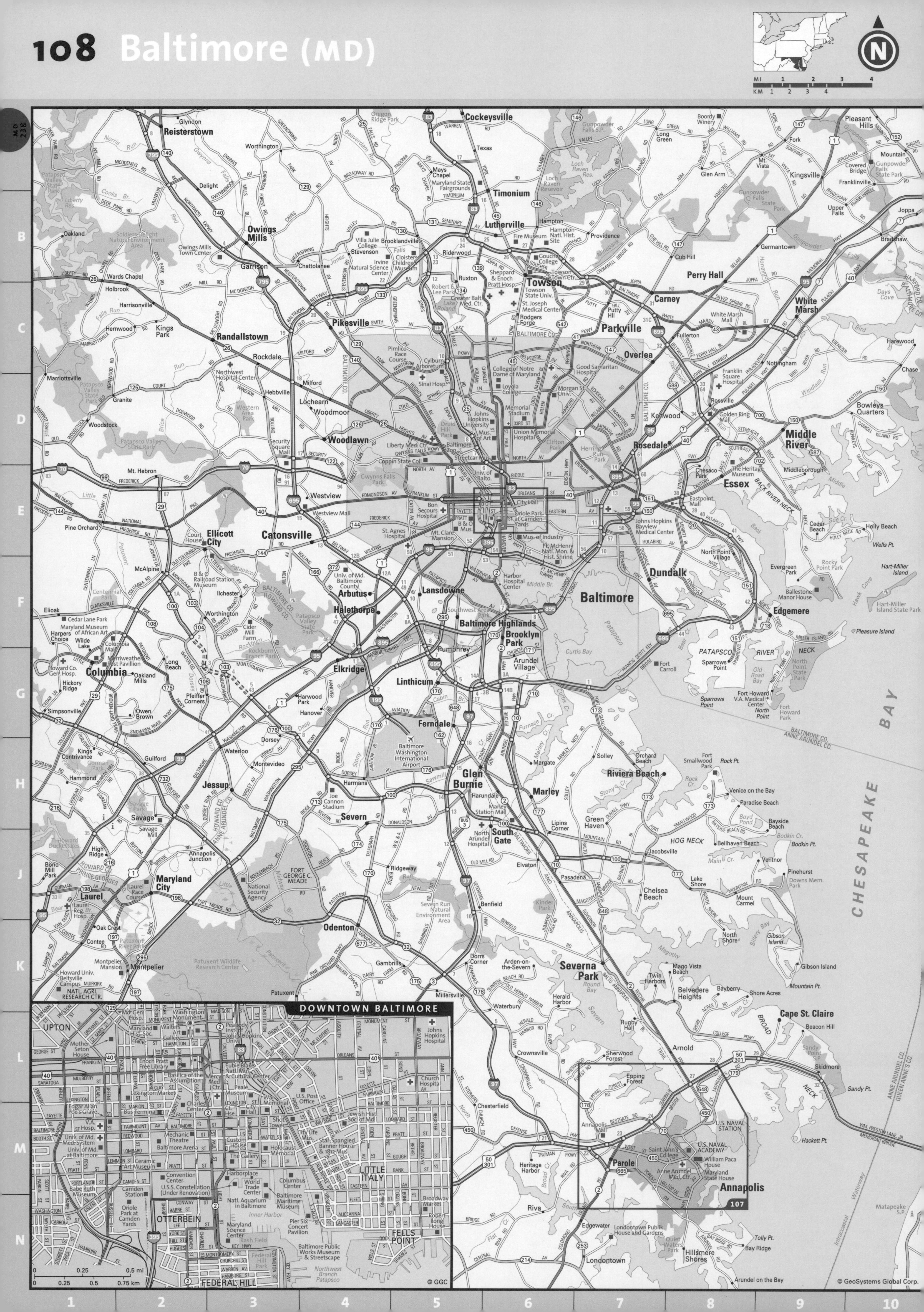

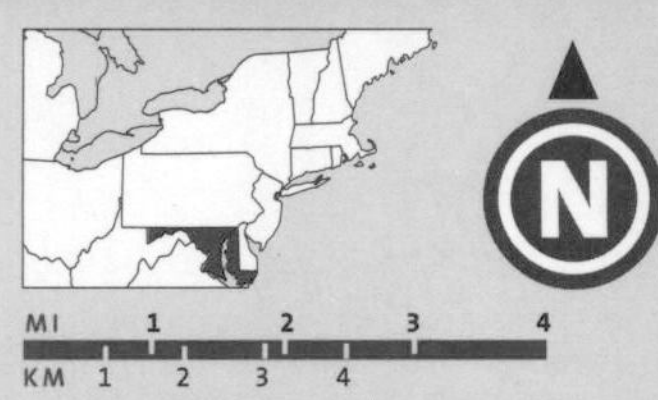

Reisterstown
Glyndon
Worthington
Cockeysville
Texas
Timonium
Mays Chapel
Lutherville
Owings Mills
Garrison
Pikesville
Randallstown
Towson
Perry Hall
Carney
Parkville
Overlea
White Marsh
Kingsville
Long Green
Glen Arm
Fork
Mt. Vista
Pleasant Hills
Joppa
Germantown
Cub Hill
Providence
Rockdale
Milford
Lochearn
Woodmoor
Woodlawn
Hebbville
Granite
Woodstock
Marriottsville
Oakland
Wards Chapel
Holbrook
Harrisonville
Hernwood
Kings Park
Mt. Hebron
Westview
Catonsville
Ellicott City
Pine Orchard
McAlpine
Arbutus
Halethorpe
Lansdowne
Baltimore Highlands
Brooklyn Park
Pumphrey
Arundel Village
Linthicum
Elkridge
Baltimore
Rosedale
Kenwood
Rossville
Middle River
Bowleys Quarters
Essex
Dundalk
Edgemere
Sparrows Point
Fort Carroll
Columbia
Wilde Lake
Harpers Choice
Long Reach
Oakland Mills
Hickory Ridge
Simpsonville
Owen Brown
Pfeiffer Corners
Harwood Park
Hanover
Dorsey
Ferndale
Glen Burnie
Waterloo
Montevideo
Guilford
Kings Contrivance
Hammond
Jessup
Harmans
Severn
Marley
Riviera Beach
Orchard Beach
Solley
Green Haven
Lipins Corner
South Gate
Savage
High Ridge
Bond Mill Park
Annapolis Junction
Maryland City
Laurel
Oak Crest
Contee
Montpelier
Odenton
Gambrills
Benfield
Elvaton
Pasadena
Chelsea Beach
Lake Shore
Mount Carmel
North Shore
Severna Park
Arden-on-the-Severn
Dorrs Corner
Millersville
Patuxent
Waterbury
Herald Harbor
Crownsville
Rugby Hall
Sherwood Forest
Arnold
Cape St. Claire
Skidmore
Epping Forest
Chesterfield
Annapolis
Parole
Heritage Harbor
Riva
Edgewater
Londontown
Hillsmere Shores
Bay Ridge
Arundel on the Bay
CHESAPEAKE BAY

DOWNTOWN BALTIMORE

Upton
Little Italy
Fells Point
Otterbein
Federal Hill

© GGC

© GeoSystems Global Corp.

MI 2 4
KM 2 4

MA 238
Wilmington
Nutting Lake
Lynnfield
Peabody
Beverly
Beverly Harbor
Pinehurst
Reading
Burlington
Wakefield
Salem
Marblehead
Woburn
Bedford
Stoneham
Saugus
Lynn
Swampscott
Lexington
Winchester
Melrose
Malden
Nahant Bay
Nahant
Medford
Arlington
Everett
Revere
Broad Sound
Belmont
Somerville
Chelsea
ATLANTIC OCEAN
Waltham
Winthrop
Massachusetts Bay
Weston
Watertown
Cambridge
Logan International Airport
Boston Harbor
Newton
Boston
Brookline
Hull
Wellesley
Hingham Bay
Needham
Quincy Bay
Quincy
Milton
Dedham
Hingham
Weymouth
Braintree
Randolph
Holbrook
Rockland
Stoughton
Avon
Abington
Brockton
Whitman
Hanson
North Easton
DOWNTOWN BOSTON
CHARLESTOWN
NORTH END
WEST END
BEACON HILL
FINANCIAL DISTRICT
CHINATOWN
SOUTH BOSTON
© GGC
© GeoSystems Global Corp.
B
C
D
E
F
G
H
J
K
L
M
N
1
2
3
4
5
6
7
8
9
10

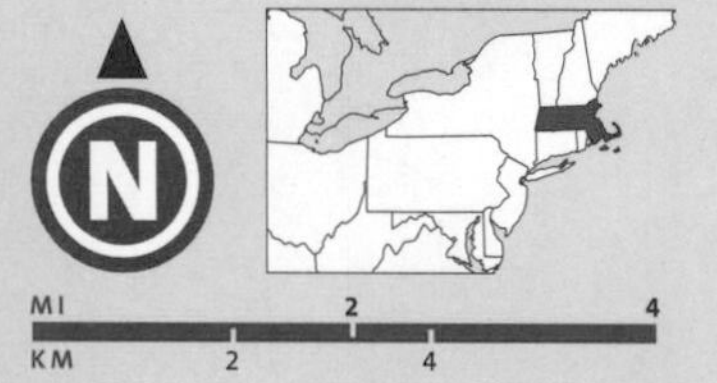

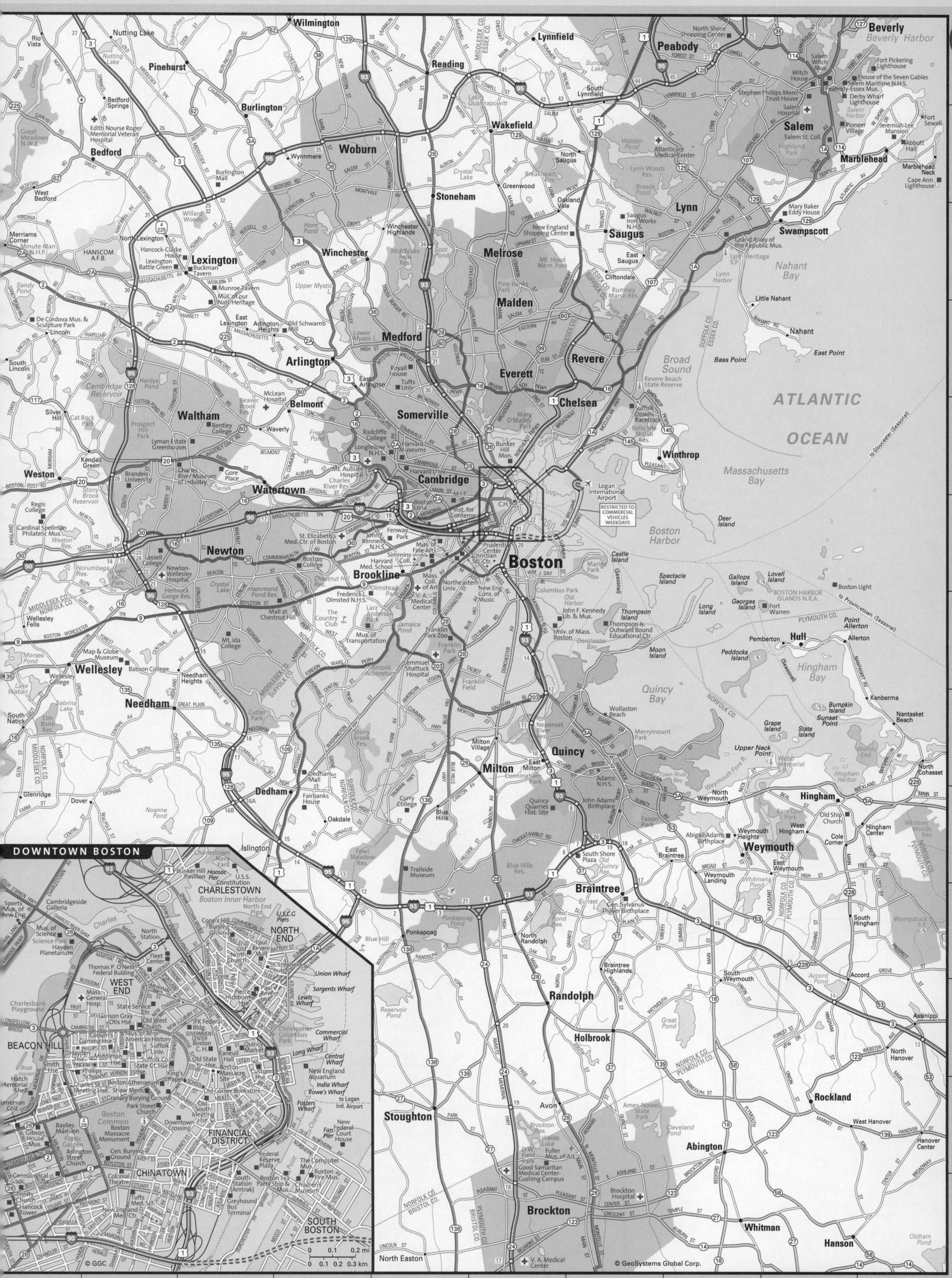

TOURISM:
800.447.6277
617.727.3201

ROAD CONDITIONS:
617.374.1234

MI 5 10 15
KM 5 10 15

SPRINGFIELD

WORCESTER

NEW BEDFORD–FALL RIVER

© GGC

LOWELL
Lowell
Dracut
Chelmsford
North Billerica
Tewksbury
Boston
ATLANTIC OCEAN
Massachusetts Bay
Cape Cod Bay
Cape Cod
Nantucket Sound
Martha's Vineyard
Nantucket Island
Rhode Island Sound
Buzzards Bay
Providence
Worcester
Fall River
New Bedford
Brockton
Plymouth
Lynn
Quincy
Cambridge
Gloucester
Haverhill
Lawrence
Newburyport
Salem
Hyannis
Provincetown
Newport
© GeoSystems Global Corporation
© GGC

TOURISM:
888.784.7328

ROAD CONDITIONS:
313.872.3342

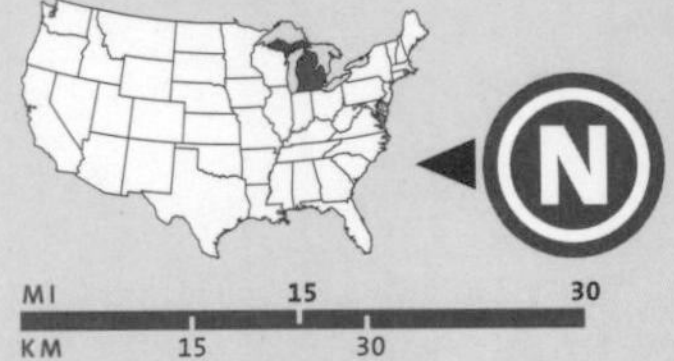

NORTHWESTERN MICHIGAN

SAGINAW

ISLE ROYALE NATIONAL PARK

LAKE HURON
Saginaw Bay
LAKE MICHIGAN
LAKE ERIE
Lake St. Clair
CANADA
UNITED STATES
LANSING
Detroit
Grand Rapids
Lansing
East Lansing
Flint
Saginaw
Bay City
Midland
Kalamazoo
Battle Creek
Jackson
Ann Arbor
Toledo
Port Huron
Sarnia
Windsor
Muskegon
Holland
South Bend
Chicago
Gary
Cadillac
Manistee
Ludington
Sheboygan
Manitowoc
Two Rivers
Mt. Pleasant
Owosso
Pontiac
Warren
Livonia
Dearborn
Westland
Southfield
Sterling Hts.
Ypsilanti
Monroe
Adrian
Hillsdale
Coldwater
Sturgis
Three Rivers
Portage
Niles
Elkhart
Mishawaka
Goshen
Michigan City
La Porte
Benton Harbor
St. Joseph
South Haven
Grand Haven
Hastings
Charlotte
Ionia
Greenville
Alma
St. Johns
Howell
Brighton
Marshall
Albion
Angola
Wauseon
Port Clinton
Kingsville
Leamington
Tecumseh
Essex
Wallaceburg
Marysville
St. Clair
Lapeer
Fenton
Bad Axe
Caro
Vassar

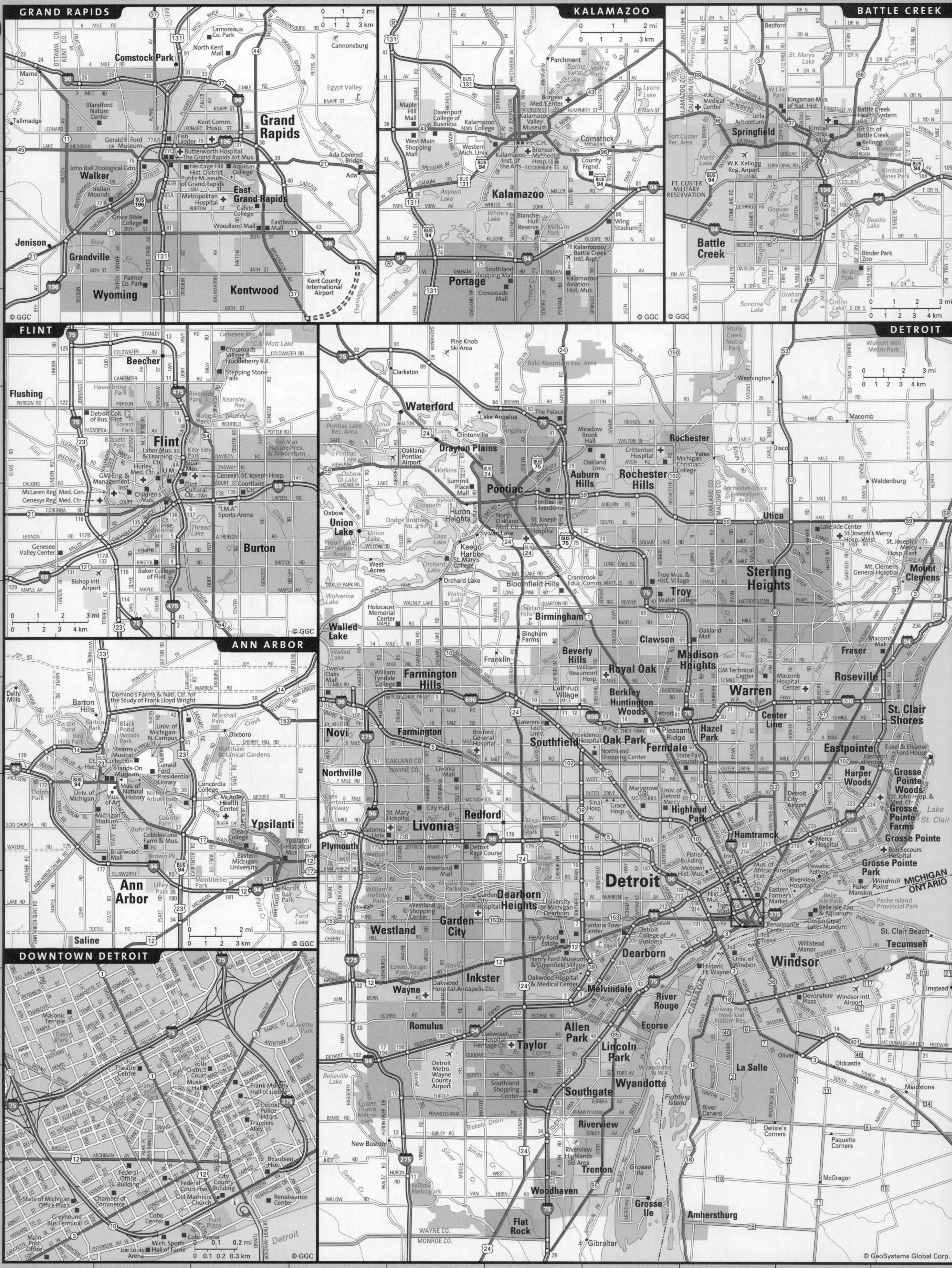

GRAND RAPIDS

KALAMAZOO

BATTLE CREEK

FLINT

DETROIT

ANN ARBOR

DOWNTOWN DETROIT

N
MI 1 2 3
KM 1 2 3 4

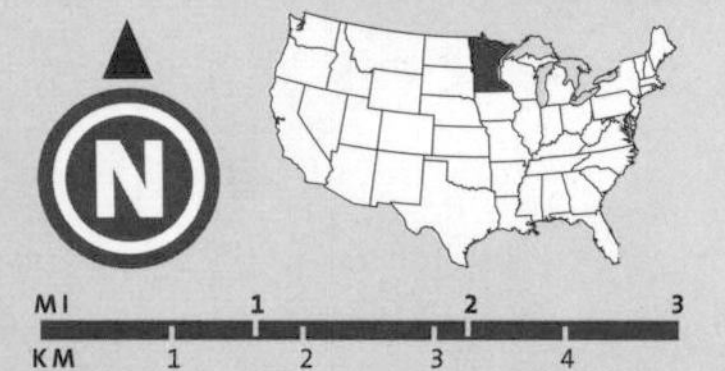

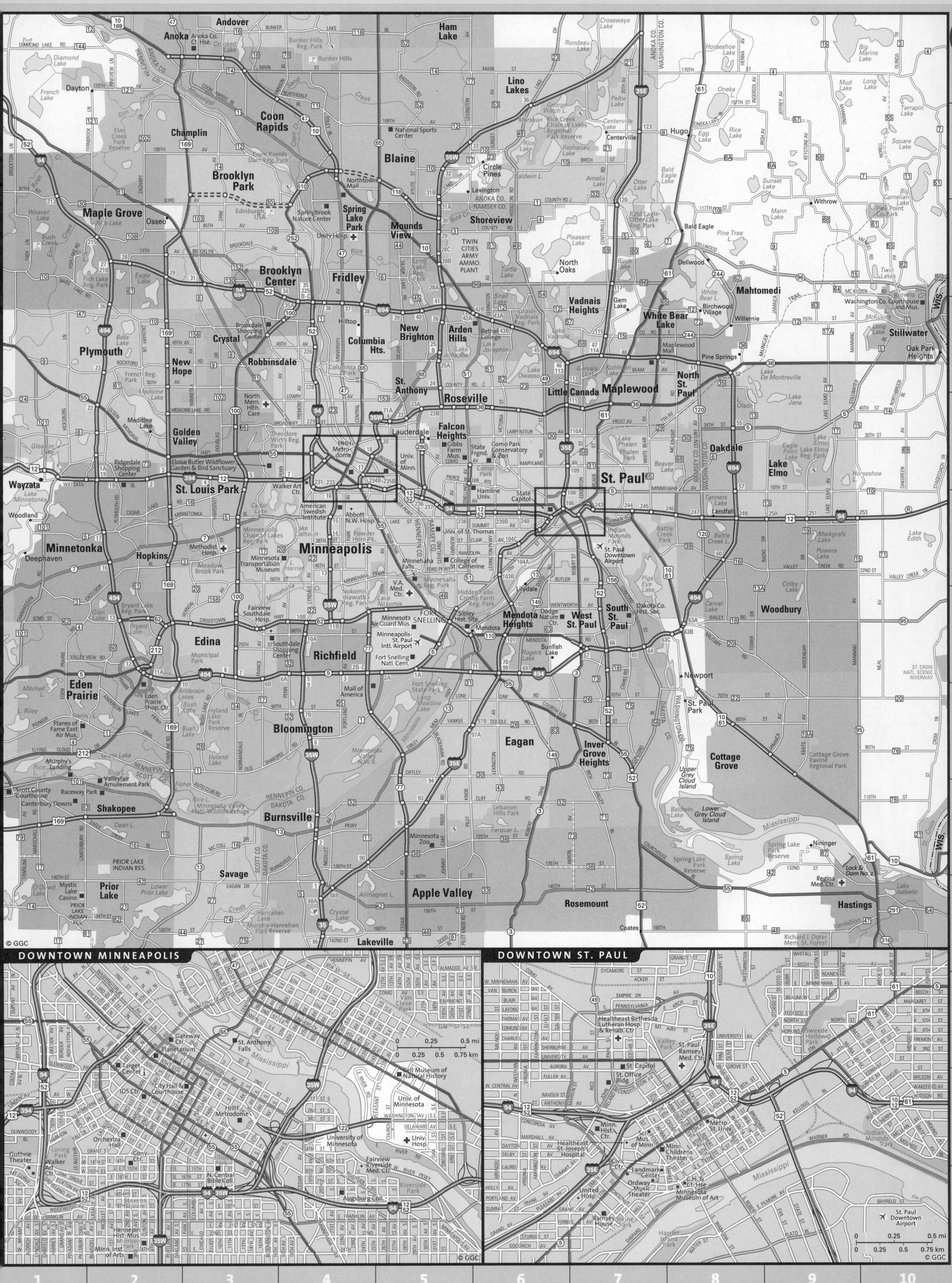

Andover
Anoka
Ham Lake
Lino Lakes
Hugo
Coon Rapids
Champlin
Dayton
Blaine
Brooklyn Park
Maple Grove
Osseo
Spring Lake Park
Mounds View
Shoreview
North Oaks
Brooklyn Center
Fridley
Mahtomedi
Vadnais Heights
White Bear Lake
Stillwater
Oak Park Heights
Plymouth
Crystal
New Hope
Robbinsdale
Columbia Hts.
New Brighton
Arden Hills
St. Anthony
Roseville
Little Canada
Maplewood
North St. Paul
Golden Valley
Falcon Heights
Oakdale
Lake Elmo
Wayzata
St. Louis Park
St. Paul
Minnetonka
Hopkins
Minneapolis
Deephaven
Woodbury
Mendota Heights
West St. Paul
South St. Paul
Edina
Richfield
Eden Prairie
Bloomington
Eagan
Inver Grove Heights
Newport
St. Paul Park
Cottage Grove
Shakopee
Burnsville
Savage
Prior Lake
Apple Valley
Rosemount
Hastings
Lakeville
Coates
Mississippi
WIS.
© GGC
DOWNTOWN MINNEAPOLIS
DOWNTOWN ST. PAUL
0 0.25 0.5 0.75 mi
0 0.25 0.5 0.75 km
0.5 mi
1 2 3 4 5 6 7 8 9 10
B C D E F G H J K L M N

TOURISM:
800.657.3700
612.296.5029

ROAD CONDITIONS:
800.542.0220
612.405.6030

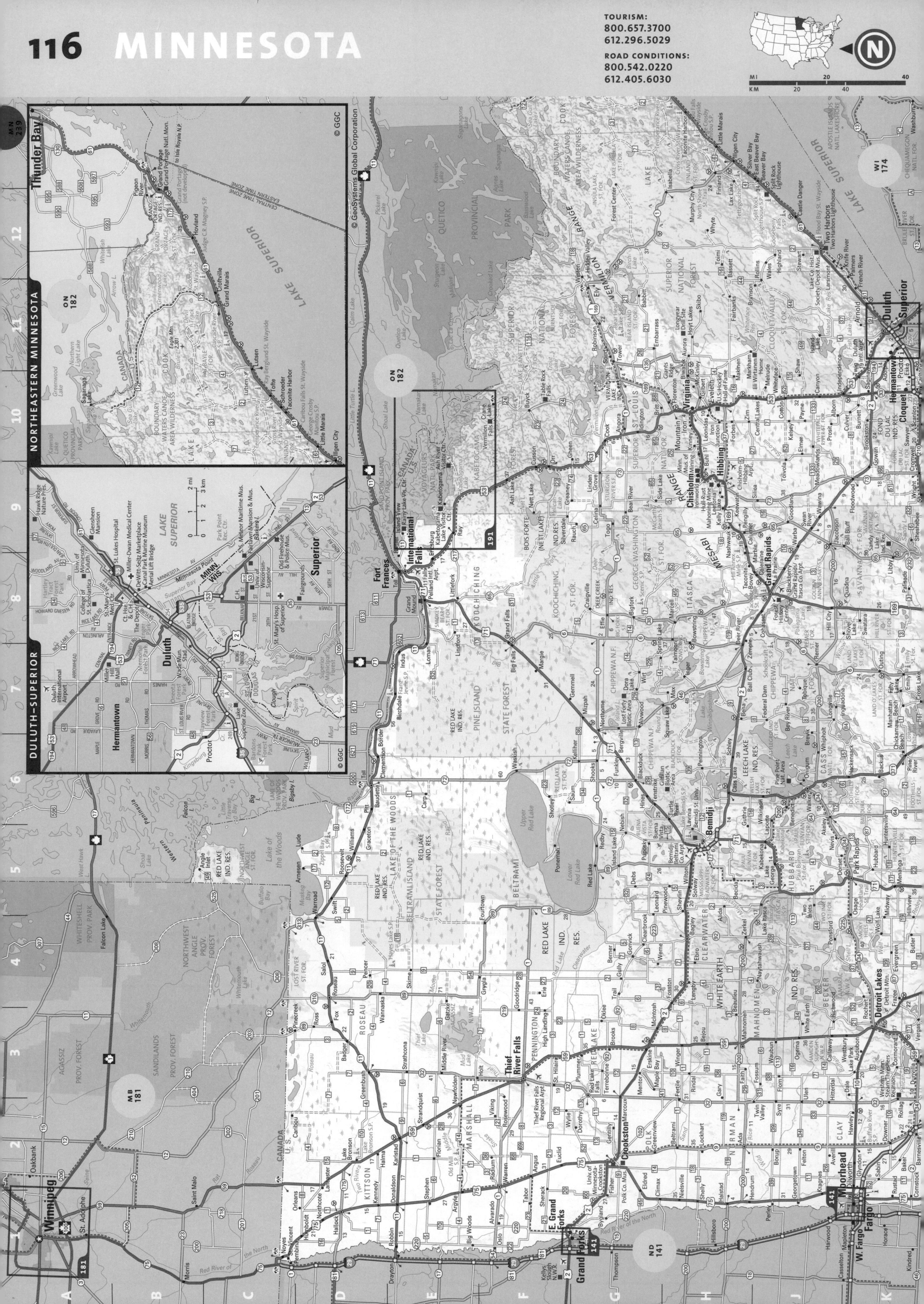

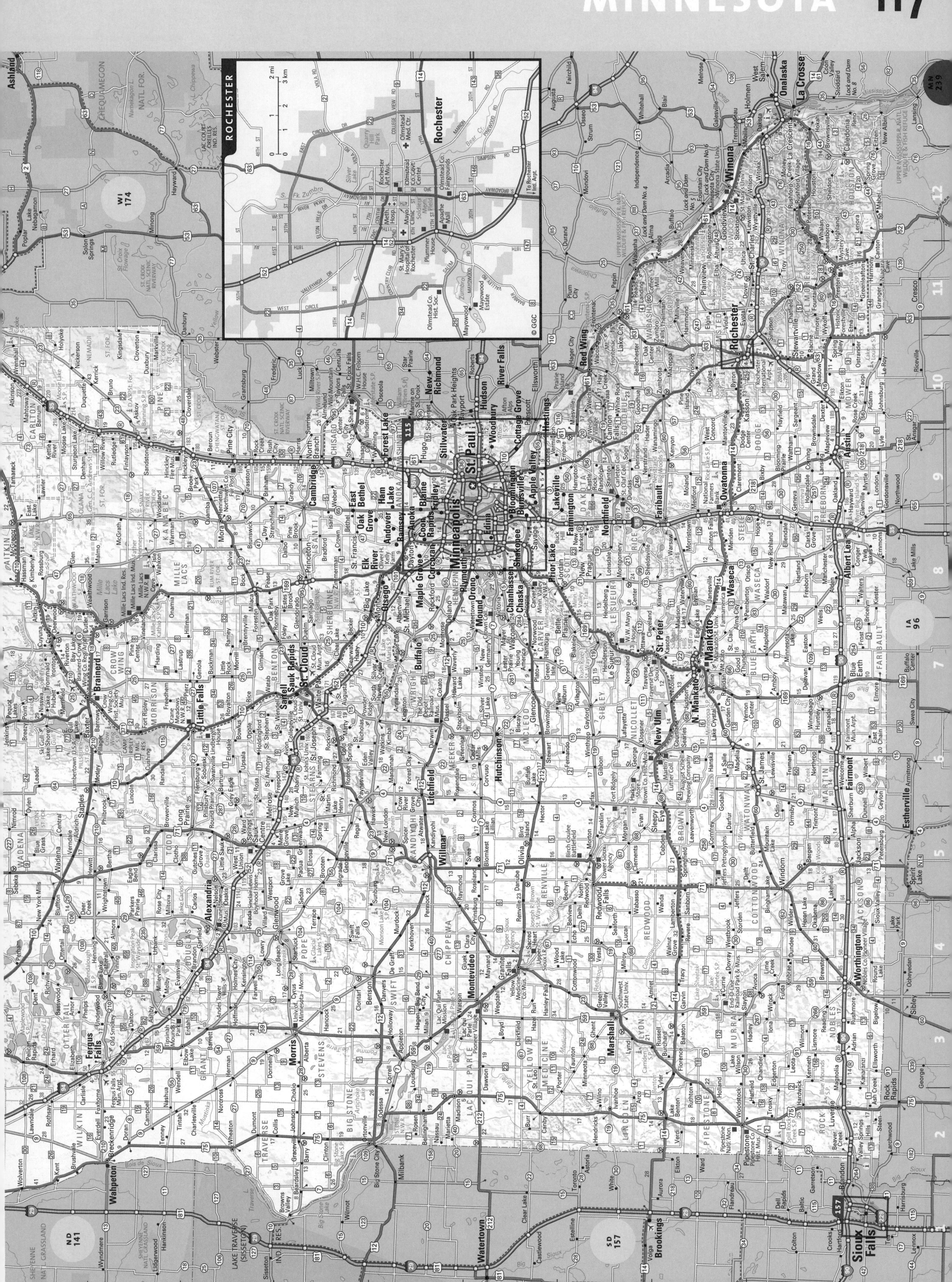
ROCHESTER
Rochester
Minneapolis
St. Paul
St. Cloud
Duluth
Mankato
Winona
La Crosse
Sioux Falls
Fergus Falls
Alexandria
Brainerd
Willmar
Marshall
Worthington
Albert Lea
Austin
Owatonna
Faribault
Red Wing
Hastings
Stillwater
Hudson
Little Falls
Morris
Montevideo
Hutchinson
Litchfield
New Ulm
Fairmont
Watertown
Brookings
Wahpeton
Breckenridge
ND 141
SD 157
IA 96
WI 174
MN 239
© GGC

TOURISM:
800.927.6378
601.359.3297

ROAD CONDITIONS:
601.987.1212

MI 0 25 50
KM 0 25 50

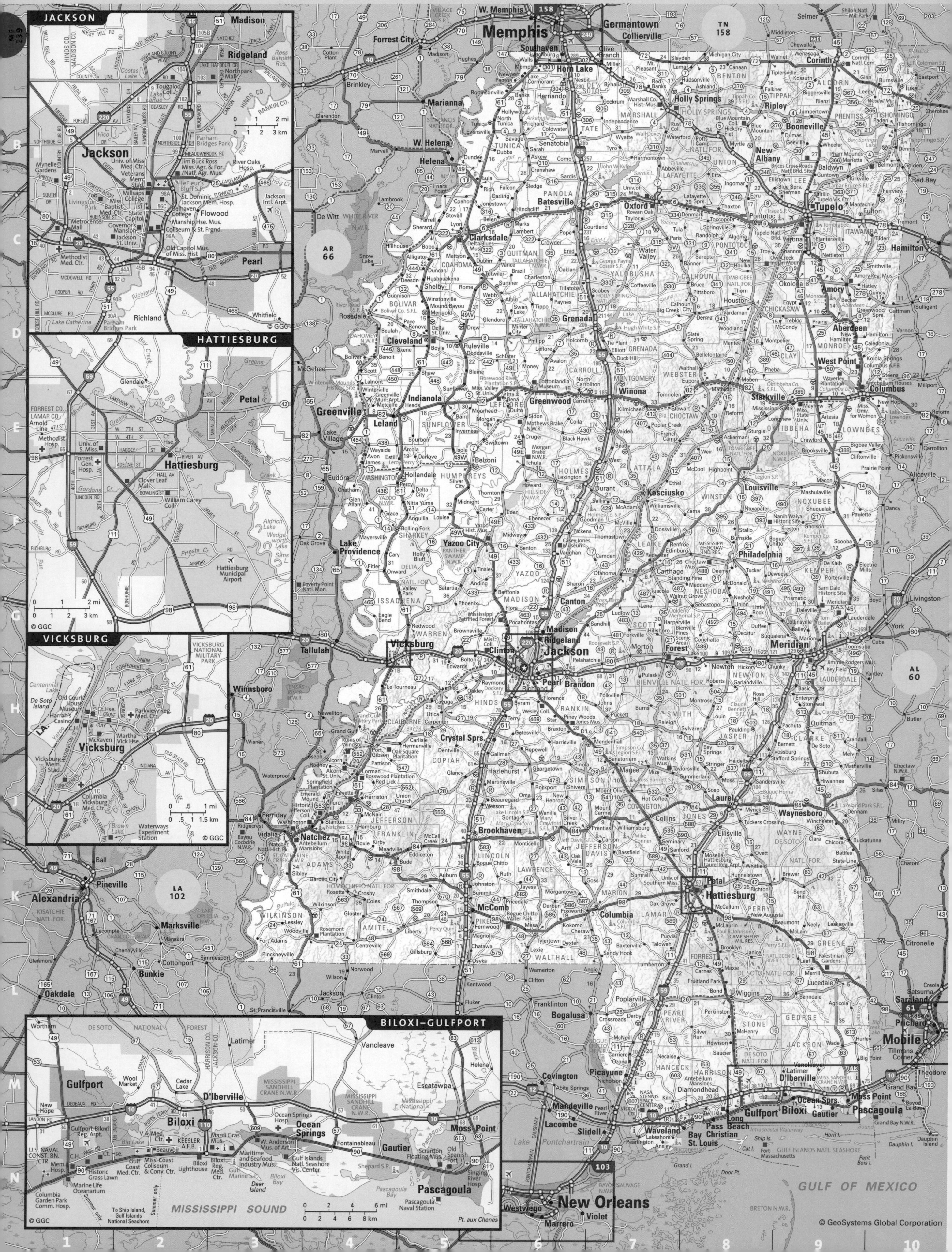

JACKSON

HATTIESBURG

VICKSBURG

BILOXI-GULFPORT

GULF OF MEXICO

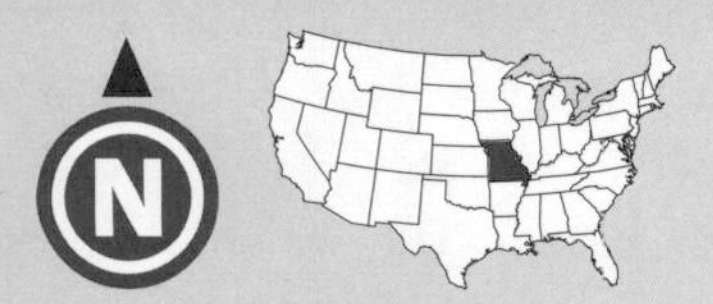

KANSAS CITY

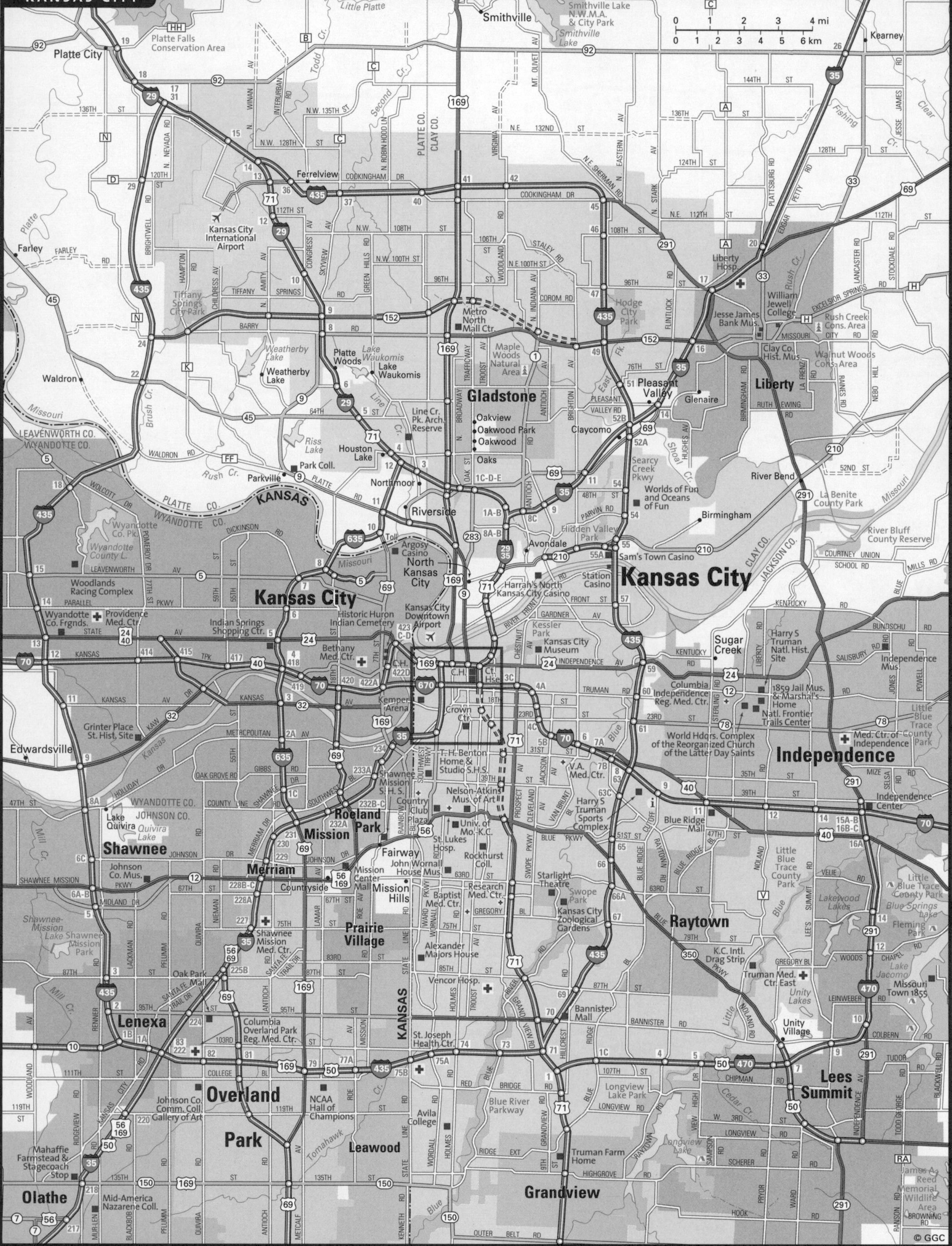

DOWNTOWN KANSAS CITY

ST. JOSEPH

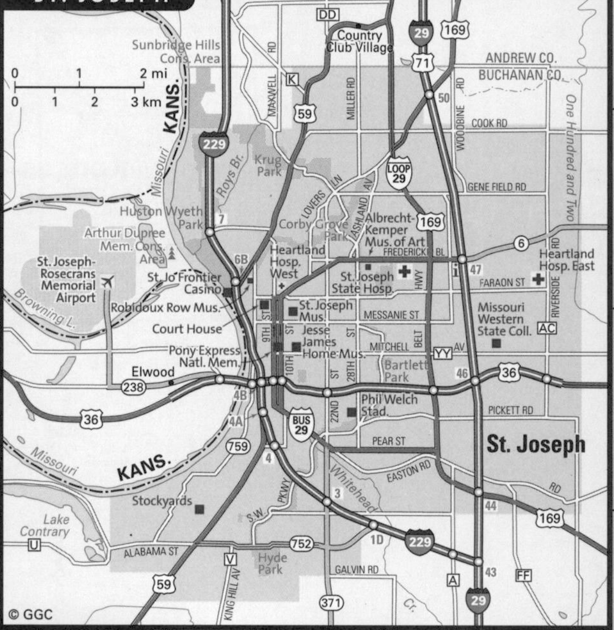

JOPLIN

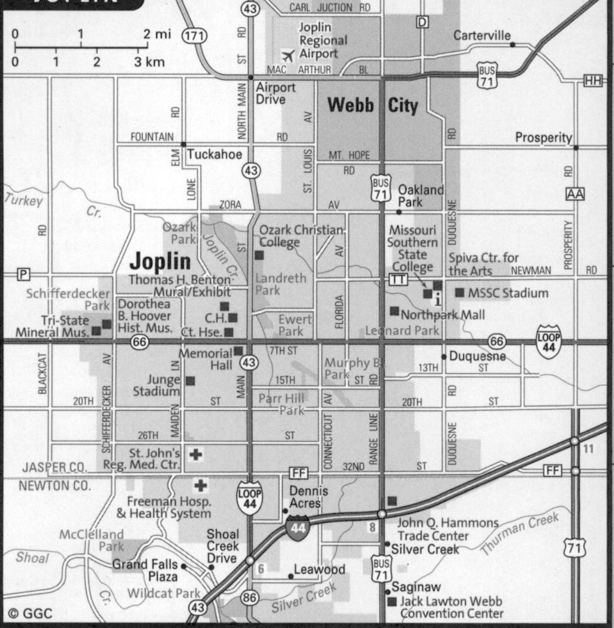

BRANSON

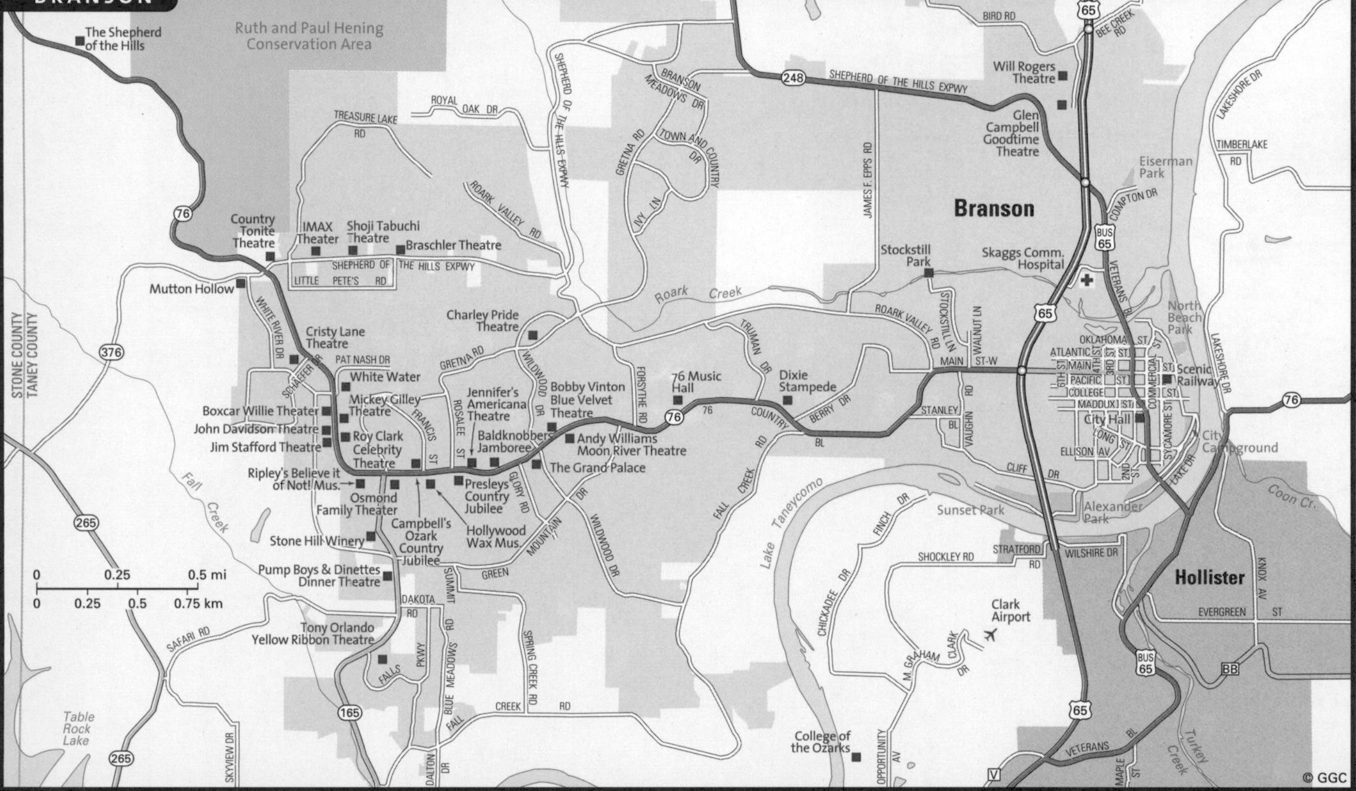

SPRINGFIELD

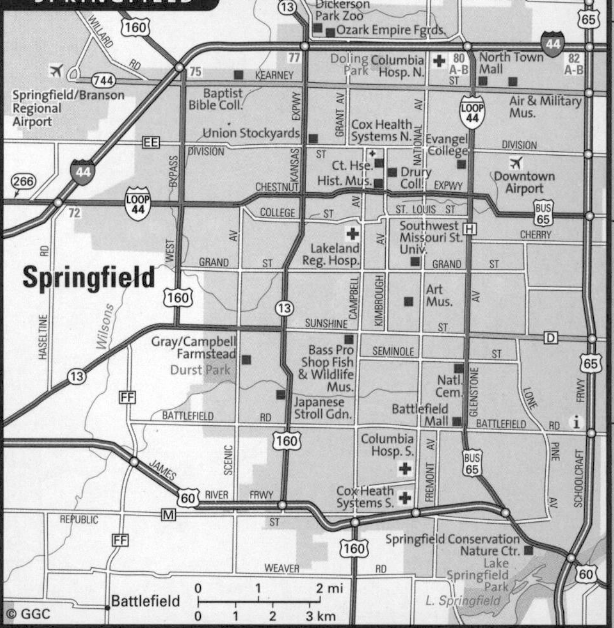

120
MISSOURI
TOURISM:
800.877.1234
573.751.4133
ROAD CONDITIONS:
800.222.6400 (MO)
573.526.8828
N
MI 20 40
KM 20 40

ST. LOUIS
DOWNTOWN ST. LOUIS
JEFFERSON CITY
COLUMBIA
St. Louis
St. Charles
St. Peters
Florissant
Chesterfield
Kirkwood
Webster Groves
East St. Louis
Belleville
Granite City
Alton
Edwardsville
Collinsville
Jefferson City
Columbia
Cape Girardeau
Carbondale
Poplar Bluff
Sikeston
© GeoSystems Global Corporation

TOURISM:
800.847.4868
406.444.2654

ROAD CONDITIONS:
800.332.6171
406.444.6339

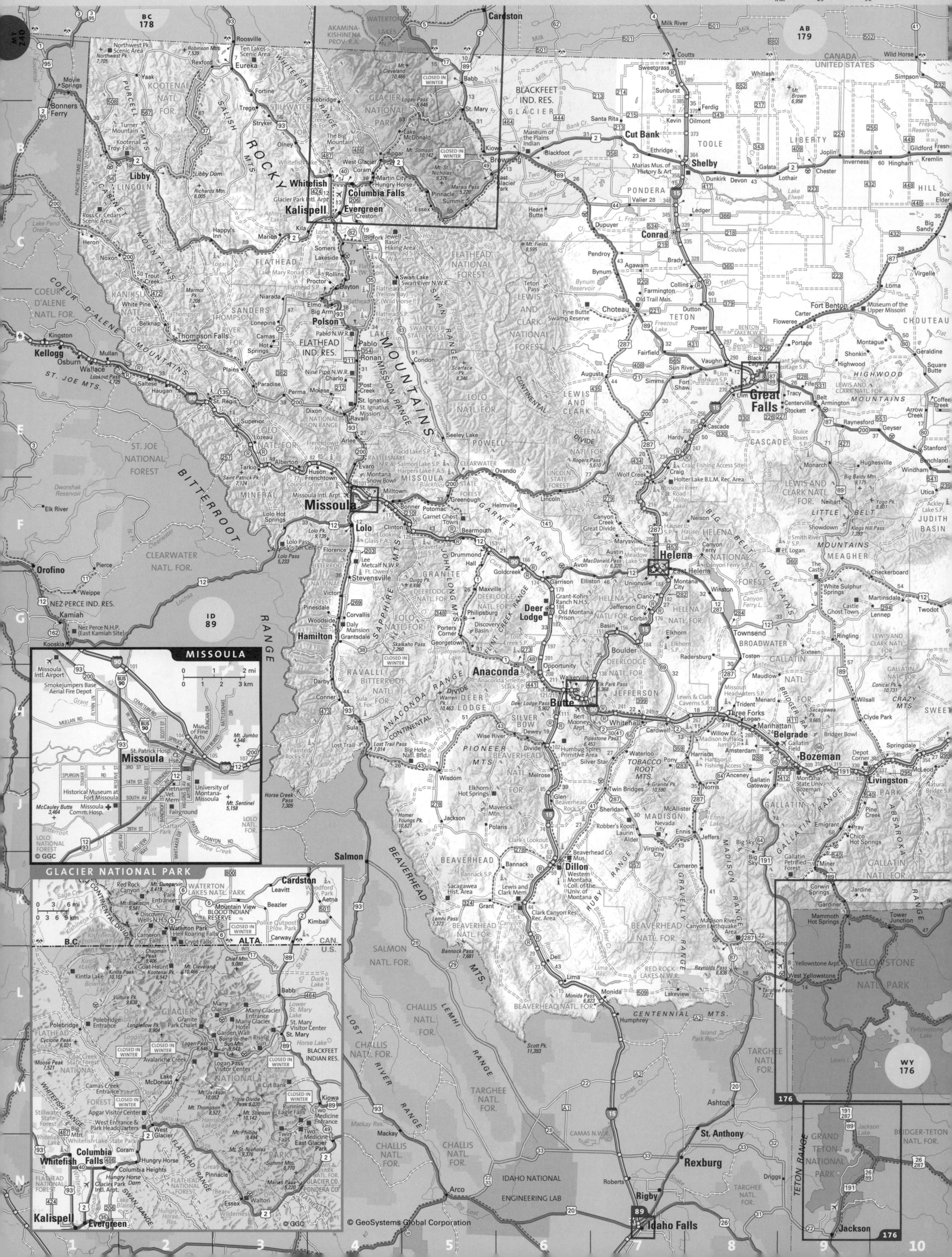

MI 0 25 50
KM 0 25 50

MISSOULA

GLACIER NATIONAL PARK

Havre
Chinook
Malta
Glasgow
Wolf Point
Scobey
Plentywood
Williston
Sidney
Circle
Jordan
Glendive
Lewistown
Roundup
Miles City
Baker
Forsyth
Hardin
Billings
Laurel
Colstrip
Broadus
Red Lodge
Sheridan
Powell
Cody
Belle Fourche
FORT PECK IND. RES.
FORT BELKNAP IND. RES.
CROW INDIAN RESERVATION
NORTHERN CHEYENNE INDIAN RES.
CHARLES M. RUSSELL NATIONAL WILDLIFE REFUGE
CENTRAL TIME ZONE
MOUNTAIN TIME ZONE
CANADA
UNITED STATES
BUTTE
HELENA
GREAT FALLS
BILLINGS
Butte
Helena
Great Falls
© GGC

TOURISM:
800.228.4307
402.471.3796

ROAD CONDITIONS:
800.906.9069 (NE)
402.471.4533

ROAD CONSTRUCTION:
402.479.4512

GRAND ISLAND
LINCOLN
OMAHA–COUNCIL BLUFFS
Grand Island
Lincoln
Omaha
Council Bluffs
Sioux City
Norfolk
Columbus
Fremont
Kearney
Hastings
Beatrice
Yankton
SD 157
IA 96
MO 120
KS 98

TOURISM:
800.638.2328

ROAD CONDITIONS:
702.486.3116
(SOUTH—LAS VEGAS)
702.793.1313
(NORTHWEST—RENO)
702.738.8888
(NORTHEAST—ELKO)

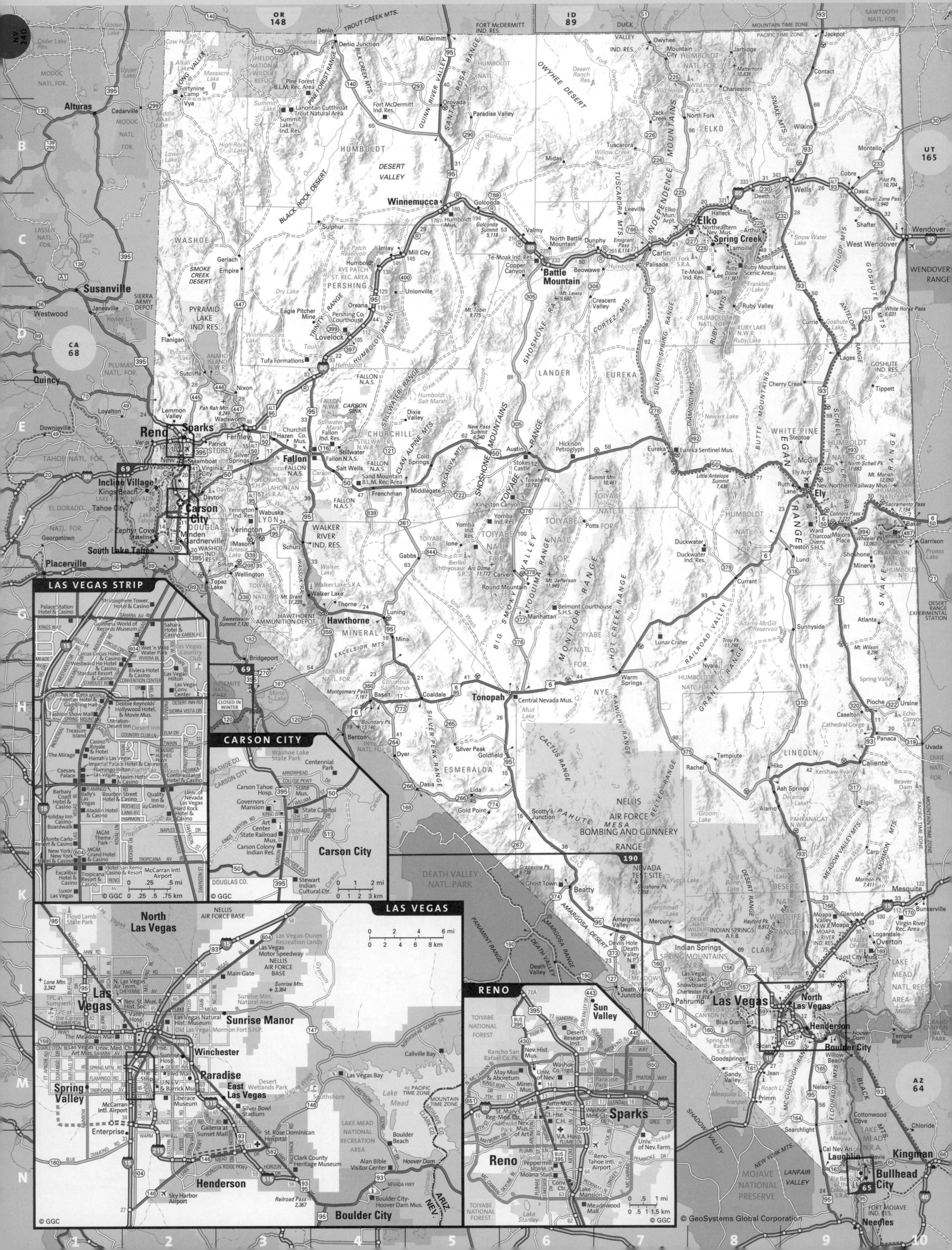

TOURISM:
800.386.4664
603.271.2666

ROAD CONDITIONS:
800.918.9993 (NH)
603.271.6900

MI 20 40
KM 20 40

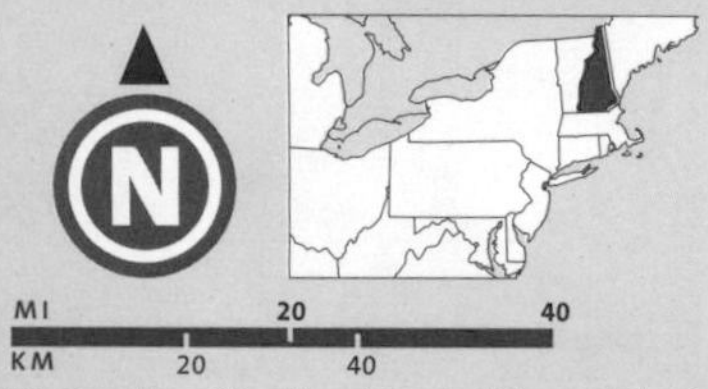

ROCHESTER

PORTSMOUTH

CONCORD

MANCHESTER

NASHUA

ATLANTIC OCEAN

TOURISM:
800.537.7397
609.292.2470

ROAD CONDITIONS:
732.247.0900
(NJ TURNPIKE)
732.727.5929
(GARDEN STATE PARKWAY)

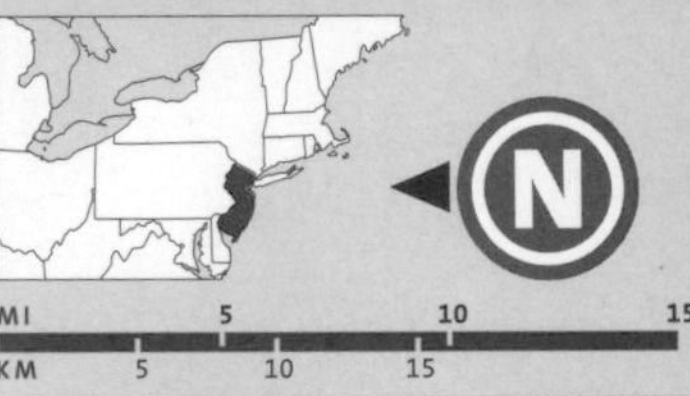

MI 0 5 10 15
KM 0 5 10 15

ATLANTIC CITY
DOWNTOWN ATLANTIC CITY
ATLANTIC OCEAN
DELAWARE BAY
Philadelphia
Camden
Wilmington
Dover
Atlantic City
Vineland
Millville
Bridgeton
Cape May
PINE BARRENS
© GeoSystems Global Corporation
© GGC
PA 150
DE 80

TOURISM:
800.545.2040
800.733.6396
ROAD CONDITIONS:
800.432.4269
505.827.5118
MI 25 50
KM 25 50
N
NM 241
OK 146
TX 160
CO 76
UT 165
AZ 64
CENTRAL TIME ZONE
MOUNTAIN TIME ZONE
Santa Fe
Albuquerque
Las Vegas
Raton
Clayton
Tucumcari
Clovis
Portales
Roswell
Santa Rosa
Fort Sumner
Taos
Espanola
Los Alamos
Farmington
Aztec
Bloomfield
Shiprock
Kirtland
Gallup
Grants
Zuni Pueblo
Socorro
Belen
Los Lunas
Rio Rancho
Bernalillo
Moriarty
Truth or Consequences
Ruidoso
Carrizozo
Durango
Cortez
Trinidad
Window Rock
Ft. Defiance
UNION
HARDING
COLFAX
MORA
SAN MIGUEL
QUAY
CURRY
ROOSEVELT
GUADALUPE
DE BACA
CHAVES
LINCOLN
TORRANCE
VALENCIA
SOCORRO
CATRON
SANDOVAL
McKINLEY
SAN JUAN
RIO ARRIBA
TAOS
CIBOLA
WHITE SANDS MISSILE RANGE
MESCALERO APACHE IND. RES.
NAVAJO IND. RES.
ZUNI IND. RES.
JICARILLA APACHE IND. RES.
UTE MOUNTAIN IND. RES.
SOUTHERN UTE IND. RES.
CIBOLA NATL FOR.
CARSON NATL FOR.
SANTA FE NATL FOR.
GILA NATL FOR.
APACHE NATL FOR.
KIOWA NATL GRASSLAND
COMANCHE NATL GRASSLAND
SAN JUAN NATL FOR.
JORNADA DEL MUERTO
TULAROSA VALLEY
PLAINS OF SAN AUGUSTIN
CONTINENTAL DIVIDE

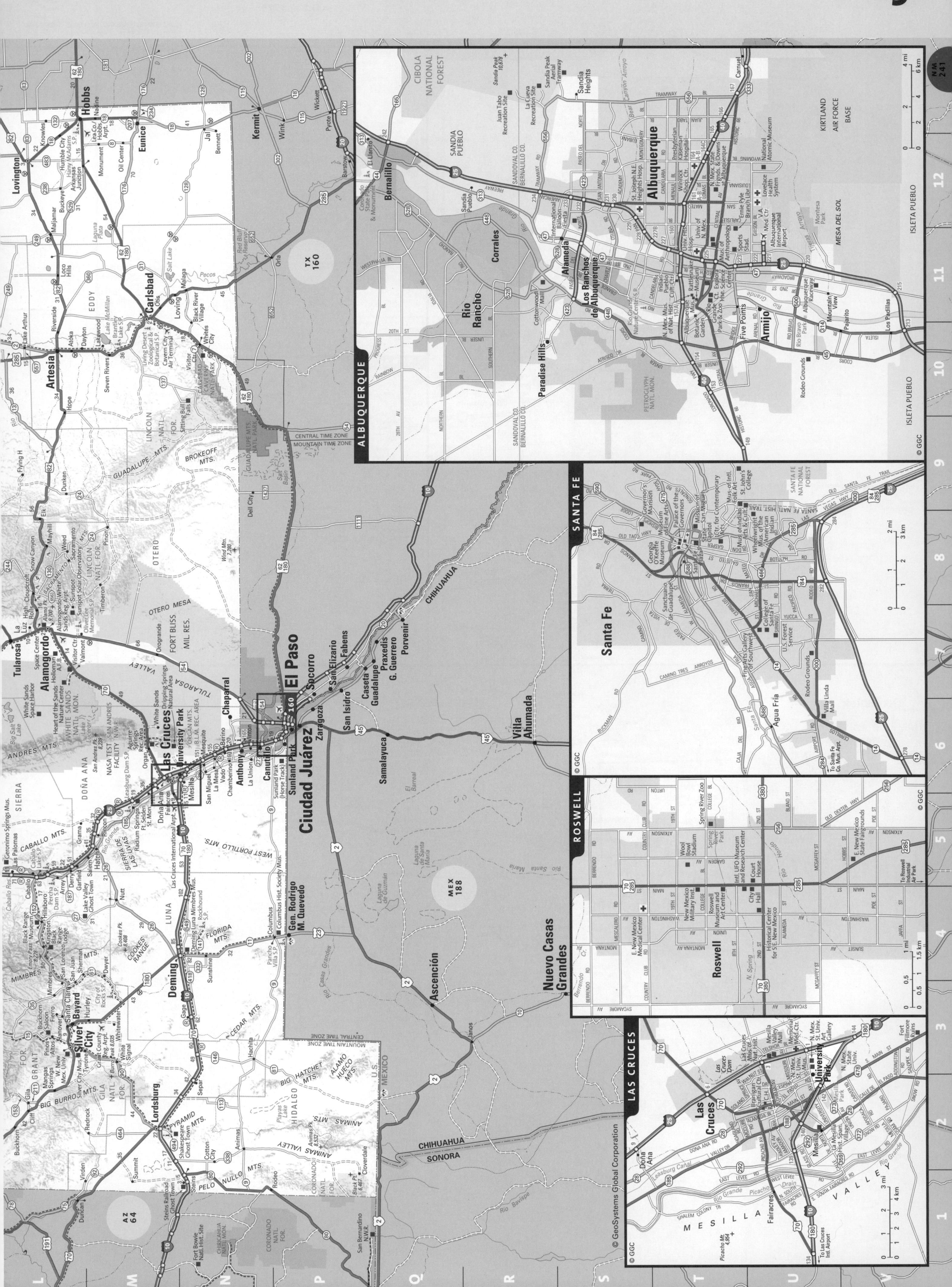
ALBUQUERQUE
SANTA FE
ROSWELL
LAS CRUCES
Albuquerque
Santa Fe
Roswell
Las Cruces
El Paso
Ciudad Juárez
Carlsbad
Hobbs
Alamogordo
Deming
Lordsburg
Silver City
Artesia
Rio Rancho
CHIHUAHUA
SONORA
CENTRAL TIME ZONE
MOUNTAIN TIME ZONE
KIRTLAND AIR FORCE BASE
© GeoSystems Global Corporation
© GGC

TOURISM:
800.225.5697

ROAD CONDITIONS:
800.847.8929

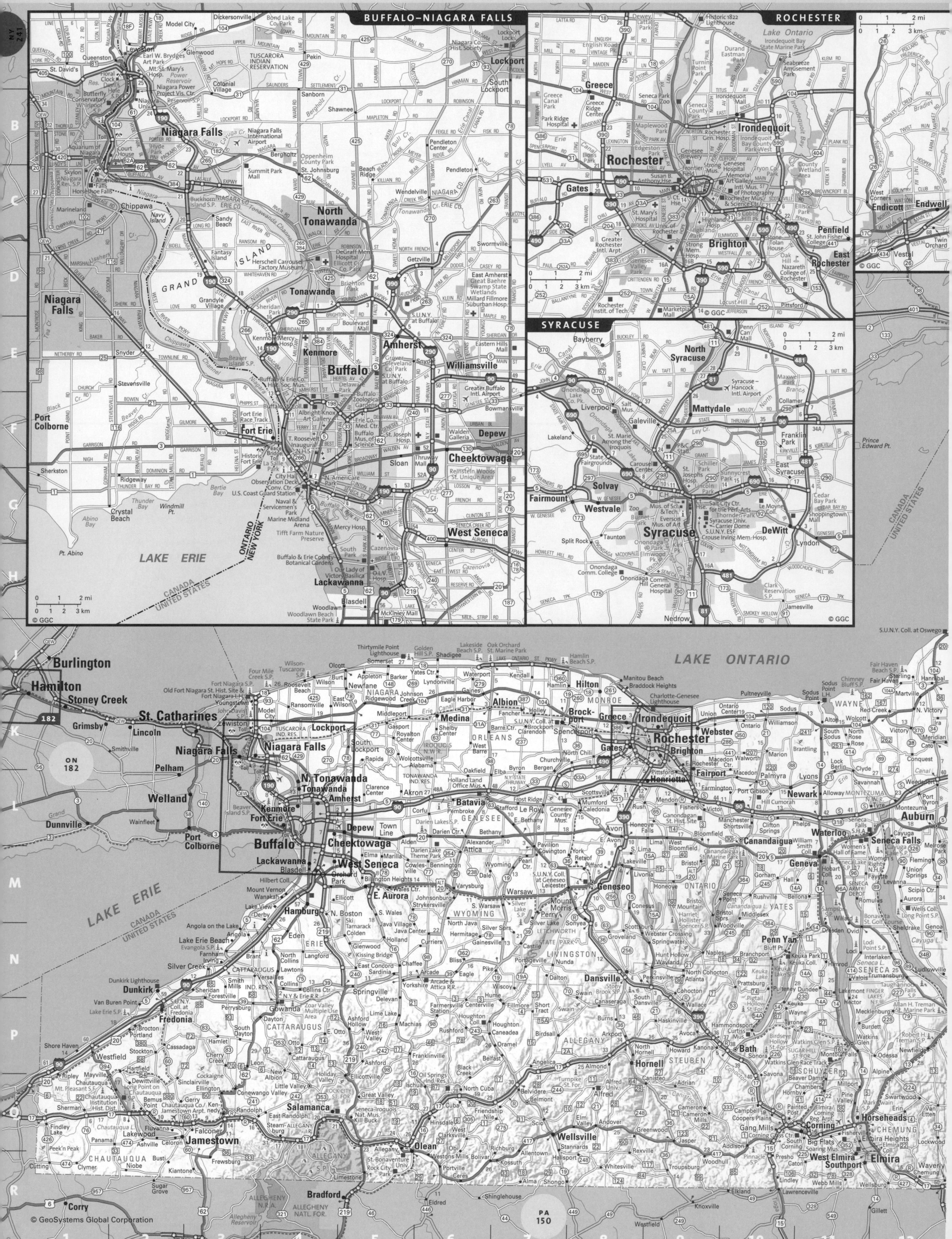

MI 15 30
KM 15 30

BUFFALO–NIAGARA FALLS

ROCHESTER

SYRACUSE

LAKE ONTARIO

LAKE ERIE

ON 182

PA 150

BINGHAMTON
ON 182
PQ 184
VT 166
MA 110
CT 78
PA 150
CANADA
UNITED STATES
Cornwall
Massena
Malone
Plattsburgh
Burlington
S. Burlington
Ogdensburg
Potsdam
Canton
Saranac Lake
Tupper Lake
Watertown
Lowville
ADIRONDACK PARK
ADIRONDACK MOUNTAINS
Oswego
Fulton
Syracuse
Rome
Utica
Oneida
Herkimer
Little Falls
Gloversville
Johnstown
Amsterdam
Saratoga Springs
Glens Falls
Schenectady
Troy
Albany
Cohoes
Cortland
Ithaca
Norwich
Oneonta
Binghamton
Johnson City
Endicott
Kingston
Hudson
Pittsfield
Middlebury
Ticonderoga
CATSKILL MTS.
FORT DRUM MIL. RES.
ST. LAWRENCE
FRANKLIN
CLINTON
ESSEX
HAMILTON
HERKIMER
LEWIS
JEFFERSON
OSWEGO
ONEIDA
ONONDAGA
MADISON
CAYUGA
CORTLAND
CHENANGO
OTSEGO
DELAWARE
SCHOHARIE
ALBANY
GREENE
FULTON
MONTGOMERY
SCHENECTADY
SARATOGA
WARREN
WASHINGTON
RENSSELAER
COLUMBIA
DUTCHESS
ULSTER
SULLIVAN
BROOME
TIOGA
TOMPKINS
13 14 15 16 17 18 19 20 21 22 23 24
A B C D E F G H J K L M N P Q R

134
NEW YORK (south)
TOURISM:
800.225.5697
ROAD CONDITIONS:
800.847.8929
MI 5 10 15
KM 5 10 15
N
NY 241
PA 150
NJ 128
136
152
CATSKILL PARK
CATSKILL MOUNTAINS
SHAWANGUNK MOUNTAINS
POCONO MTS.
KITTATINNY MOUNTAIN
DELAWARE WATER GAP N.R.A.
SULLIVAN
DELAWARE
GREENE
ULSTER
ORANGE
PUTNAM
DUTCHESS
COLUMBIA
WESTCHESTER
ROCKLAND
QUEENS
KINGS
RICHMOND
BRONX
Kingston
Poughkeepsie
Newburgh
New Paltz
Monticello
Middletown
Port Jervis
Goshen
Peekskill
Yonkers
New Rochelle
White Plains
Paterson
Newark
Jersey City
Elizabeth
New York
East Stroudsburg
Stroudsburg
Easton
Phillipsburg
Bethlehem
Edison
New Brunswick
Plainfield
Morristown
Newton
R S T U V W X Y
17 18 19 20 21 22 23

UTICA
ALBANY–SCHENECTADY–TROY
Utica
Whitesboro
Yorkville
New York Mills
New Hartford
Oriskany
Oneida County Airport
Clinton
Hamilton College
Scotia
Schenectady
Rotterdam
Niskayuna
Colonie
Latham
Cohoes
Troy
Watervliet
Loudonville
Roessleville
Westmere
Albany
Rensselaer
Delmar
Elsmere
Voorheesville
Slingerlands
Wynantskill
Torrington
Litchfield
Thomaston
Terryville
Plainville
Bristol
Southington
Waterbury
Watertown
Oakville
Naugatuck
Middlebury
Meriden
Cheshire
Wallingford
Prospect
New Milford
Danbury
Bethel
Ridgefield
Brookfield
Newtown
Southbury
Seymour
Ansonia
Derby
Shelton
Woodbridge
Hamden
North Haven
New Haven
East Haven
West Haven
Orange
Branford
Milford
Trumbull
Stratford
Bridgeport
Fairfield
Westport
Norwalk
Darien
Stamford
New Canaan
Wilton
Guilford
Madison
Clinton
Westbrook
Old Saybrook
Essex
Deep River
Chester
Haddam
Durham
New London
Groton
Waterford
Mystic
Pawcatuck
Westerly
Niantic
Fishers Island
Block Island Sound
Long Island Sound
LONG ISLAND
Orient
Greenport
Southold
Shelter Island
Sag Harbor
East Hampton
Amagansett
Montauk
Mattituck
Riverhead
Southampton
Hampton Bays
Bridgehampton
Gardiners I.
Plum I.
Port Jefferson
Stony Brook
Smithtown
St. James
Centereach
Selden
Coram
Ronkonkoma
Farmingville
Medford
Shirley
Mastic
Mastic Beach
Patchogue
E. Patchogue
Sayville
Holbrook
Central Islip
Brentwood
Hauppauge
Commack
Huntington
Huntington Station
Northport
East Northport
Syosset
Plainview
Jericho
Hicksville
Westbury
Levittown
Bethpage
East Meadow
Hempstead
Freeport
Merrick
Massapequa
Massapequa Park
Copiague
Lindenhurst
Babylon
W. Babylon
Bay Shore
W. Islip
E. Islip
Deer Park
Oceanside
Lido Beach
FIRE ISLAND NATL. SEASHORE
ATLANTIC OCEAN
© GeoSystems Global Corporation

MI 2 4
KM 2 4
N
NJ
NY
Oakland
Franklin Lakes
Wyckoff
Waldwick
Midland Park
Pompton Lakes
Pompton Plains
Hillsdale
Old Tappan
Northvale
Norwood
Rockleigh
Harrington Park
Westwood
Emerson
Oradell
Washington Township
Closter
Haworth
Demarest
Dumont
Cresskill
Alpine
Dobbs Ferry
Hastings-on-Hudson
Greenville
Tuckahoe
Bronxville
Yonkers
Mount Vernon
North Haledon
Hawthorne
Ridgewood
Glen Rock
Paramus
Haledon
Prospect Pk.
Fair Lawn
River Edge
New Milford
Bergenfield
Tenafly
Paterson
Elmwood Park
Rochelle Park
Maywood
Saddle Brook
Lincoln Park
Totowa
West Paterson
Little Falls
Garfield
Lodi
Hackensack
Teaneck
Bogota
Englewood
Englewood Cliffs
Fairfield
North Caldwell
Cedar Grove
Clifton
Passaic
Hasbrouck Hts.
Wallington
Wood Ridge
Leonia
Ridgefield Park
Palisades Park
Fort Lee
West Caldwell
Caldwell
Verona
East Rutherford
Rutherford
Little Ferry
Moonachie
Ridgefield
Cliffside Pk.
Montclair
Nutley
Carlstadt
North Bergen
Fairview
Bronx
West Orange
Glen Ridge
Bloomfield
Lyndhurst
Belleville
North Arlington
Guttenberg
West New York
Livingston
Orange
East Orange
Secaucus
Weehawken
Kearny
Union City
Hoboken
South Orange
Harrison
Manhattan
Millburn
Maplewood
Irvington
Newark
New York
Springfield
Union
Hillside
Jersey City
Kenilworth
Roselle Park
Westfield
Cranford
Elizabeth
Bayonne
Garwood
Roselle
Brooklyn
Clark
Linden
Rahway
Staten Island
Carteret
Iselin
Avenel
Colonia
Menlo Park
Woodbridge
Sewaren
Port Reading
Fords
Perth Amboy
Keasbey
South Amboy
Sayreville
Upper New York Bay
Lower New York Bay
Raritan Bay
Jamaica Bay
1 2 3 4 5 6 7 8 9 10
B C D E F G H J K L M N

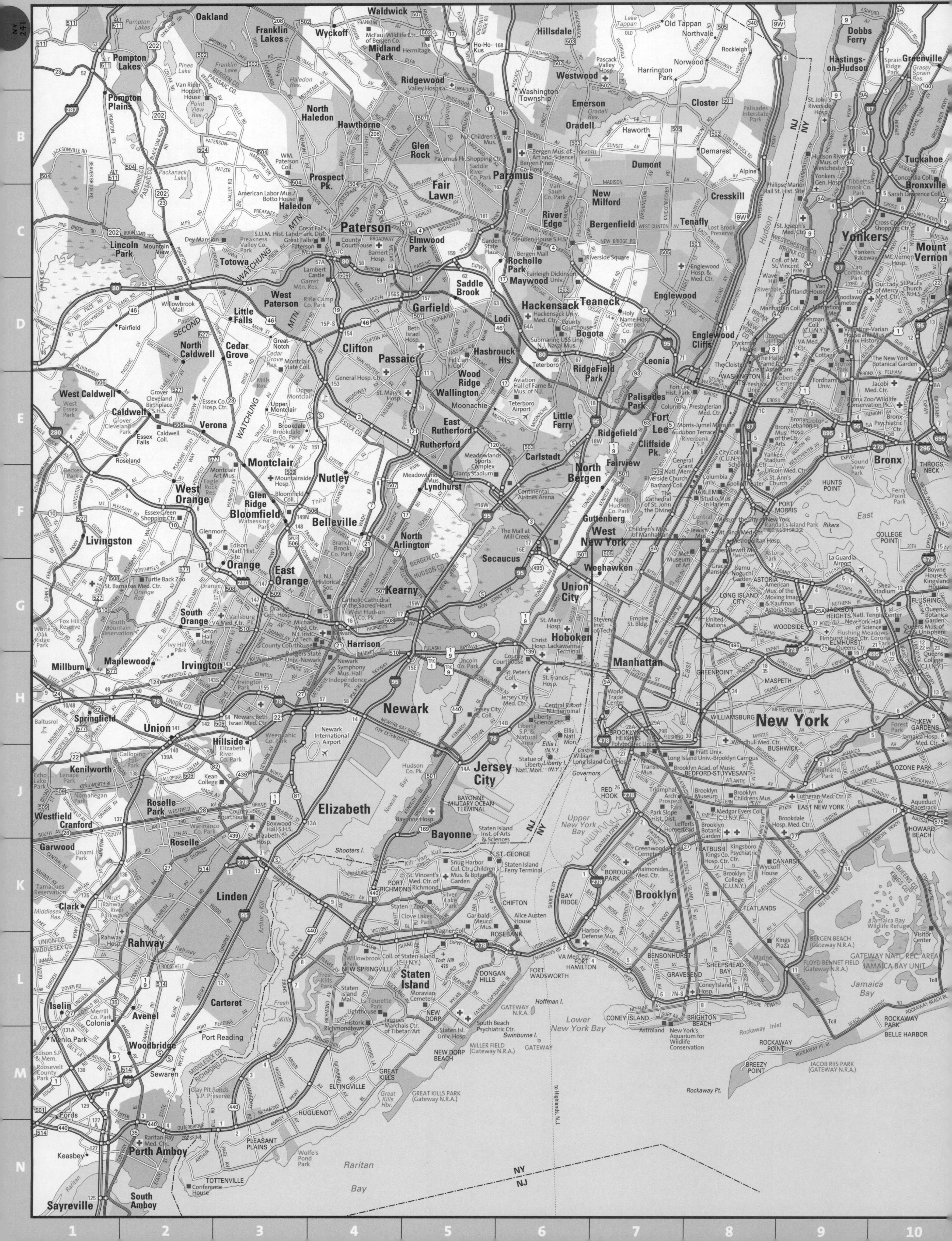

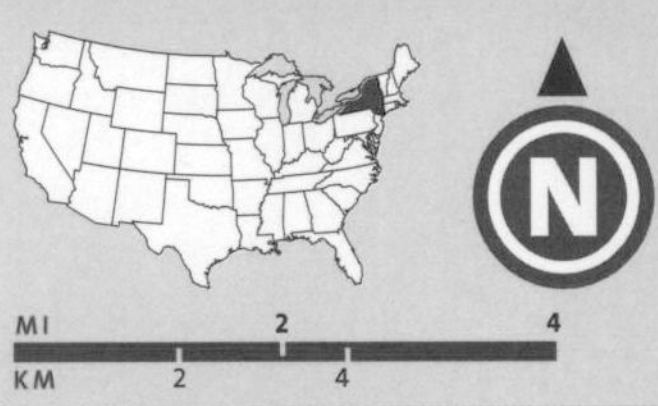

MANHATTAN
West New York
Union City
Weehawken
NEW JERSEY
HUDSON
UPPER WEST SIDE
UPPER EAST SIDE
Central Park
CLINTON
MIDTOWN
TURTLE BAY
FASHION CENTER
MURRAY HILL
CHELSEA
Manhattan
GRAMERCY PARK
STUYVESANT TOWN
WEST VILLAGE
GREENWICH VILLAGE
EAST VILLAGE
SOHO
LITTLE ITALY
TRIBECA
CHINATOWN
LOWER EAST SIDE
BATTERY PARK CITY
Brooklyn
BROOKLYN HEIGHTS
FORT GREENE
WILLIAMSBURG
GREENPOINT
LONG ISLAND CITY
Queens
Roosevelt Island
EAST
Scarsdale
White Plains
West Chester
Port Chester
Harrison
Eastchester
Rye
New Rochelle
Mamaroneck
Larchmont
Pelham
Pelham Manor
Long Island Sound
Glen Cove
Sea Cliff
Manorhaven
Port Washington
Great Neck
Manhasset
Roslyn Hts
Mineola
New Hyde Park
Garden City
Floral Park
Elmont
Franklin Square
North Valley Stream
Lakeview
Queens
Valley Stream
Malverne
Lynbrook
Rockville Centre
South Valley Stream
Hewlett
East Rockaway
Woodmere
Cedarhurst
Inwood
Lawrence
Long Beach
ATLANTIC OCEAN
© GeoSystems Global Corp.
© GGC
0 0.25 0.5 mi
0 0.25 0.5 0.75 km
11 12 13 14 15 16 17 18 19 20
B C D E F G H J K L M N

TOURISM:
800.847.4862
919.733.4171

ROAD CONDITIONS:
919.549.5100, EXT. 7623
919.733.3861

MI 10 20 30
KM 10 20 30 40

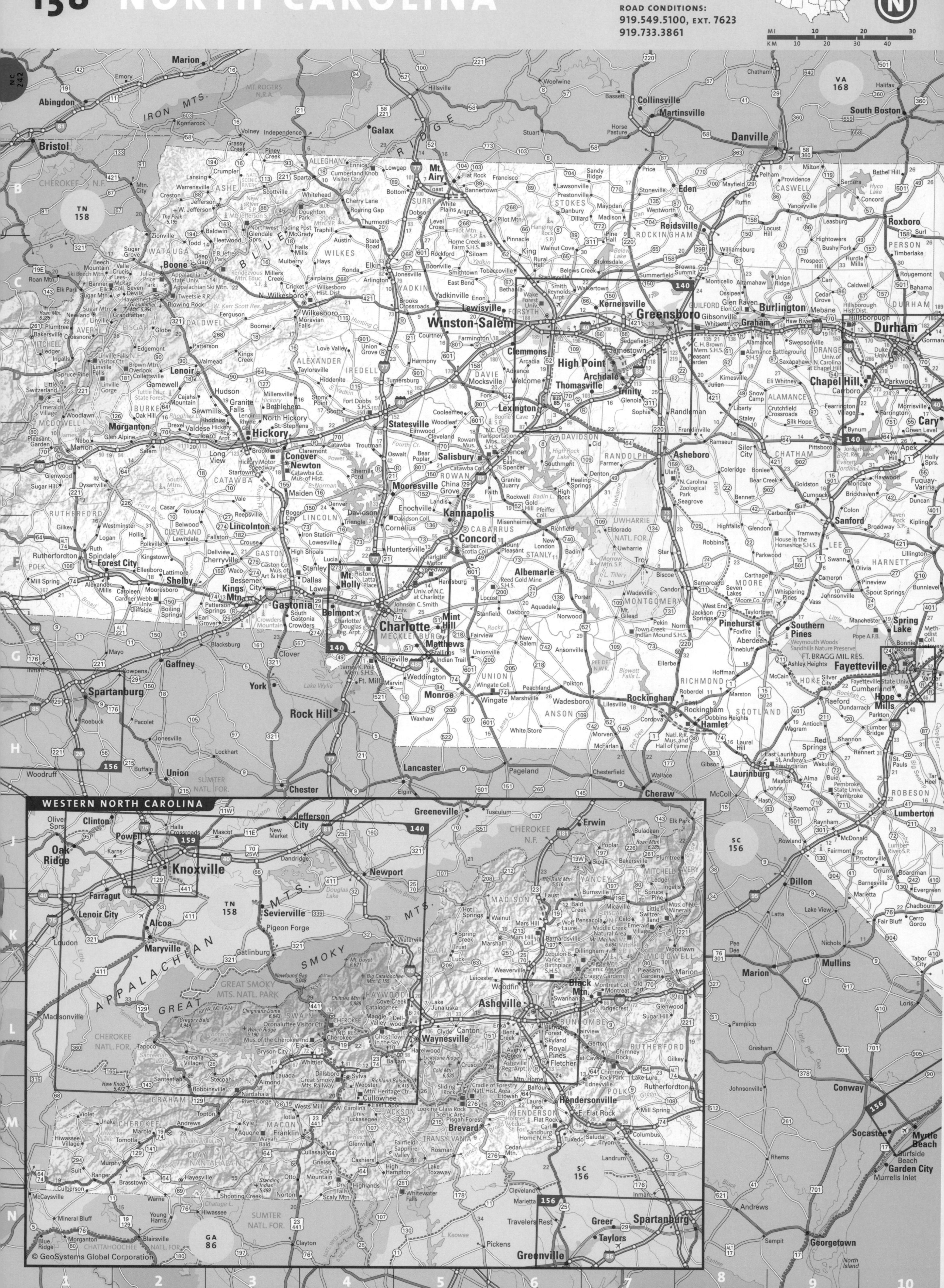

NC 242
167
VA 168
Suffolk
Chesapeake
Emporia
Franklin
Roanoke Rapids
Henderson
Oxford
Raleigh
Garner
Wake Forest
New Hope
Rocky Mount
Tarboro
Wilson
Greenville
Williamston
Washington
Plymouth
Edenton
Elizabeth City
Kill Devil Hills
Manteo
Smithfield
Goldsboro
Kinston
New Bern
Havelock
Morehead City
Beaufort
Jacksonville
Half Moon
Clinton
Dunn
Whiteville
Wilmington
Seagate
OUTER BANKS
ATLANTIC OCEAN
Onslow Bay
Long Bay
FAYETTEVILLE
Fayetteville
Hope Mills
ASHEVILLE
Asheville
WILMINGTON
© GeoSystems Global Corporation
© GGC
11
12
13
14
15
16
17
18
19
20
B
C
D
E
F
G
H
J
K
L
M
N

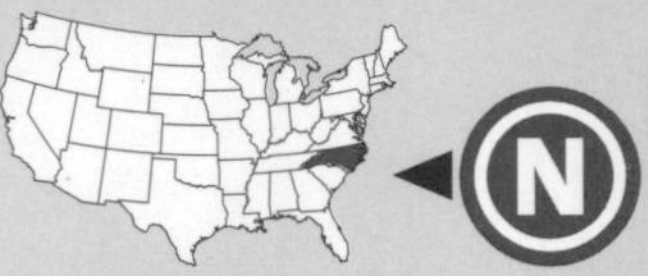

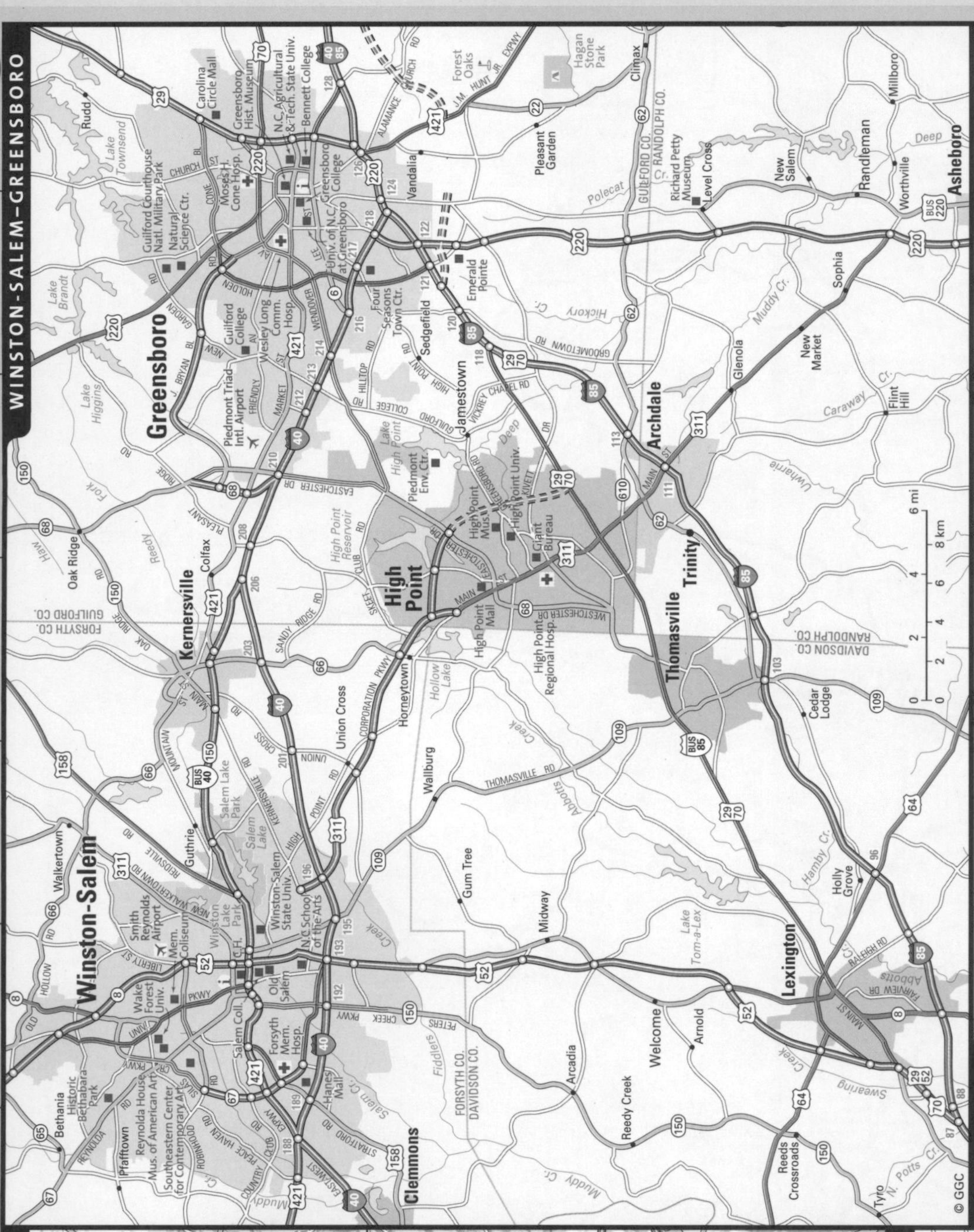

WINSTON-SALEM–GREENSBORO
Greensboro
High Point
Winston-Salem
Kernersville
Thomasville
Lexington
Archdale
Trinity
Asheboro

CHARLOTTE
Charlotte
Mint Hill
Matthews
Belmont
Mount Holly

GREAT SMOKY MTS. AREA
Knoxville
Maryville
Gatlinburg
Sevierville
Pigeon Forge
Waynesville
Newport
Oak Ridge
GREAT SMOKY MOUNTAINS NATIONAL PARK

RALEIGH–DURHAM
Raleigh
Durham
Cary
Chapel Hill
Carrboro
Garner

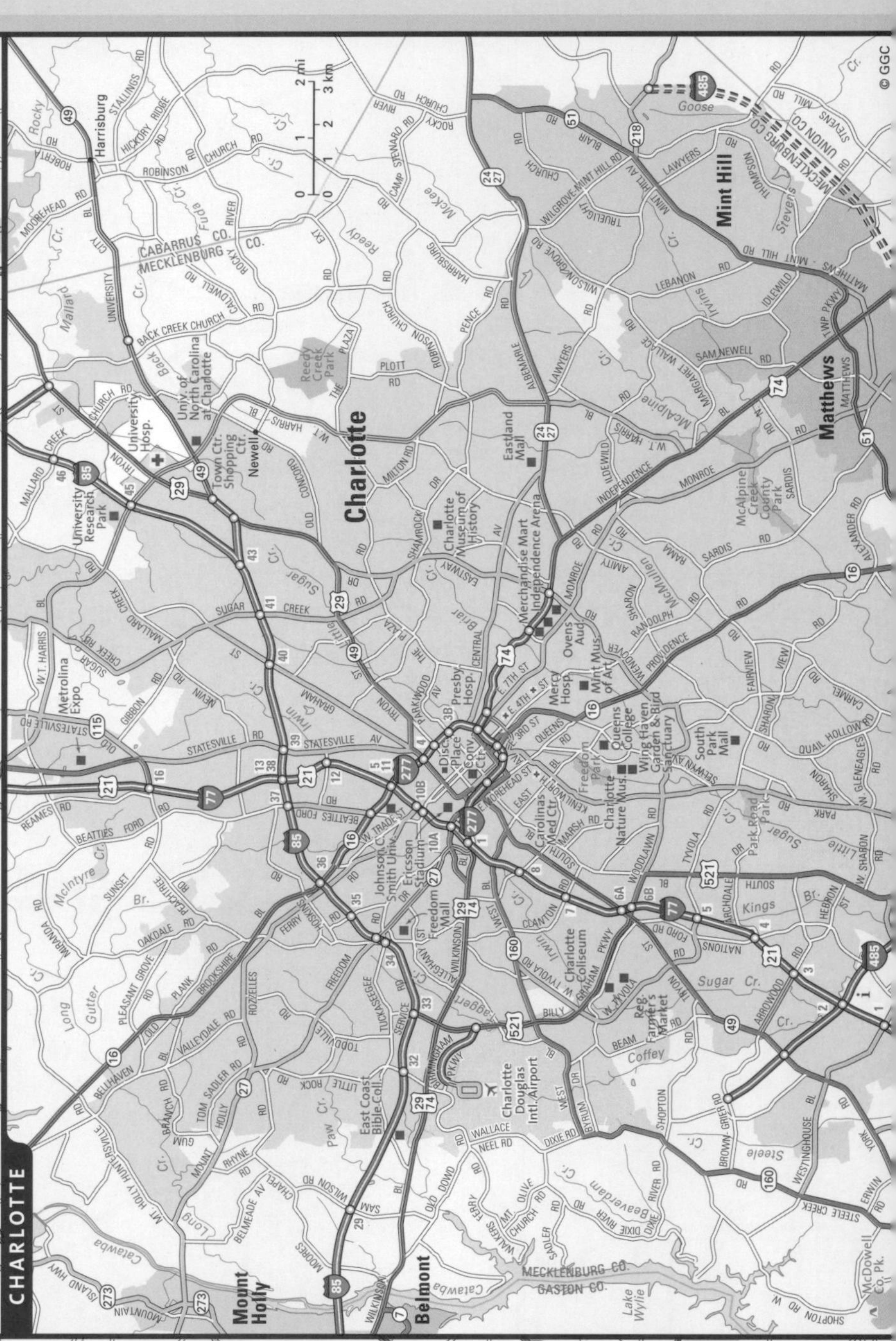

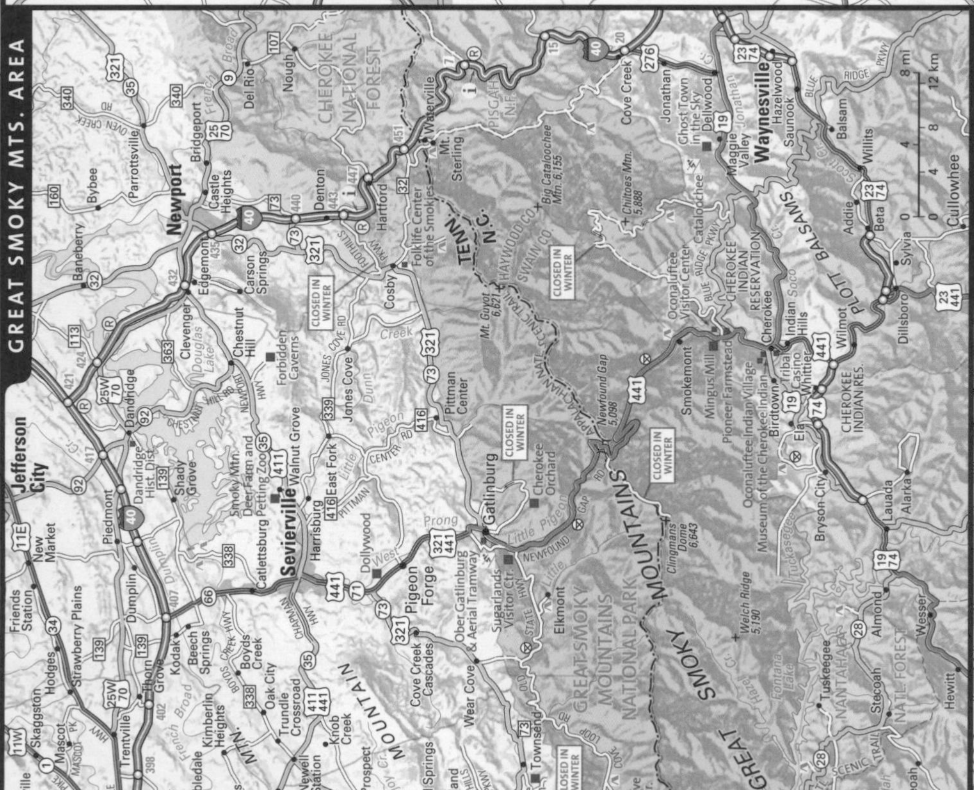

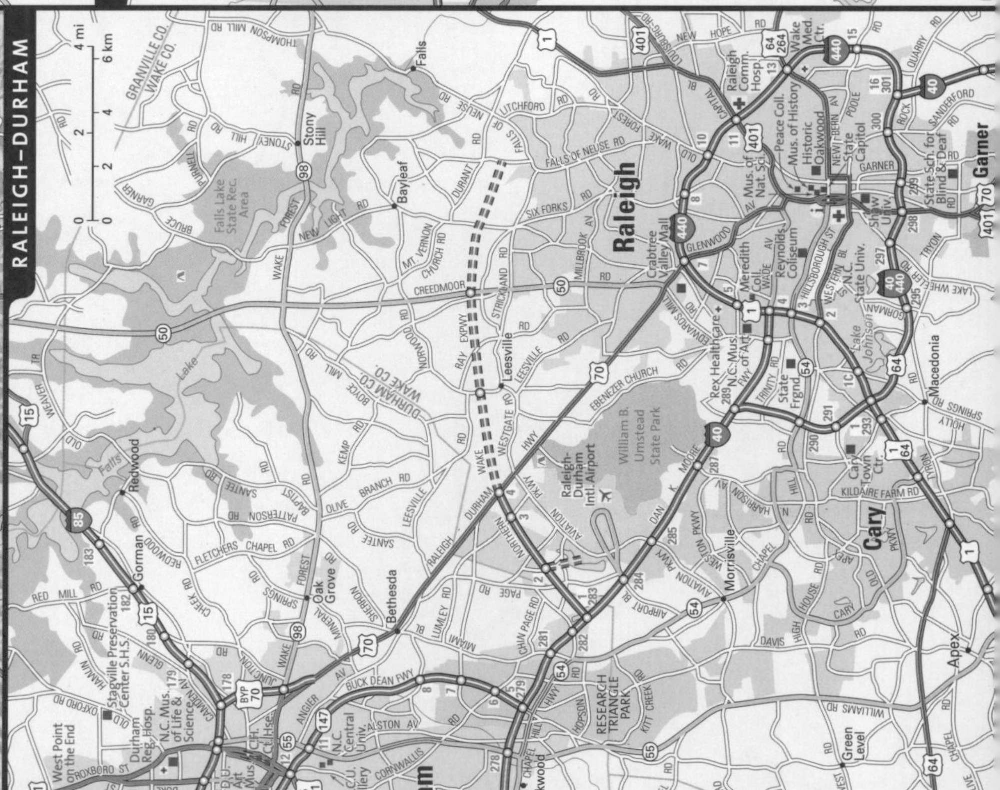

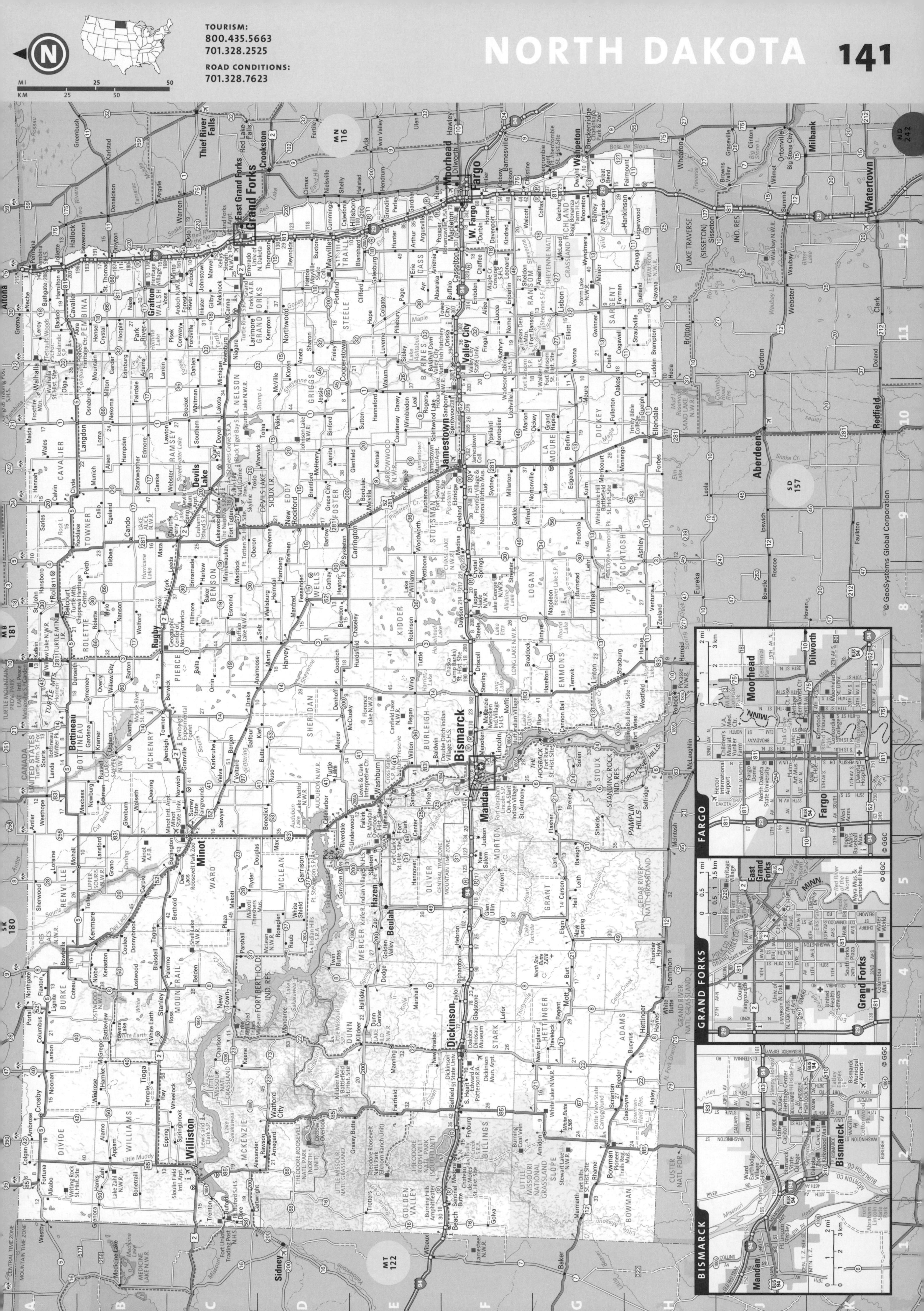
TOURISM:
800.435.5663
701.328.2525
ROAD CONDITIONS:
701.328.7623
MI 25 50
KM 25 50
© GeoSystems Global Corporation

142 OHIO (north)
TOURISM:
800.282.5393
ROAD CONSTRUCTION:
614.466.7170
MI 10 20
KM 10 20
TOLEDO
AKRON
CANTON–MASSILLON
© GGC
MICHIGAN
Sylvania
Toledo
Rossford
Northwood
Oregon
Maumee
Perrysburg
Walbridge
Ottawa Hills
Franklin Park Mall
Toledo Firefighters Museum
Toledo Botanical Garden
Univ. of Toledo
Ohio Baseball Hall of Fame
Wolcott House Museum
Battle of Fallen Timbers State Memorial
Fort Meigs
Lime City
Stony Ridge
Moline
Cuyahoga Falls
Stow
Munroe Falls
Silver Lake
Akron
Fairlawn
Tallmadge
Copley
Norton
Barberton
Portage Lakes
Mogadore
Lakemore
Goodyear World of Rubber
Akron Zoo Park
To Akron-Canton Regional Airport
North Canton
Canton
Louisville
Massillon
Perry Heights
Middlebranch
McDonaldsville
Crystal Springs
Hills and Dales
Pro Football Hall of Fame
McKinley Mus. & Nat'l Mem.
Canton Classic Car Mus.
Waco
Massillon Psychiatric Ctr.
Richville
Lambertville
Temperance
Sylvania
Toledo
Oregon
Northwood
Rossford
Maumee
Perrysburg
Waterville
Whitehouse
Bowling Green
Port Clinton
Sandusky
Fremont
Clyde
Bellevue
Tiffin
Fostoria
Findlay
Willard
Angola
Auburn
Fort Wayne
New Haven
Decatur
Portland
Union City
Winchester
Bryan
Wauseon
Archbold
Napoleon
Defiance
Paulding
Van Wert
Ottawa
Delphos
Lima
Celina
St. Marys
Wapakoneta
Ada
Kenton
Upper Sandusky
Bucyrus
Galion
Marion
Bellefontaine
Sidney
Piqua
Troy
Greenville
Urbana
Marysville
Delaware
Westerville
Worthington
Dublin
Hilliard
Upper Arlington
Columbus
Gahanna
Huber Ridge
145
WILLIAMS
FULTON
LUCAS
OTTAWA
DEFIANCE
HENRY
WOOD
SANDUSKY
SENECA
PAULDING
PUTNAM
HANCOCK
VAN WERT
ALLEN
WYANDOT
CRAWFORD
MERCER
AUGLAIZE
HARDIN
MARION
MORROW
LOGAN
SHELBY
DARKE
MIAMI
CHAMPAIGN
UNION
DELAWARE
CANADA
UNITED STATES
Maumee Bay
Lake Erie
Grand Lake (St. Marys)
Indian Lake S.P.
IN 94
MI 112
OH 243
1 2 3 4 5 6 7

CLEVELAND
DOWNTOWN CLEVELAND
LAKE ERIE
Cleveland
Akron
Canton
Youngstown
Warren
© GeoSystems Global Corporation

TOURISM:
800.282.5393

ROAD CONSTRUCTION:
614.466.7170

MI 0 10 20
KM 0 10 20

OH 243

IN 94

KY 100

CINCINNATI

DAYTON

0 2 4 mi
0 2 4 6 km

0 1 2 mi
0 1 2 3 km

© GGC

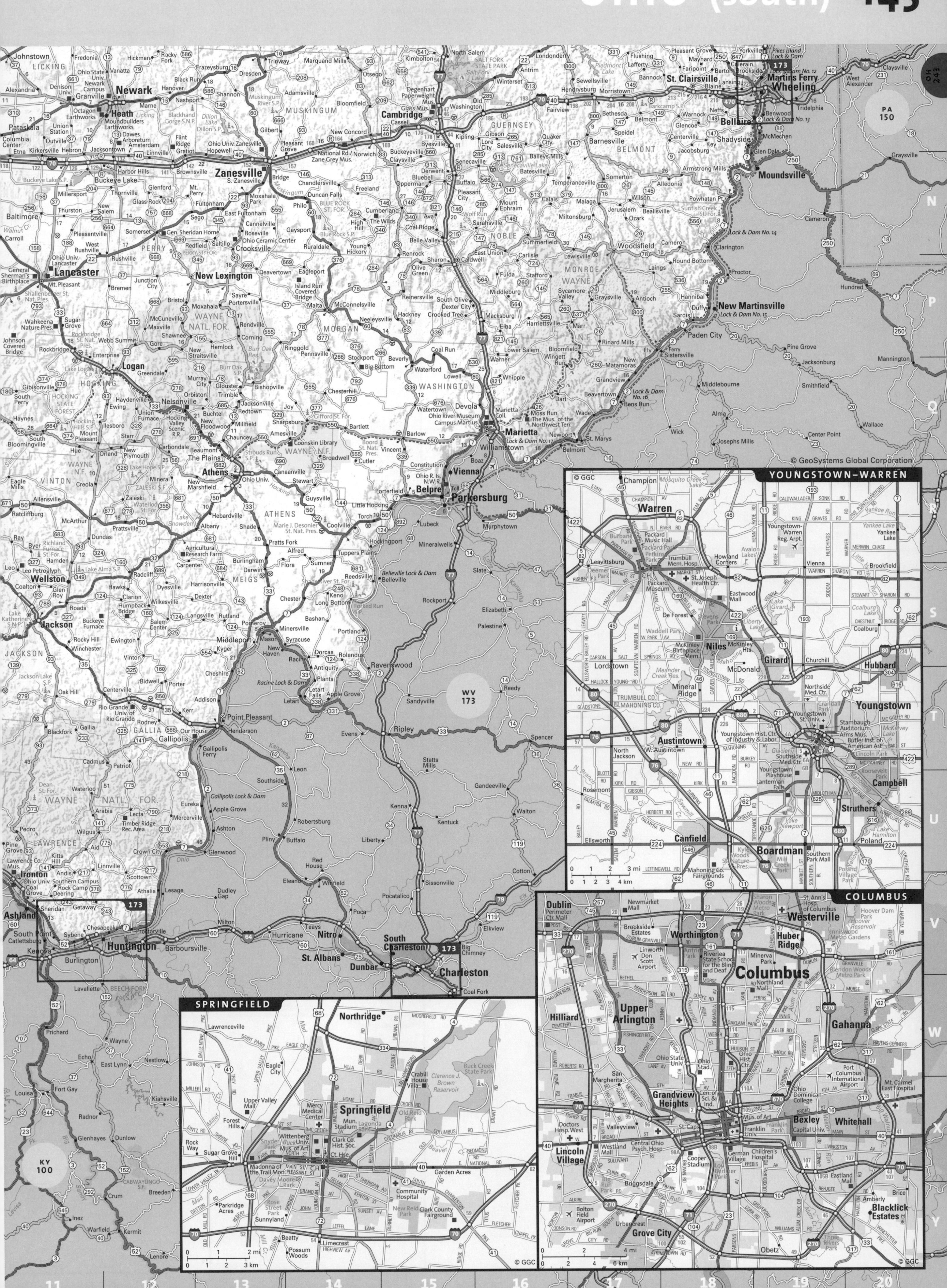
YOUNGSTOWN–WARREN
SPRINGFIELD
COLUMBUS
© GeoSystems Global Corporation
Newark
Zanesville
Cambridge
St. Clairsville
Martins Ferry
Wheeling
Bellaire
Moundsville
Lancaster
New Lexington
Logan
Nelsonville
Athens
Marietta
Parkersburg
Belpre
Vienna
New Martinsville
Wellston
Jackson
Gallipolis
Point Pleasant
Ironton
Ashland
Huntington
Nitro
St. Albans
South Charleston
Charleston
Warren
Niles
Youngstown
Austintown
Boardman
Canfield
Girard
Hubbard
Campbell
Struthers
Springfield
Northridge
Westerville
Worthington
Columbus
Upper Arlington
Hilliard
Gahanna
Grandview Heights
Bexley
Whitehall
Lincoln Village
Grove City
Blacklick Estates
PA 150
WV 173
KY 100

TOURISM:
800.652.6552
405.521.2409

ROAD CONDITIONS:
405.425.2385

ROAD CONSTRUCTION:
405.521.2554

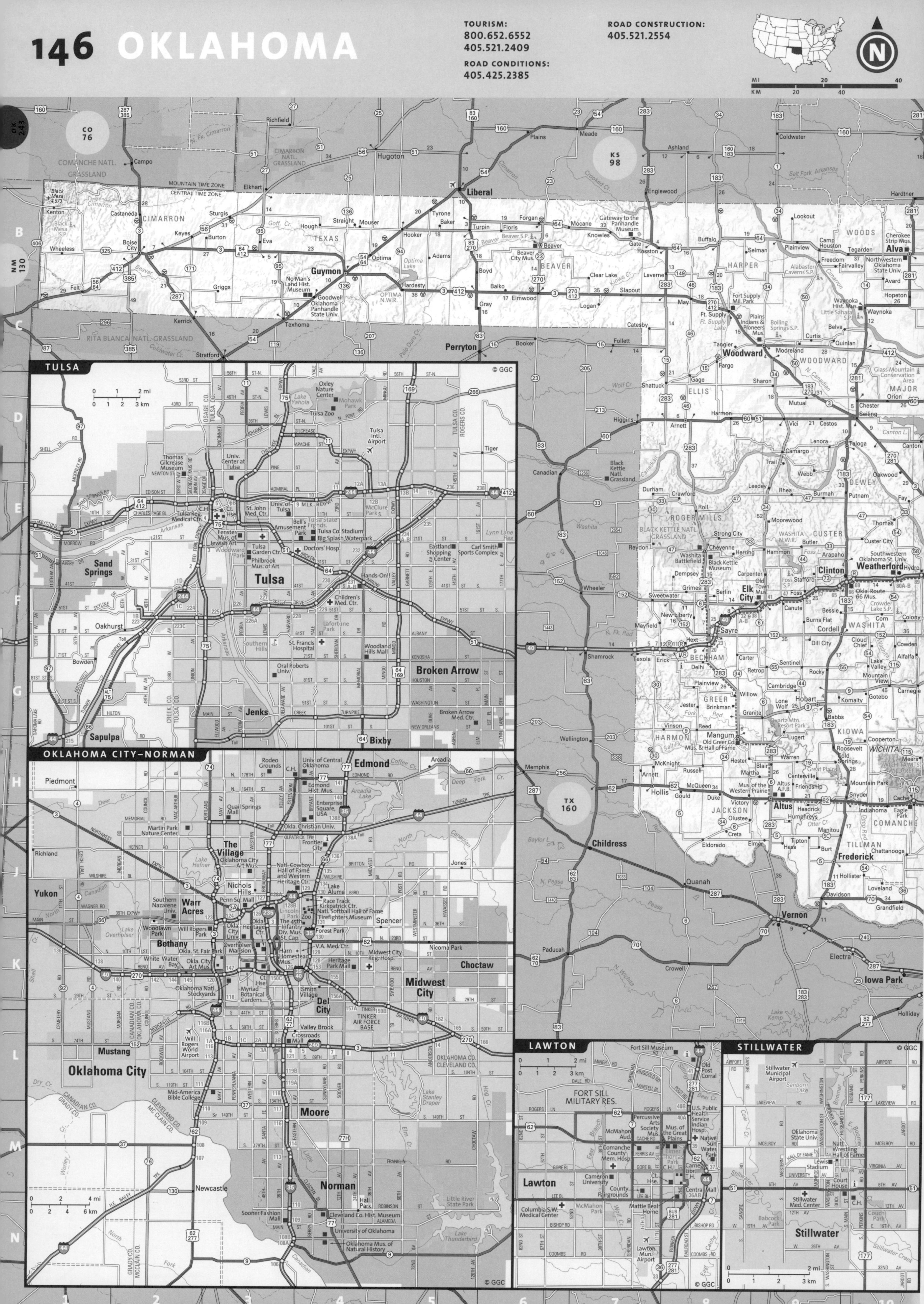

KS 98
MO 120
AR 66
TX 160
OK 243
Wellington
Winfield
Arkansas City
Independence
Coffeyville
Parsons
Joplin
Carthage
Neosho
Miami
Blackwell
Ponca City
Bartlesville
Vinita
Enid
Pryor
Claremore
Owasso
Tulsa
Sand Sprs.
Jenks
Broken Arrow
Sapulpa
Glenpool
Bixby
Coweta
Wagoner
Tahlequah
Stillwater
Cushing
Guthrie
Edmond
Oklahoma City
El Reno
Yukon
Bethany
Mustang
Midwest City
Moore
Norman
Shawnee
Tecumseh
Seminole
Henryetta
Okmulgee
Muskogee
Checotah
Sallisaw
Van Buren
Fort Smith
Siloam Springs
Springdale
Fayetteville
Bentonville
Bella Vista
Poteau
Eufaula
McAlester
Chickasha
Anadarko
Lawton
Duncan
Pauls Valley
Ada
Ardmore
Durant
Atoka
Hugo
Idabel
Mena
Wichita Falls
Burkburnett
Denison
Sherman
Gainesville
Paris
Bonham
Denton
McKinney
Frisco
The Colony
Lewisville
Plano
Carrollton
Richardson
Grapevine
Garland
Rockwall
Irving
Dallas
Fort Worth
Arlington
Mesquite
Greenville
Commerce
Sulphur Springs
Mt. Pleasant
New Boston
Mineral Wells
Graham
Weatherford
Terrell
BOSTON MTS.
OUACHITA MTS.
KIAMICHI MTS.
SANS BOIS MTS.
© GeoSystems Global Corporation
11
12
13
14
15
16
17
18
19
20

TOURISM:
800.547.7842

ROAD CONDITIONS:
800.977.6368 (OR)
541.889.3999

PORTLAND
SALEM
EUGENE
CRATER LAKE NATL. PARK
Richland
Pasco
Kennewick
Walla Walla
Pendleton
La Grande
Baker City
Ontario
Burns
Portland
Salem
Eugene
Springfield
Gresham
Beaverton
Crater Lake
© GeoSystems Global Corporation

TOURISM:
800.847.4872

ROAD CONDITIONS:
800.331.3414 (PA)
717.939.9551 (PA TURNPIKE)

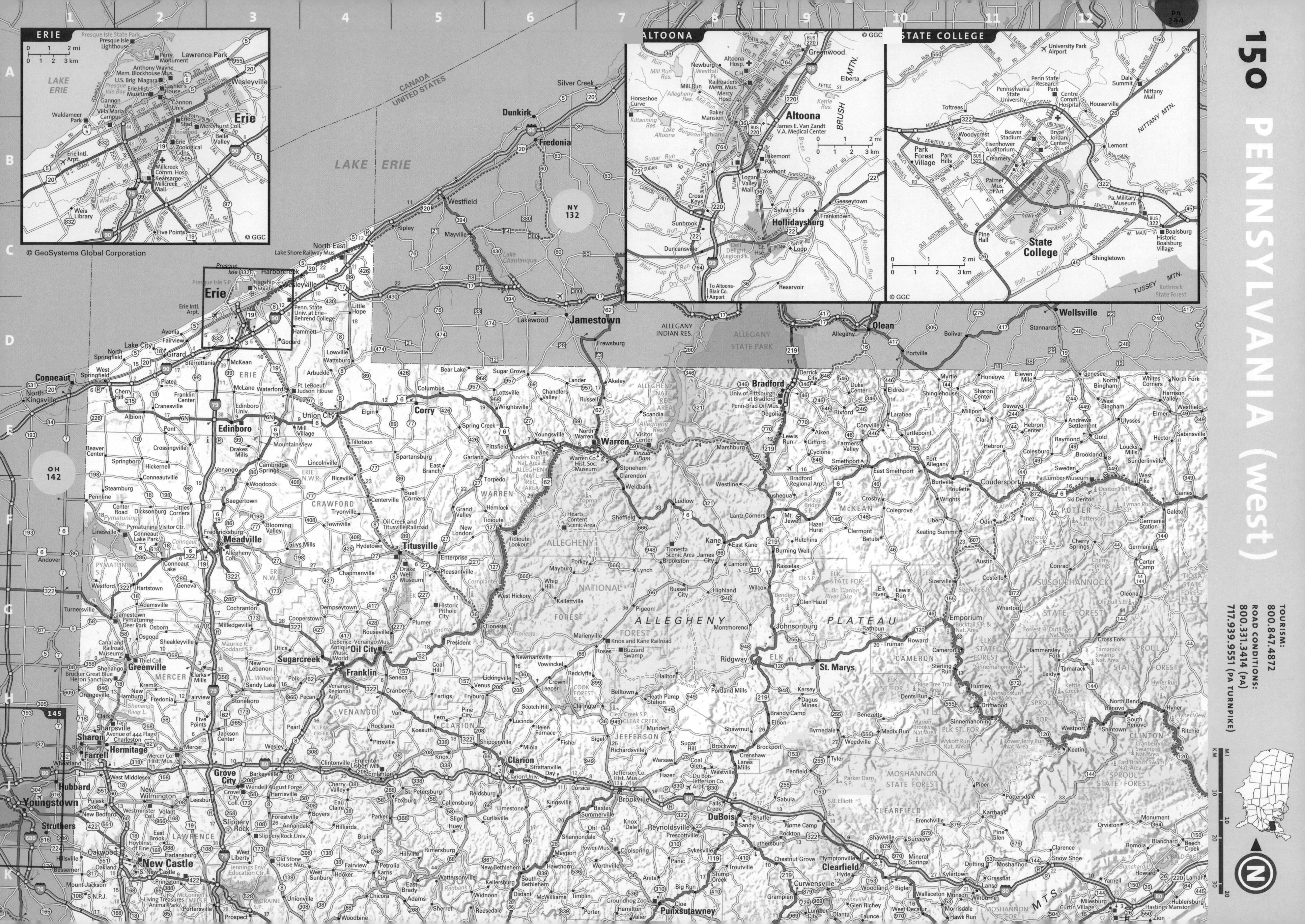

TOURISM:
800.847.4872

ROAD CONDITIONS:
800.331.3414 (PA)
717.939.9551 (PA TURNPIKE)

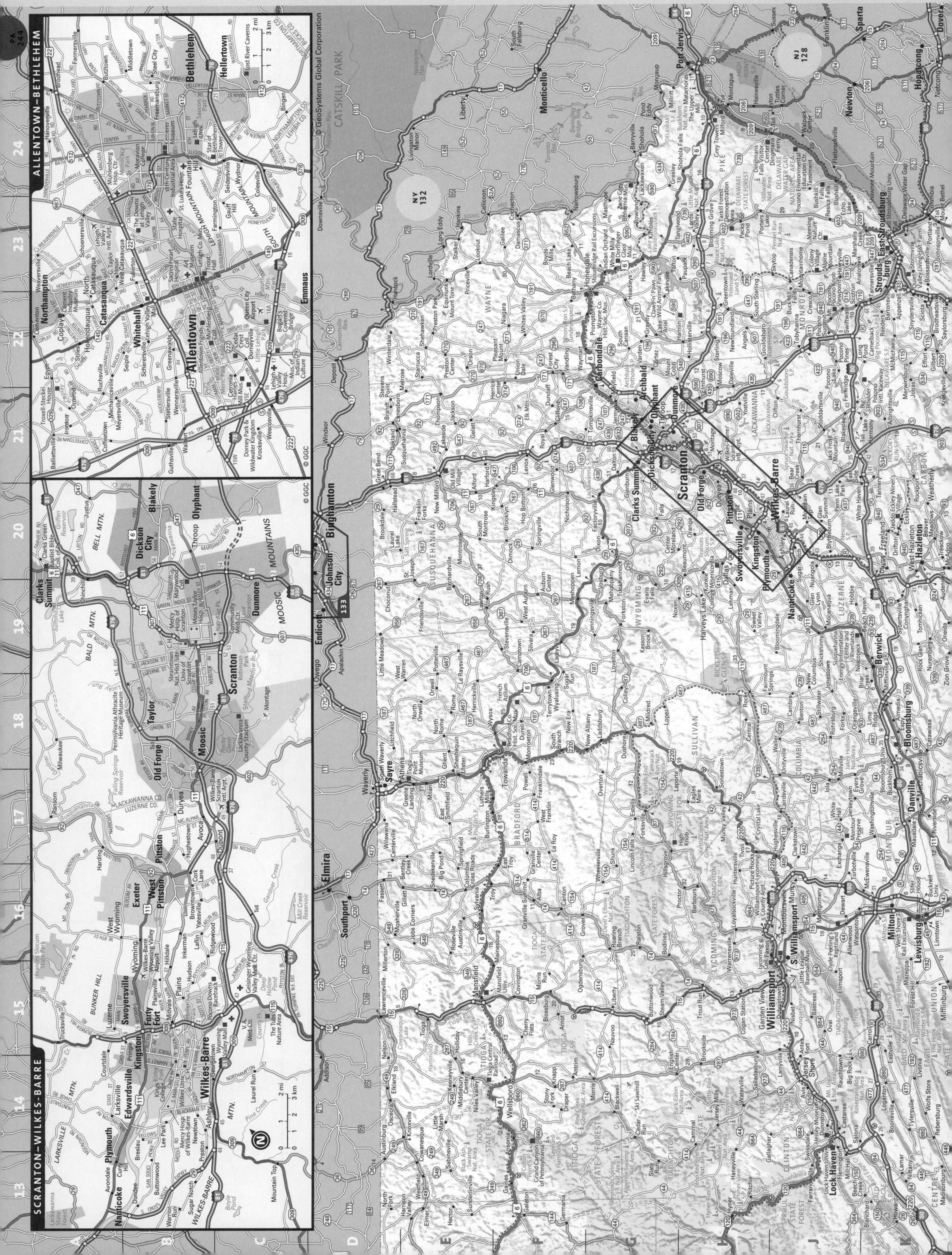

ALLENTOWN–BETHLEHEM

SCRANTON–WILKES-BARRE

© GeoSystems Global Corporation

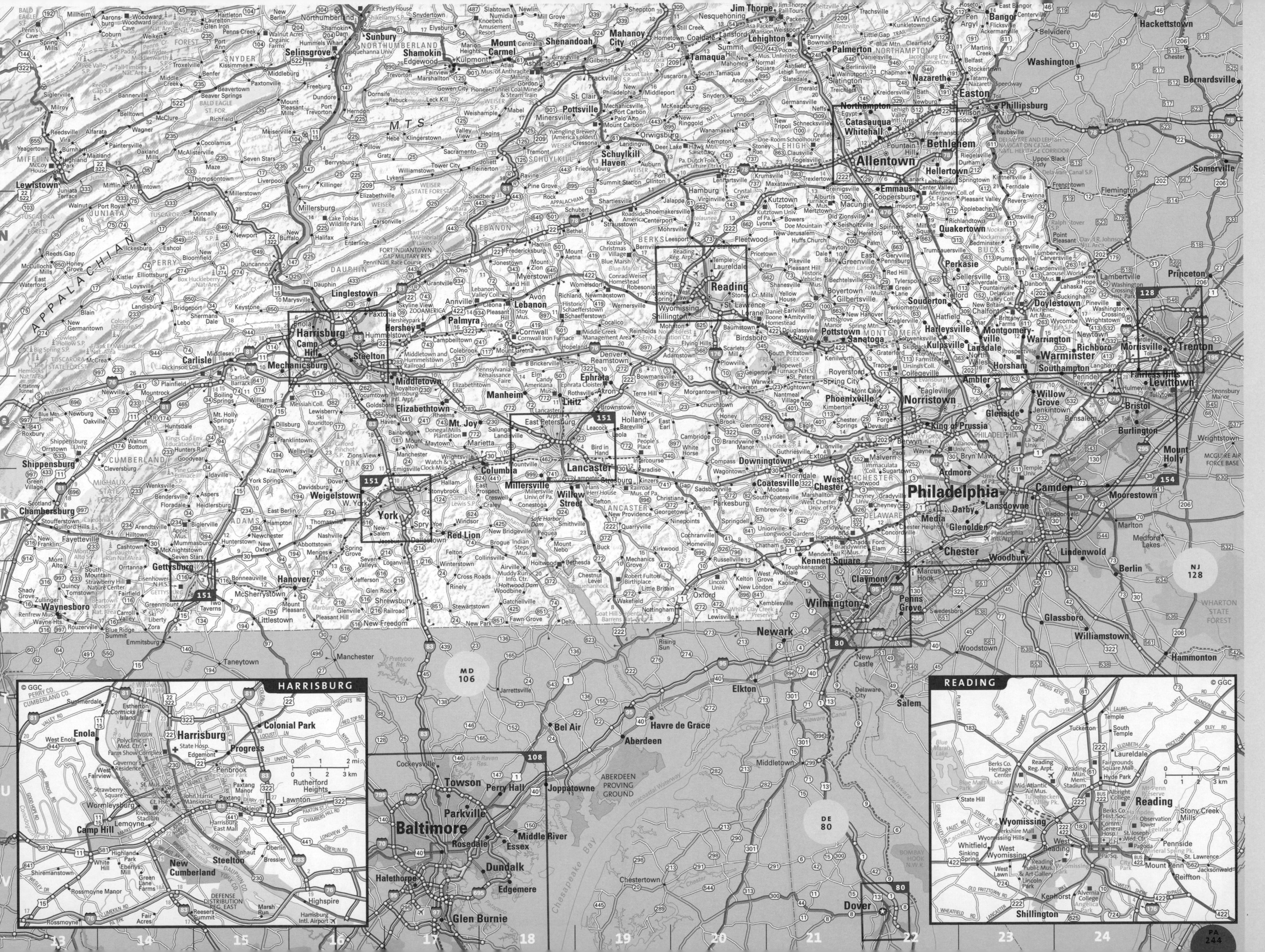
HARRISBURG
READING
Philadelphia
Baltimore
Allentown
Reading
Lancaster
York
Harrisburg
Wilmington
Camden
Trenton

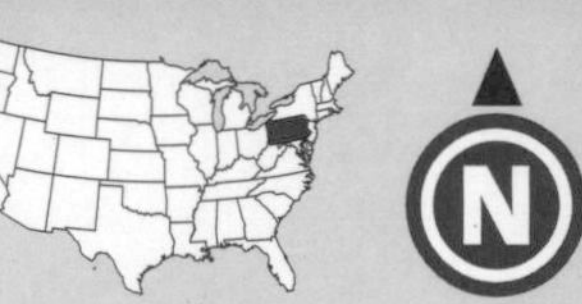

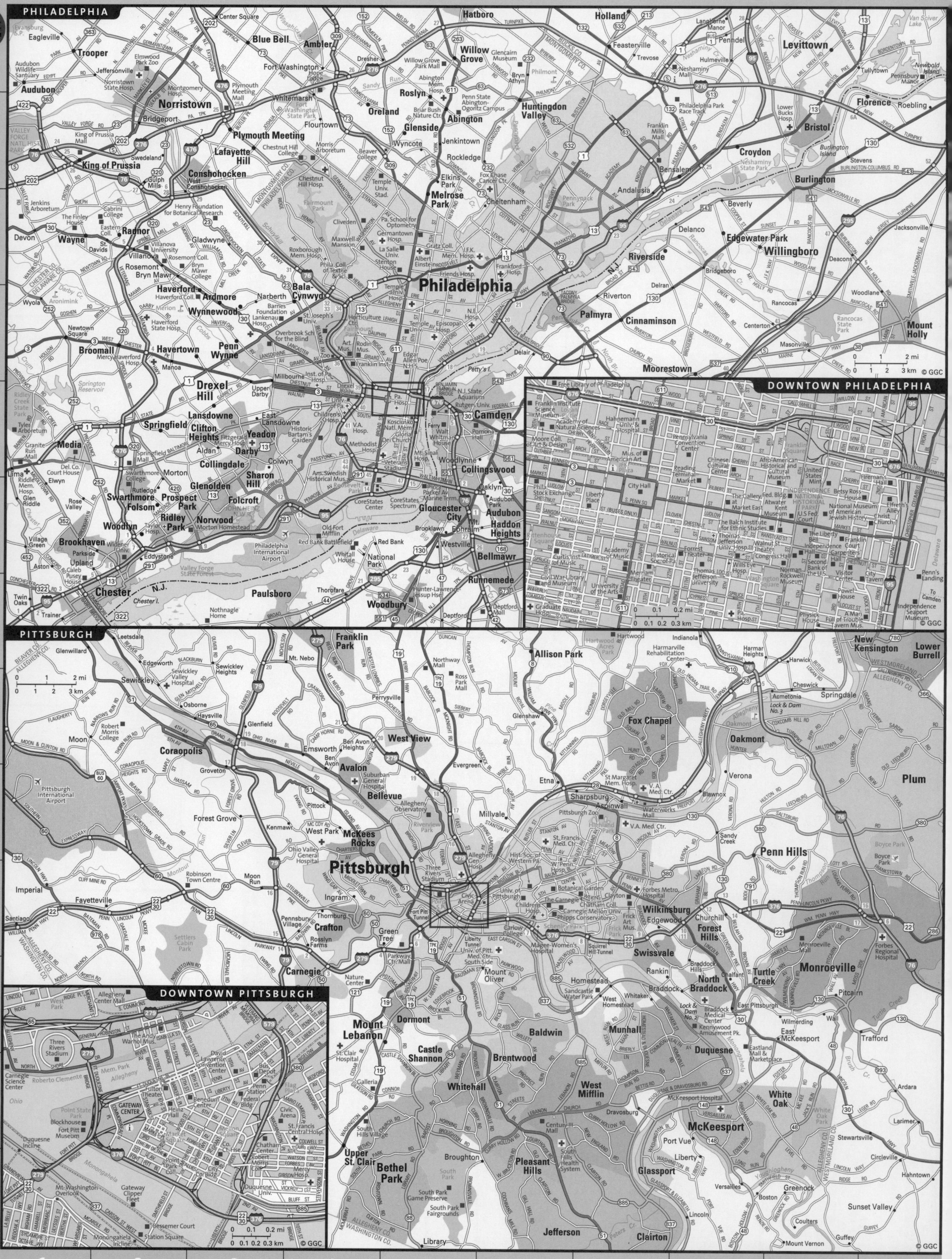

PHILADELPHIA
Philadelphia
Camden
Norristown
King of Prussia
Conshohocken
Drexel Hill
Chester
Willingboro
Levittown
Bristol
Burlington
Cherry Hill
DOWNTOWN PHILADELPHIA
City Hall
Independence National Historical Park
PITTSBURGH
Pittsburgh
McKees Rocks
Fox Chapel
Penn Hills
Monroeville
McKeesport
Bethel Park
West Mifflin
Mount Lebanon
Wilkinsburg
Coraopolis
DOWNTOWN PITTSBURGH
Gateway Center
Point State Park
Three Rivers Stadium
Civic Arena
© GGC

TOURISM:
800.556.2484
ROAD CONDITIONS:
800.354.9595
PROVIDENCE
NEWPORT
ATLANTIC OCEAN
Rhode Island Sound
Block Island Sound
Providence
Pawtucket
East Providence
Cranston
Warwick
West Warwick
Woonsocket
Newport
Bristol
Westerly
Kingston
Fall River
New Bedford
Attleboro
Block Island
© GeoSystems Global Corporation

TOURISM:
800.872.3505
803.734.0122

ROAD CONDITIONS:
803.896.9621
(COLUMBIA AREA)

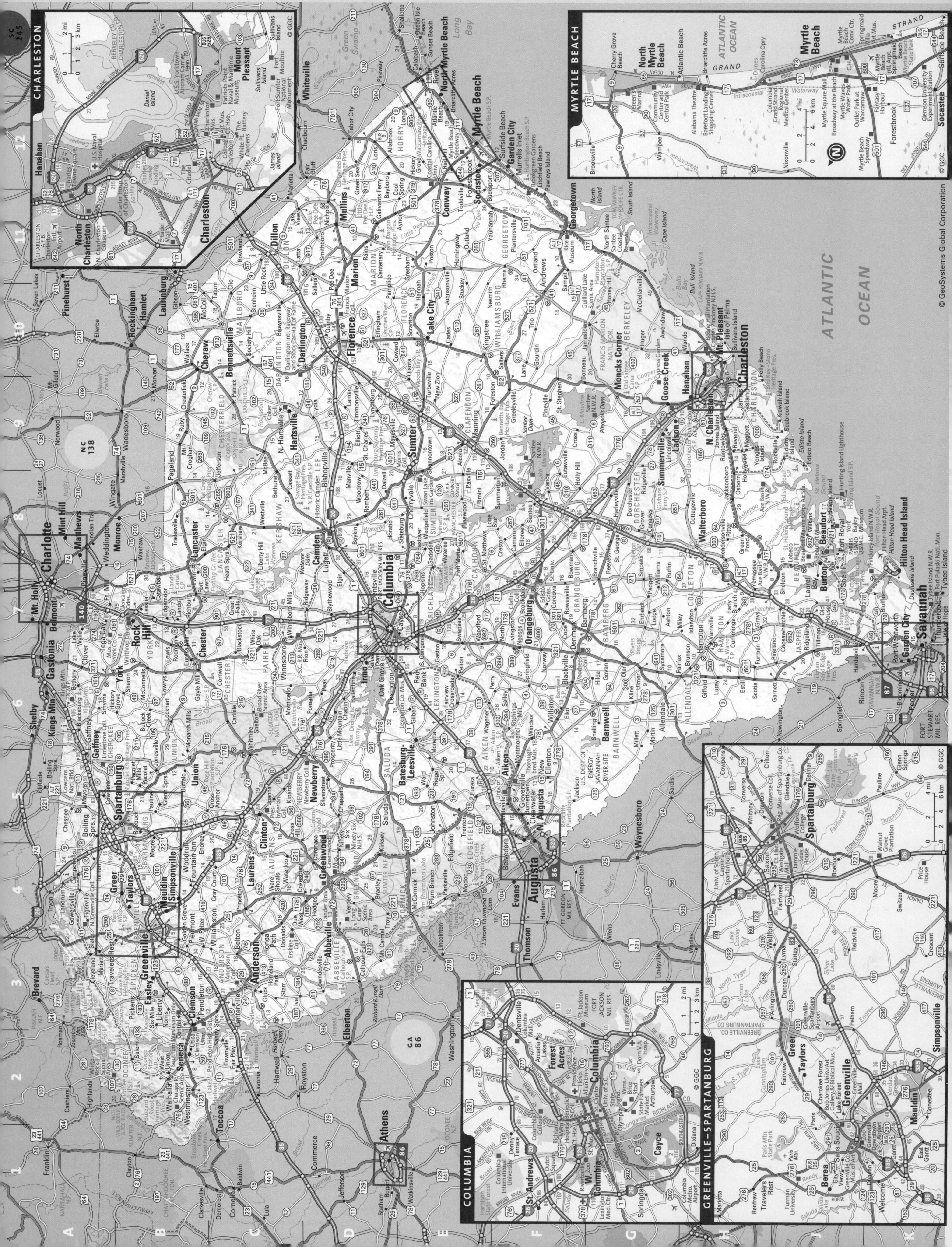

TOURISM:
800.732.5682
ROAD CONDITIONS:
605.626.2282
605.394.2255
605.367.5707 (FLOODING)
SOUTH DAKOTA
157
PIERRE
SIOUX FALLS
RAPID CITY
BLACK HILLS–SOUTH
BLACK HILLS–NORTH
Sioux Falls
Rapid City
Pierre
Aberdeen
Watertown
Brookings
Huron
Mitchell
Yankton
Vermillion
Mobridge
Spearfish
Sturgis
Lead
Deadwood
Custer
Hot Springs
Belle Fourche
Winner
Redfield
Madison
Milbank
Sisseton
Lemmon
Box Elder
Brandon
Canton
Sioux City
Valentine
Chadron
Newcastle
Sundance
STANDING ROCK IND. RES.
CHEYENNE RIVER IND. RES.
PINE RIDGE IND. RES.
ROSEBUD IND. RES.
CROW CREEK IND. RES.
CUSTER NATL. FOR.
BLACK HILLS NATIONAL FOREST
Custer State Park
WIND CAVE NATIONAL PARK
CENTRAL TIME ZONE
MOUNTAIN TIME ZONE
MN 116
IA 96
NE 124
WY 176
MT 122
ND 141
© GeoSystems Global Corporation
© GGC

TOURISM:
800.836.6200
615.741.2158

ROAD CONDITIONS:
800.342.3258

MI 10 20 30
KM 10 20 30 40

KY 100

MO 120

AR 66

MS 118

AL 60

Memphis, Jackson, Clarksville, Columbia, Union City, Martin, Paris, Dyersburg, Covington, Millington, Bartlett, Germantown, Collierville, Bolivar, Savannah, Lawrenceburg, Pulaski, Florence, Sheffield, Tuscumbia, Muscle Shoals, Corinth, Decatur, Athens, Booneville, Russellville, Mayfield, Murray

MEMPHIS

Memphis, West Memphis, Bartlett, Southaven, Horn Lake, Olive Branch, ARKANSAS, MISSISSIPPI

0 2 4 mi
0 2 4 6 km

© GGC

NASHVILLE

Nashville, Hendersonville, Brentwood, Forest Hills, Oak Hill, Belle Meade

0 1 2 mi
0 1 2 3 km

© GGC

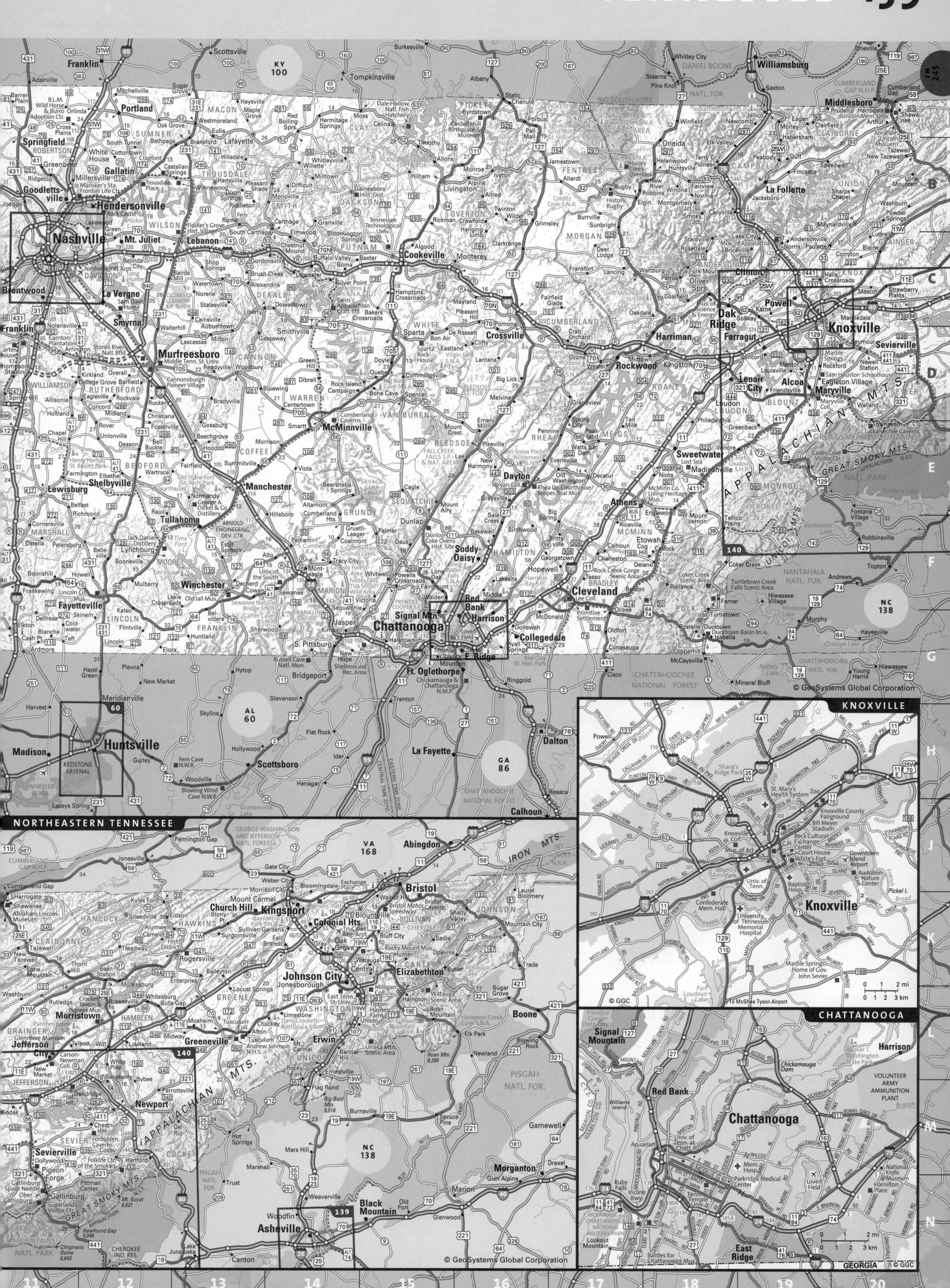
NORTHEASTERN TENNESSEE
KNOXVILLE
CHATTANOOGA
Nashville
Knoxville
Chattanooga
Murfreesboro
Cookeville
Clarksville
Cleveland
Huntsville
Johnson City
Kingsport
Bristol
Asheville
APPALACHIAN MTS.
GREAT SMOKY MTS.
© GeoSystems Global Corporation
© GGC

160 TEXAS (west)
TOURISM:
800.888.8839
ROAD CONDITIONS:
800.452.9292
AMARILLO
LUBBOCK
ODESSA–MIDLAND
EL PASO

AUSTIN
ABILENE
WACO
McALLEN
© GeoSystems Global Corporation

TOURISM:
800.888.8839
ROAD CONDITIONS:
800.452.9292
MI 25 50
KM 25 50
BEAUMONT
AR 66
LA 102
OK 146

DOWNTOWN SAN ANTONIO
CORPUS CHRISTI
SAN ANTONIO
LAREDO
GULF OF MEXICO
PADRE ISLAND NATIONAL SEASHORE
NUECES PLAINS
Houston
San Antonio
Corpus Christi
Laredo
Nuevo Laredo
Brownsville
Matamoros
Reynosa
Victoria
Galveston
Port Arthur
MEX 188
TX 246
© GeoSystems Global Corporation

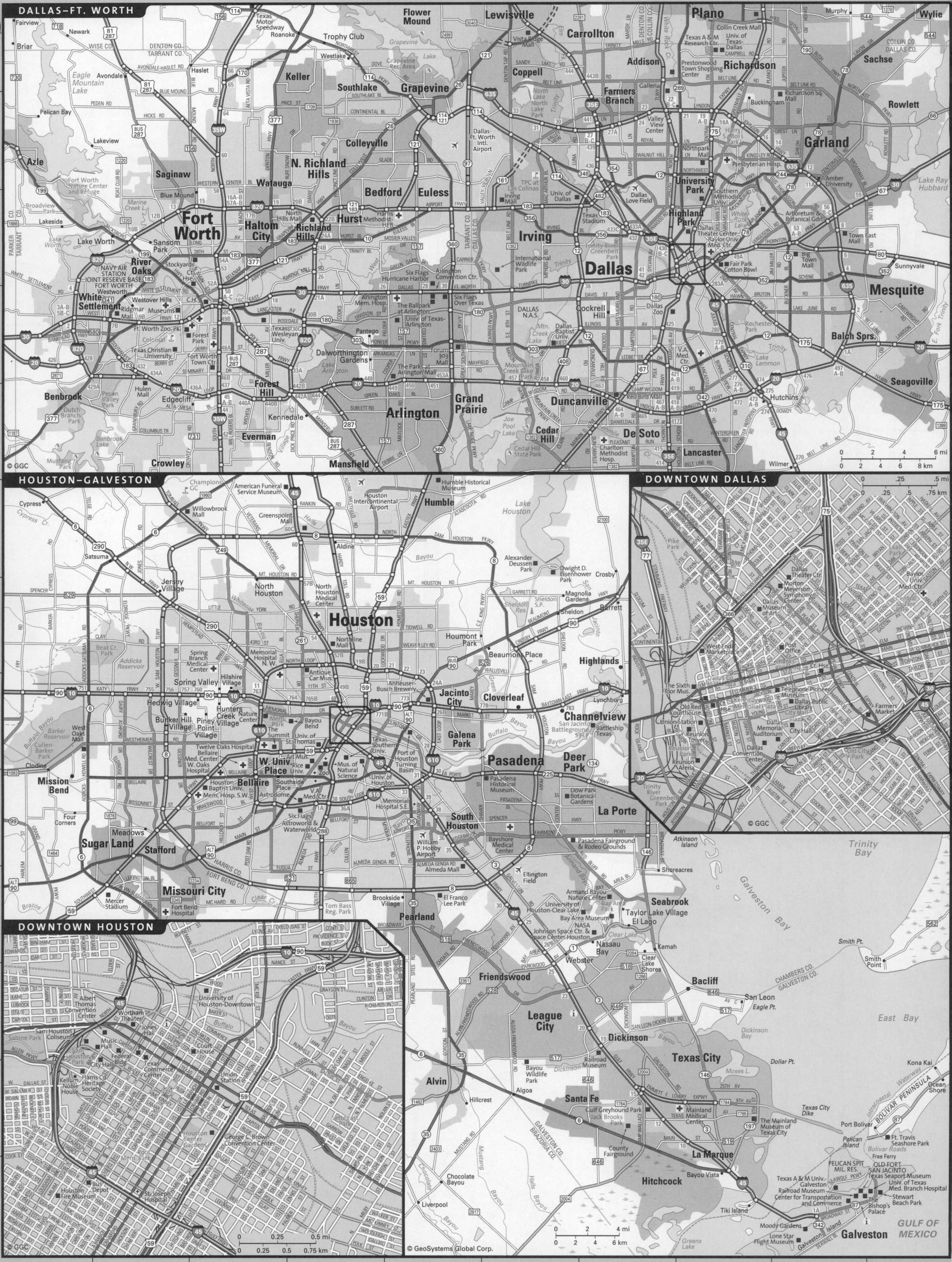

DALLAS–FT. WORTH

0 2 4 6 mi
0 2 4 6 8 km

HOUSTON–GALVESTON

0 2 4 mi
0 2 4 6 km

DOWNTOWN DALLAS

0 .25 .5 mi
0 .25 .5 .75 km

DOWNTOWN HOUSTON

0 0.25 0.5 mi
0 0.25 0.5 0.75 km

TOURISM:
800.200.1160
801.538.1030

ROAD CONDITIONS:
801.964.6000

MI 30 60
KM 30 60

ZION NATL. PARK

PROVO

OGDEN

SALT LAKE CITY

BRYCE CANYON N.P.

TOURISM:
800.837.6668
802.828.3236

ROAD CONDITIONS:
800.429.7623 (WINTER, VT)
802.828.2648

CHARLOTTESVILLE
Charlottesville
Woodbrook
Northfields
Fashion Square Mall
Colthurst
Meadow Creek Park
McIntire Municipal Park
Pen Park
Bellair
Rivanna
Darden Towe Park
Univ. of Virginia
Rotunda
Scott Stadium
Martha Jefferson Hosp.
Univ. of Va. Med. Ctr.
Tonsler Park
Virginia Discovery Museum
Riverview Park
Azalea Park
Monticello
Michie Tavern
Ash Lawn-Highland
PETERSBURG
Colonial Heights
Hopewell
Weston Plantation
City Point Unit (Petersburg Natl. Btfld.)
South Park Mall
Violet Bank Civil War Mus.
Virginia State University
Ettrick
Matoaca
Centre Hill Mansion
Quartermaster Museum
Petersburg Natl. Bfld.
Ft. Lee Mil. Res.
Old Blandford Church & Cemetery
Court House
Prince George
Central St. Hosp.
Petersburg
Pamplin Civil War Park
Softball Hall of Fame
Blackwater Swamp
WASHINGTON, DC AREA
Leesburg
Gaithersburg
Quince Orchard
Darnestown
Dufief
Rockville
Derwood
Aspen Hill
Colesville
Rossmoor Leisure World
Countryside
Sugarland Run
Ashburn
Copenhaver
Potomac
Wheaton
Kensington
Sterling
Dranesville
Great Falls
Bethesda
Silver Spring
Takoma Park
Herndon
Reston
Chevy Chase
Washington Dulles International Airport
Pleasant Valley
Spring Hill
McLean
Langley
Tysons Corner
Vienna
Pimmit Hills
Chantilly
Oakton
Falls Church
Arlington
Washington
Merrifield
Seven Corners
Fairfax
Centreville
Bull Run
Annandale
Baileys Crossroads
Kings Park West
Kings Park
Burke
Alexandria
West Gate of Lomond
Manassas Park
Yorkshire
Manassas
North Springfield
Springfield
West Springfield
Franconia
Rose Hill
Groveton
Hybla Valley
Fort Foote Village
Newington
Manassas Natl. Battlefield Park
NORFOLK–VIRGINIA BEACH–NEWPORT NEWS
Newport News
Poquoson
Hampton
Norfolk
Portsmouth
Virginia Beach
Chesapeake
Suffolk
Smithfield
Carrollton
Hobson
Longview
Grafton
Tabb
Fort Eustis Military Reservation
Mulberry Island
Plum Tree Island N.W.R.
N.A.S.A. Research Center
Langley A.F.B.
Fort Monroe
Fort Monroe Military Reservation
Chesapeake Bay
Atlantic Ocean
Norfolk Naval Base
Little Creek U.S. Naval Amphibious Base
Ft. Story Military Res.
Cape Henry Memorial
Old Cape Henry Lighthouse
Oceana N.A.S.
Camp Pendleton
U.S. Naval Amphibious Base
Dam Neck U.S. Naval Fleet Training Center
Great Dismal Swamp N.W.R.
Back Bay N.W.R.
Nansemond N.W.R.
U.S. Naval Transmitter Station
Lake Tecumseh
Stumpy Lake
Oak Grove
Lynnhaven Roads
COLONIAL NATL. HIST. PARK
Williamsburg
College of William and Mary
Colonial Williamsburg
Camp Peary
Five Forks
Water Country U.S.A.
Yorktown Naval Weapons Station
Yorktown
Gloucester Point
Jamestown Settlement
Jamestown Island
Kingsmill
Busch Gardens
Newport News
© GeoSystems Global Corp.

TOURISM:
800.932.5827

ROAD CONDITIONS:
800.367.7623

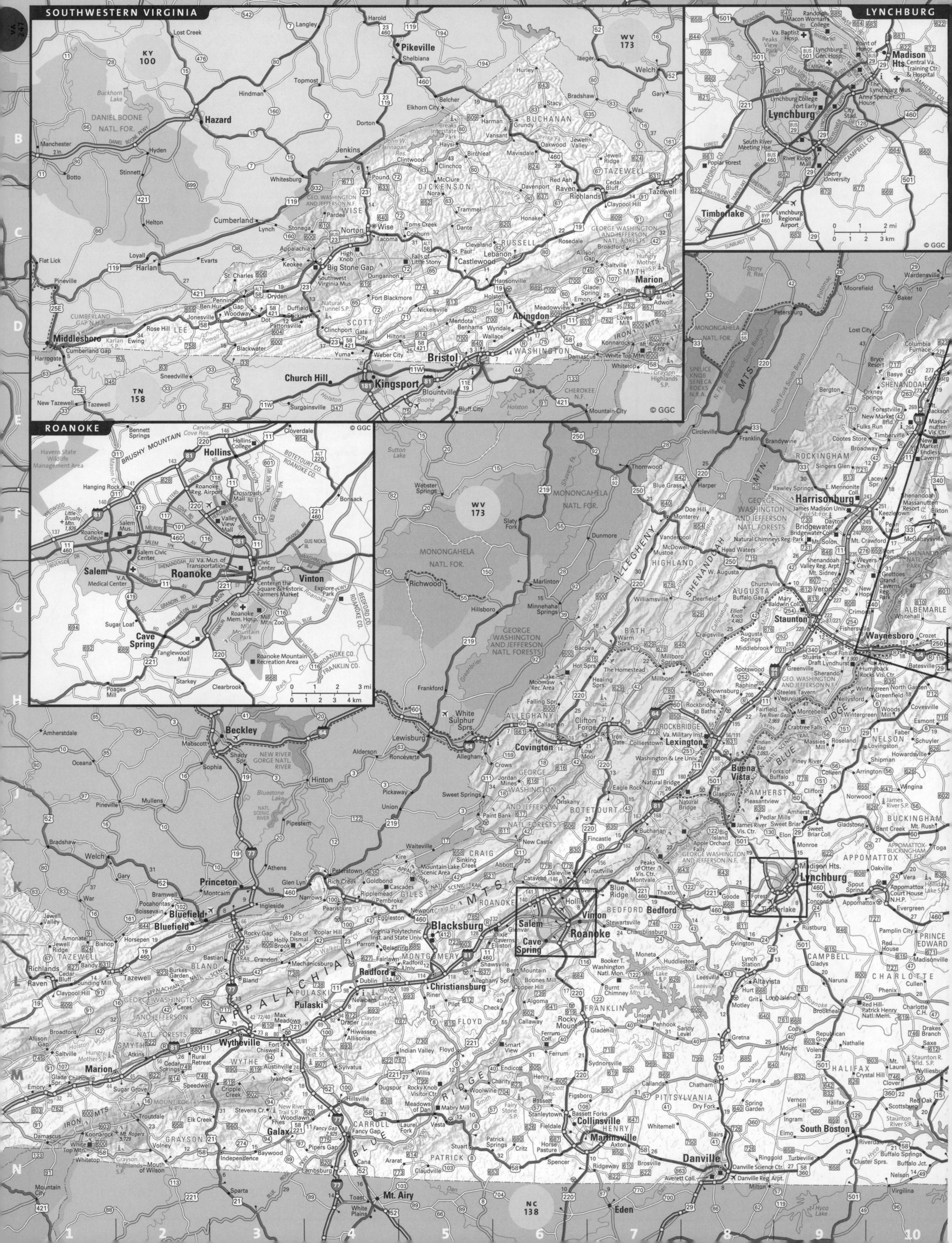

MI 10 20 30
KM 10 20 30

SOUTHWESTERN VIRGINIA

© GGC

LYNCHBURG

© GGC

ROANOKE

© GGC

RICHMOND
Washington
Baltimore
Arlington
Alexandria
Annapolis
Towson
Dundalk
Columbia
Frederick
Hagerstown
Martinsburg
Winchester
Front Royal
Leesburg
Rockville
Gaithersburg
Wheaton
Bethesda
Reston
Centreville
Manassas
Woodbridge
Dale City
St. Charles
La Plata
Fredericksburg
Culpeper
Charlottesville
Richmond
Lakeside
Mechanicsville
Bon Air
Chester
Ashland
Petersburg
Colonial Hts.
Hopewell
Williamsburg
Poquoson
Hampton
Newport News
Norfolk
Portsmouth
Virginia Beach
Chesapeake
Suffolk
Franklin
Emporia
Farmville
Salisbury
Cambridge
Chincoteague
Pocomoke City
Crisfield
Chesapeake Bay
ATLANTIC OCEAN
Roanoke Rapids
© GeoSystems Global Corporation

TOURISM:
800.544.1800
ROAD CONDITIONS:
888.766.4636 (WA)
206.368.4499

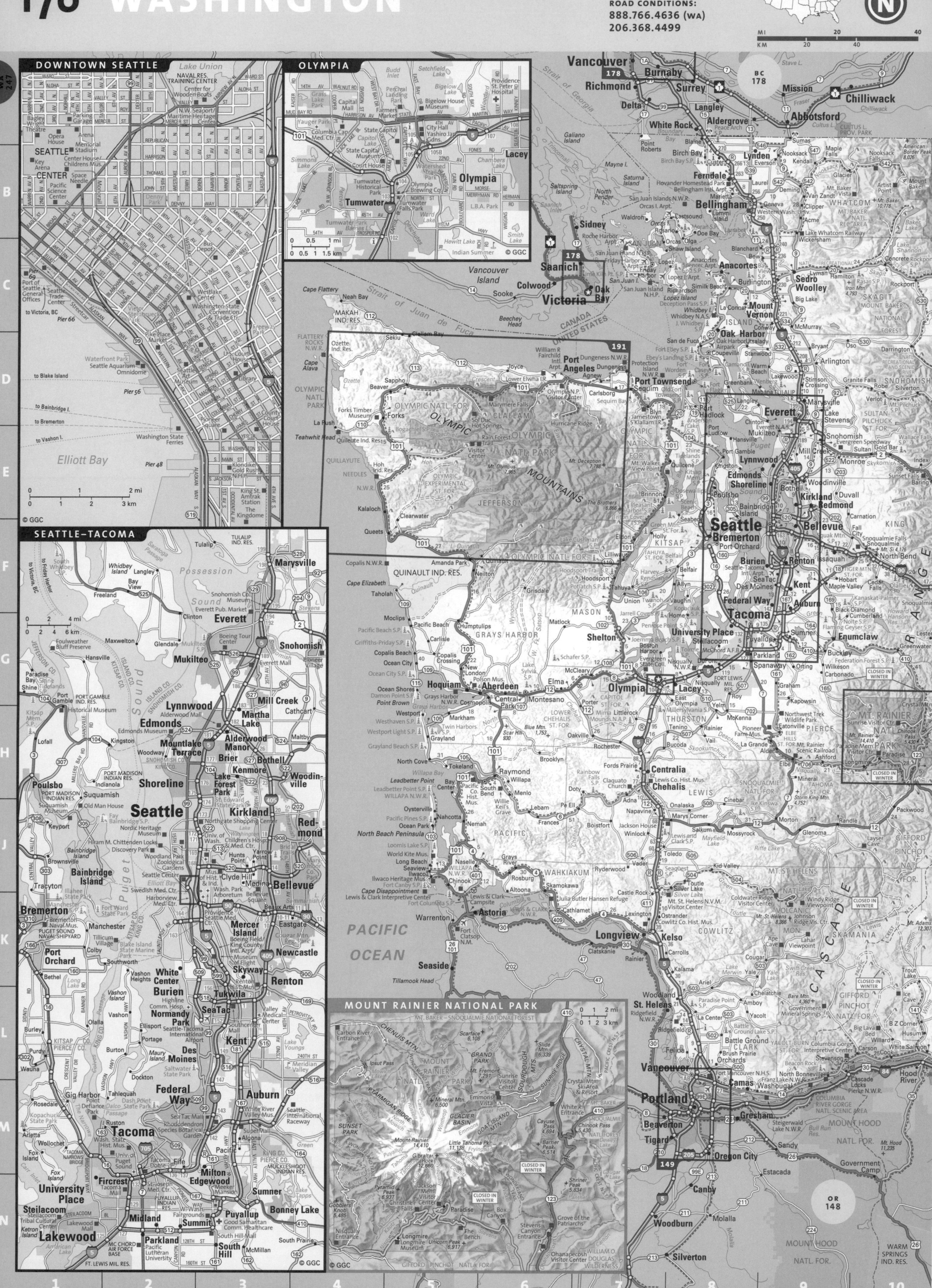

Spokane
Country Homes
Veradale
Opportunity
Cheney
Wenatchee
Ellensburg
Yakima
Richland
Pasco
Kennewick
Walla Walla
College Place
Moses Lake
Ephrata
Pullman
Clarkston
Lewiston
Moscow
Coeur d'Alene
Post Falls
The Dalles
Pendleton
Hermiston
Milton-Freewater
Omak
Okanogan
Colville
Sunnyside
Grandview
Toppenish
Selah
YAKIMA
SPOKANE
BC 178
ID 89
OR 148
WA 247
CANADA
UNITED STATES

TOURISM:
800.422.8644

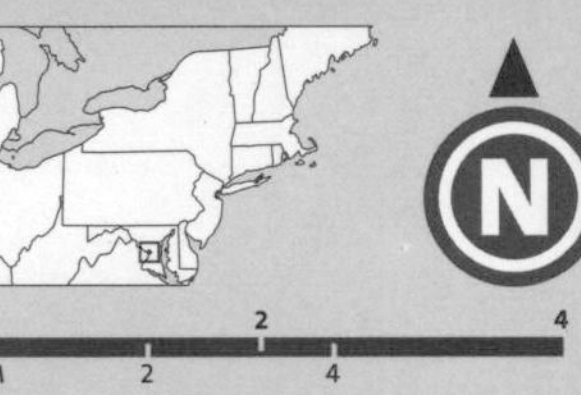

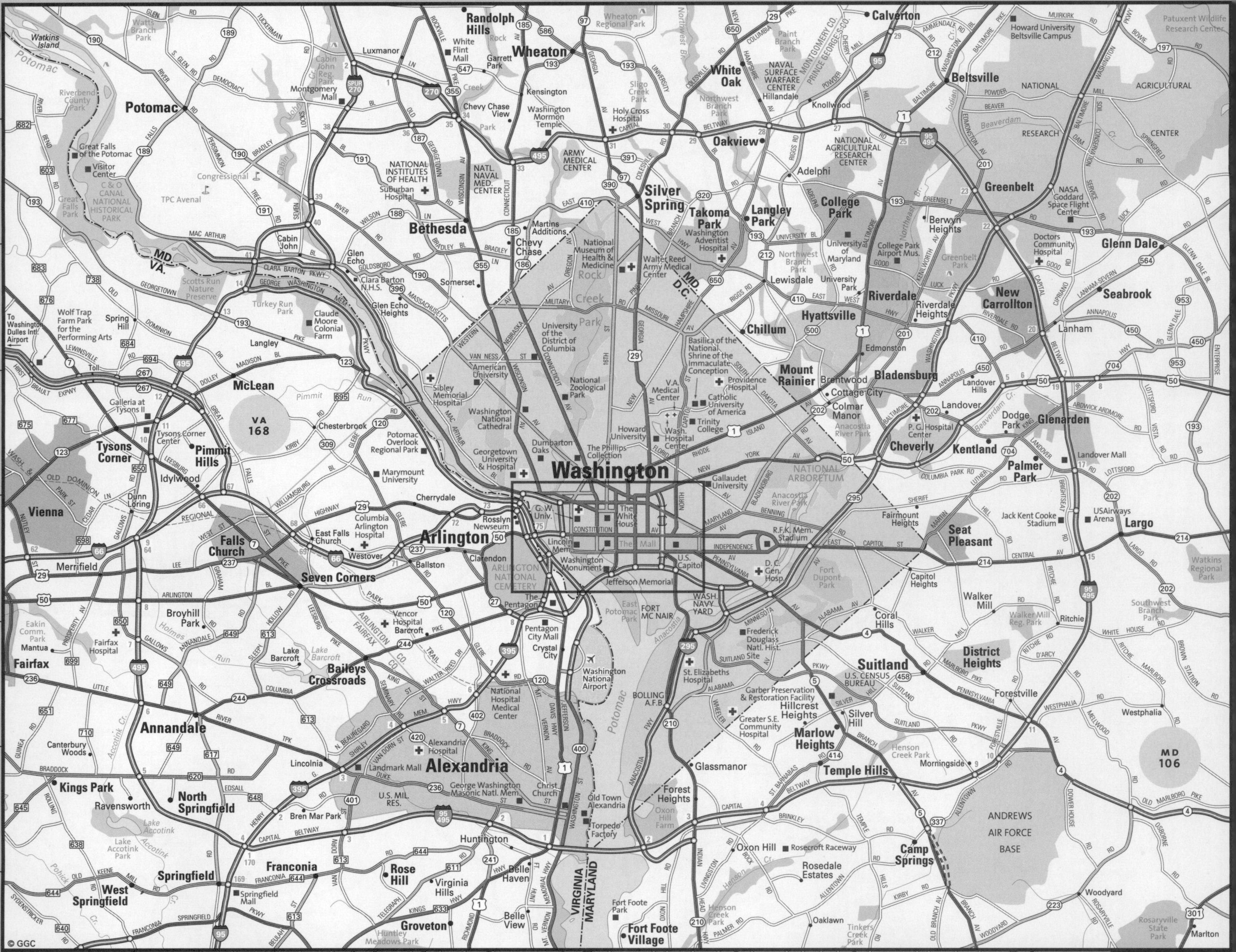

THE MALL

TOURISM:
800.225.5982
304.558.2286
ROAD CONDITIONS:
304.558.2889

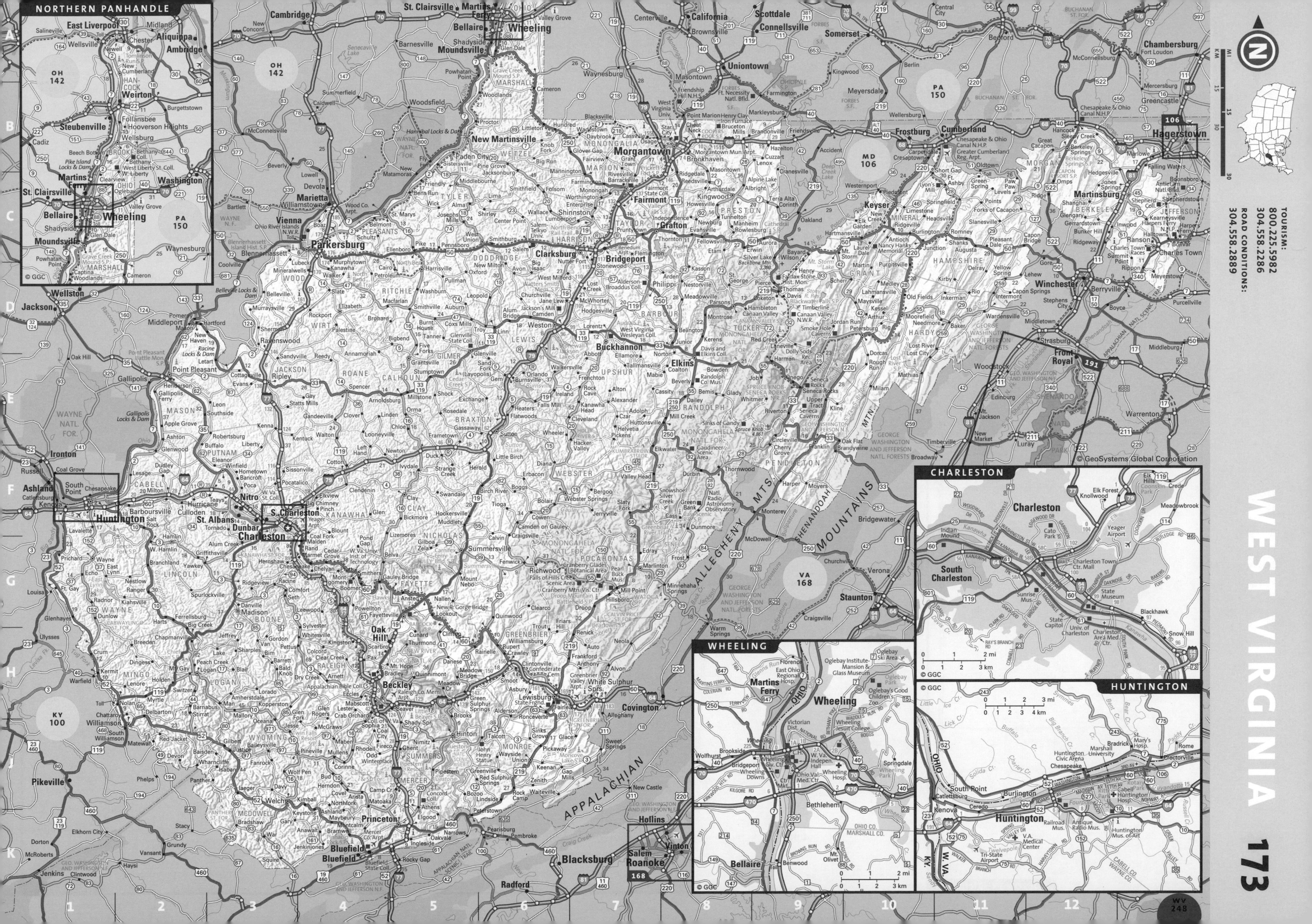

TOURISM:
800.432.8747

ROAD CONDITIONS:
800.762.3947 (WI)
608.246.7580

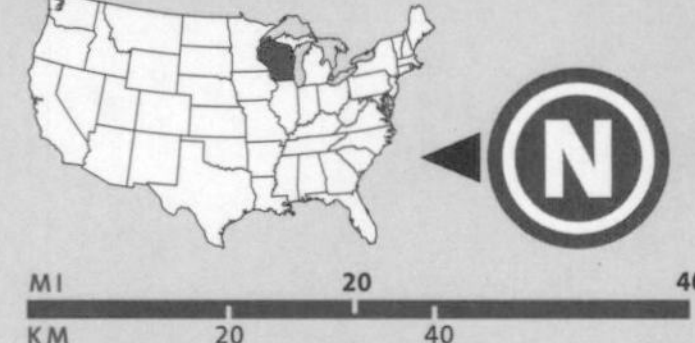

EAU CLAIRE
MADISON
MILWAUKEE
DOWNTOWN MILWAUKEE
LAKE MICHIGAN
Milwaukee
Madison
Chicago
Green Bay
Appleton
Oshkosh
Manitowoc
Sheboygan
Fond du Lac
La Crosse
Eau Claire
Racine
Kenosha
Janesville
Beloit
Rockford
Dubuque
Gary
Joliet
© GeoSystems Global Corporation

TOURISM:
800.225.5996
307.777.7777

ROAD CONDITIONS:
307.635.9966

YELLOWSTONE NATL. PARK

GRAND TETON NATL. PARK

CASPER

CHEYENNE

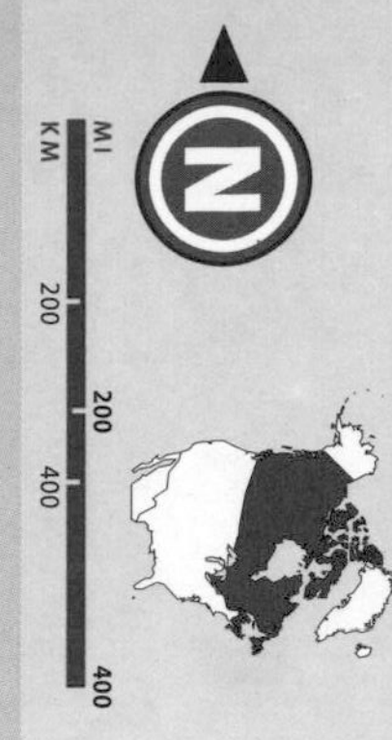

DISTANCES BETWEEN CITIES ARE COMPUTED IN KILOMETERS OVER MAIN HIGHWAYS AND INCLUDE FERRY DISTANCES

	BOSTON, MA	BRANDON, MB	CALGARY, AB	CHARLOTTETOWN, PE	CHICAGO, IL	DAWSON CREEK, BC	EDMONTON, AB	FREDERICTON, NB	HALIFAX, NS	KENORA, ON	MINNEAPOLIS, MN	MONTRÉAL, PQ	NEW YORK, NY	NORTH BAY, ON	OTTAWA, ON	PRINCE GEORGE, BC	QUÉBEC, PQ	REGINA, SK	ST. JOHN'S, NF	SASKATOON, SK	SAULT STE. MARIE, ON	SEATTLE, WA	THUNDER BAY, ON	TORONTO, ON	VANCOUVER, BC	VICTORIA, BC	WHITEHORSE, YT	WINDSOR, ON	WINNIPEG, MB
BANFF, AB	4470	1258	129	5078	2904	1018	428	4705	5120	1669	2190	3871	4447	3313	3681	632	4142	893	6481	748	2887	1081	2179	3562	928	1033	2513	3369	1464
BOSTON, MA		3212	4341	999	1593	4953	4362	652	920	2801	2254	545	328	1104	735	5076	629	3577	2402	3834	1583	4917	2291	907	5398	5503	6394	1158	2953
BRANDON, MB			1130	3863	1646	1741	1150	3446	3862	410	932	2613	3189	2055	2423	1865	2883	365	5223	623	1628	2339	920	2304	2187	2291	3236	2111	206
CALGARY, AB				4930	2776	890	299	4557	4972	1540	2061	3743	4319	3184	3553	761	4013	764	6333	619	2758	1210	2050	3434	1057	1162	2385	3241	1335
CHARLOTTETOWN, PE					2576	5553	4962	373	280	3401	3057	1199	1353	1757	1389	5677	959	4177	1448	4434	2183	5810	2891	1738	5998	6103	7047	2111	3606
CHICAGO, IL						3387	2796	2203	2618	1236	661	1369	1344	1152	1229	3511	1640	2011	3979	2269	726	3324	1070	830	3833	3937	4882	465	1440
DAWSON CREEK, BC							590	5187	5603	2151	2673	4354	4930	3796	4164	405	4624	1376	6956	1118	3369	1318	2661	4045	1202	1307	1495	3852	1947
EDMONTON, AB								4597	5012	1561	2082	3763	4339	3205	3574	714	4034	785	6365	528	2779	1360	2071	3455	1244	1348	2085	3261	1356
FREDERICTON, NB									415	3036	2692	833	1009	1392	1023	5311	586	3812	1776	4069	1818	5445	2526	1372	5633	5738	6682	1738	3241
HALIFAX, NS										3451	3107	1249	1278	1807	1438	5726	981	4227	1503	4484	2233	5860	2941	1788	6048	6153	7097	2153	3656
KENORA, ON											708	2203	2779	1644	2013	2275	2473	776	4804	1033	1205	2750	510	1894	2597	2701	3646	1701	204
MINNEAPOLIS, MN												1858	2005	1300	1669	2796	2129	1297	4460	1554	874	2663	560	1493	2811	2709	4167	1128	726
MONTRÉAL, PQ													613	558	190	4478	270	2978	2601	3236	985	4611	1693	539	4799	4904	5849	904	2407
NEW YORK, NY														1146	777	5054	864	3554	2759	3812	1561	4668	2269	885	5413	5517	6462	1136	2983
NORTH BAY, ON															368	3920	829	2420	3160	2677	426	3879	1134	335	4141	4346	5278	700	1849
OTTAWA, ON																4288	460	2788	2792	3046	795	4471	1503	399	4610	4714	5659	764	2217
PRINCE GEORGE, BC																	4748	1500	7080	1242	3480	912	2785	4169	796	901	1900	3976	2071
QUÉBEC, PQ																		2349	2362	3506	1255	4882	1963	809	5070	5174	6119	1175	2677
REGINA, SK																			5580	257	1981	1974	1286	2669	1821	1926	2870	2476	571
ST. JOHN'S, NF																				5837	3586	7213	4294	3141	7401	7602	8450	3514	5009
SASKATOON, SK																					2238	1829	1543	2927	1677	1781	2613	2734	829
SAULT STE. MARIE, ON																						3453	708	676	3802	3907	4851	581	1422
SEATTLE, WA																							3260	4072	232	130	2812	3707	2545
THUNDER BAY, ON																								1384	3107	3212	4156	1289	714
TORONTO, ON																									4490	4595	5527	365	2098
VANCOUVER, BC																										105	2697	4298	2232
VICTORIA, BC																											2801	4402	2336
WHITEHORSE, YT																												5347	3524
WINDSOR, ON																													1905
WINNIPEG, MB																													

Nunavut, currently the eastern portion of the Northwest Territories, will become an established territory in 1999.

CAN 249

TOURISM:
800.663.6000
250.387.1642
604.663.6000 (BC)

ROAD CONDITIONS:
604.420.4997

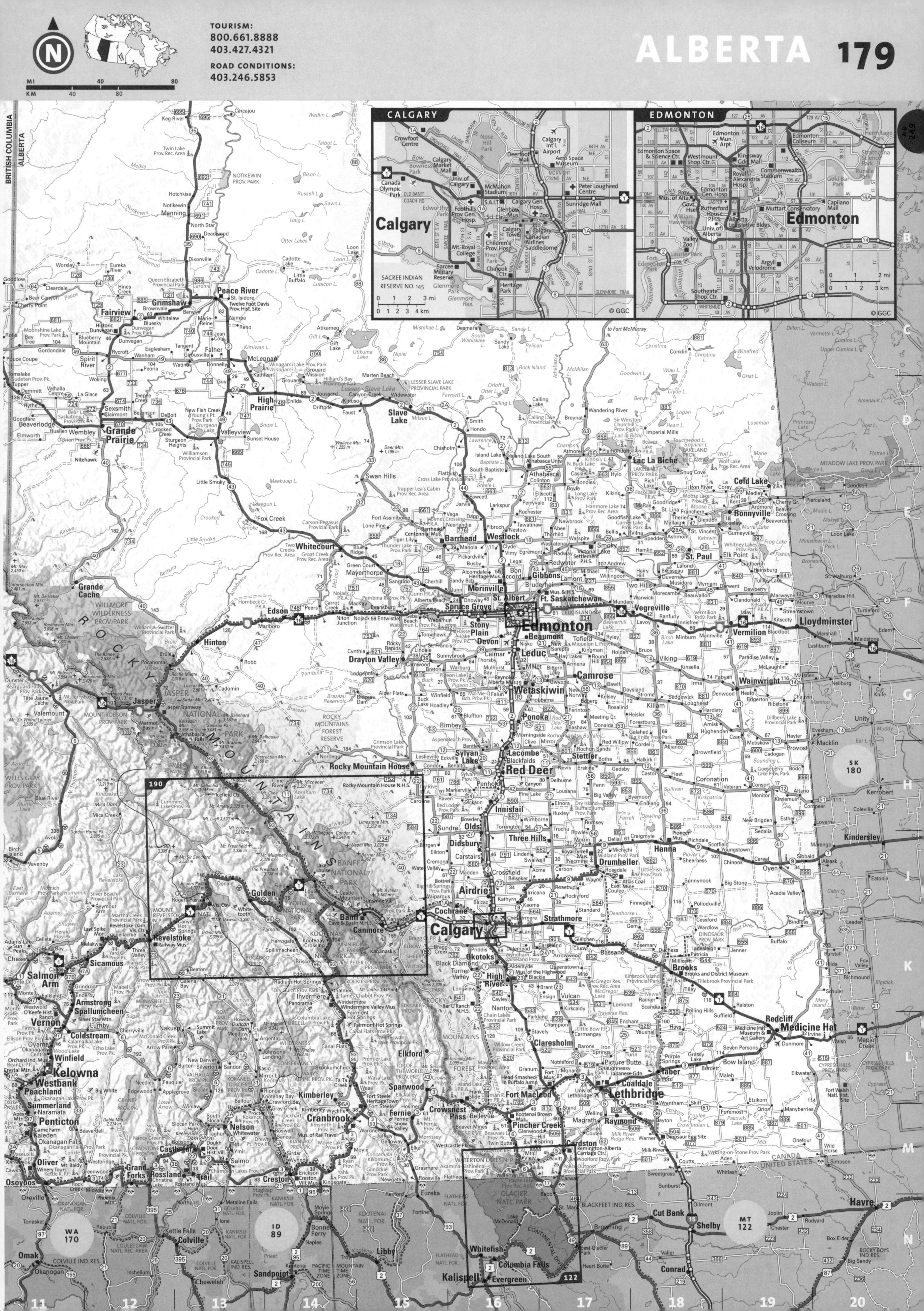
TOURISM:
800.661.8888
403.427.4321
ROAD CONDITIONS:
403.246.5853
CALGARY
EDMONTON
Calgary
Edmonton
Peace River
Grande Prairie
High Prairie
Slave Lake
Fort McMurray
Lac La Biche
Cold Lake
Bonnyville
Athabasca
Whitecourt
Barrhead
Westlock
St. Albert
Spruce Grove
Stony Plain
Ft. Saskatchewan
Vegreville
Lloydminster
Vermilion
Leduc
Wetaskiwin
Camrose
Wainwright
Edson
Hinton
Jasper
Grande Cache
Drayton Valley
Ponoka
Lacombe
Red Deer
Rocky Mountain House
Sylvan Lake
Innisfail
Olds
Three Hills
Didsbury
Drumheller
Hanna
Airdrie
Cochrane
Canmore
Banff
Okotoks
High River
Strathmore
Brooks
Medicine Hat
Claresholm
Fort Macleod
Lethbridge
Taber
Pincher Creek
Cardston
Crowsnest Pass
Golden
Revelstoke
Salmon Arm
Vernon
Kelowna
Penticton
Oliver
Nelson
Cranbrook
Kimberley
Fernie
Sparwood
Trail
Castlegar
Creston
Whitefish
Kalispell
Columbia Falls
Libby
Cut Bank
Shelby
Havre
Sandpoint
Colville
Omak
ROCKY MOUNTAINS
BRITISH COLUMBIA
ALBERTA
SK 180
MT 122
WA 170
ID 89
190
UNITED STATES
CANADA

TOURISM:
800.667.7191
306.787.2300

ROAD CONDITIONS:
306.787.7623

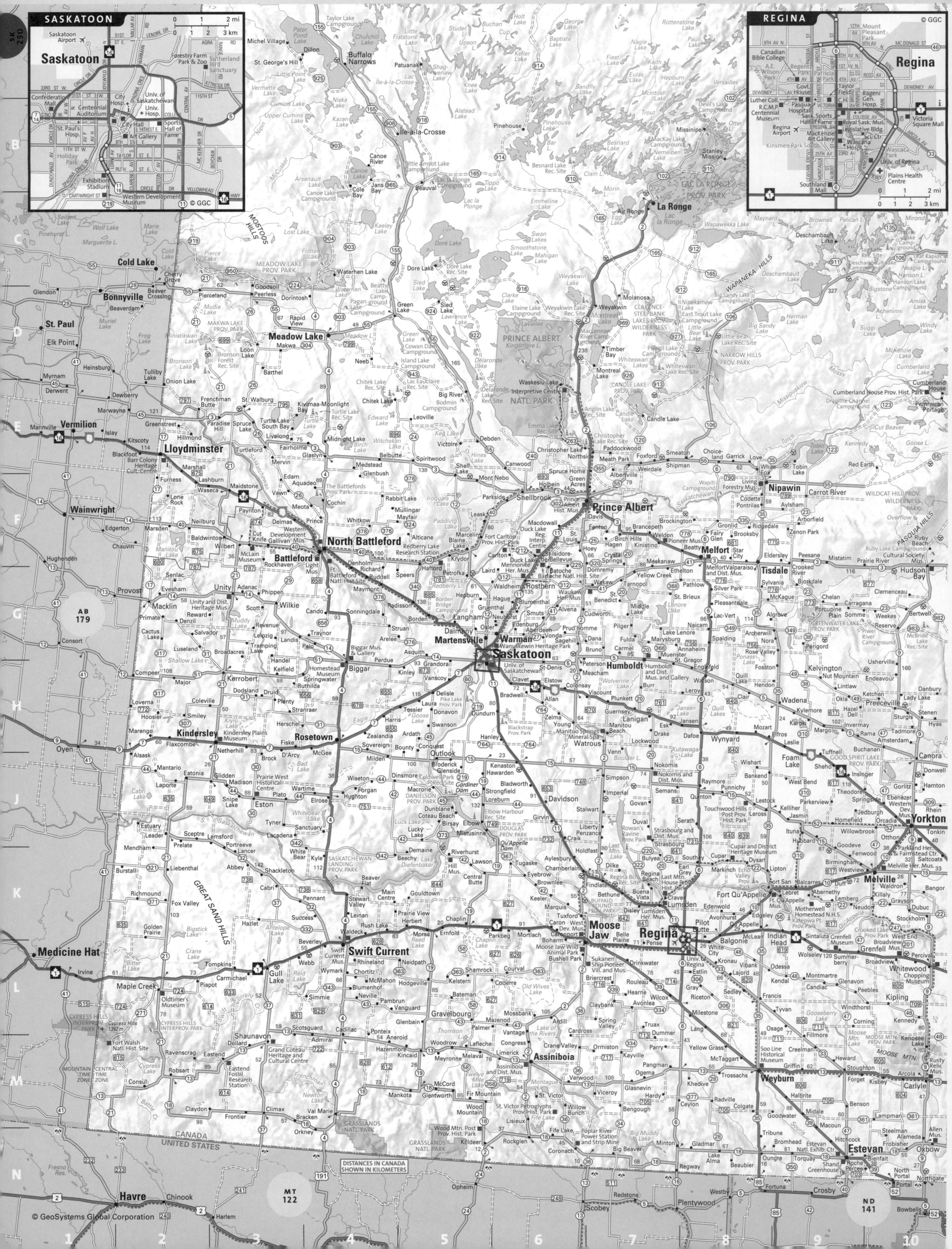

MI 0 30 60
KM 0 30 60

SK 250

SASKATOON

REGINA

AB 179

MT 122

ND 141

DISTANCES IN CANADA SHOWN IN KILOMETERS

CANADA
UNITED STATES

MOUNTAIN / CENTRAL TIME ZONE

GREAT SAND HILLS

TOURISM
204.945.3777
ROAD CONDITIONS
204.945.3704

MI 30 60
KM 30 60

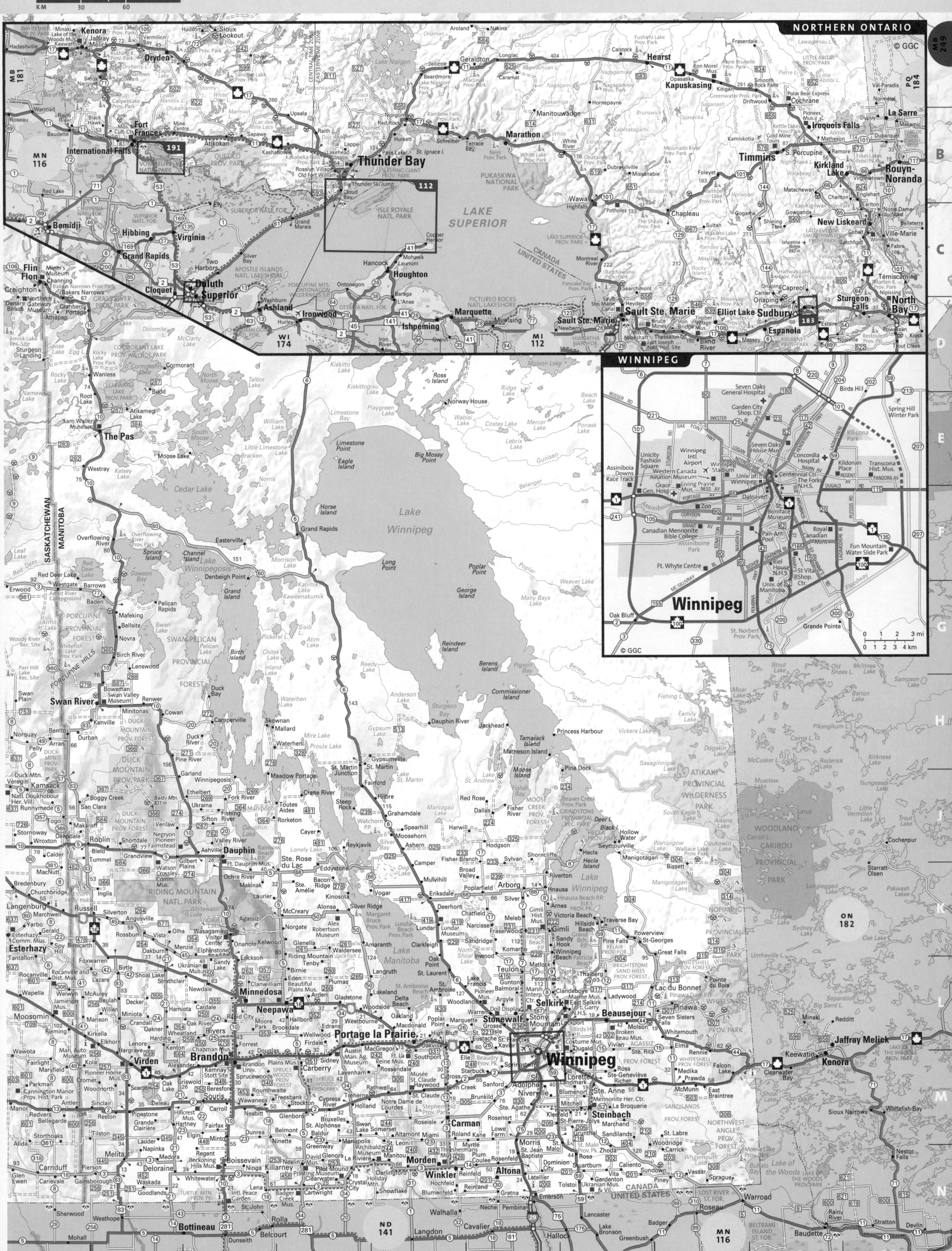

TOURISM:
800.668.2746
416.314.0944
ROAD CONDITIONS:
416.235.1110

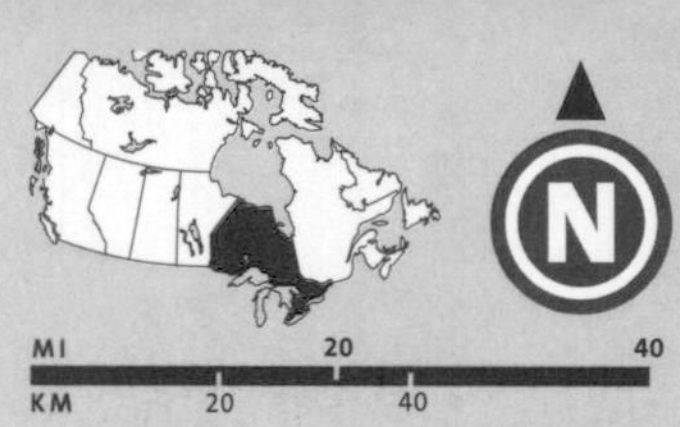

DISTANCES IN CANADA SHOWN IN KILOMETERS

TRAVEL NOTE: Reclassification of Ontario roads at time of publication may result in highway number changes.

HAMILTON

LONDON

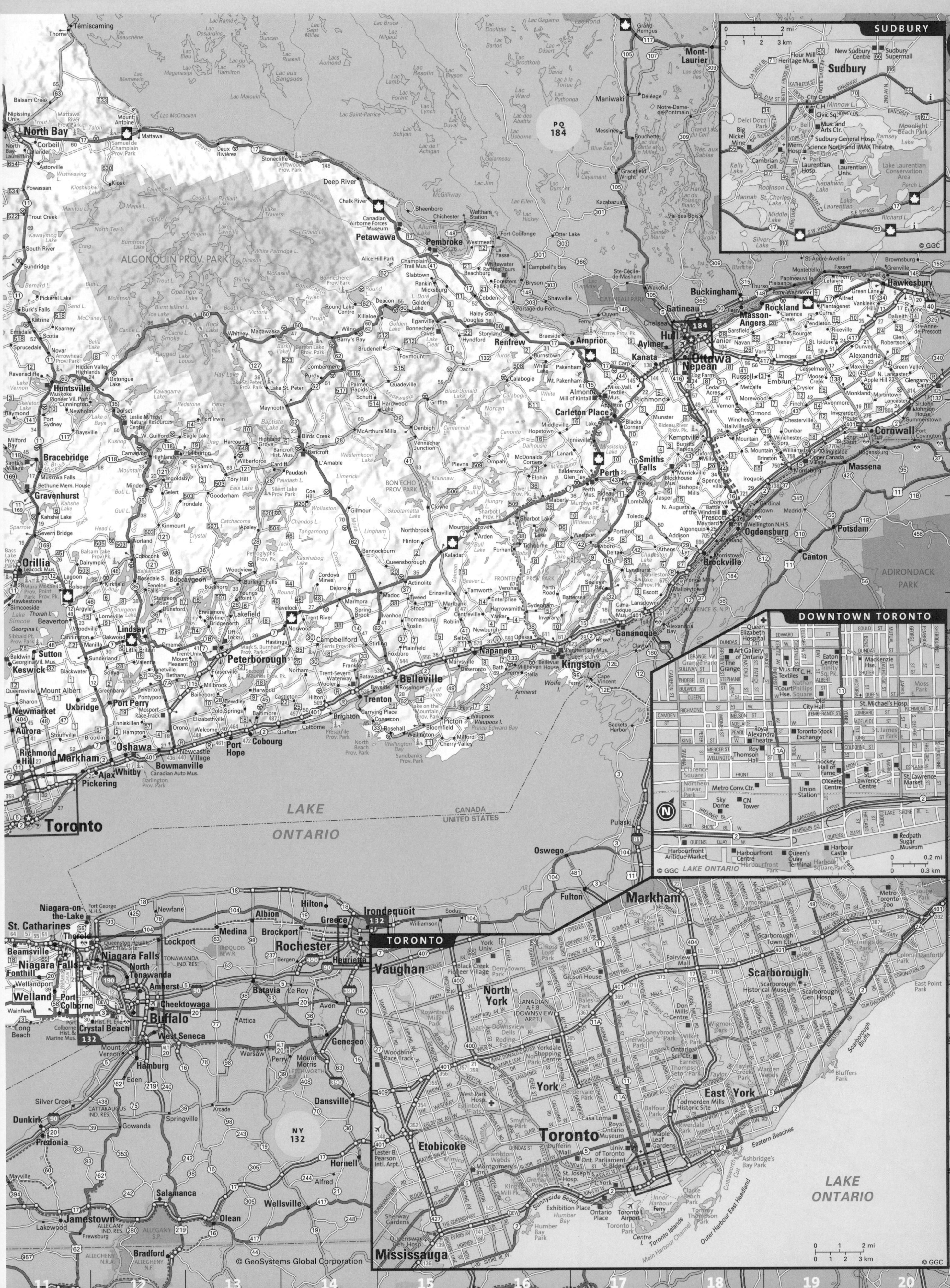
SUDBURY
DOWNTOWN TORONTO
TORONTO
LAKE ONTARIO
CANADA
UNITED STATES
ALGONQUIN PROV. PARK
ADIRONDACK PARK
PQ 184
NY 132
ON 249
North Bay
Huntsville
Bracebridge
Gravenhurst
Orillia
Barrie
Lindsay
Peterborough
Belleville
Trenton
Napanee
Kingston
Gananoque
Brockville
Prescott
Cornwall
Hawkesbury
Ottawa
Hull
Gatineau
Nepean
Kanata
Arnprior
Renfrew
Pembroke
Petawawa
Deep River
Mattawa
Perth
Smiths Falls
Carleton Place
Kemptville
Ogdensburg
Massena
Potsdam
Canton
Oshawa
Whitby
Ajax
Pickering
Markham
Newmarket
Aurora
Uxbridge
Port Perry
Cobourg
Port Hope
Bowmanville
Toronto
Vaughan
North York
Scarborough
York
East York
Etobicoke
Mississauga
St. Catharines
Niagara Falls
Welland
Buffalo
Rochester
Oswego
Batavia
Lockport
Jamestown
Olean
Dunkirk
Fredonia
Salamanca
Hornell
Dansville
Geneseo
© GeoSystems Global Corporation

TOURISM:
800.363.7777
514.873.2015

ROAD CONDITIONS:
514.873.4121

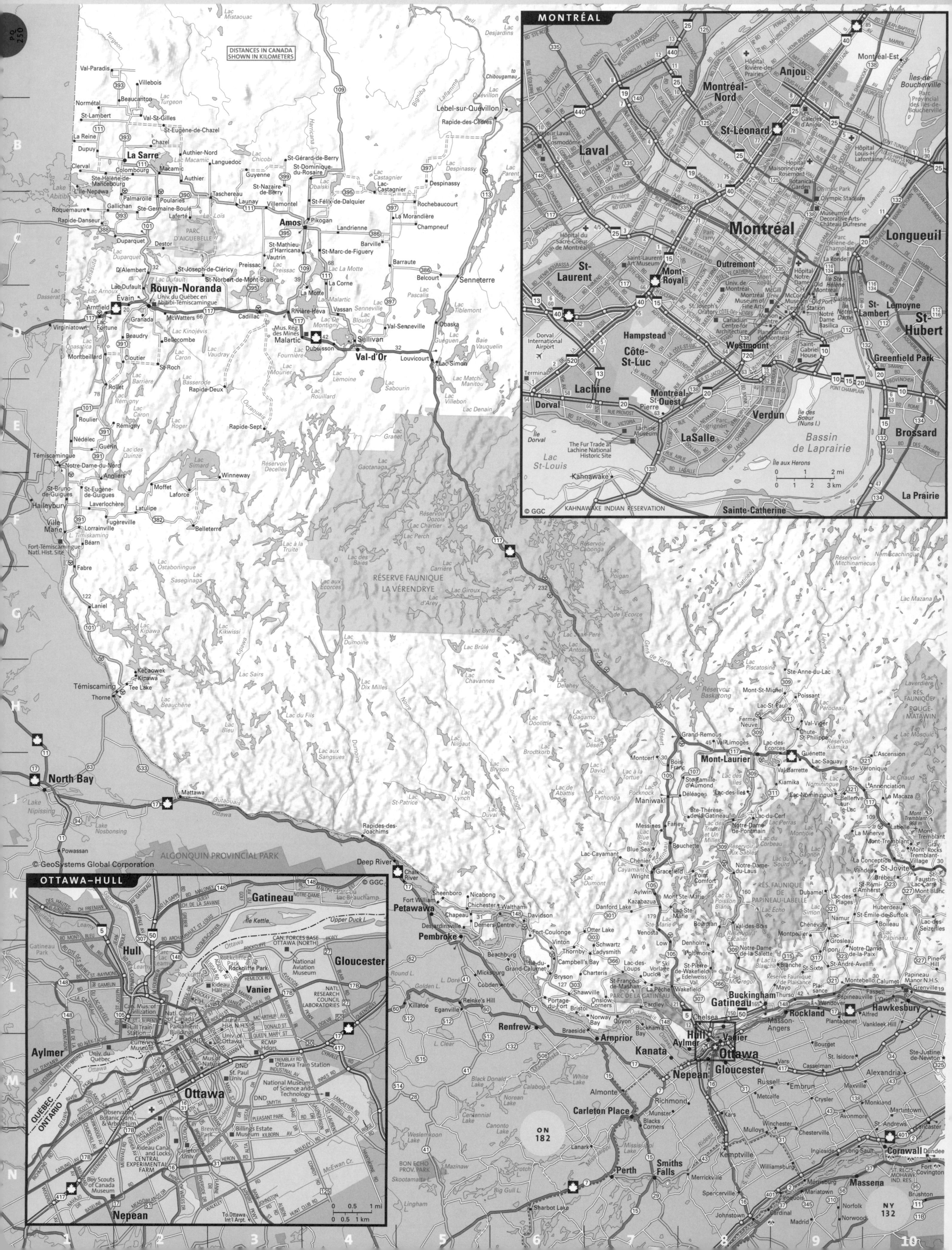

MONTRÉAL

OTTAWA–HULL

DISTANCES IN CANADA SHOWN IN KILOMETERS

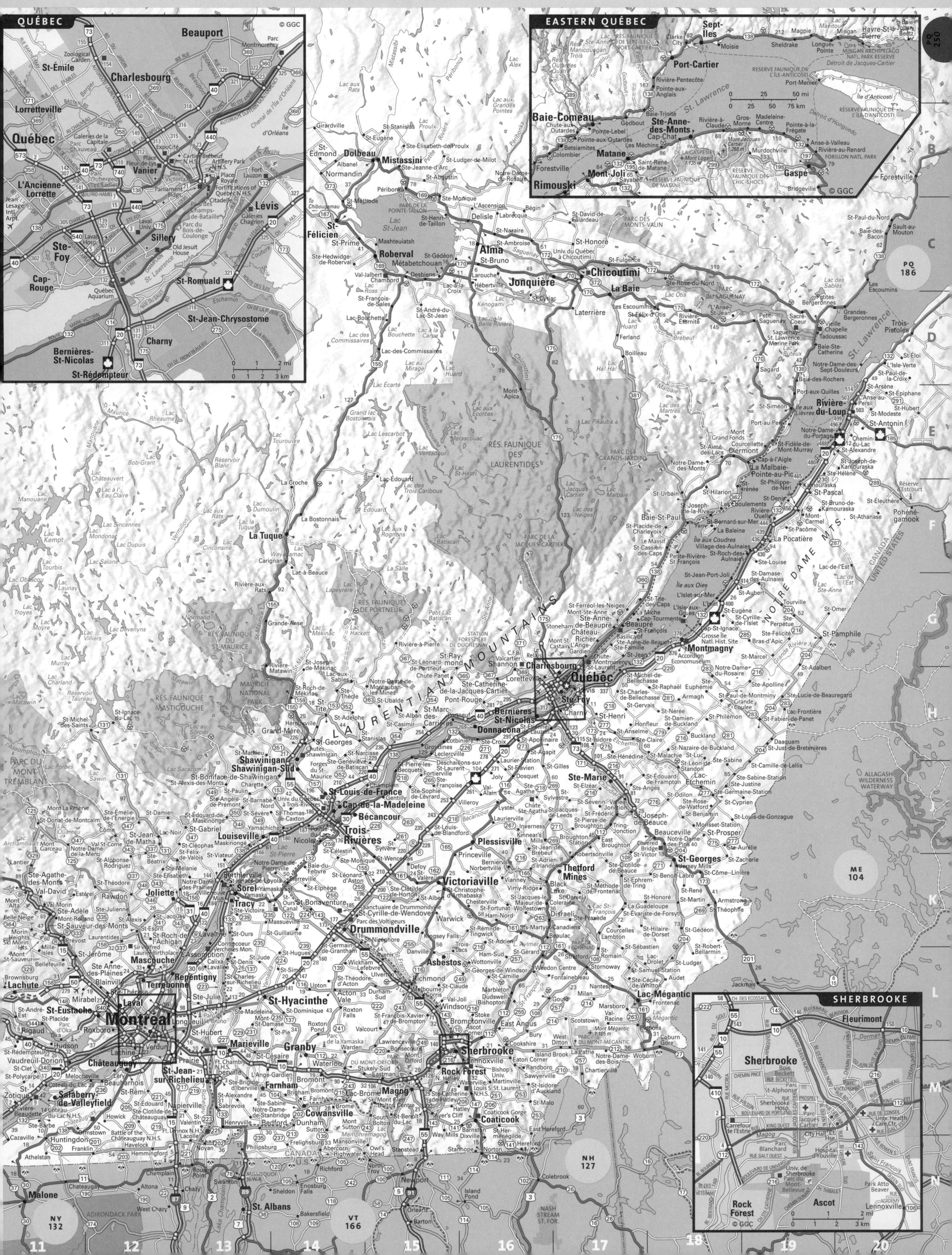
QUÉBEC
© GGC
Beauport
Charlesbourg
Lorretteville
St-Émile
Québec
Vanier
L'Ancienne-Lorrette
Lévis
Ste Foy
Sillery
Cap-Rouge
St-Romuald
St-Jean-Chrysostome
Charny
Bernières-St-Nicolas
St-Rédempteur
EASTERN QUÉBEC
Sept-Îles
Port-Cartier
Baie-Comeau
Ste-Anne-des-Monts
Matane
Mont-Joli
Rimouski
Gaspé
SHERBROOKE
Fleurimont
Sherbrooke
Rock Forest
Ascot
Lennoxville
PQ 186
PQ 250
ME 104
NH 127
VT 166
NY 132
Dolbeau
Mistassini
St-Félicien
Roberval
Alma
Jonquière
Chicoutimi
La Baie
La Tuque
Shawinigan
Shawinigan-Sud
Trois-Rivières
Cap-de-la-Madeleine
Bécancour
Victoriaville
Drummondville
Sorel
Joliette
Montréal
Laval
St-Hyacinthe
Granby
Sherbrooke
Magog
Thetford Mines
Ste-Marie
St-Georges
Lac-Mégantic
Rivière-du-Loup
Montmagny
La Malbaie
Baie-St-Paul
Valleyfield
Salaberry-de-Valleyfield
St-Jean-sur-Richelieu
Châteauguay
Cowansville
Coaticook
Malone
St. Albans
Newport
RÉS. FAUNIQUE DES LAURENTIDES
LAURENTIAN MOUNTAINS
NOTRE DAME MTS.
St. Lawrence
CANADA
UNITED STATES
B C D E F G H J K L M N
11 12 13 14 15 16 17 18 19 20

NEW BRUNSWICK
TOURISM:
800.561.0123
ROAD CONDITIONS:
800.561.4063

PRINCE EDWARD ISLAND
TOURISM:
800.463.4734
ROAD CONDITIONS:
902.368.4770

MI 25 50
KM 25 50

QUÉBEC
GASPÉ PENINSULA
NEW BRUNSWICK
Gulf of St. Lawrence
Bay of Fundy
Gulf of Maine
ATLANTIC OCEAN
CANADA
UNITED STATES
EASTERN TIME ZONE
ATLANTIC TIME ZONE

NOVA SCOTIA TOURISM:
800.565.0000

ROAD CONDITIONS:
902.424.3933

NEWFOUNDLAND TOURISM:
800.563.6353
709.729.2830

ROAD CONDITIONS:
709.729.2391 (ST. JOHN'S, DEC–MAR)
709.466.4160 (CLARENVILLE)
709.292.4300 (GRAND FALLS)

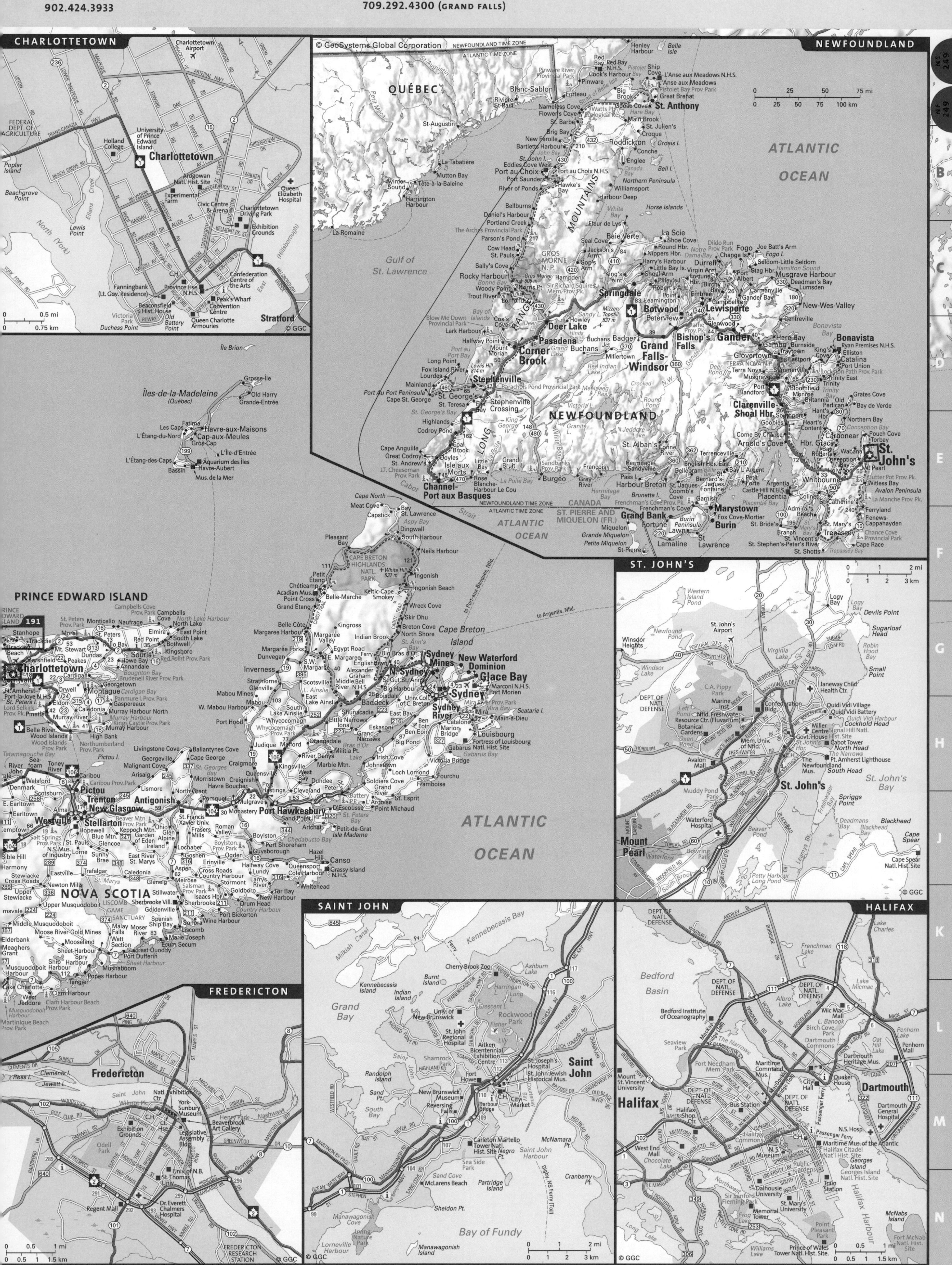

TOURISM:
800.446.3942

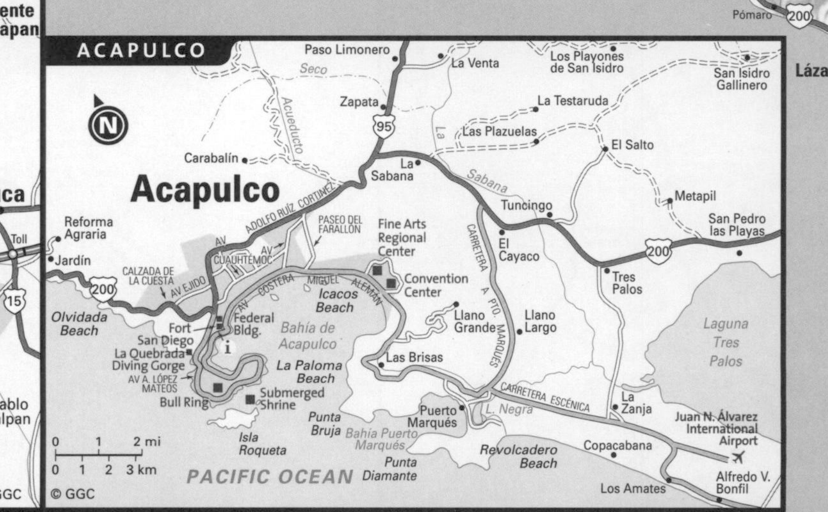

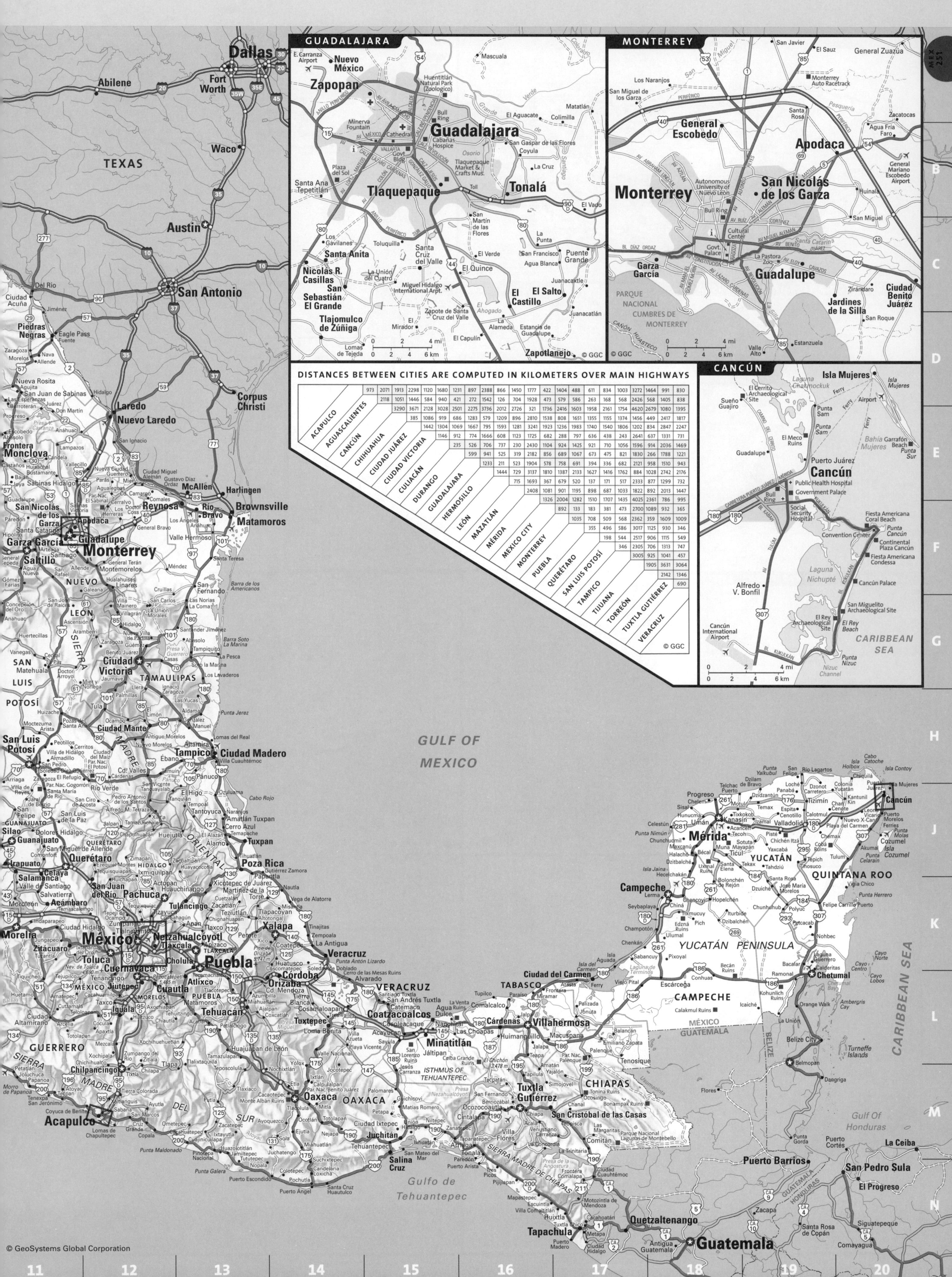

DISTANCES BETWEEN CITIES ARE COMPUTED IN KILOMETERS OVER MAIN HIGHWAYS

	Aguascalientes	Cancún	Chihuahua	Ciudad Juárez	Ciudad Victoria	Culiacán	Durango	Guadalajara	Hermosillo	León	Mazatlán	Mérida	Mexico City	Monterrey	Puebla	Querétaro	San Luis Potosí	Tampico	Tijuana	Torreón	Tuxtla Gutiérrez	Veracruz
ACAPULCO	973	2071	1913	2298	1120	1680	1231	897	2388	866	1450	1777	422	1404	488	611	834	1003	3272	1464	991	830
AGUASCALIENTES		2118	1051	1446	584	940	421	272	1542	126	704	1928	473	579	586	263	168	568	2426	568	1405	838
CANCÚN			3290	3671	2128	3028	2501	2275	3736	2012	2726	321	1736	2416	1603	1958	2161	1754	4620	2679	1080	1395
CHIHUAHUA				385	1086	919	686	1283	579	1209	896	2810	1538	808	1651	1355	1155	1374	1456	449	2417	1817
CIUDAD JUÁREZ					1442	1304	1069	1667	795	1593	1281	3241	1923	1236	1983	1740	1540	1806	1202	834	2847	2247
CIUDAD VICTORIA						1146	912	774	1666	608	1123	1725	682	288	797	636	438	243	2641	637	1331	731
CULIACÁN							235	526	706	737	230	2430	1104	924	1425	921	710	1056	1596	914	2036	1469
DURANGO								599	941	525	319	2182	856	689	1067	673	475	821	1830	266	1788	1221
GUADALAJARA									1233	211	523	1904	578	758	691	394	336	682	2121	958	1510	943
HERMOSILLO										1444	729	3137	1810	1387	2133	1627	1416	1762	884	1028	2742	2176
LEÓN											715	1693	367	679	520	137	171	517	2333	877	1299	732
MAZATLÁN												2408	1081	901	1195	898	687	1033	1822	892	2013	1447
MÉRIDA													1326	2004	1282	1510	1707	1435	4025	2361	786	995
MEXICO CITY														892	133	183	381	473	2700	1089	932	365
MONTERREY															1035	708	509	568	2362	359	1609	1009
PUEBLA																355	496	586	3017	1125	930	346
QUERÉTARO																	198	544	2517	906	1115	549
SAN LUIS POTOSÍ																		346	2305	706	1313	747
TAMPICO																			3005	925	1041	457
TIJUANA																				1905	3631	3064
TORREÓN																					2142	1346
TUXTLA GUTIÉRREZ																						690

© GGC

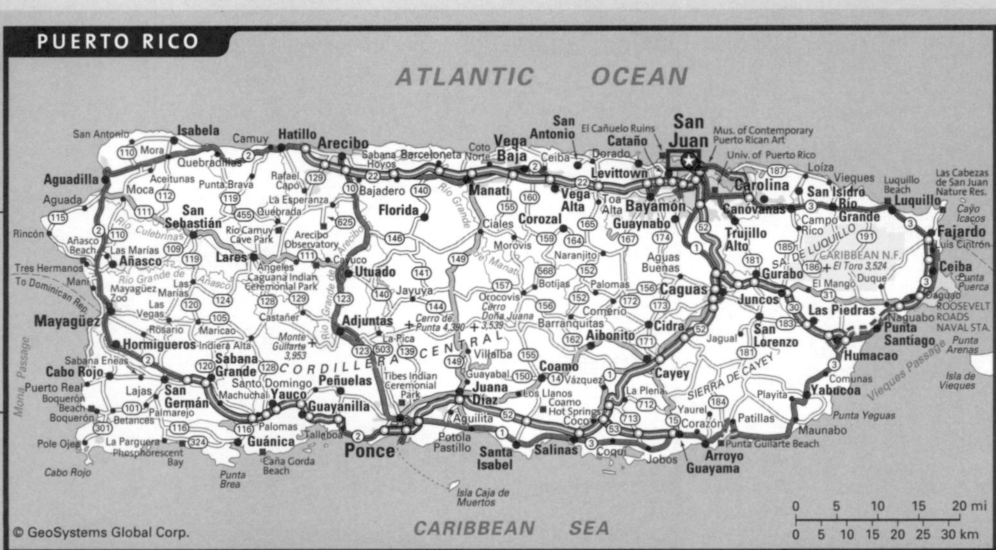

PUERTO RICO
ATLANTIC OCEAN
CARIBBEAN SEA
San Juan
Aguadilla
Isabela
Arecibo
Mayagüez
Ponce
Caguas
Bayamón
Carolina
Fajardo
Humacao
Guayama
Cabo Rojo
© GeoSystems Global Corp.

SAN JUAN
ATLANTIC OCEAN
Bahía De San Juan
Castillo San Felipe del Morro
La Fortaleza
Capitol
Maritime Museum
Customs House
La Puntilla
COMANDANTE FERNANDO RIVAS DOMINICCI AIRPORT (Isla Grande)
© GGC

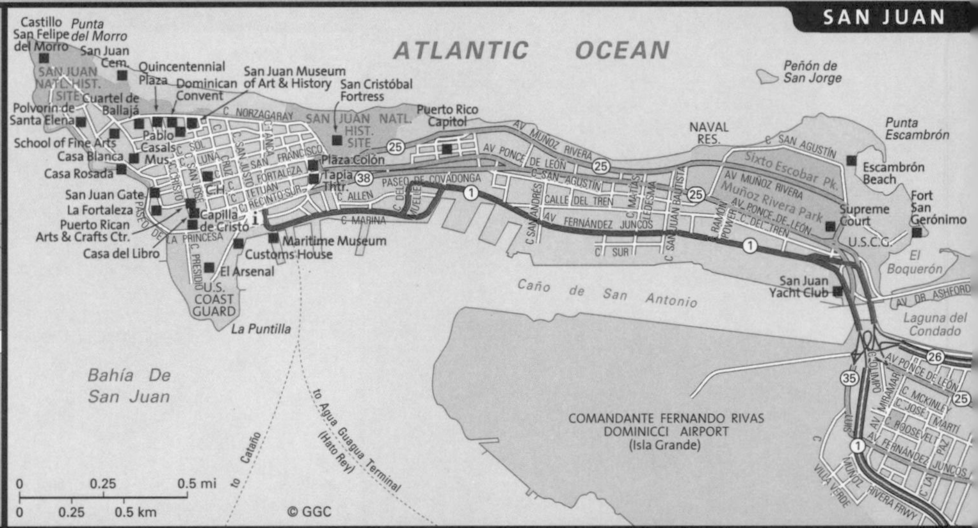

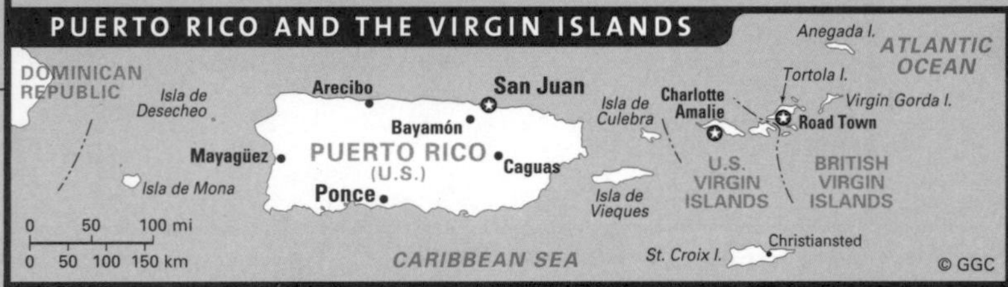

PUERTO RICO AND THE VIRGIN ISLANDS
DOMINICAN REPUBLIC
PUERTO RICO (U.S.)
San Juan
Arecibo
Bayamón
Caguas
Mayagüez
Ponce
Isla de Mona
Isla de Culebra
Isla de Vieques
U.S. VIRGIN ISLANDS
BRITISH VIRGIN ISLANDS
Charlotte Amalie
Road Town
Tortola I.
Virgin Gorda I.
Anegada I.
Christiansted
St. Croix I.
ATLANTIC OCEAN
CARIBBEAN SEA
© GGC

VIRGIN ISLANDS
Jost Van Dyke I.
Cane Garden Bay
Tortola I.
St. Thomas I.
Hans Lollik I.
Charlotte Amalie
Cyril E. King Arpt.
Savana Island
VIRGIN ISLANDS N.P.
Coral Harbor
Cruz Bay
St. John I.
CARIBBEAN SEA
Salt River Bay N.H.P. and Ecological Pres.
BUCK ISLAND REEF N.M.
Christiansted
Fredensborg
Frederiksted
Whim Greathouse Museum
Alexander Hamilton Arpt.
St. Croix Island
© GGC

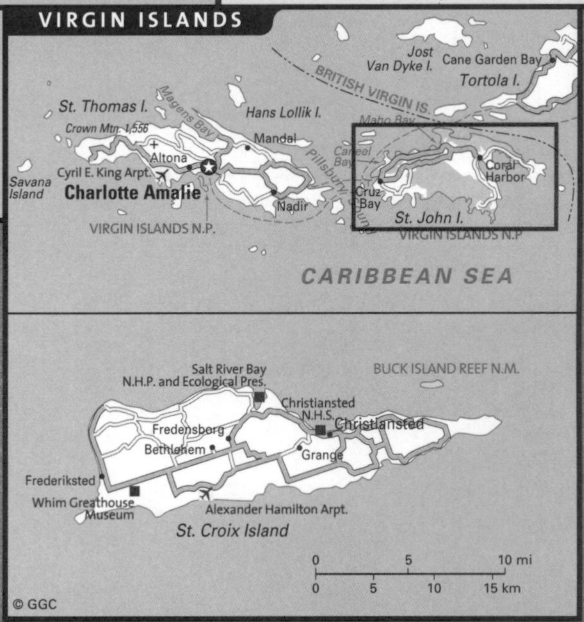

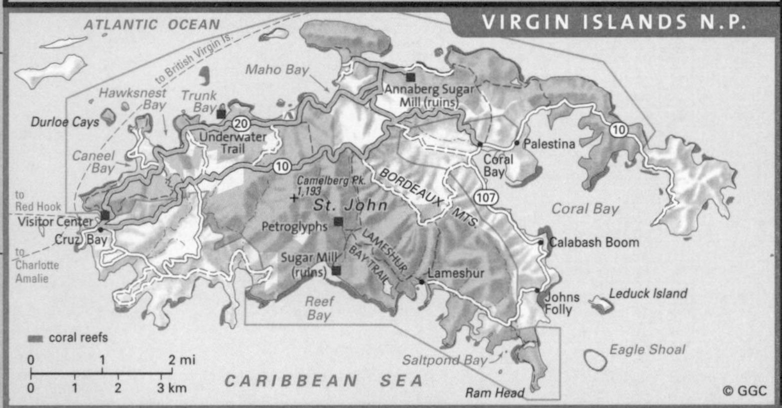

VIRGIN ISLANDS N.P.
ATLANTIC OCEAN
Maho Bay
Annaberg Sugar Mill (ruins)
Durloe Cays
Caneel Bay
Palestina
Coral Bay
St. John
Cruz Bay
Calabash Boom
Lameshur
Leduck Island
Eagle Shoal
Reef Bay
Saltpond Bay
Ram Head
CARIBBEAN SEA
coral reefs
© GGC

ARCHES NATL. PARK
KLONDIKE BLUFFS
Devils Garden
Landscape Arch
Skyline Arch
Broken Arch
FIERY FURNACE
Delicate Arch
ARCHES NATIONAL PARK
Panorama Point
Balanced Rock
Double Arch
THE WINDOWS SECTION
PETRIFIED DUNES
Tower of Babel
COURTHOUSE TOWERS
La Sal Mts. Viewpoint
Visitor Center
© GGC

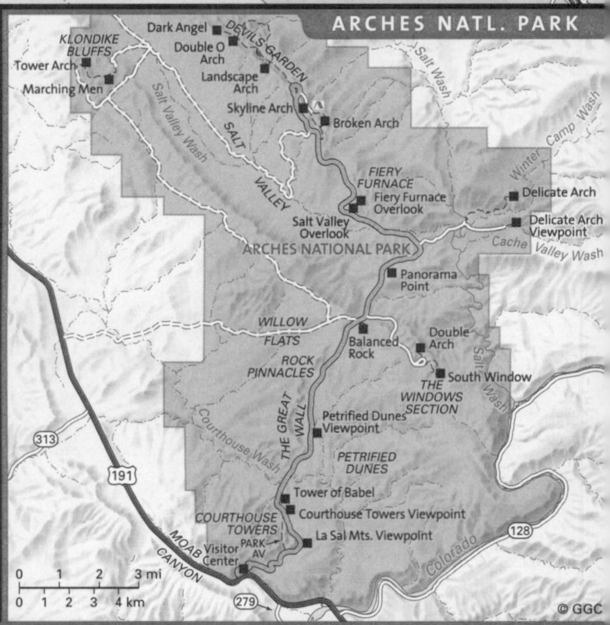

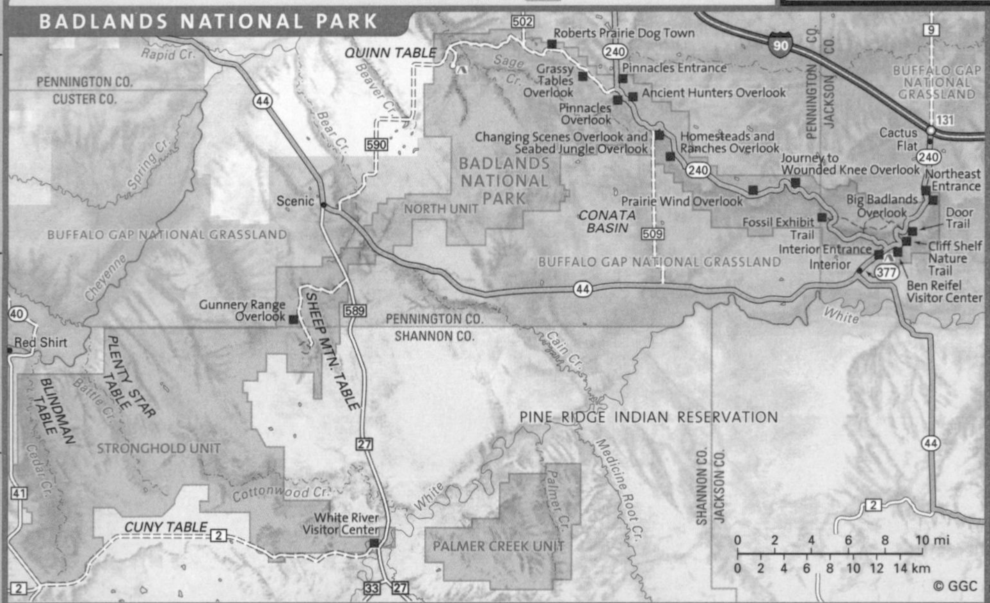

BADLANDS NATIONAL PARK
Roberts Prairie Dog Town
Pinnacles Entrance
BADLANDS NATIONAL PARK
BUFFALO GAP NATIONAL GRASSLAND
NORTH UNIT
CONATA BASIN
Scenic
Interior
Ben Reifel Visitor Center
PINE RIDGE INDIAN RESERVATION
STRONGHOLD UNIT
PALMER CREEK UNIT
White River Visitor Center
CUNY TABLE
© GGC

BANFF NATL. PARK
JASPER N.P.
ROCKY MOUNTAINS
SELKIRK MTS.
GLACIER NATL. PARK
MOUNT REVELSTOKE NATL. PARK
YOHO NATL. PARK
BANFF NATIONAL PARK
KOOTENAY NATL. PARK
PURCELL MTS.
Golden
Revelstoke
Lake Louise
Banff
Canmore
Field
Radium
© GGC

BIG BEND NATIONAL PARK
Persimmon Gap Visitor Center
ROSILLOS MOUNTAINS
DAGGER FLAT
CHRISTMAS MOUNTAINS
Terlingua
Study Butte
Panther Jct.
BURRO MESA
CHISOS MOUNTAINS
BIG BEND NATIONAL PARK
Rio Grande Village
Castolon
Santa Elena Canyon Overlook
MEXICO
CHIHUAHUA
COAHUILA
TEXAS
© GGC

DEATH VALLEY NATL. PARK
Scotty's Castle
Ubehebe Crater
INYO MOUNTAINS
SALINE VALLEY
The Racetrack
DEATH VALLEY NATIONAL PARK
PANAMINT RANGE
Stovepipe Wells
Furnace Creek
Badwater
Beatty
Rhyolite (Ghost town)
NELLIS AIR FORCE BOMBING AND GUNNERY RANGE
CHINA LAKE NAVAL WEAPONS CENTER
Lone Pine
Death Valley Junction
© GGC

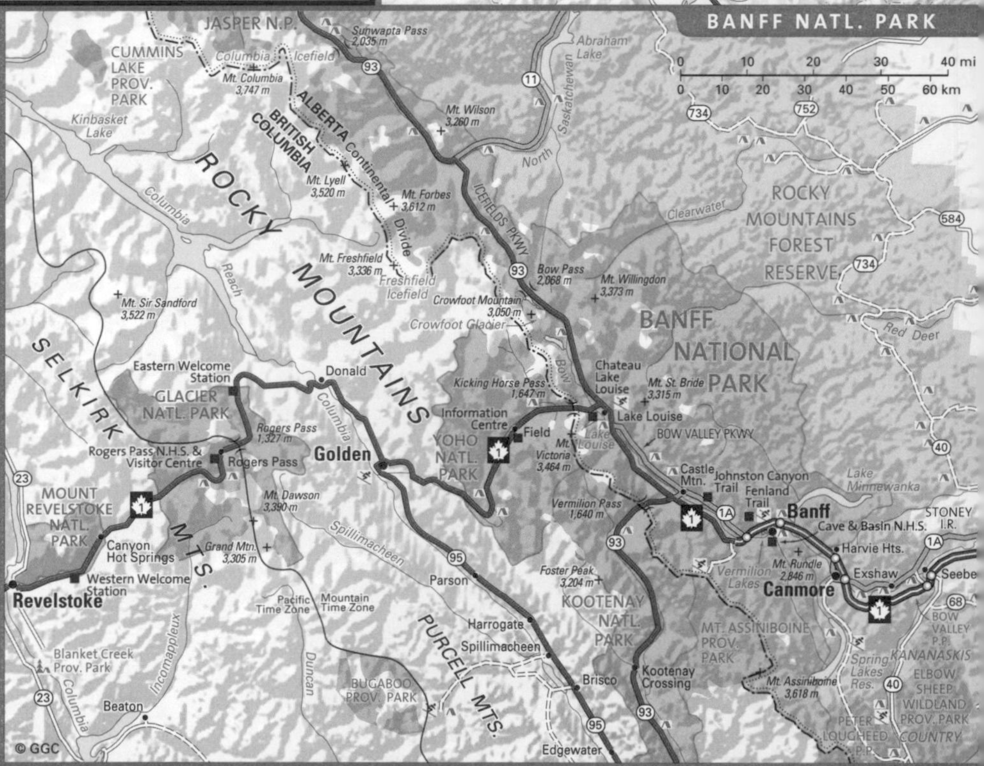

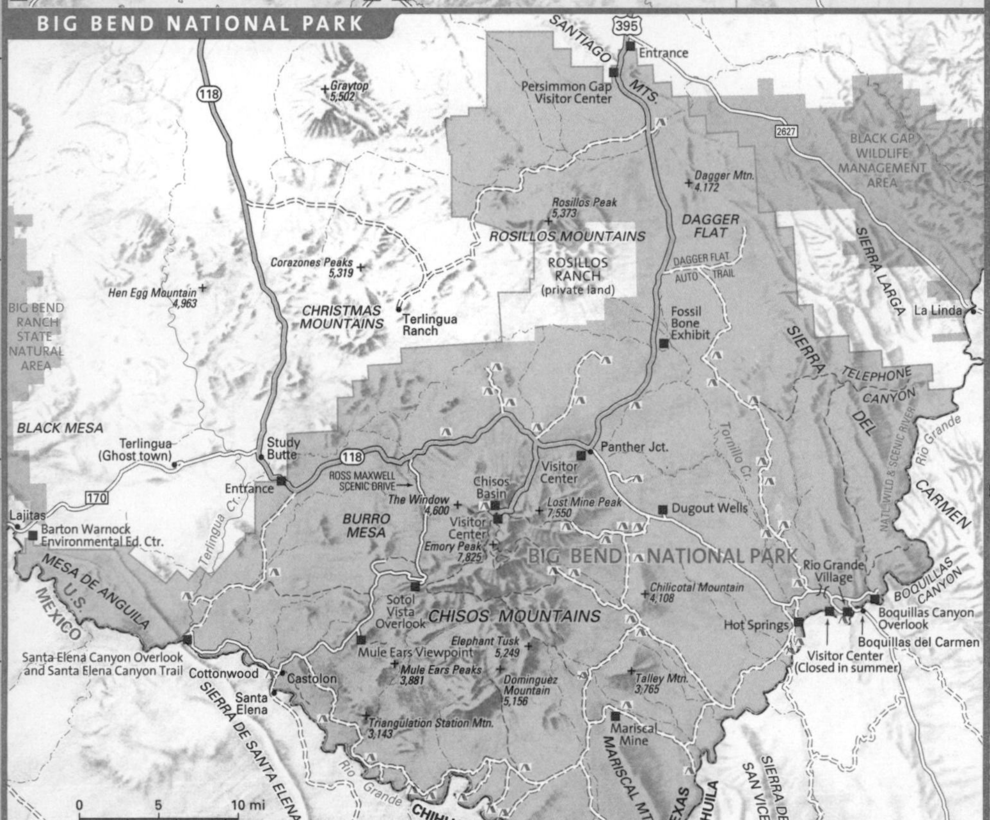

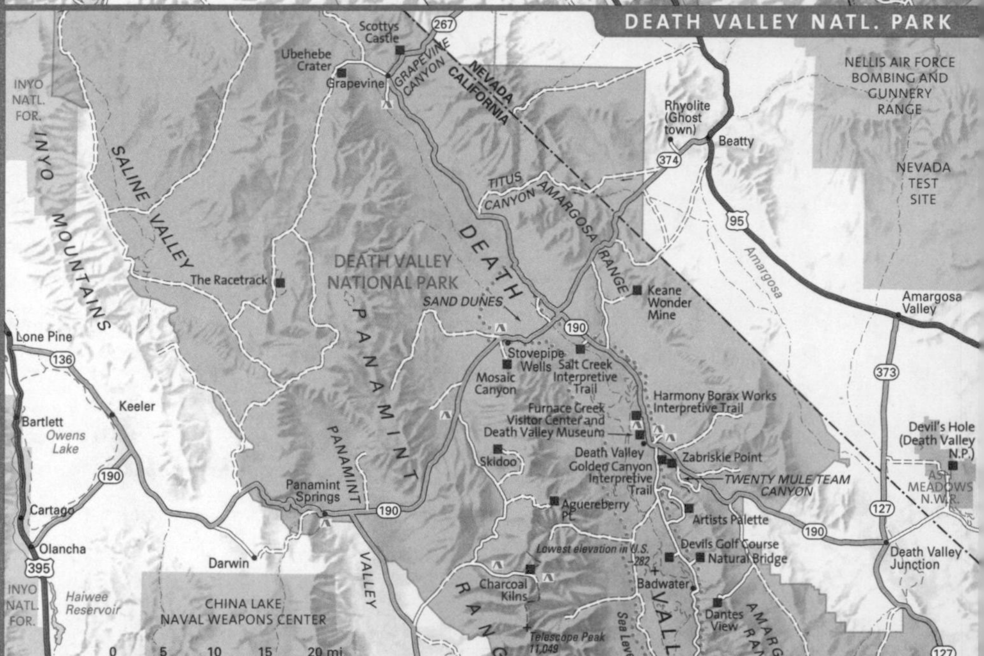

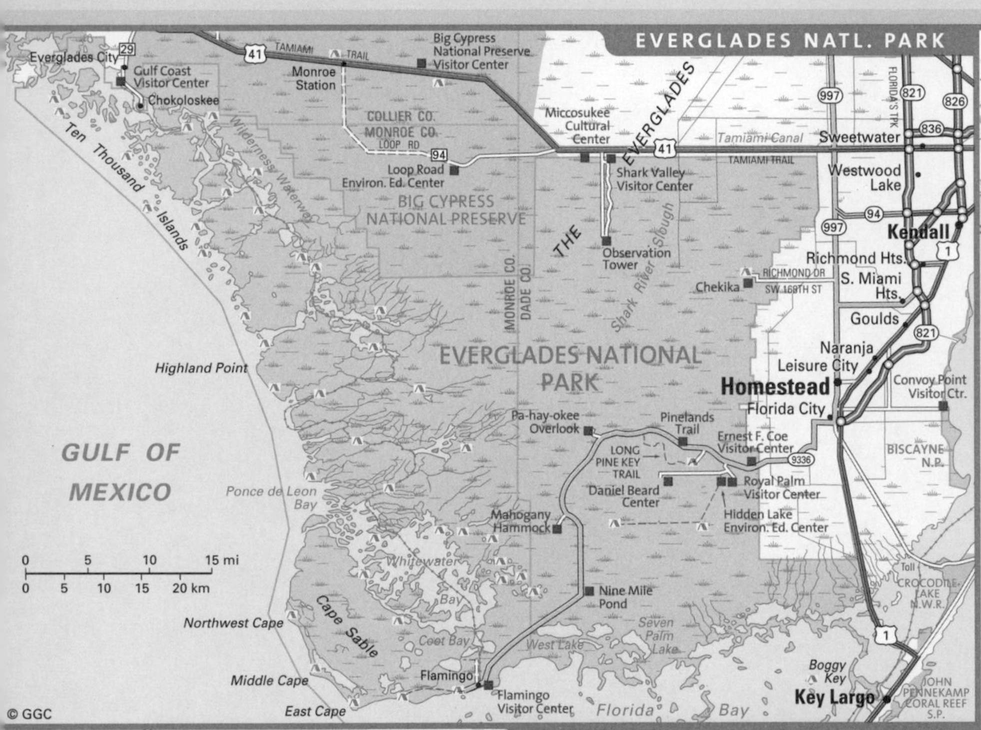
EVERGLADES NATL. PARK
Everglades City
Gulf Coast Visitor Center
Chokoloskee
Ten Thousand Islands
Big Cypress National Preserve Visitor Center
Monroe Station
COLLIER CO.
MONROE CO.
Loop Road Environ. Ed. Center
BIG CYPRESS NATIONAL PRESERVE
THE EVERGLADES
Miccosukee Cultural Center
Shark Valley Visitor Center
Observation Tower
Tamiami Canal
Sweetwater
Westwood Lake
Kendall
Richmond Hts.
S. Miami Hts.
Chekika
Goulds
Naranja
Leisure City
Homestead
Florida City
Convoy Point Visitor Ctr.
Highland Point
EVERGLADES NATIONAL PARK
Pa-hay-okee Overlook
Pinelands Trail
Ernest F. Coe Visitor Center
Royal Palm Visitor Center
Daniel Beard Center
Hidden Lake Environ. Ed. Center
BISCAYNE N.P.
GULF OF MEXICO
Ponce de Leon Bay
Mahogany Hammock
Nine Mile Pond
Northwest Cape
Cape Sable
Middle Cape
East Cape
Flamingo
Flamingo Visitor Center
Florida Bay
Key Largo
JOHN PENNEKAMP CORAL REEF S.P.
0 5 10 15 mi
0 5 10 15 20 km
© GGC

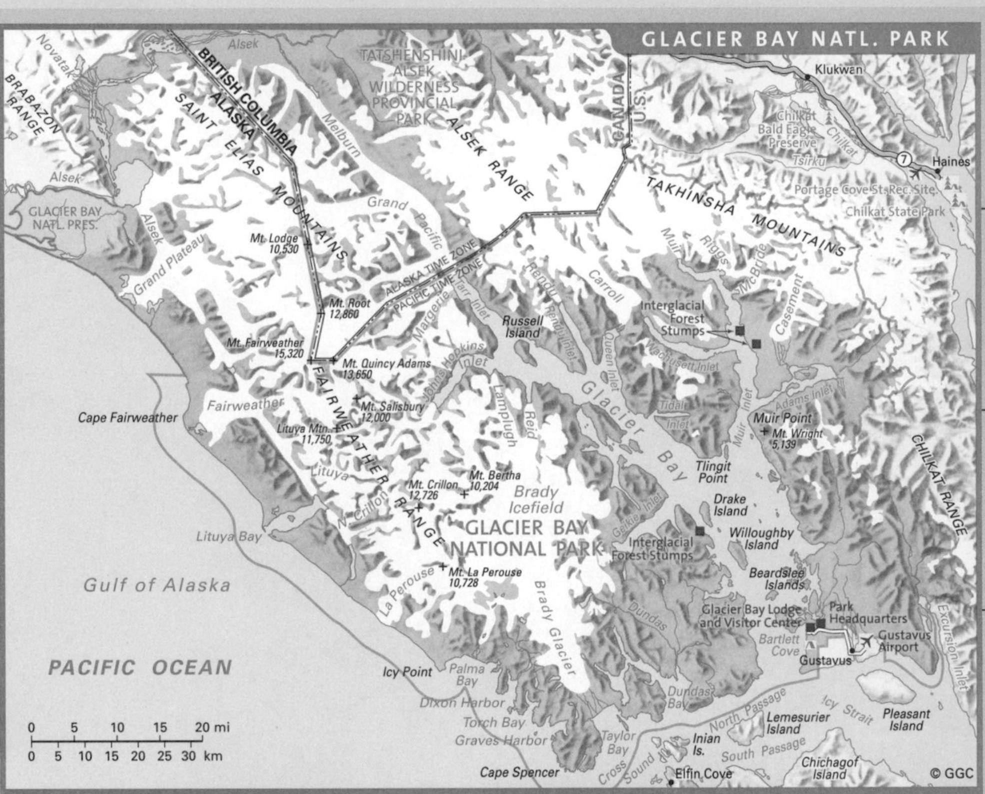
GLACIER BAY NATL. PARK
BRITISH COLUMBIA
ALASKA
TATSHENSHINI-ALSEK WILDERNESS PROVINCIAL PARK
ALSEK RANGE
SAINT ELIAS MOUNTAINS
GLACIER BAY NATL. PRES.
Mt. Lodge 10,530
Mt. Root 12,860
Mt. Fairweather 15,320
Mt. Quincy Adams 13,650
Mt. Salisbury 12,000
Lituya Mtn. 11,750
FAIRWEATHER RANGE
Mt. Crillon 12,726
Mt. Bertha 10,204
Brady Icefield
GLACIER BAY NATIONAL PARK
Mt. La Perouse 10,728
Cape Fairweather
Lituya Bay
Gulf of Alaska
PACIFIC OCEAN
Icy Point
Palma Bay
Dixon Harbor
Torch Bay
Graves Harbor
Cape Spencer
Elfin Cove
Klukwan
Chilkat Bald Eagle Preserve
Haines
Portage Cove St. Rec. Site
Chilkat State Park
TAKHINSHA MOUNTAINS
Interglacial Forest Stumps
Russell Island
Glacier Bay
Muir Point
Mt. Wright 5,139
Tlingit Point
Drake Island
Willoughby Island
Beardslee Islands
Glacier Bay Lodge and Visitor Center
Park Headquarters
Gustavus
Gustavus Airport
Bartlett Cove
Dundas Bay
Inian Is.
Lemesurier Island
Pleasant Island
Icy Strait
Chichagof Island
CHILKAT RANGE
0 5 10 15 20 mi
0 5 10 15 20 25 30 km
© GGC

HAWAII VOLCANOES NATL. PARK
Mauna Loa Observatory
MAUNA LOA FOREST RESERVE
NORTHEAST RIFT ZONE
Steaming Cone 11,787
HAWAII VOLCANOES N.P.
Mauna Loa Summit Cairn 13,677
Mauna Loa Cabin
Mokuaweoweo Caldera
Lookout Shelter
PUU MAKAALA NATURAL AREA RESERVE
OLAA FOREST
KILAUEA FOREST RESERVE
Bird Park (Kipuka Puaulu)
Steam Vents
Kilauea Visitor Center
Glenwood
Volcano
Kilauea Caldera
Thurston Lava Tube
Kilauea Iki Crater
Devastation Trail
Halemaumau Crater
KAPAPALA FOREST RESERVE
SOUTHWEST RIFT ZONE
KAOIKI PALI
KAHAUALEA NATURAL AREA RESERVE
EAST RIFT ZONE
Kalalua 2,181
PUNA FOREST RESERVE
Makaopuhi Crater
Napau Crater
Mauna Ulu
HAWAII VOLCANOES N.P.
KAU DESERT
Hilina Pali Overlook Shelter
HILINA PALI
HOLEI PALI
Puu Loa Petroglyphs
Wahaula Heiau
Lae Apuki (Ancient village)
Holei Sea Arch
Kaena Point
Apua Point
KAU FOREST RESERVE
Wood Valley
Great Crack
PACIFIC OCEAN
0 2 4 6 mi
0 2 4 6 8 km
© GGC

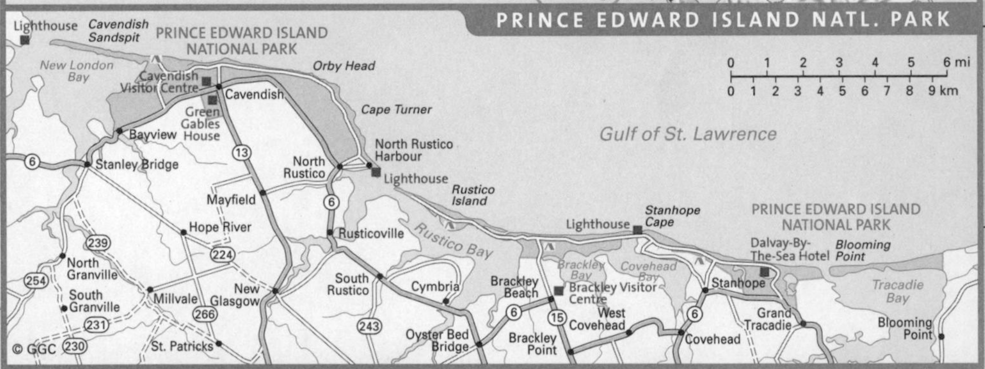
PRINCE EDWARD ISLAND NATL. PARK
Lighthouse
Cavendish Sandspit
PRINCE EDWARD ISLAND NATIONAL PARK
Orby Head
New London Bay
Cavendish Visitor Centre
Cavendish
Green Gables House
Cape Turner
North Rustico Harbour
Bayview
Stanley Bridge
North Rustico
Rustico Island
Gulf of St. Lawrence
Mayfield
Hope River
Rusticoville
Rustico Bay
Stanhope Cape
Dalvay-By-The-Sea Hotel
Blooming Point
North Granville
South Granville
Millvale
New Glasgow
South Rustico
Cymbria
Brackley Beach
Brackley Visitor Centre
Stanhope
Tracadie Bay
Grand Tracadie
Oyster Bed Bridge
Brackley Point
West Covehead
Covehead
Blooming Point
St. Patricks
0 1 2 3 4 5 6 mi
0 1 2 3 4 5 6 7 8 9 km
© GGC

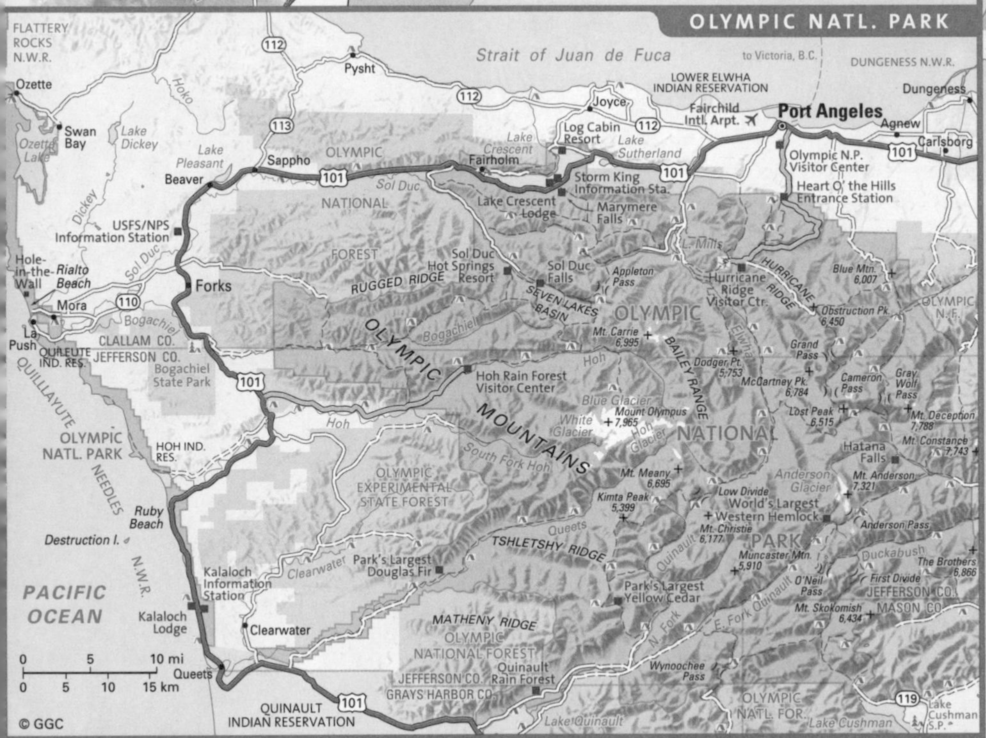
OLYMPIC NATL. PARK
FLATTERY ROCKS N.W.R.
Strait of Juan de Fuca
to Victoria, B.C.
DUNGENESS N.W.R.
Ozette
Pysht
LOWER ELWHA INDIAN RESERVATION
Joyce
Fairchild Intl. Arpt.
Port Angeles
Dungeness
Agnew
Carlsborg
Lake Crescent
Log Cabin Resort
Sappho
Beaver
Fairholm
Storm King Information Sta.
Olympic N.P. Visitor Center
Heart O' the Hills Entrance Station
Marymere Falls
USFS/NPS Information Station
Hole-in-the-Wall
Rialto Beach
Mora
La Push
Forks
Sol Duc Hot Springs Resort
RUGGED RIDGE
SEVEN LAKES BASIN
OLYMPIC NATIONAL
Hurricane Ridge Visitor Ctr.
Bogachiel State Park
CLALLAM CO.
JEFFERSON CO.
QUILLAYUTE NEEDLES
OLYMPIC NATL. PARK
Hoh Rain Forest Visitor Center
OLYMPIC MOUNTAINS
Mount Olympus 7,965
HOH IND. RES.
Ruby Beach
Destruction I.
OLYMPIC EXPERIMENTAL STATE FOREST
PACIFIC OCEAN
Kalaloch Information Station
Kalaloch Lodge
Clearwater
Park's Largest Douglas Fir
TSHLETSHY RIDGE
Park's Largest Yellow Cedar
Queets
MATHENY RIDGE
OLYMPIC NATIONAL FOREST
JEFFERSON CO.
GRAYS HARBOR CO.
Quinault Rain Forest
QUINAULT INDIAN RESERVATION
Lake Quinault
Lake Cushman
0 5 10 mi
0 5 10 15 km
© GGC

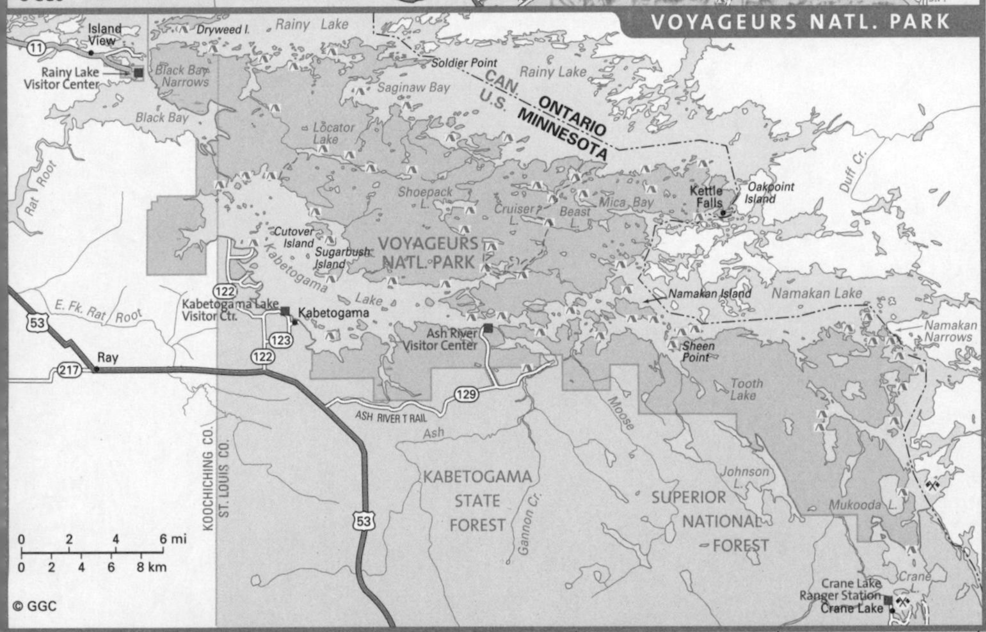
VOYAGEURS NATL. PARK
Island View
Rainy Lake
Rainy Lake Visitor Center
Black Bay Narrows
Soldier Point
Saginaw Bay
CAN.
U.S.
ONTARIO
MINNESOTA
Black Bay
Locator Lake
Kettle Falls
Oakpoint Island
Cutover Island
Sugarbush Island
VOYAGEURS NATL. PARK
Kabetogama Lake Visitor Ctr.
Kabetogama
Namakan Island
Namakan Lake
Ray
Ash River Visitor Center
Sheen Point
KOOCHICHING CO.
ST. LOUIS CO.
KABETOGAMA STATE FOREST
SUPERIOR NATIONAL FOREST
Crane Lake Ranger Station
Crane Lake
0 2 4 6 mi
0 2 4 6 8 km
© GGC

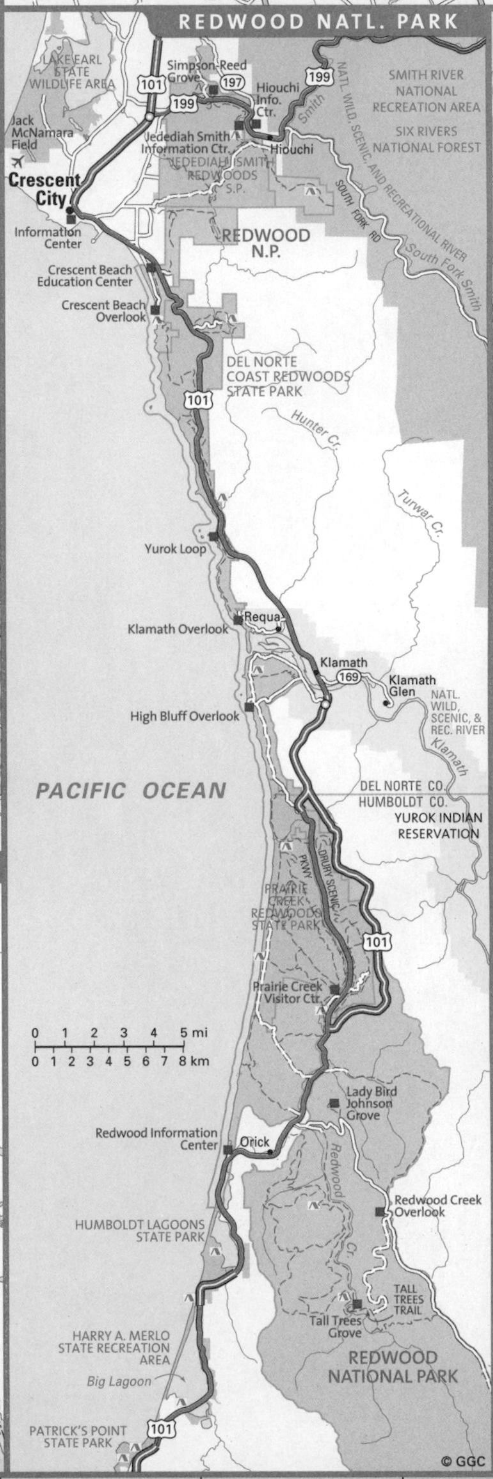
REDWOOD NATL. PARK
LAKE EARL STATE WILDLIFE AREA
Simpson-Reed Grove
Hiouchi Info. Ctr.
SMITH RIVER NATIONAL RECREATION AREA
SIX RIVERS NATIONAL FOREST
Jack McNamara Field
Jedediah Smith Information Ctr.
Hiouchi
JEDEDIAH SMITH REDWOODS S.P.
Crescent City
Information Center
REDWOOD N.P.
Crescent Beach Education Center
Crescent Beach Overlook
DEL NORTE COAST REDWOODS STATE PARK
Yurok Loop
Klamath Overlook
Requa
Klamath
Klamath Glen
High Bluff Overlook
PACIFIC OCEAN
DEL NORTE CO.
HUMBOLDT CO.
YUROK INDIAN RESERVATION
PRAIRIE CREEK REDWOODS STATE PARK
Prairie Creek Visitor Ctr.
Lady Bird Johnson Grove
Redwood Information Center
Orick
Redwood Creek Overlook
HUMBOLDT LAGOONS STATE PARK
TALL TREES TRAIL
Tall Trees Grove
HARRY A. MERLO STATE RECREATION AREA
REDWOOD NATIONAL PARK
Big Lagoon
PATRICK'S POINT STATE PARK
0 1 2 3 4 5 mi
0 1 2 3 4 5 6 7 8 km
© GGC

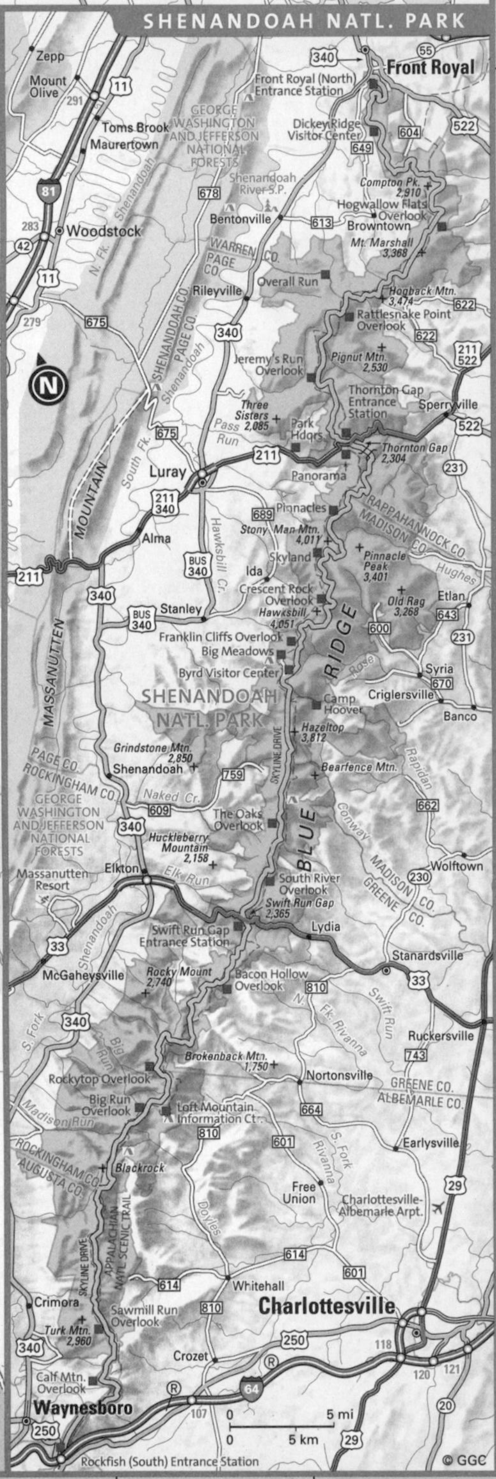
SHENANDOAH NATL. PARK
Front Royal
Front Royal (North) Entrance Station
Zepp
Mount Olive
Toms Brook
Maurertown
Dickey Ridge Visitor Center
Woodstock
Compton Pk. 2,909
Hogwallow Flats Overlook
Browntown
Mt. Marshall 3,368
Bentonville
Overall Run
Rileyville
Hogback Mtn. 3,474
Rattlesnake Point Overlook
Jeremy's Run Overlook
Pignut Mtn. 2,530
Thornton Gap Entrance Station
Sperryville
Three Sisters 2,085
Park Hdqrs.
Luray
Panorama
Thornton Gap 2,304
Pinnacles
Stony Man Mtn. 4,011
Skyland
Alma
Pinnacle Peak 3,401
Old Rag 3,268
Etlan
Crescent Rock Overlook
Hawksbill 4,051
Stanley
Franklin Cliffs Overlook
Big Meadows
Byrd Visitor Center
Syria
Criglersville
SHENANDOAH NATL. PARK
Camp Hoover
Hazeltop 3,812
Banco
Grindstone Mtn. 2,850
Shenandoah
Bearfence Mtn.
BLUE RIDGE
MASSANUTTEN MOUNTAIN
The Oaks Overlook
Huckleberry Mountain 2,158
Elkton
Massanutten Resort
South River Overlook
Swift Run Gap 2,365
Lydia
Wolftown
Swift Run Gap Entrance Station
Stanardsville
McGaheysville
Rocky Mount 2,740
Bacon Hollow Overlook
Ruckersville
Brokenback Mtn. 1,750
Rockytop Overlook
Nortonsville
Big Run Overlook
Loft Mountain Information Ct.
Earlysville
Blackrock
Free Union
Charlottesville-Albemarle Arpt.
Whitehall
Crimora
Sawmill Run Overlook
Charlottesville
Turk Mtn. 2,980
Crozet
Calf Mtn. Overlook
Waynesboro
Rockfish (South) Entrance Station
0 5 mi
0 5 km
© GGC

National Parks

NATIONAL PARKS

For more information on specific parks, see NATIONAL GEOGRAPHIC'S GUIDE TO THE NATIONAL PARKS OF THE UNITED STATES, which features detailed travel information on 54 parks, including itineraries and sight-by-sight tours.

Crimson blueberry bushes near Wonderland Trail

Morning mist over tidal flats at Sand Beach

Turret Arch in The Windows Section, with La Sal Mountains in the distance

North Unit clay stone pinnacles in summer

ACADIA

Central coastal Maine
Established February 26, 1919
35,000 acres

Headquarters
Acadia National Park
P.O. Box 177
Bar Harbor, ME 04609
207.288.3338
www.nps.gov/acad

Visitor Centers
Hulls Cove Visitor Center (207.288.3338), Rte. 3 just before entrance to Park Loop Road, open daily mid-Apr to end of Oct. Mt. Desert Island Information Center (207.288.3411), at Thompson Island, on Rte. 3 just before driving onto Mt. Desert Island, open daily mid-May to mid-Oct.

Entrance Fees
$10 per vehicle for 7-day permit. $5 per person on foot or bicycle for 7 days.

Accommodations
Two campgrounds on Mt. Desert Island. Blackwoods, open year-round, with facilities closed from mid-Nov to mid-Apr. Reservations required June 15 to Sept 15. Seawall, open late May to late Sept, is first-come, first-served (lines begin to form early in the morning). Five lean-to shelters at Duck Harbor Campground (207.288.3338), on Isle au Haut, are available by reservation from May 15 to Oct 15.

When to Go
Like all of New England, the Maine coast has notoriously fickle weather. During summer, the most popular time to visit, temperatures seldom rise above 80°F (although traffic can cause personal temperatures to rise much higher), and fog is common. The shoulder months of May and Sept are good times to avoid crowds and cold. For the heartier souls who don't mind bone-chilling winds and frigid temperatures, the off-season can be a rewarding time to visit: The park stays open year-round (though all but a 2-mile section of the 27-mile Park Loop Road is closed when there's snow or ice).

Acadia National Park covers about half of Mount Desert Island, a rocky bite of land just off Maine's coast, north of Penobscot Bay. About five times larger than Manhattan, the island includes five large lakes and more than a dozen mountains, including Cadillac Mountain, whose 1,530-foot summit high above Frenchman Bay is the highest Atlantic coastal point north of Rio de Janeiro. The rugged summit of this peak, with its granite outcrops and blueberry bushes, is the first place in the United States to be lit by the morning sun. For the more than three million visitors each year, the park *is* Maine: A place where pine-scented evergreen forests and stark granite cliffs meet crashing surf and teeming tidal pools.

Carved by the last continental glacier, Mount Desert Island began to form about 500 million years ago. Its major valleys run north and south, and each holds one or two lakes scooped out by the glacier, while boulders lie stranded erratically where the huge ice sheet dropped them. Somes Sound, a true fjord, bisects the island into two lobes, with most of the park's sites on the eastern side. The Wabanaki called Mount Desert Island *Pemetic*, "the sloping land." Shell heaps in the park indicate Native American encampments dating back 5,000 years, and the first Europeans to encounter Maine's coastal peoples described a culture that lived off the land.

The French explorer and founder of Québec, Samuel de Champlain, whose travels took him nearly everywhere along the northeast coast, sailed by Mount Desert in 1604, 16 years before the Pilgrims arrived at Plymouth Rock. Champlain wrote in his journal: "The Mountain summits are all bare and rocky . . . I name it Isles des Monts Desert" – Island of Barren Mountains. Nine years later, Jesuits established the first French mission in America on what is now Fernald Point, near the entrance to Somes Sound. The short-lived settlement was part of the French province of Acadia, from which the park obtained its name. Today's busy summer retreat came into being during the latter part of the 19th century, when many of America's wealthiest families built mansions on Mount Desert. Although numerous estates were destroyed in a fire in 1947, some still remain and now provide tony lodgings for visitors to the park. Some of the "summer people" helped protect the island from development by donating land to the park – John D. Rockefeller, Jr., built the island's 57 miles of gravel carriage roads, banning automobiles from them, and gave more than 11,000 acres to the park.

Acadia lies at a transition between two biological communities, which for armchair naturalists means a thrilling abundance of sea and bird life: 300 species of birds have been sighted in or near Acadia. Common eiders live year-round at the park, feeding on barnacles, crabs, and sea urchins. As Maine's trademark fishing boats haul their lobster and crab traps, herring gulls circle, waiting for a handout. Peregrine falcons nest in cliffs from which they can drop on prey with lightning speed and amazing accuracy. Seals bask on the rocks of nearby Baker Island, while northern starfish and green sea urchins dwell in the tidal pools.

The best way to see the park is the popular – and in summer, overcrowded – 27-mile Park Loop Road. Among the top attractions on the road are Sand Beach, a swimming beach made up of finely ground shells and sand (be warned that the parking lot fills up early in the summer); Great Head, one of the highest sheer Atlantic headlands in the country; Thunder Hole, where water rushes into a coastal cave with a roar; and Cadillac Mountain. There are more than 120 miles of hiking trails, ranging from short, level walks along the ocean to steep, grueling climbs. The self-guided, one-mile Jordan Pond Nature Trail, which begins and ends at the Jordan Pond House on the Loop Road, winds along the lakeshore and through fields and woods. For a tougher hike, try the Cadillac Mountain South Ridge Trail. This 7.4-mile round-trip route to the summit of the mountain begins just south of Blackwoods Campground and climbs through woods and then above the tree line, where blueberry picking offers a pleasant summer distraction from spectacular ocean views.

A number of shops in the touristy summer town of Bar Harbor rent bikes to ride on the park's carriage roads, which are closed to motor vehicles, or on the Park Loop Road (which can be a bit nerve-racking in heavy traffic). Paradise Hill Loop is maintained especially for bicycles, and Eagle Lake has a fine 5.8-mile loop. Wildwood Stables, near Jordan Pond, offers a variety of horse-drawn carriage rides on the carriage roads from mid-June through Columbus Day. Two small mountains known as The Bubbles and the eastern shore's Otter Cliffs are popular spots for rock climbing.

Schoodic Peninsula and Isle au Haut are sections of Acadia National Park located off Mount Desert Island. A 7.2-mile shore drive that leads to Schoodic Point, at the tip of the peninsula, while a bit less dramatic than the Park Loop Road, has excellent scenery, rocks to climb on, and far fewer crowds. More than half of Isle au Haut, a tiny island eight miles off the Deer Isle town of Stonington, is preserved as part of the park, which maintains numerous hiking trails and Duck Harbor Campground. The island is accessible only by mail boat from Stonington (207.367.5193). The drive from Bar Harbor to Stonington takes approximately one and a half hours.

ME 104
PARK 105

ARCHES

Eastern Utah
Established November 12, 1971
73,379 acres

Headquarters
Arches National Park
P.O. Box 907
Moab, UT 84532
435.259.8161
www.nps.gov/arch

Visitor Center
Arches National Park Visitor Center (435.259.8161), on U. S. Rte. 191 at park entrance, open daily, except Christmas.

Entrance Fees
$10 per vehicle for 7 days.

Accommodations
Devils Garden Campground, open all year on a first-come, first-served basis. Arrive early because campground usually fills by early morning. No lodging in park. For group campground reservations, call 435.259.4351. For other accommodations, contact Moab/Green River Visitor Information (800.635.6622 or 435.259.8825).

When to Go
Because the park is located in the desert, weather conditions can be extreme, with highs exceeding 100°F in summer and dropping below 32°F in winter. Spring and fall are the ideal times to visit, especially for high-desert hiking. Colorful wildflowers bloom from Apr to June.

With slabs of stone rising up like natural skyscrapers, bridges and arches of stone perched atop slickrock shelves, and perfectly balanced rock piles that resemble animals and even humans, it's hard not to think of Arches National Park as a giant funland for the gods. One can imagine titans playing for eons in this high-desert sandbox, arranging and rearranging giant red rock heaps into windows, tables, and bridges. Then one day, the giants departed, leaving this isolated corner of desert as it exists today – a natural phenomenon with one of the largest concentrations of sandstone arches in the world. The extraordinary spires, pinnacles, pedestals, and stone arches have been sculpted by wind and rain for 150 million years. In the Jurassic period, a 300-foot layer of soft red sand, called the Entrada Sandstone, was first deposited here. As underlying salt deposits dissolved, it buckled and weathered into a jumble of slabs called fins – leading to the more than 2,000 natural arches seen today.

This is a visitor-friendly park, with a number of short, well-maintained trails that lead directly to the major attractions. Most visitors are content to see the park by taking the 18-mile scenic drive (one-way), and perhaps settling for at least one short hike to get a close look at one of the arches. From the visitor center, the road climbs up from the floor of Moab Canyon through a slickrock expanse known as the Petrified Dunes, where ancient sand berms long ago turned to stone. Continue over the paved road to The Windows Section, where you can see and photograph eight immense arches and some smaller formations as well. This is also a good spot for a short hike – just a quarter mile to South Window. A half-mile trail affords a dramatic close-up of Double Arch, a formerly solid, huge rock – one of its openings is the third largest in the park.

The road ends at the Devils Garden Trail. If you're only going to take one hike, this should be it. The two-and-a-quarter-mile route gives you views of up to 12 arches, including Landscape Arch, a long, seemingly gravity-defying thin ribbon of stone that is considered one of the most beautiful arches in the park. Although the park is essentially a desert area with little vegetation, about 130 species of birds have been spotted here, making it a popular spot for bird-watching. Outfitters from nearby Moab also run river trips, jeep tours, and horseback trips in the park vicinity.

UT 165
PARK 190

BADLANDS

Southwestern South Dakota
Established November 10, 1978
244,300 acres

Headquarters
Badlands National Park
P.O. Box 6
Interior, SD 57750
605.433.5361
www.nps.gov/badl

Visitor Centers
Ben Reifel Visitor Center (605.433.5361), at Cedar Pass on Badlands Loop Rd./Rte. 240, open daily except major holidays. White River Visitor Center (605.455.2878), in the Stronghold District via Rte. 27, open June through Aug.

Entrance Fees
$10 per vehicle for 7 days. $5 per bicycle or motorcycle plus $5 per passenger. In the off-season, fees collected at visitor centers.

Accommodations
Cedar Pass and Sage Creek campgrounds are open all year on a first-come, first-served basis. No running water at Sage Creek. Cedar Pass Lodge (605.433.5460) is the only lodging inside the park; open mid-Apr through mid-Oct.

When to Go
Summer is most popular, but daytime temperatures can reach 100°F and thunderstorms with high winds are not unusual. Spring and fall are more pleasant, with clear, cool days and fewer crowds. Winter is bitterly cold.

The Lakota called the ghostly buttes and spires that rise out of the rolling Great Plains prairie *mako sica* – "bad land." Col. George Custer called the fantastic pinnacles and tortuous gullies hell without the fire. No matter how you describe the landscape, it is unlike anyplace else on earth, thanks to 65 million years of erosion from wind and rain. Here, where the Lakota danced their last Ghost Dance atop Stronghold Table in 1890, is a harsh, arid environment, with frequent droughts and a winter that lasts half the year. Though viewed as a wasteland by most 19th-century pioneers who passed through quickly in their search for farm and grazing land, the area is nonetheless a geologic and ecological wonder. Sharply eroded buttes and colorful spires are just part of the largest protected mixed-grass prairie in the United States. Nearly 50 kinds of wild grasses and 200 types of wildflowers grow in the Badlands. Below the surface is the world's richest repository of fossils from the Oligocene epoch, dating 23 to 35 million years ago. Paleontologists have unearthed the remains of saber-toothed cats, three-toed horses, and early ancestors of the hog, camel, and rhinoceros.

The easiest way to view the park is by driving the 32-mile Badlands Loop, which swoops down from I-90 along South Dakota Route 240 before exiting the North Unit of the park at the Pinnacles Entrance. Just inside the park's Northeast Entrance you'll come to the Big Badlands Overlook, giving you your first view of The Wall, the park's focal point. This 100-mile-long spine of pastel-colored stone serves as a dramatic backdrop for the herds of bison, pronghorn, and bighorn sheep that wander the lower prairie. Further along the highway is the Windows Overlook, which serves as the trailhead for three short nature trails – the Door, Window, and Notch Trails. Door Trail is an easy three-quarter-mile walk leading through a natural doorway in The Wall into an otherworldly landscape. The even shorter Window Trail leads to a natural window overlooking a deeply cut canyon. And the more difficult Notch Trail takes you along the side of a gully to a break in the rocks, where you can look out over the White River and the Pine Ridge Reservation, part of which lies in the South Unit of the park, added in 1976. With few roads and access only with the permission of private landowners, the undeveloped South Unit is difficult to explore. Stronghold Table in the South Unit, site of the last Ghost Dance before Wounded Knee, is a sacred place for the Lakota.

SD 157
PARK 190

ALBERTA

Babel Creek at Consolation Basin

Peyto Lake and the Waputik Mountains, north of Lake Louise

TEXAS

Sotol Vista in the Chisos Mountains

UTAH

Rock spires called hoodoos at Sunset Point

BANFF

Southwestern Alberta, Canada
Established November 28, 1885
1,640,960 acres

Headquarters
Banff National Park
Box 900
Banff, Alberta
Canada T0L 0C0
403.762.1500
www.worldweb.com/parkscanada-banff

Visitor Centers
Banff Park Information Centre (403.762.1550), 224 Banff Ave., in the town of Banff, and Lake Louise Information Centre (403.522.1200), in the hamlet of Lake Louise, open daily year-round.

Entrance Fees
C$5 for adults per day; C$4 for seniors; C$2.50 for children 6 to 16, under 6 free; C$10 for a group of 2 to 10 people, per day.

Accommodations
There are 13 campgrounds and a total of more than 2,000 campsites in Banff National Park. All sites are awarded on a first-come, first-served basis. Tunnel Mountain Village II, Lake Louise Trailer, and Mosquito Creek are open year-round. The resort towns of Banff and Lake Louise are located in the park and offer a wide range of lodging facilities; call Banff-Lake Louise Tourism Bureau (403.762.8421).

When to Go
The park is open year-round, but travel can be restricted in winter due to road closures. Most people come in July and Aug. Some of the best wildlife viewing is possible in the fall, when herds of elk and deer move to winter grounds. Winter sports are popular Dec to Apr in many areas of the park. Not until mid-July are the majority of the park's passes open and dry. Regardless of the time of year, come prepared for snow – even in Aug.

The Canadian Rockies that run up the middle of Banff and neighboring Jasper national parks are a bit deceiving. Massive hulks of glacially tormented mountains burst upward like huge frozen explosions, seeming to the naked eye to dwarf Colorado's southern Rockies in scale and grandeur. In truth, Rocky Mountain National Park reaches higher into the sky, topped by 14,255-foot Longs Peak. Part of the optical illusion can be explained by the fact that the Canadian Rockies rise from much lower elevations; another, perhaps, by the park's glaciation. The visitor center at Colorado's Estes Park is at 7,890 feet, while, by comparison, Banff townsite, the unofficial gateway to Canada's Rockies, sits in Bow Valley at a humble 4,500 feet.

The first and probably most famous of Canada's national parks, Banff is bejeweled with strings of turquoise-colored lakes, pristine alpine meadows, and wild, powerful rivers that rush through forested valleys. From its famous elk to rarer grizzly and caribou, wildlife abounds in these mountains, and the largest ice deposit south of Alaska, the vast Columbia Icefield, caps the range – 125 square miles wide and more than a thousand feet thick.

The park had its beginnings in 1883, when three railway workers stumbled across a cave and basin containing hot springs on the eastern slopes of Alberta's Rocky Mountains, near the Bow River. "It's like some fantastic dream from a tale of the *Arabian Nights*," declared one of the discoverers, William McCardell, who also imagined that by establishing a bathing resort he and his partners could bring attention and tourism to the area. So began Canada's national parks system, in the town of Banff. Today, a cluster of hotels, restaurants, and shops have made this old Canadian Pacific railroad town into the seat of the park, yet the peaks towering overhead, a bounty of bike trails, the evergreen forest, and the swift Bow River prevent it from seeming stifling or overcrowded. Today, the park's residents do not own land, but only lease it from the park. In the townsites, it's not uncommon to encounter elk wandering around, munching serenely on potted pansies or cropped hedges.

About an hour's drive north is the park's other major center, Lake Louise, which in winter is one of Canada's top ski resorts. To see the lake itself, named for Queen Victoria's youngest daughter, take Highway 1A across the river to the usually jam-packed Chateau Lake Louise, a massive cream-colored resort on the lake's eastern shore. In summer, rent a canoe and paddle the blue-green glacial waters; the lake rests beneath high, gnarled peaks and runs up against the sheer face of Mount Victoria.

Both of the townsites have popular gondola rides that whisk visitors, in a matter of minutes, from valley floors up to overlooks and trailheads that allow further exploration of the high country. Just south of Banff, next to Upper Hot Springs, is the Sulphur Mountain Gondola; and across the Trans-Canada Highway from Lake Louise is the Lake Louise Gondola, which rises partway up Mount Whitehorn.

Banff is bisected by a number of scenic routes that offer good chances of seeing elk, deer, bighorn sheep, mountain goats, moose, black bears, and even grizzly bears. The Icefields Parkway, a magnificent 143-mile drive between Lake Louise and Jasper townsite, is a must. One of Canada's highest roads, with an average elevation of 5,100 feet, it skirts lakes and forested river valleys, rising, falling, and penetrating into the Columbia Icefield. A good stop is Bow Lake, where Crowfoot Glacier adorns the rugged face of Crowfoot Mountain. Rising to the chilly 6,787-foot Bow Summit, the parkway pauses at an overlook for a stunning view of Peyto Lake. Dropping again, the parkway visits a graceful canyon cut by the Mistaya River and travels alongside the North Saskatchewan River before crossing into Jasper National Park. Three hours north of Banff, near Sunwapta Pass, there is a chance (weather permitting) to walk onto Athabasca Glacier, a four-mile swath of ice marked by deep crevasses and towering blue ice pillars. Closer to Jasper townsite, the thundering Athabasca Falls are also a memorable stop. The entire Icefields Parkway can be completed in several hours, or for a more leisurely tour, try stretching it into an overnight trip, with a stop at the cozy Num-Ti-Jah Lodge near Bow Lake.

The specially designed, 30-mile Bow Valley Parkway scenic drive, between Banff and Lake Louise, features a number of marked trails and interpretive areas along the way, giving visitors a good overview of the park's topography and natural history. One of the best is the Johnston Canyon Trail, where a three-and-a-half-mile round-trip trail, veering out over swift currents on catwalks, leads to two spectacular falls. There are also a number of walking and hiking trails near Banff townsite. The Fenland Trail is only minutes from town but takes you through marsh and forest inhabited by beaver, muskrat, and waterfowl. The Vermilion Lakes, immediately west of town, are famous for their scenic views of Mount Rundle and for migrating wildfowl and beaver families.

With snow conditions often good well into May, skiers can take advantage of off-season rates in the spring. Sunshine Village offers the highest alpine skiing in Canada, as well as Banff's only slopeside accommodations.

AB 179
PARK 190

BIG BEND

Southwestern Texas
Established June 12, 1944
801,163 acres

Headquarters
Big Bend National Park
P.O. Box 129
Big Bend National Park, TX 79834
915.477.2251
www.nps.gov/bibe

Visitor Centers
Panther Junction Visitor Center (915.477.2251), 26 miles from Persimmon Gap entrance, open year-round. Persimmon Gap (915.477.2393) and Chisos Basin Visitor Centers (915.477.2264), open most of the year, staff permitting. Rio Grande Village Visitor Center (915.477.2271), 20 miles south of Panther Junction, open Nov to Apr.

Entrance Fees
$10 per vehicle for 7 days. $5 per person on foot, bicycle, motorcycle, or bus.

Accommodations
Three developed campgrounds, all available first-come, first-served only. Chisos Mountain Lodge (915.477.2291) is operated by the National Parks Concession.

When to Go
The park is usually free of crowds until spring break, generally the second or third week in March; the week between Christmas and New Year's Day can be very busy. If it rains enough, the desert blooms beautifully during the spring.

Not only did the mighty Rio Grande give this park its name (it's situated where the river makes a sharp turn – or Big Bend – along the U. S.–Mexican border), but it also helps define its three main elements: The river, the desert, and the mountains. The river flows for 118 miles along the southern boundary of the park, cutting through dramatic limestone canyons. Most of the park north of the Rio Grande consists of Chihuahuan desert vegetation – cactus, yucca, creosote bush, and the like – but there are also lush floodplains and the Chisos Mountains with their stands of juniper, pine, and oak.

Because of the park's surprising topography, there is a remarkable diversity of life, with some 1,000 plant species and 400 species of birds, including the rare, lyrical Colima warbler, whose only known nesting places are here and in Mexico. There are deer and mountain lions in the mountains, *javelina* (wild boar) and kit fox in the hills, and coyotes and lizards just about everywhere. The park's remoteness can make visiting problematic, depending on where you're coming from: It's 410 miles west of San Antonio and 300 miles southeast of El Paso. Hiking is really the best way to experience, enjoy, and appreciate Big Bend (there are over 350 miles of trails). One of the most popular hikes is through Santa Elena Canyon, a massive boxlike gorge on the southwest edge of the park. A moderate one-and-three-quarter-mile trail goes along a rocky ledge into the canyon mouth, rewarding you with striking views of sculpted limestone cliffs.

After your hike, stop at the Santa Elena Canyon Overlook for great views of the 1,500-foot-deep canyon that was worn away by the abrasive silt and gravel carried by the Rio Grande. About six miles east along the road is an overlook onto the adobe houses of Castolon, a pioneer settlement established by a mixture of Mexican farmers, American cattlemen, and the U. S. Cavalry. Although no commercial river rafters are based inside the park, float trips down the Rio Grande into Big Bend are available through outfitters at Terlingua and other nearby towns. Two-day trips include overnight camping on a sandbar in Boquillas Canyon or Santa Elena Canyon.

TX 160
PARK 190

BRYCE CANYON

South-central Utah
Established September 15, 1928
35,835 acres

Headquarters
Bryce Canyon National Park
P.O. Box 170001
Bryce Canyon, UT 84717
435.834.5322
www.nps.gov/brca

Visitor Center
Bryce Canyon National Park Visitor Center (435.834.5322), on main road just inside park boundary on State Rte. 63, open year-round, except major holidays.

Entrance Fees
$10 per vehicle for 7 days.

Accommodations
The park has two campgrounds, North and Sunset, available on a first-come, first-served basis. Bryce Canyon Lodge (435.834.5361) is open Apr to Oct.

When to Go
One of the park's big attractions is its more than 160 bird species, which appear in the greatest numbers between May and Sept. Small crowds and lots of wildflowers make spring and early summer particularly good times to visit. Crowds peak in July and Aug and are at their lowest Dec to Feb. During some winters, Alaskan cold fronts descend onto the Colorado Plateau and bring temperatures as low as 20°F below zero.

Two things make Bryce Canyon unusual among parks: Its relatively compact size, and the beautiful fingers of worn limestone, sandstone, and mudstone called hoodoos, which were described by original inhabitants of the land as "red rocks standing like men." Perhaps a better name for the park would be Hoodoo Plateau, as Bryce Canyon is not a canyon at all but a series of amphitheaters carved out of a high land called Paunsaugunt Plateau, which in turn is one of many plateaus that extend from the Mesa Verde cliff dwellings in the east to the canyonlands of Utah in the west, known collectively as the Colorado Plateau. Ponderosa pines, high-elevation meadows, and spruce and fir forests border the rim of Paunsaugunt Plateau, while panoramic views of three states spread beyond the park's boundaries.

Because of the park's small size, you can drive from one end to the other in less than three hours – except then you'd miss out on some of the 50 miles of trails that explore thousands of colorful spires, fins, pinnacles, and mazes that make this park special. Think of Bryce as basically a day-hike park with a number of connecting trails that allow you to customize the length and duration of your outing. One of the easiest trails is the half-mile section of Rim Trail starting at Sunrise Point. As the name suggests, this is a popular spot to catch the first rays of the sun as it paints the fluted walls and sculptured spires warm yellows, oranges, and reds. Another favorite place to watch the sunrise is Bryce Point, one of the highest overlooks along the rim of Bryce Amphitheater, the most striking of 12 bowl-shaped canyons where the hoodoo formations cluster in dense stands.

To explore more, combine the Queen's Garden and Navajo Trails for a moderately strenuous two-to-three-hour hike that loops from Sunset Point to Sunrise Point. This is a good walk for viewing the canyon's scenery and the park's many wildflowers in spring and early summer. In the summer, rangers lead nature walks. If you camp, participate in the night sky programs – the area boasts some of the nation's best air quality. This, coupled with the lack of nearby light sources, creates wonderful opportunities for stargazing. On clear days, on the rim of Bryce Canyon, long-distance views of more than 100 miles can be enjoyed. Spring through fall, wranglers lead horseback rides into Bryce Amphitheater along a dedicated horse trail. In winter, the chill is offset by high-altitude sun, bountiful snow, cross-country skiing, and snowshoeing.

UT 165
PARK 165

CALIFORNIA/NEVADA

Wind-propelled rock in a former lake bed called The Racetrack

ALASKA

Toklat River between Stony Hill and Polychrome Pass

Cloud-embraced Tokosha Mountains, as seen from Denali State Park

FLORIDA

Coastal glade along Snake Bight Trail

DEATH VALLEY

Eastern California; southwestern Nevada
Established October 31, 1994
3.3 million acres

Headquarters
Death Valley National Park
P.O. Box 579
Death Valley, CA 92328
760.786.2331
www.nps.gov/deva

Visitor Center
Furnace Creek Visitor Center, off Rte. 190 in the center of the park, open daily.

Entrance Fees
$10 per vehicle for 7 days.

Accommodations
Furnace Creek Campground is open year-round; reservations required. Three campgrounds – Texas Springs, Sunset, and Stovepipe Wells – are open Oct through Apr and are first-come, first-served. Mesquite Springs campground, near Scottys Castle, is open year-round, first-come, first-served. Other lodging includes the Furnace Creek Inn (760.786.2361), the Furnace Creek Ranch (800.528.6367 or 760.786.2345), and the Stovepipe Wells Village Motel (760.786.2387).

When to Go
Not in summer. Even nighttime lows often top 100°F. The climate is best Nov to Apr, with temperatures ranging between 39 and 75°F.

Surely the forbidding name given to this desert valley seems ludicrous to anyone who has ever spent a lovely spring day here when the sky was blue, the wildflowers in bloom, and the temperature a very reasonable 80°F. But all it takes is opening your car window on a sweltering summer afternoon to recall the party of nine intrepid pioneers who likely perished while trying to cross the basin back in the 1850s. The nation's largest national park south of Alaska, Death Valley is a land of extremes. The geological term for the area is a graben, a sunken section of the earth's crust. Its barren, silent depths contain the lowest point in the Western Hemisphere – 282 feet below sea level, at Badwater. Also, North America's highest temperature – 134°F – was recorded here; and with two inches of rainfall annually, it is the continent's driest spot. Despite its foreboding name, Death Valley offers crisp air and lonely, fascinating landscapes, from the sand dunes near Stovepipe Wells Village to the mudstone badlands beyond Zabriskie Point.

The popular belief that nothing lives in Death Valley is discounted by the diverse animal and plant life that has tenaciously adapted to the burning heat and dryness. In fact, nearly a thousand species of plants and trees, including ferns, lilies, and orchids, flourish inside the park. More elusive are the many animals, most of which emerge only at night. But you can spot bighorn sheep between Telescope Peak and Badwater.

Death Valley can be explored on some 290 miles of paved roads and 300 more of dirt. Most of the area's unique attractions lie no more than an easy stroll from one of them. The area is also gaining popularity with bicyclists, drawn to its relatively flat roads and good weather. South of the visitor center you'll find a number of must-see natural wonders, including the Devil's Golf Course, which is really the remains of an ancient lake, and Artists Palette, a curious terrain of yellow, red, orange, and even green rocks that appears to be painted into the side of a canyon. Dante's View, on the crest of the Black Mountains, is one of the most spectacular scenic overlooks in the United States. And don't miss Scottys Castle, at the northern end of the park. Built in the 1920s by a legendary character known as Death Valley Scotty, the flamboyant Spanish-Moorish house cost $2 million and took ten years to complete. Horseback riding is available seasonally out of the Furnace Creek Ranch.

CA 68
NV 126
PARK 190

DENALI

Central Alaska
Established as Mt. McKinley National Park on February 26, 1917
6,028,091 acres

Headquarters
Denali National Park & Preserve
P.O. Box 9
Denali Park, AK 99755
907.683.2294
www.nps.gov/dena

Visitor Centers
Visitor Access Center (VAC), eastern border of park, open daily Apr to late Sept. Eielson Visitor Center, center of park, open early June to mid-Sept.

Entrance Fees
$10 per family and $5 per person for 7 days. Varying fees charged for shuttle and tour bus services; call 800.622.7275.

Accommodations
Seven campgrounds open mid-May to mid-Sept. Riley Creek (open year-round), Savage River, and Teklanika River are open to private vehicles; reservations required. Denali Park Hotel is the only lodging within the park; open mid-May to early Sept (800.276.7234).

When to Go
Though the park is open year-round, car travel is restricted. By lottery, 400 private cars per day are allowed to drive the park road over a 4-day period, scheduled for a different time each year. The annual road lottery takes place each fall. Contact park headquarters to apply; applications accepted in July. Mosquitoes are worst in June and early July; after Aug 15, the atmosphere is crisp, but the annoying bugs are gone.

Imagine a park larger than Massachusetts and you'll start to get an idea of how immense Denali National Park & Preserve really is. While it has quickly become the most popular park in Alaska, only a few visitors ever see much more than a tiny swath of untamed wilderness on either side of the 85-mile park road that runs from the Visitor Access Center on the eastern border to Wonder Lake in Denali's center. Beyond the lake, the vast roadless and largely trailless wilderness continues on for many miles in every direction. Biologist and naturalist Olaus Murie, overwhelmed by the expansiveness and range of natural wonders at Denali, called it "the greatest scenic experience on the North American continent."

Known originally as Mount McKinley National Park (the name given to it by gold prospector William L. Dickey in 1896), the area was renamed by Congress in 1980, when it was enlarged to over three times its original size. Denali, meaning "the high one," is what early Athapaskan Indians called the snowcapped mountain. Encompassing hundreds of lakes and rivers, acres of spruce and birch forests, and a complete subarctic ecosystem with untold numbers of large mammals – grizzly bears, wolves, Dall sheep, moose – the park's greatest spectacle continues to be mighty Mount McKinley, which rises from a valley only 1,000 feet above sea level to an altitude of 20,320 feet, making it the tallest peak in North America. Even at a distance of 26 miles (the closest approach by car), it overshadows the other wilderness attractions that are themselves reason enough for a visit.

Unfortunately, Mount McKinley can be almost as tough to spot as a wolf – on average, one in every five visitors sees a wolf, while one in every three sees McKinley. In summer the frequent cloudy, rainy weather (caused by the mountain itself) prevents many visitors from ever seeing the towering spire. Your best bet is to try and catch a glimpse early in the morning (don't forget that there are 16 to 20 hours of daylight this far north in the summer, so when we say early, we're talking about 3 or 4 a.m.). August is popular as a viewing month, but don't get your hopes up.

Whether or not you spy Mount McKinley, there's plenty else to see. Because the park limits the number of private vehicles inside (and they are restricted to the Savage River Check Station, at mile 14), the best way to see the park is by shuttle or tour bus. Though it's only 85 miles from the park's eastern boundary to Wonder Lake, at the western end of the road, it's a good 11-hour journey round-trip, thanks to the winding, primitive character of the road and its 35 mph speed limit. If you take the shuttle bus you can get off virtually anywhere along the route and wait for a bus going the opposite way. If any wildlife wanders by, the driver stops so passengers can take pictures. While there's never any guarantee of wildlife spottings, on a good day the drive along the park highway can be like a visit to an outdoor zoo. As the bus crosses the Savage River Bridge, you might spot Dall sheep clinging to the mountainsides. Just beyond, in a marshy flat with odd spruce trees sprouting in all directions, moose sometimes linger. At Sable Pass, 40 miles from the park entrance, grizzly bears have occasionally been so numerous that park officials forbid you to leave the roadway. These awe-inspiring creatures, feeding on roots, berries, and other plants in the area, are a favorite with photographers. And caribou herds numbering in the dozens often graze below the Eielson Visitor Center.

Despite the great size of Denali, there are few official trails for hikers. But, as most of the park is open tundra, you can hike just about anywhere (although some areas are regularly closed by park officials to prevent habitat damage and to protect wildlife), making it possible to select a destination and then to walk directly toward it. Some good areas for day hikes include Savage River, Primrose Ridge, Polychrome Pass, and Wonder Lake. The roughly one-hour round-trip Horseshoe Lake Trail, an easy family hike near the park entrance, winds gently through a lovely forest of spruce and aspen to an old oxbow of the Nenana River. For something a little more strenuous, try the six-mile round-trip Triple Lakes Trail, where you'll be afforded marvelous views of the Alaska Range, including Mount Fellows and Pyramid Mountain. You're also welcome to hike farther into the wilderness and stay overnight, though you'll need to get a use permit, issued on a first-come, first-served basis, at the Visitor Access Center. Popular backcountry hiking areas abound in the park; check with a ranger to find one that matches your interests and abilities.

The most serious – and challenging – sport in the park is mountaineering. Because of the difficulty involved in sumitting, the park has several restrictions on climbing. Climbers must register 60 days in advance and there is a required $150 fee per climber. A reference book by the park's mountaineering rangers is a must-read for expeditions: It includes mandatory requirements, general information, equipment suggestions, and medical information.

Several companies offer guided float trips down the Nenana River, along the George Parks Highway and the park's eastern border. Trips last from two hours to four days. Surprisingly, fishing is not very good in most of the park rivers because of the milky, pulverized silt that the waters usually carry. Your best bet for casual fishing is Wonder Lake. Popular winter activities include dogsled tours, cross-country skiing, and snowshoeing.

AK 62
PARK 62

EVERGLADES

Southern Florida
Established December 6, 1947
1,509,000 acres

Headquarters
Everglades National Park
40001 State Road 9336
Homestead, FL 33034
305.242.7700
www.nps.gov/ever

Visitor Centers
The Ernest F. Coe Visitor Center, 12 miles west of Homestead and Florida City. Royal Palm Visitor Center, 4 miles past the Coe Visitor Center. Flamingo Visitor Center, 38 miles past the Coe Visitor Center. Shark Valley Visitor Center, on northern end of park, 30 miles west of the Florida Turnpike on U. S. 41. Gulf Coast Visitor Center, 3 miles south of U. S. 41 on Hwy. 29. All open daily.

Entrance Fees
$10 per vehicle for 7 days.

Accommodations
Three developed campgrounds, all open year-round, free during July and Aug. Reservations accepted up to 5 months in advance for stays between Dec 15 and Apr 30 for Long Pine Key and Flamingo. Chekika is first-come, first-served.

When to Go
During the dry season, Dec to Apr, the weather is generally clear and pleasant, and temperatures are moderate.

This vast swath of wetlands and rivers, described as a "river of grass" by conservationist Marjory Stoneman Douglas, is the first national park designated primarily to protect an ecosystem rather than for its scenic or historic value. A wetland of international importance, the 1.5 million acres of watery wilderness include dense cypress domes and mangrove swamps; a saw-grass prairie that ripples in the wind; and shadowy hardwood islands called hammocks, thick with mahogany and other tropical trees.

South Florida itself surfaced only since the last, or Pleistocene, ice age, and the rock beneath the park has only been exposed for a mere 6,000 to 8,000 years. No point in the Everglades is higher than eight feet above sea level, and the sole source of water for the subtropical region is the rain that falls on it. The park itself comprises just one-fifth of the total mass of the Everglades, and the rains are being siphoned away by extensive canal and levee systems, creating an artificial drought that threatens the park's wildlife and ecological balance. Also, pollutants from agricultural runoff are contaminating the plants, animals, and fish that live in the wetlands. To fight these trends, Congress, in one of the world's largest ecosystem restoration projects, has extended the park boundary to help protect delicate areas.

Today, the Everglades are home to more than a dozen threatened and endangered species, as well as to hundreds of subtropical plants and animals found nowhere else in the United States. The endangered wood stork makes its home here – in decreasing numbers – as do alligators, snowy egrets, a few remaining Florida panthers, and 26 species of snakes. From May through August hundreds of female loggerhead sea turtles come ashore to lay their eggs on the Florida beaches. A colorful assemblage of migratory birds, like numerous warblers, peregrine falcons, and wading birds, use the park as a wintering area and a migration stopover.

The sprawling park has several distinctive sections: Everglades City, its western saltwater gateway; Shark Valley, which encompasses the Shark River Slough as well as the saw-grass prairie; and the area near the historic town of Flamingo, on the Florida Bay. Boardwalks and trails lead off from the 38-mile-long main park road, which connects the Ernest F. Coe Visitor Center with Flamingo. Though much of the park is accessible only by boat or canoe, a car tour on this road can work well for short visits. Also, tram tours from Shark Valley are a good bet for wildlife sightings.

FL 82
PARK 191

Icebergs on Glacier Bay's Muir Inlet

Redbud tree on a stone bar in Deer Creek

View from Point Imperial, North Rim

Rare July snowfall graces 13,770-foot Grand Teton

GLACIER BAY

Southeastern Alaska
Established December 2, 1980
3,280,198 acres

Headquarters
Glacier Bay National Park & Preserve
P.O. Box 140
Gustavus, AK 99826
907.697.2230
www.nps.gov/glba

Visitor Centers
Information centers near the dock at Bartlett Cove (907.697.2627) and at Glacier Bay Lodge (907.697.2661); open May to Sept.

Entrance Fees
None.

Accommodations
A primitive campground is available at Bartlett Cove, no fee; open all year, first-come, first served. The only lodging inside the park is Glacier Bay Lodge (800.451.5952).

When to Go
The best time to enjoy a cruise along this marine highway is from May to mid-Sept, when days are long and temperatures cool. Sept is often rainy and windy; May and June tend to be more sunny and pleasant.

Sitting about 90 miles northwest of Juneau, in the Fairweather Range of the St. Elias Mountains, is one of Alaska's most dramatic sites, Glacier Bay. A window into the Ice Age and a continuing study in glacial retreat, Glacier Bay did not exist 200 years ago: It lay covered by a sheet of ice many miles wide and thousands of feet thick. In one of the fastest known glacial retreats, the shifting ice has unveiled a bay and left behind an entire ecosystem, thriving with everything from a rain forest to ocean waters teeming with life. More than 20 tremendous glaciers and many equally impressive smaller ones, including tidewater glaciers, spread across an area of over three million acres – most of it trailless and maintained only by wild animals. A dramatic range of plant communities, from rocky terrain recently uncovered by ice to lush, temperate rain forest, and a large variety of animals, including bears, mountain goats, humpback and killer whales, harbor seals, and bald eagles, can be found within the park. Also included are Mount Fairweather, the highest peak in southeastern Alaska, and the American portion of the Alsek River.

Think of Glacier Bay as an ocean highway. A good way to explore the park is from the deck of a cruise ship, from the daily tour boat that runs in the summer, or – for the hardy – from the waterline of a sea kayak. Bartlett Cove, on the southern end of the park, is a hub of activity where you'll find the park's only three maintained trails. In summer, rangers lead hikes through Bartlett Cove's luxuriant spruce and hemlock rain forest, starting from the Glacier Bay Lodge. The Forest Loop Trail is an easy one-mile walk through the forest to Blackwater Pond. Bartlett Cove is also a popular starting point for one-day kayak trips out among the Beardslee Islands, a maze of shorelines and quiet waterways. Guided kayak trips are also available. In the remote northwestern corner of the park, rafting trips down the Alsek River can be arranged.

The highlight of any visit to Glacier Bay is a close look at the star performers – the glaciers themselves. During the summer months, Glacier Bay Lodge operates day-tour boat trips that take you up the western arm of the bay to see the highest mountains and the most active tidewater glaciers in the park, conditions permitting. At Tarr Inlet, the glaciers Margerie and Grand Pacific can be seen calving huge icebergs into the water in a magnificent setting that includes Mount Quincy Adams, which rises 13,650 feet above the inlet.

AK 62
PARK 191

GRAND CANYON

Northern Arizona
Established February 26, 1919
1,218,375 acres

Headquarters
Grand Canyon National Park
P.O. Box 129
Grand Canyon, AZ 86023
520.638.7888
www.nps.gov/grca

Visitor Centers
South Rim Visitor Center (520.638.7888), in Grand Canyon Village, open year-round. North Rim Contact Station (520.638.7864), open mid-Oct through mid-May.

Entrance Fees
$20 per vehicle for 7 days; $10 per person on foot or bicycle.

Accommodations
Three campgrounds, all with 7-day limits; 2 on South Rim and 1 on North Rim. Mather Campground, open year-round, is handled on a first-come, first-served basis from Dec 1 to Mar 1. Amfac Parks & Resorts operates 7 hotels and lodges inside the park (South Rim only), from the showpiece El Tovar Hotel, in the village, to Phantom Ranch, at the bottom of the canyon. All in-park lodging is available through Grand Canyon National Park Lodges; for advance reservations, call 303.297.2757.

When to Go
Facilities on the South Rim are open all year, but congestion is heavy in summer, and air pollution and hazy days can drop visibility considerably. The best time to visit is spring or fall, when crowds are slight. For river rafters, prime season is Apr through Oct.

All Americans feel as if they know the Grand Canyon, even if they've never been within a thousand miles of it. Its precipitous rim and colorful geological landmarks are as much a national icon as the Statue of Liberty. Even so, nothing can prepare you for actually standing on the edge of Yavapai Point on the South Rim and seeing it for the first time – it literally takes your breath away. Panoramic IMAX images give no more than an inkling of the canyon's vastness. On a clear day, when visibility seems unlimited, you'll see a picture of the earth that seems to reveal the beginning of time. Stretching 277 miles across northern Arizona, the canyon measures 18 miles across at its widest spot, and is, on average, a mile deep – making it at once an unfathomable, shadowy abyss and a bright panorama of buttes and sand spires. At its bottom, some of the oldest rock in the world sits exposed, dating back 1.7 billion years. Awed after his first visit to the Grand Canyon, in 1903, Teddy Roosevelt called it "one of the great sights which every American ... should see." Some think his words too modest.

For thousands of years, the canyon was home to ancient people who lived high in the cliffs. The first European visitors were Spanish soldiers who, in 1540, passed by the canyon in search of the mythical Seven Cities of Cibola. For the next 300 years it remained largely unexplored until John Wesley Powell, a one-armed adventurer, rode down the mighty Colorado River in 1869. But it wasn't until the Santa Fe Railroad completed a line to the South Rim in 1901 – followed by the opening of the world-famous El Tovar Hotel in 1905 – that the era of tourism began. Today, close to five million visitors come here annually, though almost 90 percent never go further than the two popular scenic drives on the canyon's south side. The less visited North Rim is only 10 miles away by air, but 215 by car. Adventurous travelers who make it to this side of the canyon are rewarded with pristine forests, rolling meadows, and superb, uncluttered panoramas. Unfortunately, the North Rim is open only from mid-May through mid-October; its higher elevation often means heavy snowfall. Because of the heavy crowds at the Grand Canyon during spring, summer, and fall, it is imperative that overnight visitors make camping and lodging reservations well in advance.

Most visitors enter the park at the South Entrance Station, near the village of Grand Canyon and the Visitor Center. A free shuttle runs eight miles west along the rim on the West Rim Drive to the limestone curio shop at Hermits Rest, stopping along the way at key points for stunning views of the main canyon (the shuttle runs from Memorial Day to early October). During peak season, the West Rim Drive is closed to private vehicles, but the shuttles operate at frequent intervals. The 23-mile East Rim Drive offers several fine views of the Colorado River; turn off at Yaki Point to see the darkly glowing innermost canyon, Granite Gorge.

Hiking in the Grand Canyon is the reverse of mountain climbing; first you go down and then you come up. It's important to remember this, since it generally takes twice as much time – and energy – to come back up from a hike as to go down. One of the best family hikes is the South Rim Nature Trail, an easy 1.5-mile trek from the Yavapai Museum, set on the brink of the canyon, to the El Tovar Hotel. The trail is paved and nearly level the whole way. Hikers who want to penetrate the canyon can descend the steep South Kaibab Trail, which switchbacks down to the Colorado River (it can be three miles round-trip if you end at Cedar Ridge; otherwise it's best as an overnight trip). One of the most beautiful hikes is the North Kaibab Trail. Start in the cool forests of the North Rim, then descend through the woods into Roaring Springs Canyon. Off the East Rim Drive, Grandview Trail is a steep but scenic walk to Horseshoe Mesa, where copper ore was mined around the turn of the century. A number of unmaintained trails of the South Rim's inner canyons lead to some beautiful corners of the park, where you'll find solitude and spectacular views.

An easier way down to the canyon floor is to go by mule on one of the popular two-day trips from the South Rim. Overnight riders stay and eat at Phantom Ranch. Trips can be booked as early as 11 months in advance; call early. A shorter one-day trip that goes partway to the river is also offered. If you're not interested in seeing the inner canyons, you can rent gentle horses at Moqui Lodge in the village of Tusayan. A number of commercial white-water trips through the Grand Canyon begin at Lee's Ferry, a two-and-a-half-hour drive from the South Rim, and range from three days to three weeks. Some companies also offer trips starting from or ending at Phantom Ranch. River trips operate April through October. Most trips stop for day hikes at waterfalls, Indian ruins, and interesting side canyons. A gentler one-day smooth-water raft trip on the Colorado River runs from the town of Page to Lee's Ferry. Helicopter and airplane tours from Grand Canyon Airport can give you the big picture, though flights are no longer allowed below the rim because of safety and noise concerns.

AZ 64
PARK 65

GRAND TETON

Northwestern Wyoming
Established February 26, 1929
309,590 acres

Headquarters
Grand Teton National Park
P.O. Drawer 170
Moose, WY 83012
307.739.3300
www.nps.gov/grte

Visitor Centers
Moose Visitor Center (307.739.3399), at park's southern end, open daily except Christmas. Colter Bay Visitor Center (307.739.3594), on Jackson Lake, open mid-May to end of Sept. Jenny Lake Visitor Center (307.739.3392), open June to Sept.

Entrance Fees
$20 per vehicle for 7 days (also good for Yellowstone)

Accommodations
Five campgrounds. Jenny Lake has 7-day limit; all others, 14-day limit. All open from May to Sept or Oct, except Lizard Creek, open mid-June to early Sept. All first-come, first-served, except Colter Bay Trailer Village; call Grand Teton Lodge Co. (800.628.9988 or 307.543.2811), which also runs three lodges and cabins in park.

When to Go
High season runs July to Aug, when day temperatures are in the 70s and 80s, nights in the 40s, though fishing is best in Sept. First heavy snow falls by Nov and continues through Mar.

Without any foothills impeding its 7,000-foot ascent from the Jackson Hole valley floor, the Teton Range is a stunning sight. Twelve of its craggy, rock-faced peaks top 12,000 feet, and Grand Teton alone stands at 13,770 feet. While the oldest rocks at the tops of the mountains are more than half the age of this planet, the range itself is geologically young, thanks to its place on an active fault. For nine million years, Jackson Hole has sunk and the jagged Tetons risen skyward. Below, in the 50-mile-long valley bisected by the Snake River, sagebrush flats and forests of lodgepole pine and spruce make ideal habitats for pronghorn, deer, elk, and even moose. The Tetons take their name from lonely 19th-century French-Canadian trappers who imagined a likeness to breasts in the snowy peaks: Teton is an archaic French word for cow's teats.

More than 200 miles of marked trails offer an unlimited choice of hiking or cross-country skiing excursions, depending on the season. If you're on a tight schedule, drive the Signal Mountain Summit Road, which takes you 800 feet above the valley for panoramic views of the entire Teton Range, Jackson Lake, and most of Jackson Hole. A half-day excursion runs from the Moose Visitor Center to Jenny Lake Scenic Drive, which many consider to be the visual heart of the Tetons offering majestic views of the central peaks. Cathedral Group Turnout is a good lookout. Jenny Lake is also an excellent spot for a hike. A good family walk takes you to outstanding views of the glacially carved lake. A longer, six-mile hike joins the Cascade Canyon Trail to the spectacular Hidden Falls and Inspiration Point. A passenger boat departs from the southern end of the lake and gets you to within a half mile of the falls. The Jenny Lake Ranger Station is the center for mountaineering in the area. Mountain guides offer training that has beginners crawling up sheer cliffs their first day. Two days of instruction are required to go on the guided overnight climbs of Mount Owen, Mount Moran, or Grand Teton. Parkway concessionaires and operators provide a variety of floating and fishing trips on the Snake River. Half-day trips from Pacific Creek usually include a lunch at Deadman's Bar. Horseback rides are offered out of Colter Bay and Jackson Lake Lodge. Better riders can spend a full day on the high trails or arrange pack trips through guest ranches in the valley. Winter, though harsh, is a good time for sports like cross-country skiing, snowshoeing, dogsledding, and snowmobiling and for spotting large herds of elk moving across the open flats to their wintering area south of the park.

WY 176
PARK 176

NORTH CAROLINA/TENNESSEE

Tipton barn at Cades Cove

Sunset view from Clingman's Dome, the highest point in the park

HAWAII

New lava flow from Kilauea meets the ocean

ARKANSAS

Oak forest along West Mountain Trail

GREAT SMOKY MOUNTAINS

Western North Carolina; eastern Tennessee
Established June 15, 1934
520,409 acres

Headquarters
Great Smoky Mountains National Park
107 Park Headquarters Road
Gatlinburg, TN 37738
423.436.1200
www.nps.gov/grsm

Visitor Centers
Oconaluftee Visitor Center, 2 miles north of main park entrance near Cherokee, NC, open year-round. Cades Cove Visitor Center, 12 miles south of Townsend, TN, open mid-Mar to Dec. Sugarlands Visitor Center, 2 miles south of Gatlinburg, TN, on Newfound Gap Rd., open year-round.

Entrance Fees
None.

Accommodations
Ten campgrounds, with a total of 997 campsites. Elkmont, Cades Cove, and Smokemont require advance reservations for May 15 to Oct 31. All others on first-come, first-served basis. Length of stay is limited in high season. Advance reservations are required for Le Conte Lodge (423.429.5704), accessible by foot or on horseback only; open mid-Mar to late Nov.

When to Go
Although summer is the most popular time of year, spring and fall are great seasons to visit. Summer can be hot, humid, and crowded. Spring can be wet, but is an ideal time for blooming wildflowers. Fall, when the hardwood forests put on their magnificent foliage display, is often very crowded, but temperatures are much cooler. Park roads close in icy conditions.

Named for the distinctive smokelike haze that envelops them, the Great Smoky Mountains are the stately ceiling of the Appalachian Highlands, encompassing 16 peaks that rise more than 6,000 feet above sea level. The mountains' dense nests of brush and trees, packed with leaves that exude water, oxygen, and hydrocarbons, are responsible for the "smoky" air that is especially visible after rain or in the early morning. Its persistent blue haze only adds to the mystique of the Smokies, a jumble of old mountains whose pioneer history lives on in the churches, barns, and cabins left behind by hardscrabble mountain people.

The Great Smoky Mountains make up a small portion of the Appalachian Mountains, which extend over 2,000 miles from Maine to Georgia (the Appalachian Trail follows the crest of the Great Smokies for 68 miles). The rocks that make up the Smokies are mostly sedimentary, formed by deposits of soil, silt, sand, and gravel. As sediments were deposited, they became layers of hard rock – some more than 50,000 feet thick. For most of the rocks here, this process occurred more than 600 million years ago. The Great Smoky Mountains are rounder and lower in elevation than younger mountain ranges; but even though hundreds of millions of years of wind and rain have diminished their size, their lofty isolation remains.

The park, which straddles North Carolina and Tennessee, is one of the largest protected land areas east of the Rocky Mountains. A United Nations International Biosphere Reserve and World Heritage Site, it has more than 1,600 kinds of flowering plants, the largest stand of old-growth forest in the East, and the highest peaks east of the Rockies. Among the park's special features are its several historic districts. These Appalachian heritage sites, plus the fact that the park is within 550 miles for one-third of the U. S. population, make it the most visited in the National Park System.

The earliest inhabitants of the region are thought to be Paleo-Indians who lived here some 12,000 years ago. Spanish explorer Hernando de Soto led the first European expedition through the area in 1540, encountering Mississippian peoples. In the late 1700s, European immigrants settled the mountains. In 1838, the U. S. government, under a Removal Act signed by President Andrew Jackson, forced 13,000 Cherokee to march to Oklahoma along what has become known as the Trail of Tears. Descendants of a few who disobeyed the order now live on the Cherokee Indian Reservation along the park's southern boundary. In later years, the mountains were home to farmers and timber companies, who, by the 1930s, had logged off all but the most inaccessible areas in what is now the park.

In the park's central section, the transmountain Newfound Gap Road (U. S. 441) links the Sugarlands and Oconaluftee Visitor Centers and is one of the park's two main arteries, climbing from 2,000 feet to 5,048 feet and providing spectacular views of the surrounding peaks. Just past the Oconaluftee Visitor Center, in the southern section of the park, is Mountain Farm Museum, a collection of farm buildings where costumed interpreters re-enact pioneer farm life (summer through late October). At nearby Mingus Mill, a costumed miller demonstrates how pioneers ground grain. In the western section, at Cades Cove, an isolated valley first settled in 1819, the rangers maintain a historical and cultural preserve of log cabins, churches, and other buildings. Cable Mill is an operating water-powered gristmill. The one-way, 11-mile Cades Cove Loop Road passes by the remains of homes, barns, and community buildings erected in the early to mid 19th century by settlers who, under a treaty with the Cherokee, cleared the broad, high valley here.

With 800 miles of trails in the Smokies, ranging from short paths to a 68-mile-long segment of the Appalachian Trail, getting out of the car and walking is a great way to dip into what is referred to as a "little bit of the world as it once was" – and something that surprisingly few visitors opt to do. Among the easiest hikes are several gentle, quarter-mile paths called Quiet Walkways. An eight-mile round-trip hike along the Appalachian Trail between Newfound Gap and Charlies Bunion passes through a spruce forest and provides mountain vistas. The paved, two-and-a-half-mile round-trip Laurel Falls Trail, the most popular waterfall trail in the park, meanders through stands of pine and oak, while the strenuous, eight-mile round-trip Ramsay Cascade Trail leads to the park's highest waterfall. Sugarlands Valley Nature Trail, off Newfound Gap Road, is a 3,000-foot loop paved to accommodate visitors with disabilities. Among the self-guided nature trails are the one-mile Sugarlands route, which introduces visitors to the history of the Smokies, and the five-mile Alum Cave Bluffs Trail, which passes through a "bald" (treeless) swath of mountain laurels and rhododendrons.

Both Cades Cove and Cataloochee Valley are popular routes for bicyclists. Many of the park streams permit fishing for rainbow and brown trout all year (a state fishing license is required). Streams popular with anglers include Abrams Creek below Cades Cove; Big Creek near I-40 at the park's northeastern end; Little River, near Elkmont Campground; and Fontain Lake, along the park's southern boundary. The Smokies have some of the best horseback-riding country in the East. Contact park headquarters for a listing of stables.

NC 138
TN 158
PARK 140

HAWAII VOLCANOES

Southeastern Hawaii Island
Established August 1, 1916
229,177 acres

Headquarters
Hawaii Volcanoes National Park
P.O. Box 52
Hawaii National Park, HI 96718
808.985.6000
www.nps.gov/havo

Visitor Centers
Kilauea Visitor Center, a quarter mile inside the park entrance off Hwy. 11, and the Thomas A. Jaggar Museum, on Crater Rim Dr., 3 miles from park entrance, both open year-round.

Entrance Fees
$10 per vehicle for 7 days; $5 per person on foot or bicycle.

Accommodations
One campground, open year-round, first-come, first-served, 7-day limit. Inside the park, lodging available at the Volcano House (808.967.7321), on the rim of Kilauea, or the Namakani Paio Cabins (808.967.7321).

When to Go
The weather is moderate year-round, so crowds can always be a problem. It rains all year, though Sept and Oct are generally the driest months. While the park's coast is warm and breezy, Kilauea's 4,000-foot summit tends to be rainy and chilly, and it snows occasionally atop 13,677-foot Mauna Loa.

For sheer drama, it's hard for any park in the country to top this one. Here, on an island animated by the spiritual traditions and myths of an ancient culture, lie two of the most active volcanoes on the planet: Kilauea and Mauna Loa, both believed by native Hawaiians to be the homes of the goddess Pele.

The two turbulent mountains are quite different from one another, despite their proximity. Kilauea, at about 4,000 feet high and still growing, abuts the southeastern slope of Mauna Loa, its much older and larger sibling, which rises to 13,677 feet above the Pacific. Measured from its base, 18,000 feet below sea level, Mauna Loa exceeds Mount Everest in height and is the world's most massive volcano. While the park stretches from sea level to Mauna Loa's rugged summit, most visitors come to Kilauea, which offers easier access for viewing the caldera, lava tubes, and regrowth of trees and ferns around recent flows. At the bottom of its southwestern slope, Kilauea meets the sea; periodic eruptions send brilliant molten lava cascading toward the waves, and the two forces connect with awesome displays of steam. Here, at the earth's most continuously active volcano, scientists gain insights on the birth of the Hawaiian Islands while visitors get close-up views of dramatic volcanic landscapes.

A trip to the park often begins at the Kilauea Summit and Crater Rim Drive. Near the Kilauea Visitor Center is the historic Volcano House hotel – step inside the lobby for a staggering picture-window view of the desolate caldera. The 11-mile loop then takes you past rain forest, steam vents, and sheer lava cliffs to scenic turnouts at Thurston Lava Tube and craters such as Kilauea Iki ("little Kilauea"). Continue on to Devastation Trail, a short walk through an *ohia* forest choked by cinder in 1959.

For a closer look at current volcanic activity, take the turnoff to the Chain of Craters Road. Winding 20 miles one way from the summit to the sea, it passes trailheads, craters, and petroglyphs (ancient rock carvings) as it follows the active East Rift Zone of Kilauea. Where the road ends, covered by a 1995 lava flow, you'll know you're standing on some of the freshest land in the world. Wear sturdy shoes and walk out over hardened, cooled flows to watch – if you're lucky and the timing is right – a fireworks display, as active red lava, white-capped waves, and black beach intersect in a crashing, violent climax.

HI 88
PARK 191

HOT SPRINGS

Western Arkansas
Established March 4, 1921
5,549 acres

Headquarters
Hot Springs National Park
P.O. Box 1860
Hot Springs, AR 71902
501.624.3383, ext. 640
www.nps.gov/hosp

Visitor Center
Fordyce Bathhouse Visitor Center (501.624.3383, ext. 640), in the middle of Bathhouse Row, open daily except major holidays.

Entrance Fees
None, but donations are accepted. Concession fees charged for the thermal baths.

Accommodations
Gulpha Gorge campground, open year-round, first-come, first-served. Hot-springs water is piped into the Arlington Hotel (501.623.7771); the Downtowner Hotel (501.624.5521); the Majestic Hotel (501.623.5511); the Hot Springs Park Hilton (501.623.6600); the Leo N. Levi Arthritis Hospital (501.624.1281); and Hot Springs Health Spa (501.321.9664).

When to Go
Spring is mild and begins in Feb, when four-petaled bluets, the first of many wildflowers, begin to bloom. Summers are hot and very humid, and July is the most crowded month. Try going in late fall, when mountains in the area produce spectacular foliage.

Hernando de Soto may get credit for discovering the springs in 1541, but don't tell that to the Native American tribes that had been taking advantage of the curative powers of the hot flowing water long before he came on the scene. The 47 hot springs that flow from the southwestern slope of Hot Springs Mountain at a temperature of 143°F came to the attention of President Andrew Jackson in 1832, which is when he set aside the area as a "special reservation." Some think this makes the park the oldest in the National Park System, predating Yellowstone's establishment by 40 years.

Hot Springs' main attraction has always been its magnificent bathhouses, many of them built in the 1930s and '40s, when a million people per year would come to soak in the mineral-rich waters. Eight historic bathhouses have been preserved along a stretch of Central Avenue dubbed Bathhouse Row, but only one – the Buckstaff – still offers the traditional treatment, including a hot pack, steam cabinet, and needle shower. Even if you don't feel like a soak, stop by the Fordyce Bathhouse, which now serves as the park's visitor center. This restored "temple of health and beauty" contains three floors of fountains, stained-glass windows, authentic furnishings, and elegant statuary.

But the hot springs aren't the park's only attraction. There are approximately 26 miles of day-use hiking trails through beautiful woodlands – all the more remarkable when one considers that the park is basically in the center of a busy city (former home of Bill Clinton, the 42nd president of the United States). From De Soto Rock, near the corner of Central Avenue and Fountain Street, follow the trail to the Hot Water Cascade. The flowing water here began its journey as long as 4,000 years ago, when rainfall seeped through fractures in the earth. The tufa rocks you see here, a result of the water's mineral content, are building up at the rate of about one-eighth inch a year. Nearby, running behind the bathhouses, along a wooded hillside, the Grand Promenade is a landscaped, brick walkway that leads to walking trails, concealed springs, and pleasant views of the downtown skyline.

AR 66
PARK 66

Rain-soaked Historic Entrance to Mammoth Cave

Cliff Palace on Chapin Mesa

Mosses in Sol Duc Valley

Sunset at Kalaloch Creek

MAMMOTH CAVE

South-central Kentucky
Established July 1, 1941
52,830 acres

Headquarters
Mammoth Cave National Park
P.O. Box 7
Mammoth Cave, KY 42259
502.758.2328
www.nps.gov/maca

Visitor Center
At the center of the park is Mammoth Cave Visitor Center (502.758.2328), open daily year-round except Christmas.

Entrance Fees
None; a variety of fees are charged for cave tours; advance reservations recommended.

Accommodations
Three campgrounds, all on a first-come, first-served basis, except Maple Springs Group Campground (502.758.2251), which accommodates horses and requires reservations. All open Mar to Nov, except Houchins Ferry, open year-round. Mammoth Cave Hotel (502.758.2225).

When to Go
The park is least crowded before Memorial Day and after Labor Day, although these times can be cold and wet. Mid-Mar to mid-Apr, when the redbud and dogwood trees are in bloom, is a popular time to visit. Summers tend to be hot, humid, and buggy. The temperature in the cave is a steady 54°F year-round.

The world's largest known cave system, Mammoth has more than 350 mapped miles of underground passages. The ten miles of cave open to the public offer a rare glimpse of a beautiful subterranean world, including stalagmites and stalactites, canyons, and mineral-encrusted chambers.

Above the cave is a rugged country of second-growth forest and wetlands providing sanctuary to almost a thousand plant species. The Green River flows for 27 miles through the park and has played an important part in Mammoth's formation. Beginning more than 200 million years ago, rainwater made acidic by deposits of carbon dioxide in the area's soil drained to the ever-lowering Green River channel. As the water emptied, it passed through an upper layer of sandstone and infiltrated millions of tiny cracks and crevices in underground limestone ridges, which were the remnants of deep beds of shell fragments on the floor of a shallow sea that covered the area until about 280 million years ago. This acidic water slowly dissolved the limestone, creating the caves. At depths of up to 360 feet below the surface, cave streams are still forming passages today.

As the caves spread, numerous aquatic species began to adapt to cave habitats. Of the approximately 130 species that use the cave on a regular basis, 12 are unique troglodytes (eyeless, colorless cave dwellers) found only in Mammoth Cave and its immediate vicinity. Three endangered species – the Kentucky cave shrimp, the Indiana bat, and the gray bat – also make their homes here. Above ground, sharp-eyed visitors may spot the endangered Michigan lily, sundrops, and silky aster that grow here.

Native Americans discovered the cave system approximately 4,000 years ago and mined minerals, including gypsum and selenite, from it over the next 2,000 years. In the early 1800s, settlers rediscovered the cave, and during the War of 1812, slaves mined saltpeter to use in the manufacture of gunpowder. Local entrepreneurs began giving tours in 1816. Now the park offers a variety of interpretive tours of varying lengths and difficulty. Among the more popular are the two-hour, two-mile Historic Tour, focusing on the area's human history; the two-hour, three-quarter-mile Frozen Niagara Tour which explores the pits, domes, and decorative dripstone formations of the Frozen Niagara section of Mammoth Cave; and the very strenuous, six-hour, five-and-a-half-mile Wild Cave Tour (limited to people 16 or over with a hip or chest size of no more than 42 inches).

KY 100
PARK 100

MESA VERDE

Southwestern Colorado
Established June 29, 1906
52,074 acres

Headquarters
Mesa Verde National Park
P.O. Box 8
Mesa Verde, CO 81330
970.529.4465
www.nps.gov/meve

Visitor Centers
Far View Visitor Center (970.529.4543), at northwest end of park, open daily mid-Apr to mid-Oct. Chapin Mesa Museum (970.529.4475), at southern end of park, open daily year-round.

Entrance Fees
$10 per vehicle for 7 days. Tickets for tours of Cliff Palace, Balcony House, and Long House for sale at Far View Visitor Center.

Accommodations
Morefield Campground is open mid-Apr through mid-Oct, first-come, first-served. Lodging available at Far View Lodge (800.449.2288 or 970.529.4421), closed in winter.

When to Go
With wildflowers in bloom, Apr through Sept is best. Many facilities and cliff dwellings are closed in winter, though cross-country skiers have access to parts of Ruins Road, conditions permitting.

Mesa Verde, Spanish for "green table," was the first cultural park set aside by the United States. It's a stirring experience to walk through ancient dwellings and numerous mesa-top villages built by Ancestral Puebloan peoples between A.D. 600 and 1300. Though abandoned villages were first recorded by a U. S. Army lieutenant in 1849, and scientific examinations of the sites occurred in 1874, it wasn't until two local cowboys tracked stray cattle after a December 1888 snowfall that the most magnificent and largest of the ruins – Cliff Palace – was discovered. Though many of the inhabitant's secrets have been learned since, the answer to the biggest mystery, why the Mesa Verde people abandoned their ancestral home, may never be known.

A short trip to Mesa Verde should include a stop at the Chapin Mesa Archeological Museum, located at the Spruce Tree House Trailhead, followed by a drive over the Mesa Top Loop Road. The museum contains excellent dioramas that help bring the Mesa Verde people to life. There's also a good collection of Mesa Verde pottery, decorated in signature black geometric designs against a white background. The 12-mile Mesa Top Loop Road winds through Chapin Mesa's fragrant piñon-juniper woodland. This area contains the largest concentration of sites. Plan to visit Cliff Palace, the largest cliff dwelling in North America, which once housed more than 100 Ancestral Puebloan peoples. Because of ladders and staircases at Cliff Palace, it is not recommended for visitors with disabilities. Other highlights on the loop include the Square Tower House overlook: A short trail leads to a dramatic viewpoint above the park's tallest tower, the four-story remnant of an even larger, multitiered structure. Another good stop is the Sun Temple, a strange, doorless structure that was never inhabited, but may have been a ceremonial center.

Because of the fragile nature of the sites and the emphasis on the cultural aspects of Mesa Verde, hiking is somewhat restricted in the area. But if you're up for it, take the 2.8-mile Petroglyph Point Trail, a self-guided nature walk that leads from the museum around the base of the cliff on the east side of Spruce Tree House and Navajo Canyon. Register at the museum before you go. Before leaving Mesa Verde, be sure to stop at 8,571-foot-high Park Point fire lookout. The highest spot in the park, it affords open views into Arizona, Utah, New Mexico, and Colorado, which all meet at nearby Four Corners.

CO 76
PARK 76

OLYMPIC

Western Washington
Established June 29, 1938
922,000 acres

Headquarters
Olympic National Park
600 East Park Avenue
Port Angeles, WA 98362
360.452.4501
www.nps.gov/olym

Visitor Centers
Olympic National Park Visitor Center (360.452.0330, ext. 230), in Port Angeles, take Race St. off U.S. 101, open and staffed year-round. Hurricane Ridge Visitor Center, 13 miles past visitor center in Port Angeles, and Hoh Rain Forest Visitor Center (360.374.6925), 19 miles east of U.S. 101 on the west side of park, open year-round (road and weather conditions permitting), but may be self-service fall through spring, dependent on staffing.

Entrance Fees
Permits and passes (valid for 7 consecutive days) are sold spring though fall at entrance stations for $10 per vehicle, $5 per person on bicycle or bus. The $10 fee is also collected in the winter at Heart o' the Hills entrance station en route to Hurricane Ridge. Season passes are $20 for a calendar year.

Accommodations
The National Park Service operates 16 campgrounds, for a total of 910 sites, available on a first-come, first-served basis. Some campgrounds are open in the winter. A nightly fee of $8-$12 is charged, depending on the facility; call 360.452.0330 for more information.

Four lodges and resorts also operate inside the park. For information on these and other nearby accommodations outside the park, call the North Olympic Visitors and Convention Bureau (800.942.4042).

When to Go
Olympic National Park is open 24 hours a day, 365 days a year. December and January are the quietest months, but some roads may be subject to winter closure due to snow; for visitors, proper weather gear is a must. Late spring, when colorful subalpine meadows are beginning to bloom and the craggy mountain peaks are still bedecked with snow, is an ideal time for a visit. Summer weekends have heavy traffic (call ahead for road conditions, even in Apr and May).

A dizzying and diverse labyrinth of soaring peaks, moss-covered forests, lush meadows, alpine lakes, and fog-shrouded coastline, Olympic National Park encompasses three ecosystems and almost a million acres as it stretches its wet, green tendrils from glacier to coast. Occupying the central portion of the Olympic Peninsula, as well as a narrow 63-mile strip of land along the Pacific coastline, the park lies near the north-westernmost tip of the lower 48 – a silent, thriving, wondrous place that can be as eerie as it is awesome.

Before the first Europeans set foot here – probably Juan de Fuca, in 1592, though George Vancouver made the first intensive investigation of the waterways 200 years later – Northwest Indians spent thousands of years in what is now the park. Today, just as when native peoples lived here, it remains a place of solitude and discovery. These characteristics are preserved in part due to its immense size, but also because of its isolation – still crowned by alpine glaciers and surrounded on three sides by water. Indeed, this is a place intrinsically tied to the water. Glaciers gouged out Puget Sound and Hood Canal to the east and the Strait of Juan de Fuca to the north, isolating the peninsula from the main-land. The rock of the Olympic Mountains developed under the ocean; marine fossils are embedded in the summits. This string of peaks forming the centerpiece of the park is not comparatively high – the tallest, Mount Olympus, is just under 8,000 feet – but the mountains rise almost from the water's edge and their nearly circular pattern is contoured by 13 rivers. The mountains so effectively trap marine moisture that the western slopes boast the wettest climate in the lower 48 states.

Just as dramatic as the mountains themselves are the ocean beaches, river valleys, and dense forests that make up the rest of the park. More than 60 miles of Pacific Ocean coastline invite exploration: Wild shoreline, thunderous surf, arches and sea stacks, mesmerizing tidal pools, and the calls of gulls, bald eagles, and black oystercatchers. The rain forest, protected in three park valleys, inspires awe – a misty and magical place soaked with more than 140 inches of rainfall each year.

To undertake a visit to this often overwhelming park, plan to spend at least two days. Stroll subalpine meadows at Hurricane Ridge in sight of the peaks and glaciers in the distance; on a clear day you can see as far north as the mountains just north of Vancouver, British Columbia. Watch for black-tailed deer and for Olympic marmots, which whistle when approached (one of several animals unique to the Olympics). Drive on to lovely Lake Crescent, carved by a glacier (although Indian legend says that the angered Mount Storm King created it when he hurled a boulder at two fighting tribes). Boating and fishing for trout are popular here. At Sol Duc (Native American for "sparkling waters") Hot Springs, you can soothe tired muscles in natural mineral waters, where travelers have bathed since a resort was first established here in 1912.

The temperate rain forests in the valleys of the Quinault, Queets, and Hoh Rivers contain some spectacular examples of Sitka spruce as well as Douglas fir, western red cedar, big-leaf maple, red alder, vine maple, and black cottonwood. Make a visit to the Hoh Rain Forest, where trees enrobed in club moss and licorice ferns stretch 300 feet to the sky. Ranger-guided or independent walks lead you deep into the woods, where you can stop to contemplate the 200-foot-high Sitka spruces, estimated to be more than 500 years old. Although Roosevelt elk shy away from humans, keep your eyes peeled. The protection of these beasts, named for Teddy, is one of the main reasons that the park came to be. On the western shores of the park, stop to walk the trails to Ruby or Rialto Beaches for good examples of wild, windswept beaches complete with sea otters, puffins, and harbor seals, plus migrating gray whales in spring and fall.

Most roads end shortly after entering the park land, so access to the majority of Olympic National Park is on foot. With more than 600 miles of trails, hiking in the Olympics can range from short nature walks to rugged backcountry hikes to the ascent of Mount Olympus. Inquire about hiking options as well as climbing, white-water rafting, sea kayaking, fishing, cross-country skiing, and snowshoeing, all of which are possible in the park.

WA 170
PARK 191

PRINCE EDWARD ISLAND

Sandstone cliffs at sunset

CALIFORNIA

Rhododendrons in Lady Bird Johnson Grove

COLORADO

Never Summer Mountains, near the park's western border

VIRGINIA

Wintery Skyline Drive

PRINCE EDWARD ISLAND

Prince Edward Island, Canada
Established 1937
10 square miles

Headquarters
Parks Canada
2 Palmer's Lane
Charlottetown, PE
Canada C1A 5V6
902.672.6350
parkscanada.pch.gc.ca/parks/pei/pei_np/pei_npe.htm

Visitor Centers
Cavendish Visitor Centre (902.963.2391), junction Hwys. 6 and 13, and Brackley Visitor Centre (902.672.7474), junction Hwys. 6 and 15, both open May to mid-Oct. Dalvay Administration Office (902.672.6350), along Gulf Shore Pkwy. off Hwy. 6, open year-round.

Entrance Fees
Adults, C$3; children, C$1.50; senior citizens, C$2; or family, C$6.50 (whichever is cheaper).

Accommodations
Campgrounds: Cavendish, open early June to Sept, first-come, first-served; Stanhope and Rustico Island, open June to Labor Day, reservations recommended. Dalvay-by-the-Sea Hotel (902.672.2048).

When to Go
Summer is, of course, the best time for the beach but also the most crowded season. In early autumn, migrating birds stop at the beaches. Winter offers cross-country skiing and snowshoeing.

Located in Canada's smallest province, and separated from the mainland by the Northumberland Strait, this park – compact, tidy, and green, like Prince Edward Island itself – boasts some of the most beautiful beaches in the Maritimes. Before the 7.9-mile Confederation Bridge from Cape Tormentine, New Brunswick, opened in 1997, the island (and park) were only accessible by ferry. Some lament the loss of its splendid isolation and fear that the island paradise of carefully tended potato, vegetable, and dairy farms; pristine beaches; and red rock shores will be ruined by a rolling wave of rubber tires.

Prince Edward Island National Park comprises a 25-mile sliver of coast along the island province's north shore, overlooking the Gulf of St. Lawrence. Its trademark sand dunes, covered by marram grass, rise to 59 feet high. In addition to protecting an ecosystem of dunes, freshwater ponds, saltwater marshes, and woodlands, the park also features several cultural landmarks including Green Gables, the house and farm that inspired Lucy Maud Montgomery's famous novels about Anne of Green Gables; and the Victorian Dalvay-by-the-Sea, completed in 1896 by an American industrialist as a private seaside retreat and now a restaurant and hotel.

Archaeologists date the earliest habitation here to A.D. 1400. At one time it was home to the Mi'kmaq, who named the crescent-shaped island Abegweit, "land cradled on the waves." The first European settlers, Acadians, who were farmers and fishermen, arrived in 1720. The island, fought over by France, the American colonies, and Britain between 1745 and 1758, finally fell to the British, who deported 3,500 Acadians back to France. Today's Acadians on Prince Edward Island are ancestors of those who either escaped the deportation or who later returned. By the late 1800s, the island had become a popular tourist destination, famed for its pristine beaches and bucolic little villages.

Most of the trees that originally covered the island were cut and cleared for farming, settlement, and industry by the early 1900s. The majority of trees now growing (pines for windbreaks, hardwoods for shade) have been planted or transplanted since 1941. With its woods, dunes, streambeds, and tide pools, the park provides a home for red fox, raccoons, snowshoe hare, mink, and muskrat. More than 200 species of birds, including the long-legged great blue heron and the endangered piping plover, live in the park's woodland and along the shore and can be spotted at places like Brackley Marsh and alongside the sand dunes.

PE 186
PARK 191

REDWOOD

Northwestern California
Established October 2, 1968
105,516 acres (including three state parks)

Headquarters
Redwood National Park
1111 Second Street
Crescent City, CA 95531
707.464.6101
www.nps.gov/redw

Visitor Centers
Crescent City Information Center (707.464.6101, ext. 5064), at northern end of park, and Redwood Information Center (707.464.6101, ext. 5265), at southern end of park, open year-round except major holidays.

Entrance Fees
None for national park. $5 day-use fee in developed areas at state parks inside border.

Accommodations
Four state-run campgrounds are inside the park. All open year-round, except Mill Creek, open Apr to Oct. Reservations required, except for Gold Bluffs Beach, first-come, first-served.

When to Go
Redwood draws big crowds June through Sept, so the best bet is to visit in fall, when the deciduous trees change color. In winter, the park is cool and often drenched with rain. Rhododendrons flourish during the spring, and migrating birds bring the big trees to life in both spring and fall.

It's hard to imagine that anyone ever said a tree is a tree – especially once you have visited the glorious old-growth groves of Redwood National Park. Called "ambassadors from another time" by John Steinbeck, redwoods are almost immortal. Their 6- to 8-inch thick bark repels fire and insects; they cannot be killed by disease, and when one falls, new sprouts regenerate from its stump and trunk. In the park, acres of the earth's tallest living things cluster around you, bearing silent witness to thousands of years of both human and natural history. The hundreds of groves stretching along the northernmost reaches of the California coast are remnants of a magnificent primeval forest that once covered two million acres. Today, only a fraction of that remains. In 1978, Congress expanded the park by an additional 48,000 acres, but most of the new land had already been logged, leaving one park official to describe it as having the "look of an active war zone." Since then, many acres have been replanted and logging roads eliminated, but it will take at least another two or three centuries for the slow-growing seedlings to reach even modest size.

The aptly named Tall Trees Grove is accessible by car, via a 16-mile drive that takes about 30 minutes (30 free permits are given out per day for car access to the grove). You'll want to walk down the trailhead to Redwood Creek for some close-up time with these giants. The star is the National Geographic Society Tree, which soars up more than 365 feet from the forest floor. The world's tallest tree, it's estimated to be between 600 and 800 years old.

More than 160 miles of hiking trails in the park include several shorter, looped nature trails with exhibits, all near roadside pullovers. One of the best is a mile-long walk through the Lady Bird Johnson Grove, leading to the 1968 National Park dedication site. Kids enjoy the cool, moist air around the trees and are fascinated by the hollowed-out redwoods that continue to live and grow. These living caves once sheltered the fowl and livestock of early settlers. For a more active look at the area, take one of the kayak tours of the Klamath River estuary. The half-day expeditions usually encounter otters, seals, sea lions, whales, and even beavers. Canoeing, freshwater and ocean fishing, and horseback riding are also available in the summer.

CA 68
PARK 191

ROCKY MOUNTAIN

Northern Colorado
Established January 26, 1915
265,727 acres

Headquarters
Rocky Mountain National Park
Estes Park, CO 80517
970.586.1206
www.nps.gov/romo

Visitor Centers
Headquarters Visitor Center, U. S. 36 at east entrance, and Kawuneeche Visitor Center, U. S. 34 north of Grand Lake, open year-round. Alpine Visitor Center, on U. S. 34, and Moraine Park Museum and Visitor Center, on Bear Lake Rd., south of Beaver Meadows entrance, open May to mid-Oct. Lily Lake Visitor Center, 7 miles south of Estes Park on Hwy. 7, open June to Aug.

Entrance Fees
$10 per private vehicle; $5 per person on foot or bicycle.

Accommodations
Five campgrounds: Longs Peak, Aspenglen, and Timber Creek are first-come, first-served; Moraine Park and Glacier Basin, reservations required. Longs Peak, Moraine Park, and Timber Creek, open year-round; others, June to Sept.

When to Go
Half of the roughly 3 million annual visitors come mid-June to mid-Aug. Sept may be the best time to visit; elk move to lower elevations, where visitors can hear their mating bugles.

Congress had two goals in mind when it established Rocky Mountain National Park in 1915. First, to protect the rugged environment and dwindling stocks of wildlife, and second, to promote the recreational opportunities of a land so high that the tallest summits are perpetually capped in snow and even the valleys are 8,000 feet above sea level. For hundreds of years the land's high altitude and extreme weather made it off limits to all but the boldest of travelers. With the construction of mountain roads and a grand hotel near Estes Park around the turn of the century, unrestricted development seemed inevitable – until the fiery pioneer naturalist Enos Mills enlisted the aid of John Muir to lobby for the creation of a new park.

Straddling the Continental Divide, the park contains the source of the Colorado River, which flows south and west into the Gulf of California, and the headwaters of the Cache la Poudre and Big Thompson Rivers sit in the alpine peaks on the east side. Within the park's 415 square miles are 78 peaks higher than 12,000 feet; 20 of them over 13,000 feet. The tallest, Longs Peak, rises 14,255 feet, and acted as a guidepost to pioneers. With 147 lakes to enjoy, and more than 350 miles of trail, the park is an outdoor-lover's dream, particularly for those willing to take on the backcountry, where you're likely to encounter more mule deer than humans.

Even if you never leave your car and stick only to the Trail Ridge Road, it would be worth the visit. Trail Ridge Road follows an ancient path where Native Americans once hunted elk, deer, and beaver. This road ascends to an elevation of 12,183 feet, making it the highest continuous paved road in the U. S. For 11 miles you travel above timberline, winding through the alpine tundra of delicate grasses and wildflowers. A short, five-minute nature trail, Tundra World, begins at the Forest Canyon overlook, where you can peer into a glacier-carved valley 2,500 feet below.

The park offers trails suited to every hiking ability, but because of the high elevations, be alert to altitude sickness and don't attempt any strenuous hikes before acclimating yourself for at least a day. Families might consider the easy Sprague Lake hike, located off Bear Lake Road. It's a half-mile nature walk with spectacular views of Continental Divide peaks. There's also excellent rock climbing in the park. One of the most popular areas is Lumpy Ridge, a subalpine outcrop of sheer rock faces two miles north of Estes Park.

CO 76
PARK 75

SHENANDOAH

Northern Virginia
Established December 26, 1935
196,000 acres

Headquarters
Shenandoah National Park
3655 U. S. Highway 211E
Luray, VA 22835
540.999.3500
www.nps.gov/shen

Visitor Centers
Dickey Ridge Visitor Center (540.635.3566), 4 miles south of the Front Royal Entrance Station, and Harry F. Byrd, Sr., Visitor Center (540.999.3283), mile 51 on Skyline Drive, open Apr to Nov. Mileposts, numbered from north to south on Skyline Drive, help visitors locate park facilities, services, and areas of interest.

Entrance Fees
$10 per vehicle for 7 days; $5 per person on foot, bicycle, or motorcycle, for 7 days.

Accommodations
Four developed campgrounds, open from between early Apr and late May to Oct., all first-come, first-served except Big Meadows; reservations suggested. Two lodges and one cabin complex inside park; reservations essential. Contact ARAMARK Virginia Skyline Company (800.999.4714).

When to Go
Portions of Skyline Drive may be closed temporarily in winter. Fall foliage offers the most spectacular scenery.

Shenandoah National Park sits in the northern part of Virginia's Blue Ridge Mountains, a flank of the Appalachian Mountains that was inhabited by farmers for more than a century. Skyline Drive, a two-lane road that rides the crest of the Blue Ridge Mountains for 105 miles through the length of the park, offers views of the Shenandoah River and Massanutten Mountain to the west, and the rolling Virginia Piedmont country to the east. The Appalachian Trail, a 2,100-mile-long footpath that stretches from Maine to Georgia, roughly parallels about 95 miles of Skyline Drive. For hikers on the trail, or motorists wending their way along the drive, Shenandoah offers the sense of traveling high above the world in a separate and serene environment – especially during the dazzling mountain laurel and azalea displays of late spring and early summer.

Human habitation can be traced back approximately 11,000 years. The first European settlers arrived soon after Governor Alexander Spotswood of Virginia led an expedition of 63 men across the Blue Ridge in 1716. By 1800, the lowlands had been settled by farmers who spread into the mountains as valley farmland became scarce. By the 20th century, those who had cleared the land began to leave as both game animals and the soil thinned. In dedicating the park in 1936, President Franklin D. Roosevelt committed the federal government to something new in land management – returning to forest a huge tract of acreage that had been used for farming, grazing, and timbering.

The experiment was successful: Today, there are some 1,100 native plant species in Shenandoah. More than 270 species grow at Big Meadows alone, the largest treeless area in the park, an excellent place to spot wildlife, pick blueberries and huckleberries, and see flowers and plants such as deerberry bushes and red osier dogwood. Rocks that exhibit columnar jointing, a phenomenon created by the rapid cooling of molten lava, can be seen at numerous points, including Compton Peak (mile 10.4) and Franklin Cliffs (mile 49). There are a number of spectacular waterfalls: 93-foot Overall Run (mile 22.2) is the park's highest. There are over 500 miles of trails in the park. From mile 52.5, hike the two-mile Mill Prong Trail to Camp Hoover, named for and used by the former president as a retreat until he donated it to the park. A popular spot for rock climbing is Old Rag Mountain.

VA 168
PARK 191

Trunk Bay and, in the distance, the British Virgin Islands

Crane Lake in October

Mountain goat near Logan Pass

Towers of the Virgin, near the South Entrance

VIRGIN ISLANDS

St. John, U. S. Virgin Islands
Established August 2, 1956
12,909 acres

Headquarters
Virgin Islands National Park
6310 Estate Nazareth
Charlotte Amalie,
St. Thomas, USVI 00802
340.775.6238
www.nps.gov/viis

Visitor Center
Cruz Bay Visitor Center (340.776.6201), a 5-minute walk from the public ferry dock, open daily year-round.

Entrance Fees
None.

Accommodations
Cinnamon Bay Campground has bare tent sites, tent-covered platforms, and cottages. The facility fills up quickly in winter months. For reservations, contact Cinnamon Bay Campground, P.O. Box 720, St. John, VI 00831, (340.776.6330).

When to Go
St. John – and all of the U. S. Virgin Islands – are among the Caribbean's dry islands, which means little rain and warm, sunny days. The average winter temperature ranges from the low 70s to the mid-80s; summer, ranges from the upper 70s to the mid-90s. Even the rainy months, Sept through Jan, are not very wet.

St. John, one of the U. S. Virgin Islands, which include St. Thomas and St. Croix, is an off-the-beaten-path volcanic island whose formation dates back 100 million years to the late Cretaceous period. St. John is part of a submarine mountain range that includes the larger islands of the Greater Antilles and the remainder of the Virgin Islands, as well as many of the smaller volcanic islands of the Lesser Antilles.

Indians migrating northward in canoes from South America lived on St. John as early as 710 B.C. In 1717, the Danes took formal possession of St. John in order to cultivate sugarcane, establishing the island's first permanent European settlement. By 1733, much of the island was taken up by cane and cotton plantations. That same year, West African slaves rose in one of the Caribbean's bloodiest revolts. The emancipation of slaves in 1848 and a weakening of worldwide demand for sugar brought on the decline of the plantations. Now, the vegetation has reclaimed the hills where cane once grew. The United States purchased this portion of the Virgin Islands from Denmark in 1917 (part of the chain is still a British possession). Little changed – today, natives still recall a time when mules were the main mode of transportation – until resort developer and conservationist Laurence Rockefeller arrived in the 1950s and bought up great swaths of land, then donated most of it to the United States government for the formation of a park. More than half of St. John is currently National Park land, including the low-key but luxurious Caneel Bay Plantation resort, which Rockefeller built.

Today's St. John is a glorious mix of tropical dry and moist second-growth forests and pristine beaches. With stunning hideaways like Hawksnest and Trunk Bays, St. John is widely said to have the best beaches in the Caribbean. Though the island is dry and desertlike in places, it has abundant plant life, including the teyer palm (St. John's only native palm tree), the bay rum tree, and brilliantly colored wild orchids. The island's largest blossom, the vanilla-scented night-blooming cereus, is pollinated by bats. For most travelers, the park's greatest wildlife attraction is its stunning array of tropical reef fish. More than a third of the park's acreage lies underwater, with coral reefs, mangrove shorelines, and sea-grass beds providing food and shelter for everything from eagle rays to parrot fish and queen conchs. These reefs also provide some of the best diving and snorkeling in the Caribbean. The 225-yard, self-guided underwater trail at Trunk Bay is a dream for novices.

VI 190
PARK 190

VOYAGEURS

Northern Minnesota
Established April 8, 1975
218,054 acres

Headquarters
Voyageurs National Park
3131 Highway 53
International Falls, MN 56649
218.283.9821
www.nps.gov/voya

Visitor Centers
Rainy Lake Visitor Center (218.286.5258), east of International Falls off Hwy. 11, open year-round. Kabetogama Lake Visitor Center (218.875.2111), off U. S. Rte. 53 on County Rd. 123/Gappa Rd., open May to Sept. Ash River Visitor Center (218.374.3221), off Ash River Trail, open daily Memorial Day to Labor Day.

Entrance Fees
None; Minnesota boat license and fishing license required.

Accommodations
Kettle Falls Hotel (888.534.6835) is accessible by boat only. The park has 180 primitive campsites suitable for tent camping and houseboating, most accessible only by boat. No fee, first-come, first-served. Houseboats can be rented; resorts border the park.

When to Go
The waterways begin to open in late April. Migratory birds return to the park in summer, and fall is an ideal time to enjoy the foliage. The fishing is best late May to June and Sept to Oct; boating is best midsummer and early fall.

One of the country's least visited national parks is this 55-mile-long swath of boreal forest, glacier-carved lakes, and pine-covered islands that straddles the Minnesota–Ontario border. Named for the 18th- and early-19th-century French-Canadian fur traders who canoed and trapped in the region, it is the only part of the National Park System wholly within the Arctic watershed of Hudson Bay. The labyrinth of waterways and marshes consists primarily of four large lakes and the park's centerpiece, Kabetogama Peninsula, a rugged and roadless area of small lakes, ponds, bogs, and meadows.

The area has a rich and varied history. First inhabited by Native Americans who lived off the land, the area was crisscrossed in the late 18th and early 19th centuries by voyageurs in birch-bark canoes who worked primarily for fur trade companies. They were followed by miners, after gold was discovered on Little American Island in Rainy Lake in 1893. By 1910, the miners had deserted the generally unsuccessful mines, and loggers moved in to cut millions of white and red pine, spruce, and fir. By 1920, virtually all of the virgin timber had been cut and the loggers, too, moved on. Commercial fishing for sturgeon, walleye, northern pike, and whitefish, which began around the time of the gold rush, reached its peak in the 1930s. Now, this watery retreat has been left to anglers, campers, and boaters attracted by its splendid isolation.

The park is in the heart of the only region in the continental United States where the eastern timber wolf survives. Among national parks, it is the best bet in the lower 48 for seeing bald eagles, who nest along the shores. Since water covers one-third of the park's surface, aquatic animals such as beaver and otter thrive, as do water birds such as cormorants, kingfishers, great blue herons, and loons.

Boating is one of the major activities in the park. Two concessionaires offer tours, and houseboats can be rented. (Contact park headquarters for a list.) The National Park Service provides free use of boats and canoes on the following lakes: Locator, Quill, Ek, Cruiser, Shoepack and Little Shoepack, Brown, and Peary. Watercraft are available on a first-come, first-served basis; reservations can be made one week in advance at a park visitor center. An angler's dream, the waters are world-renowned for walleye, northern pike, and smallmouth bass – ice fishing is also popular. Cross-country skiing, snowshoeing, and winter camping are popular from late December to late March. Snowmobile trails on the frozen lake surfaces are part of a regional network of trails.

MN 116
PARK 191

WATERTON–GLACIER

Southwestern Alberta, Canada; northwestern Montana
Established June 18, 1932
Glacier, 1,013,572 acres
Waterton Lakes, 73,800 acres

Headquarters
Glacier National Park
West Glacier, MT 59936
406.888.7800
www.nps.gov/glac

Waterton Lakes National Park
Waterton Park, Alberta
Canada T0K 2M0
403.859.2224
www.worldweb.com/parkscanada-waterton

Visitor Centers
Waterton Information Centre (403.859.5133); Apgar Visitor Center (406.888.7939), inside West Entrance; Logan Pass Visitor Center; and St. Mary Visitor Center, all open May to Sept.

Entrance fees
Waterton, C$8 per vehicle until 4 p.m. the next day; Glacier, $10 per vehicle for 7 days.

Accommodations
In Waterton, 3 campgrounds, 14-day limits, open May to Sept. In Glacier, 13 campgrounds, 14- and 7-day limits, open late spring to mid-fall. Apgar and St. Mary open all year.

When to Go
While winter draws intrepid cross-country skiers from Dec to June, Waterton–Glacier is best in summer. Trails at lower elevations are often clear of snow by June.

Though Waterton–Glacier International Peace Park still holds 48 small glaciers, it owes its name to vast flows of ice that carved, millennia ago, what naturalist John Muir called "the best care-killing scenery on the continent." He was likely not the first to think so. Drawn by the sheltered valleys and bountiful resources, people have used these mountains for more than 8,000 years. Primitive native tribes tracked buffalo across the plains and fished the lakes; and the Blackfeet Indians controlled the land well into the 19th century. Known for the sheer walls and horned summits of its tightly packed peaks, Glacier is also home to more than 600 stunning lakes and thousands of miles of rivers and streams. At the bottom of stark cliffs sit forested valley floors and tranquil meadows. Of its six large lakes, Lake McDonald is the biggest, stretching ten miles from the park's edge into its core. During summer, runoff from glaciers like Grinnell – the largest, at 150 acres – cascade off the mountains, plunging into the deep, ice-cold lakes. With such awesome spectacles, it's little wonder the Blackfeet called the area sacred.

Rich in plant life and wildlife, thanks to its varied habitats, Glacier is one of few parks where you can still find grizzly bears and gray wolves. Other fauna includes eagles, elk, mountain lions, mink, and mountain goats known for precarious snacking on cliff sides. Mackinaw trout and northern pike may be fished at Two Medicine Lake in Two Medicine Valley, in the park's southeastern section. In addition to Glacier's bounty of hiking trails, visitors can enjoy the popular all-day horseback trips that depart from Many Glacier Valley. For river lovers, raft floats of anywhere from a half-day to six-days' time explore the north and middle forks of the Flathead River. Glacier also offers what many consider the best scenic drive in America. The aptly named Going-to-the-Sun Road, open mid-June to mid-October, traverses the Continental Divide on 52 miles of unforgettable highway, complete with snowmelt spilling over sheer cliffs, hairpin turns, and 17 scenic overlooks. Skirting St. Mary Lake, on the park's east side, the road twists up to 6,646-foot Logan Pass, where a popular trailhead leads along a part-boardwalk trail. Views include Triple Divide Peak, where mountain waters divide and head to either the Arctic, the Atlantic, or the Pacific Ocean. The road descends to Lake McDonald, where visitors can swim and take boat tours from a historic mountain lodge. Other park highlights include Red Eagle Lake, with its beautiful falls and gorge, and a scenic drive on Chief Mountain International Highway.

MT 122
AB 179
PARK 122

ZION

Southwestern Utah
Established November 19, 1919
146,559 acres

Headquarters
Zion National Park
Springdale, UT 84767
435.772.3256
www.nps.gov/zion

Visitor Centers
Zion Canyon Visitor Center (435.772.3256), near the southern entrance on Utah Rte. 9, and Kolob Canyons Visitor Center (435.586.9548), in the northwest corner of the park via Exit 40 off I-15, both open year-round except major holidays.

Entrance Fees
$10 per vehicle for 7 days; $5 per person on foot, bicycle, or motorcycle.

Accommodations
Three campgrounds, all first-come, first-served; 14-day limits from Apr 15 to Oct 15, 30-day limits off-season. Watchman open all year; South open May to Sept; Lava Point open May to Oct, depending on weather. Accommodations available at Zion Lodge (435.772.3213), off Utah Rte. 9.

When to Go
The park is busiest Apr to Oct. Mild spring and fall temperatures make hiking more pleasant, and rain showers moderate the summer heat, rolling in spectacularly and creating new waterfalls on the sheer cliffs. Snow closes higher hiking trails in winter.

Mormon pioneers who first saw the sculptured rocks and multicolored walls rising above the Virgin River in Utah's high-plateau country named the area Zion, after the heavenly city of God. Thereafter, a Methodist pastor, the Reverend Frederick Fisher, on an expedition to the canyon in 1916 also gave religious names to the more spectacular natural wonders, like the towering 2,400-foot monolith called Great White Throne or the Three Patriarchs (Abraham, Isaac, and Jacob), sheer faces carved by wind and water from Navajo sandstone. Zion is, indeed, a bit of heaven on earth, a park with such magnificent scenery that it has been variously referred to as Yosemite in color and as a vertical little Grand Canyon.

The highlight of the park is Zion Canyon, a half-mile deep slash formed by the Virgin River cutting through the sandstone. Some say the main drive to view the area is among the most spectacular in the country, a bit like driving through the bottom of the Grand Canyon. The Zion Canyon Scenic Drive is a narrow paved road with colorful vistas of looming cliffs, domes, and mountains, ending at the Temple of Sinawava, named for the Paiute wolf god or good spirit. Another fork road into the park, a stretch of Utah Highway 9 called Zion–Mount Carmel Highway, passes through mile-long Zion Tunnel, 800 feet above the canyon floor, where windowlike galleries gouged in the rock let you look out on scenic wonders like East Temple and the 400-foot-high Great Arch. In summer both of these roads can be clogged with traffic; consider taking the open-air tram tours which run up and down the canyon several times a day in summer, offering narrated tours, photo stops, and many of the best sights.

The best way to experience the park, though, is by going on a hike. Zion has an extensive trail system and a wide range of choices. Weeping Rock Trail is one of three easy, self-guided nature trails. The quarter-mile-long hike climbs a hundred feet to a lovely area of hanging gardens. Another popular trail is the Riverside Walk, an easy two-mile round-trip ramble that begins at the end of the Zion Canyon Scenic Drive and takes you past golden columbine and stands of shady cottonwood and ash. More difficult is the Angels Landing Trail, a five-mile round-trip workout with steep drop-offs, a 1,500-foot elevation gain, and one of the best overall views of the park.

There are almost 250 species of birds in the park, making it a favorite location for bird-watching. Zion is known for southern birds at the northern limit of their range, including gray vireos and the black hawk.

UT 165
PARK 165

Lupine flowers carpet Buffalo Flats, a high alpine meadow

Travertine terraces of Mammoth Hot Springs

Upper Pines in winter, near the east end of Yosemite Valley

A view from Glacier Point of Half Dome and Nevada Fall

YELLOWSTONE

Northwestern Wyoming, with portions extending into southwestern Montana and eastern Idaho
Established March 1, 1872
2,221,766 acres

Headquarters
Yellowstone National Park
P.O. Box 168
Yellowstone National Park, WY 82190
307.344.7381
www.nps.gov/yell

Visitor Centers
Albright Visitor Center (307.344.2263), in Mammoth Hot Springs, open year-round. Old Faithful Visitor Center (307.545.2750), open mid-Apr to late Oct and mid-Dec to mid-Mar. Canyon Visitor Center (307.242.2550), Fishing Bridge Visitor Center (307.242.2450), and Grant Village Visitor Center (307.242.2650), all open mid-May through Sept. West Thumb Information Station, open early June to Sept.

Entrance Fees
$20 per vehicle for 7 days (also good for Grand Teton); $15 per snowmobile or motorcycle; $10 per person on foot, bicycle, or skis; $40 for annual pass.

Accommodations
Seven campgrounds are operated by the National Park Service on a first-come, first-served basis: Mammoth, Norris, Indian Creek, Lewis Lake, Pebble Creek, Slough Creek, and Tower Fall. Five campgrounds are operated by a concessionaire and accept reservations: Bridge Bay, Canyon, Grant Village, Madison, and Fishing Bridge RV Park. Lodging accommodations range from rustic cabins to luxury suites. For camping and lodging reservations, call Amfac Parks and Resorts, Inc. (307.344.7311).

When to Go
Yellowstone has truly become a year-round park, though most visitors continue to come in the summer months. In winter, except for the route from the North Entrance at Gardiner, Montana, to the Northeast Entrance at Cooke City, Montana, all roads are passable only by over-snow vehicles, making visits limited for all but snowmobilers.

Yellowstone is a land of superlatives: The nation's first national park has the world's greatest concentration of geysers, mud pots, fumaroles, and hot springs; the largest number of free-roaming wildlife in the lower 48, including bison, grizzly bears, and recently reintroduced gray wolves; more land than Rhode Island and Delaware combined; and one of North America's largest mountain bodies of water, Yellowstone Lake. In 1872, President Ulysses S. Grant convinced Congress to set aside 3,472 square miles of land for a national park, largely because of the area's strange and beautiful hydrothermal wonders. Back then, wildlife was considered merely a commodity for food or income, and the wilderness – mountain ranges, glorious canyons, expansive forests, large lakes – was viewed as an obstacle to travel and settlement. There was no gold or other precious metals in the area (or so people thought; now, a controversial gold mine development less than three miles from the northeast corner of the park is attracting great attention), and the climate was too severe for any serious ranching or farming ventures. In short, Yellowstone (which got its name from the 671-mile-long river that begins just south of the park and flows into the Missouri River) was considered worthless – except for these strange geysers and hot springs. An early visitor, fur trapper Joe Meek, described the whole area as "country that was smoking with vapor from boiling springs and burning with gasses issuing from small craters, each of which was emitting a sharp, whistling sound."

Fur trappers weren't the only early visitors to Yellowstone. Archaeological evidence suggests the park has been home to Native Americans at least since the end of the last ice age, 8,500 years ago. The Blackfeet, Crow, Shoshone, and other tribes all visited the area, particularly in summer, though the only permanent residents were the Tukudikas. In 1869, 1870, and 1871, expeditions were sent to explore Yellowstone. Their members were instrumental in convincing Congress of the need to establish Yellowstone as a national park, a radical concept when the idea of "parks" for the public was unheard of. More than 125 years later, Yellowstone is host to more than three million visitors each year (more than saw the park in the first 60 years of its existence). Its vast forests and varied wildlife are no longer thought worthless but are considered natural treasures.

The park's major scenic attractions are located along the Grand Loop Road, the roughly figure-eight-shaped road in the center of the park. The total mileage around the loop is 142 miles. Many of the most famous geysers and hot springs are located on the west side of the loop, including Old Faithful, whose eruption intervals range from 30 to 120 minutes (recent earthquake activity has lengthened the current average interval to 79.1 minutes) and Fountain Paint Pot, whose hot springs vary in color depending on the presence of bacteria and algae, as well as the composition of the surrounding rock. More recent geyser gazing has focused on the Upper Geyser Basin north of Old Faithful, where Giant Geyser has shown signs of rejuvenation after about 40 years of near dormancy.

On the east side of Grand Loop Road, from Canyon Village north to Tower Junction, is the Grand Canyon of the Yellowstone, whose golden-hued cliffs were created by thermal water acting on volcanic rock. Here, the Yellowstone River plunges 1,200 feet. A three-mile hike up Mount Washburn, whose slopes are carpeted with wildflowers in June and July, takes you to a summit where, on a clear day, you can view Yellowstone Lake and the Tetons to the south and the Beartooth Range to the east. Yellowstone's Roosevelt Country, at the northeast top of the loop, is known for its rolling hills covered with sagebrush, fir, pine, and aspen, and its sparkling streams teeming with trout. The southern end of the loop includes Lake Country. Formed by the forces of volcanoes and glaciers, Yellowstone Lake is a prime habitat for a variety of birds and mammals, as well as being spectacular scenery.

There are some 97 trailheads in Yellowstone, giving hikers and backpackers access to about 1,200 miles of trails, with some of the most appealing in the Mammoth area. The five-mile Beaver Ponds Loop Trail takes you through an area of considerable wildlife, where mule deer, moose, the occasional bear, and, of course, beaver, might be spied. It is impossible to predict the best locations for viewing wildlife, but the Hayden Valley is a popular gathering spot for moose, bison, and coyotes, while mule deer often congregate in the Geyser, Lake, and Canyon areas. Herds of elk often wander through meadows in Mammoth Hot Springs, particularly in the early morning and evening. Bighorn sheep sometimes congregate in the Mount Washburn area. Native cutthroat trout abound in Yellowstone Lake, as well as in Sylvan, Trout, Shrimp, and Buck Lakes. One- and two-hour horseback rides are available at Mammoth, Tower-Roosevelt, and Canyon stables. In winter, Yellowstone is open for snowmobiling and cross-country skiing.

WY 176
MT 122
ID 89
PARK 176

YOSEMITE

East-central California
Established October 1, 1890
747,956 acres

Headquarters
Yosemite National Park
P.O. Box 577
Yosemite, CA 95389
209.372.0200
www.nps.gov/yose

Visitor Centers
Yosemite Valley Visitor Center (209.372.0299), Yosemite Valley, open year-round. Wawona Information Station (209.375.9501), open May to Sept. Big Oak Flat Information Station (209.379.1899), near park entrance at Hwy. 120, open June to Aug. Tuolumne Meadows Visitor Center (209.372.0263), on Tioga Rd., open in summer with opening of Tioga Pass.

Entrance Fees
$20 per vehicle for 7 days; $10 per person on foot, bicycle, motorcycle, or bus; $40 for annual pass.

Accommodations
Five campgrounds in Yosemite Valley: Must reserve for Upper Pines, North Pines, and Lower Pines. Sunnyside, first-come, first-served; Backpacker's Camp available with a wilderness permit for 1 night's stay before or after hiking trip. At Tuolumne Meadows, half the sites are first-come, first-served; half are by reservation. Crane Flat has some first-come, first-served campsites, but most are by reservation. Wawona and Hodgdon Meadow campgrounds by reservation, open year-round. Bridalveil Creek campground, first-come, first-served; open June to Sept. Tamarack Flat, first-come, first-served; open July to Sept. The Ahwahnee Hotel and Yosemite Lodge are open year-round; four other lodging options in the park are open seasonally. Lodging information and reservations, 209.252.4848.

When to Go
Summer draws the heavy traffic to Yosemite, but late spring, when its famous waterfalls are at their peak, or autumn, when oaks turn golden and herds of wild deer migrate through the valley, are the best times for a visit. Avoid holiday weekends and expect filled campgrounds June to Aug.

Yosemite is often labeled the most beautiful of the national parks. And, though some may beg to differ, what cannot be questioned is our love for this spectacular park, which receives more than four million adoring fans to its portals every year. They come for its glacially polished granite cliffs, alpine meadows, groves of giant sequoias, but most of all they come to stand and gape at its stunning waterfalls, like Yosemite Falls, which, at 2,425 feet, is the highest waterfall in North America and the fifth highest in the world (taller than the Sears and Eiffel Towers combined). Other park waterfalls, cascading over granite faces, include Bridalveil, Vernal, Silver Strand, Nevada, Staircase, Ribbon, and Sentinel.

John Muir, hailed as the father of the national park system, was so enamored with Yosemite that this peripatetic traveler said he was "willing to stay forever in [Yosemite] like a tree." The Ahwahneechee, who named the land *Ahwahnee*, meaning wide-gaping mouth or deep, grassy valley, were one group of early residents, fishing the streams, gathering Black Oak acorns, and hunting the plentiful game in summer. It remained largely unvisited by interlopers until 1851, when the U. S. Cavalry's Mariposa Battalion tracked renegade Indians into the valley. According to one story, Yosemite is a mispronunciation of the native Miwok word *yohemite*, meaning "there are killers among us" – presumably said in reference to the Indians hiding from the cavalry. Alternately, it is the white settlers' mispronunciation of *uzumati*, which means grizzly bear, the park's most dominant denizen.

In 1864, President Lincoln made Yosemite a protected reserve; in 1890 it became a national park. Ever since, it has drawn throngs of visitors, anxious to see for themselves one of the great natural wonders of the world. But beauty and popularity come at a cost: Some say Yosemite is being loved to death, particularly in summer, when the valley floor, which comprises only eight square miles of the park's 1,169-square-mile area, draws over 70 percent of the visitors. On busy weekends, one-way traffic between major attractions resembles the rush-hour scene in Los Angeles, and the smog can be even worse. Plans are slowly being implemented to "de-develop" Yosemite, a goal that was ironically helped along by massive floods in 1997, which washed out several valley campgrounds and other lodging facilities that won't be replaced.

There are two simple tricks to getting the most out of a trip to Yosemite: Plan a visit in early spring or late fall – only about 30 percent of Yosemite's guests arrive between November and April (and no matter what time of year, try to come on weekdays if at all possible). Secondly, take the time to explore attractions beyond the heavily visited valley. The magnificent Mariposa Grove of giant sequoias lies near the park's south entrance, 37 miles from the valley. Here, you'll find 200-foot-tall sequoias that are among the largest and oldest of all living things. Nearby Wawona was once an Indian encampment and is now the setting for the Pioneer Yosemite History Center, a collection of relocated historic buildings and horse-drawn coaches. At Glacier Point you'll get the most spectacular view of the entire valley, from Yosemite Falls on the north wall of the valley to the sheared granite wall of Half Dome, looming 4,748 feet above the valley's east end. In winter, the road to the point is closed at Badger Pass ski area; Glacier Point is also a favorite destination of cross-country skiers. Some of the most rugged, sublime alpine scenery can be found in the Tuolumne Meadows and high country of the eastern part of the park. The Tioga Road, closed in winter, offers a 39-mile scenic drive through an area of sparkling lakes, delicate meadows, and lofty peaks that was once under glacial ice. Hetch Hetchy, 40 miles from Yosemite Valley, is also home to spectacular scenery and is the starting point for many less-used backcountry trails.

While many Yosemite sights, like Half Dome and El Capitan – one of the world's largest naked rock monoliths – can be viewed without ever leaving your car, it's a mistake not to hit the trail. Easy half-mile hikes to lower Yosemite Falls and Bridalveil can be accomplished by almost everyone. A good family hike to Vernal Falls starts at Curry Village. More strenuous but vastly rewarding hikes treat you to panoramic views of the valley from the Upper Yosemite Falls Trail and the Four Mile Trail up to Glacier Point. To really get away from it all, head into the backcountry. Tuolumne Meadows is the gateway to the alpine wilderness (wilderness permits are required for all overnight trips). Just off Tioga Road are a number of trails that lead through wildflower-filled meadows (the park is home to more than 1,400 flowering plants), brilliant blue lakes, and innumerable creeks and tributaries. Other options include horseback riding and biking, both available only in summer. Yosemite is also a natural magnet for rock climbers; a mountaineering school runs summer classes that include lessons in bouldering and rappelling. In the winter, there's skiing at Badger Pass, California's first ski area, as well as ranger-led snowshoe tours and Nordic ski instruction.

CA 68
PARK 69

NATIONAL PARKS LOCATOR MAP

Abbreviations

IHS	International Historic Site
NB	National Battlefield
NBP	National Battlefield Park
NBS	National Battlefield Site
NHP	National Historical Park
NHP & PRES	National Historical Park & Preserve
NH RES	National Historical Reserve
NHS	National Historic Site
NL	National Lakeshore
NM	National Monument
NM & PRES	National Monument & Preserve
NMP	National Military Park
N MEM	National Memorial
NP	National Park
NP & PRES	National Park & Preserve
N PRES	National Preserve
NR	National River
NRA	National Recreation Area
NRR	National Recreational River
NRRA	National River & Recreation Area
N RES	National Reserve
NS	National Seashore
NSR	National Scenic River/Riverway
NST	National Scenic Trail
PKWY	Parkway
SRR	Scenic and Recreational River
WR	Wild River
WSR	Wild & Scenic River

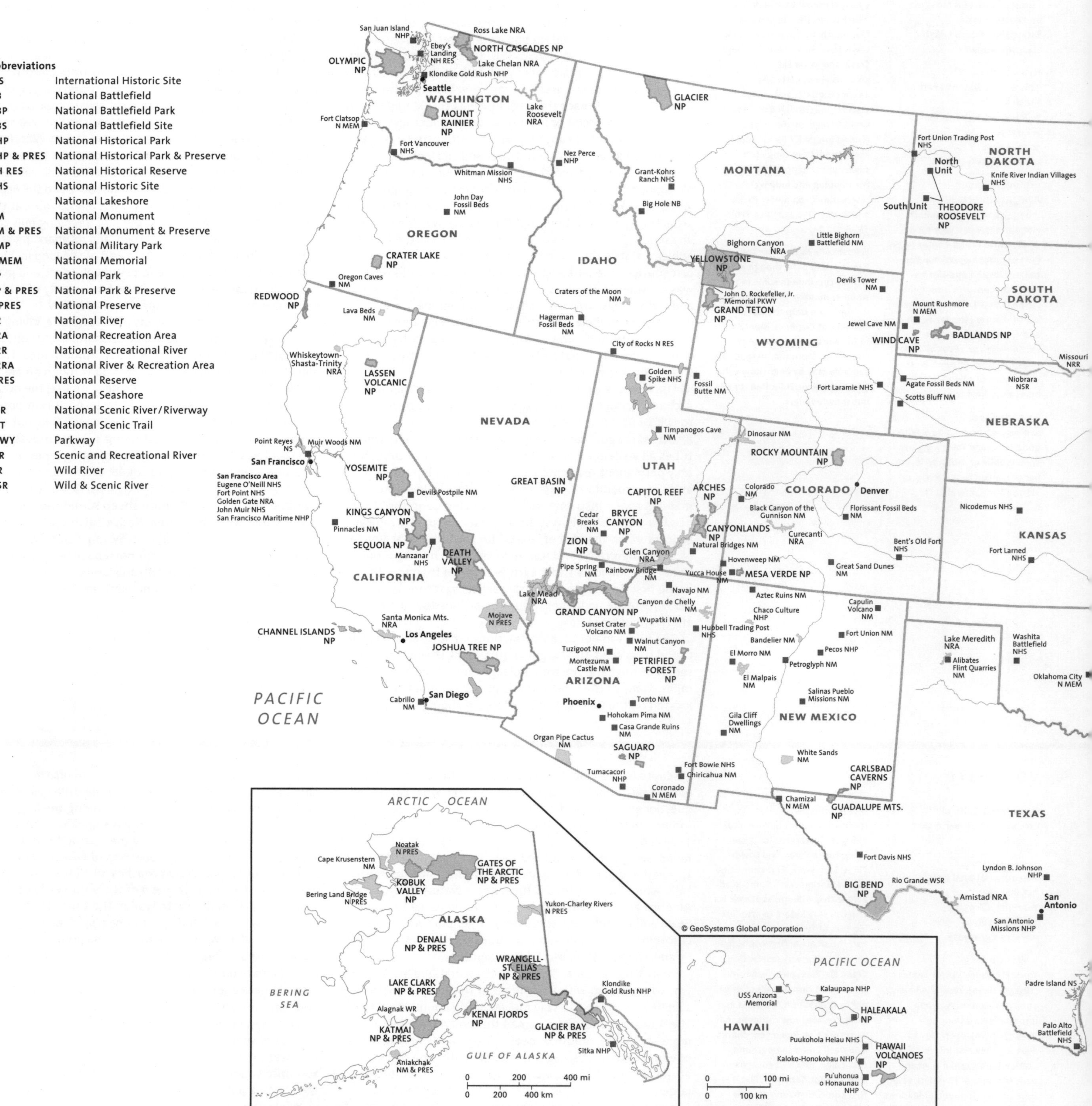

NATIONAL PARK SYSTEM GUIDE

The National Park System protects areas of natural and historical importance across the U.S., from scenic rivers, lakeshores, and seashores to historic battlefields and buildings. Included here is a list of administrative offices as well as a complete list of the National Parks.

Remember to plan ahead and contact parks in advance about reservations, permits, regulations, activities, and services. A note on reservations: The National Park Service's central reservation system has been temporarily suspended. To make reservations at indicated campgrounds, contact respective parks directly.

National Park Service Offices

National Park Service
Office of Public Inquiries
P.O. Box 37127
Washington, D.C. 20013
202.208.4747

Alaska Region
National Park Service
2525 Gambell St., Rm. 107
Anchorage, AK 99503
907.271.2737 (tourist information), 907.257.2696

Intermountain Region
National Park Service
P.O. Box 25287
Denver, CO 80225
303.969.2000

Midwest Region
National Park Service
1709 Jackson St.
Omaha, NE 68102
402.221.3471

National Capital Region
National Park Service
1100 Ohio Dr. SW
Washington, D.C. 20242
202.619.7222

Northeast Region
National Park Service
200 Chestnut St.
Philadelphia, PA 19106
215.597.7018

Pacific West Region
National Park Service
600 Harrison St., Ste. 600
San Francisco, CA 94107
415.556.0560

Southeast Region
National Park Service
Building 1924
100 Alabama St.
Atlanta, GA 30303
404.562.3123

National Parks

Acadia National Park
P.O. Box 177
Bar Harbor, ME 04609
207.288.3338

Arches National Park
P.O. Box 907
Moab, UT 84532
435.259.8161

Badlands National Park
P.O. Box 6
Interior, SD 57750
605.433.5361

Big Bend National Park
P.O. Box 129
Big Bend National Park, TX 79834
915.477.2251

Biscayne National Park
P.O. Box 1369
Homestead, FL 33090
305.230.7275

Bryce Canyon National Park
P.O. Box 170001
Bryce Canyon, UT 84717
435.834.5322

Canyonlands National Park
2282 S. West Resource Blvd.
Moab, UT 84532
435.259.7164

Capitol Reef National Park
HC 70 Box 15
Torrey, UT 84775
435.425.3791

Carlsbad Caverns National Park
3225 National Parks Hwy.
Carlsbad, NM 88220
505.785.2232

Channel Islands National Park
1901 Spinnaker Dr.
Ventura, CA 93001
805.658.5730

Crater Lake National Park
P.O. Box 7
Crater Lake, OR 97604
541.594.2211

Death Valley National Park
P.O. Box 579
Death Valley, CA 92328
760.786.2331

Denali National Park & Preserve
P.O. Box 9
Denali Park, AK 99755
907.683.2294

Dry Tortugas National Park
P.O. Box 6208
Key West, FL 33041
305.242.7700

Everglades National Park
40001 State Rd. 9336
Homestead, FL 33034
305.242.7700

Gates of the Arctic National Park & Preserve
P.O. Box 74680
Fairbanks, AK 99707
907.692.5494

Glacier Bay National Park & Preserve
P.O. Box 140
Gustavus, AK 99826
907.697.2230

Glacier National Park
P.O. Box 128
West Glacier, MT 59936
406.888.7800

Grand Canyon National Park
P.O. Box 129
Grand Canyon, AZ 86023
520.638.7888

Grand Teton National Park
P.O. Drawer 170
Moose, WY 83012
307.739.3300

Boston Area
Adams NHS
Boston African American NHS
Boston Harbor Islands NRA
Boston NHP
Frederick Law Olmstead NHS
John F. Kennedy NHS
Longfellow NHS
Lowell NHP
Minute Man NHP
Salem Maritime NHS
Saugus Iron Works NHS

New York City Area
Castle Clinton NM
Edison NHS
Federal Hall N MEM
General Grant N MEM
Hamilton Grange N MEM
Sagamore Hill NHS
Saint Paul's Church NHS
Statue of Liberty NM
Theodore Roosevelt Birthplace NHS

Philadelphia Area
Edgar Allan Poe NHS
Independence NHP
Thaddeus Kosciuszko N MEM

Baltimore Area
Ft. McHenry NM and Historic Shrine
Hampton NHS

District of Columbia
Constitution Gardens
Ford's Theatre NHS
Franklin Delano Roosevelt Memorial
Frederick Douglass NHS
Korean War Veterans Memorial
Lincoln Memorial
L.B. Johnson Memorial Grove
Mary McLeod Bethune Council House NHS
National Mall
Pennsylvania Avenue NHS
Rock Creek Park
Theodore Roosevelt Island
Thomas Jefferson Memorial
Vietnam Veterans Memorial
Washington Monument
White House

Maryland
Chesapeake and Ohio Canal NHP
Clara Barton NHS
Fort Washington Park
Greenbelt Park
Monocacy NB
Piscataway Park
Potomac Heritage NST

Virginia
Arlington House
George Washington Memorial PKWY
Wolf Trap Farm Park

The National Park of American Samoa and the War in the Pacific NHP are also administered by the National Park Service but are not shown on this map.

Great Basin National Park
Baker, NV 89311
702.234.7331

Great Smoky Mountains National Park
107 Park Headquarters Rd.
Gatlinburg, TN 37738
423.436.1200

Guadalupe Mountains National Park
HC 60 Box 400
Salt Flat, TX 79847
915.828.3251

Haleakala National Park
P.O. Box 369
Makawao, HI 96768
808.572.9306

Hawaii Volcanoes National Park
P.O. Box 52
Hawaii National Park, HI 96718
808.985.6000

Hot Springs National Park
P.O. Box 1860
Hot Springs, AR 71902
501.624.3383

Isle Royale National Park
800 E. Lakeshore Dr.
Houghton, MI 49931
906.482.0984

Joshua Tree National Park
74485 National Park Dr.
Twentynine Palms, CA 92277
760.367.5500

Katmai National Park & Preserve
P.O. Box 7
King Salmon, AK 99613
907.246.3305

Kenai Fjords National Park
P.O. Box 1727
Seward, AK 99664
907.224.2132

Kobuk Valley National Park
P.O. Box 1029
Kotzebue, AK 99752
907.442.3890

Lake Clark National Park & Preserve
4230 University Dr., Ste. 311
Anchorage, AK 99508
907.781.2218

Lassen Volcanic National Park
38050 Hwy. 36 E
Mineral, CA 96063
916.595.4444

Mammoth Cave National Park
P.O. Box 7
Mammoth Cave, KY 42259
502.758.2328

Mesa Verde National Park
P.O. Box 8
Mesa Verde National Park, CO 81330
970.529.4465

Mount Rainier National Park
Tahoma Woods, Star Rte.
Ashford, WA 98304
360.569.2211

National Park of American Samoa
Pago Pago, AS 96799
684.633.7082

North Cascades National Park
2105 State Rte. 20
Sedro Woolley, WA 98284
360.856.5700

Olympic National Park
600 E. Park Ave.
Port Angeles, WA 98362
360.452.4501

Petrified Forest National Park
P.O. Box 2217
Petrified Forest National Park, AZ 86028
520.524.6228

Redwood National Park
1111 Second St.
Crescent City, CA 95531
707.464-6101

Rocky Mountain National Park
Estes Park, CO 80517
970.586.1206

Saguaro National Park
3693 S. Old Spanish Trail
Tucson, AZ 85730
520.733.5153

Sequoia & Kings Canyon National Parks
Three Rivers, CA 93271
209.565.3341

Shenandoah National Park
3655 U.S. Highway 211 E
Luray, VA 22835
540.999.3500

Theodore Roosevelt National Park
P.O. Box 7
Medora, ND 58645
701.623.4466

Virgin Islands National Park
6310 Estate Nazareth,
Charlotte Amalie,
St. Thomas, VI 00802
340.775.6238

Voyageurs National Park
3131 Hwy. 53
International Falls, MN 56649
218.283.9821

Wind Cave National Park
RR 1, Box 190
Hot Springs, SD 57747
605.745.4600

Wrangell-St. Elias National Park & Preserve
P.O. Box 439
Copper Center, AK 99573
907.822.5234

Yellowstone National Park
P.O. Box 168
Yellowstone National Park, WY 82190
307.344.7381

Yosemite National Park
P.O. Box 577
Yosemite, CA 95389
209.372.0200

Zion National Park
Springdale, UT 84767
801.772.3256

Scenic Drives

For detailed descriptions of hundreds more scenic drives, see NATIONAL GEOGRAPHIC'S GUIDE TO SCENIC HIGHWAYS AND BYWAYS and NATIONAL GEOGRAPHIC'S DRIVING GUIDES TO AMERICA series, which includes the titles CALIFORNIA AND NEVADA AND HAWAII; FLORIDA AND THE SOUTHEAST; GREAT LAKES; THE HEARTLAND; NEW ENGLAND; NEW YORK AND PENNSYLVANIA AND NEW JERSEY; PACIFIC NORTHWEST; THE ROCKIES; SOUTHWEST; TEXAS AND LOUISIANA, MISSISSIPPI, ARKANSAS AND OKLAHOMA; WASHINGTON, D.C., AND VIRGINIA, WEST VIRGINIA, MARYLAND, AND DELAWARE; and CANADA.

323 miles | 1½ days

GEORGE PARKS HIGHWAY

ALASKA

Road Notes

Linking the state's two largest cities – Anchorage and Fairbanks – with Denali National Park & Preserve, this highway travels through the kind of scenery that defines the Alaskan interior: tundra and muskeg, the continent's highest peaks, glaciers, forests, wild rivers, and lonely expanses inhabited only by moose, grizzlies, foxes, wolves, and a wealth of birds. Unless you enjoy subzero temperatures, come here during the brief bloom of the Alaskan summer, when daylight lasts as long as 21 hours.

AK 62
AK 232

The George Parks Highway begins at its junction with the Glenn Highway and then heads west to Wasilla. For testimonials to the self-sufficiency and isolation of this area's old-time bush communities in the days before the Parks was built, visit the Dorothy G. Page Museum (907.373.9071). The nearby Iditarod Trail Committee Headquarters (907.376.5155) has a museum and sled-dog rides.

Leaving Wasilla, the highway soon picks up the Little Susitna River (mile 57.1), thronged by migrating salmon in late spring and midsummer. At mile 70.8 the Willow Creek Parkway offers access to riverside wetlands flanking the Susitna River's Delta Islands. Hatcher Pass Junction Road at mile 71.2 leads to the Willow Creek State Recreation Area (907.745.3975), noted for its profusion of wildflowers.

Denali National Park & Preserve

Weather permitting, northbound views of 20,320-foot Mount McKinley, the highest peak in North America, begin about mile 76. Also called Denali– meaning the "high one" in an Athapaskan dialect – the peak rises 15,000 feet above the surrounding terrain.

Exit at mile 98.7 and follow the 14.5-mile road to Talkeetna, now a popular staging area for climbing expeditions to Mount McKinley. About 28 miles north of the Talkeetna turnoff, the highway enters Denali State Park (907.745.3975). This primitive 324,240-acre state preserve shares the natural wonders but not the crowds of the adjoining national park.

Few McKinley views match the one from the turnout at mile 135.2, where signs identify various Alaska Range landmarks. In another 20 miles you will be able to see Eldridge Glacier, just six miles west of the road. Turnouts along here lead to creeks, beaver ponds, and good fishing spots.

At mile 174, the road crosses the bridge above 260-foot-deep Hurricane Gulch, then continues north to Broad Pass (mile 201.3), whose summit marks a watershed divide: From here, northflowing streams drain into the Yukon River and south-flowing into Cook Inlet.

Traffic builds near the entrance to Denali National Park & Preserve (mile 237.3; 907.683.2294; see pg. 199). North of the park entrance, the highway negotiates the steep Nenana River Canyon. Scan the heights above Moody Bridge (mile 242.9) for Dall sheep.

In the sleepy town of Nenana (mile 304.5), the highway rejoins the Nenana River at its confluence with the 440-mile Tanana River.

Between Nenana and Fairbanks, far horizons suggest the scale of Alaskan terrain. The plain extending west from mile 318 includes Minto Flats Game Refuge (907.459.7200), a primordially pristine wildlife sanctuary. The Parks ends near downtown Fairbanks (907.456.5774), at the junction with Route 2.

67 miles | 4 hours

MOUNT ADAMS DRIVE

WASHINGTON

Road Notes

This drive in southern Washington feels almost like a hike, as it follows a series of paved and unpaved roads deep into the Gifford Pinchot National Forest. Along the way, it passes lakes, rivers and creeks, old-growth forests, and memorable mountain views. Don't hurry through this beautiful country – there are a number of good campsites right along the roadside, and if you have basic backpacking gear the road runs past trailheads with access to the subalpine wildflower meadows and mountain views of the Mount Adams and Goat Rocks Wildernesses.

WA 170
WA 247

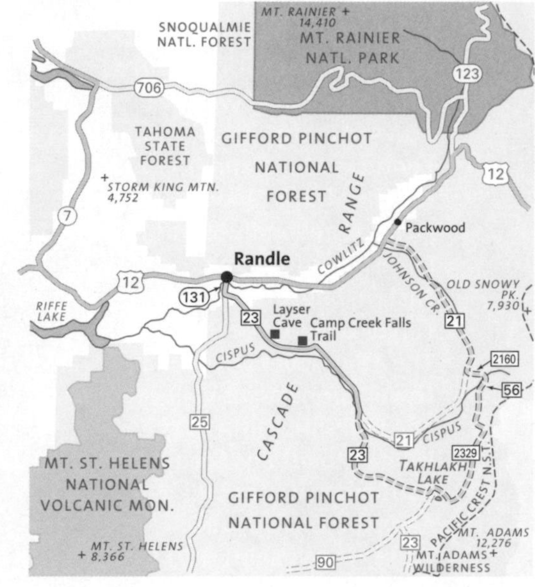

From Randle, turn south on Route 131. After going two miles, make a left turn onto Cispus Road. You'll pass a bucolic blend of small ranches, farms, and orchards for several miles until you cross into the Gifford Pinchot National Forest (Randle Ranger District, 360.497.1100; Packwood Ranger District, 360.494.0600).

Once in the national forest, the drive, now FR 23, tunnels through a classic western Cascades old-growth forest that is anchored by massive Douglas firs. To appreciate the size of these evergreen skyscrapers, walk up to one. Its trunk will be bigger across than you are tall.

Hiking trails branch off FR 23 in this area; stretch your legs on the quarter-mile Camp Creek Falls Trail, seven or eight miles from the Layser Cave turnoff. Camp Creek Falls itself plunges 30 feet over a rocky ledge, and along the trail, you might see a six-inch banana slug chomping on leaves, or a newt stepping in slow motion across the forest floor.

From here, the road soon picks up the Cispus River. For the next 15 miles, you stay with the river as it meanders down the valley. You'll see a snow-draped peak in the southeast; that's Mount Adams, the 12,307-foot volcano for which this route is named.

A couple of miles farther on, you leave FR 23 and turn left onto FR 2329, which soon brings you to Takhlakh Lake. The large, tree-lined lake – one of Washington's best camping spots – is exquisitely backdropped by Mount Adams. Just beyond the lake is the trailhead for the five-mile path to Adams Creek/Killen Creek Meadows, a beautiful high-country area that's ablaze with wildflowers all summer.

FR 2329 then follows along the northern edge of the Mount Adams Wilderness. Along the way, Mount Adams frequently punctuates the southern sky, while 14,410-foot Mount Rainier rises far to the north. Shimmering ribbons of icy, clear water flow from the nearby mountainsides.

Some ten miles past Takhlakh Lake, turn right onto FR 56 and follow it along the Cispus River for about a mile, then turn left on FR 2160. After two miles, turn right on FR 21. Passing several more groves of enormous Douglas firs, the road tightropes along a mountainside high above Johnson Creek for several miles before it ends at the junction with U.S. 12.

Mount Rainier

120 miles | ½ day

ROGUE UMPQUA SCENIC BYWAY

OREGON

Road Notes

This byway in southwest Oregon offers the rare opportunity to drive alongside two of the country's federally designated Wild and Scenic Rivers – the North Umpqua and the Rogue – both a feast of rapids, waterfalls, gorges, and serene stretches of cold, clear mountain water. These rivers are the stuff of fly-fishing legend, with salmon and steelhead runs that still bear some resemblance to the explosion of life that Zane Grey made famous in the 1930s with his stories. Both rivers are favorites with white-water rafters as well. Also on the itinerary is spectacular Crater Lake National Park. Summer is the prime time to experience all of these southern Oregon experiences, and at Crater Lake in particular you should be prepared for crowds.

OR 148
OR 244

From the quiet town of Roseburg, head east on Route 138. For the next 16 miles the road passes through farmland on its way to the North Umpqua River, which stages a dramatic entrance in the town of Glide. Below the town's Colliding Rivers Viewpoint, the North Umpqua and the Little River meet.

Leaving Glide, the road follows the North Umpqua up into the forests of the Cascade Range. A half mile beyond mile 21.5, stop at Swiftwater Park. The 79-mile North Umpqua Trail, good for backpacking and mountain biking, begins across the river here.

Among fly-fishing enthusiasts the next 30 miles of the North Umpqua are world famous for summer steelhead runs. Much of this stretch is framed by the towering basaltic cliffs of the North Umpqua River Canyon. Some nine miles past Swiftwater Park you enter the Umpqua National Forest (541.672.6601). Trails are plentiful here, often leading to waterfalls. Near the Toketee Ranger Station, the gorgeous half-mile trail to 120-foot-high Toketee Falls winds above a narrow, rocky gorge resounding with the North Umpqua's turbulence. The trail ends at a viewing platform high above the falls.

Rogue River, Crater Lake National Park

About 18 miles farther on, a detour takes you to capacious Diamond Lake, backdropped by thick coniferous forests and the snow-covered peaks of the Cascades, including 8,363-foot Mount Bailey. A detour of about two miles on Route 138 leads to Crater Lake National Park (541.594.2211). Inky blue Crater Lake, the deepest lake in the nation, fills the caldera of dormant Mount Mazama.

To continue, head right off Route 230. In three miles, you'll enter the Rogue River National Forest (541.858.2200). For a view of the Crater's rim, stop at Crater Rim Viewpoint, a couple of miles into the national forest.

For about the next 20 miles, Route 230 descends past trees and occasional lava flows almost two million years old; dropping into the canyon of the Rogue River (541.479.3735), the road meanders alongside the river. Route 230 soon ends, and you join Route 62 south. In 1.5 miles you'll come to Union Creek, a historic Civilian Conservation Corps center that is now a tiny hamlet. At Natural Bridge, a mile south of Union Creek, another short trail offers more great views of the Rogue. At one point, the river actually disappears underground for some 200 feet through an ancient lava tube.

Continuing four mor through stands of loo pines, ponderosa pine Douglas firs, the roa Mammoth Pines N

The drive ends a farther on, when it small logging tow

65 miles | 2 hours 

LOST COAST

CALIFORNIA

Road Notes

The Lost Coast is California's longest completely undeveloped stretch of wild shoreline, and its hallmarks – steeply pitched mountains rising out of the sea, clad with dense old-growth redwoods and wreathed almost perpetually in thick fog – are more in keeping with the Pacific Northwest than with the sunny imagery we associate with the Golden State. Many of the natural wonders of this area are beyond the reach of the automobile; indeed, backpacking the cobblestoned, black-sand beaches of the Lost Coast is one of the most remote wilderness treks you can manage in the lower 48. However, driving this little-traveled road, and stopping in two interesting, friendly settlements, will give you a feel for the place.

Begin in the Eel River Valley at Ferndale (707.786.4477), an 1852 town that grew rich from creameries. An ideally timed visit to Ferndale would coincide with May's World Champion Kinetic Sculpture Race, in which whimsically designed human-powered vehicles compete over a course that travels both land and water.

Follow Mattole Road out of town, zigzagging up slopes wooded with maples and evergreens. After four miles, a wide view opens across forested valleys, then grassy hills appear. This stretch is called Wildcat Ridge, but the animals you're likely to see are hawks overhead and cows in the windswept pastures. The road descends to the Bear River and a ranch at Capetown, a former stage stop. A precipitous stretch continues on to Cape Mendocino. Here, three large tectonic plates grind together just off the coast, creating one of the continent's most active earthquake zones. For some five miles you drive beside a tidal zone that rose about four feet during the April 1992 earthquake, giving the appearance of a perpetual low tide.

Ahead, there's a five-mile side trip on Lighthouse Road to the shore; from there, a 3.5-mile trail leads to an old lighthouse. Here, at the mouth of the Mattole River, is where backpackers set out into the wilds of the Lost Coast; the southern terminus of the trek is the tiny fishing and vacation-home village of Shelter Cove. You're on the northern margin of the King Range National Conservation Area (707.986.7731), whose steep terrain, including 4,088-foot King Peak, defies highway engineers.

Humboldt Redwoods State Park

Return to Mattole Road and drive on to Honeydew, no more than a store yawning in the shade. The road climbs, crossing the Mattole and then Panther Gap as you enter Humboldt Redwoods State Park (707.946.2409) and Rockefeller Forest, which hold more than 40 percent of the world's remaining old-growth redwoods. Because some sections of the Avenue of the Giants have been turned into commercial tourist attractions, you may want to consider getting into the backcountry of this park, where there are plenty of old-growth trees in their primeval state. The Eel River, an excellent canoeing and fishing stream that has numerous swimming holes, runs through the park.

Ahead, in South Fork, the road joins U.S. 101 and Avenue of the Giants. The latter, one of the most famous scenic routes in the country, runs from Phillipsville north to Pepperwood and will take you through touristy hamlets, magnificent forests, and yes, even a living redwood you can drive your car through.

CA 68

CA 233

123 miles | 6 hours 

CALIFORNIA 1 SOUTH

CALIFORNIA

Road Notes

Along this coastline, central California preserves its natural beauty and remembers its roots. The drive starts in historic Monterey, visits the art colony of Carmel, and threads through Big Sur, where the rocky, chaparral peaks of the Santa Lucias plunge into the Pacific in one of the planet's most dramatic encounters between land and sea. Overnighting amid Big Sur's towering redwoods is popular, but both beds and campsites are scarce – make reservations well in advance. Farther south, the landscape mellows to oak-studded hills as the road passes Hearst Castle on its way to Morro Bay. Temperatures are cool along the coast year round; winter sees more rain, and summer often brings thick coastal fog.

Join Route 1 in Monterey (408.649.1770). Visit touristy Fisherman's Wharf and Cannery Row, home of the celebrated Monterey Bay Aquarium (408.648.4888), where the world's largest window (15 feet high by 54 feet long) looks onto an indoor ocean. Also worth taking in is the Path of History, a tour of historic adobe buildings that celebrates Monterey's heritage as a fishing boomtown and capital of Spanish California.

Big Sur coastline

Drive three miles south on Route 1 to Carmel-by-the-Sea (408.624.2522), an upscale village of quaint cottages, inns, restaurants, art galleries, and shops. From Carmel, drive 3.5 miles south to the magical Point Lobos State Reserve (408.624.4909), which encompasses coves, rocky headlands, meadows, and the nation's first undersea ecological reserve. On land, trails offer sightings of black-tailed deer, playful sea otters, and noisy sea lions.

A few miles south of Point Lobos you'll pass the affluent Carmel Highlands and enter wild Big Sur (408.667.2100). Nine miles south is the graceful, much photographed Bixby Creek Bridge. Ahead, the road passes Hurricane Point, a place of big views, and the mouth of the Little Sur River. Looking inland, you'll see 3,709-foot-high Pico Blanco. Toward the sea, sand dunes soon appear, rolling toward the 1889 Point Sur Light Station (408.625.4419), a state historic park. In three miles you reach Andrew Molera State Park (408.667.2315), whose redwood forests and broad beach are a hiker's paradise.

Along the five miles of urban Big Sur you'll pass the entrance to Pfeiffer Big Sur State Park (408.667.2315), with a large public campground and hiking trails that run past old-growth redwoods and cool swimming holes. A half mile beyond is Big Sur Station (408.667.2315), a backcountry information center. Next, keep your eyes peeled for an unmarked road (the second right after the station) leading west toward Pfeiffer Beach, where the surf roars through arched rocks.

After nearly two miles you reach Nepenthe (408.667.2345), a mountaintop restaurant famous for its jaw-dropping view. Another eight miles along is Julia Pfeiffer Burns State Park (408.667.2315), whose terrain ranges from 3,000-foot-high ridges to an underwater preserve.

After 35 miles of hairpin turns through southern Big Sur, the landscape settles down to hills and pastureland. Next stop is San Simeon, a staging area for the five-mile bus ride to Hearst Castle (805.927.2020).

Continue about seven miles to Cambria, an arty town nestled against hills; on the ocean side of the highway, at Moonstone Beach, look for moonstones and California jade. The route ends at Morro Bay (800.231.0592), easily identified by its landmark Morro Rock, an ancient volcanic cone.

CA 68

CA 233

27 miles | 2 hours

OAK CREEK CANYON DRIVE

ARIZONA

Road Notes

On the southern edge of the great Colorado Plateau that produced such marvels as Grand, Zion, and Bryce Canyons lies an equally stunning, but far more intimate spot – Oak Creek Canyon. For the past three million years, Oak Creek has carved a 12-mile-long, 2,000-foot-deep slice along the fault line into the ancient geologic past. From the ponderosa pines of Flagstaff to the red-rock desertscape of Sedona, the Oak Creek Canyon Drive reveals layers of dazzling red sandstone, tan limestone, and purple siltstone, all eroded into curious shapes. The numerous camping and picnic grounds along the short route are very popular – come in fall, when the crowds have thinned and the cottonwoods turn a fiery yellow.

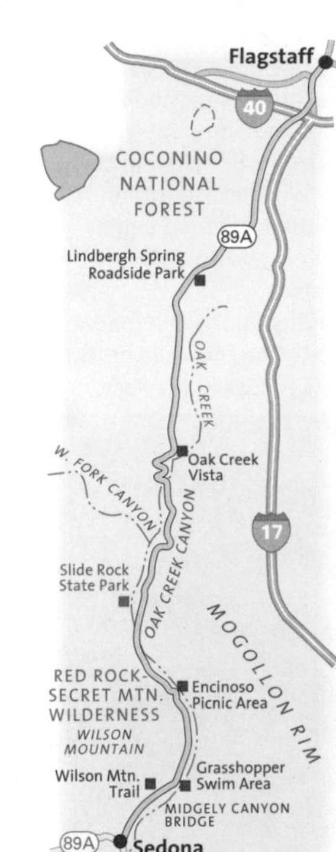

Route 89A leaves the bustle of Flagstaff, a former lumber town in the shadows of the rugged San Francisco Mountains, and travels through the thick ponderosa pines of the Coconino National Forest (520.527.3600). After three miles the road passes the small Lindbergh Spring Roadside Park, a good spot for a close-up look at ponderosas. Their clusters of three long needles distinguish them from other pine species.

After eight miles atop the plateau, the road comes to the Oak Creek Vista on the left, at the lip of a great escarpment known as the Mogollon Rim. Thirty million years ago, seismic forces thrust this section of the earth's crust thousands of feet above the surrounding land.

A short loop trail, where Native Americans sell crafts, brings you to the edge of a sheer drop. From this 6,400-foot vantage point, you'll see a diversity of plant life resulting from the dramatic elevation changes and relative abundance of water. Water-loving trees, such as alder, willow, oak, and walnut, thrive along the creek. Dense brush dominates the dry hillsides. Where the canyon widens, desert plants appear.

From the overlook, the road – which began as a cattle trail and was later adapted to wagons – switchbacks precipitously downward for two miles to the Pumphouse Wash Bridge. About 17 miles south of Flagstaff, a day-use area leads to the canyon's most popular hike, the West Fork Trail, a moderate three-mile walk under sheer walls into West Fork Canyon, past fern forests and sandy beaches.

The road continues, passing campsites and picnic grounds along the Oak Creek. Above, layers of sedimentary rock mark the rock walls. In age and composition they are like the rocks in the top third of the Grand Canyon.

Halfway through the canyon drive, Slide Rock State Park (520.282.3034) appears on the right. Beyond the orchard and down some steps, a path leads to the site of the park's most popular activity. Here, the creek bubbles through a shoot of smooth Coconino sandstone, and the air fills with shouts as people ride the natural slide. (Be sure to bring water socks and jeans – the ride can be bumpy.) In summer you must arrive before 11 a.m. to park. Not far beyond Slide Rock is Oak Creek's other popular swim spot, Grasshopper Swim Area, with deep pools and soaring cliffs.

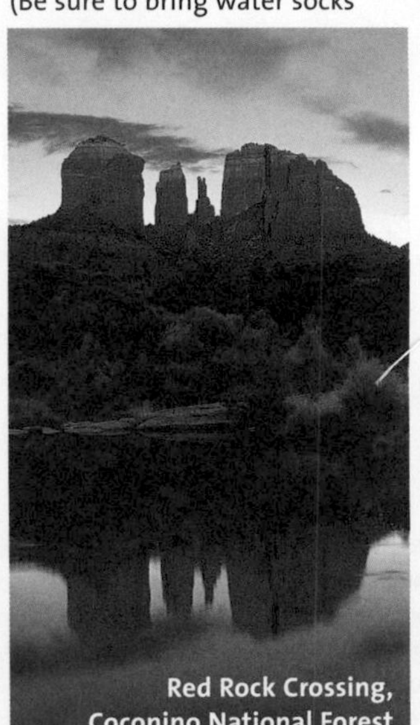
Red Rock Crossing, Coconino National Forest

Just after this swim area, a pull-off on the north side of Midgely Bridge serves as the trailhead for the Wilson Mountain Trail, which pushes west into the Red Rocks–Secret Mountain Wilderness. Though strenuous – the trail rises 2,300 feet in 5.6 miles – the spectacular views extend several hundred miles and encompass Verde Valley, Sedona, and Oak Creek Canyon. An equally strenuous alternative is the North Wilson Trail, which starts north of the Encinoso Picnic Area and joins the Wilson Mountain Trail. Two miles from Midgely Bridge, the road passes out of the canyon and into Sedona, an arts community set among spectacular red-rock formations.

AZ 64

AZ 232

118 miles | ½ day

GILA SCENIC BYWAY

NEW MEXICO

NM 130
NM 241

Road Notes

Within the high-desert forests of Gila National Forest, this southwestern New Mexico route penetrates some of the nation's largest and most remote tracts of wilderness. It passes a couple of Old West towns, winds to ancient cliff dwellings, and skirts an immense open-pit copper mine. The tortuous road is all but impassable to RVs and trailers, and is slow going for anyone – make an early start to ensure you'll have time to explore the cliff dwellings.

The route begins at Silver City, a mining town that boomed in the 1870s, when silver was discovered. The town's colorful history is told at the Silver City Museum (505.538.5921).

From town, the route climbs north on Route 15 for six miles into the Pinos Altos Range and reaches the town of Pinos Altos, or "tall pines," which hugs the Continental Divide at 7,840 feet. The famous bar at the Buckhorn Saloon (505.538.9911), which also has a fine restaurant, keeps the sleepy town alive.

After Pinos Altos the road narrows considerably as it winds through the Pinos Altos Range, heading up Cherry Creek past a couple of rustic picnic areas shaded by ponderosa pines and cottonwoods. Eighteen miles after Pinos Altos, the route drops steeply to Sapillo Creek, where Route 15 intersects with Route 35. Continue north for 17 miles to the Gila Cliff Dwellings National Monument. On its way up to the cliff dwellings, the road climbs through a series of switchbacks, passing the Senator Clinton P. Anderson Wilderness Overlook after about six miles. The Gila River Canyon lies 2,000 feet below, while spectacular vistas of the Gila Wilderness spread to the horizon. After the overlook, Route 15 crosses a level ridge with open views and then descends sharply to a bridge across the Gila River.

Four miles later, the road reaches Gila Cliff Dwellings National Monument (505.536.9344). The road to the dwellings passes the Lower Scorpion Campground, which features a small cave dwelling. (The short paved path to the right ends at a series of ancient red pictographs.) Parking for the major cliff dwellings lies just beyond the campground. A one-mile loop climbs 175 feet to the dwellings on the southeast-facing cliff. Five caves contain a remarkable series of 42 rooms. Some 40 to 50 Mogollon people lived in these dwellings in the late 13th century.

Retrace the route to Sapillo Creek and take Route 35 southeast for four miles to pine-hemmed Lake Roberts. As the road winds around the lake, it passes Vista Village, an archaeological site undergoing excavation. It's believed that prehistoric Native Americans occupied an 18- to 25-room pueblo here. The road continues up a wide valley and again crests the Continental Divide before reaching the Mimbres River Valley and the

Gila National Forest

Mimbres Ranger District (505.536.2250) outside the town of Mimbres.

Near the town of San Lorenzo, the route intersects Route 152, which heads west 8.5 miles to the overlook of the Phelps Dodge Santa Rita Copper Mine, an immense hole in the earth. Continue on to Santa Clara, where U.S. 180 takes you back to Silver City.

54 miles | 2 hours

TALIMENA SCENIC BYWAY

OKLAHOMA/ARKANSAS

OK 146
AR 66
OK 243
AR 232

Road Notes

Built in the late 1960s expressly for grand views, this two-lane highway ripples over the gentle Ouachita Mountains, which straddle the Oklahoma–Arkansas border. Evergreen and deciduous trees shoulder the road, the latter making for gorgeous floral displays in spring and brilliant color in autumn. The byway's name derives from a combination of the towns that form its two endpoints – Talihina and Mena. It runs through the 1.7-million-acre Ouachita National Forest (501.321.5202), the South's oldest (established in 1907) and largest national forest. Ouachita is a Native American word meaning either "good hunting grounds" or "hunting trip," and these woods still hold plentiful deer, squirrel, and other wildlife.

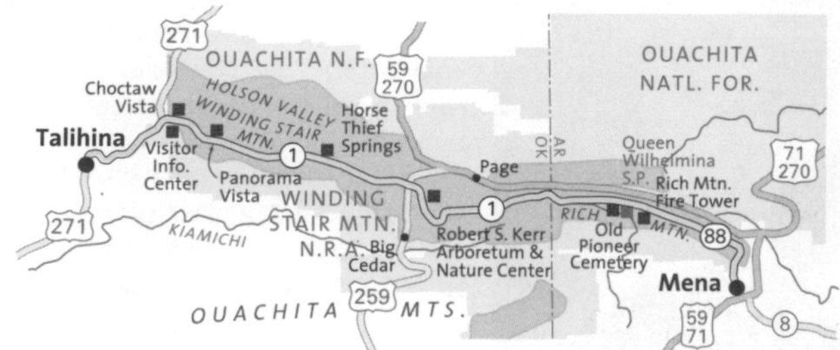

Begin in Talihina, a town founded by missionaries in the late 1880s, when the Frisco Railway came through the mountains (its name is Choctaw for "iron road"). A Visitor Information Station about seven miles to the northeast, at the junction of U.S. 271 and Oklahoma 1, marks the start of the designated byway. Just 0.3 mile past the information station you come to Choctaw Vista, on the west end of Winding Stair Mountain, part of the Ouachita Mountains. From here you can look out on the beautiful dark blue hills and valleys through which the Choctaw traveled west from Mississippi, in compliance with the 1830 Indian Removal Act.

For the next several miles the road cuts through a forest of shortleaf pine and scrub oak. The east-west lay of the Ouachita Mountains has created separate plant communities on either side: Post oak, blackjack, and serviceberry cover southern slopes, while the rich soil of the northern slopes supports white oak, hickory, dogwood, and papaw.

Past the forest entrance, stop at Panorama Vista for sweeping views of the mountains and the small farming villages tucked into the Holson Valley. Hang-glider enthusiasts often launch from here. Golden eagles, vultures, and hawks also soar on the updrafts.

Continue on to Horse Thief Springs (mile 16). The road now swoops back and forth down Winding Stair Mountain, giving you constantly shifting views. The Ouachita Mountains once extended to the Appalachians, before the Mississippi separated the ranges. The 300-million-year-old sandstones and shales of the Ouachitas were thrust up, folded, and faulted. Fault lines are visible in places along the drive, including the area around Robert S. Kerr Arboretum and Nature Center.

For several miles past the nature center the byway follows the crest of Rich Mountain through a forest of dwarf oak stunted by severe ice storms and southerly winds. Oklahoma 1 changes to Arkansas 88 as you cross the state line. At about mile 40, the Old Pioneer Cemetery holds the graves of 23 people who homesteaded here between the mid-19th and the mid-20th centuries.

Two miles beyond, the Queen Wilhelmina State Park (501.394.2863) features dramatic southerly views from the crest of Rich Mountain. The park centers around a rustic stone lodge. Originally constructed at the turn of the century and since rebuilt, the lodge was named for the queen of Holland, whose country held a substantial stake in the local railroad.

Three miles east of the park stands the highest point on the drive, Rich Mountain Fire Tower (2,681 feet). From this vantage, you have fine views of the forested mountains.

The drive ends in Mena, a timber and cattle town that sprang to life in 1896 when the first train of the Kansas City Southern Railroad came chugging through the mountains.

Winding Stair Mountain

236 miles | 1–2 days

SAN JUAN SKYWAY

COLORADO

CO 76
CO 233

Road Notes

As its fanciful name implies, the San Juan Skyway flirts with the heights, climbing to more than 10,000 feet three times as it charts a ragged loop through the mountains and high deserts of southwestern Colorado. Starting at Ridgway, this spectacular route heads south over the crest of the San Juan Mountains and passes through historic mining towns, red-rock canyons, and Mesa Verde National Park, where you can walk through 800-year-old Ancestral Puebloan cliff dwellings. The drive is beautiful year-round, but keep in mind that the mountain passes close sometimes after heavy winter snows.

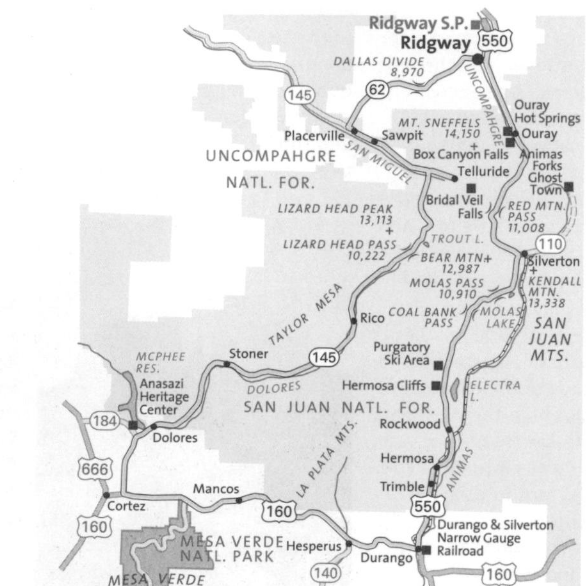

Begin four miles north of town, at Ridgway State Park (970.626.5822), where U.S. 550 tops a dry hill and the southern skyline fills with the jagged crest of the San Juans. Cross the valley floor to Ridgway, at the base of 14,150-foot Mount Sneffels, then continue south along the Uncompahgre River.

At Ouray, multicolored cliffs squeeze the valley against the base of 14,000-foot peaks. Ouray Hot Springs, a municipal pool, steams at the north end of downtown Ouray's ornate 1880s buildings. U.S. 550 next switchbacks up into the mountains, offering splendid vistas back down to Ridgway. Waterfalls and creeks spill from side canyons and high cliffs in Uncompahgre Gorge. Next, just drive up the short series of hairpin turns, top the rim of the gorge, and let your pulse soar. Vivid crimson peaks burst into view, with broad smears of orange and red gravel streaming down into the dark surrounding evergreens. It's an astonishing, surrealistic sight, and yet the peaks carry mundane labels: Red Mountain No. 1, No. 2, and No. 3. You climb nearly to tree line before arriving at 11,008-foot Red Mountain Pass, and then the road begins its ten-mile, 1,700-foot descent into Silverton.

Continuing south, the road winds along the contours of the mountains to Coal Bank Pass, then tilts downward toward the plateau and canyon country around Durango, an 1880s railroad town. From Durango, follow U.S. 160 west through a rolling terrain of minor canyons and mesas. About eight miles beyond Mancos is Mesa Verde National Park (970.529.4461; see pg. 205).

Continue along U.S. 160 toward Cortez, then turn north onto Route 145, which follows the Dolores River back into the San Juan Mountains. About ten miles from Rico, you'll see 13,113-foot Lizard Head Peak off to the left. Lizard Head Pass (10,222 feet) offers more incredible views of the San Juans, then the road descends over some miles to a T-intersection. Turn right and drive into Telluride. Its mint Victorian downtown is nestled in a pocket valley beneath the San Juans, and 365-foot Bridal Veil Falls drops from the cliffs behind town. Follow Route 145 to Placerville, turn right on Route 62, and after crossing the pass of Dallas Divide, you'll glide back down to Ridgway.

San Juan Mountains

122 miles | ½–1 day

UTAH

UTAH 12 SCENIC BYWAY

Road Notes

Some of Utah's most outstanding high-desert scenery unfolds along this route, which begins near the pale orange spires of Bryce Canyon and ends amid the immense sandstone domes of Capitol Reef. Between these two national parks, this remote highway snakes along narrow ridge tops, carves through red-rock canyons past prehistoric Native American ruins, and ascends 11,000-foot Boulder Mountain for breathtaking views.

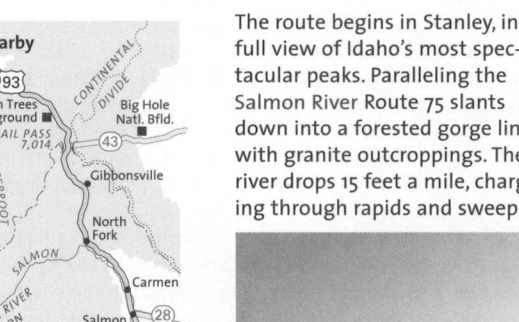

From its western terminus at U.S. 89, Route 12 soon enters Dixie National Forest (435.865.3700) and rolls through Red Canyon, a fairylike world of sculptured limestone formations colored brilliant red by iron oxides and accented by ponderosa pines.

At 12 miles, Route 63 branches off to the south and enters Bryce Canyon National Park (435.834.5322; see pg. 197). The road along the rim skirts 12 huge amphitheaters that drop a thousand feet.

Back on Route 12, the next stop, about 13 miles past the small town of Tropic, is a pullout with stunning views of the salmon-colored cliffs of 10,188-foot Powell Point. The road continues east across Table Cliff Plateau and reaches Escalante State Park and Visitor Center (435.826.4466). Wide Hollow Reservoir offers trout fishing, while a 1.5-mile nature trail leads to a petrified forest and a view of the early Mormon town of Escalante.

Highway 12 next crosses Calf Creek near the Calf Creek Campground (435.826.5499), where a 5.5-mile trail leads to 126-foot Calf Creek Falls. In this area, the road twists along the crest of a narrow ridge with spectacular views of Calf Creek far below. Continue on six miles to Boulder, where Anasazi State Park (435.335.7308) offers a re-created dwelling and a museum of the Anasazi, who, along with the Fremont Indians, occupied this region in prehistoric times.

North of Boulder, Route 12 enters a landscape of sagebrush and piñon pines. It ascends Boulder Mountain, which sits on the Aquarius Plateau, one of the continent's highest timbered plateaus. In fall, stands of fire-yellow aspens play against the evergreens. Views from several overlooks, such as Point Lookout, are exceptional. The road descends to the junction with Route 24 near Torrey.

Turn right onto Route 24 and enter Capitol Reef National Park (435.425.3791), which preserves a portion of the Waterpocket Fold, a great wrinkle in the earth's crust. Exposed edges of the uplift have eroded into a dramatic slickrock wilderness of massive domes, cliffs, and a maze of twisted canyons. Stop at the Visitor Center to plan your park visit.

Red Canyon, Dixie National Forest

UT 165
UT 247

184 miles | ½ day

IDAHO

SALMON RIVER SCENIC ROUTE

Road Notes

This scenic route follows central Idaho's largest river north from its headwaters in the Sawtooth Range through desert canyons to the tiny town of North Fork, where the waters swerve suddenly to the west and leave all roads far behind. The drive then heads back into the mountains, following the path of Lewis and Clark over Lost Trail Pass and down into the Bitterroot Valley. It's a gorgeous drive and one that touches on major historical themes – exploration, fur trapping, mining, settlement, and Native American conflicts.

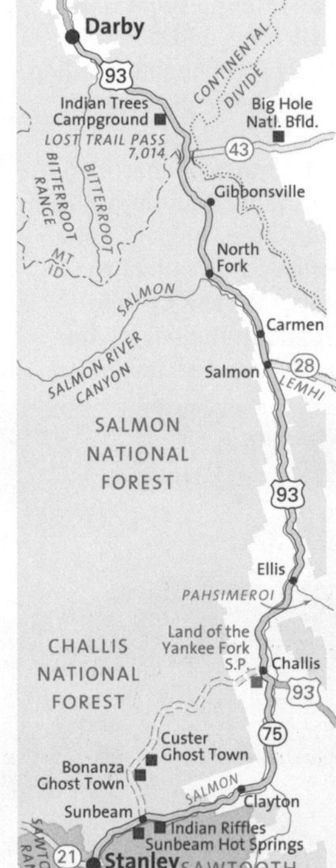

The route begins in Stanley, in full view of Idaho's most spectacular peaks. Paralleling the Salmon River Route 75 slants down into a forested gorge lined with granite outcroppings. The river drops 15 feet a mile, charging through rapids and sweeping past hot-spring pools. The best known, Sunbeam Hot Springs, trickles down a rocky slope about 11 miles from Stanley. Less than a mile beyond the springs, the river stalls out in deep pools of emerald green at the crossroads town of Sunbeam.

Follow the river 2.5 miles east to Indian Riffles. The road continues along the Salmon River through small canyons that widen as you descend. Beyond Clayton, the river bends northeast and runs through a valley surrounded by high-desert hills.

Approaching the junction with U.S. 93, you pass under a towering cliff of rust-colored rock. Bighorn sheep frequent the area. A sign at the Bison Jump Archaeological Site describes how Native Americans drove small herds of the animals over the cliff.

At the junction of Route 75 and U.S. 93, stop at the Land of the Yankee Fork Visitor Center (208.879.5244) to see exhibits on the region's geology, history, and mining methods.

Soon you cross the Pahsimeroi River and round the northern flank of the Lemhi Range. About 18 miles past Challis, both road and river punch through a narrow gorge that widens into a spectacular canyon whose walls soar hundreds of feet.

Follow U.S. 93 to Salmon, an 1860s mining town and now a center for ranchers, loggers, and river runners. Heading north, the road runs through yet another canyon carved by the Salmon. Look for great blue herons, cliff swallows, deer, pronghorn, and maybe even river otters. At North Fork the river plunges west into the Salmon River Canyon and rushes across the vast wilderness of central Idaho.

U.S. 93 tunnels through dense forests to Lost Trail Pass, 7,014 feet, named in 1805 by the bewildered northbound party of Lewis and Clark. In 1877, during their epic flight for freedom, the Nez Perce also crossed east through these mountains. At the Big Hole National Battlefield (15 miles east on Route 43; 406.689.3205), you can walk over the ground where the Nez Perce beat back the U.S. Army.

From the pass, you descend into Bitterroot Valley. Stop at Indian Trees Campground to admire stands of mature ponderosa pines. The drive ends in Darby.

Salmon River, Sawtooth Range

ID 89
ID 234

162 miles | 1 day

WYOMING

CENTENNIAL SCENIC BYWAY

Road Notes

One of the finest drives in the Rockies, the Centennial Scenic Byway charts a long, doglegging course through the mountains and river valleys of northwest Wyoming. Along the way, it passes nearly every major sight in the region – the Wind River Range, the Tetons, the Snake River, and the Green River Valley. Get an early start so you can catch the morning light on the Tetons and still make Pinedale in time to watch the sun set on the Winds. The drive is spectacular year-round, though winter snows occasionally close Togwotee Pass.

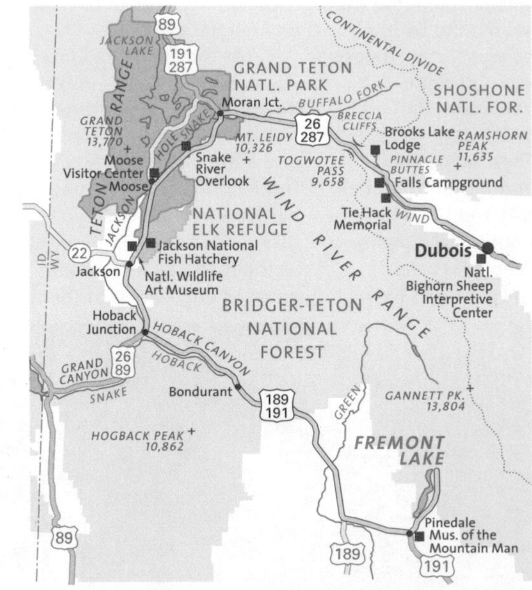

The byway begins at Dubois, where the surrounding terrain shifts from colorful badlands to forested mountain slopes. As U.S. 26 climbs from town, look to the northeast to see 11,635-foot Ramshorn Peak, part of the volcanic Absaroka Range. Beside the road, the Wind River curves over beds of cobblestones, sliding past evergreens and aspens.

About 20 miles from town, the Pinnacle Buttes burst over the treetops. Stop at Falls Campground to stroll the rim of the waterfall.

U.S. 26 rises steadily through a pine forest. In meadows rife with wildflowers, be on the lookout for moose, elk, deer, even bear. Soon, you cross Togwotee Pass (9,658 feet) and descend to Teton Range Overlook, with its incomparable view of Wyoming's best known mountains.

Drive out of the mountains onto the floodplain of the Buffalo Fork River, and you're soon in Grand Teton National Park (307.739.3600; see pg. 201). At Moran Junction, Route 26 turns south and passes through a wetland area. Look for moose, elk, and bison along here. Continue south to the Snake River Overlook, with one of the classic views of the Teton Range. Bald eagles and ospreys sometimes glide over the river. From here, the drive heads south through Jackson Hole to Moose Junction, where you'll find the main park Visitor Center (307.739.3399). About six miles south of Moose, a fence encloses the National Elk Refuge, where nearly 10,000 elk gather every winter. Sleigh rides among the elk (307.733.0277) start from refuge headquarters.

Soon you arrive in Jackson, a former ranch town turned tourist mecca. Avoid the town's traffic by taking the truck route and follow U.S. 189/191 south. Seven miles from Jackson you'll hit the Snake River; follow it to Hoback Junction. Here, the Hoback River joins the Snake, and their combined waters send raging white water through the Grand Canyon of the Snake River.

Southeast of Bondurant, the road drops out of the mountains onto the sagebrush flats of the Green River Valley. Stop at the Museum of the Mountain Man (307.367.4101), on Route 189/191. End your tour by following Fremont Lake Road out of Pinedale to Fremont Lake.

Snake River, Grand Teton National Park

WY 176
WY 248

ND 141
ND 242

14 miles | ¾ hour

NORTH DAKOTA

OXBOW OVERLOOK SCENIC BYWAY

Road Notes

Meandering through the magnificent badlands of western North Dakota so beloved by Theodore Roosevelt, this park road traverses the length of the 24,000-acre North Unit of the Theodore Roosevelt National Park. Traffic tends to be light for a national park, and you have ample opportunities for viewing wide prairies, wildlife, and, above all, the wonderful badlands rock formations. Pullouts en route have interpretive plaques and hiking trails.

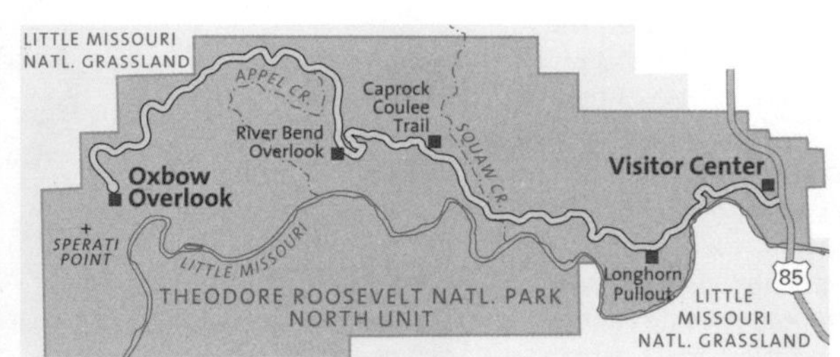

The drive begins at the Theodore Roosevelt National Park's visitor center (701.623.4466), a worthwhile stop with good displays and films and a friendly staff. The park was named for the man whose experiences in North Dakota helped mold him into a world leader. Roosevelt first visited the badlands in 1883 to hunt bison and other big game. A vigorous conservationist, he set aside a tremendous amount of land for parks, forests, and wildlife refuges during his terms as President (1901–9).

The Longhorn Pullout (mile 2) is situated on the edge of a prairie where a small herd of longhorn steer graze. Longhorn in the area date from an 1884 Texas trail drive that pushed 4,000 head into an open range vacated by dwindling bison. Thousands of longhorn followed in subsequent drives, but in 20 years they too had gone, victims of overgrazing and hard winters.

The scenery that captured Roosevelt's imagination is evident at every bend in the road. Climbing through hills laced with juniper trees, the road soars above the canyons and ravines characteristic of the badlands. Watch for wildlife, often not far from the road – mule deer, prairie dogs, bison, and more. The Caprock Coulee Nature Trail (mile 7) takes about an hour (or longer if you make a loop) and offers an up-close examination of the local geology. Interpretive brochures are available at the trailhead.

River Bend Overlook (about mile 8) affords splendid views of peaks and rounded buttes and the cottonwood-lined Little Missouri far below. The multicolored rock formations are layers of sandstone, clay, shale, and petrified wood deposited millions of years ago. Easily eroded by the elements, the rocks have infinitely varied shapes – from drip castles to capped pillars and buttes. In 1864, Gen. Alfred Sully described the region as "hell with the fires out." The fires sometimes still burn when seams of lignite coal catch fire from lightning and bake the surrounding clay a sienna red.

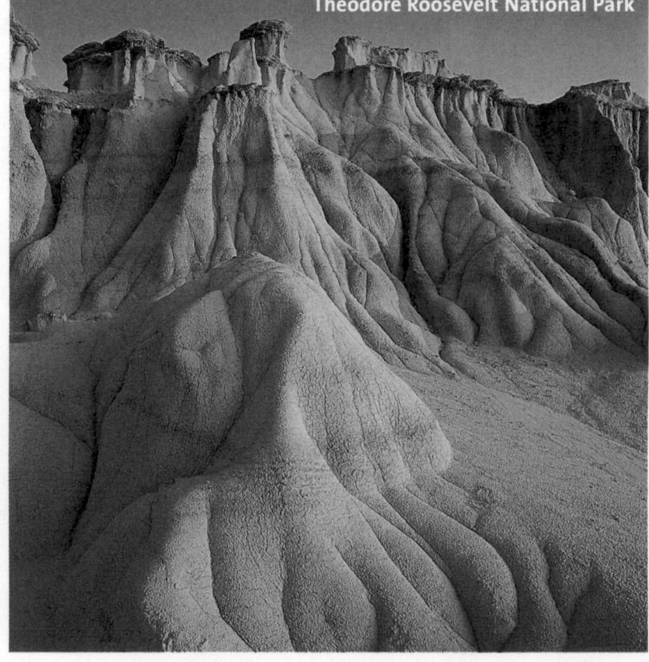
Theodore Roosevelt National Park

The road ends at Oxbow Overlook, another breathtaking vantage point. Here you can see where the Little Missouri once flowed north toward Hudson Bay. Forced by a glacier to find a new course, the river turned east to the Mississippi during the last ice age.

SD 157
SD 245

33 miles | 1½ hours

SOUTH DAKOTA

CUSTER SCENIC BYWAY

Road Notes

First-time visitors to southwestern South Dakota will probably experience an odd sense of déjà vu. It's an elemental Old West landscape, and we have been here before – through the magic of the movies, anyway. The bison you'll see during this drive through the heart of the Black Hills may have been extras in *Dances With Wolves*, and amid the hoodoos and ponderosa pines it's easy to sense the lingering presence of the legends who once walked this land – Crazy Horse, Wild Bill Hickok and Calamity Jane, and Colonel Custer are a few. Today the most colorful time to be here is in August, when more than 100,000 Harley-Davidson enthusiasts stream into the area to attend the Sturgis Motorcycle Rally and Races.

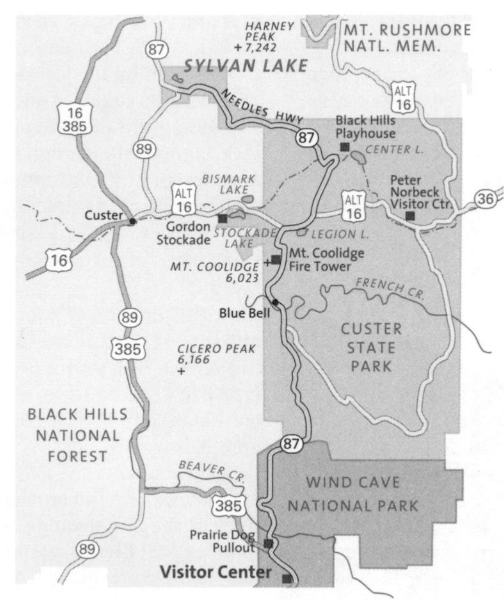

Throughout history, the Black Hills, called Paha Sapa ("hills that are black") by the Lakota, were sacred ground to the Cheyenne, Arapaho, Kiowa, and Lakota – a place to seek visions, to purify one's spirit, and a neutral site where warring tribes could meet. With the discovery of gold here in 1874, the passage of the Black Hills from Native American to white hands ran its inevitable course. Colonel Custer and Sitting Bull, Little Bighorn and Wounded Knee are part of lasting American myth. There is still a strong Lakota presence in the area; they continue to fight in court to regain the Black Hills.

The drive begins at Wind Cave National Park (605.745.4600), where extensive subterranean architecture has been sculptured over the eons in the porous limestone surrounding the Black Hills. The 81-mile maze of caverns, only partially explored, are rife with interesting formations; guided tours are available. Above ground, in the park's mixed-grass prairies and pine forests, wildlife includes coyotes, bison, pronghorn, and mule deer.

Heading north along Route 87 from its junction with U.S. 385, stop at the Prairie Dog Pullout. If you stay in the car, you'll have more to watch; cars don't spook the rodents but people do. Farther along is Custer State Park (605.255.4515), contiguous with the national park. The park has four jewellike lakes – Sylvan, Center, Stockade, and Legion Lakes – all offering swimming, fishing, boating, and camping.

Route 87 soon begins winding up through dense pine forest. Near Mount Coolidge you'll notice vast tracts of charred forest from the 1988 and 1990 fires that devastated the park. For a 360-degree panorama of the Black Hills, take the 1.3-mile gravel road (on the left) to the Mount Coolidge Fire Tower.

The 14.5-mile section of Route 87 north of U.S. 16A is known as the Needles Highway (closed winters), and it's a thrilling finish to the drive. Around you rise the needles, or upthrust pylons of granite, in the heart of the Sioux holy land; amazing views seem magically to appear before your windshield. The drive ends at Sylvan Lake. Above its north shore rises Harney Peak, which, at 7,242 feet, is the highest mountain east of the Rockies.

Custer State Park

MO 120
MO 239

44 miles | 1 hour

MISSOURI

MISSOURI OZARKS

Road Notes

Coursing through the peaceful farm country and upland forests of southeastern Missouri, this winding road passes near a large section of the Mark Twain National Forest and crosses the Ozark National Scenic Riverways wilderness area. Protected in this wilderness are the Current and Jacks Fork Rivers, beautiful recreational rivers offering excellent fishing, canoeing, swimming, and camping opportunities. Most popular in spring and fall, the highway boasts redbud and dogwood trees in pink and white and a palette of brilliant autumn colors. Wildflowers, from last cold-front to first frost, enhance the beauty of the roadsides.

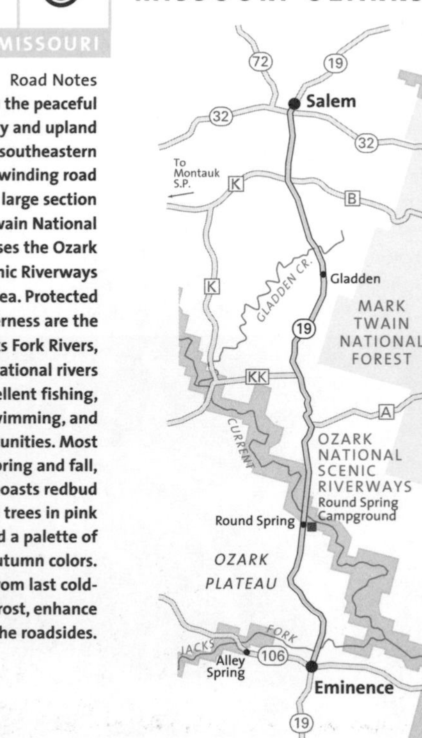

From Salem, seat of Dent County, head south past the courthouse (on your left) on Route 19. The first several miles envelop you in the big, undulant pastures typical of the region. Roads at four and seven miles lead east to the Salem and Potosi Districts of the 1.5-million-acre Mark Twain National Forest (573.364.4621). If you take a right turn off Route 19 at the road at four miles, you'll be on your way west to Montauk State Park (573.548.2201), where seven cold springs form the headwaters of the Current River, which is regularly stocked with rainbow trout. The park has campsites, motel rooms, and cabins.

Back on Route 19 about ten miles from Salem, the wide, green fields begin yielding to thick forests. Cross Gladden Creek and continue on the windy road through shadowed glens and grassy meadows. A brief stretch of mobile homes and shacks gives way to woods and long views of the misty blue-green Ozarks.

Traveling up now through the hardwood forest, Route 19 ascends the Ozark Plateau, an eroded tableland spreading from northern Arkansas to southern Missouri and west to northeastern Oklahoma. Continue south into the Ozark National Scenic Riverways (573.323.4236), a National Park Service unit protecting more than 134 miles of the Current and Jacks Fork Rivers. A smooth, fast-flowing river with deep pools, the Current offers excellent bass fishing and will be a memorable trip for novice canoeists and those who just want to float it on an inner tube.

Cross the sparkling Current River and make a left into the Round Spring campground and picnic area. Here you can explore one of the area's many caves, tucked into the high limestone bluff; park rangers offer a two-mile guided tour. Continue south as the road begins climbing again to good views of the valley and hills. In about three miles you pass a tract of virgin pine. About nine miles farther, a pullout lets you savor the southern panorama of forested mountains. To get into the heart of these mountains, stop at Coldwater Ranch (573.226.3723) for guided horseback rides.

Ozark National Scenic Riverways

Route 19 next descends steeply to the Jacks Fork River; just beyond is the town of Eminence, which has outfitters for river expeditions and other activities. Five miles west of Eminence along Route 106 in Alley Spring is a one-room schoolhouse and a historic roller mill that used to grind corn and wheat. If you have time to continue on, check out the town of Van Buren, 21 miles southeast of Eminence via Route 19 and U.S. 60; there are more canoe- and tube-rental outfitters here, and a few miles south of town is Big Spring, the nation's largest single-outlet spring. It discharges 227 million gallons of water per day into the Current River.

150 miles | 3 hours

NORTH SHORE LAKE SUPERIOR DRIVE

MINNESOTA

Road Notes

Skirting the jagged, glacier-worn Sawtooth Mountains, this winding road follows the rocky shoreline of Lake Superior, passing lighthouses and cascading streams and penetrating the only part of the continental United States where a boreal forest ecology thrives. The route is at its best from spring through fall. The seaway is frozen throughout winter, a sublime sight for off-season travelers.

Begin the drive in Duluth, and take in the eclectic mix of museums known as The Depot (218.727.8025), housed in a restored 1892 railway station. Head northeast on Route 61 (the old one, not the four-lane expressway). About four miles beyond downtown, at Lester River, walks, overlooks, and stairways reveal the lake's immensity.

Grand Marais

Beyond Two Harbors, the road climbs, twists, and tunnels through Silver Cliff and Lafayette Bluff. Ancient volcanoes created the North Shore's bedrock, which was then sculpted by the same glaciers that carved out the Great Lakes. The centerpiece of Gooseberry Falls State Park (218.834.3855) – the first of eight extraordinary state parks along the drive – is a stunning cascade that tumbles into Lake Superior.

The road continues east to Split Rock Lighthouse State Park (218.226.6377), and its restored 1910 lighthouse. The Split Rock History Center (218.226.6372) has exhibits on shipwrecks and commercial lake fishing. Beyond Silver Bay, Tettegouche State Park (218.226.6365) has 17 miles of trails.

Continue on to Superior National Forest – home to moose, wolves, black bears, and loons – and then through Lutsen to Cascade River State Park (218.387.3053).

About five miles ahead is Grand Marais and the beginning of the most magnificent stretch of this drive. A sense of remoteness envelops the road as it continues deeper into the realm of the early fur trappers and missionaries. Just past the second intersection with Route 14, the Moose Area sign marks one of the best spots to see these impressive animals.

The road continues through Hovland and enters the Grand Portage Indian Reservation, home of the Ojibwa. Regional lore is recounted at Grand Portage National Monument (218.387.2788).

Beyond Grand Portage, the road climbs to a crest near 1,348-foot Mount Josephine. From a scenic overlook take in superb views of the lake, the Susie Islands, and Wauswaugoning Bay. The drive continues across the international border into Canada, where it officially ends at Thunder Bay.

MN 116
MN 239

96 miles | 3 hours

CHERRY ORCHARDS DRIVE

MICHIGAN

Road Notes

Prolific cherry trees, handsome summer resort towns, stunning fall foliage, and Lake Michigan vistas highlight this eastern lakeshore drive. Once trod by Indians, French fur traders, and Jesuit missionaries, the route is most enjoyable from spring through fall.

From Cross Village, Route 119 begins a lovely 27-mile traverse that traces Michigan's rugged shoreline through an area known as *l'arbre croche*, the crooked tree, named by early voyageurs who used a lone gnarled fir on the shore as a landmark.

Just past a golf course is Harbor Springs, whose small downtown has a pleasant cluster of shops and restaurants. Nearby, Thorne Swift Nature Preserve (616.526.6401) offers a sampling of dunes, wetlands, and stands of trees. Route 119 wends southeast around Petoskey State Park (616.347.2311) and then ends. Continue west on U.S. 31 to Bay View, a charming Victorian town overlooking the bay. In Petoskey an exhibit at the Little Traverse History Museum (616.347.2620) honors Ernest Hemingway, who spent 20 summers in the area.

When you see the tip of Lake Charlevoix, you'll know the community of Charlevoix is a short distance ahead. Hop aboard the two-and-a-quarter-hour ferry ride to Beaver Island (616.448.2254), in Lake Michigan, where you'll find sandy beaches, hiking trails, and the Marine Museum (616.448.2254).

As U.S. 31 continues south, the woods give way to rolling farmland and panoramic views of Grand Traverse Bay and the forested hills of Leelanau Peninsula. Just before Atwood there are groves of cherry trees.

Charlevoix Lighthouse

North of the town of Torch Lake, look for Barnes County Park, located west on Barnes Park Road, with its secluded beach on Grand Traverse Bay. Get a close-up view of Torch Lake – once fished at night by Native Americans – by detouring east from U.S. 31 onto Barnes Road, about three miles south of town. Veer right on West Torch Lake Drive and follow it to Campbell Road, back to U.S. 31. An M-DOT Roadside Park 2.5 miles south offers a spacious picnic spot at Birch Lake.

Detour at the lakeside resort town of Traverse City onto Route 37, which meanders north through the nation's greatest concentration of cherry trees, to the 1870 Old Mission Light, located just south of the 45th parallel – halfway between the Equator and the North Pole.

MI 112
MI 238

53 miles | 1 hour

GREAT RIVER ROAD

WISCONSIN

Road Notes

Squeezing between steep, lush bluffs and the Mississippi River, this segment of the Great River Road (Route 35) passes through river towns dating back to before the days of steamboats and Mark Twain. The drive is at its most scenic during fall foliage.

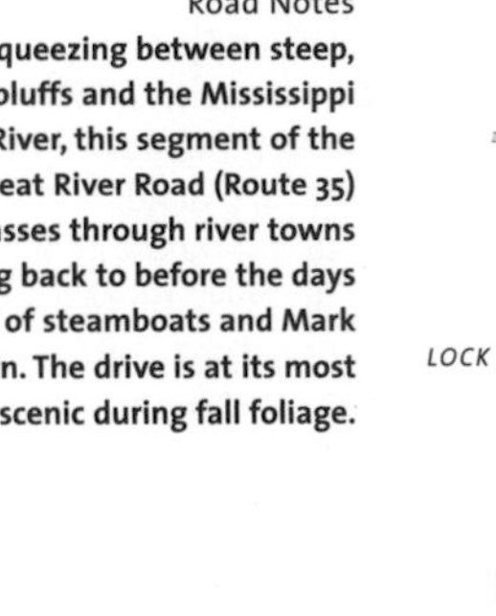

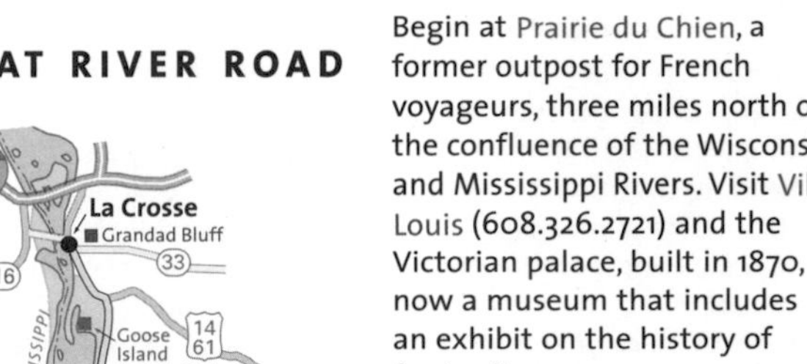

Begin at Prairie du Chien, a former outpost for French voyageurs, three miles north of the confluence of the Wisconsin and Mississippi Rivers. Visit Villa Louis (608.326.2721) and the Victorian palace, built in 1870, now a museum that includes an exhibit on the history of fur trading.

Wisconsin River Valley, near Prairie du Chien

Outside city limits, Route 35 wanders through cornfields and dairy country. About five miles from the city, it wraps around high sandstone bluffs – forested with sumacs, sugar maples, and oaks. After about three miles the Mississippi appears, dotted with wooded islands that create a maze of marshes and ponds. The rich bottomland is home to a wide variety of birds, mammals, and fish species. Protected by the Upper Mississippi River National Wildlife and Fish Refuge (507.452.4232), it stretches 260 miles from Wabasha, Minnesota to Rock Island, Illinois.

About six miles north, Lock and Dam Number 9 creates a beautiful pool that edges close to the bluffs, with the road snaking between. Similar pools to the north make this a virtually continuous lakeside drive.

Over the next 40 miles, Route 35 passes through a string of fishing villages, including Ferryville, perhaps the nation's longest one-street village, and De Soto, named for the Spanish explorer who crossed the Mississippi in the 1540s. Further up is Victory, site of the Battle of Bad Axe, which ended the Black Hawk War.

Genoa, seven miles north of Victory, was renamed in 1868 by Italian settlers, though the town little resembles its Mediterranean namesake. Just south is Lock and Dam Number 8, with an informative wayside park. About three miles north of Genoa, Old Settlers Overlook yields a breathtaking view of the river from atop a 500-foot bluff.

The road continues through the town of Stoddard, with a river beach at Stoddard Park, and by Goose Island County Park (608.785.9770), a recreational area on several islands. Five miles north is La Crosse, at the confluence of the La Crosse, Black, and Mississippi Rivers, considered one of Wisconsin's loveliest cities. Named by French settlers for a Winnebago Indian game, La Crosse is notable for its startling topography. (Buffalo Bill Cody found it so appealing that he bought part of Barron's Island.) For a taste of older days, catch a ride on a paddle wheeler, or visit the Italianate Hixon House (608.782.1980), preserved exactly as it was in the 1880s. Or take in the valley view (which looks on three states) from atop 600-foot-tall Grandad Bluff.

WI 174
WI 248

OH 142
OH 243

48 miles	2 hours

OHIO

COVERED BRIDGE SCENIC BYWAY

Road Notes

The route traverses a pastoral corner of southeastern Ohio through Wayne National Forest, alternately snaking along the muddy Little Muskingum River and climbing onto steep, forested bluffs. Along the way are tiny towns, century-old covered bridges, and weathered barns. The drive is best from spring through fall; heavy snows may close the road in winter.

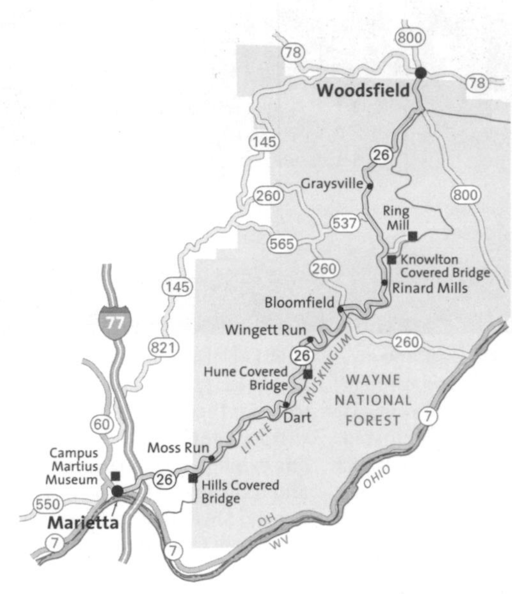

Begin the drive at Marietta, site of the first permanent organized settlement in the Northwest Territory. After studying outpost history at the Campus Martius Museum (740.373.3750), a modern building that incorporates part of the original fort, head north on Route 26 through the city's outskirts.

About four miles ahead, the road twists along a wooded ridge overlooking hilly fields, deep hollows, and tree-covered highlands, then descends to the Little Muskingum valley floor. Along the river's floodplain are small corn and hay fields and some of the nation's oldest oil wells.

Detour a half mile east on Route 333 to Hills Covered Bridge Built in 1878, it's one of more than 2,000 bridges – covered to protect the main structural timbers from inclement weather – that once spanned Ohio's rivers.

Back on Route 26, the Little Muskingum River soon appears on the right, in the shade of sycamores, box elders, and silver maples. The river's name is a Native American word meaning "muddy river." Popular in spring and fall with canoeists, the river lures anglers with more than 40 species of fish.

The drive continues along the river valley, rising occasionally to traverse bluffs and winding through small towns. Watch for Hune Covered Bridge, built in 1879. Cross it to hike a portion of the North Country National Scenic Trail, which one day will link New York and North Dakota.

After Route 26 leaves the river, beyond Rinard Mills, look for Knowlton Covered Bridge, built in 1887 and set in a tangle of wildflowers and native grasses. Three miles east on gravel Route 68 is Ring Mill, a historic house and former mill in use between 1846 and 1921, with a lovely riverside park. Back on Route 26, continue through hilly farm country. At the junction with Route 800, head north three miles to Woodsfield, a quiet little town at the end of the drive.

Buckeye Furnace Bridge

KY 100
KY 237

30 miles	1 hour

KENTUCKY

KENTUCKY HEARTLAND

Road Notes

This rolling rural drive follows a former buffalo trace – a pathway regularly used by the great beasts, which were exterminated from this part of the country even before they vanished from the plains – and an early 19th-century Shaker toll road. The route then traverses Kentucky's famed bluegrass region and the rugged terrain of the Kentucky River Gorge.

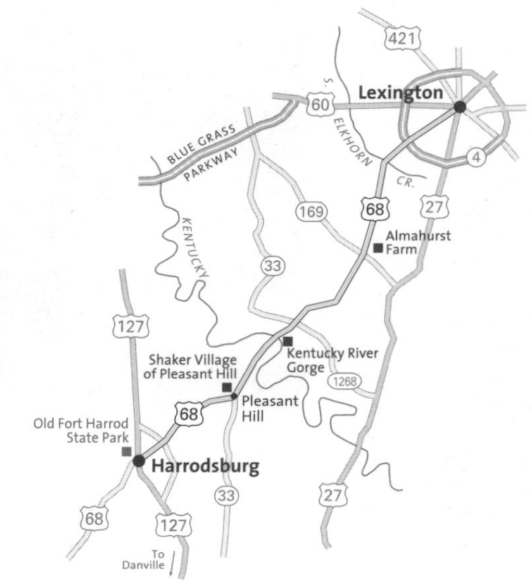

Begin the drive in Lexington, home of the Kentucky Horse Park (800.568.8813), which features two museums and an array of annual equestrian events. Head south from downtown on South Broadway (U.S. 68). Soon after passing South Elkhorn Creek, urban development yields to modest plots of burley tobacco and lush pastures dotted with cows and hay bales.

The most prominent feature of this region is its miles of black-and-white fences, behind which thoroughbred horses graze in manicured meadows. This is the heart of Kentucky Bluegrass country, where the world's finest racing stock is bred. One of the most famous horse farms along the route is Almahurst Farm, ten miles outside of Lexington, which can be recognized by its cream-colored barns trimmed in forest green and burgundy. Beyond the farm, U.S. 68 winds past more horse farms, roadside stands, and weather-beaten tobacco barns.

Several miles after entering Jessamine County, the drive begins its descent into a narrow side valley of the Kentucky River Gorge. After 1.5 miles, the road crosses the Brooklyn Bridge, which spans the Kentucky River; from the bridge there's a fabulous view of the river's 300-foot-high limestone palisades. After several miles the land opens up into rough, rolling farmland.

Soon the buildings of the Shaker Village of Pleasant Hill (606.734.5411) appear. Although the colony effectively disbanded in 1910, many of the gray and pastel-colored Shaker buildings have been restored and are open for tours. Savor traditional Kentucky fare in the excellent dining hall of the Trustees Office.

The drive continues another seven miles, past more rolling pastureland, groves of walnut and oak trees, and antebellum mansions, before ending in Harrodsburg. Kentucky's oldest permanent settlement began as a fenced village in 1775, built to protect settlers from hostile Native Americans. A reproduction of the fort can be seen at Old Fort Harrod State Park (606.734.3314), near the original site.

From Harrodsburg, return to Lexington on U.S. 68 or take U.S. 127 to Danville, another fine old Kentucky town.

Bluegrass country, Lexington

MS 118
MS 239

270 miles	1–2 days

MISSISSIPPI

NATCHEZ TRACE PARKWAY

Road Notes

This two-lane parkway, administered by the National Park Service, parallels the original Natchez Trace – one of the United States' most famous frontier trails. From buffalo paths used by prehistoric hunters, the trace evolved into a series of Native American trails later trod by French and Spanish trappers, traders, missionaries, and soldiers – not to mention a few cutthroats and vagabonds. The parkway, in its entirety, stretches for 445 miles from Nashville, Tennessee, to Natchez, Mississippi. This drive begins at the Natchez Trace Parkway Visitor Center (mile 270) and goes south to Natchez (mile 0). Mileposts record mileages in reverse.

Begin at the Natchez Trace Parkway Visitor Center (800.305.7417), which offers exhibits and an audiovisual presentation about the trace.

The Chickasaw Village (mile 261.8) marks the former Native American settlement and provides interpretations of Chickasaw life. The open country along this part of the drive, called the Black Belt for the color of its soil, is the remnant of a vast prairie. Enter an oak, hickory, and pine woods that is part of the Tombigbee National Forest (601.285.3264). Take a stretch under the fragrant pines at magical Witch Dance before heading south, past Bynum Mounds – remains of the prehistoric culture of the Mound Builders.

The next 40 miles offer a changing landscape of farms, pastureland, and forests. Jeff Busby Site (mile 193.1) has the only services along the drive and offers a view from 603-foot Little Mountain. From here, the trace soon crosses a bottomland of shrubs, which turns swampy for the next few miles, through Cole Creek and River Bend (mile 122.6). Just beyond, a boardwalk trail penetrates the eerie forest of bald cypress and tupelo at Cypress Swamp. The parkway follows the scenic Ross Barnett Reservoir for eight miles before reaching the Mississippi Crafts Center at Ridgeland (601.856.7546). Further south, the parkway is interrupted; detour on I-55 to I-220 south to I-20 west toward Vicksburg, then follow signs to rejoin the trace.

Mississippi's gracious capital, Jackson (601.960.1891), offers a walking tour of its historic downtown, which features stunning gardens and excellent museums.

Crossing Big Bayou Pierre four times, you get a view of its cultivated floodplain before reaching peaceful Mangum Site and Grindstone Ford. Now the parkway sweeps south past farms and wetlands, passing the Sunken Trace, a short trail along an eroded portion of the old trace, at mile 41.5. Here, the road begins to climb a ridge forested with hardwood and pine. The only inn remaining on the trace, Mount Locust (mile 15.5), built in 1810, is one of the oldest structures in the state. The parkway winds to its current southern terminus two miles farther on, when it intersects U.S. 61. Seven miles southwest lies Natchez (800.647.6724), an elegant vestige of the Old South containing a wealth of historic homes and estates.

Longwood Estate, Natchez

103 miles | 4 hours

FLORIDA PANHANDLE SCENIC DRIVE

FLORIDA

Road Notes

Lush vegetation, Old World architecture, dazzling white sand, emerald waters, and ultrakitsch await the visitor to Florida's Panhandle, which stretches 200 miles between Tallahassee and the Alabama border along the Gulf of Mexico. This drive hugs the Gulf shore from Pensacola to Panama City, meandering through live oak thickets and the ubiquitous tourist strips. Short of a hurricane, inclement weather is rare. The sun usually blazes, and a swimsuit is as much a necessity as a toothbrush.

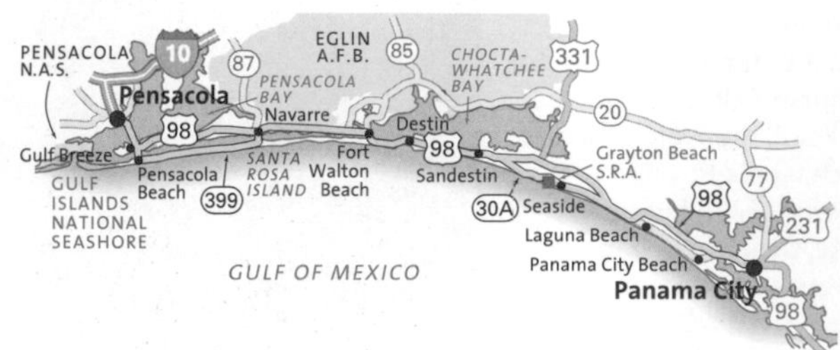

Begin the drive in Pensacola, site of the National Museum of Naval Aviation (800.327.5002), which has Skylab on display as well as an IMAX theater. The Pensacola Historical Museum (850.433.1559) has exhibits explaining why this city has flown five different flags. Bougainvillea-draped Seville Square Historic District, one of three, reflects a bit of the Old South's rural charm, and Historic Pensacola Village includes several fine buildings open to the public: The 1815 French Creole-style Lavalle House; Dorr House, a Greek Revival affair built in 1871; and the unpretentious Julee Cottage, owned by a free black woman in the early 1800s. In this historic district you'll also find a collection of oddities on the third floor of the T. T. Wentworth, Jr. Florida State Museum (850.595.5990), including stuffed Kodiak bears, a petrified cat, and a size 37 shoe.

Head east on Main Street (Bayfront Parkway / U. S. 98), past Pensacola Harbor and Pensacola Bay to where the road crosses three-mile-long Pensacola Bay Bridge heading out to Gulf Breeze. Here the road forks. You can continue east on U. S. 98 through the Naval Live Oaks Area, a trail-laced thicket of live oaks purchased in 1828 by the federal government to preserve the trees. The area is part of the 150-mile-long Gulf Islands National Seashore (850.934.2600). Another option is to pick up Route 399 and cross the Bob Sikes Bridge – watch for the much-loved '50s-era neon welcome sign – to Santa Rosa Island, a barrier island that is also part of the national seashore and offers unspoiled miles of live oaks, sea oats, and billowing sand dunes. The Blackbird Marsh Nature Trail passes through a teeming ecosystem of exotic flora and fauna, including blue herons.

Grayton Beach State Recreation Area

The two roads reconvene in the town of Navarre, the beginning of a stretch of hotels, amusement parks, and condominiums that continues to Panama City. Beyond the town of Fort Walton Beach, U. S. 98 returns to Santa Rosa Island and a recreation area on Choctawatchee Bay, which offers swimming and boating. The road cuts through a scenic stretch of pine-dotted dunes with Gulf vistas before crossing the mouth of the Choctawatchee Bay and entering the town of Destin, immensely popular with charter-fishing enthusiasts.

Continue east through pine thickets and urban development; small side streets lead to lovely sandy beaches. Three miles east of Sandestin, detour onto Route 30A, a secondary road that angles 20 miles past lily-dotted lakes, pine thickets, and tiny towns. Highlights include Grayton Beach State Recreation Area (850.231.4210) and the resort village of Seaside.

About nine miles beyond Seaside, Route 30A joins U. S. 98 for the last brassy stretch to Panama City and its 27 miles of sandy beaches.

FL 82
FL 234

81 miles | 2 hours

SEA ISLANDS

GEORGIA

Road Notes

Georgia's shoreline is so interlaced with marshes, swamps, mudflats, and sloughs that no single coastal road can reveal all its beauty. The route that comes closest to the ideal is U. S. 17, which runs a few miles from the shore but winds through grassy tidal estuaries, pine thickets, and quaint shrimping villages. Traveling up the coast from Jekyll Island, this drive ends in Savannah, whose antebellum charm lingers in open squares, live oaks, and historic inns. Along the way, causeways and bridges branch off to a few of the state's "golden isles" – subtropical barrier islands where luxurious resorts jostle against salt marshes.

Begin the drive at Jekyll Island, purchased in 1886 by 50 business magnates – among them Rockefellers, Pulitzers, and Vanderbilts – to be used as their exclusive winter playground. Their sumptuous homes are in the Jekyll Island Historic District (912.635.2119).

Take Jekyll Island Causeway (Route 520), pick up U. S. 17, and head north across the Brunswick River to Brunswick, founded in 1771 and one of Georgia's largest ports. To the north and east of Brunswick lie the green and fecund environs of the Marshes of Glynn. The ground teems with crabs, shrimps, oysters, fish, and alligators. A short boardwalk at the marshes' Overlook Park (junction of U. S. 17 and Route 25) provides a good vantage on marsh life.

Three of Georgia's barrier islands cluster together just east of Brunswick: Little St. Simons, accessible only by boat, and St. Simons and Sea Island, a quick jaunt across the F. J. Torras Causeway. Just before the causeway is the Brunswick-Golden Isles Welcome Center (800.933.2627). At St. Simons Island, visit Fort Frederica National Monument (912.638.3639), an 18th-century town, now a scenic ruin. The hub of exclusive Sea Island is the Cloister (912.638.3611), a Mediterranean-style resort built in the 1920s.

Back on U. S. 17, continue for ten miles to Hofwyl-Broadfield Plantation State Historic Site (912.264.7333), dotted with camellias, magnolias, and ancient live oaks. Rice fields crossed with dikes and floodgates testify to the area's rich rice culture.

The drive continues across the flood delta of the Altamaha River, part of the 27,078-acre Altamaha State Waterfowl Management Area, a haven for herons, egrets, and other wading birds. On the river's north bank is Darien, founded in 1736 and renowned for its annual April blessing of the shrimp fleet. The road to the right, immediately after the Darien Welcome Center (912.437.6684), leads to Fort King George State Historic Site (912.437.4770), a reconstruction of the British Empire's southernmost continental North American outpost.

St. Simons Island Lighthouse, Little St. Simons

From Darien, continue on U. S. 17 through more coastal plain scenery. Or follow Route 99, a country road that passes Thicket, with its ruins of a sugar mill and a rum distillery. Route 99 rejoins U. S. 17 at Eulonia. Eight miles farther, detour seven miles east on Harris Neck Road to Harris Neck National Wildlife Refuge (912.652.4415), where as many as 30,000 wading birds congregate in late summer and fall. Back on U. S. 17, continue to the town of Midway and the Midway Museum (912.884.5837), filled with colonial furnishings and documents. The drive ends 30 miles farther, in Savannah, the embodiment of classic southern charm.

GA 86
GA 234

80 miles | 2 hours

EASTERN SHORE

MARYLAND

Road Notes

Separating the Chesapeake Bay and the Atlantic Ocean, the peninsula portion of Maryland is a land of broad tidal rivers, tranquil farmlands, and historic manors. Famous for its oysters, crabs, and clams, the Eastern Shore's shellfish abundance has in recent years been threatened with depletion, prompting government intervention. Consequently, it is now illegal to harvest oysters except from wooden boats called skipjacks – which explains why these rather antiquated vessels are still in use. The route begins in Chesapeake City and terminates at Dogwood Harbor on Tilghman Island, where the skipjack fleet docks.

Chesapeake Bay

Begin the drive in Chesapeake City, a handsomely restored 19th-century town near the western end of the Chesapeake and Delaware Canal, built in 1829. The enormous waterwheel used through the early 1900s to regulate water levels is on view in the Old Lock Pump House (410.885.5621). The drive south along Route 213 passes by fields of corn and soybeans, two staples of the Delmarva (Delaware, Maryland, Virginia) Peninsula. Within the first 15 miles, the route crosses the Bohemia and Sassafras Rivers, which, during the 1700s, were indispensable thoroughfares for the great tobacco plantations of the area.

Continue to Chestertown, founded in 1706, with its stately Georgian and gaily painted Victorian homes, and some fine examples of pre-revolutionary architecture. Afternoon tea is served at the White Swan Tavern B&B (410.778.2300) on High Street. Just a mile past its intersection with U. S. 50, Route 213 ends at Wye Mills (410.827.6909), a 17th-century waterpowered gristmill. South of the mill, on Route 662, is 400-year-old Wye Oak, said to be the country's largest white oak tree.

Continue south on U. S. 50 toward Easton, where the 1684 Third Haven Friends Meeting House (410.822.0293) offers a glimpse of the town's Quaker heritage. Nearby, at the mouth of the Wye River, is Wye House (private), once the seat of a vast plantation where the abolitionist Frederick Douglass spent his boyhood as a slave. Near Easton, turn right onto Route 322, then right again onto Route 33 east and continue for 11 miles to St. Michaels, a charming harbor town with tidy inns, restaurants, and the excellent Chesapeake Bay Maritime Museum (410.745.2916), dedicated to the history and workaday lore of the bay. The museum even has a lighthouse to explore.

Thirteen miles past St. Michaels, a tiny bridge leads over Knapps Narrows to Tilghman Island, home for centuries to hardy individuals who harvest the bay's bounty. Less than a half mile from the bridge, turn left on Dogwood Harbor Road to view Chesapeake Bay skipjacks, wooden sailing vessels ranging from 25 to 60 feet in length, which are usually docked here. The venerable craft are used in the local oyster industry.

At the fork, 2.5 miles farther on, bear right for a view of the bay along Black Walnut Point Road. The road ends in a half mile, at the gate of the Black Walnut Point Inn (410.886.2452), one of the most secluded B&Bs on the Eastern Shore.

MD 106
MD 238

39 miles | 1 hour

FINGER LAKES DRIVE

NEW YORK

NY 132
NY 241

Road Notes

Few topographical features are more aptly named than the Finger Lakes, which fan across the Allegheny Plateau like the outstretched digits of an enormous hand. This drive winds along the shoreline of the longest of them, 40-mile Cayuga Lake, where pleasant towns and fine wineries accent the countryside. Late spring through mid-fall the drive is best – wineries harvest at the end of summer.

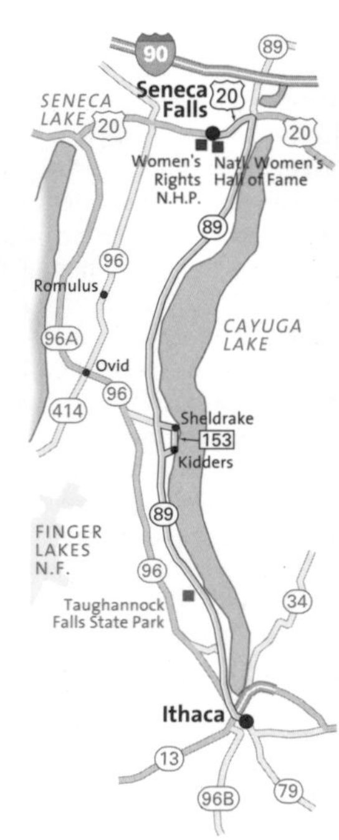

Begin in Ithaca, at the southern end of Cayuga Lake. As Route 89 heads north it first winds past Ithaca's outlying suburbs before cutting through Taughannock Falls State Park (607.387.6739), ten miles outside town. In addition to the falls, there are boat launches and rentals and a beach. At 215 feet, Taughannock is higher than Niagara, but there's no roaring cascade. The narrow white ribbon of water changes seasonally, needling down into a cold, green pool at the center of a vast natural amphitheater of shale.

Continue north past the falls, where Route 89 passes through tranquil lakeside farmland, with occasional views of Cayuga Lake and its eastern shore. The Finger Lakes region ranks as the largest wine-producing area in the East, and almost a dozen wineries are located just off the road here. In fact, this leg of Route 89 has been dubbed the Cayuga Wine Trail. Most of the wineries offer tours and on-site purchasing. Several roadside apiaries also sell honey.

For a pleasant side trip with outstanding lake views, turn right eight or nine miles north of Taughannock Falls onto Deerlick Springs Road, then left on Route 153, which winds through the small towns of Kidders and Sheldrake. Other than a few restaurants and B&Bs, the route is uncommercialized, passing gracious Victorian homes framed by big weeping willows whose branches drape out across the water. The shore road, now called Weyers Point Road, loops up and rejoins Route 89 after 4.5 miles, but the panoramas of the lake continue to the east. To the west, farmlands, orchards, and the occasional small town occupy the gently rising pillow of land that reaches across to the shores of Seneca Lake. Two of the rural communities here, Ovid and Romulus, typify the local penchant in the early 1800s for naming towns after people and places of classical antiquity.

Taughannock Falls State Park

The road hugs Cayuga Lake quite closely along much of the northern half of the route and ends in Seneca Falls, just west of Cayuga Lake on U. S. 20. Seneca Falls is home to several archives of women's history. Here, in the mid-19th century, Elizabeth Cady Stanton and Lucretia Mott laid the groundwork for the modern feminist movement by organizing the 1848 Women's Rights Convention in Declaration Park. The Elizabeth Cady Stanton House is preserved in the Women's Rights National Historical Park (315.568.2991). Exhibits at the National Women's Hall of Fame (315.568.8060) tell the stories of distinguished American women. And the Seneca Falls Historical Society (315.568.8412), a Queen Anne mansion, contains original documents of feminism's first wave.

92 miles | 2½ hours

THE ADIRONDACKS

NEW YORK

NY 132
NY 241

Road Notes

A favorite retreat of mobsters and millionaires alike, the Adirondack Mountains are among the Northeast's last great wildernesses, with 42 peaks rising higher than 4,000 feet. At the heart of the region is the six-million-acre Adirondack Park, a harmonious blending of pristine lakes, dense forests, and picturesque villages. Turn-of-the-century industrialists built great camps as summer retreats on the shores of some of the more remote lakes. In fall, the foliage is magnificent. Roads can be extremely icy during winter storms, and visibility poor at higher elevations in snow and fog.

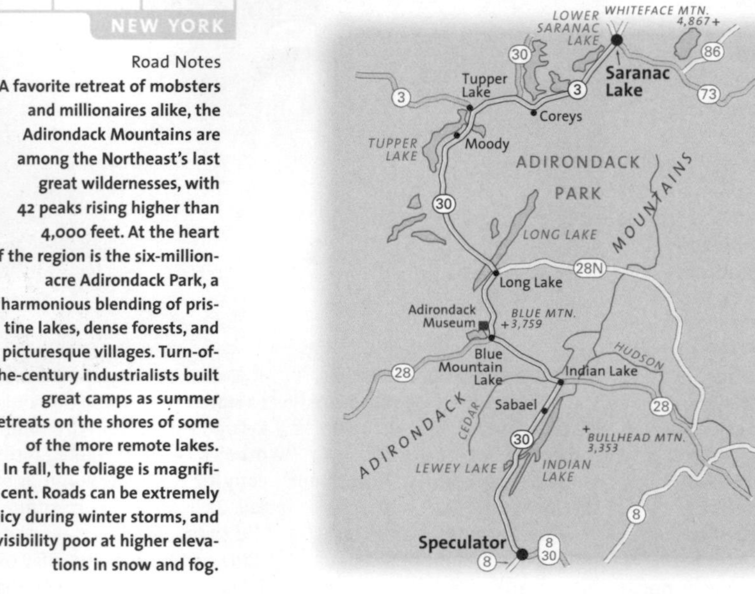

Begin at the intersection of Routes 8 and 30 in the village of Speculator, a hunting, fishing, and skiing center. Along Route 30 north, the mountains rise gradually and the forests of maple, beech, and birch explode with color in the fall. After 12 miles, just past Lewey Lake and the entrance to Lewey Lake Campground (518.457.2500), the road crosses a stream linking Lewey Lake with Indian Lake, which forms part of the Hudson River's headwaters. Following along the shore of Indian Lake, views of the distant peaks of the northern Adirondacks open up. After seven miles, a scenic turnoff takes in 3,353-foot Bullhead Mountain and surrounding peaks.

A mile past the turnoff, make a left at the T-junction in Indian Lake and continue on Route 30 across the Cedar River. Thirteen miles past Indian Lake is the small resort town of Blue Mountain Lake, home to a shop that sells the wooden slat chairs named for the region. Turn right and continue on Route 30. Ahead is the lake from which the town takes its name and, on the right, Blue Mountain itself. Its 3,759-foot summit is accessible by a 2.2-mile trail that begins about a mile north of town. Before the trailhead is the Adirondack Museum (518.352.7311), one of the country's finest regional museums, whose collection includes antique guideboats, furniture, and mementos of early resort life.

Town of Saranac Lake, Lower Saranac Lake

From the museum, the road descends through forests to Long Lake, which offers excellent trout fishing. Turn left at the town of Long Lake and continue on Route 30. After a 20-mile drive through the forest, follow Route 30/3 through the town of Tupper Lake, notable for its early 20th-century facades. As the road crests a hill on the east side of town, 4,867-foot Whiteface Mountain, one of the highest peaks in the Adirondacks, looms ahead.

Bear right onto Route 3 about five miles past Tupper Lake and follow a forested, mountainous road that opens onto spectacular views of Lower Saranac Lake. Just beyond is the town of Saranac Lake, where gingerbread cottages line the shore. Famous a century ago for its tuberculosis sanatorium, the town is now the largest community in the Adirondack Park and a hub for outdoor recreation. The drive ends at the intersection of Routes 3 and 86.

56 miles | 2 hours

LOWER CONNECTICUT VALLEY

CONNECTICUT

CT 78
CT 233

Road Notes

The towns and harbors along the lower reaches of the Connecticut River have hummed with activity for more than 300 years – but the valley still possesses many lovely undeveloped stretches. This drive explores the natural and human-made environments that inspired the Nature Conservancy to designate the tidelands of the Connecticut River one of the hemisphere's "last great places." The route is most scenic from May through October.

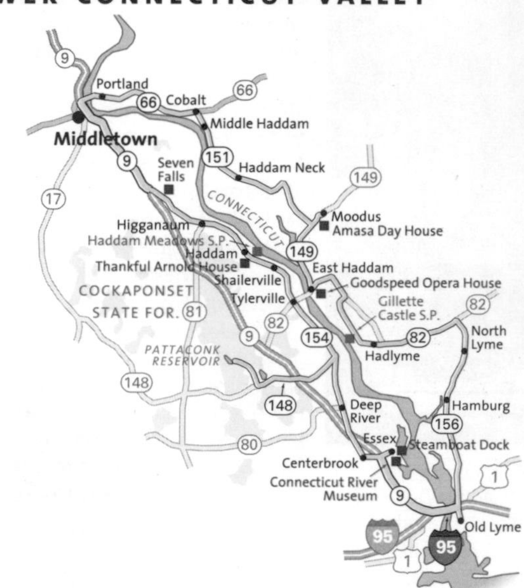

Begin in Middletown, home to Wesleyan University (860.685.2000), at the junction of Routes 9 and 66. Head east on Route 66 across the river into Portland, once a brownstone quarrying center. Five miles farther, in the village of Cobalt, turn right on Route 151 and head south for eight miles, then east on 149 to Moodus, where the 1816 Amasa Day House (860.873.8144) boasts federal and Empire furnishings.

Connecticut River Museum, Essex

Backtrack and head south on Route 149, to East Haddam, where musical performances and scheduled tours are offered at the Victorian Goodspeed Opera House (860.873.8668). From the junction of Routes 149 and 82 in East Haddam, head east on 82 to Route 156. Head south to the township of Old Lyme, once a vital shipbuilding hub and inspiration to painters of the American Barbizon school. South over the Connecticut River on I-95, take the first exit to Route 9, and the second exit off 9 to Route 154.

One mile north is Essex, settled in 1690. The first Connecticut warship, the *Oliver Cromwell*, was built here in 1775. Steamboat Dock, built in 1640 at the end of Main Street, is New England's oldest continuously operating wharf. Turn off onto Route 9 and follow signs past the 1776 Griswold Inn (860.767.1776), with its famed Tap Room, to the historic waterfront and the Connecticut River Museum (860.767.8269), home of a reproduction of the 1775 *American Turtle*, the first submarine.

North on Route 154, past the junction with Route 9, is the Essex Steam Train & Riverboat Ride (860.767.0103). Further north, detour west on Route 148 for about five miles, then right on Cedar Lake Road to Pattaconk Reservoir and the 16,000-acre Cockaponset State Forest (860.345.8521), which boasts a number of New England's few tulip trees. Continue north on Route 154 to Haddam, and turn left at Walkley Hill Road to visit the 1794 Thankful Arnold House (860.345.2400), with its delightful vegetable and herb gardens. Return to Route 154 and continue north to Haddam Meadows State Park, a meadowland in the river's floodplain. The scenic portion of Route 154 ends some four miles ahead, at a pretty waterfall in Seven Falls State Highway Park. Just past the falls on the left, the stone slabs of Bible Rock are poised on edge like an open book. About a mile from the park is an entrance to Route 9 northwest back toward Middletown.

120 miles | 1 day

THE BERKSHIRES

MASSACHUSETTS

Road Notes

The Berkshire Hills of Massachusetts have long been a favorite rustic retreat – and the city dwellers who summer here have made them a major venue for art, music, and dance. This drive takes in Herman Melville's home and the Boston Symphony Orchestra, and joins Shaker simplicity with Gilded Age grandeur. The best (though busiest) times of year to tour the Berkshires are fall foliage season and summer; reserve accommodations well in advance if visiting during Tanglewood or other festivals.

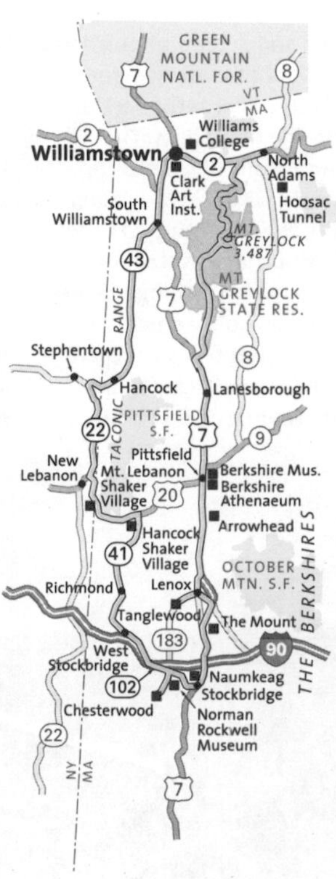

Start at Williamstown (413.458.9077), home to the Sterling and Francine Clark Art Institute (413.458.9545), renowned for its collection of paintings by American masters and French Impressionists. The Williams College Museum of Art (413.597.2429) highlights American art, while the Chapin Library of Rare Books, on the college grounds, contains Revolutionary War-era documents.

Head south on U.S. 7 and Massachusetts 43, along the Green River West Branch. Dipping into New York State, the route pushes south on New York 22 to U.S. 20. You're now in Shaker country. Mount Lebanon Shaker Village (518.794.9500) looks much as it did in the 19th century. Back over the border in Massachusetts, the fully restored Hancock Shaker Village (413.443.0188) is a testament to Shaker ingenuity.

Take Massachusetts 41/102/183 south to the Norman Rockwell Museum (413.298.4100). Tour guides, some of whom modeled for America's favorite illustrator as children, regale visitors with anecdotal tidbits. Down the road, turn onto Mohawk Lake Road for Chesterwood (413.298.3579), the summer home of sculptor Daniel Chester French. In the high-ceilinged studio, French labored over his greatest work, the Lincoln Memorial.

Congregation Church, Williamstown

Backtrack to Massachusetts 102 and head east into Stockbridge (413.298.5200), Rockwell's inspiration, and the setting for Arlo Guthrie's classic song, "Alice's Restaurant." Nearby is the shingle-style mansion Naumkeag (413.298.3239), designed by Stanford White. Its stunning gardens by Fletcher Steele were 30 years in the making.

Continue north on U.S. 7 toward Lenox, to the junction of Massachusetts 7A and The Mount (413.637.1899). Designed by novelist Edith Wharton, this turn-of-the-century mansion reflects the author's love of balance and symmetry. In the resort town of Lenox (413.637.3646), head out West Street (Massachusetts 183) to Tanglewood (413.637.1600), the summer home of the Boston Symphony Orchestra.

Further north on U.S. 7 is the turn for Arrowhead (413.442.1793), Herman Melville's home from 1850 to 1863. The classic *Moby Dick* was written in the upstairs room. Further north on U.S. 7, in Pittsfield (413.443.9186), the Herman Melville Memorial Room in the Berkshire Athenaeum (413.499.9486) contains a fine collection of his personal memorabilia. The Berkshire Museum (413.443.7171) features paintings by American masters such as Albert Bierstadt.

At Lanesborough, turn right onto North Main Street for Mount Greylock State Reservation (413.499.4262) and the state's highest peak. An observation tower offers views of the Berkshire Valley and the Taconic Range. Descend Mount Greylock via scenic Notch Road, then take Massachusetts 2 east to Western Gateway Heritage State Park (413.663.8059). Here, an exhibit recounts the dramatic story of the nearby Hoosac Tunnel. Completed in 1875, the 25,000-foot engineering feat cost \$20 million and almost 200 lives.

Return to Williamstown on Route 2, the "Mohawk Trail," which follows the trek made by Native Americans between the lush Connecticut and Hudson River Valleys.

MA 110

MA 238

130 miles | ½–1 day

WHITE MOUNTAINS SCENIC DRIVE

NEW HAMPSHIRE

Road Notes

New Hampshire's White Mountains, named for the white granite embedded in the hills, are the rooftop of New England and the centerpiece of the 800,000-acre White Mountain National Forest. Although most tourists (skiers excepted) explore this lofty realm in spring, summer, and fall, roads are generally well maintained throughout the year. Travel early in the day – and on weekdays in summer – to avoid heavy traffic that can slow down driving on popular routes such as the Kancamagus Highway. Weekends in fall foliage season attract a lot of traffic to the mountains, and winter is a season of famously unpredictable weather.

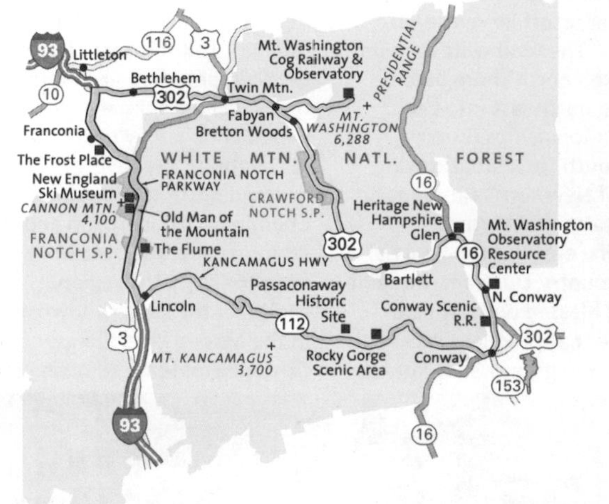

Frost Place, Franconia

Start at the junction of U.S. 302 and I-93, just south of Littleton. At Franconia, a narrow dirt road leads to the battered mailbox marking The Frost Place (603.823.5510), a simple white farmhouse where poet Robert Frost once lived. It's now a museum with first editions and Frost memorabilia.

South of town, I-93 merges with the nearly nine-mile Franconia Notch Parkway, cutting through Franconia Notch. On a clear day you can look far into Vermont and Maine from the top of 4,100-foot Cannon Mountain. An aerial tramway (603.823.5563) is the quickest way to the summit. The New England Ski Museum (603.823.7177), at the base of the mountain, traces the sport's history. Farther south, stop at Profile Lake for a great view of the natural stone formation known as the Old Man of the Mountain. Just ahead lies the Flume, a 180-million-year-old natural gorge whose granite walls rise up to 90 feet.

Just outside Lincoln, pick up the Kancamagus Highway, a National Forest Scenic Byway that meanders east for 37 miles through pristine wilderness and climbs to nearly 3,000 feet as it traverses the flank of Mount Kancamagus. The Swift River forms natural pools at the Rocky Gorge Scenic Area, a popular swimming spot.

Turn north on Route 16 to North Conway and check the weather conditions atop Mount Washington at the Mount Washington Observatory Resource Center (603.356.8345). Just north of the Route 16–U.S. 302 junction in Glen, Heritage New Hampshire (603.383.9776) reviews the state's history from 1634 to the present.

The six-mile stretch of U.S. 302 through Crawford Notch State Park offers spectacular views of the Presidential Range. In Bretton Woods, just beyond Crawford Notch, is the 1902 Mount Washington Hotel (800.258.0330). Modeled after a luxury cruise ship, it's the largest wooden building in New England.

With its rack rails and valiant little cog-driven locomotives, the nearby Mount Washington Cog Railway (800.922.8825) has been hauling passengers to the 6,288-foot summit since 1869. Only three miles long, the railway is also one of the steepest. Up top, you can visit Mount Washington Observatory museum, and on a clear day you can see forever – all the way to the ocean at Portland, Maine.

At the turn of the century, the pure air of Bethlehem (603.869.2151), farther west on U.S 302, made the town a popular destination for hay fever sufferers. The main street is lined with old hotels. Continue west on U.S. 302 to return to I-93.

NH 127

NH 240

100 miles | ½ day

ROUTE 100

VERMONT

Road Notes

Route 100 is the Main Street of Vermont's Green Mountains, running alongside the state's rugged spine from Massachusetts almost to Québec. This drive covers one of the most scenic portions of the route, terminating in Smugglers' Notch, where peregrine falcons nest beneath rugged thousand-foot cliffs. The drive is most scenic from late spring through mid-fall, with fall foliage peaking earlier in the north. Traffic can be heavy in high summer and foliage season.

Begin in Weston, considered one of Vermont's prettiest villages and home to Weston Playhouse (802.824.5288) and the Vermont Country Store (802.824.3184). Bear right 3.5 miles north of Weston and follow Route 100 for seven hilly miles into Ludlow, a former mill town turned into a lively agglomeration of shops and restaurants.

Continue on Route 100 back into rural Vermont. On the right, Lake Rescue soon comes into view, followed by Echo and Amherst Lakes – all strung together by the Black River. Continue for three miles, past the northern end of Amherst Lake and detour onto Route 100A for a two-mile side trip into tiny Plymouth Notch, where Calvin Coolidge became president. The hamlet's houses, barns, and old Coolidge-family store are now part of the President Calvin Coolidge State Historic Site (802.672.3773).

Stowe

Return to Route 100 and continue north along the Black River Valley, reaching U.S. 4 at West Bridgewater. The Ottauquechee River here once turned the wheels of Bridgewater's woolen mills. Route 100 and U.S. 4 merge along the river, climbing in elevation as they pass the Killington Ski Area (802.422.3333), which spans seven mountains.

When the routes diverge, bear right on Route 100, which enters a wooded stretch of mountainous terrain, with the northern section of the Green Mountain National Forest on the left. Continue north to Rochester, one of the loveliest towns along this stretch. The route passes through the steep-sided White River Valley to the Granville Reservation. Look to the left for lovely Moss Glen Falls, cascading down a sheer rock wall 1.4 miles into the reservation. Continue for three miles, to Route 100 and the Mad River Valley – more ski country.

In Irasville, detour left onto Route 17 to the Sugarbush and Mad River Glen Ski Areas. The 12-mile stretch of Route 100 between Waitsfield and Waterbury is largely farmland with fine mountain views.

Just a mile past the point where Route 100 crosses I-89 is one of Vermont's most popular attractions, Ben & Jerry's Ice Cream Factory (802.244.8687). Three miles beyond, at the Cold Hollow Cider Mill (802.244.8771), visitors can watch cider being made. Ten miles north of Waterbury is Stowe, a town long synonymous with skiing and the famous Trapp Family Lodge (802.253.8511). The tiny town is clustered around the 1833 Green Mountain Inn (802.253.7301). In the center of town, Route 108 leads to Mount Mansfield – at 4,393 feet, the highest point in Vermont and a skiing center, with Stowe Mountain Resort and Smugglers Notch Ski Area. Smugglers Notch is a scenic natural pass that saw considerable action during Prohibition. Backtrack to I-89 to continue east or west.

VT 166

VT 281

NS 186
NS 249
PQ 184
PQ 250
AK 62
YT 177
AK 232
YT 253

CAPE BRETON

108 miles | 1–2 days

NOVA SCOTIA

Road Notes

The finest scenic drive in Canada's maritime provinces winds around Cape Breton's northern shores overlooking the Gulf of St. Lawrence, and climbs into the moody highlands of Cape Breton National Park – one of Canada's most magnificent wilderness areas. The route then follows the Atlantic coast to South Gut St. Ann's, site of North America's only Gaelic college.

Begin the drive in Baddeck, the adopted home of Alexander Graham Bell, one of the founders of the National Geographic Society. The Alexander Graham Bell National Historic Site (902.295.2069) presents an exciting, interactive walk through his world, and houses the most complete collection of his memorabilia, artifacts, and equipment. Drive a few miles west on Trans-Canada 105 to join the famous Cabot Trail – named for explorer John Cabot. Then head north to North East Margaree through the narrow wooded valley of the Middle River, a favorite among salmon and trout anglers. After about 32 kilometers, stop by the Margaree Salmon Museum (902.248.2848), housed in an old schoolhouse.

As the route winds north along the river valley to the coast, the landscape becomes more rugged, remote, and barren, and the communities become smaller and more scattered. Up the hill, in St. Joseph du Moine, stop by the whimsical Gallery La Bella Mona Lisa (902.224.2560), a fine collection of provincial folk art. At Chéticamp, gateway to the highlands, the landmark St. Peter's Church (1893) was built of stone from Chéticamp Island. The Acadian Museum (902.224.2170) features the local cottage industry – hooked rugs.

The moody highlands loom ahead at the entrance to Cape Breton Highlands National Park (902.224.2306, 902.285.2691), the rugged roof of Nova Scotia. To take advantage of pulloffs, detours, and serendipitous diversions, allow at least five hours for this 106-kilometer park drive. Among the highlights: The towering walls of Chéticamp Canyon, MacKenzie Mountain look-off, the ascent up 475-meter North Mountain (watch for moose), and the fishing villages and narrow, isolated beaches along the Atlantic coast. Drive on to the Ingonish area. Just outside town, Cape Smokey Lodge (902.285.2778) operates a chairlift up a 300-meter vertical slope to the top of Old Smokey Mountain. Continue south along the coast for about 80 kilometers to South Gut St. Ann's, settled by Highland Scots. The Gaelic College of Celtic Arts and Crafts (902.295.3411) has exhibits on Scottish history and culture and offers demonstrations of traditional weaving, music, and dance. The craft shop stocks nearly 300 tartans. Continue south on the Cabot Trail to return to Baddeck.

Cape Breton, Nova Scotia

EASTERN TOWNSHIPS

240 miles | 1–2 days

QUÉBEC

Road Notes

This drive begins in Montréal, the world's second largest French-speaking city, then heads through pastoral Montérégie into the region called either Cantons-de-l'Est, by French-speaking Quebecois, or the Eastern Townships, by Anglophones, of which there are several significant pockets – reflecting early 19th-century British settlement – in this part of Québec. Along the way, the route passes through picturesque wine country.

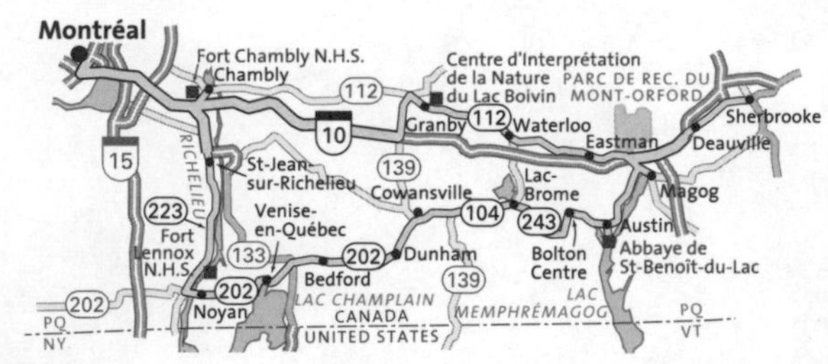

Begin in Montréal (800.363.7777), located on an island in the St. Lawrence River. The cosmopolitan city, founded by France as a missionary colony in 1642, retains a decidedly French flair. Adjacent to the hilltop Parc du Mont-Royal, designed by Frederick Law Olmsted, is the huge copper-domed Oratoire Saint-Joseph (514.733.8211), a popular religious shrine. The Biodôme de Montréal (514.868.3000), a unique environmental museum, re-creates four distinct ecosystems.

Head south on Route 10 across Pont Champlain. Exit at Chambly and continue through town to historic Chambly Canal, where keepers manually operate the old locks. Fort Chambly National Historic Site (514.658.1585) preserves the site of a 1665 French stockade, replaced in 1709 by a stone fortification. Proceed south on Route 223 through the Richelieu Valley. Just beyond Saint-Paul-de-l'Île-aux-Noix is the British fortification at Fort Lennox National Historic Site (514.291.5700). A ferry transports visitors to l'Île-aux-Noix, the small island on which the fort stands.

Head south on Route 223 to pick up Route 202 east, la Route des Vignobles (the "vintners trail"), which traverses rolling wine country. Lac Champlain comes into view near the modest summer resort of Venise-en-Québec. The road winds around the lake's north shore before veering northeast into the Eastern Townships (800.355.5755). Look south for a breathtaking view of New York's Adirondack Mountains and Vermont.

To the east lies the heart of wine country, Dunham, a quaint village blessed with a microclimate that produces excellent apples and grapes. Take Routes 202, 104, 243, and 245 to Bolton Centre, detouring toward Austin and following the signs to the Abbaye de Saint-Benoît-du-Lac (819.843.4080), situated above Lac Memphrémagog. Several times daily, monks at the Benedictine abbey recite prayers in Gregorian chant.

Head north to Magog via Chemin Nicholas-Austin and take Route 112 east to Sherbrooke (800.561.8331), the regional capital of the Eastern Townships. In the Magog River Gorge, Centrale Frontenac (819.821.5406), Québec's oldest operating hydroelectric plant, offers interactive exhibits, guided tours, and the interpretive Magog River Trail. Head west on Route 112. In Deauville, continue west to return to Magog (800.267.2744) at the head of Lac Memphrémagog, a pristine 48-kilometer-long body of water that extends south between wooded shores into Vermont. Continue on Route 112 through Waterloo, on the Yamaska River, which sprang to prominence with the arrival of the railway. A part of the original line has been converted into Estriade Cycle Path, providing bikers with a scenic link to Granby's Lake Boivin. In Granby, the Granby Zoo (514.372.9113) is home to some one thousand animals of 225 different species. The Centre d'Interprétation de la Nature du Lac Boivin (514.375.3861) provides some of the best bird-watching vantage points in Québec. Return to Montréal via Route 112 or Route 10, a limited-access expressway.

Place Jacques Cartier, Montréal

THE ROUTE TO KLONDIKE GOLD

253 miles | 3–5 days

ALASKA / YUKON TERR.

Road Notes

As resonant a part of frontier history as any event, the 1897–98 Klondike gold rush brought tens of thousands of prospectors into a ferociously wild, hard land by way of one of two 33-mile-long, brutally steep foot trails and then a float trip of some 500 miles up the Yukon River. This drive follows the first part of the stampeders' journey toward the goldfields. Beginning in the former boomtown port of Skagway, in Alaska, the drive climbs over White Pass on a highway that roughly parallels the trail the sourdoughs used, then stops near Whitehorse, the capital of the Yukon Territory. Finally, the route heads west to the Kluane Lake area, arguably the most spectacular part of the 1,400-mile Alaska Highway.

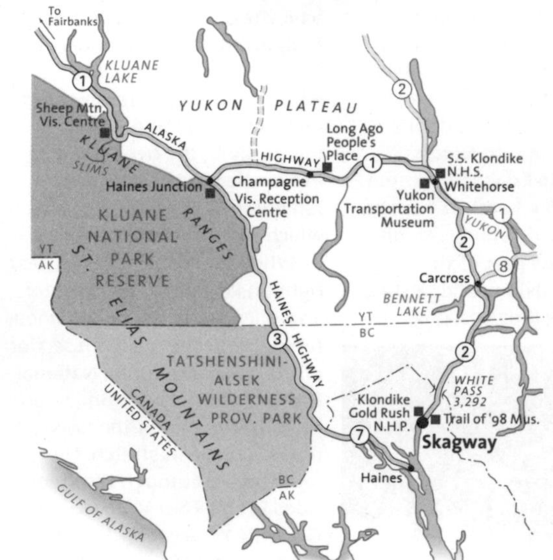

Once a major gateway for the Klondike gold rush, Skagway (907.983.2855) lies at the mouth of a slender canyon. Brush up on gold rush history at the Visitor Center for the Klondike Gold Rush National Historical Park (907.983.2921).

Follow Highway 2 north out of Skagway. Soon, you climb out of the gorge and top 3,292-foot White Pass, where you'll descend into the gentler landscape of this part of the Yukon interior, with its immense lakes. Whitehorse (867.667.7545) sprang to life as a gold rush transportation hub connecting Dawson City and Skagway.

Downtown, along the startling blue waters of the Yukon River, is the S.S. *Klondike* National Historic Site (867.667.3910), where a guided tour of the gleaming 1930s paddle wheeler offers riverboat lore. Near the airport is the Yukon Transportation Museum (867.668.4792), with a time line of the region's history. Heading west from Whitehorse, the Alaska Highway glides over the southern fringe of the Yukon Plateau. For thousands of years, this region has been home to the Southern Tutchone people – Athapaskans who had no direct contact with Europeans until the mid-19th century. Stop at the Long Ago People's Place (867.667.6375), just east of Champagne, where you can learn how the Tutchone tanned hides, dried fish, and hunted with ingenious traps and tools. Beyond Champagne lie the jaw-dropping ramparts of the Kluane Ranges. This abrupt line of glaciated peaks stands above a sprawling valley and extends along the entire eastern front of Kluane National Park Reserve (867.634.7250). Hidden behind this imposing wall lies the heart of the park – an intensely wild landscape with one of the world's largest nonpolar ice fields, the St. Elias Mountains. In Haines Junction, stop at the park's excellent Visitor Reception Centre. To the north is 40-mile-long Kluane Lake. North across the mudflats of the Slims River Delta is the Sheep Mountain Visitor Centre, dedicated to Dall sheep, Kluane's most abundant large mammal. From here, the Alaska Highway continues on to Alaska, where you can follow the highway to its terminus in Fairbanks or take the Tok cutoff to Anchorage. If you want to return to Skagway, return to Haines Junction and follow the Haines Highway to Haines, where a ride on an Alaska Marine Highway ferry (800.642.0066) will complete your journey.

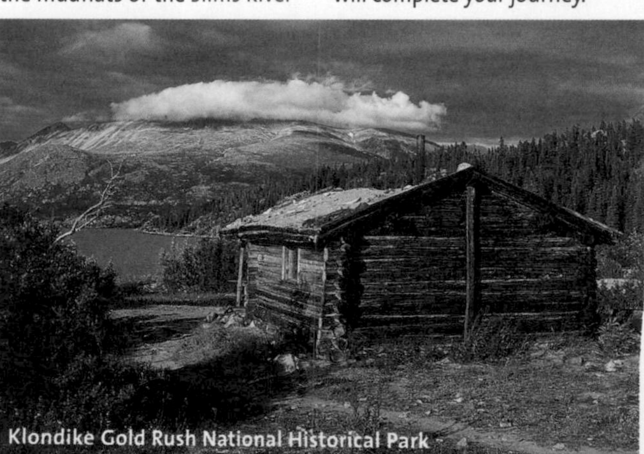
Klondike Gold Rush National Historical Park

70 miles | 3 hours

BAJA'S GOLD COAST

MEXICO HIGHWAY 1 SOUTH

Road Notes

Northern Baja's craggy coastline is home to a strange hybridized culture of Moorish castles, tiny fishing villages, and luxury resort developments. Once you've crossed the border from San Ysidro, the road curves around the *playas*, or beaches, of Tijuana, past the grand "Bullring-by-the-Sea." If you take the toll road (Mexico 1-D), the modern highway hugs the coast of the Mexican Riviera, a booming stretch of high-rise hotels, condominiums, and golf courses. Tolls are collected at three points for a total of about six dollars. The free two-lane road (Mexico 1) winds through a mountainous area for 16 kilometers before crossing the toll road at Rosarito. Both roads follow the coast for the next 50 kilometers before the free road turns inland again at La Misión. Mexico 1-D is dotted with kilometer markers from Tijuana (K0) to Ensenada (K112).

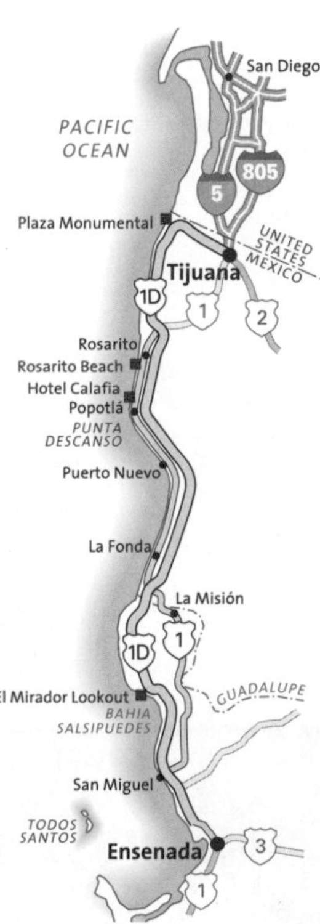

Tijuana (66.881685) is the second largest city along the Pacific Coast after Los Angeles. For a quick visit, focus on Avenida Revolución, the city's main drag. Hucksters beckon you to look at their cheap leather sandals outside stores selling Luis Vuitton luggage. At the southern end of the street is the landmark Frontón Palacio – the jai alai stadium. From Avenida Revolución, follow signs for Carretera Cuota (a toll road) to avoid having to navigate through downtown Tijuana.

Mexico 1-D, the toll highway, climbs out of the smoky valley that encloses Tijuana and skirts a residential area along the city's beaches. The most visible sight is the Plaza Monumental, ten kilometers west of town, which is the second largest bullring in the world. Bullfights run from May through September. South of the border, at kilometer 29 (K29), is Rosarito Beach (800.962.2252), a popular resort destination. In the center of town is the Rosarito Beach Hotel (800.343.8582), once frequented by Hollywood stars like Lana Turner, Mickey Rooney, and Rita Hayworth. A dozen other hotels and condominiums are perched on cliffs above the huge, white-sand beach.

From Rosarito, you can continue south on either the toll road or the free road since they follow essentially the same route. The toll road is less congested and gives you better views of the coast, but there are only a few places to pull over. About ten kilometers south of Rosarito Beach is the Hotel Calafia, a sprawling resort perched on cliffs high above the beach. The ocean-view restaurant is a great place for whale watching. The Spanish galleon perched on an outside deck is a bar and nightclub.

As you continue south, look for the Puerto Nuevo exit sign at about K44. This tiny seaside town with the dirt roads is Baja's lobster capital, with more than 20 restaurants, all specializing in Puerto Nuevo-style lobster, where the *langosta* is lightly fried in oil before being briefly grilled.

Matador, cape men, and bull, Tijuana

Just past La Fonda, at K65, the free road turns inland again and weaves its way through mountains before joining Mexico 1-D just north of Ensenada at San Miguel. The toll road continues to hug the coast. Stop at El Mirador Lookout, at K84, for dramatic views of tranquil Bahia Salsipuedes and the glittering shoreline that is often referred to as Baja's Big Sur. If it's a clear day, you'll spot two craggy outcroppings some 20 kilometers offshore. This is Isla de Todos Santos, a popular spot for both anglers and surfers. From here it's another 25 kilometers to the bustling port city of Ensenada, known for its seafood taco stands and tourist bars, including the landmark Hussong's Cantina (6.678.3210), which has been selling cold *cerveza* since 1892.

MEX 188

MEX 251

50 miles | 6 hours

MAUI

HANA HIGHWAY

Road Notes

Known as one of Hawaii's most scenic routes, the Hana Highway winds along the coast past waterfalls and rocky streams, through rain forests, and among tropical blossoms and fruit trees. The twisting "highway," built in 1927 by convict laborers, is well paved but narrow, with around 600 curves and many stops while oncoming traffic crosses one-lane bridges. Set out early in the day, pull over for restless drivers behind you, and take it easy. It's the trip that counts here, not the destination.

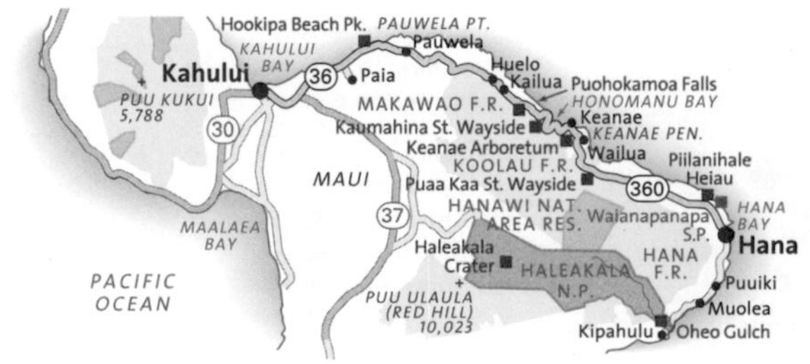

Route 36 begins in Kahului. A surf-laced coastline and sugarcane fields appear alongside you on the seven miles to Paia, the last place before Hana to fill your gas tank and picnic basket. Paia is a laid-back colony of hippies, craftspeople, and windsurfers, who show their stuff at Hookipa Beach Park, near the nine-mile marker past town.

Just past the 16-mile marker, the road is renumbered at Route 360, and mile markers go back to zero. This is the start of the "real" Hana Highway. Gardens and mailboxes sprout up when you reach tiny Kailua, where many residents work on the ditches that carry rainwater from the wet uplands to the dry cane fields of central Maui. Along this stretch, guava trees and mountain apples are common.

Past the nine-mile marker, stop at the short Waikamoi Ridge Trail to stroll among tall eucalyptus trees, their trunks twined with South American taro vines. On the road just ahead are Waikamoi Falls and Puohokamoa Falls, the latter a fine picnic spot with pools to swim in. Then continue just over a mile to Kaumahina State Wayside Park and its expansive view over the coastline.

The road runs along several hundred feet above the sea, then skirts U-shaped Honomanu Bay (entrance just past the 14-mile marker). After you climb the bay's far side, there is a small pullout with a stunning view back over the bay.

In about two miles you reach the Keanae Arboretum, where trails lead to native and introduced plants (taro, breadfruit, banana, bamboo, ti, and ginger). Just ahead is the road down to the Keanae Peninsula, an extension of land created by lava that spilled down from Haleakala, the dormant volcano that dominates eastern Maui. Down in quiet Keanae village, whose residents are mainly native Hawaiians, there is a restored 1860 stone church and cultivated patches of taro, the source of poi. You can get a good view of the peninsula from the small, unmarked Keanae Overlook, just past the 17-mile marker.

Now comes a stretch where the road climbs high above the ocean. Above this region, Haleakala's slopes receive an average of 390 inches (and sometimes as much as 500 inches) of rain yearly, which accounts for the many waterfalls through here. One of the prettiest is beyond the 22-mile marker at the wayside park of Puaa Kaa.

Waterfall on Haleakala

Stop at Waianapanapa State Park, which offers a black-sand beach and caves formed of collapsed lava tubes. The water inside sometimes turns red – some say because of clouds of small shrimp, while others cite the legend of a slain Hawaiian princess whose blood tinges the water.

Within a few miles you reach the pastoral town of Hana, which is quiet and unspectacular, though its setting between Hana Bay and the green hills is lovely and its mood timeless. The main businesses are ranching and the upscale Hotel Hana-Maui (808.248.8211), started in 1946. Do see the Hawaiian artifacts and crafts on display at the Hana Cultural Center (808.248.8622) and visit the 1838 Wananalua Church, built of lava rock.

HI 88

HI 234

165 miles | 1–3 days

PUERTO RICO

RUTA PANORÁMICA

Road Notes

The best known of the island's rural routes connects Yabucoa in the southeast with Mayagüez on the west coast, passing through the Cordillera Central, Puerto Rico's mountainous backbone. From the east, the route climbs quickly into the hills, often reaching heights of more than 900 meters. Ahead, a network of roads provides views of magnificent tropical scenery and glimpses of traditional rural lifestyles. The verdant terrain – a refuge for hundreds of bird species – includes *flamboyan*, *yagrumo*, and mango trees, bamboo, sierra palms, and giant luminescent tree ferns. One-day trips are recommended at right. A good map, with the route highlighted, is essential. Plant and bird guidebooks are also useful.

Day 1: From Yabucoa to Cayey. The loop around Yabucoa and Maunabo – coastal towns where camping on the beach is permitted – offers lovely views of the ocean and sugarcane fields. The route then ascends into the Sierra de Cayey and bisects the Carite Forest Reserve, which borders a lake of the same name. The 6,000-acre state forest, just an hour from San Juan, is the natural habitat of 50 species of birds, including the Puerto Rico tanager, a brilliantly colored songbird, as well as the golden *coquí*, a native Puerto Rican tree frog. Waterfalls and intensely blue pools, like the small Charco Azul, are scattered throughout the forest.

Day 2: From Cayey to Adjuntas. The spectacular San Cristóbal Canyon, wedged between the towns of Aibonito (the highest town on the island) and Barranquitas, was formed by volcanic processes during Puerto Rico's rise from the ocean floor. A scenic overlook at Degetau Rock provides magnificent views of valleys and mountains, bursting with flowers and tropical growth. In Barranquitas, visit the Muñoz Mausoleum and Muñoz Rivera Library Museum (787.857.0230), which memorialize the island's 19th-century patriot Luís Muñoz Rivera.

Continuing on toward Adjuntes, the highest lake on the island, Guineo Reservoir, and the tallest peak, 4,390-foot Cerro de Punta, sit in the lush Toro Negro State Forest. The scenery here is a blend of stunning mountain terrain, that overlooks both the Atlantic and the Caribbean, and junglelike forests of sierra palms. Detour on Route 140 to reach the town of Jayuya, on the northern border of Toro Negro, which is noted for its skilled and meticulous wood-carvers.

Day 3: From Adjuntas to Mayagüez. Former coffee estates and coffee groves surround the town of Adjuntas, a leading producer of *cintrón*. West of Adjuntas the route crosses the dam of Lake Garzas and ascends to remote Guilarte State Forest, where woodpeckers, cuckoos, and hawks nest in mahogany, *tabanuco*, and trumpet trees. A short, often slippery trail leads to the summit of Monte Guilarte. Beyond are several villages in the heart of coffee country.

The Maricao Fish Hatchery (787.838.3710), in the town of Maricao, raises some 25,000 fish each year to stock farm fishponds and island lakes. The hatchery, set in tropical gardens, is part of the Maricao State Forest, home to numerous bird species. A stone observation tower reveals long vistas of the western coast and the Mona Passage, which separates Puerto Rico from the rest of the Greater Antilles. Finish the route at Mayagüez, Puerto Rico's third largest city.

Sierra de Cayey

PR 190

PR 251

UNITED STATES

Alabama
Alabama Bureau of Tourism & Travel
401 Adams Ave., P.O. Box 4927
Montgomery, AL 36103
800.252.2262, 334.242.4169
www.touralabama.org

Alaska
Alaska Div. of Tourism
P.O. Box 110801
Juneau, AK 99811
907.465.2010
www.state.ak.us/local/akpages/COMMERCE/tour.htm

Arizona
Arizona Office of Tourism
2702 N. Third St., Ste. 4015
Phoenix, AZ 85004
800.842.8257, 602.230.7733
www.arizonaguide.com

Arkansas
Arkansas Dept. of Parks & Tourism
One Capitol Mall
Little Rock, AR 72201
800.628.8725, 501.682.7777
www.1800natural.com

California
California Div. of Tourism
P.O. Box 1499
Sacramento, CA 95812
800.862.2543, 916.322.2881
www.gocalif.ca.gov

Colorado
Colorado Travel & Tourism Authority
707 17th St., Ste. 3500
Denver, CO 80202
800.265.6723, 303.296.3384
www.state.co.us/visit_dir/visitormenu.html

Connecticut
Connecticut Office of Tourism
505 Hudson St.
Hartford, CT 06106
800.282.6863, 860.270.8080
www.state.ct.us/tourism

Delaware
Delaware Tourism Office
99 Kings Highway
Dover, DE 19901
800.441.8846, 302.739.4271
www.state.de.us/tourism/intro.htm

Florida
Florida Tourism Industry Marketing Corporation
P.O. Box 1100
Tallahassee, FL 32302
888.735.2872, 850.488.5607
www.flausa.com

Georgia
Georgia Dept. of Industry, Trade & Tourism
P.O. Box 1776
Atlanta, GA 30301
800.847.4842, 404.656.3590
www.itt.state.ga.us

Hawaii
Hawaii Visitors & Convention Bureau
2270 Kalakaua Ave., Ste. 801
Honolulu, HI 96815
800.464.2924, 808.923.1181
www.visithawaii.com

Idaho
Idaho Dept. of Commerce
Box 83720
Boise, ID 83720
800.847.4843, 208.334.2470
www.idoc.state.id.us

Illinois
Illinois Bureau of Tourism
100 W. Randolph St., Ste. 3-400
Chicago, IL 60601
800.226.6632, 312.814.4732
www.enjoyillinois.com

Indiana
Indiana Tourism
1 N. Capitol Ave.
Indianapolis, IN 46024
800.759.9191
www.state.in.us/tourism/index.html

Iowa
Iowa Div. of Tourism
200 E. Grand Ave.
Des Moines, IA 50309
800.345.4692, 515.242.4705
www.state.ia.us/tourism/index.html

Kansas
Kansas Travel & Tourism Development Div.
700 S.W. Harrison, Ste. 1300
Topeka, KS 66603
800.252.6727, 785.296.2009
www.kansascommerce.com

Kentucky
Kentucky Dept. of Travel
Capital Plaza Tower
500 Mero St., Ste. 22
Frankfort, KY 40601
800.225.8747
www.state.ky.us/tour/tour.htm

Louisiana
Louisiana Office of Tourism
P.O. Box 94291
Baton Rouge, LA 70804
800.695.4064, 504.342.8100
www.louisianatravel.com

Maine
Maine Publicity Bureau
P.O. Box 2300
Hallowell, ME 04347
800.533.9595, 207.623.0363
www.visitmaine.com

Maryland
Maryland Office of Tourism Development
217 E. Redwood St.
Baltimore, MD 21202
800.445.4558, 410.767.3400
www.mdisfun.org

Massachusetts
Massachusetts Office of Travel & Tourism
100 Cumming Center
Beverly, MA 01915
800.447.6277, 617.727.3201
www.mass-vacation.com

Michigan
Michigan Travel Bureau
P.O. Box 30226
Lansing, MI 48909
888.784.7328, 517.373.0670
www.michigan.org

Minnesota
Minnesota Office of Tourism
500 Metro Square
121 Seventh Place
St. Paul, MN 55101
800.657.3700, 612.296.5029
www.exploreminnesota.com

Mississippi
Mississippi Div. of Tourism
P.O. Box 1705
Ocean Spring, MS 39556
800.927.6378, 601.359.3297
www.decd.state.ms.us/tourism.htm

Missouri
Missouri Div. of Tourism
301 W. High St., P.O. Box 1055
Jefferson City, MO 65102
800.877.1234, 573.751.4133
www.missouritourism.org

Montana
Travel Montana
1424 Ninth Ave.
Helena, MT 59620
800.847.4868, 406.444.2654
www.travel.mt.gov

Chugach Mountains, AK

Nebraska
Nebraska Travel & Tourism
P.O. Box 94666
Lincoln, NE 68509
800.228.4307, 402.471.3796
www.ded.state.ne.us/tourism.html

Nevada
Nevada Commission on Tourism
5151 S. Carson St.
Carson City, NV 89701
800.638.2328, 702.687.4322, 800.237.0774
www.travelnevada.com

New Hampshire
New Hampshire Office of Travel & Tourism Development
172 Pembroke Rd., P.O. Box 1856
Concord, NH 03302
800.386.4664, 603.271.2666
www.visitnh.gov

New Jersey
New Jersey Div. of Travel & Tourism
20 W. State St., P.O. Box 826
Trenton, NJ 08625
800.537.7397, 609.292.2470
www.state.nj.us/travel

New Mexico
New Mexico Dept. of Tourism
491 Old Santa Fe Trail
Santa Fe, NM 87503
800.545.2040, 800.733.6396
www.newmexico.org

New York
New York State Div. of Tourism
One Commerce Plaza
Albany, NY 12245
800.225.5697, 518.474.4116
www.iloveny.state.ny.us

North Carolina
North Carolina Div. of Tourism, Film & Sports Development
301 N. Wilmington St.
Raleigh, NC 27601
800.847.4862, 919.733.4171
www.visitnc.com

North Dakota
North Dakota Tourism
604 E. Boulevard Ave.
Bismarck, ND 58505
800.435.5663, 701.328.2525
www.ndtourism.com

Ohio
Ohio Div. of Travel & Tourism
77 S. High St., 29th Fl.
Columbus, OH 43215
800.282.5393
www.ohiotourism.com

Oklahoma
Oklahoma Dept. of Tourism & Recreation
P.O. Box 60789
Oklahoma City, OK 73146
800.652.6552, 405.521.2409
www.otrd.state.ok.us

Oregon
Oregon Tourism Commission
775 Summer St. NE
Salem, OR 97310
800.547.7842, 503.986.0000
www.traveloregon.com

Pennsylvania
Pennsylvania Office of Travel, Tourism & Film Promotion
Rm. 404, Forum Building
Harrisburg, PA 17120
800.847.4872, 717.787.5453
www.state.pa.us/visit

Rhode Island
Rhode Island Tourism Div.
1 W. Exchange St.
Providence, RI 02903
800.556.2484
www.visitrhodeisland.com

South Carolina
South Carolina Dept. of Parks, Recreation & Tourism
P.O. Box 71
Columbia, SC 29201
800.872.3505, 803.734.0122
www.prt.state.sc.us/sc

South Dakota
South Dakota Dept. of Tourism
711 E. Wells Ave.
Pierre, SD 57501
800.732.5682
www.state.sd.us/state/executive/tourism/tourism.html

Tennessee
Tennessee Dept. of Tourist Development
320 Sixth Ave. N
Rachel Jackson Building
Nashville, TN 37243
800.836.6200, 615.741.2158
www.state.tn.us/tourdev

Texas
Texas Dept. of Economic Development, Tourism Div.
P.O. Box 12728
Austin, TX 78711
800.888.8839, 512.462.9191
www.traveltex.com

Utah
Utah Travel Council
Council Hall/Capitol Hill
Salt Lake City, UT 84114
800.200.1160, 801.538.1030
www.utah.com

Vermont
Vermont Dept. of Tourism & Marketing
134 State St., Box 1471
Montpelier, VT 05601
800.837.6668, 802.828.3236
www.travel-vermont.com

Virginia
Virginia Tourism Corporation
901 E. Byrd St.
Richmond, VA 23219
800.932.5827, 804.786.4484
www.virginia.org

Washington
Dept. of Community Trade & Economic Development, Washington State Tourism Div.
P.O. Box 42500
Olympia, WA 98504
800.890.5493, 800.544.1800
www.tourism.wa.gov

Garden of the Gods, CO

Washington, D.C.
WCVA Visitors Services
1212 New York Ave. NW, Ste. 600
Washington, D.C. 20005
800.422.8644, 202.789.7000
www.washington.org

West Virginia
West Virginia Div. of Tourism
2101 Washington St. E
Charleston, WV 25305
800.225.5982, 304.558.2286
www.state.wv.us/tourism

Wisconsin
Wisconsin Dept. of Tourism
P.O. Box 7976
Madison, WI 53707
800.432.8747
tourism.state.wi.us

Wyoming
Wyoming Div. of Tourism
I-25 at College Dr.
Cheyenne, WY 82002
800.225.5996, 307.777.7777
www.state.wy.us/state/tourism/tourism.html

UNITED STATES TERRITORIES

Puerto Rico
Puerto Rico Tourism Company
Old San Juan Station
P.O. Box 4435
San Juan, PR 00902
800.223.6530, 787.721.2400
www.discoverpuertorico.com

Virgin Islands
U.S. Virgin Islands Dept. of Tourism
P.O. Box 6400
St. Thomas, VI 00804
340.774.8784
www.usvi.net

CANADA

Alberta
Travel Alberta
10155 102nd St., 3rd Fl.
Edmonton, AB, Canada T5J 4G8
800.661.8888, 403.427.4321
www.discoveralberta.com

British Columbia
Super, Natural British Columbia
Box 9830
Stn. Prov. Govt.
Victoria, BC, Canada V8W 9W5
800.663.6000, 250.387.1642
www.tbc.gov.bc.ca

Manitoba
Travel Manitoba
7-155 Carlton St.
Winnipeg, MB, Canada R3C 3H8
800.665.0040, ext. SG8, 204.945.3777
www.gov.mb.ca/itt/travel

New Brunswick
Tourism New Brunswick
P.O. Box 12345
Woodstock, NB, Canada E0J 2B0
800.561.0123
www.gov.nb.ca/tourism

Newfoundland
Newfoundland & Labrador Tourism Marketing
P.O. Box 8730
St. John's, NF, Canada A1B 4K2
800.563.6353, 709.2830
www.gov.nf.ca/tourism

Nova Scotia
Tourism Nova Scotia
P.O. Box 519
Halifax, NS, Canada B3J 2R5
800.565.0000, 902.424.4247
www.explore.gov.ns.ca/virtualns

Ontario
Ontario Tourism
Queen's Park, 900 Bay St.
Toronto, ON, Canada M7A 2E1
800.668.2746, 416.314.0944
www.travelinx.com

Prince Edward Island
Dept. of Economical Development & Tourism
P.O. Box 940
Charlottetown, PE, Canada C1A 7M5
800.463.4734, 902.368.4444
www.gov.pe.ca/vg/index.asp

Québec
Tourisme Québec
P.O. Box 979
Montréal, PQ, Canada H3C 2W3
800.363.7777, 514.873.2015
www.tourisme.gouv.qc.ca

Saskatchewan
Tourism Saskatchewan
Albert St., Ste. 500
Regina, SK, Canada S4P 4L9
800.667.7191, 306.787.2300
www.sasktourism.com

MEXICO

Mexico Ministry of Tourism
Mariano Escobedo, No. 726
Col. Nueva Anzures
11590 Mexico City, D.F. Mexico
800.446.3942
www.mexico-travel.com

STATE POLICE

Telephone numbers for information on road conditions and construction are available in the Road Map chapter. The numbers below may be used for nonemergency roadside assistance and travel safety advisories. Many state police authorities are divided into districts; in such cases, calls will be referred to the most appropriate local office.

Alabama State Troopers
334.242.4378

Alaska State Troopers
907.428.7200

Arizona Dept. of Public Safety
602.223.2000

Arkansas State Police
501.618.8000

California Highway Patrol
916.445.1865

Colorado State Patrol
303.239-4501

Connecticut Dept. of Public Safety
860.685.8190

Delaware State Police
302.739.5931

Florida Highway Patrol
904.488.5370

Georgia State Patrol
404.657.9300

Hawaii Motor Vehicle Safety Office
808.832.5824

Idaho State Police
208.884.7120

Illinois State Police
217.786.6677

Indiana State Police
317.897.6220

Iowa State Patrol
515.281.5824

Kansas Highway Patrol
785.296.3102

Kentucky State Police
502.695.6300

Louisiana State Police
504.754.8500

Maine State Police
207.624.7000

Maryland State Police
410.653.4200

Massachusetts State Police
508.820.2121

Michigan State Police
517.332.2521

Minnesota Dept. of Public Safety
612.297.3935

Mississippi State Highway Patrol
601.987.1212

Missouri State Highway Patrol
573.751.3313

Montana Highway Patrol
406.444.7000

Nebraska State Police
402.479.4952

Nevada Highway Patrol
702.687.5300

New Hampshire State Police
603.271.3636

New Jersey State Police
609.882.2000

New Mexico State Police
505.827.9300

New York State Police
518.457.6811

North Carolina State Highway Patrol
919.733.7952

North Dakota Highway Patrol
701.328.2455

Ohio State Highway Patrol
614.466.2660

Oklahoma Highway Patrol
405.425.2043

Oregon Dept. of State Police
503.378.2575

Pennsylvania State Police
717.787.7777

Rhode Island State Police
401.444.1000

South Carolina State Patrol
803.896.9621

South Dakota Highway Patrol
605.773.3536

Tennessee Highway Patrol
615.741.2060

Texas Dept. of Public Safety
800.525.5555

Utah Highway Patrol
801.576.8606

Vermont State Police
802.244.8727

Virginia State Police
804.674.2000

Off Route 1, north of Big Sur, CA

Washington State Patrol
360.753.6540

Washington, D.C. Police Dept.
202.727.1010

West Virginia State Police
304.746.2100

Wisconsin State Patrol
608.266.3212

Wyoming Highway Patrol
307.777.4321

WEATHER

Alabama
Birmingham 205.945.7000
Huntsville 205.837.5655
Mobile 334.478.6666

Alaska
Anchorage 907.936.2525
So. AK hwys. 907.936.2626
Fairbanks 907.452.3553
Juneau 907.586.3997

Arizona
Flagstaff 520.774.3301
Phoenix 602.265.5550
Tucson 520.881.3333

Arkansas
Fort Smith 501.785.9000
Little Rock 501.371.7777

California
Eureka (north coast) 707.443.7062
Los Angeles (and Oxnard) 805.988.6610
Monterey (San Francisco Bay area) 408.656.1725
Redding 916.221.5613
Sacramento 916.646.2000
San Diego 619.289.1212
San Francisco 510.562.8573
San Joaquin Valley 805.393.2340
209.584.8047

Colorado
Denver and Boulder 303.398.3964
Grand Junction 970.243.0914
Pueblo 719.948.3371

Connecticut
Southern New England 508.822.0634

Delaware
Mount Holly, NJ (area office) 609.261.6600

Florida
Daytona Beach 904.252.8000
Jacksonville 904.387.4545
Melbourne 407.255.2900
Miami 305.229.4522
Orlando 407.851.7510
Pensacola 904.476.1313
Tallahassee 904.422.1212
Tampa Bay 813.645.2506

Georgia
Atlanta 770.486.8834
Macon 912.755.1300
Savannah 912.964.1700

Hawaii
Honolulu 808.973.4380
Oahu 808.973.4381

Idaho
Boise 208.334.9860
208.342.6569
Lewiston 208.743.3841
Pocatello 208.233.0137

Illinois
Chicago 815.834.0675
Lincoln (central IL) 217.732.3089
Peoria 309.697.8620
Rockford 815.963.8518
Springfield 217.522.0642

Indiana
Fort Wayne 219.424.5050
Indianapolis 317.635.5959
South Bend 219.234.1504

Iowa
Des Moines 515.270.2614
Quad Cities 319.386.3976

Kansas
Dodge City 316.227.3311
Northwest KS 913.899.7119
Topeka 913.234.2592
Wichita 316.942.3102

Kentucky
Jackson 606.666.8000
Louisville 502.968.6025
Paducah 502.744.6331

Louisiana
Baton Rouge 504.387.5411
Lake Charles 318.478.4810
New Orleans 504.828.4000
Shreveport 318.635.7575

Maine
Portland 207.688.3210

Maryland
Washington, D.C. (area office) 703.260.0307
Northern MD and VA mountains 703.260.0705

Massachusetts
Southern New England 508.822.0634

Michigan
Detroit 248.620.2355
Gaylord (north-central lower MI) 517.732.6242
Grand Rapids 616.949.4253
Marquette 906.475.5212

Minnesota
Duluth 218.729.6697
Minneapolis/St. Paul 612.512.1111

Mississippi
Jackson 601.354.3333
Meridian 601.693.5311

Missouri
Kansas City 816.540.6021
Springfield 417.869.4491
St. Louis 314.441.8467

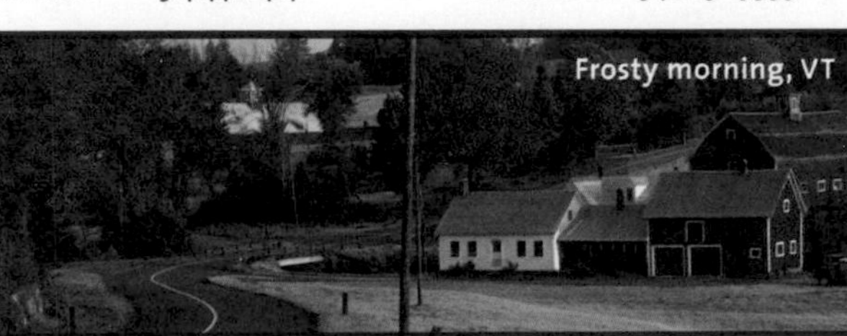
Frosty morning, VT

Montana
Billings 406.652.1916
Glasgow 406.228.9625
Great Falls 406.453.5469
Helena 406.443.5151
Missoula 406.755.4829

Nebraska
Hastings 402.462.4287
North Platte 308.532.5592
Omaha 402.392.1111

Nevada
Elko 702.738.3018
Ely 702.289.2403
Las Vegas 702.263.9744
Reno and Lake Tahoe 702.831.6677
Winnemucca 702.623.2203

New Hampshire
Portland, ME 207.688.3210

New Jersey
Mount Holly, NJ (area office) 609.261.6600

New Mexico
Albuquerque 505.821.1111
Roswell 505.347.5700

New York
Albany 518.476.1111
Binghamton 607.729.1597
Buffalo 716.565.0204

North Carolina
Morehead City (eastern NC) 919.223.5737

North Dakota
Bismarck 701.223.3700
Grand Forks (eastern ND) 701.772.0720
Williston 701.572.2351

Ohio
Cincinnati 513.241.1010
Cleveland 216.265.2370
Columbus 614.281.8211
Dayton 937.499.1212

Oklahoma
Norman 405.478.3377
Tulsa 918.743.3311

Oregon
Astoria 503.861.2722
Eugene 541.688.9041
Klamath Falls 541.882.5060
Medford 541.779.5990
Pendleton 541.276.0103
Portland 503.243.7575
Salem 503.363.4131

Pennsylvania
Mount Holly, NJ (area office) 609.261.6600
Pittsburgh 412.262.2170

Rhode Island
Southern New England 508.822.0634

South Carolina
Charleston 803.744.3207
Columbia 803.822.8135

South Dakota
Aberdeen 605.225.6173
Rapid City 605.341.7531
Sioux Falls 605.330.4444

Tennessee
Memphis 901.522.8888
Nashville 615.737.2255

Texas
Abilene 915.698.8484
Amarillo 806.354.2278
Brownsville 956.546.5378
Corpus Christi 512.289.1861
El Paso 915.562.4040
Dallas / Fort Worth 972, 817, or 214.787.1111
Galveston 409.740.7272
Houston 713.529.4444
Lubbock 806.745.1058
Midland 915.563.9292
San Angelo 915.949.8586
San Antonio 210.225.0404
Victoria 512.572.9999
Wichita Falls 940.692.9999

Utah
Salt Lake City 801.575.7246

Vermont
Burlington 802.862.2475

Virginia
Roanoke/Lynchburg 540.552.0497
Richmond 804.268.1212
Washington, D.C. (area office) 703.260.0307
VA mountains and northern MD 703.260.0705

Washington
Olympia 360.357.6453
Seattle 206.526.6087
Spokane 509.244.6395

Washington, D.C.
703.260.0307

West Virginia
Charleston 304.345.2121

Wisconsin
Green Bay 920.494.2363
La Crosse 608.784.7294
Milwaukee / Sullivan 414.744.8000

Wyoming
Cheyenne 307.635.9901

BORDER CROSSING

Canada

Visiting Canada requires neither a passport nor visa; however, individuals should be prepared to demonstrate proof of United States citizenship at the port of entry. They should carry U.S. birth certificates or naturalization papers; medical cards or credit cards accompanied by photo identification may also be accepted. Alien residents of the U.S. must show their Alien Registration Receipt Cards. Individuals under 18 must provide a letter from a legal guardian stating permission for their travel in Canada.

Automobiles entering Canada are admitted free of payments or duty fees for up to 12 months. No special insurance is required; however, motorists are advised to carry vehicle registration cards with them as well as documents establishing proof of insurance and vehicle ownership. A yellow Non-Resident Inter-Provincial Motor Vehicle Liability Insurance Card can be obtained from most U.S. insurance companies. The card indicates the insurance company's agreement to provide the minimum legal coverage required in all Canadian provinces and territories.

United States (from Canada)

Canadian citizens visiting the U.S. are not required to present passports or visas for visits lasting less than six months. Individuals should be prepared, however, to demonstrate proof of citizenship at their port of entry. A photo identification accompanied by a valid birth certificate or citizenship card should suffice. For visits exceeding six months valid passports or visas are required, obtainable from the U.S. Immigration and Naturalization Service.

Automobiles may enter the U.S. free of payments or duty fees. Drivers need only provide customs officials with valid proof of vehicle registration, ownership, and insurance.

Mexico

Visiting Mexico requires neither a passport nor visa, but individuals must prove their United States citizenship at border crossing points. Naturalized citizens must show naturalization certificates or a U.S. passport. Alien residents of the U.S. must carry Tourist Cards, which can be obtained from the nearest Mexican Consulate or Mexican Tourist Office.

Vehicles traveling from the U.S. to Mexico require permits if traveling more than 13 miles beyond the border. Permits are not required for travel within the Baja Peninsula, or in Puerto Peñasco and El Golfo de Santa Clara in the State of Sonora. Permit holders must be of 18 years of age. Permits may be obtained from the Mexican Customs Office at border crossing points as long as the original and two copies of the following documents are provided:

Valid proof of driver's citizenship (passport or birth certificate) or tourist card

Valid vehicle registration in driver's name

Valid driver's license in driver's name

Major U.S.- or Canadian-issued credit card in driver's name (Visa, MasterCard, American Express, Diners Club)

Permits require a fee of U.S. $12.00, payable by credit card only, and are valid for 180 days. They must be returned at the border when leaving Mexico.

U.S. and Canadian auto insurance policies are not valid in Mexico, and buying short-term tourist insurance is required. Many U.S. insurance companies sell Mexican auto insurance. American Automobile Association (for members only) and Sanborn's Mexico Insurance (800.638.9423) are popular companies with offices at most U.S. border crossings.

SUNSHINE

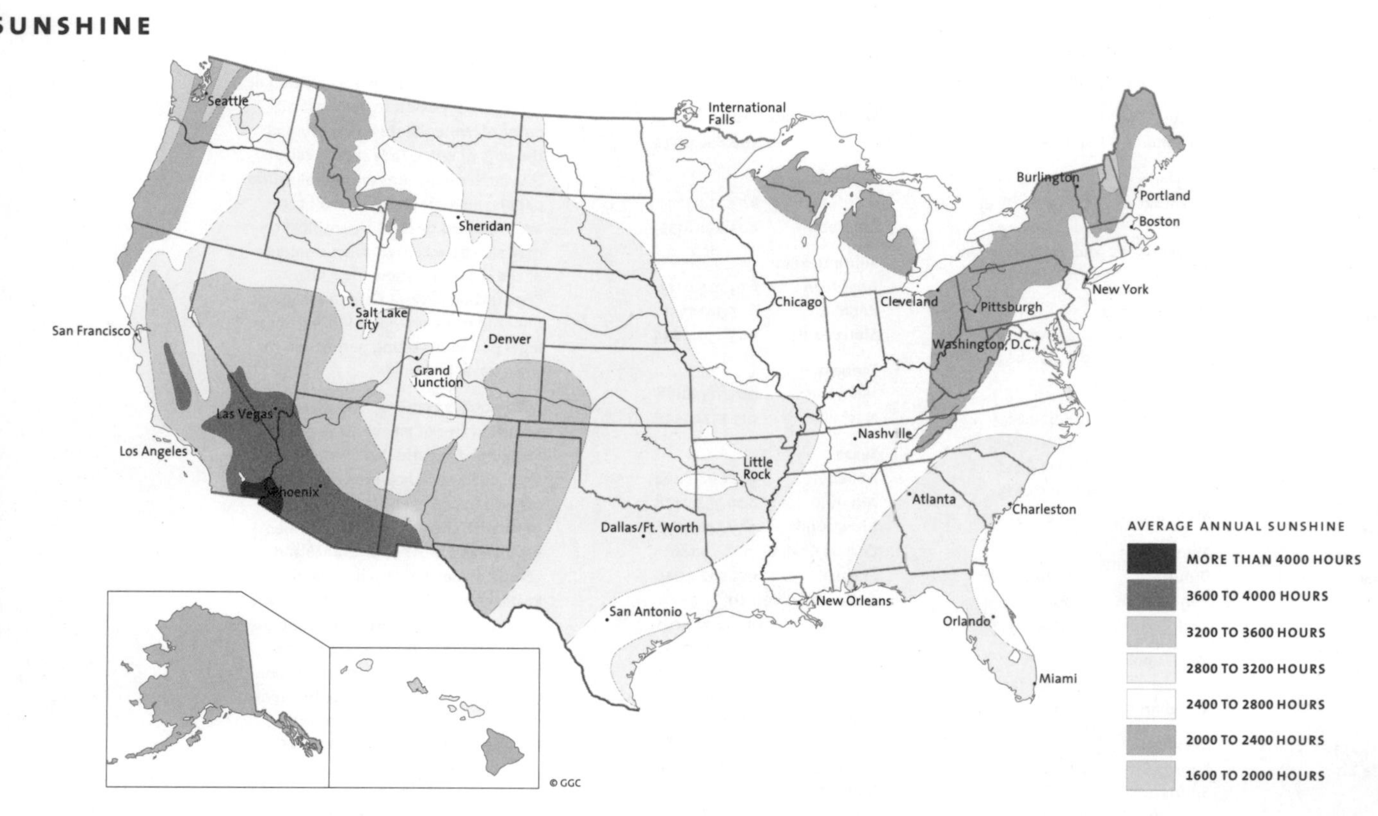

CITY	DAYS OF SUNSHINE
Las Vegas, NV	211.1
Phoenix, AZ	211.0
Los Angeles, CA	186.0
San Francisco, CA	160.3
Grand Junction, CO	136.6
Dallas/Fort Worth, TX	135.5
Salt Lake City, UT	125.0
Little Rock, AR	118.7
Denver, CO	115.2
Atlanta, GA	110.4
New York, NY	106.7
San Antonio, TX	106.1
Nashville, TN	102.9
Charleston, SC	102.3
New Orleans, LA	101.4
Portland, ME	101.3
Boston, MA	98.4
Washington, DC	96.7
Sheridan, WY	95.8
Orlando, FL	89.9
Chicago, IL	83.8
International Falls, MN	76.7
Miami, FL	75.1
Seattle, WA	71.0
Cleveland, OH	66.4
Pittsburgh, PA	58.3
Burlington, VT	57.9

RAINFALL

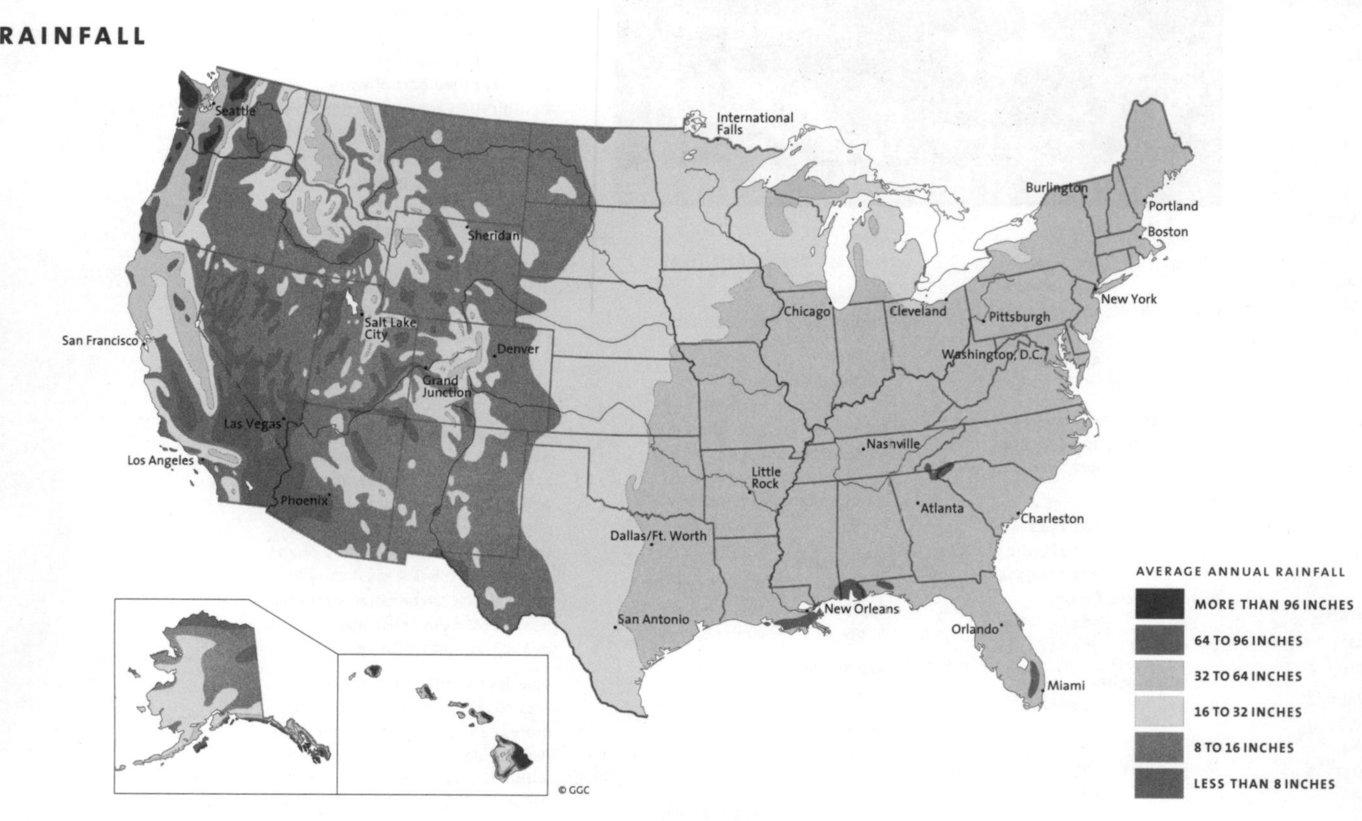

CITY	DAYS OF RAINFALL
Cleveland, OH	156.0
Burlington, VT	154.0
Pittsburgh, PA	153.3
Seattle, WA	150.4
International Falls, MN	131.3
Miami, FL	129.5
Portland, ME	128.5
Boston, MA	126.5
Chicago, IL	126.3
New York, NY	120.6
Nashville, TN	118.6
Orlando, FL	115.8
Atlanta, GA	115.1
New Orleans, LA	114.5
Charleston, SC	112.9
Washington, DC	112.3
Sheridan, WY	106.8
Little Rock, AR	104.5
Salt Lake City, UT	90.6
Denver, CO	89.1
San Antonio, TX	82.1
Dallas/Fort Worth, TX	78.9
Grand Junction, CO	72.8
San Francisco, CA	62.0
Phoenix, AZ	36.5
Los Angeles, CA	35.2
Las Vegas, NV	26.5

SNOWFALL

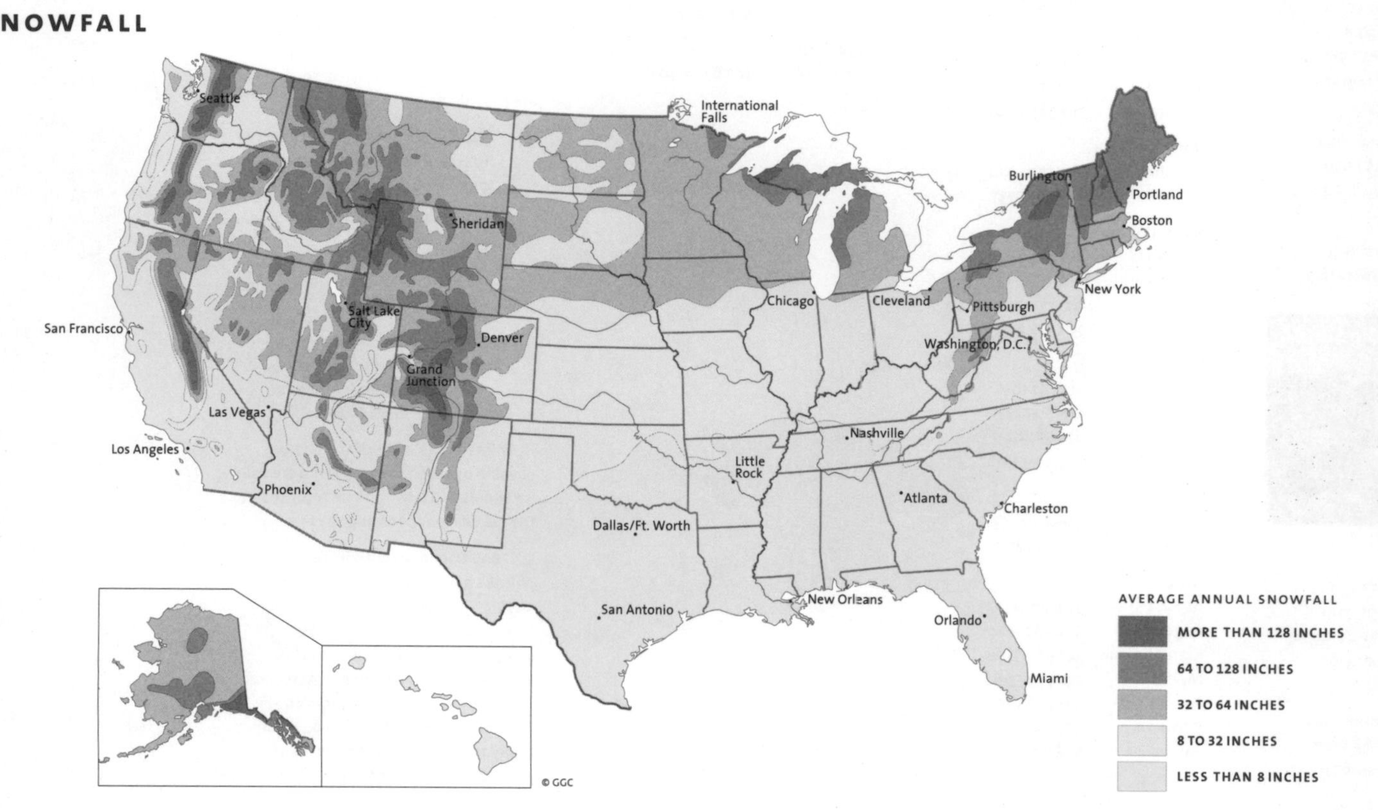

CITY	DAYS OF SNOWFALL
Sheridan, WY	23.6
Burlington, VT	22.0
International Falls, MN	19.5
Cleveland, OH	18.4
Denver, CO	17.9
Salt Lake City, UT	17.8
Portland, ME	17.3
Pittsburgh, PA	12.8
Chicago, IL	11.6
Boston, MA	10.7
Grand Junction, CO	8.7
New York, NY	7.9
Washington, DC	4.6
Nashville, TN	3.5
Seattle, WA	2.4
Little Rock, AR	1.9
Dallas/Fort Worth, TX	1.1
Atlanta, GA	0.6
Las Vegas, NV	0.4
Charleston, SC	0.2
San Antonio, TX	0.2
New Orleans, LA	rare
San Francisco, CA	rare
Los Angeles, CA	0.0
Miami, FL	0.0
Orlando, FL	0.0
Phoenix, AZ	0.0

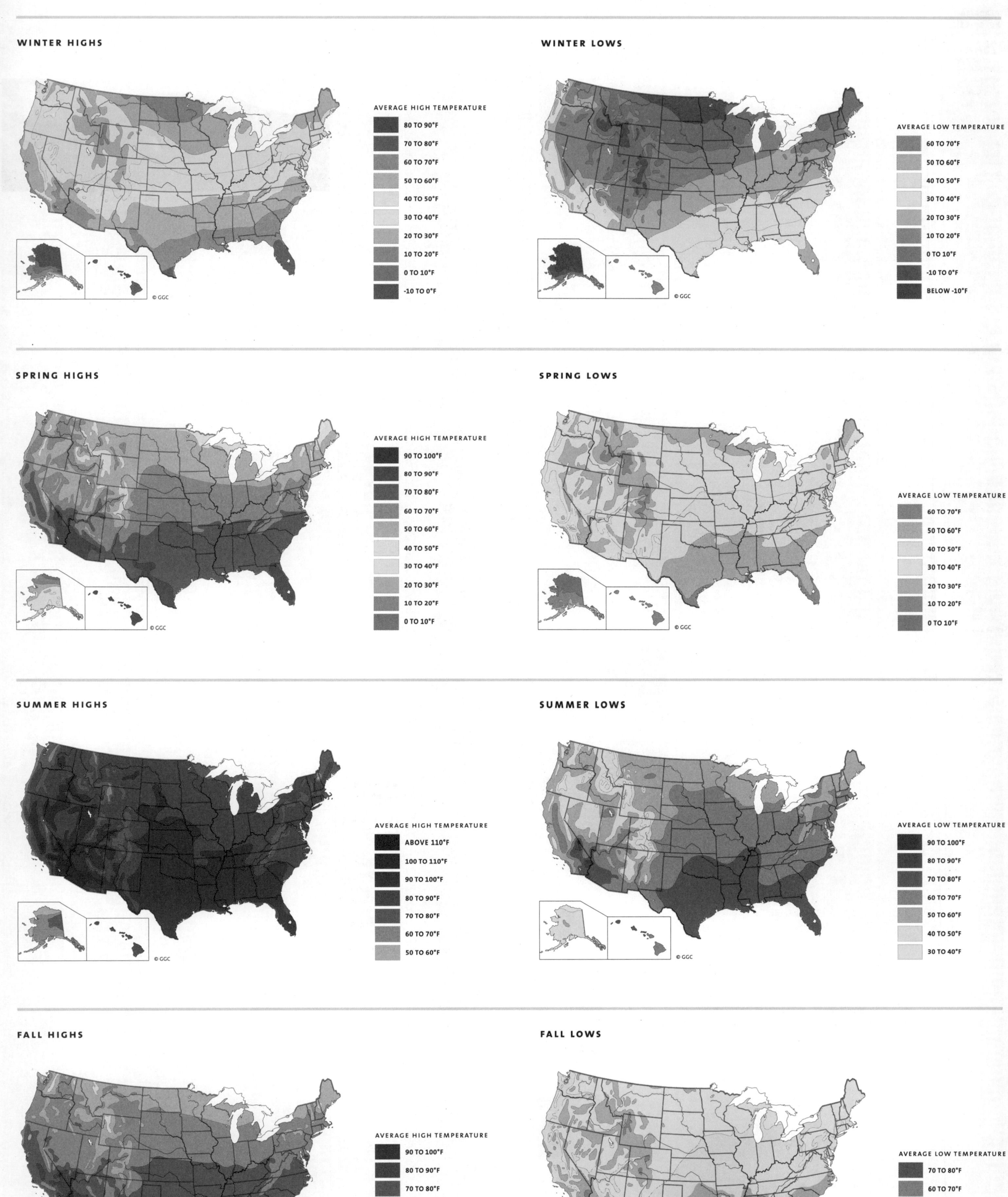
WINTER HIGHS
AVERAGE HIGH TEMPERATURE
80 TO 90°F
70 TO 80°F
60 TO 70°F
50 TO 60°F
40 TO 50°F
30 TO 40°F
20 TO 30°F
10 TO 20°F
0 TO 10°F
-10 TO 0°F
© GGC
WINTER LOWS
AVERAGE LOW TEMPERATURE
60 TO 70°F
50 TO 60°F
40 TO 50°F
30 TO 40°F
20 TO 30°F
10 TO 20°F
0 TO 10°F
-10 TO 0°F
BELOW -10°F
© GGC
SPRING HIGHS
AVERAGE HIGH TEMPERATURE
90 TO 100°F
80 TO 90°F
70 TO 80°F
60 TO 70°F
50 TO 60°F
40 TO 50°F
30 TO 40°F
20 TO 30°F
10 TO 20°F
0 TO 10°F
© GGC
SPRING LOWS
AVERAGE LOW TEMPERATURE
60 TO 70°F
50 TO 60°F
40 TO 50°F
30 TO 40°F
20 TO 30°F
10 TO 20°F
0 TO 10°F
© GGC
SUMMER HIGHS
AVERAGE HIGH TEMPERATURE
ABOVE 110°F
100 TO 110°F
90 TO 100°F
80 TO 90°F
70 TO 80°F
60 TO 70°F
50 TO 60°F
© GGC
SUMMER LOWS
AVERAGE LOW TEMPERATURE
90 TO 100°F
80 TO 90°F
70 TO 80°F
60 TO 70°F
50 TO 60°F
40 TO 50°F
30 TO 40°F
© GGC
FALL HIGHS
AVERAGE HIGH TEMPERATURE
90 TO 100°F
80 TO 90°F
70 TO 80°F
60 TO 70°F
50 TO 60°F
40 TO 50°F
30 TO 40°F
20 TO 30°F
© GGC
FALL LOWS
AVERAGE LOW TEMPERATURE
70 TO 80°F
60 TO 70°F
50 TO 60°F
40 TO 50°F
30 TO 40°F
20 TO 30°F
10 TO 20°F
© GGC

Alabama–Arkansas

Note: State populations are 1996 estimates from the U.S. Bureau of the Census. All other figures derived from latest available official population data.

ALABAMA
PG. 60–61

CAPITAL
Montgomery

NICKNAME
Heart of Dixie

POPULATION
4,273,084, rank 23

AREA
51,705 sq mi, rank 29

Counties

Autauga, 34222 ....J-6
Baldwin, 98280 ....R-4
Barbour, 25417 ....M-10
Bibb, 16576 ....H-5
Blount, 39248 ....D-7
Bullock, 11042 ....L-10
Butler, 21892 ....M-6
Calhoun, 116034 ....E-9
Chambers, 36876 ....H-10
Cherokee, 19543 ....D-10
Chilton, 32458 ....J-7
Choctaw, 16018 ....M-2
Clarke, 27240 ....M-3
Clay, 13252 ....G-9
Cleburne, 12730 ....F-10
Coffee, 40240 ....N-9
Colbert, 51666 ....B-3
Conecuh, 14054 ....P-5
Coosa, 11063 ....H-8
Covington, 36478 ....P-7
Crenshaw, 13635 ....N-8
Cullman, 67613 ....D-6
Dale, 49633 ....N-10
Dallas, 48130 ....L-5
De Kalb, 54651 ....C-9
Elmore, 49210 ....J-8
Escambia, 35518 ....P-6
Etowah, 99840 ....D-8
Fayette, 17962 ....E-4
Franklin, 27814 ....C-3
Geneva, 23647 ....Q-9
Greene, 10153 ....H-3
Hale, 15498 ....H-4
Henry, 15374 ....N-11
Houston, 81331 ....Q-11
Jackson, 47796 ....A-8
Jefferson, 651525 ....F-6
Lamar, 15715 ....E-3
Lauderdale, 79661 ....A-4
Lawrence, 31513 ....C-4
Lee, 87146 ....J-11
Limestone, 54135 ....A-6
Lowndes, 12658 ....L-6
Macon, 24928 ....K-9
Madison, 238912 ....A-7
Marengo, 23084 ....L-3
Marion, 29830 ....D-3
Marshall, 70832 ....C-7
Mobile, 378643 ....Q-2
Monroe, 23968 ....N-5
Montgomery, 209085 ....L-8
Morgan, 100043 ....C-6
Perry, 12759 ....J-5
Pickens, 20699 ....G-3
Pike, 27595 ....M-9
Randolph, 19881 ....G-10
Russell, 46860 ....L-11
St. Clair, 50009 ....E-8
Shelby, 99358 ....G-7
Sumter, 16174 ....K-2
Talladega, 74107 ....F-8
Tallapoosa, 38826 ....H-9
Tuscaloosa, 150522 ....G-4
Walker, 67670 ....E-5
Washington, 16694 ....P-2
Wilcox, 13568 ....L-5
Winston, 22053 ....C-4

Cities and Towns

Abbeville, 3173 ....N-11
Aberfoil, 125 ....L-10
Abernant, 175 ....G-5
Ackerville L-6
Ada L-8
Adamsville, 5161 ....F-6
Addison, 626 ....D-5
Akron, 468 ....H-4
Alabaster, 14732 ....G-6
Alberta, 175 ....L-5
Albertville, 14507 ....C-8
Alexander City, 14917 ....H-9
Aliceville, 3009 ....G-2
Allgood, 464 ....E-7
Alma, 250 ....N-4
Almond, 50 ....G-10
Altoona, 960 ....D-8
Andalusia, 9269 ....P-7
Anderson, 339 ....A-5
Annemanie L-5
Anniston, 26623 ....F-9
Ansley, 70 ....M-8
Arab, 6321 ....C-7
Ardmore, 1090 ....A-6
Argo, 930 ....E-7
Ariton, 743 ....N-9
Arkadelphia, 100 ....E-6
Arley, 338 ....D-5
Ashby, 125 ....H-6
Ashford, 1926 ....P-11
Ashland, 2034 ....G-9
Ashridge C-4
Ashville, 1494 ....E-8
Athens, 16901 ....A-6
Atmore, 8046 ....Q-4
Attalla, 6859 ....D-8
Atwood C-3
Auburn, 33830 ....J-10
Autaugaville, 681 ....K-7
Avon, 462 ....P-11
Awin M-6
Axis, 400 ....Q-3
Babbie, 576 ....P-8
Baileyton, 352 ....C-7
Baker Hill, 90 ....M-11
Bangor, 90 ....D-6
Banks, 195 ....M-9
Bankston, 80 ....E-4
Barfield G-9
Barnett Crossroads P-5
Barton, 400 ....B-3
Dry Forks C-6
Bashi, 30 ....M-3
Bass A-9
Batesville, 10 ....L-11
Bay Minette, 7168 ....Q-3
Bayou La Batre, 2456 ....S-2
Bayview S-10
Bear Cr., 813 ....C-4
Beatrice, 455 ....N-5
Beaverton, 319 ....E-3
Belgreen, 150 ....C-3
Belk, 255 ....F-4
Bellamy, 600 ....K-2
Belleville N-5
Benevola G-3
Benton, 48 ....K-6
Bermuda N-5
Berry, 1218 ....E-4
Bertha N-10
Bessemer, 33497 ....F-6
Bexar, 60 ....D-3
Bigbee N-2
Billingsley, 150 ....J-7
Birmingham, 265968 ....F-6
Black, 174 ....Q-8
Black Rock M-7
Blacksher, 10 ....P-4
Bladon Sprs. M-2
Blanche, 20 ....C-10
Bleecker, 150 ....J-11
Blountsville, 1527 ....D-7
Blue Mtn., 221 ....E-8
Blue Ridge, 1151 ....K-8
Blue Sprs., 108 ....N-10
Bluff E-3
Boaz, 6928 ....D-8
Boligee, 268 ....J-3
Bolinger M-2
Bolling, 80 ....N-7
Bomar D-10
Bon Air, 91 ....G-8
Bon Secour S-4
Booth, 80 ....K-7
Borden Sprs., 20 ....E-10
Boyd, 125 ....J-2
Bradley, 40 ....Q-7
Braggs, 80 ....L-6
Branchville, 370 ....F-7
Brantley, 1015 ....N-8
Brandley K-6
Bremen, 250 ....D-6
Brent, 2776 ....H-5
Brewton, 5885 ....P-6
Bridgeport, 2936 ....A-9
Brighton T-10
Brilliant, 751 ....D-4
Brooklyn, 30 ....P-6
Brooks, 60 ....N-7
Brookside, 1365 ....F-6
Brooksville, 100 ....D-7
Brookwood, 658 ....G-5
Browns, 20 ....K-5
Brownsville, 30 ....F-4
Brundidge, 2472 ....M-9
Bryant A-10
Bucks, 40 ....Q-3
Burkville, 30 ....K-7
Burnsville, 175 ....K-6
Burnt Corn, 90 ....N-5
Butler, 1872 ....L-2
Butler Sprs. M-6
Bynum, 1917 ....F-9
Cahaba Hts., 4778 ....F-7
Calera, 2136 ....G-6
Calhoun, 100 ....L-7
Calvert P-3
Camden, 2414 ....M-5
Camp Hill, 1415 ....H-10
Campbell, 10 ....M-3
Canoe Q-5
Capps N-11
Carbon Hill, 2115 ....E-4
Cardiff, 72 ....R-10
Carlowville, 40 ....L-6
Carlton, 10 ....P-3
Carns B-9
Carolina, 201 ....P-7
Carrollton, 1170 ....G-3
Castleberry, 669 ....P-5
Catalpa M-9
Catherine, 50 ....L-4
Cecil, 70 ....K-9
Cedar Bluff, 1174 ....D-10
Center Pt., 22658 ....F-7
Center Star A-5
Centerville P-6
Central, 125 ....J-8
Central City P-8
Centre, 2893 ....D-10
Centreville, 2508 ....H-5
Chalkville, 3900 ....E-8
Chancellor, 200 ....P-9
Chandler Sprs. G-8
Chapman, 100 ....N-7
Chastang, 70 ....Q-3
Chatom, 1094 ....N-2
Chelsea, 1329 ....G-7
Cherokee, 1479 ....B-3
Chestnut M-5
Chickasaw, 6651 ....R-3
Childersburg, 4579 ....G-8
Chrysler, 40 ....N-4
Chunchula, 300 ....Q-2
Citronelle, 3671 ....Q-2
Claiborne, 40 ....N-4
Clanton, 7669 ....H-7
Claud J-8
Clay E-7
Clayhatchee, 411 ....P-9
Clayton, 1564 ....M-10
Cleveland, 739 ....D-7
Clinton, 175 ....H-3
Clio, 1365 ....N-10
Clopton, 20 ....N-10
Cloverdale, 150 ....A-4
Coal Fire F-3
Coaling, 600 ....G-5
Coatopa, 20 ....K-3
Cochrane, 20 ....H-2
Coden S-2
Coffee Sprs., 294 ....P-9
Coffeeville, 431 ....M-3
Coker, 650 ....G-4
Cole Spr. C-6
Collinsville, 1429 ....C-9
Collinsville, 1429 ....C-9
Collirene L-6
Colony, 298 ....E-6
Columbia, 922 ....P-11
Columbiana, 2968 ....G-7
Columbus City C-8
Conecuh L-10
Cooper, 250 ....J-7
Cordova, 2623 ....E-5
Corona E-4
Cottondale, 2000 ....G-4
Cottonton, 20 ....L-11
Cottonwood, 1385 ....Q-11
County Line, 189 ....E-7
County Line, 127 ....F-8
Courtland, 803 ....B-5
Cowarts, 1400 ....P-11
Crafton, 90 ....G-10
Crane Hill D-5
Crawford, 250 ....K-11
Creola, 1896 ....Q-3
Crews F-3
Cromwell, 30 ....L-2
Crooked Oak B-3
Cropwell F-8
Crosby, 10 ....Q-11
Crossville, 1350 ....C-9
Crossville, 150 ....K-3
Cuba, 390 ....K-2
Cullman, 13367 ....D-6
Cullomburg, 175 ....N-2
Curry, 125 ....F-9
Cusseta, 125 ....J-11
Cypress, 60 ....H-4
Dadeville, 3276 ....H-9
Daleville, 5117 ....P-10
Dancy, 100 ....H-2
Daphne, 11290 ....R-3
Dauphin Island, 824 ....S-3
Davenport L-7
Daviston, 261 ....H-10
Davisville K-10
Dawson C-9
Dayton, 77 ....K-4
DeArmanville, 700 ....F-9
Deatsville, 350 ....J-8
Decatur, 49917 ....B-6
Deer Park, 30 ....P-2
Delmar D-4
Delta, 90 ....G-10
Demopolis, 7512 ....K-3
Deposit A-7
Detroit, 281 ....D-2
Dickinson, 250 ....M-4
Dixie P-7
Dixons Mills, 400 ....L-3
Dixonville, 30 ....Q-5
Dodge City, 467 ....D-6
Dora, 2214 ....E-6
Dozier N-10
Double Sprs., 1138 ....D-5
Douglas, 474 ....D-8
Downing P-5
Dozier, 483 ....N-8
Dry Forks M-5
Dublin L-8
Duke E-9
Duncanville, 175 ....H-4
Dutton, 243 ....B-9
E. Brewton, 2579 ....Q-6
Echo, 50 ....N-10
Echola G-4
Eclectic, 1087 ....J-8
Eddy C-7
Edgewater S-10
Edwardsville, 118 ....E-10
Edwin N-11
Elamville N-10
Elba, 4011 ....P-9
Elberta, 458 ....S-4
Eldridge, 225 ....E-4
Elgin A-5
Eliska N-4
Elkmont, 389 ....A-6
Elkwood A-7
Ellisville D-10
Elmore, 550 ....J-8
Elrod, 150 ....G-3
Elsanor S-4
Emelle, 44 ....J-2
Enterprise, 20123 ....P-9
Epes, 243 ....J-2
Equality, 60 ....J-8
Ethelsville, 52 ....F-2
Eufaula, 13220 ....M-11
Eunola, 169 ....P-9
Eutaw, 2281 ....H-3
Eva, 438 ....C-6
Evansville H-11
Evergreen, 3911 ....N-6
Ewell P-10
Excel, 571 ....P-5
Fackler, 175 ....A-8
Fadette D-10
Fairfield, 12200 ....F-6
Fairfield, 60 ....P-3
Fairford P-3
Fairhope, 8490 ....S-3
Fairview, 383 ....C-7
Fairview J-7
Falkville, 1337 ....C-6
Fatama M-5
Faunsdale, 96 ....K-4
Fayette, 4909 ....E-3
Fayetteville, 200 ....G-7
Fisk A-7
Five Points, 200 ....H-10
Five Points C-5
Flat Rock, 175 ....B-9
Flatwood, 10 ....L-4
Flomaton, 1811 ....Q-5
Florala, 2075 ....Q-8
Florence, 36426 ....A-4
Little River P-4
Foley, 4937 ....S-4
Forest Home, 20 ....M-6
Forestdale, 10395 ....S-11
Forkland, 667 ....J-3
Forkville C-4
Forney, 50 ....D-10
Ft. Davis, 80 ....L-10
Ft. Deposit, 1240 ....M-7
Ft. Mitchell, 200 ....K-11
Ft. Morgan, 350 ....T-3
Ft. Payne, 11838 ....C-9
Fosters, 200 ....G-4
Fostoria L-6
Fountain, 50 ....N-5
Francisco A-8
Franklin, 30 ....M-5
Franklin, 152 ....K-8
Franklinville, 125 ....N-2
Fredonia H-11
Freemanville, 450 ....Q-4
Frisco City, 1581 ....N-5
Fruitdale, 125 ....P-2
Fruithurst, 177 ....E-10
Fulton, 384 ....M-4
Fultondale, 6400 ....F-6
Furman, 20 ....M-6
Fyffe, 1094 ....C-9
Gadsden, 42523 ....D-8
Gainestown P-4
Gainesville, 449 ....H-2
Gallion, 100 ....K-4
Gantt, 265 ....P-7
Garden City, 578 ....D-6
Gardendale, 9251 ....F-6
Garland, 40 ....N-6
Gasque, 350 ....T-3
Gaylesville, 149 ....C-10
Geiger, 270 ....H-2
Geneva, 4681 ....Q-9
Georgetown, 300 ....Q-2
Georgiana, 1933 ....N-7
Geraldine, 801 ....C-8
Gilbertown, 235 ....M-2
Glen Allen, 350 ....E-4
Glencoe, 4670 ....D-9
Glenville, 30 ....L-11
Glenwood, 208 ....N-8
Goldville, 61 ....G-9
Good Hope, 1700 ....D-6
Good Sprs. A-5
Goodwater, 1840 ....H-8
Goodway N-5
Gordo, 1918 ....G-3
Gordon, 493 ....P-11
Gordonsville L-7
Gorgas, 40 ....F-5
Goshen, 302 ....N-8
Gosport N-4
Grady, 100 ....M-8
Graham, 125 ....F-11
Grand Bay, 3383 ....S-2
Grangeburg, 10 ....Q-11
Grant, 638 ....C-8
Graysville, 2241 ....E-6
Green Pond, 200 ....G-5
Greensboro, 3047 ....J-4
Greenville, 7492 ....N-7
Grove Hill, 1551 ....N-3
Gu-Win, 243 ....D-4
Guin, 2464 ....D-3
Gulf Crest, 90 ....Q-2
Gulf Shores, 3261 ....T-4
Guntersville, 7038 ....C-8
Gurley, 1007 ....B-8
Hackleburg, 1161 ....C-3
Hackneyville H-9
Hacoda, 50 ....Q-8
Haleburg, 97 ....P-11
Haleyville, 4452 ....C-4
Halsell, 30 ....L-2
Hamilton, 6171 ....D-3
Hammondville, 420 ....B-10
Hanceville, 2246 ....D-6
Hanover H-8
Hardaway, 40 ....K-9
Harpersville, 772 ....G-7
Harrisburg H-5
Hartford, 2448 ....Q-10
Hartselle, 11114 ....C-6
Harvest, 1922 ....A-6
Hatchechubbee, 40 ....K-11
Hatton, 400 ....B-5
Havana H-4
Hayden, 385 ....E-6
Hayneville, 969 ....L-7
Hazel Green, 2208 ....A-7
Hazen, 62 ....L-5
Headland, 3266 ....P-11
Heath, 182 ....P-7
Heflin, 2906 ....F-10
Helena, 3918 ....G-6
Henagar, 1934 ....B-9
Henderson N-8
Hendrix, 175 ....D-7
Henson Sprs. D-3
Hepzibah P-9
Heron Bay, 550 ....S-2
Higdon A-10
Highland Home, 125 ....M-8
Highland Lake, 304 ....E-7
Hightogy E-3
Hillsboro, 587 ....B-5
Hissop H-8
Hoboken Q-3
Hodges, 272 ....C-3
Hokes Bluff, 3739 ....D-9
Hollins Crossroads, 225 ....F-10
Holly Pond, 602 ....D-7
Hollytree, 50 ....A-8
Hollywood, 916 ....B-9
Holt, 4125 ....G-4
Homewood, 22922 ....F-6
Honoraville, 90 ....M-7
Hoover, 39788 ....F-6
Horn Hill, 255 ....P-8
Horton, 30 ....C-8
Houston D-5
Hueytown, 15280 ....F-6
Huguley, 3161 ....H-11
Hulaco, 400 ....C-7
Hunter, 20 ....K-7
Huntsville, 159789 ....B-7
Hurtsboro, 707 ....L-10
Huxford, 80 ....P-4
Hybart, 20 ....N-5
Ider, 671 ....B-10
Indian Sprs. Vil., 1234 ....G-6
Inverness L-9
Irondale, 9454 ....F-7
Isbell, 200 ....C-4
Isney M-1
Jachin L-2
Jack, 90 ....N-9
Jackson, 5819 ....N-3
Jacksons Gap, 789 ....H-9
Jacksonville, 10283 ....E-9
Jamestown C-10
Jasper, 13553 ....E-5
Jemison, 1898 ....H-6
Jenifer, 550 ....F-9
Johns, 70 ....F-5
Jones Chapel, 50 ....D-6
Jordan K-8
Keener, 150 ....D-9
Kellerman G-5
Kellyton H-9
Kennedy, 523 ....F-3
Kent, 175 ....J-8
Killen, 1047 ....A-4
Kimberly, 1096 ....E-6
Kimbrough, 70 ....L-3
Kingville E-3
Kinston, 595 ....P-8
Knoxville, 20 ....H-3
Koenton P-2
La Place K-9
Lacey's Spr., 750 ....B-7
Ladonia, 2905 ....K-11
Lafayette, 3150 ....H-10
Lanett, 8567 ....J-11
Lamison, 50 ....L-4
Land, 30 ....L-2
Landersville, 150 ....C-5
Lanett, 8985 ....H-11
Langston, 207 ....B-8
Lapine M-8
Lavaca, 100 ....L-3
Lawley, 125 ....H-6
Lawrenceville N-11
Lebanon C-9
Leeds, 9946 ....F-7
Leesburg, 218 ....D-9
Leighton, 1084 ....B-4
Leroy N-3
Lester, 89 ....A-5
Letohatchee, 175 ....L-7
Level Plains, 1473 ....P-9
Lexington, 821 ....A-5
Liberty E-7
Libertyville, 133 ....P-7
Lillian, 350 ....S-5
Lim Rock, 30 ....B-8
Lincoln, 3262 ....F-8
Linden, 2548 ....K-3
Lineville, 2394 ....G-9
Lipscomb, 2892 ....F-6
Lisman, 481 ....L-2
Little River P-4
Littleville, 925 ....B-4
Livingston, 3530 ....J-2
Loachapoka, 259 ....J-10
Lockhart, 484 ....Q-8
Locust Fork, 342 ....E-7
Lomax, 150 ....H-7
London P-5
Long Island, 80 ....A-10
Louisville, 728 ....M-10
Lower Peach Tree, 100 ....M-4
Lowndesboro, 139 ....K-7
Loxley, 1161 ....R-4
Lugo M-11
Luverne, 2555 ....N-8
Lyeffion N-6
Lynn, 611 ....D-4
Macedonia, 290 ....P-2
Madison, 14904 ....B-7
Madrid, 211 ....Q-10
Magnolia L-4
Magnolia Sprs. S-3
Malbis R-3
Malcolm P-3
Malone, 30 ....G-10
Malvern, 570 ....P-10
Manack, 30 ....K-7
Maplesville, 725 ....J-6
Margaret, 616 ....F-7
Marion, 4211 ....J-5
Marion Jct., 50 ....K-5
Martling C-8
Marvel, 70 ....G-6
Marvyn K-10
Maylene G-6
Maysville B-7
Maytown, 651 ....S-8
McCalla G-6
McCullough, 200 ....P-4
McIntosh, 250 ....P-3
McKenzie, 464 ....N-7
McMullen, 112 ....G-2
McVay L-3
McWilliams, 125 ....M-5
Megargel, 90 ....P-4
Mellow Valley G-9
Melvin, 60 ....M-1
Memphis, 54 ....G-2
Mentone, 474 ....B-10
Mendenhilla, 2852 ....A-7
Mexia N-5
Midfield, 5559 ....F-6
Midland City, 1819 ....P-10
Midway, 455 ....L-10
Midway, 10 ....N-6
Mifflin S-4
Millbrook, 6050 ....K-8
Miller, 40 ....L-3
Millers Ferry, 20 ....L-5
Millerville, 200 ....G-9
Millport, 1203 ....E-3
Millry, 781 ....N-2
Milstead, 10 ....K-9
Minter, 60 ....L-6
Mitchell L-9
Mobile, 199973 ....R-3
Molloy E-2
Mon Louis S-2
Monroeville, 6993 ....N-5
Montevallo, 4239 ....G-6
Montgomery, 187543 ....K-8
Montrose R-3
Moody, 4921 ....F-7
Moores Bridge, 10 ....F-3
Mooresville, 54 ....B-6
Moreland C-6
Morgan City, 550 ....C-7
Morris, 1136 ....E-6
Morvin M-3
Mosses, 1072 ....L-7
Moulton, 3248 ....C-5
Moundville, 1348 ....H-4
Mt. Andrew, 40 ....M-10
Mt. Carmel A-9
Mt. Hebron H-3
Mt. Olive H-8
Mt. Rozell K-5
Mt. Sterling L-2
Mt. Vernon, 902 ....Q-3
Mt. Willing L-7
Mtn. Brook, 19810 ....F-6
Mtn. Cr., 300 ....J-7
Mountainboro, 261 ....D-8
Mulga, 261 ....K-10
Munford, 500 ....F-9
Muscle Shoals, 9611 ....B-4
Myrtlewood, 197 ....L-3
Nanafalia L-3
Natural Bridge, 90 ....D-4
Nauvoo, 240 ....D-4
Nectar, 238 ....D-7
Needham, 99 ....M-2
New Brockton, 1184 ....P-9
New Hope, 2248 ....B-8
New Lexington F-4
New Market, 1094 ....A-7
New Site, 669 ....H-9
Newbern, 222 ....J-4
Newell F-10
Newton, 1580 ....P-10
Newtonville, 40 ....F-3
Newville, 531 ....P-11
Nixburg H-8
N. Courtland, 973 ....B-5
N. Johns, 177 ....F-5
Northport, 17366 ....G-4
Notasulga, 979 ....J-10
Oak Bowery J-10
Oak Gr., 436 ....K-2
Oak Hill, 28 ....M-6
Oak Level E-10
Oakland A-5
Oakman, 846 ....E-5
Oakville C-5
Odenville, 796 ....E-8
Ohatchee, 1042 ....E-8
Old Spr. Hill K-3
Old Texas M-5
Oleander C-7
Oneonta, 4844 ....E-7
Onycha, 150 ....P-8
Opelika, 22122 ....J-10
Opp, 6985 ....P-8
Orange Beach, 2253 ....S-4
Orion, 30 ....M-9
Orrville, 234 ....K-5
Overbrook, 400 ....G-8
Owassa N-6
Owens Crossroads, 695 ....B-7
Oxford, 9362 ....F-9
Ozark, 12922 ....N-10
Paint Rock, 214 ....B-8
Palmetto F-3
Panola, 90 ....H-2
Pansey P-11
Parkdale C-8
Parrish, 1433 ....E-5
Patsburg M-8
Pea Ridge, 175 ....G-6
Pelham, 9765 ....G-6
Pell City, 8118 ....F-8
Pennington, 302 ....L-3
Perdido, 400 ....P-4
Perdido Beach S-4
Perdue Hill N-4
Perote, 10 ....M-10
Perryville K-5
Peterman N-5
Peterson, 450 ....G-5
Petersville, 800 ....A-4
Petrey, 80 ....M-8
Phenix City, 25312 ....K-12
Phil Campbell, 1317 ....C-4
Pickensville, 169 ....G-2
Piedmont, 5288 ....E-10
Pigeon Cr. N-7
Pike Road, 20 ....K-8
Pikeville D-3
Pinckard, 618 ....P-10
Pine Apple, 385 ....M-6
Pine Flat J-6
Pine Hill, 481 ....M-4
Pine Level, 100 ....L-8
Pine Orchard N-5
Pine Ridge, 227 ....C-9
Pinson, 2100 ....E-7
Pisgah, 652 ....B-9
Pittsview, 70 ....L-11
Plantersville, 300 ....J-6
Pleasant Gr., 8458 ....F-6
Pleasant Groves, 454 ....A-9
Pleasant Hill L-6
Pleasant Hill V-9
Pleasant Ridge H-3
Pleasant Site, 50 ....B-3
Pletcher, 90 ....J-6
Plevna, 50 ....A-7
Poarch Q-4
Pt. Clear, 2125 ....S-3
Pollard, 100 ....Q-5
Pondville, 60 ....H-5
Poplar Sprs. D-3
Portersville, 30 ....C-8
Powell, 762 ....B-9
Prairieville J-4
Prattville, 19587 ....K-7
Priceville, 1323 ....C-6
Prichard, 34311 ....R-3
Princeton A-8
Providence, 307 ....K-3
Putnam L-3
Pyriton, 70 ....G-9
Rabun, 100 ....Q-4
Ragland, 1807 ....E-8
Rainbow City, 7673 ....E-8
Rainsville, 3875 ....C-9
Ralph, 40 ....G-4
Ramer, 100 ....L-8
Ranburne, 447 ....F-11
Randolph, 30 ....H-6
Range, 80 ....P-5
Red Bank B-5
Red Bay, 3451 ....C-3
Red Hill, 250 ....J-8
Red Level, 588 ....P-7
Reece City, 657 ....D-8
Reform, 2105 ....F-3
Rehobeth, 769 ....Q-10
Repton, 293 ....P-5
Republic E-11
Richmond L-6
Ridgewood, 40 ....J-8
Ridgeville, 178 ....D-8
Ripley B-5
River Falls, 710 ....P-7
Riverside, 1004 ....F-8
Riverton A-3
Riverview, 90 ....Q-6
Roanoke, 6362 ....G-10
Robertsdale, 2401 ....S-4
Robinsonville G-4
Rock Mills G-11
Rock Run E-10
Rockford, 461 ....H-8
Rockledge, 600 ....D-8
Rocky Head N-9
Rogersville, 1125 ....A-5
Rome Q-7
Rosa, 139 ....D-7
Rosalie, 400 ....B-9
Roseball A-3
Russell Q-2
Russellville, 7812 ....C-4
Rutledge, 473 ....N-8
Saco, 100 ....M-9
Safford, 30 ....K-5
Saginaw, 300 ....G-6
St. Elmo S-2
St. Florian, 388 ....A-4
St. Stephens, 60 ....N-3
Saints Crossroads B-4
Saks, 11138 ....E-9
Salem, 125 ....J-11
Salitpa, 150 ....N-3
Samantha, 70 ....F-4
Samson, 2190 ....Q-9
Sand Rock, 438 ....C-9
Sandy Ridge, 20 ....L-7
Sanford, 282 ....P-8
Santuck J-8
Saraland, 11784 ....R-3
Sardis, 80 ....K-6
Sardis City, 1301 ....D-8
Satsuma, 5194 ....R-3
Sawyerville, 50 ....J-4
Scottsboro, 13786 ....B-8
Seale, 225 ....K-11
Searight N-8
Section, 777 ....B-9
Sellers L-8
Selma, 23755 ....K-6
Selmont, 1100 ....K-6
Seman J-8
Semmes, 2250 ....R-2
Shawmut, 2181 ....H-11
Shady Gr., 40 ....M-8
Shady Gr. C-4
Shannon U-11
Sheffield, 10380 ....B-4
Shiloh, 252 ....C-9
Shorter, 400 ....K-9
Shorterville, 80 ....N-11
Shottsville C-3
Silas, 245 ....M-2
Silverhill, 556 ....S-3
Simcoe C-5
Sims Chapel, 80 ....P-2
Sipsey, 668 ....E-6
Skipperville N-10
Skyline, 740 ....A-8
Slocomb, 1906 ....Q-10
Smiths, 3456 ....J-11
Smut Eye, 40 ....M-10
Snead, 632 ....D-8
Snow Hill, 10 ....M-6
Snowdoun, 400 ....L-8
Society Hill, 10 ....K-10
Somerville, 211 ....C-6
Southside, 5580 ....E-9
Spanish Ft., 3327 ....R-3
Speigner, 1700 ....J-8
Sprague, 50 ....L-8
Spr. Hill, 150 ....N-9
Spr. Valley B-4
Springville, 1910 ....E-7
Sprott, 10 ....J-5
Stanton, 70 ....J-6
Stapleton, 400 ....R-3
State Line N-1
Steele, 1046 ....E-8
Sterrett, 350 ....F-7
Stevenson, 2046 ....A-9
Stewartville, 450 ....H-8
Stockton, 225 ....Q-4
Stroud, 60 ....H-11
Sulligent, 1886 ....E-3
Sulphur Sprs. C-9
Summit, 2604 ....C-8
Summerdale, 559 ....S-4
Summit, 125 ....D-7
Summit Farm V-10
Suncoast C-5
Sunflower P-3
Sunny South, 200 ....M-4
Surginer, 150 ....L-4
Susan Moore, 658 ....D-7
Suttle, 10 ....J-5
Swaim A-8
Sweet Water, 243 ....L-3
Sycamore, 500 ....G-8
Sylacauga, 12520 ....G-8
Sylvania, 932 ....B-9
Talladega, 18175 ....F-8
Tallassee, 5112 ....J-9
Tanner, 900 ....B-6
Tanner Williams R-2
Tarrant, 8046 ....F-6
Taylor, 1352 ....Q-10
Taylorville V-2
Tennant, 70 ....G-10
Tensaw, 20 ....P-3
Texasville, 30 ....M-10
Thach, 175 ....A-6
Theodore, 6509 ....S-2
Thomaston, 497 ....K-4
Thomasville, 4301 ....M-4
Thornton J-9
Thorsby, 1465 ....H-7
Three Notch L-10
Tibbie, 50 ....P-2
Tillmans Corner, 17988 ....R-2
Titus J-8
Town Cr., 1379 ....B-5
Townley E-5
Toxey, 211 ....M-2
Trafford, 739 ....E-6
Trenton B-8
Triana, 499 ....B-6
Trinity, 1380 ....B-5
Troy, 13051 ....M-9
Trussville, 8266 ....F-7
Tumbleton P-11
Tunnel Sprs., 80 ....N-5
Tuscaloosa, 77759 ....G-4
Tuscumbia, 8413 ....B-4
Tuskegee, 12257 ....K-10
Tyler, 30 ....K-6
Union A-7
Union, 321 ....H-3
Union Gr., 119 ....C-7
Union Gr. K-7
Union Hill C-7
Union Sprs., 3975 ....L-9
Uniontown, 1730 ....K-4
Uriah N-4
Uriah, 200 ....P-4
Valhermoso Sprs. C-7
Valley, 9556 ....H-11
Valley Cr., 150 ....F-6
Valley Head, 577 ....B-10
Vance, 248 ....G-5
Verbena, 250 ....J-7
Vernon, 2247 ....E-3
Vestavia Hills, 19749 ....F-6
Victoria N-9
Vidette M-8
Village Sprs., 550 ....E-7
Vina, 356 ....C-3
Vincent, 1767 ....F-7
Vinegar Bend, 30 ....P-2
Vineland L-4
Vinemont, 543 ....C-6
Vredenburgh, 313 ....M-5
Wadley, 517 ....G-10
Wagarville, 100 ....N-3
Waldo, 309 ....F-9
Walker Sprs., 50 ....N-3
Wallsboro, 200 ....J-9
Walnut Gr., 717 ....D-8
Walnut Hill J-9
Ward, 30 ....K-2
Warrior, 3280 ....E-6
Warsaw H-2
Waterloo, 250 ....A-3
Watson R-11
Wattsville F-8
Waverly, 152 ....J-10
Weaver, 2715 ....E-9
Webb, 1039 ....P-11
Wedgeworth H-4
Wedowee, 796 ....G-10
Wellington, 250 ....E-9
Weogufka, 70 ....H-8
Weoka J-8
W. Blocton, 1468 ....G-5
W. End, 2400 ....K-9
W. Greene H-3
W. Jefferson, 388 ....F-6
W. Point, 257 ....C-6
Wetumpka, 4670 ....J-8
Whatley, 125 ....N-4
White City K-7
White Hall, 814 ....K-7
Whitfield, 50 ....K-3
Wilmer, 494 ....R-2
Wilsonville, 1185 ....G-7
Wilton, 602 ....H-6
Windham Sprs., 100 ....F-4
Winfield, 3689 ....E-3
Wing, 50 ....Q-7
Woodland, 189 ....G-10
Woodstock, 300 ....G-5
Woodville, 687 ....B-8
Wren, 100 ....C-5
Wright A-3
Yantley, 125 ....K-2
Yarbo, 70 ....N-2
Yellow Bluff, 245 ....M-4
Yellow Pine, 70 ....P-2
York, 3160 ....K-2

ALASKA
PG. 62

CAPITAL
Juneau

NICKNAME
Great Land

POPULATION
607,007, rank 48

AREA
591,004 sq mi, rank 1

Cities and Towns

Adak, 4633 ....K-3
Akhiok, 77 ....H-9
Akiachak, 481 ....F-7
Akiak, 285 ....F-7
Akutan, 589 ....F-8
Alakanuk, 544 ....E-3
Aleknagik, 185 ....F-4
Allakaket, 170 ....C-7
Ambler, 311 ....C-5
Amchitka K-2
Anaktuvuk Pass, 259 ....B-6
Anchor Pt., 866 ....F-7
Anchorage, 226338 ....F-7
Anderson, 628 ....D-7
Angoon, 638 ....G-10
Aniak, 540 ....F-4
Anvik, 82 ....E-4
Arctic Vil., 96 ....B-7
Atka, 73 ....J-5
Atqasuk, 216 ....A-5
Attu J-1
Barrow, 3469 ....A-5
Beaver, 103 ....C-7
Bethel, 4674 ....F-4
Bettles, 36 ....C-6
Big Delta, 400 ....D-7
Brevig Mission, 198 ....C-3
Buckland, 318 ....C-4
Cantwell, 147 ....E-7
Central, 52 ....D-7
Chalkyitsik, 90 ....C-8
Chefornak, 320 ....F-3
Chevak, 598 ....E-3
Chignik, 188 ....H-4
Chitina, 49 ....F-8
Circle, 73 ....C-8
Clarks Pt., 60 ....G-5
Coffman Cove, 186 ....H-11
Cold Bay, 148 ....H-3
College, 11249 ....D-7
Copper Ctr., 449 ....E-7
Cordova, 2537 ....F-7
Craig, 1260 ....H-11
Deadhorse, 26 ....B-7
Deering, 157 ....C-4
Delta Jct., 652 ....D-7
Dillingham, 2017 ....G-4
Diomede, 178 ....C-3
Dutch Harbor J-2
Eagle, 168 ....D-8
Eek, 254 ....G-4
Egegik, 122 ....G-5
Ekwok, 77 ....G-5
Elim, 264 ....D-4
Emmonak, 642 ....D-3
Fairbanks, 30843 ....D-7
False Pass, 69 ....H-3
Flat E-5
Ft. Yukon, 580 ....C-7
Fox, 275 ....D-7
Galena, 833 ....D-5
Gambell, 525 ....D-2
Glennallen, 451 ....E-7
Golovin, 127 ....D-4
Goodnews Bay, 241 ....F-4
Grayling, 208 ....E-4
Gulkana, 103 ....E-8
Gustavus, 258 ....G-10
Haines, 1238 ....F-10
Healy, 487 ....D-7
Hollis, 111 ....H-11
Holy Cross, 277 ....E-4
Homer, 3660 ....F-6
Hoonah, 795 ....G-10
Hooper Bay, 845 ....E-3
Hope, 161 ....F-7
Houston, 697 ....E-6
Hughes, 54 ....C-6
Huslia, 207 ....D-5
Hydaburg, 384 ....H-11
Hyder, 99 ....H-12
Igiugig, 33 ....G-5
Iliamna, 94 ....G-5
Juneau, 26751 ....G-10
Kake, 700 ....G-11
Kaktovik, 224 ....A-8
Kaltag, 240 ....D-5
Kantishna B-11
Kasigluk, 425 ....F-4
Kenai, 6327 ....F-6
Ketchikan, 8263 ....H-11
Kiana, 385 ....C-5
King Cove, 451 ....H-3
King Salmon, 696 ....G-5
Kipnuk, 470 ....F-3
Kivalina, 317 ....B-4
Klawock, 722 ....H-11
Klukwan, 129 ....F-10
Kobuk, 69 ....C-5
Kodiak, 6365 ....G-6
Kokhanok, 152 ....G-5
Koliganek, 181 ....F-5
Kotlik, 461 ....E-4
Kotzebue, 2751 ....C-4
Koyuk, 231 ....D-4
Koyukuk, 126 ....D-5
Kwethluk, 558 ....F-4
Larsen Bay, 147 ....G-5
Levelock, 105 ....G-5
Lime Vil., 42 ....F-5
Lower Kalskag, 291 ....E-4
Manley Hot Sprs., 96 ....D-6
Manokotak, 385 ....G-5
Marshall, 273 ....E-4
McCarthy, 25 ....F-8
McGrath, 528 ....E-5
McKinley Park, 171 ....E-7
Mekoryuk, 177 ....F-3
Mentasta Lake, 96 ....E-8
Metlakatla, 1407 ....H-11
Minto, 218 ....D-7
Moose Pass, 81 ....F-7
Mountain Vil., 674 ....E-4
Nabesna E-8
Naknek, 575 ....G-5
Napakiak, 318 ....F-4
Napaskiak, 328 ....F-4
Nenana, 393 ....D-7
New Stuyahok, 391 ....F-5
Newhalen, 160 ....F-5
Newtok, 207 ....F-3
Nikiski, 2743 ....F-6
Nikolai, 109 ....E-6
Nikolski, 35 ....J-1
Ninilchik, 456 ....F-6
Noatak, 333 ....B-4
Nome, 3500 ....D-3
Nondalton, 178 ....F-5
Noorvik, 531 ....C-4
N. Pole, 1456 ....D-7
Northway, 123 ....E-8
Nuiqsut, 354 ....A-6
Nulato, 359 ....D-5
Old Harbor, 284 ....H-6
Ophir E-5
Ouzinkie, 209 ....G-6
Palmer, 2866 ....F-7
Paxson E-7
Pelican, 222 ....G-10
Petersburg, 3207 ....G-11
Petersville D-11
Pilot Pt., 53 ....G-5
Pilot Sta., 463 ....E-4
Pt. Hope, 639 ....B-4
Pt. Lay, 139 ....A-4
Poorman D-5
Port Alexander, 119 ....H-10
Port Heiden, 119 ....H-4
Port Lions, 222 ....G-6
Prudhoe Bay, 47 ....A-7
Quinhagak, 501 ....G-4
Rampart, 68 ....C-6
Ruby, 170 ....D-5
Russian Mission, 246 ....E-4
Sagwon B-7
St. George, 138 ....G-2
St. Marys, 441 ....E-4
St. Michael, 295 ....D-4
St. Paul, 763 ....G-2
Sand Pt., 878 ....H-4
Savoonga, 519 ....D-2
Scammon Bay, 343 ....E-3
Selawik, 596 ....C-5
Seldovia, 316 ....G-6
Seward, 2699 ....F-7
Shageluk, 139 ....E-4
Shaktoolik, 178 ....D-4
Sheldon Pt., 109 ....E-3
Shishmaref, 456 ....C-3
Shungnak C-5
Sitka, 8588 ....G-10
Skagway, 692 ....F-10
Slana, 63 ....E-8
Sleetmute, 106 ....F-5
Soldotna, 3482 ....F-6
Stebbins, 400 ....D-4
Stevens Vil., 102 ....C-7
Summit B-13
Talkeetna, 250 ....E-6
Tanacross, 106 ....E-8
Tanana, 345 ....D-6
Tatitlek, 119 ....F-7
Teller, 151 ....C-3
Tenakee Sprs., 94 ....G-10
Tetlin, 87 ....E-8
Thorne Bay, 569 ....H-11
Togiak, 613 ....G-4
Tok, 935 ....E-8
Toksook Bay, 420 ....F-3
Trapper Cr., 296 ....E-6
Tununak, 316 ....F-3
Unalakleet, 714 ....D-4
Unalaska, 3089 ....J-2
Valdez, 4068 ....F-7
Venetie, 182 ....C-7
Wainwright, 492 ....A-5
Wales, 161 ....C-3
Wasilla, 4028 ....F-7
White Mtn., 180 ....D-4
Whittier, 243 ....F-7
Wonder Lake B-11
Wrangell, 2479 ....G-11
Yakutat, 705 ....F-9

ARIZONA
PG. 63–65

CAPITAL
Phoenix

NICKNAME
Grand Canyon State

POPULATION
4,428,068, rank 21

AREA
114,000 sq mi, rank 6

Counties

Apache, 61591 ....E-12
Cochise, 97624 ....P-12
Coconino, 96591 ....D-7
Gila, 40216 ....J-9
Graham, 26554 ....L-11
Greenlee, 8008 ....K-12
La Paz, 13844 ....J-3
Maricopa, 2122101 ....K-6
Mohave, 93497 ....D-3
Navajo, 77658 ....E-10
Pima, 666880 ....N-7
Pinal, 116379 ....M-8
Santa Cruz, 29676 ....Q-9
Yavapai, 107714 ....H-6
Yuma, 106895 ....K-3

Cities and Towns

* City indexed to pg. 63

Agua Caliente, 50 ....L-4
Ajo, 2919 ....N-5
Ak Chin, 150 ....N-7
Ak-Chin, 353 ....L-7
Ali Chuk, 450 ....P-6
Alpine, 60 ....J-13
Amado, 125 ....P-9
Anegam, 175 ....N-7
Apache, 20 ....P-13
Apache Jct., 18100 ....K-8
Aquila, 90 ....J-5
Aravaipa L-10
Arizona G-10
Arivaca, 100 ....Q-8
Arizola, 550 ....M-8
Arizona City, 1940 ....M-8
Arlington, 90 ....K-5
Artesia, 200 ....M-12
Ash Fork, 450 ....F-6
Avondale, 17595 ....K-6
Aztec, 20 ....M-4
Bagdad, 1858 ....G-5
Bapchule, 70 ....L-7
Beardsley, 10 ....K-6
Bellemont E-7
Benson, 3824 ....P-10
Bidahochi, 20 ....E-11
Big Sprs. B-6
Bisbee, 6288 ....Q-11
Bitter Sprs., 30 ....B-8
Black Canyon City, 1811 ....H-7
Blaisdell, 30 ....M-2
Blue, 30 ....J-13
Blue Gap C-11
Bonita, 10 ....M-11
Bosque, 100 ....M-5
Bouse, 250 ....J-3
Bowie, 550 ....N-12
Brenda, 50 ....K-3
Bridgeport, 30 ....G-7
Buckeye, 5038 ....K-6
Bullhead City, 21951 ....F-2
Bylas, 1219 ....L-10
Cactus Flat, 550 ....M-12
Cactus Forest, 20 ....L-8
Calva, 50 ....K-10
Cameron, 493 ....D-8
Camp Cr., 80 ....J-7
Camp Verde, 6243 ....G-7
Cane Beds, 30 ....A-5
Canelo, 60 ....Q-10
Canyon Day, 857 ....J-11
Canyon Diablo F-9
Carefree, 1666 ....J-7
Carrizo, 150 ....H-10
Casa Blanca, 350 ....L-7
Casa Grande, 19082 ....M-7
Cascabel, 50 ....N-10
Cashion E-4
Castle Hot Sprs. H-6
Catalina, 4864 ....N-9
Cave Cr., 2395 ....J-7
Cedar Cr., 70 ....J-11
Cedar Ridge, 225 ....C-8
Central, 400 ....M-11
Chambers, 250 ....E-12
Chandler, 125000 ....K-7
Chandler Hts., 950 ....L-8
Charleston Q-11
Chilchinbito, 250 ....B-11
Childs, 20 ....H-5
Chinle, 5059 ....C-12
Chino Valley, 4837 ....G-6
Chloride, 175 ....E-3
Christmas, 70 ....L-10
Chuichu, 330 ....M-7
Cibecue, 1254 ....H-10
Cibola J-2
Circle City *A-2
Clarkdale, 2144 ....G-7
Clay Sprs., 250 ....G-10
Claypool, 1942 ....K-9
Cleator, 10 ....H-6
Clifton, 2840 ....L-12
Cochise, 40 ....P-11
Colorado City, 2426 ....A-5
Concho, 50 ....G-12
Congress, 175 ....H-5
Constellation, 100 ....H-6
Coolidge, 6927 ....L-8
Cornfields, 300 ....D-12
Cornville, 2089 ....G-7
Cortaro, 1700 ....N-9
Cottonwood, 12956 ....G-7
Cottonwood, 10 ....C-11
Cove, 125 ....B-12
Covered Wells, 60 ....N-7
Cow Sprs., 225 ....C-9
Cowlic, 100 ....P-7
Crown King, 60 ....H-6
Crystal, 100 ....A-9
Curtiss, 40 ....P-11
Cutter, 10 ....K-10
Date, 10 ....H-5
Dateland, 70 ....M-4
Dennehotso, 616 ....A-11
Desert View, 10 ....C-7
Dewey, 70 ....G-7
Dilkon, 650 ....E-10
Dolan Sprs., 1090 ....D-2
Dome, 20 ....M-2
Dos Cabezas, 40 ....P-12
Double Adobe, 125 ....Q-12
Douglas, 13908 ....Q-12
Dragoon, 70 ....P-11
Dudleyville, 1356 ....M-9
Duncan, 662 ....M-13
Eagar, 4025 ....H-12
Eden, 70 ....L-11
Ehrenberg, 1226 ....J-2
El Mirage, 5001 ....*C-4
Elfrida, 500 ....P-12
Elgin, 50 ....Q-10
Eloy, 7211 ....M-8
Flagstaff, 45857 ....E-8
Florence, 7819 ....L-8
Florence Jct., 250 ....K-8
Forest Lakes, 90 ....H-9
Ft. Apache, 100 ....J-11
Ft. Defiance, 4489 ....D-13
Ft. Grant, 800 ....M-11
Ft. McDowell J-8
Ft. Thomas, 125 ....L-11
Fountain Hills, 10030 ....J-7
Franklin, 70 ....M-13
Fredonia, 1207 ....A-6
Fresnal Canyon, 20 ....P-8
Friendly Corners, 20 ....M-8
Gadsden, 300 ....N-1
Ganado, 1257 ....D-12
Geronimo, 10 ....L-11
Gila Bend, 1747 ....L-5
Gilbert, 29149 ....K-7
Gisela, 300 ....H-8
Glendale, 182615 ....K-6
Glenbar, 30 ....L-11
Globe, 6062 ....K-9
Golden Shores F-2
Goodyear, 6258 ....K-6
Grand Canyon, 1499 ....C-7
Granville, 10 ....K-12
Grasshopper H-10
Gray Mtn., 90 ....D-8
Greasewood, 196 ....E-12
Greaterville, 60 ....P-10
Green Valley, 13231 ....P-9
Greer, 30 ....H-12
Groom Cr., 250 ....G-6
Gu Oidak, 150 ....P-7
Gu Vo, 175 ....N-6
Guadalupe, 5458 ....*E-6
Gunsight, 200 ....N-5
Guthrie L-12
Hackberry, 20 ....E-4
Haivana Nakya, 200 ....P-8
Hannagan Meadow, 10 ....J-12
Happy Jack G-8
Harcuvar, 40 ....J-4
Hawley Lake H-11
Hayden, 909 ....L-9
Heber, 225 ....G-10
Hereford Q-11
Hickiwan, 30 ....N-6
Higley, 450 ....*F-8
Hillside, 100 ....G-5
Hilltop, 20 ....P-13
Holbrook, 4686 ....F-11
Hope, 20 ....J-4
Horn, 150 ....L-4
Hotevilla, 869 ....D-10
Houck, 10 ....E-12
Huachuca City, 1782 ....P-10
Humboldt, 500 ....G-6
Hunters Pt., 400 ....E-13
Hyder, 40 ....L-4
Iron Sprs. G-6
Jackrabbit, 20 ....M-7
Jacob Lake B-7
Jakes Corner, 10 ....H-8
Jeddito, 125 ....D-11
Jerome, 403 ....G-7
Johnson N-11
Joseph City, 1000 ....F-10
Kaibab, 40 ....A-6
Kaibito, 641 ....B-9
Kaihon Kug, 10 ....P-7
Katherine E-2
Kayenta, 4372 ....B-10
Keams Canyon, 393 ....D-11
Kearny, 2262 ....L-9
Kelvin, 150 ....L-9
Kingman, 13208 ....E-3
Kinlichee, 20 ....D-12
Kirkland, 40 ....G-6
Kirkland Jct., 10 ....H-6
Klagetoh, 50 ....E-12
Klondyke, 50 ....M-10
Kohatk, 150 ....M-7
Kohls Ranch H-9
Komatke, 1116 ....K-7
Kykotsmovi, 773 ....D-10
La Palma, 100 ....L-8
Lake Havasu City, 24363 ....G-2
Lake Montezuma, 1841 ....G-7
Laveen, 850 ....K-7
Lees Ferry, 100 ....A-8
Leupp, 857 ....E-9
Leupp Corner, 100 ....E-9
Liberty, 250 ....K-6
Ligurta, 10 ....M-2
Linden, 60 ....H-11
Litchfield Park, 3303 ....*D-3
Little Tucson, 30 ....P-7
Littlefield, 20 ....A-3
Lochiel Q-10
Low Mtn., 175 ....D-11
Lukachukai, 113 ....B-12
Lukeville, 125 ....P-5
Lupton, 400 ....E-13
Madera Canyon, 70 ....P-9
Mammoth, 1845 ....M-10
Many Farms, 1294 ....C-12
Marana, 2565 ....N-8
Marble Canyon, 100 ....B-8
Maricopa, 800 ....L-7
Maricopa Vil. K-6
Mayer, 850 ....G-6
McNary, 355 ....H-11
McNeal, 100 ....Q-12
Meadview, 10 ....D-3
Mesa, 289199 ....K-7
Mexican Water, 60 ....A-12
Miami, 2018 ....K-9
Mobile, 40 ....L-6
Moccasin, 80 ....A-5
Moenkopi, 924 ....C-8
Mohave Valley, 6962 ....F-2
Mohawk M-3
Morenci, 1799 ....L-12
Mormon Lake, 50 ....F-8
Morristown, 80 ....H-6
Mt. Trumbull C-4
Mountainaire, 700 ....F-8
Munds Park, 300 ....F-8
Naco, 791 ....Q-11
Navajo, 10 ....E-12
Navajo Sta., 80 ....E-11
Nazlini, 20 ....D-12
Nelson E-4
New River, 300 ....J-7
Nicksville, 450 ....Q-11
Nogales, 19489 ....Q-9
N. Komelik, 100 ....M-7
N. Rim C-7
Nutrioso, 40 ....H-13
Oatman, 150 ....F-2
Octave, 50 ....H-5
Oljato, 60 ....A-10
Oracle, 3043 ....M-9
Oracle Jct., 550 ....N-9
Oro Valley, 9024 ....N-9
Overgaard, 175 ....G-10
Page, 6598 ....A-9
Palo Verde, 100 ....K-6
Palomas L-4
Palominas Q-11
Pan Tak, 40 ....P-8
Pantano, 350 ....P-10
Paradise, 20 ....P-13
Paradise Valley, 11903 ....*D-6
Parker, 2897 ....H-2
Parks, 20 ....F-7
Patagonia, 888 ....Q-10
Paul Spur, 20 ....Q-12
Paulden, 250 ....F-6
Payson, 8377 ....H-8
Peach Sprs., 787 ....E-4
Pearce, 20 ....P-12
Peeples Valley, 100 ....H-6
Peoria, 51080 ....K-7
Peridot, 957 ....K-10
Perkinsville, 10 ....F-7
Perryville *E-3
Phoenix, 988015 ....K-7
Pia Oik, 450 ....P-6
Picacho, 500 ....M-8
Pima, 1725 ....L-11
Pine, 400 ....G-8
Pine Sprs. E-12
Pinedale, 100 ....H-10
Pinetop-Lakeside, 2422 ....H-11
Pinon, 468 ....C-10
Pirtleville, 1364 ....Q-12
Pisinimo, 341 ....P-6
Polacca, 1108 ....D-10
Pomerene, 40 ....P-10
Portal, 20 ....P-13
Poston, 480 ....H-2
Prescott, 26455 ....G-6
Prescott Valley, 8858 ....G-6
Punkin Ctr. J-8
Quartzsite, 1876 ....J-2
Queen Cr., 2667 ....L-8
Queens Well N-5
Quijotoa, 150 ....N-7
Quivero, 10 ....P-7
Rainbow Valley, 20 ....K-6
Randolph, 250 ....L-8
Red Lake, 225 ....E-7
Red Mesa, 175 ....A-12
Red Rock, 10 ....N-8
Red Rock, 10 ....B-13
Red Rock, 10 ....Q-13
Redington, 30 ....N-10
Rio Rico Q-9
Rock Pt., 450 ....B-12
Rock Sprs., 20 ....J-7
Roll, 70 ....M-3
Roosevelt, 30 ....J-9
Rough Rock, 523 ....B-11
Round Rock, 80 ....B-12
Rye, 40 ....H-8
Sacaton, 1452 ....L-7
Safford, 7112 ....L-11
Sahuarita, 1629 ....P-9
St. David, 1468 ....P-11
St. Johns, 3294 ....G-12
St. Michaels, 1119 ....D-13
Salado, 125 ....G-12
Salina, 150 ....D-11
Salome, 70 ....J-4
San Carlos, 2918 ....K-10
San Luis, 4212 ....N-1
San Luis, 60 ....N-7
San Manuel, 4009 ....M-10
San Miguel, 80 ....Q-7
San Pedro N-8
San Simon, 125 ....N-13
San Xavier, 50 ....P-9
Sanders, 200 ....E-12
Santa Cruz *G-5
Santa Maria *E-5
Santa Rosa, 493 ....N-7
Sasabe, 20 ....Q-8
Sawmill, 507 ....D-13
Schuchk, 50 ....N-8
Scottsdale, 130099 ....K-7
Second Mesa, 929 ....D-10
Sedona, 7720 ....F-7
Seligman, 500 ....E-5
Sells, 2750 ....P-7
Sentinel, 30 ....L-4
Sheldon, 30 ....M-13
Shonto, 710 ....B-10
Show Low, 5019 ....H-11
Shumway, 125 ....G-11
Shungopavi, 730 ....D-10
Sierra Vista, 32983 ....Q-10
Sil Nakya, 125 ....N-7
Silver Cr. H-11
Skull Valley, 60 ....G-6
Smoke Signal, 20 ....D-11
Snowflake, 3679 ....G-11
Solomon, 500 ....M-12
Somerton, 5293 ....M-1
Sonoita, 50 ....P-10
S. Komelik, 90 ....P-7
S. Tucson, 5093 ....N-9
Springerville, 1802 ....H-12
Stanfield, 600 ....L-7
Star Valley, 550 ....H-8
Stargo L-12
Steamboat Canyon, 1100 ....D-11
Strawberry, 400 ....G-8
Summerhaven, 20 ....N-9
Sun City, 38126 ....J-6
Sun City West, 15997 ....*C-3
Sun Lakes, 6578 ....L-7
Sun Valley, 20 ....F-11
Sunizona, 200 ....P-12
Sunrise Sprs., 40 ....E-12
Sunset, 80 ....M-1
Sunsites P-11
Supai, 423 ....C-6
Superior, 3468 ....K-9
Surprise, 7122 ....J-6
Sweetwater, 225 ....A-12
Swift Trail Jct., 1203 ....M-12
Tacna, 90 ....M-3
Tanque, 40 ....M-12
Tanque Verde, 1800 ....N-10
Taylor, 2418 ....G-11
Teec Nos Pos, 317 ....A-13
Tees Toh, 20 ....E-10
Tempe, 141865 ....K-7
Temple Bar, 20 ....C-2
Thatcher, 3763 ....M-12
The Gap, 175 ....C-8
Three Points, 2175 ....N-8
Tolleson, 4436 ....*E-4
Toltec, 20 ....M-8
Tombstone, 1220 ....P-11
Tonalea, 225 ....B-9
Tonopah, 10 ....K-5
Tonto Vil. H-9
Topawa, 150 ....P-7
Topock G-2
Tortilla Flat, 40 ....K-8
Toyei, 70 ....D-11
Truxton, 30 ....E-4
Tsaile, 1043 ....C-12
Tuba City, 7323 ....C-8
Tubac, 450 ....Q-9
Tucson, 415444 ....N-9
Tumacacori, 400 ....Q-9
Turkey Flat M-11
Tusayan, 400 ....D-7
Two Guns F-9
Vail, 1200 ....N-10
Valentine, 20 ....E-4
Valley Farms, 300 ....L-8
Vamori, 60 ....P-7
Vaya Chin, 70 ....N-6
Ventana, 70 ....M-6
Vernon, 10 ....H-12
Vicksburg, 20 ....J-3
Wagoner, 10 ....H-6
Warren, 20 ....Q-11
Wellton, 1066 ....M-3
Wenden, 450 ....J-4
White Cone, 20 ....D-11
Whiteriver, 3775 ....J-11
Why, 225 ....N-5
Wickenburg, 4515 ....H-6
Wikieup, 20 ....G-4
Wilhoit, 125 ....G-6
Willaha E-6
Willcox, 3122 ....N-11
Williams, 2532 ....E-7
Willow Beach, 30 ....D-2
Window Rock, 3306 ....D-13
Winkelman, 676 ....L-9
Winona, 10 ....E-8
Wintergarden, 10 ....E-8
Winterburg, 125 ....K-5
Wittmann, 550 ....J-6
Woodruff, 150 ....G-11
Yampai, 10 ....E-5
Yarnell, 500 ....H-5
York, 50 ....L-13
Young, 80 ....H-9
Youngtown, 2542 ....*C-4
Yucca, 100 ....F-3
Yuma, 54923 ....M-2

ARKANSAS
PG. 66–67

CAPITAL
Little Rock

NICKNAME
Natural State

POPULATION
2,509,793, rank 33

AREA
53,187 sq mi, rank 27

Counties

Arkansas, 21653 ....H-12
Ashley, 24319 ....M-11
Baxter, 31186 ....B-8
Benton, 97499 ....B-4
Boone, 28297 ....B-7
Bradley, 11793 ....M-10
Calhoun, 5826 ....L-8
Carroll, 18654 ....B-6
Chicot, 15713 ....M-12
Clark, 21437 ....K-7
Clay, 18107 ....B-14
Cleburne, 19411 ....E-10
Cleveland, 7781 ....K-10
Columbia, 25691 ....M-7
Conway, 19151 ....F-8
Craighead, 68856 ....C-14
Crawford, 42493 ....E-4
Crittenden, 49939 ....E-15
Cross, 19225 ....E-14
Dallas, 9614 ....K-8
Desha, 16798 ....K-12
Drew, 17369 ....L-11
Faulkner, 60006 ....F-9
Franklin, 14897 ....E-5
Fulton, 10037 ....B-11
Garland, 73397 ....H-7
Grant, 13948 ....J-9
Greene, 31804 ....C-14
Hempstead, 21621 ....K-6
Hot Spring, 26115 ....J-7
Howard, 13569 ....J-5
Independence, 31192 ....C-12
Izard, 11364 ....C-11
Jackson, 18944 ....D-13
Jefferson, 85487 ....H-10
Johnson, 18221 ....D-6
Lafayette, 9643 ....M-6
Lawrence, 17457 ....C-12
Lee, 13053 ....G-13
Lincoln, 13690 ....K-11
Little River, 13966 ....K-4
Logan, 20557 ....E-5
Lonoke, 39268 ....G-11
Madison, 11618 ....C-6
Marion, 12001 ....B-9
Miller, 38467 ....M-5
Mississippi, 57525 ....D-15
Monroe, 11333 ....H-13
Montgomery, 7841 ....G-6
Nevada, 10101 ....L-6
Newton, 7666 ....C-7
Ouachita, 30574 ....K-8
Perry, 7969 ....G-8
Phillips, 28838 ....H-13
Pike, 10086 ....J-6
Poinsett, 24664 ....E-13
Polk, 17347 ....H-4
Pope, 45883 ....D-7
Prairie, 9518 ....G-11
Pulaski, 349660 ....G-9
Randolph, 16558 ....B-13
St. Francis, 28497 ....F-14
Saline, 64183 ....G-8
Scott, 10205 ....F-5
Searcy, 7841 ....D-8
Sebastian, 99590 ....F-4
Sevier, 13637 ....J-4
Sharp, 14109 ....B-12
Stone, 9775 ....D-10
Union, 46719 ....N-8
Van Buren, 14008 ....D-8
Washington, 113409 ....C-4
White, 54676 ....E-11
Woodruff, 9520 ....F-12
Yell, 17759 ....F-6

Cities and Towns

Abbott, 50 ....F-5
Acorn G-5
Adona, 146 ....F-8
Agnos, 50 ....B-11
Alabam, 40 ....C-6
Albion E-11
Alco, 50 ....C-9
Alexander, 201 ....G-9
Alicia, 157 ....C-13
Alix, 200 ....E-6
Alleene, 80 ....K-4
Allison C-10
Allport, 188 ....H-11
Alma, 2959 ....E-4
Almond, 50 ....D-11
Almyra, 311 ....H-12
Alpena, 319 ....B-7
Alpine, 80 ....J-7
Altheimer, 972 ....H-11
Altus, 433 ....E-6
Amagon, 108 ....D-13
Amity, 526 ....J-6
Amy, 100 ....K-8
Anderson, 160 ....J-7
Aplin, 50 ....F-8
Appleton, 200 ....E-8
Arden, 100 ....K-4
Arkadelphia, 10014 ....J-7
Arkansas City, 523 ....L-13
Arkinda, 40 ....K-4
Armorel, 100 ....C-16
Ash Flat, 667 ....B-12
Ashdown, 5150 ....K-4
Athens H-5
Atkins, 2834 ....E-8
Atlanta, 10 ....M-7
Attica B-13
Aubrey, 204 ....G-13
Augusta, 2759 ....E-12
Austin, 510 ....F-10
Auvergne, 80 ....E-13
Avoca, 269 ....B-5
Back Gate, 70 ....K-12
Bald Knob, 2653 ....E-12
Banks, 88 ....L-10
Barber, 30 ....D-11
Barling, 4078 ....E-4
Barton, 175 ....H-14
Bassett, 199 ....D-15
Bates, 125 ....F-4
Batesville, 8187 ....D-11
Bauxite, 412 ....H-9
Bay, 1660 ....D-14
Bayou Meto, 40 ....H-11
Bear Cr. Sprs. B-7
Bearden, 1021 ....K-9
Beaver, 57 ....A-6
Bee Branch, 60 ....E-9
Beebe, 4455 ....F-11
Beedeville, 141 ....E-13
Beirne, 30 ....K-7
Bella Vista, 9083 ....A-5
Bellefonte, 361 ....B-8
Belleville, 390 ....F-6
Ben D-11
Ben Hur, 20 ....D-8
Ben Lomond, 157 ....K-5
Benton, 18177 ....H-9
Bentonville, 11257 ....B-5
Bergman, 324 ....B-8
Berryville, 3212 ....B-6
Bethel Hts., 281 ....B-5
Bethesda, 150 ....D-11
Biggers, 337 ....B-14
Big Flat, 72 ....C-9
Big Fork, 60 ....H-5
Bigelow, 340 ....F-9
Biscoe, 537 ....G-12
Birdeye E-14
Birta F-7
Biscoe, 484 ....G-12
Bismarck, 225 ....H-7
Black Fork, 10 ....G-4
Black Oak, 277 ....D-15
Black Rock, 736 ....C-13
Black Sprs., 97 ....H-5
Blackton, 70 ....G-13
Blackwell, 125 ....E-8
Blakemore G-10
Blevins, 253 ....K-6
Blue Ball, 50 ....G-6
Blue Eye, 28 ....A-7
Blue Mtn., 146 ....F-6
Bluff City L-7
Blytheville, 22906 ....C-16
Board Camp, 40 ....H-5
Bodcaw, 161 ....L-6
Boles, 100 ....G-5
Bonanza, 520 ....E-4
Bono, 1220 ....C-14
Booker J-9
Booneville, 3804 ....F-5
Boswell, 30 ....C-10
Botkinburg, 50 ....D-9
Boxley C-7
Boydell, 20 ....M-12
Bradford, 874 ....E-12
Bradley, 585 ....M-6
Branch, 299 ....E-5
Brashears D-6
Brentwood, 50 ....C-5
Brickeys, 30 ....G-14
Bright Star, 60 ....M-5
Brinkley, 4234 ....G-13
Brockwell, 175 ....B-11
Brookland, 819 ....C-14
Bruno C-8
Bryant, 5940 ....H-9
Buckner, 325 ....M-6
Buena Vista, 30 ....M-5
Buffalo City B-9
Bull Shoals, 1534 ....A-9
Burdette, 148 ....D-16
Burlington, 30 ....B-7
Bussey, 50 ....M-6
Butterfield, 125 ....H-8
Cabot, 8319 ....F-10
Caddo Gap, 150 ....H-6
Caddo Valley, 389 ....J-7
Calamine C-12
Caldwell, 334 ....F-14
Cale, 70 ....K-7
Calico Rock, 938 ....C-10
Calion, 558 ....M-9
Camden, 14380 ....L-8
Cammack Vil., 828 ....G-9
Camp, 50 ....B-11
Campbell Sta., 247 ....D-12
Canaan C-8
Canfield, 70 ....M-5
Caraway, 1356 ....D-15
Carlisle, 2253 ....G-11
Carthage, 452 ....J-9
Casa, 200 ....E-7
Cash, 214 ....D-13
Casscoe, 90 ....H-12
Cauthron, 90 ....F-4
Cave City, 1809 ....D-12
Cave Sprs., 920 ....B-5
Cecil, 70 ....E-5
Cedar Cr., 60 ....G-5
Cedarville D-4
Center, 20 ....C-12
Center Hill, 100 ....E-11
Center Pt. J-5
Center Ridge, 150 ....E-9
Centerton, 491 ....B-4
Centerville, 225 ....F-7
Central City, 419 ....E-4
Charleston, 2128 ....E-5
Charlotte D-12
Chatfield, 70 ....F-15
Cherokee Vil., 900 ....B-12
Cherry Valley, 659 ....E-14
Chester, 125 ....D-5
Chickalah, 100 ....E-6
Chicot, 10 ....M-13
Chicot Jct. M-13
Chidester, 489 ....K-8
Chismville, 30 ....F-5
Clarendon, 2072 ....G-12
Clarkedale, 80 ....E-15
Clarkridge, 60 ....B-9
Clarksville, 5833 ....E-6
Cleveland, 30 ....E-8
Clifty, 100 ....B-6
Clinton, 2213 ....D-9
Clow, 30 ....K-6
Coal Hill, 912 ....E-6
College City, 339 ....C-13
Collins, 40 ....L-11
Colt, 334 ....F-14
Compton, 30 ....C-7
Concord, 262 ....D-11
Conway, 26481 ....F-9
Cord, 70 ....D-12
Corinth, 63 ....F-7
Corley, 50 ....F-6
Cornerville, 100 ....K-11
Corning, 3323 ....B-14
Cotter, 867 ....B-8
Cotton Plant, 1150 ....F-12
Cove, 346 ....H-4
Coy, 142 ....H-11
Crawfordsville, 617 ....F-15
Crocketts Bluff, 40 ....H-13
Cross Roads J-9
Crossett, 6282 ....M-11
Crystal Sprs., 20 ....H-7
Curtis, 350 ....K-7
Cushman, 428 ....C-11
Daisy, 122 ....J-6
Dalark, 20 ....J-8
Dalton, 20 ....B-13
Damascus, 306 ....E-9
Danville, 1585 ....F-7
Dardanelle, 3722 ....F-7
Datto, 120 ....B-14
De Ann, 50 ....K-5
De Luce J-13
De Queen, 4633 ....J-4
De Valls Bluff, 702 ....G-12
De Witt, 3553 ....J-12
Decatur, 918 ....B-4
Deckerville, 60 ....E-15
Deer, 100 ....D-7
Delaney C-5
Delaplaine, 146 ....B-14
Delaware, 125 ....E-7
Delight, 311 ....J-6
Dell, 258 ....C-16
Denmark E-12
Dennard, 150 ....D-9
Dermott, 4715 ....L-12
Des Arc, 2001 ....F-12
Desha, 650 ....D-11
Dewitt J-12
Diamond City, 601 ....B-8
Diaz, 1363 ....D-12
Dierks, 1263 ....J-5
Dixie, 70 ....E-8
Doddridge, 40 ....M-5
Dogpatch B-7
Dolph C-10
Donaldson, 291 ....J-8
Dover, 1055 ....E-7
Dowdy C-12
Drasco, 100 ....D-11
Driggs, 100 ....E-6
Driver, 80 ....D-16
Dumas, 5520 ....K-12
Dyer, 502 ....E-4
Dyess, 466 ....D-15
Eagle Mills, 60 ....L-8
Eagleton, 20 ....G-4
Earle, 3393 ....E-15
E. Camden, 783 ....L-8
Edmondson, 286 ....F-15
Egypt, 123 ....C-13
El Dorado, 23146 ....M-9
El Paso, 150 ....F-10
Elaine, 846 ....J-13
Elkins, 692 ....C-5
Elliott, 150 ....L-8
Elm Sprs., 893 ....B-5
Elm Store B-13
Emerson, 317 ....M-7
Emmet, 446 ....K-6
England, 3351 ....H-10
Enola, 179 ....F-10
Ethel, 20 ....J-13
Etowah, 352 ....D-15
Eudora, 3155 ....M-13
Eureka Sprs., 1900 ....B-6
Evansville, 60 ....D-4
Evening Shade, 437 ....C-12
Evening Shade, 100 ....E-6
Everton, 150 ....B-8
Fairfield Bay, 2043 ....D-10
Fairview M-13
Faith, 125 ....J-10
Fargo, 150 ....G-12
Farmington, 1322 ....C-4
Fayetteville, 42099 ....C-5
Felsenthal, 95 ....N-10
Felton, 70 ....G-14
Ferndale, 80 ....G-8
Fifty-Six, 156 ....C-10
Fisher, 245 ....E-13
Fitzhugh, 30 ....E-12
Flippin, 1006 ....B-9
Floral, 70 ....D-11
Florence, 60 ....L-11
Floyd, 150 ....F-10
Fomby K-5
Fordyce, 4729 ....K-9
Foreman, 1267 ....K-4
Formosa, 150 ....E-9
Forrest City, 13364 ....F-14
Ft. Douglas D-7
Ft. Smith, 72798 ....E-4
Forum B-6
Fouke, 634 ....M-5
Fountain Hill M-11
Fourche, 55 ....F-8
Fourche Jct. F-9
Fox, 60 ....D-10
Franklin, 205 ....B-11
Friendship, 160 ....J-8
Fulton, 269 ....L-5
Galloway G-10
Garland, 175 ....M-5
Garfield, 308 ....A-5
Garland, 415 ....M-6
Garner, 191 ....E-11
Gassville, 1167 ....B-9
Gateway, 65 ....A-5
Genoa, 70 ....M-5
Gentry, 1726 ....B-4
Georgetown, 126 ....E-12
Gethsemane H-11
Gibson, 60 ....D-14
Giesick F-13
Gilbert, 43 ....C-8
Gillett, 883 ....J-12
Gillham, 210 ....H-4
Gilmore, 331 ....E-15
Glen Rose J-8
Glencoe, 160 ....B-11
Glendale, 200 ....K-11
Glenwood, 1354 ....H-6
Goodwin, 100 ....F-13
Goshen, 589 ....C-5
Gosnell, 4345 ....C-16
Gould, 1470 ....K-12
Grady, 586 ....J-11
Grannis, 557 ....J-4
Grapevine, 50 ....J-9
Gravel Ridge, 3846 ....G-10
Gravelly, 60 ....G-6
Gravette, 1412 ....B-4
Grays, 80 ....F-13
Green Forest, 2050 ....B-7
Greenbrier, 2130 ....F-9
Greenfield, 125 ....D-14
Greenland, 757 ....C-5
Greenway, 212 ....B-15
Greenwood, 3984 ....F-4
Greers Ferry, 724 ....D-10
Gregory, 70 ....F-12
Grider D-16
Griffithville, 237 ....F-11
Grubbs, 528 ....D-13
Guion, 93 ....C-11
Gum Sprs., 157 ....J-7
Gurdon, 2199 ....K-7
Guy, 241 ....E-9
Hackett, 490 ....F-4
Hagarville, 50 ....E-7
Halley, 90 ....L-12
Halliday, 100 ....C-15
Hamburg, 3098 ....M-11
Hampton, 1562 ....L-9
Hanover, 50 ....D-10
Hardy, 538 ....B-12
Harmony, 50 ....D-6
Harrell, 258 ....L-9
Harriet, 60 ....C-9
Harrisburg, 1943 ....D-14
Harrison, 9922 ....B-7
Hartford, 721 ....F-4
Hartman, 498 ....E-6
Harvey, 40 ....G-6
Haskell, 2118 ....H-9
Hasty B-7
Hatfield, 414 ....H-4
Hattieville, 60 ....E-8
Havana, 358 ....F-6
Haynes, 268 ....G-14
Hazen, 1668 ....G-12
Heber Sprs., 5628 ....E-10
Hector, 476 ....E-8
Helena, 7491 ....H-14
Hempwallace H-7
Henderson, 60 ....B-10
Hermitage, 639 ....L-10
Hickory, 50 ....J-11
Hickory Plains, 80 ....F-11
Hickory Ridge, 436 ....E-13
Higden, 92 ....D-10
Higgins F-11
Higginson, 255 ....F-11
Highfill, 84 ....B-4
Highland, 90 ....B-11
Hillemann, 10 ....F-13
Hindsville, 69 ....C-5
Hiwasse, 300 ....B-4
Holland, 100 ....F-9
Holly Gr., 675 ....H-13
Holly Sprs., 70 ....K-8
Hollywood, 80 ....J-7
Hon, 150 ....F-5
Hooker B-14
Hope, 9643 ....L-6
Horatio, 793 ....K-4
Horseshoe Bend, 2239 ....B-11
Horseshoe Lake, 298 ....G-15
Hot Sprs., 37431 ....H-7
Hot Sprs. Vil., 6361 ....G-8
Houston, 149 ....F-8
Howell, 30 ....E-12
Hoxie, 2798 ....C-13
Hughes, 1810 ....G-15
Humnoke, 311 ....H-11
Humphrey, 443 ....H-11
Hunt D-6
Hunter, 137 ....F-13
Huntington, 715 ....F-4
Huntsville, 1605 ....C-6
Hurricane Gr. H-6
Huttig, 831 ....N-10
Ico, 80 ....B-7
Imboden, 616 ....B-13
Immanuel H-12
Indian K-12
Ingalls, 60 ....M-9
Ink, 125 ....H-5
Ione F-5
Ivan, 90 ....K-8
Jacksonport, 264 ....D-12
Jacksonville, 29101 ....G-10
Japton, 60 ....C-6
Jasper, 332 ....C-7
Jefferson, 175 ....H-10
Jennette, 184 ....F-14
Jennie, 40 ....M-12
Jenny Lind, 650 ....F-4
Jericho, 213 ....E-15
Jerome, 47 ....L-12
Jersey, 30 ....L-9
Jerusalem, 150 ....E-8
Jessieville, 200 ....G-7
Johnson, 599 ....C-5
Johnsville M-10
Joiner, 618 ....D-15
Jonesboro, 46535 ....D-14
Joy E-11
Judsonia, 1915 ....E-11
Jct. City, 674 ....N-8
Kedron, 175 ....J-10
Keiser, 805 ....D-15
Kelso, 80 ....K-13
Kensett, 1741 ....F-11
Kent, 90 ....J-8
Keo, 154 ....H-10
Kibler, 60 ....E-5
Kibler, 931 ....E-4
Kingsland, 395 ....K-9
Kingston, 60 ....C-6
Kirby, 225 ....H-6
Knobel, 317 ....B-14
Knoxville, 376 ....E-7
Lacey, 90 ....L-11
Ladd, 90 ....J-10
Ladelle, 50 ....L-11
Lafe, 315 ....B-14
LaGrange, 108 ....G-14
Lake City, 1833 ....D-15
Lake Hamilton, 1331 ....H-7
Lake View, 526 ....H-14
Lake Vil., 2791 ....M-12
Lakeview, 485 ....B-8
Lamar, 1257 ....E-7
Lamartine L-7
Lambrook, 30 ....J-13
Landis, 40 ....J-9
Langley, 90 ....H-5
Lavaca, 1253 ....E-4
Lawson, 100 ....M-8
Leachville, 1763 ....C-15
Lead Hill, 283 ....B-8
Lee Cr. D-4
Leola, 476 ....J-9
Lepanto, 2033 ....D-15
Leslie, 446 ....D-8
Letona, 218 ....E-11
Lewisville, 1424 ....M-6
Lexa, 295 ....G-14
Light C-14
Limestone, 50 ....C-6
Lincoln, 1463 ....C-4
Little Flock, 944 ....B-5
Little Rock, 175795 ....G-9
Lockesburg, 608 ....K-5
Locust Bayou L-8
Locust Gr., 150 ....C-11
Lodge Corner, 10 ....J-12
London, 825 ....E-7
Lonoke, 4022 ....G-11
Lonsdale, 127 ....H-8
Louann, 156 ....M-8
Lowell, 1224 ....B-5
Luxora, 1338 ....D-16
Lynn, 299 ....C-12
Macedonia, 125 ....M-7
Macon, 1100 ....F-10
Madison, 1263 ....F-14
Magazine, 799 ....F-6
Magness, 158 ....D-12
Magnolia, 11151 ....M-7
Malvern, 9256 ....H-8
Mammoth Spr., 1097 ....A-12
Mandeville, 700 ....L-5
Manila, 2635 ....C-15
Manning, 30 ....J-8
Mansfield, 1018 ....F-4
Marble, 40 ....C-6
Marianna, 5910 ....G-14
Marie, 129 ....D-16
Marion, 4405 ....E-15
Marked Tree, 3100 ....D-15
Marmaduke, 1164 ....B-15
Marshall, 1318 ....C-9
Martinville, 40 ....F-9
Marvell, 1545 ....H-13
Maumelle, 6714 ....G-9
Mayflower, 1415 ....F-9
Maynard, 354 ....B-13
Maysville, 50 ....B-4
McCaskill, 80 ....K-6
McCrory, 1971 ....E-13
McDougal, 208 ....B-15
McGehee, 4997 ....L-12
McKamie, 10 ....M-6
McMillan Corner L-12
McNab, 95 ....L-5
McNeil, 686 ....M-7
McRae, 669 ....F-11
Melbourne, 1562 ....C-11
Mellwood, 10 ....J-13
Mena, 5475 ....H-4
Menifee, 355 ....F-8
Metalton, 30 ....B-6
Midland, 220 ....F-4
Midway B-9
Mineral Sprs., 1004 ....K-5
Minturn, 124 ....C-13
Mist, 50 ....M-11
Mitchell B-10
Mitchellville, 513 ....K-12
Moark, 125 ....A-14
Moko, 60 ....B-11
Monette, 1115 ....C-15
Monroe, 100 ....G-13
Montcello, 8116 ....L-11
Montrose, 528 ....M-12
Moorefield, 160 ....D-11
Moreland, 225 ....E-8
Morganton, 80 ....E-9
Morrilton, 6551 ....F-8
Morrison Bluff, 84 ....E-6
Moscow, 50 ....J-11
Mountain Pine, 772 ....H-7
Mtn. Home, 11102 ....B-10
Mtn. View, 2439 ....D-10
Mountainburg, 488 ....D-5
Mt. Holly, 150 ....M-8
Mt. Ida, 775 ....H-6
Mt. Olive C-10
Mt. Pleasant, 422 ....C-11
Mt. Vernon, 192 ....E-10
Mulberry, 1448 ....E-5
Murfreesboro, 1542 ....J-6
Myron, 40 ....B-11
Nashville, 4639 ....K-5
Nathan, 60 ....K-5
Natural Dam, 60 ....D-4
Nebo, 10 ....E-4
Neddmore G-5
New Edinburg, 50 ....K-10
New London, 20 ....M-9
Newark, 1159 ....D-12
Newburg, 125 ....C-11
Newhope, 90 ....J-5
Newport, 8459 ....D-12
Nimmons, 96 ....B-15
Norfork, 394 ....B-10
Norman, 382 ....H-6
Norphlet, 706 ....M-9
N. Crossett, 3358 ....M-11
N. Little Rock, 61741 ....G-10
Number Nine C-16
Oak Gr., 331 ....B-7
Oak Gr. Hts., 513 ....C-14
Oakhaven, 35 ....K-5
Oakland, 100 ....B-9
Oden, 126 ....G-5
Ogden, 264 ....L-5
Ogeman, 80 ....L-8
Oil Trough, 208 ....D-12
O'Kean, 250 ....B-14
Okolona, 113 ....K-7
Ola, 1090 ....F-7
Old Lexington, 20 ....B-13
Olvey, 200 ....B-8
Olyphant, 20 ....E-12
Omaha, 175 ....A-7
Oneida, 702 ....H-14
Onyx, 10 ....G-7
Oppelo, 50 ....F-8
Osage, 60 ....B-7
Osceola, 9165 ....D-16
Ozan, 50 ....K-5
Ouachita, 90 ....K-8
Owensville, 70 ....G-8
Oxford, 562 ....B-11
Ozark, 3330 ....E-5
Palestine, 711 ....F-14
Pangburn, 630 ....E-11
Paragould, 18540 ....C-14
Paris, 3674 ....E-6
Parkdale, 393 ....M-12
Parkers, 250 ....N-7
Parkin, 1847 ....F-14
Parks, 220 ....F-5
Patmos, 72 ....M-6
Patterson, 445 ....E-13
Paynneway, 225 ....D-14
Pea Ridge, 1620 ....B-5
Peach Orchard, 187 ....B-14
Pearcy, 175 ....H-7
Pearson, 70 ....E-10
Peel, 80 ....B-9
Pelsor, 10 ....D-7
Perry, 228 ....F-8
Perrytown, 248 ....K-6
Perryville, 1261 ....F-8
Pettigrew, 30 ....D-6
Pettus H-11
Piggott, 3777 ....B-15
Pike City, 40 ....J-6
Pindall, 50 ....C-9
Pine Bluff, 57140 ....J-10
Pine Gr. K-8
Pine Ridge, 30 ....G-5
Pine Ridge D-9
Piney, 20 ....F-7
Pinnacle, 350 ....G-9
Plainview, 695 ....F-6
Pleasant Plains, 256 ....E-11
Plumerville, 832 ....F-8
Pocahontas, 6151 ....B-13
Pollard, 229 ....B-15
Ponca, 30 ....C-7
Poplar Gr., 350 ....H-14
Portia, 540 ....C-13
Portland, 560 ....M-12
Possum Grape, 150 ....E-12
Potter, 90 ....H-4
Pottsville, 1079 ....E-7
Poughkeepsie C-12
Powhatan, 51 ....C-13
Poyen, 303 ....J-9
Prairie Gr., 1761 ....C-4
Prairie View, 80 ....E-6
Prattsville, 251 ....H-9
Prescott, 3673 ....K-7
Prim, 40 ....D-10
Princeton K-9
Proctor E-15
Providence E-11
Provo, 100 ....J-5
Pyatt, 185 ....B-8
Quitman, 632 ....E-10
Ralph C-9
Ramsey, 40 ....K-9
Ratcliff, 180 ....E-5
Ravenden, 330 ....B-12
Ravenden Sprs., 131 ....B-13
Rea Valley B-9
Reader, 56 ....K-7
Readland, 125 ....M-13
Rector, 2268 ....B-15
Red Star, 10 ....C-6
Redfield, 1082 ....H-10
Reed, 355 ....K-12
Reydell J-12
Reyno, 467 ....B-14
Rhea, 100 ....C-4
Richmond, 60 ....L-4
Rison, 1258 ....K-10
Riverside, 40 ....B-15
Rivervale, 80 ....D-15
Rockport, 368 ....H-8
Rockwell, 2514 ....H-7
Rocky H-4
Roe, 135 ....G-12
Rogers, 24692 ....B-5
Rohwer, 150 ....K-12
Roland, 200 ....G-9
Rondo, 283 ....G-14
Rondo, 50 ....M-5
Rose Bud, 156 ....E-10
Rosebud, 150 ....H-11
Rosston, 262 ....L-7
Round Pond F-14
Rover, 175 ....F-7
Rudd B-7
Rudy, 45 ....E-4
Rule, 10 ....D-11
Rupert, 100 ....D-8
Rushing D-10
Russell, 180 ....E-12
Russellville, 21260 ....E-7
Rye, 100 ....K-10
Sage, 60 ....C-11
St. Charles, 169 ....H-12
St. Francis, 201 ....B-15
St. James, 126 ....D-11
St. Joe, 150 ....C-8
St. Paul, 88 ....C-6
Salado, 350 ....D-12
Salem, 1474 ....B-11
Salem, 2950 ....G-9
Salesville, 374 ....B-10
Salus, 30 ....D-7
Saratoga K-5
Scott, 70 ....G-10
Scottsville, 60 ....E-7
Scranton, 218 ....E-6
Searcy, 15180 ....E-11
Sedgwick, 86 ....C-13
Selma, 50 ....L-12
Shannon Hills, 1755 ....G-9
Sheridan, 3098 ....J-9
Sherrill, 55 ....H-11
Sherwood, 18893 ....H-9
Shirley, 363 ....D-9
Sidney, 271 ....C-11
Sidon, 40 ....E-11
Siloam Sprs., 8151 ....B-4
Sims, 100 ....G-6
Smackover, 2232 ....M-8
Smithton, 10 ....K-7
Smithville, 86 ....C-12
Snow Lake, 40 ....J-13
Snowball, 40 ....C-8
Snyder, 80 ....M-12
Social Hill, 80 ....H-8
S. Lead Hill, 96 ....B-8
Sparkman, 622 ....K-8
Spr. Hill, 30 ....L-5
Spr. Valley, 50 ....B-5
Springdale, 29941 ....B-5
Springfield, 90 ....F-9
Springtown, 115 ....B-4
Stacy D-14
Stamps, 2478 ....M-6
Star City, 2138 ....K-11
Staves, 125 ....D-13
Stephens, 1137 ....L-7
Stepnock, 50 ....E-11
Stonewall, 70 ....B-14
Story, 40 ....G-6
Strawberry, 273 ....C-12
Strong, 624 ....M-9
Sturkie, 70 ....A-11
Stuttgart, 10420 ....H-12
Subiaco, 538 ....E-6
Success, 170 ....B-14
Sulphur Rock, 356 ....D-12
Sulphur Sprs., 523 ....A-4
Summers, 225 ....C-4
Summit, 480 ....B-9
Sumpter L-11
Sunnydale, 60 ....E-11
Sunset, 571 ....E-15
Swan Lake J-11
Sweet Home M-18
Swifton, 830 ....C-13
Taylor, 564 ....N-6
Tarry, 250 ....J-11
Taylor, 621 ....E-5
Texarkana, 22631 ....M-5
Thida, 100 ....D-12
Thornton, 502 ....L-9
Three Creeks, 30 ....M-8
Tichnor, 10 ....J-12
Tillar, 221 ....L-11
Tilly D-8
Tilton, 90 ....E-14
Tinsman, 69 ....L-9
Tokio, 30 ....K-5
Tollette, 316 ....K-5
Tomato, 30 ....C-16
Tontitown, 460 ....B-4
Traskwood, 488 ....H-9
Trumann, 6304 ....D-14
Tuckerman, 2020 ....D-13
Tulip J-9
Tull, 313 ....H-9
Tupelo, 208 ....E-13
Turrell, 988 ....E-15
Twin Groves, 299 ....E-9
Tyro, 40 ....L-11
Tyronza, 858 ....E-15
Ulm, 193 ....H-12
Umpire, 100 ....H-5
Uniontown, 150 ....D-4
Urbana, 90 ....M-9
Urbanette, 175 ....B-6
Valley Sprs., 200 ....B-8
Van Buren, 14979 ....E-4
Vandervoort, 111 ....H-4
Vanndale, 300 ....E-14
Vick, 30 ....M-10
Victoria, 110 ....C-15
Village, 125 ....M-7
Vilonia, 1133 ....F-10
Vimy Ridge, 600 ....H-9
Viola, 330 ....B-11
Violet Hill, 70 ....C-11
Wabash, 50 ....H-14
Wabbaseka, 322 ....H-11
Walcott, 60 ....C-14
Waldenburg, 71 ....E-14
Waldo, 1489 ....M-7
Waldron, 3024 ....G-5
Walnut Ridge, 4388 ....C-13
Ward, 2160 ....F-10
Warm Sprs., 40 ....B-12
Warren, 6611 ....L-10
Washington, 148 ....K-6
Washita H-6
Watalula D-5
Watson, 282 ....K-13
Waveland E-6
Webb City, 200 ....E-5
Weiner, 738 ....D-14
Weldon, 100 ....E-12
Wesley, 175 ....C-6

THE WESTIN ALYESKA PRINCE HOTEL AND SKI RESORT, AK

GUNTERSVILLE LAKE, AL

CALIFORNIA PG. 68–75

3MBC123

CAPITAL
Sacramento

NICKNAME
Golden State

POPULATION
31,878,234, rank 1

AREA
158,706 sq mi, rank 3

Counties

COLORADO PG. 75–77

AB1234 COLORADO

CAPITAL
Denver

NICKNAME
Centennial State

POPULATION
3,822,676, rank 25

AREA
104,091 sq mi, rank 8

Counties

BUFFALO NATIONAL RIVER, AR

CONNECTICUT PG. 78–79

CONNECTICUT 123·ABC ·CONSTITUTION STATE

CAPITAL
Hartford

NICKNAME
Constitution State

POPULATION
3,274,238, rank 28

AREA
5,018 sq mi, rank 48

Counties

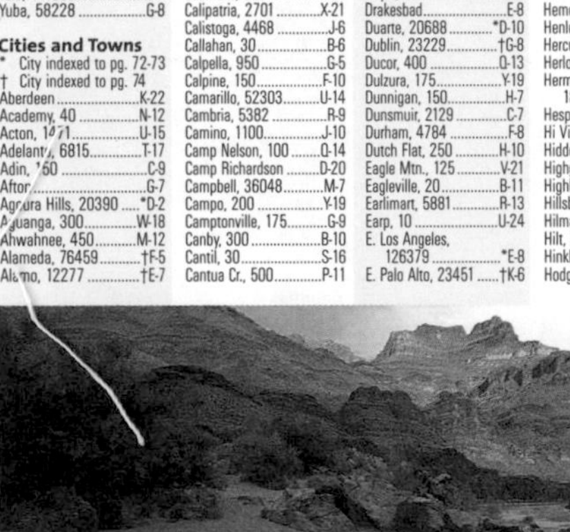

BASS TRAIL, GRAND CANYON NATIONAL PARK, AZ

Wilton, 2000 J-4
Winchester Ctr., 250 B-6
Windermere Vil. C-11
Windham, 1000 D-13
Windsor, 3600 C-10
Windsor Locks, 12358 B-10
Windsorville C-11
Winnipauk J-4
Winsted, 8254 B-7
Winthrop, 400 H-11
Wolcott, 4000 E-7
Woodbridge, 1400 H-7
Woodbury, 1212 F-6
Woodmont, 1770 J-7
Woodstock, 400 B-15
Woodstock Valley, 750 B-14
Woodville, 225 D-5
Wrightville C-6
Yalesville, 3600 F-9
Yantic F-14

DELAWARE
PG. 80

CAPITAL
Dover

NICKNAME
First State

POPULATION
724,842, rank 46

AREA
2,044 sq mi, rank 49

Counties
Kent, 110993 G-2
New Castle, 441946 E-2
Sussex, 113229 K-4

Cities and Towns
Adamsville, 90 J-2
Andrewsville, 150 J-2
Angola L-5
Arden, 477 B-3
Ardencroft, 282 B-3
Ardentown, 325 A-10
Argos Corner, 550 J-4
Atlanta K-2
Bacons M-2
Bay View Beach D-2
Bayard M-5
Bayville M-6
Bear C-2
Bellefonte, 1243 B-3
Bethany Beach, 326 L-6
Bethel, 178 L-2
Big Pine J-2
Big Stone Beach H-4
Blackbird, 700 E-2
Blackiston E-2
Blades, 834 L-2
Blue Ball B-3
Bowers Beach, 179 H-4
Brandywine B-3
Bridgeville, 1210 K-3
Broadkill Beach, 70 J-5
Brookside, 15307 C-2
Brownsville J-2
Bryans Store L-4
Camden, 1899 G-3
Cannon, 175 K-2
Canterbury, 1200 H-3
Capitol Park, 700 G-3
Carrcroft A-9
Centerville B-2
Cheswold, 321 F-2
Clarksville, 900 L-5
Claymont, 9800 B-3
Clayton, 1163 F-2
Collins Park, 8300 D-8
Columbia M-2
Concord L-3
Coverdale Crossroads K-3
Cowgills Corner K-10
Dagsboro, 398 L-5
Delaware City, 1682 D-2
Delmar, 962 M-3
Dewey Beach, 204 K-6
Dover, 27630 G-3
Downs Chapel F-2
Dublin Hill K-2
Dunleith, 9100 C-8
Edgemoor, 5853 B-3
Ellendale, 313 K-3
Elsmere, 5935 B-2
Fairfax, 2300 A-8
Fairmount L-5
Farmington, 122 J-3
Felton, 683 H-3
Fenwick Island, 186 M-6
Fieldsboro E-2
Five Points K-5
Frankford, 591 M-5
Frederica, 761 H-3
Georgetown, 3732 K-4
Glasgow, 2500 C-1
Gravel Hill K-4
Greenville B-2
Greenville J-2
Greenwood, 578 K-2
Gumboro, 300 M-4
Guyencourt A-8
Hamilton Park C-8
Harbeson, 350 K-4
Hardscrabble L-3
Hares Corner D-7
Harrington, 2311 J-3
Hartly, 107 G-2
Hazlettville, 450 G-2
Hearns Crossroads M-3
Henlopen Acres, 107 K-6
Hickman J-2
Hitchens Crossroads L-3
Hockessin, 4000 B-2
Hollandsville H-2
Hollyville L-5
Houston, 487 J-3
Jimtown, 175 K-5
Johnson M-5
Kenton, 232 F-2
Kirkwood, 1800 D-2
Kitts Hummock, 250 G-4
Laurel, 3226 L-3
Lebanon, 1400 G-3
Leipsic, 236 F-3
Lewes, 2295 K-5
Lincoln, 950 J-3
Little Cr., 167 G-3
Little Heaven, 1400 H-3
Llangollen Estates, 5600 C-2
Lowes Crossroads M-4
Lynch Hts., 550 H-3
Magnolia, 211 H-3
Marydel G-2
Masseys Landing L-5
Mastens Corner, 175 H-2

POINT LOBOS STATE RESERVE, CA

McClellandville, 2400 C-1
Middletown, 3834 E-2
Midway, 1500 K-5
Milford, 6040 J-3
Millsboro, 1643 L-4
Millville, 206 L-5
Milton, 1417 K-4
Minquadale C-8
Mission L-4
Montchanin A-8
Mt. Pleasant D-2
Nassau, 1600 K-5
New Castle, 4837 C-3
Newark, 25098 C-1
Newport, 1240 C-2
Oak Orchard, 750 L-6
Oakley J-3
Ocean View, 606 L-6
Odessa, 303 E-2
Old Furnace L-3
Omar M-5
Owens, 125 K-3
Pepper M-3
Pepperbox M-3
Petersburg, 225 H-2
Pine Tree Corners E-2
Pinetown, 1100 K-5
Piney Gr. L-4
Port Mahon G-4
Port Penn D-2
Portsville L-2
Primehook Beach, 30 J-5
Red Lion C-2
Redden K-3
Reeves Crossing, 450 H-3
Rehoboth Beach, 1234 K-6
Reliance L-2
Rising Sun, 2500 G-3
Rockland A-8
Rodney Vil., 1745 M-8
Rosedale Beach, 750 L-5
Roseville Park, 6200 C-2
Roxana, 350 M-5
St. Georges D-2
Sandtown, 350 H-2
Seaford, 5689 L-2
Selbyville, 1335 M-5
Shaft Ox Corner M-4
Slaughter Beach, 114 J-4
Smyrna, 5231 F-3
S. Bethany, 148 M-6
S. Bowers H-4
Stanton, 5028 C-2
Star Hill, 600 H-3
Staytonville J-3
Stockley L-4
Swann Keys, 700 M-5
Sycamore L-3
Talleys Corner A-9
Talleyville, 6346 B-3
Taylors Bridge, 20 E-2
Thompsonville H-4
Townsend, 322 E-2
Vernon H-2
Viola, 153 H-3
Ward M-3
Warwick L-5
Westover Hills B-8
Whiteleysburg H-2
Whitesville, 125 M-4
Williamsville, 350 M-5
Williamsville, 300 M-5
Willow Gr. H-2
Wilmington, 71529 B-3
Wilmington Manor, 8568 C-2
Winterthur A-8
Woodenhawk, 200 K-2
Woodland L-2
Woodland Beach, 100 F-3
Woodside, 140 H-3
Workmans Corners, 400 L-4
Wyoming, 977 G-3
Yorklyn B-2

DISTRICT OF COLUMBIA
PG. 172

POPULATION
543,213

AREA
69 sq mi

Washington, 543213 D-5

FLORIDA
PG. 81–84

CAPITAL
Tallahassee

NICKNAME
Sunshine State

POPULATION
14,399,985, rank 4

AREA
58,664 sq mi, rank 22

Counties
Alachua, 181596 G-15
Baker, 18486 E-15
Bay, 126994 E-7
Bradford, 22515 F-15
Brevard, 398978 L-19
Broward, 1255488 R-19
Calhoun, 11011 E-7
Charlotte, 110975 P-16
Citrus, 93515 J-14
Clay, 105986 F-16
Collier, 152099 R-17
Columbia, 42613 E-14
Dade, 1937094 S-19
De Soto, 23865 N-16
Dixie, 10585 G-13
Duval, 672971 F-16
Escambia, 262798 D-2
Flagler, 28701 G-17
Franklin, 8967 F-9
Gadsden, 41105 E-9
Gilchrist, 9667 G-14
Glades, 7591 P-17
Gulf, 11504 F-8
Hamilton, 10930 E-13
Hardee, 19499 N-16
Hendry, 25773 Q-18
Hernando, 101115 K-14
Highlands, 68432 M-17
Hillsborough, 834054 M-15
Holmes, 15778 D-6
Indian River, 90208 M-19
Jackson, 41375 D-8
Jefferson, 11296 E-11
Lafayette, 5578 F-13
Lake, 152104 J-17
Lee, 335113 Q-16
Leon, 192493 E-10
Levy, 25923 H-14
Liberty, 5569 F-9
Madison, 16569 E-12
Manatee, 211707 N-15
Marion, 194833 H-15
Martin, 100900 P-19
Monroe, 78024 T-18
Nassau, 43941 E-16
Okaloosa, 143776 D-4
Okeechobee, 29627 N-18
Orange, 677491 K-18
Osceola, 107728 L-18
Palm Beach, 863518 Q-19
Pasco, 281131 K-14
Pinellas, 851659 L-14
Polk, 405382 L-17
Putnam, 65070 G-16
St. Johns, 83829 F-17
St. Lucie, 150171 N-19
Santa Rosa, 81608 D-3
Sarasota, 277776 N-15
Seminole, 287529 K-18
Sumter, 31577 K-15
Suwannee, 26780 F-13
Taylor, 17111 F-11
Union, 10252 F-15
Volusia, 370712 J-18
Wakulla, 14202 F-9
Walton, 27760 D-5
Washington, 16919 E-6

Cities and Towns
* City indexed to pg. 81
Alachua, 4529 G-14
Alcoma, 125 M-17
Alford, 472 D-7
Allandale C-16
Allentown, 40 D-3
Alliance, 80 E-8
Altamonte Sprs., 34879 K-17
Altha, 497 E-8
Alton, 80 F-12
Altoona, 650 J-16
Alturas, 400 M-16
Alva, 1036 Q-17
Amelia City, 1300 E-17
American Beach, 800 E-17
Anna Maria, 1744 N-14
Anthony, 1600 H-15
Apalachicola, 2602 G-8
Apollo Beach, 6025 *D-5
Apopka, 13512 K-17
Arcadia, 6488 N-16
Archer, 1372 G-14
Argyle, 350 D-5
Aripeka, 650 K-14
Arredondo, 1400 G-15
Ashton I-18
Ashville, 90 E-12
Astatula, 981 K-16
Astor, 1273 H-17
Astor Park, 175 H-17
Athena, 20 F-12
Atlantic Beach, 11636 E-17
Atlantis, 1653 *D-9
Auburn, 400 D-5
Auburndale, 8858 L-16
Aventura, 14914 *K-9
Avon Park, 8042 M-17
Azalea Park, 8926 *P-3
Babcock, 50 P-16
Babson Park, 1125 M-17
Bagdad, 1457 D-3
Baker, 300 D-4
Bakers Mill, 10 E-13
Bal Harbour, 3045 *K-9
Baldwin, 1450 E-16
Balm M-15
Barberville, 200 H-17
Barrineau Park, 60 D-2
Bartow, 14716 M-16
Bascom, 90 D-8
Basinger, 50 N-18
Bay Harbor Islands, 4703 *K-9
Bay Hill, 5346 J-2
Bay Lake, 100 L-6
Bay Pines, 4171 *D-2
Bay Sprs., 50 D-2
Bayonet Pt., 21860 K-14
Bayou George, 800 E-7
Bayport, 50 K-5
Bayshore, 750 Q-16
Bayshore Gardens, 17062 *F-9
Bayview, 1500 B-5
Beacon Hill, 100 F-7
Becker, 40 E-6
Bee Ridge, 6406 N-14
Bell, 267 G-13
Bellair, 9100 M-7
Bellair Bluffs, 2128 *C-1
Bellair Shore, 100 *C-1
Belle Glade, 16177 Q-19
Belle Isle, 5272 J-4
Belleair, 3968 *C-1
Belleair Beach, 2070 M-13
Belleview, 2666 J-15
Bellview, 19386 B-2
Bellwood, 450 K-19
Bennett E-7
Bereah, 30 M-17
Berry G-3
Berrydale, 50 D-3
Bertha G-6
Betmar Acres, 4000 L-15
Beverly Beach, 312 G-18
Beverly Hills, 6163 J-14
Big Coppitt Key, 2388 V-17
Big Pine V-17
Bithlo, 4834 K-18
Blackman, 20 D-4
Blanton, 200 K-15
Bloomingdale, 13912 *C-6
Blountstown, 2404 E-8
Bloxham, 450 E-9
Bluff Sprs., 225 D-3
Boca Grande, 700 Q-15
Boca Raton, 61492 Q-21
Bogia, 50 D-3
Bokeelia, 550 Q-15
Bonifay, 2612 D-7
Bonita Beach T-14
Bonita Sprs., 13600 R-16
Bostwick, 350 G-16
Boulogne, 150 D-16
Bowling Green, 1836 M-16
Boyd, 175 F-12
Boyette, 70 M-15
Boynton Beach, 46194 Q-21
Bradenton, 43779 N-14
Bradenton Beach, 1657 N-14
Bradfordville, 1100 E-10
Bradley Jct., 850 M-16
Brandon, 57985 L-15
Branford, 670 F-13
Bratt, 225 C-2
Brent, 21624 E-3
Brewster M-16
Brighton, 20 N-18
Briny Breezes, 400 Q-21
Bristol, 937 E-8
Bronson, 875 H-14
Brooker, 312 G-15
Brooksville, 7440 K-15
Brownsville B-2
Brownsville N-16
Bruce, 30 E-6
Bryceville, 100 E-16
Buckhead Ridge, 1279 N-18
Buena Ventura Lakes, 14148 L-4
Bunnell, 1873 H-17
Bushnell, 1998 K-15
Butler Beach, 3377 G-17
Callahan, 946 E-16
Callaway, 12253 F-7
Campbell, 3884 L-17
Campbellton, 202 D-7
Campton, 150 D-5
Campville, 200 G-15
Canal Pt., 500 P-19
Cannon Town, 125 D-4
Cantonment, 2300 D-3
Cape Canaveral, 8014 K-19
Cape Coral, 74991 Q-16
Capps, 40 E-11
Captiva, 225 Q-15
Carol City, 53331 R-20
Carrabelle, 1200 G-9
Carrollwood, 7195 *B-4
Caryville, 631 D-6
Cassadaga, 650 J-18
Casselberry, 20736 K-17
Cedar Gr., 1479 F-7
Cedar Key, 668 H-13
Center Hill, 735 K-16
Century, 1989 C-3
Chaires, 300 E-10
Charlotte Beach, 1600 P-15
Charlotte Harbor, 3327 P-15
Chassahowitzka, 700 K-14
Chattahoochee, 4382 D-9
Cherry Lake, 80 E-12
Chiefland, 1917 H-13
Chipley, 3866 D-7
Chipola Park F-8
Chokoloskee, 300 S-17
Christmas K-18
Chuluota, 1441 K-18
Citra, 800 H-15
Citrus Ctr. P-18
Citrus Sprs., 2213 J-14
Clarcona G-2
Clarksville E-8
Clearwater, 98784 L-14
Clermont, 6910 K-16
Cleveland, 2896 P-16
Clewiston, 6085 P-18
Cocoa, 17722 K-19
Cocoa Beach, 12123 K-19
Cocoa West, 6160 C-18
Coconut Cr., 27485 *F-9
Cody's Corner H-17
Coleman, 857 J-15
Columbia, 550 F-14
Compass Lake, 200 E-7
Concord E-10
Conway, 13159 J-5
Cooks Hammock, 20 F-12
Cooper City, 20791 *J-8
Copeland, 80 S-17
Coral Cove N-14
Coral Gables, 40091 S-20
Coral Sprs., 79443 R-20
Corkscrew Q-17
Cornwell, 70 N-18
Cortez, 4509 N-14
Cottage Hill, 1300 D-3
Cottondale, 900 D-7
Crawford E-16
Crawfordville, 750 F-10
Creels, 10 D-3
Crescent Beach, 1081 G-17
Crescent City, 1859 H-17
Crestview, 9886 D-5
Crooked Lake Park, 1575 M-17
Cross City, 2041 G-13
Crows Bluff, 30 J-17
Crystal Beach, 4000 *C-1
Crystal Lake, 20 E-7
Crystal River, 4044 J-14
Crystal Sprs., 700 L-15
Cudjoe, 300 V-17
Curlew, 5900 *B-2
Cutler Ridge, 21268 S-20
Cypress Quarters, 1343 N-19
Dade City, 5633 K-15
Dahoma E-14
Dalkeith, 125 F-8
Dallas, 350 J-15
Dania, 13024 *J-9
Darlington, 175 D-6
Davenport, 1529 L-17
Davie, 47217 R-20
Day, 90 F-13
Daytona Beach, 61921 H-18
Daytona Beach Shores, 2335 H-18
De Bary, 9327 J-17
De Funiak Sprs., 5120 D-6
De Land, 16491 J-17
De Leon Sprs., 1481 H-17
De Soto City, 550 M-17
Deanville H-17
Deer Park, 60 L-18
Deerfield Beach, 46325 R-21
Deerland D-5
Dekle Beach, 20 G-12
Dellwood, 125 D-8
Delray Beach, 47181 Q-21
Deltona, 49429 J-18
Denaud, 300 P-17
Denham L-14
Destin, 8080 E-5
Doctor Phillips, 7963 K-2
Doctors Inlet, 1400 F-16
Dover, 2606 L-15
Dowling Park, 650 F-13
Drifton, 200 E-11
Duette, 10 N-15
Dukes, 70 F-15
Dundee, 2335 L-17
Dunedin, 34012 L-14
Dunnellon, 1624 J-14
Dupont, 20 H-18
Durbin, 10 F-17
E. Naples, 22951 R-16
E. Palatka, 1989 G-17
Eastlake Weir, 150 J-16
Eastpoint, 1577 G-8
Eaton Park, 3000 L-16
Eatonville, 2170 G-4
Ebro, 255 E-6
Edgewater, 15337 J-18
Edgewood, 1062 J-4
El Portal, 2457 *L-9
Elfers, 12356 L-14
Ellaville, 10 E-13
Ellenton, 2573 *F-4
Ellzey, 60 H-14
Englewood, 15025 P-15
Englewood Beach, 1000 P-15
Ensley, 16362 E-3
Enterprise, 125 J-17
Eridu, 40 E-11
Espanola, 40 G-17
Estero, 3177 Q-16
Esto, 253 D-7
Eucheeanna, 40 D-6
Eureka, 450 H-16
Eustis, 12967 J-16
Eva K-16
Everglades City, 321 S-17
Fairbanks, 750 G-15
Fairview Shores, 13192 G-4
Fairvilla H-4
Falmouth, 30 E-13
Fanning Sprs., 493 G-13
Favoretta, 650 H-18
Felda, 300 Q-17
Fellsmere, 2179 M-19
Fenholloway, 20 F-12
Fern Park, 8294 F-5
Fernandina Beach, 8765 E-17
Ferry Pass, 26301 E-3
Flagler Beach, 3820 H-18
Flamingo, 200 U-18
Flamingo Bay R-13
Florahome, 400 G-16
Floral City, 2609 J-15
Florida City, 5806 T-20
Foley, 225 F-12
Forest City, 10638 F-3
Forest Hills, 600 J-17
Ft. Basinger, 20 N-18
Ft. Drum, 150 M-19
Ft. Green, 40 M-16
Ft. Lauderdale, 149377 R-20
Ft. McCoy H-16
Ft. Meade, 5151 M-16
Ft. Myers, 45206 Q-16
Ft. Myers Beach, 9284 Q-16
Ft. Myers Shores, 5460 Q-16
Ft. Myers Villas, 8500 Q-16
Ft. Ogden, 225 P-16
Ft. Pierce, 36830 N-20
Ft. Walton Beach, 21471 E-4
Ft. White, 268 F-14
Fountain, 225 E-7
Franklintown J-10
Freeport, 843 E-6
Frink, 20 E-8
Frontenac, 1900 B-18
Frostproof, 2808 M-17
Fruit Cove, 5904 F-17
Fruitland Park, 2754 J-16
Fruitville, 9808 *H-4
Gainesville, 84770 G-15
Gardner, 30 N-16
Gaskin, 80 D-6
Geneva, 500 J-18
Genoa, 50 E-14
Georgetown, 450 H-17
Gibsonia, 5168 L-16
Gibsonton, 7706 M-15
Gifford, 6278 M-20
Glen Ridge, 207 *C-9
Glen St. Mary, 480 E-15
Glendale, 80 D-6
Golden Beach, 774 *K-9
Golden Gate, 14148 R-16
Golf, 234 Q-20
Golfview, 153 *C-9
Gonzalez, 7669 D-3
Gotha H-2
Goulds, 7284 S-20
Gower's Corner K-14
Graceville, 2675 D-7
Graham G-15
Grand Ridge, 536 D-8
Grant, 300 L-19
Green Cove Sprs., 4497 F-16
Greenacres, 18683 Q-20
Greensboro, 586 E-9
Greenville, 950 E-12
Greenwood, 474 D-8
Gretna, 1981 E-9
Griffins Corner N-16
Grove City, 2374 P-15
Groveland, 2300 K-16
Gulf Breeze, 5530 E-3
Gulf Hammock, 40 H-14
Gulf Stream, 690 Q-21
Gulfport, 11727 *E-2
Haines City, 11683 L-17
Hallandale, 30996 R-20
Hampton, 296 G-15
Hampton Sprs., 40 F-12
Hanson, 175 E-12
Harbor Bluffs, 2659 *C-1
Harbour Hts., 2523 P-16
Harlem, 2826 P-18
Harold, 80 D-4
Hastings, 595 G-17
Hatchbend, 50 G-13
Havana, 1654 E-10
Haverhill, 1058 *C-9
Hawthorne, 1305 G-15
Hedges H-9
Hernando, 2103 J-15
Hernando Beach, 1767 K-14
Hialeah, 188004 S-20
Hialeah Gardens, 7713 *K-7
High Pt., 5800 *C-2
High Sprs., 3144 G-14
Highland, 80 F-15
Highland Beach, 3209 *F-10
Highland City, 1919 L-16
Highland View, 450 G-7
Hildreth, 60 G-14
Hillcrest Hts., 221 M-17
Hilliard, 1751 D-16
Hillsboro Beach, 1748 R-21
Hines G-13
Hinson, 750 E-10
Hobe Sound, 11507 P-20
Holder, 225 J-15
Holiday, 19360 L-14
Holley, 650 E-4
Holly Hill, 11141 H-18
Hollywood, 121697 R-20
Holmes Beach, 4810 N-14
Holopaw, 400 L-18
Holt, 125 D-4
Homeland, 300 M-16
Homestead, 26866 T-20
Homosassa, 2113 J-14
Homosassa Sprs., 6271 J-14
Honeyville, 400 F-8
Horseshoe Beach, 252 H-12
Hosford, 1400 E-9
Houston, 125 F-13
Howard Cr. F-8
Hudson, 7344 K-14
Hull, 150 N-16
Hypoluxo, 830 *D-10
Immokalee, 14120 Q-17
Indialantic, 2844 L-19
Indian Harbour Beach, 6933 L-19
Indian Lake Estates, 250 M-17
Indian River Estates, 4858 N-20
Indian River Shores, 2278 N-20
Indian Rocks Beach, 3963 M-13
Indian Shores, 1405 *C-1
Indiantown, 4794 P-20
Indrio, 550 M-20
Inglis, 1241 J-14
Intercession City, 900 L-17
Interlachen, 1160 G-16
Inverness, 5797 J-15
Inwood, 6824 L-16
Islamorada, 1220 U-19
Island Gr., 100 H-15
Istachatta, 350 K-15
Izagora, 80 D-6
Jacksonville, 635230 E-16
Jacksonville Beach, 17839 E-17
Jacobs, 261 D-7
Jamestown G-6
Jamieson, 20 D-10
Jasmine Estates, 17136 L-14
Jasper, 2099 E-13
Jay, 666 D-3
Jena, 400 G-12
Jennings, 712 E-13
Jensen Beach, 9884 N-20
Jerome, 40 R-17
Juno Beach, 2121 P-21
Jupiter, 26753 P-21
Jupiter Inlet Colony, 405 P-21
Jupiter Island, 549 P-20
Kathleen, 2743 L-16
Keaton Beach, 80 G-12
Kenansville, 20 M-18
Kendall, 87271 S-20
Kendrick, 600 H-15
Kenneth City, 4462 *D-2
Kensington Park, 3026 *H-4
Kenwood G-16
Key Biscayne, 8854 S-20
Key Colony Beach, 977 V-18
Key Largo, 11336 U-20
Key West, 24832 V-16
Keystone Hts., 1315 G-16
Kinard, 30 E-8
Kings Ferry D-16
Kingsley, 450 F-16
Kissimmee, 30050 L-17
Knights, 1000 *B-7
Korona, 40 H-18
La Belle, 2703 P-17
La Crosse, 122 G-15
La Grange A-18
Lacoochee, 2072 K-15
Lady Lake, 8071 J-16
Laguna Beach, 1876 E-6
Lake Alfred, 3622 L-16
Lake Bird, 50 F-12
Lake Buena Vista, 1776 K-17
Lake Butler, 2116 F-15
Lake Cain Hills J-3
Lake City, 10005 F-14
Lake Clarke Shores, 3364 *C-10
Lake Gem J-16
Lake Harbor, 60 Q-19
Lake Helen, 2344 J-18
Lake Marian Highlands M-18
Lake Mary, 5929 J-17
Lake Panasoffkee, 2705 J-15
Lake Park, 6704 *B-10
Lake Placid, 1158 N-17
Lake Wales, 9670 M-17
Lake Worth, 28564 Q-21
Lakeland, 70576 L-16
Lakeport P-18
Lakewood Park, 7211 M-20
Lamont, 125 E-11
Lanark Vil., 550 F-9
Land O' Lakes, 7892 L-14
Lantana, 8392 Q-21
Largo, 65674 M-14
Lauderdale Lakes, 27341 *H-9
Lauderdale-by-the-Sea, 2990 *H-9
Lauderhill, 49708 *H-8
Laurel, 8245 N-14
Laurel Hill, 543 D-5
Lawtey, 676 F-15
Layton, 183 U-19
Lealman, 21748 *D-2
Lebanon, 50 H-14
Lecanto, 1243 J-14
Lee, 306 E-12
Leesburg, 14903 J-16
Lehigh Acres, 13611 Q-17
Leisure City, 19379 T-20
Leonia, 40 D-6
Liberty, 50 D-5
Lighthouse Pt., 10378 R-21
Limestone, 30 N-16
Live Oak, 6332 E-13
Lloyd, 200 E-11
Lochloosa, 125 G-15
Lockhart, 11636 J-3
Longboat Key, 5937 N-14
Longwood, 13316 K-17
Lorida, 350 N-18
Loughman, 1214 L-17
Lovett, 30 E-12
Lulu, 90 F-14
Lumberton L-15
Luraville, 10 F-13
Lutz, 10552 L-14
Lynn Haven, 9298 E-7
Macclenny, 3966 E-15
Madeira Beach, 4225 M-14
Madison, 3345 E-12
Maitland, 9110 K-17
Malabar, 1977 L-19
Malone, 765 D-8
Manalapan, 312 Q-21
Mango, 8700 *B-5
Mangonia Park, 1453 *C-10
Marathon, 8857 V-18
Marco, 9493 S-16
Margate, 42985 R-20
Marianna, 6292 D-8
Marineland, 21 G-18
Marion Oaks, 100 J-15
Martel, 400 H-15
Mary Esther, 4139 E-4
Masaryktown, 900 K-14
Mascotte, 1761 K-16
Matlacha, 750 Q-15
Mayo, 917 F-13
McAlpin, 80 F-13
McDavid, 175 C-3
McIntosh, 411 H-15
McKinnon, 50 D-2
Meadow Woods, 4876 L-4
Medart, 175 F-10
Medley, 663 *L-7
Medulla, 3977 L-16
Melbourne, 59646 L-19
Melbourne Beach, 3021 L-19
Melrose, 800 G-15
Memphis, 6760 *F-4
Merritt Island, 32886 K-19
Mexico Beach, 992 F-7
Miami, 358548 S-20
Miami Beach, 92639 S-20
Miami Lakes, 12750 *K-8
Miami Shores, 10084 *L-9
Miami Sprs., 13268 S-20
Micanopy, 612 G-15
Micco, 8757 M-19
Miccosukee, 150 E-11
Middleburg, 6223 F-16
Midway, 852 E-10
Milligan, 450 D-4
Milton, 7216 D-3
Mims, 9412 K-18
Minneola, 1515 K-16
Miramar, 40663 R-20
Miramar Beach, 1644 E-5
Molino, 1207 D-3
Monroe Sta. S-18
Montbrook, 100 H-14
Monticello, 2573 E-11
Moore Haven, 1432 P-18
Morningside Park K-4
Morriston, 125 H-14
Moss Bluff, 200 H-16
Mt. Carmel, 100 C-3
Mt. Dora, 7196 J-16
Mt. Pleasant, 150 D-9
Mt. Plymouth, 1752 J-17
Mulberry, 2988 M-16
Munson, 30 D-4
Myakka City, 200 N-15
Myrtle Gr., 17402 E-3
Naples, 19505 R-16
Naples Manor, 4574 R-16
Naples Park, 8002 R-16
Naranja, 5790 T-20
Narcoossee, 500 L-18
Nassau Vil., 1900 J-7
Nassauville H-9
Navarre, 450 E-4
Neptune Beach, 6816 E-17
New Hope, 150 E-6
New Port Richey, 14044 L-14
New River F-15
New Smyrna Beach, 16543 J-18
Newberry, 1644 G-14
Newburn, 60 F-13
Newport F-10
Niceville, 10507 E-5
Nobleton K-15
Nocatee, 700 N-16
Nokomis, 3448 P-15
Noma, 207 D-7
N. Bay Vil., 5383 *L-9
N. Ft. Myers, 30027 Q-16
N. Lauderdale, 26506 *G-8
N. Miami, 49998 S-20
N. Miami Beach, 35359 R-20
N. Naples, 13422 R-16
N. Palm Beach, 11538 P-21
N. Port, 11973 P-15
N. Redington Beach, 1135 *D-1
N. River Shores, 3250 N-20
Northdale, 10000 *A-4
Oak Gr., 100 D-2
Oak Gr., 40 D-9
Oak Hill, 917 J-18
Oakdale, 125 D-8
Oakland Park, 26326 *H-9
O'Brien, 80 F-13
Ocala, 42045 H-15
Ocean Breeze Park, 519 N-20
Ocean City, 5422 E-4
Ocean Reef Club, 1000 T-20
Ocean Ridge, 1570 *E-10
Ochopee S-17
Ocklawaha, 550 J-16
Ocoee, 12778 K-17
Odessa, 350 L-14
Okeechobee, 4943 N-19
Okeelanta, 90 Q-19
Old Myakka, 225 N-15
Old Town, 100 G-13
Oldsmar, 8361 L-14
Olustee, 150 F-15
Ona, 100 N-16
Oneco, 7500 N-14
O'Neil H-9
Opa-Locka, 15283 S-20
Orange, 10 F-8
Orange City, 5372 J-17
Orange Hts., 150 G-15
Orange Lake, 650 H-15
Orange Park, 9488 F-16
Orange Sprs., 100 G-16
Orangedale F-17
Orchid, 10 M-20
Orient Park, 4300 *B-5
Orlando, 164693 K-17
Orlovista, 5990 H-3
Ormond Beach, 29721 H-18
Ormond-by-the-Sea, 8157 H-18
Osceola J-18
Oslo, 1900 M-20
Osprey, 2597 N-14
Osteen, 450 J-18
Otter Cr., 136 H-14
Oviedo, 11114 K-18
Oxford, 350 J-16
Pace, 6277 D-3
Pahokee, 6822 P-19
Palatka, 10201 G-16
Palm Bay, 62632 L-19
Palm Beach, 9814 Q-21
Palm Beach Gardens, 24139 P-20
Palm Beach Shores, 1040 *B-10
Palm Coast, 14287 G-18
Palm Harbor, 50256 L-14
Palm River, 2700 *C-5
Palm Shores, 210 D-19
Palm Sprs., 9763 Q-20
Palm Valley, 9960 F-17
Palmdale, 175 P-17
Palmetto, 9268 N-14
Panacea, 550 F-10
Panama City, 34378 F-7
Panama City Beach, 4051 F-6
Parker, 4598 F-7
Parkland, 3558 R-20
Parrish, 550 M-15
Pasco, 100 L-15
Paxton, 600 D-5
Pedro J-15
Pembroke, 30 M-16
Pembroke Park, 4933 *J-9
Pembroke Pines, 65452 R-20
Penney Farms, 609 F-16
Pensacola, 58165 E-3
Pensacola Beach, 750 E-3
Perrine, 15576 S-20
Perry, 7151 F-12
Picnic M-15
Piedmont G-2
Pierson, 2988 H-17
Pine Barren, 150 D-3
Pine Castle, 8276 K-17
Pine Hills, 35322 H-3
Pine Island Ctr. R-12
Pine Level N-16
Pine Log, 60 E-6
Pinecrest, 900 M-15
Pinecrest S-18
Pineda, 1100 L-19
Pineland, 400 Q-15
Pinellas Park, 43426 M-14
Pineola, 100 J-15
Pinetta, 250 E-12
Pinewood, 16000 *L-8
Pioneer, 600 J-18
Pittman, 60 J-16
Placida, 300 P-15
Plant City, 22754 L-15
Plantation, 66692 R-20
Plantation, 4405 U-19
Plantation, 3618 *L-5
Polk City, 1439 L-16
Pomona Park, 663 H-17
Pompano Beach, 72411 R-20
Ponce de Leon, 406 D-6
Ponce Inlet, 1704 J-18
Ponte Vedra Beach, 1100 F-17
Port Charlotte, 41535 P-15
Port La Belle, 1512 P-17
Port Mayaca, 10 P-19
Port Orange, 35317 H-18
Port Richey, 2523 L-14
Port St. Joe, 4044 G-8
Port St. John, 8933 K-19
Port St. Lucie, 55866 N-20
Port Salerno, 7786 N-20
Portland, 300 E-5
Princeton, 7073 T-20
Prosperity, 70 E-6
Providence, 100 L-16
Providence F-15
Punta Gorda, 10747 P-16
Punta Rassa, 1493 Q-16
Putnam Hall, 400 G-16
Quincy, 7444 E-9
Raiford, 198 F-15
Raleigh, 300 H-14
Ratliff, 404 E-16
Red Head, 60 E-6
Redbay, 60 E-6
Reddick, 554 H-15
Redington Beach, 1626 M-14
Redington Shores, 2366 *D-1
Richland K-15
Richmond Hts., 8583 S-20
Ridge Manor, 1947 K-15
Rio, 1054 N-20
Riverview, 6478 M-15
Riviera Beach, 27639 P-21
Rochelle, 125 G-15
Rock Hill, 10 E-6
Rockdale *N-7
Rockledge, 16023 K-19
Romeo, 60 H-15
Roseland, 1379 M-19
Rosewood H-13
Rotonda, 3576 P-15
Round Lake, 200 D-7
Royal Palm Beach, 14589 Q-20
Ruskin, 6046 M-15
Russell, 100 F-16
Safety Harbor, 15124 L-14
St. Augustine, 11692 F-17
St. Augustine Beach, 3657 G-17
St. Augustine Shores, 4411 G-17
St. Catherine, 80 K-15
St. Cloud, 12453 L-17
St. James City, 1904 Q-15
St. Leo, 1009 K-15
St. Lucie, 584 N-20
St. Marks, 307 F-10
St. Pete Beach, 9200 M-14
St. Petersburg, 238629 M-14
St. Teresa, 20 F-10
Salem, 80 F-12
Salt Sprs., 600 H-16
Samoset, 3119 *G-3
Sampson City, 60 F-15
Samsula, 175 J-18
San Antonio, 776 K-15
San Carlos Park, 11785 Q-16
San Mateo, 1000 G-17
Sanborn, 10 F-9
Sanderson, 500 F-15
Sandy N-15
Sanford, 32387 J-17
Sanibel, 5468 Q-16
Santa Rosa Beach, 300 E-5
Sante Fe, 150 G-15
Santos, 550 J-15
Sarasota, 50961 N-14
Satellite Beach, 9889 L-19
Satsuma, 700 G-16
Sawgrass M-10
Scottsmoor, 600 J-18
Sea Ranch Lakes, 619 *G-9
Seagrove Beach, 150 E-6
Sebastian, 10205 M-19
Sebring, 8900 N-17
Seffner, 5371 *B-6
Seminole, 9251 *D-2
Seville, 500 H-17
Shady Gr., 90 E-12
Shalimar, 341 E-5
Shamrock, 200 G-13
Sharpes, 3348 K-19
Sherman N-19
Shired Island H-13
Siesta Key, 7772 N-14
Silver Sprs., 6421 H-15
Silver Sprs. Shores, 6421 H-15
Sink Cr., 50 E-8
Sirmans, 10 E-12
Sky Lake, 6202 K-4
Slavia F-6
Sneads, 1746 D-9
Solana, 1128 P-16
Sopchoppy, 367 F-10
S. Apopka, 6360 F-2
S. Bay, 3558 Q-19
S. Daytona, 12482 H-18
S. Miami, 10404 *M-8
S. Miami Hts., 30030 *N-7
S. Palm Beach, 1480 *D-10
S. Pasadena, 5644 *D-2
S. Patrick Shores, 10249 L-19
S. Ponte Vedra Beach, 150 F-17
S. Venice, 11951 P-15
Southport, 1500 E-7
Southwood, 10500 J-3
Sparr, 400 H-15
Spr. Hill, 31117 K-14
Spr. Lake K-15
Springfield, 8715 F-7
Starke, 5226 F-15
Steinhatchee, 700 G-12
Stock Island, 3613 V-16
Stuart, 11936 N-20
Sumatra, 60 F-8
Summer Haven, 70 G-18
Summerfield, 550 J-16
Summerland Key, 600 V-17
Sumterville, 250 J-15
Sun City, 175 M-14
Sun City Ctr., 8326 M-15
Sunniland R-17
Sunrise, 64407 *H-8
Surfside, 4108 *L-9
Suwannee, 450 H-13
Suwannee Sprs., 70 E-13
Sweetwater, 13909 S-20
Sylvan Shores, 2155 N-17
Taft, 2200 K-4
Tallahassee, 124773 E-10
Tallevast, 1100 *G-4
Tamarac, 44822 R-20
Tampa, 280015 L-14
Tangelo Park, 2663 K-3
Tarpon Sprs., 17906 L-14
Tavares, 7383 J-16
Tavernier, 2433 U-20
Taylor, 150 E-15
Taylor Cr., 4081 N-19
Telogia, 200 E-9
Temple Terrace, 16444 *B-5
Tenille, 10 G-12
Tequesta, 4499 P-20
Theressa, 175 G-15
Thomas City E-11
Thonotosassa, 3300 L-15
Tice, 3971 Q-16
Titusville, 39394 K-19
Tocoi G-17
Town 'n Country, 60946 *B-4
Treasure Island, 7266 M-14
Trenton, 1287 G-14
Trilby, 850 K-15
Truckland G-13
Two Egg D-8
Umatilla, 2350 J-16
Union Park, 6890 H-6
University Park *H-7
Valkaria, 200 L-19
Valparaiso, 4672 E-5
Vamo, 3325 N-14
Venice, 16922 P-15
Venice Gardens, 7701 P-15
Venus, 10 P-17
Vermont Hts., 250 G-17
Verna, 30 N-15
Vernon, 778 E-7
Vero Beach, 17350 M-20
Vicksburg, 30 E-7
Villano Beach, 1867 F-17
Vilas, 10 F-9
Villages of Oriole, 4500 Q-20
Vineland K-2
Virginia Gardens, 2212 *L-8
Wabasso, 1145 M-20
Wacissa, 350 E-11
Wakulla, 175 F-10
Wakulla Beach, 400 F-10
Waldo, 1017 G-15
Walnut Hill, 400 C-2
Walton, 100 N-20
Wannee, 125 G-13
Ward Ridge, 60 G-8
Warm Mineral Sprs., 4041 *K-6
Warrington, 16040 E-3
Watertown, 3340 F-14
Wauchula, 3253 N-16
Waukeenah, 60 E-11
Wausau, 313 E-7
Waverly, 2071 L-17
Webster, 746 K-15
Weeki Wachee, 53 K-14
Weeki Wachee Gardens, 1170 K-14
Weirsdale, 750 J-16
Welaka, 533 H-16
Wellborn, 350 F-14
Wellington, 20670 Q-20
Wesley Chapel, 1200 L-15
W. Bay, 225 E-6
W. Frostproof, 125 M-17
W. Melbourne, 8399 L-19
W. Miami, 5727 S-20
W. Palm Beach, 67643 Q-21
W. Pensacola, 22107 E-3
Westville, 257 D-6
Westwood Acres, 125 H-15
Westwood Lake, 11522 S-20
Wewahitchka, 1779 F-8
Whiskey Cr., 5061 R-14
White City, 4645 N-20
White City, 300 F-8
White Sprs., 704 E-14
Whitfield Estates, 4200 N-14
Wilbur-by-the-Sea C-17
Wildwood, 3421 J-16
Williamsburg, 3093 K-3
Willis Lodge F-16
Williston, 2179 H-15
Wilma, 10 F-9
Wilton Manors, 11804 *H-9
Wimauma, 2932 M-15
Windermere, 1371 K-17
Winfield, 225 E-14
Winston, 9118 L-16
Winter Beach, 225 M-20
Winter Garden, 9745 K-17
Winter Haven, 24725 L-16
Winter Park, 24260 K-17
Winter Sprs., 22151 K-17
Woods E-8
Woodville, 2760 E-10
Wright, 18945 E-4
Yalaha, 1168 J-16
Yankeetown, 635 J-14
Yeehaw Jct., 100 M-18
Youngstown, 40 E-7
Yulee, 6915 E-17
Yulee Hts. H-9
Zephyrhills, 8220 L-15
Zolfo Sprs., 1219 N-16

GEORGIA
PG. 85–87

CAPITAL
Atlanta

NICKNAME
Empire State of the South

POPULATION
7,353,225, rank 10

AREA
58,910 sq mi, rank 21

Counties
Appling, 15744 M-9
Atkinson, 6213 N-7
Bacon, 9566 M-9
Baker, 3615 N-4
Baldwin, 39530 H-6
Banks, 10308 D-6
Barrow, 29721 E-5
Bartow, 55911 D-3
Ben Hill, 16245 M-7
Berrien, 14153 N-7
Bibb, 149967 H-5
Bleckley, 10430 K-6
Brantley, 11077 N-10
Brooks, 15398 Q-6
Bryan, 15438 L-11
Bulloch, 43125 K-10
Burke, 20579 H-10
Butts, 15326 G-5
Calhoun, 5013 M-3
Camden, 30167 P-11
Candler, 7744 K-10
Carroll, 71422 F-2
Catoosa, 42464 B-2
Charlton, 8496 P-9
Chatham, 216935 L-12
Chattahoochee, 16934 K-2
Chattooga, 22242 C-1
Cherokee, 90204 D-3
Clarke, 87594 E-6
Clay, 3364 N-2
Clayton, 182052 F-4
Clinch, 6160 P-8
Cobb, 447745 E-3
Coffee, 29592 N-8
Colquitt, 36645 P-6
Columbia, 66031 F-9
Cook, 13456 P-6
Coweta, 53853 G-3
Crawford, 8991 J-5
Crisp, 20011 L-6
Dade, 13147 B-1
Dawson, 9429 D-4
Decatur, 25511 Q-3
De Kalb, 545837 F-4
Dodge, 17607 K-7
Dooly, 9901 L-6
Dougherty, 96311 N-4
Douglas, 71120 F-3
Early, 11854 N-3
Echols, 2334 Q-7
Effingham, 25687 K-12
Elbert, 18949 E-8
Emanuel, 20546 J-9
Evans, 8724 L-10
Fannin, 15992 B-4
Fayette, 62415 F-3
Floyd, 81251 D-2
Forsyth, 44083 D-5
Franklin, 16650 D-7
Fulton, 648951 F-3
Gilmer, 13368 C-4
Glascock, 2357 G-8
Glynn, 62496 N-11
Gordon, 35072 C-3
Grady, 20279 Q-4
Greene, 11793 G-7
Gwinnett, 352910 E-5
Habersham, 27621 C-6
Hall, 95428 D-6
Hancock, 8908 G-7
Haralson, 21966 F-2
Harris, 17788 J-3
Hart, 19712 D-7
Heard, 8628 G-2
Henry, 58741 G-5
Houston, 89208 J-6
Irwin, 8649 M-6
Jackson, 30005 D-6
Jasper, 8453 G-6
Jeff Davis, 12032 M-8
Jefferson, 17408 H-9
Jenkins, 8247 H-10
Johnson, 8329 J-8
Jones, 20739 H-6
Lamar, 13038 G-4
Lanier, 5531 P-7
Laurens, 39988 J-7
Lee, 16250 M-5
Liberty, 52745 L-11
Lincoln, 7442 E-8
Long, 6202 M-11
Lowndes, 75981 Q-6
Lumpkin, 14573 C-5
Macon, 13114 K-5
Madison, 21050 D-7
Marion, 5590 K-3
McDuffie, 20119 G-9
McIntosh, 8634 M-12
Meriwether, 22411 H-3
Miller, 6280 P-3
Mitchell, 20275 P-4
Monroe, 17113 H-5
Montgomery, 7163 L-9
Morgan, 12883 F-6
Murray, 26147 B-3
Muscogee, 179278 J-3
Newton, 41808 F-5
Oconee, 17618 E-6
Oglethorpe, 9763 F-7
Paulding, 41611 E-2
Peach, 21189 J-5
Pickens, 14432 C-4
Pierce, 13328 N-10
Pike, 10224 H-4
Polk, 33815 E-2
Pulaski, 8108 K-6
Putnam, 14137 G-6
Quitman, 2209 M-2
Rabun, 11648 B-6
Randolph, 8023 M-3
Richmond, 189719 G-10
Rockdale, 54091 F-5
Schley, 3588 K-4
Screven, 13842 H-11
Seminole, 9010 P-2
Spalding, 54457 G-4
Stephens, 23257 C-7
Stewart, 5654 L-2
Sumter, 30228 L-5
Talbot, 6524 J-4
Taliaferro, 1915 F-8
Tattnall, 17722 K-9
Taylor, 7642 J-4
Telfair, 11000 L-8
Terrell, 10653 M-4
Thomas, 38986 Q-5
Tift, 34998 N-6
Toombs, 24072 L-9
Towns, 6754 B-6
Treutlen, 5994 K-8
Troup, 55536 H-2
Turner, 8703 M-6
Twiggs, 9806 J-6
Union, 11993 B-5
Upson, 26300 H-4
Walker, 58340 B-2
Walton, 38586 F-5
Ware, 35471 P-9
Warren, 6078 G-8
Washington, 19112 H-8
Wayne, 22356 N-10
Webster, 2263 L-3
Wheeler, 4903 L-8
White, 13006 C-5
Whitfield, 72462 B-3
Wilcox, 7008 M-7
Wilkes, 10597 F-8
Wilkinson, 10228 J-7
Worth, 19745 M-5

Cities and Towns
* City indexed to pg. 85
Abbeville, 907 L-7
Acree, 200 N-5
Acworth, 4519 E-3
Adairsville, 2131 D-3
Adel, 5093 P-6
Adgateville, 30 G-6
Adrian, 615 J-8
Ailey, 579 L-8
Airline D-7
Alamo, 855 L-8
Alapaha, 812 N-7
Albany, 78122 N-4
Aldora, 127 H-4
Alexander, 125 H-10
Allenhurst, 594 M-11
Allentown, 273 J-7
Alma, 3663 N-9
Almon, 1000 F-5
Alpharetta, 13002 E-4
Alston, 160 L-9
Alto, 651 C-6
Alvaton, 125 G-3
Ambrose, 288 N-7
Americus, 16512 L-4
Amsterdam Q-4
Anderson City N-5
Andersonville, 277 L-4
Aonia F-8
Apalachee, 100 F-6
Appling, 225 F-9
Arabi, 433 M-5
Aragon, 902 E-2
Arcade, 697 E-6
Argyle, 206 P-8
Arlington, 1513 N-3
Armuchee D-2
Arnoldsville, 275 E-7
Ashburn, 4827 M-6
Athens, 86622 E-6
Atkinson, 100 P-10
Atlanta, 394017 F-4
Attapulgus, 380 Q-4
Auburn, 3139 E-5
Augusta, 186956 F-10
Austell, 4173 *E-2
Autreyville P-5
Avalon, 159 C-7
Avera, 215 G-9
Avondale Estates, 2209 *F-8
Axson, 90 N-8
Baconton, 623 N-4
Bainbridge, 10712 Q-3
Bairdstown F-7
Baldwin, 1439 C-6
Ball Ground, 905 D-4
Barnesville, 4747 H-4
Barney, 300 P-6
Barretts, 550 P-7
Bartow, 292 H-9
Barwick, 385 Q-5
Batesville C-6
Baxley, 3841 M-9
Beachton Q-4
Bellville, 192 L-10
Belmont *G-10
Belvedere, 11100 *G-8
Bemiss, 1500 P-7
Benevolence, 40 M-3
Berkeley Lake, 791 *B-9
Berlin, 480 P-6
Bethlehem, 348 E-6
Between, 82 E-5
Bibb City, 597 T-2
Bickley N-8
Birmingham D-4
Bishop, 158 E-6
Blackshear, 3263 N-9
Blacksville, 1112 G-5
Blackwells, 2200 E-4
Blaine C-3
Blairsville, 564 B-5
Blakely, 5595 N-2
Blitchton, 200 K-11
Bloomingdale, 2271 T-9
Blue Ridge, 1336 B-4
Bluffton, 138 N-3
Blythe, 300 G-9
Bogart, 1018 E-6
Bolingbroke, 250 H-5
Bonaire, 800 J-6
Boston, 1395 Q-5
Bostwick, 307 F-6
Bowdon, 1981 F-2
Bowersville, 311 D-7
Bowman, 791 D-7
Boykin, 125 P-3
Branchville P-4
Braselton, 418 E-5
Braswell, 247 E-2
Bremen, 4356 F-2
Brewton, 150 J-8
Bridgeboro, 200 N-5
Brinson, 238 P-3
Bristol N-9
Broadhurst, 20 N-10
Bronwood, 513 M-4
Brookfield, 350 N-6
Brookhaven *D-7
Brooklet, 1013 K-11
Brooklyn, 20 L-3
Brooks, 328 G-4
Brooksville M-3
Broxton, 1211 M-8
Brunswick, 16433 P-11
Buchanan, 1009 E-2
Buckhead, 176 F-6
Buena Vista, 1472 K-4
Buford, 8771 E-5
Bullard, 80 J-6
Butler, 1673 J-4
Butts J-10
Byromville, 452 K-5
Byron, 2276 J-5
Cadley, 30 G-8
Cadwell, 458 K-7
Cairo, 9035 Q-4
Calhoun, 7135 C-3
Calvary, 300 Q-4
Camak, 220 G-8
Camilla, 5008 P-4
Campbellton F-3
Canon, 737 D-7
Canton, 4817 D-4
Carl, 263 E-5
Carlton, 282 E-7
Carnegie, 60 M-3
Carnesville, 514 D-7
Carrollton, 16029 F-2
Cartecay C-4
Cartersville, 12035 D-3
Cary, 125 J-7
Cassville, 300 D-3
Cave Spr., 950 D-2
Cecil, 376 P-6
Cedar Crossing L-9
Cedar Gr. *H-7
Cedar Gr. K-8
Cedar Sprs. P-2
Cedartown, 7978 E-2
Center, 350 E-6
Centerpost, 250 C-1
Centerville, 3251 J-6
Centralhatchee, 301 G-2
Chamblee, 7668 E-4
Charing, 30 K-4
Chatsworth, 2865 C-3
Chattahoochee Plantation *B-5
Chauncey, 312 L-7
Chennault E-8
Cherry Log, 80 B-4
Chester, 1072 K-7
Chestnut Mtn., 650 D-5
Chickamauga, 2149 B-2
China Hill, 30 M-7
Chula, 175 N-6
Cisco, 450 B-3
Clarkdale *E-1
Clarkesville, 1151 C-6
Clarkston, 5385 *E-8
Claxton, 2464 L-10
Clayton, 1613 B-6
Clem, 300 F-2
Clermont, 402 C-5
Cleveland, 1653 C-5
Climax, 226 Q-4
Clinton H-6
Cloudland C-1
Clyattville, 450 Q-7
Clyo, 300 J-12
Coal Mtn., 700 D-5
Cobb L-5
Cobbtown, 338 K-10
Cochran, 4390 K-6
Cogdell, 40 N-8
Cohutta, 529 B-3
Colbert, 443 E-7
Coleman, 137 M-3
College Park, 20457 F-4
Collins, 528 L-10
Colomokee N-3
Colquitt, 1991 P-3
Columbus, 178681 J-3
Comer, 939 E-7
Commerce, 4108 D-6
Concord, 211 H-4
Constitution *H-7
Conyers, 7380 F-5
Coolidge, 610 P-5
Cooper Hts., 175 B-1
Coosa, 30 D-1
Cordele, 10321 L-5
Corinth, 136 G-2
Cornelia, 3219 C-6
Cotton, 80 P-5
Council Q-9
Covena K-9
Coverdale, 50 M-6
Covington, 10026 F-5
Cox, 60 N-11
Crabapple E-4
Crandall B-3
Crawford, 694 E-7
Crawfordville, 577 F-8
Crescent N-12
Crosland N-6
Crystal Sprs. D-2
Culloden, 242 H-5
Culverton, 80 G-8
Cumming, 2828 D-5
Cusseta, 1107 K-3
Cuthbert, 3730 M-3
Dacula, 2217 E-5
Dahlonega, 3086 C-5
Daisy, 138 L-10
Dakota, 80 M-6
Dallas, 2810 E-3
Dalton, 21761 B-2
Damascus, 290 N-3
Dames Ferry, 70 H-6
Danburg E-8
Danielsville, 318 E-7
Danville, 480 J-7
Darien, 1783 N-11
Dasher, 688 Q-7
Davisboro, 407 H-8
Dawson, 5295 M-4
Dawsonville, 467 D-5
De Soto, 258 L-5
Dearing, 547 G-9
Decatur, 17336 F-4
Deenwood, 2055 P-9
Deepstep, 111 H-7
Demorest, 1088 C-6
Denmark, 150 K-11
Denton, 335 M-8
Desser Q-3
Devereux, 100 G-7
Dewy Rose, 225 D-7
Dexter, 475 K-7
Diamond Hill E-7
Dickey N-3
Dillard, 199 B-6
Dixie, 125 Q-6
Dixie Union, 125 N-9
Dock Jct., 7094 P-11
Doctortown, 10 M-10
Doerun, 899 N-5
Doles, 100 M-5
Donalsonville, 2761 P-3
Donovan, 50 J-8
Dooling, 28 K-5
Doraville, 7626 E-4
Douglas, 10464 N-8
Douglasville, 11635 F-3
Doverel M-3
Doyle, 40 K-4
Draketown, 300 E-2
Drayton L-5
Druid Hills, 12174 *F-7
Dublin, 16312 J-8
Dudley, 430 J-7
Due West *B-1
Duluth, 9821 E-4
Dunwoody, 26302 *C-7
DuPont, 177 P-8
Durand, 175 H-3
E. Dublin, 2524 J-8
E. Ellijay, 303 C-4
E. Newnan, 1173 G-3
E. Point, 34402 F-4
Eastman, 5153 L-7
Eatonton, 6479 G-6
Edgehill H-8
Edison, 1182 N-3
Edith Q-9
Egypt, 70 K-11
Elberta J-6
Elberton, 5682 E-8
Eldorado N-6
Eldorendo, 100 P-3
Elko, 175 K-6
Ellabell, 450 L-11
Ellaville, 1724 K-4
Ellenton, 227 P-6
Ellerslie J-3
Ellijay, 1178 C-4
Elmodel, 20 N-4
Emerson, 1201 D-3
Emmalane, 125 J-10
Empire, 450 K-7
Enigma, 611 N-7
Ephesus, 324 G-2
Esom Hill, 125 E-1
Eton, 315 B-3
Eudora G-5
Euharlee, 850 D-3
Eulonia, 70 N-11
Evans, 13713 F-10
Everett, 70 N-11
Experiment, 3762 G-4
Fair Oaks, 6996 G-3
Fair Play F-3
Fairburn, 4013 F-3
Fairmount, 657 D-3
Fairview, 6444 B-2
Fargo, 414 Q-9
Farmington, 250 F-6
Fayetteville, 5827 G-4
Felton, 300 F-2
Finleyson L-6
Fitzgerald, 8612 M-7
Fitzpatrick H-6
Five Points K-4
Flat Rock G-7
Flemington, 279 M-11
Florence L-2
Flovilla, 602 G-5
Flowery Branch, 1251 D-5
Folkston, 2285 Q-10
Forest Park, 16925 *F-8
Forsyth, 4268 H-5
Ft. Gaines, 1248 M-2
Ft. Oglethorpe, 5880 B-2
Ft. Valley, 8198 J-5
Fortsonia, 125 E-8
Fowlstown, 250 Q-3
Franklin, 876 G-2
Franklin Sprs., 475 D-7

PICNIC POINT ON ASPEN MOUNTAIN, CO

Free Home, 550 D-4
Friendship, 20 L-4
Funkhouser H-7
Funston, 248 P-5
Gainesville, 17885 D-5
Garden City, 7410 L-12
Garden Valley K-4
Gardi, 150 N-10
Garfield, 255 J-10
Gay, 133 H-3
Geneva, 182 J-3
Georgetown, 913 M-2
Gibson, 679 G-8
Gillsville, 113 D-6
Girard, 195 H-11
Glennville, 3676 L-10
Glenwood, 881 L-8
Godfrey, 100 G-6
Good Hope, 181 F-6
Gordon, 2468 H-7
Gordy, 125 K-5
Gough, 225 H-9
Graham, 293 M-9
Grange, 10 H-9
Grantville, 1180 G-3
Graves M-3
Gray, 2189 H-6
Grayson, 529 E-5
Graysville, 201 B-2
Greensboro, 2860 F-7
Greenville, 1167 H-3
Gregory C-2
Gresham Park, 9000 *G-7
Gresston, 250 K-7
Griffin, 23451 G-4
Grovania K-6
Groveland, 100 L-10
Grovetown, 3596 G-9
Gum Branch, 291 M-11
Guyton, 740 K-11
Haddock, 500 H-6
Hagan, 787 L-10
Hahira, 1353 P-6
Hamilton, 454 J-3
Hampton, 2694 G-4
Hapeville, 5483 *H-5
Haralson, 139 G-3
Hardwick, 1100 H-7
Harlem, 2199 G-9
Harrietts Bluff Q-11
Harris City H-3
Harrison, 414 H-8
Harrisonville G-2
Hartsfield P-5
Hartwell, 4555 D-8
Hatley, 60 M-6
Hawkinsville, 3527 K-6
Haylow Q-8
Hayneville, 400 K-6
Hazlehurst, 4202 M-8
Helen, 300 C-6
Helena, 1256 L-8
Henderson, 125 K-5
Hephzibah, 2466 G-10
Herod, 40 M-4
Hiawassee, 547 B-6
Hickox, 200 P-10
Higdon B-4
Higgston, 274 K-9
High Falls G-5
Hillsboro, 50 G-6
Hiltonia, 402 H-11
Hilton N-2
Hinesville, 21603 M-11
Hinsonton P-5
Hiram, 1389 E-3
Hoboken, 440 P-10
Hogansville, 2976 G-3
Holland, 90 D-1
Hollingsworth D-6
Holly Sprs., 2406 D-4
Hollywood, 400 C-6
Homeland, 981 Q-10
Homer, 742 D-6
Homerville, 2560 P-8
Hopeful, 40 P-4
Hopeulikit J-10
Horns, 200 J-5
Hortense, 225 N-10
Hoschton, 642 E-5
Howard, 60 J-4
Howell, 60 Q-7
Huber, 300 J-6
Hull, 156 E-7
Ideal, 554 K-4
Ila, 297 D-7
Inman, 650 G-4
Iron City, 503 P-3
Irwinton, 641 J-7
Irwinville, 125 M-6
Isabella N-5
Isle of Hope, 2500 L-12
Ivey, 1053 H-7
Ivy Log B-5
Jackson, 4076 G-5
Jacksonville, 128 M-7
Jakin, 137 P-2
James, 150 H-6
Jasper, 1772 C-4
Jefferson, 2763 E-6
Jeffersonville, 1545 J-7
Jenkinsburg, 213 G-5
Jersey, 149 F-5
Jesup, 8958 M-10
Jonesboro, 3635 F-4
Jordan L-8
Juliette, 200 H-5
Jct. City, 182 J-4
Juniper, 20 J-3
Juno, 100 C-4
Kansas F-2
Kathleen, 650 J-6
Keithsburg, 300 D-4
Keller, 80 M-12
Kennesaw, 8936 E-3
Keysville, 284 G-9
Killarney P-2
Kingsland, 5711 Q-11
Kingston, 616 D-2
Kirkland, 20 N-8
Kite, 297 J-9
Knoxville, 60 J-5
La Fayette, 6655 C-2
La Grange, 25597 H-2
Lake Park, 500 Q-7
Lakeland, 2467 P-7
Lakemont, 350 B-6
Lavonia, 1840 D-7
Lawrenceville, 16848 E-5
Lax N-7
Leah F-9
Leary, 701 N-3
Lebanon D-4
Leesburg, 1452 M-4
Lenox, 783 N-6
Leslie, 445 L-5
Lester N-5
Lexington, 230 E-7
Lilburn, 9301 E-5
Lilly, 138 L-5
Lincolnton, 1476 F-9
Lindale, 4187 D-2
Linton, 150 H-7
Lithia Sprs., 2437 E-3
Lizella, 600 J-5
Locust Gr., 1681 G-5
Loganville, 3180 E-5
Lone Oak, 161 G-3
Long Cane H-2
Lookout Mtn., 1636 B-2
Lothair K-8
Louisville, 2429 H-9
Lovett, 70 J-8
Lowell F-2
Lucile, 20 P-2
Ludowici, 1291 M-11
Ludville, 200 C-3
Luella, 125 G-4
Lula, 1018 D-6
Lumber City, 1429 L-8
Lumpkin, 1250 L-3
Luthersville, 741 G-3
Lyerly, 493 D-1
Lyneville E-8
Lynn P-3
Lyons, 4502 K-9
Mableton, 25725 E-3
Macland *C-1
Macon, 106612 H-6
Madison, 3483 F-6
Madras, 350 G-3
Madray Sprs. M-10
Magruder H-9
Manassas, 123 L-10
Manchester, 4104 H-3
Manor, 200 P-9
Mansfield, 341 F-6
Marblehill D-4
Marietta, 44129 E-3
Marshallville, 1457 K-5
Martin, 243 C-7
Matt D-5
Mauk, 60 J-4
Maxeys, 180 F-7
Mayday, 20 Q-7
Mayfield, 150 G-8
Maysville, 728 D-6
McBean, 125 G-10
McCaysville, 1071 B-4
McDonough, 2929 F-4
McIntyre, 552 H-7
McKinnon, 70 N-10
McRae, 3007 L-8
Meansville, 250 H-4
Mechanicsville *G-8
Meigs, 1120 P-5
Mendes, 125 L-10
Menlo, 538 C-1
Meridian, 300 N-12
Merrillville, 175 P-5
Mershon, 90 N-9
Mesena, 30 G-8
Metter, 3707 K-10
Midville, 620 H-9
Midway, 863 M-11
Milan, 1056 L-7
Milford, 50 N-3
Milledgeville, 17727 H-7
Millen, 3808 J-10
Millhaven, 40 H-11
Millwood, 90 N-8
Milner, 321 H-4
Mineral Bluff, 153 B-4
Minter, 80 J-8
Mitchell, 181 G-8
Modoc, 30 J-9
Molena, 439 H-4
Moncrief Q-4
Moniac, 40 R-9
Monroe, 9759 F-6
Montezuma, 4506 K-5
Monticello, 2289 G-6
Montrose, 117 J-7
Moreland, 366 G-3
Morgan, 252 N-3
Morganton, 295 B-4
Morris, 30 M-2
Morrow, 5168 F-4
Morven, 536 P-6
Moultrie, 14865 P-5
Mt. Airy, 543 C-6
Mt. Berry, 225 D-2
Mt. Bethel *B-5
Mt. Vernon, 1914 L-8
Mt. Vernon B-2
Mt. Zion, 511 F-2
Mtn. City, 784 B-6
Mountville H-3
Munnerlyn H-10
Murphy, 70 P-5
Murrays Crossroads K-4
Murrayville D-5
Musella, 125 J-5
Nahunta, 1049 P-10
Naomi C-2
Nashville, 4782 P-7
Naylor, 111 Q-7
Needmore, 20 Q-8
Nelson, 486 D-4
New Branch, 50 L-9
New England B-1
New Georgia E-3
New Hope, 750 E-3
New Hope F-9
Newborn, 404 F-6
Newington, 319 J-11
Newnan, 12497 G-3
Newton, 703 N-4
Newtown *A-8
Nicholls, 1003 N-8
Nicholson, 535 E-6
Nicklesville, 20 J-7
Norcross, 5947 E-4
Norman Park, 711 N-6
Normantown, 225 K-9
Norristown, 100 J-9
N. Decatur, 13936 *F-7
N. Druid Hills, 14170 *E-7
N. High Shoals, 268 E-6
Norwood, 238 G-8
Nuberg D-8
Nunez, 135 J-9
Oak Park, 269 K-9
Oakdale *E-4
Oakfield, 125 M-5
Oakman, 30 C-3
Oakwood, 1464 D-5
Ochlocknee, 588 P-5
Ocilla, 3182 M-7
Oconee, 234 H-7
Odum, 388 M-10
Offerman, 300 N-10
Oglethorpe, 1302 K-5
Okefenokee P-9
Oliver, 242 J-11
Omaha, 116 L-2
Omega, 912 N-6
Orchard Hill, 239 G-4
Osierfield, 20 M-7
Oxford, 1945 F-5
Palmetto, 2612 F-3
Palmyra *L-1
Panthersville, 9874 *H-8
Parkers L-9
Parrott, 140 M-3
Patterson, 626 N-10
Pavo, 774 P-5
Peachtree City, 19027 G-3
Pearson, 1714 N-8
Pelham, 3869 P-4
Pembroke, 1503 L-11
Pendergrass, 298 D-6
Pennington F-6
Perkins, 80 H-10
Perry, 9452 K-6
Philomath, 50 F-7
Phinizy F-9
Piedmont, 30 H-4
Pine Gr. M-9
Pine Lake, 810 *F-9
Pine Log, 250 D-3
Pine Mtn., 875 H-3
Pine Mtn. Valley, 450 J-3
Pinehurst, 388 L-5
Pineview, 594 L-6
Pitts, 214 L-6
Plains, 716 L-4
Plainville, 231 D-2
Pleasant Hill *C-10
Pleasant Hill J-4
Pocataligo D-7
Pollards Corner F-9
Pooler, 4453 L-12
Port Wentworth, 4012 L-12
Portal, 522 J-10
Porterdale, 1278 F-5
Potterville, 175 J-5
Poulan, 962 N-5
Powder Sprs., 6893 E-3
Powelton, 20 G-8
Prattsburg J-4
Preston, 388 L-3
Pretoria, 30 N-4
Pridgen, 125 M-8
Primrose, 175 G-3
Pulaski, 264 K-10
Putnam K-4
Putney, 3108 N-5
Queensland, 200 M-7
Quitman, 5292 Q-6
Race Pond, 30 P-10
Radium Sprs. *N-3
Raines, 50 M-5
Raleigh, 125 H-3
Ramhurst, 400 C-3
Ranger, 153 C-3
Ray City, 603 P-7
Rayle, 107 F-8
Raymond, 300 G-3
Rebecca, 148 M-6
Red Oak *J-4
Redan, 24376 *G-10
Reed Cr., 1854 D-8
Register, 195 K-10
Rehoboth *E-8
Reidsville, 2469 L-10
Reno Q-4
Resaca, 410 C-3
Rest Haven, 176 D-5
Retreat M-11
Reynolds, 1166 K-5
Reynoldsville, 175 Q-3
Rhine, 466 L-7
Riceboro, 745 M-11
Richland, 1668 L-3
Richmond Hill, 2934 L-12
Rico F-3
Riddleville, 79 H-8
Ridgeville N-12
Rincon, 2697 K-12
Ringgold, 1675 B-2
Rising Fawn, 200 B-1
Riverdale, 9359 F-4
Roberta, 939 J-5
Robertstown C-5
Rochelle, 1510 L-6
Rock Spr., 550 B-2
Rockledge K-8
Rockmart, 3356 E-2
Rocky Ford, 197 J-10
Rocky Mt. G-3
Rome, 30326 D-2
Roopville, 218 G-2
Roscoe F-3
Rosier, 30 H-9
Rossville, 3601 B-2
Roswell, 47923 E-4
Round Oak, 30 G-6
Royston, 2758 D-7
Ruckersville E-8
Rupert, 20 K-4
Russell E-5
Rutledge, 659 F-6
Saffold Q-3
St. Clair, 20 G-9
St. George, 300 Q-10
St. Marks G-3
St. Marys, 8187 Q-11
St. Simons Island, 12026 P-12
Sale City, 324 N-5
Sand Hill F-3
Sandersville, 6290 H-8
Sandy Plains *A-4
Sandy Spr., 67842 *A-6
Sanford K-3
Santa Claus, 154 L-9
Sardis, 1116 H-11
Sargent, 700 G-3
Sasser, 335 M-4
Savannah, 137560 L-12
Scarboro, 50 J-10
Scotland, 244 L-8
Scott J-8
Scottdale, 8636 *F-8
Screven, 819 N-10
Sea Island, 80 P-12
Senoia, 956 G-3
Seville, 200 L-6
Shady Dale, 180 G-6
Shannon, 1703 D-2
Sharon, 94 F-8
Sharpsburg, 224 G-3
Shawnee, 150 J-11
Shell Bluff G-10
Shellman, 1162 M-3
Shellman Bluff, 150 M-12
Shiloh, 329 H-3
Shingler, 60 N-5
Sigsbee, 300 N-5
Silk Hope U-11
Siloam, 329 F-7
Silver City, 500 D-5
Six Mile, 175 D-2
Skidaway Island, 4495 L-12
Sky Valley, 187 B-7
Skyland *D-7
Smarr, 90 H-5
Smithville, 804 M-4
Smyrna, 32453 E-4
Snapfinger *H-9
Snellville, 12084 E-5
Snipesville, 70 M-8
Social Circle, 2755 F-6
Sonoraville D-3
Soperton, 2797 K-8
S. Newport, 20 M-12
Sparks, 1205 P-6
Sparta, 1710 G-7
Springfield, 1415 K-12
Springvale, 30 M-3
Stanleys Store L-9
Stapleton, 330 G-9
Starrs Mill, 300 G-4
Statenville, 50 Q-7
Statesboro, 20770 K-10
Statham, 1360 E-6
Stellaville G-9
Sterling, 550 N-11
Stevens Pottery, 350 H-7
Stewart, 300 G-5
Stilesboro E-3
Stillmore, 615 K-9
Stillwell, 80 K-12
Stilson, 80 K-11
Stockbridge, 3359 F-4
Stockton, 100 P-7
Stone Mtn., 6494 E-4
Suches, 50 C-5
Sugar Hill, 4557 E-5
Sugar Valley, 250 C-2
Summertown, 153 J-9
Summerville, 5025 C-2
Sumner, 209 N-5
Sumter, 60 L-4
Sunbury, 30 M-12
Sunnyside, 1506 G-4
Surrency, 253 M-9
Suttons Corner M-3
Suwanee, 2412 E-5
Swainsboro, 7361 J-9
Sycamore, 417 M-6
Sylvania, 2871 J-11
Sylvester, 5702 N-5
Talbotton, 1046 J-3
Talking Rock, 62 C-4
Tallapoosa, 2805 F-2
Tallulah Falls, 147 C-6
Talmo, 189 D-6
Talmo N-9
Tarboro, 125 P-11
Tarrytown, 130 K-9
Tarver, 450 Q-8
Tate, 500 D-4
Taylorsville, 269 E-2
Tazewell, 30 K-4
Temple, 1870 F-2
Tennga B-3
Tennille, 1552 H-8
Texas G-2
Thalmann, 125 N-11
The Rock, 88 H-4
Thomaston, 9127 H-4
Thomasville, 17457 Q-5
Thomson, 6862 G-9
Thunderbolt, 2786 L-13
Tifton, 14215 N-6
Tiger, 301 B-6
Tignall, 711 E-8
Tilton, 250 C-3
Toccoa, 8266 C-7
Toco Hills *E-7
Toomsboro, 617 J-7
Towns, 70 L-8
Townsend, 90 N-11
Trenton, 1994 B-1
Trion, 1661 C-2
Troutman J-4
Tucker, 25781 *D-9
Tunnel Hill, 970 B-3
Turman J-9
Turnerville, 150 C-6
Twin City, 1466 J-9
Twin Lakes, 750 Q-7
Ty Ty, 579 N-6
Tybee Island, 2842 L-13
Tyrone, 2724 F-3
Tyrus F-3
Unadilla, 1620 K-6
Union City, 9347 F-3
Union Pt., 1753 F-7
Uvalda, 561 K-9
Valdosta, 39806 Q-7
Van Wert E-2
Vanna D-7
Varnell, 358 B-2
Vesta, 30 E-8
Vidalia, 11078 K-9
Vidette, 90 H-9
Vienna, 2708 L-5
Villa Rica, 6542 F-2
Vinings, 7417 *D-4
Waco, 514 E-2
Wadley, 2473 H-9
Waleska, 700 D-4
Walnut Gr., 458 F-6
Walthourville, 2024 M-11
Wares Crossroads H-2
Waresboro, 125 P-9
Waresville K-?
Warm Sprs., 407 H-3
Warner Robins, 43726 J-6
Warrenton, 2056 G-8
Warthen H-8
Warwick, 501 M-5
Washington, 4279 F-8
Watkinsville, 1600 E-6
Waverly, 30 P-11
Waverly Hall, 769 J-3
Waycross, 16410 P-9
Waynesboro, 5701 H-10
Waynesville, 125 N-10
Wenona, 175 M-6
Weston, 42 L-3
Whigham, 605 Q-4
White, 542 D-3
White Oak, 125 P-11
White Plains, 286 F-7
Whitesburg, 643 F-3
Wildwood B-1
Willacoochee, 1205 N-7
Wiley, 20 B-6
Williamson, 295 G-4
Wilmington Island, 11230 L-13
Windsor, 7373 E-6
Winokur, 30 P-10
Winterville, 1102 E-7
Woodbine, 1212 P-11
Woodbury, 1429 H-3
Woodcliff J-11
Woodland, 552 J-3
Woodstock, 4361 E-4
Woodville, 415 F-7
Woolsey, 120 G-4
Wrens, 2414 G-9
Wrightsville, 2331 J-8
Yatesville, 409 H-4
Yorkville, 150 E-2
Young Harris, 604 B-5
Youth F-5
Zebulon, 1035 H-4

HAWAII
PG. 88

CAPITAL
Honolulu

NICKNAME
Aloha State

POPULATION
1,183,723, rank 41

AREA
6,471 sq mi, rank 47

Counties
Hawaii, 120317 C-9
Honolulu, 836231 A-8
Kalawao, 130 A-8
Kauai, 51177 A-7
Maui, 100374 B-9

Cities and Towns
Ahuimanu, 8387 G-5
Aiea, 8906 G-4
Anahola, 1181 B-4
Captain Cook, 2595 L-7
Eleele, 1489 C-2
Ewa, 3780 H-3
Ewa Beach, 14315 H-3
Foster Vil. G-4
Glenwood L-9
Haena A-2
Haena L-10
Haiku D-9
Hakalau K-9
Halaula, 496 J-7
Halawa C-7
Halawa Hts. G-4
Haleiwa, 2442 E-2
Haliimaile, 841 D-9
Hana, 683 E-10
Hanalei, 461 A-3
Hanamaulu, 3611 C-3
Hanapepe, 1395 C-2
Hauula, 3479 E-4
Hawi, 924 J-7
Heeia, 5010 G-5
Hilo, 37808 L-9
Holualoa, 3834 L-7
Honalo, 1926 L-7
Honaunau M-7
Honokaa, 2186 K-8
Honokahua D-7
Honokai Hale H-2
Honokohau D-7
Honokowai D-7
Honolulu, 365272 H-5
Honomu, 532 K-9
Honouliuli G-3
Honuapo N-8
Hookena M-7
Hoolehua C-5
Huehue L-7
Huelo D-9
Kaaawa, 1138 F-5
Kaanapali, 579 D-7
Kahakuloa D-8
Kahaluu, 3068 F-5
Kahana D-7
Kahana F-4
Kahua J-7
Kahuku, 2063 D-4
Kahului, 16672 D-8
Kailua, 36818 G-5
Kailua-Kona, 9126 L-7
Kaimu M-10
Kalaheo, 3592 C-2
Kalaoa, 4490 L-7
Kalaupapa C-6
Kalihiwai, 435 A-3
Kamalo D-6
Kamaole E-8
Kamooloa E-2
Kaneohe, 35448 G-5
Kapaa, 8149 B-4
Kapoho L-10
Kaumakani, 803 C-2
Kaumalapau E-6
Kaunakakai, 2658 C-6
Kaupo E-10
Kawaihae K-7
Kawailoa E-3
Kawailoa Beach E-3
Kawela, 366 D-3
Keaau, 1584 L-9
Kealakekua, 1453 L-7
Kealia B-4
Keanae D-9
Keauhou L-7
Kekaha, 3506 C-1
Keokea E-9
Keokea M-7
Kihei, 11107 E-8
Kilauea, 1685 A-3
Kipahulu E-10
Koloa, 1791 C-3
Kualapuu, 1661 C-6
Kukuihaele, 316 J-8
Kukuiula C-3
Kula E-9
Kunia G-3
Lahaina, 9073 D-7
Laie, 5577 E-4
Lanai City, 2400 E-6
Laupahoehoe, 508 K-9
Lawai, 1787 C-3
Lihue, 5536 B-4
Maalaea, 443 E-8
Maili, 6059 G-2
Makaha, 7990 F-2
Makakilo City, 9828 H-3
Makapala J-7
Makawao, 5405 E-9
Makena E-8
Mana B-1
Maunaloa, 405 C-5
Maunawili, 4847 G-5
Mililani Town, 29359 F-3
Mokuleia, 1776 E-2
Mtn. View, 3075 L-9
Muolea E-10
Naalehu, 1027 N-8
Nanakuli, 9575 G-2
Ninole K-9
Olowalu E-7
Omao, 1142 C-3
Ookala J-9
Opihikao M-10
Paauilo, 620 K-8
Pacific Palisades G-4
Pahala, 1520 M-8
Pahoa, 1027 L-10
Paia, 2091 D-9
Pakala Vil., 565 C-2
Papa M-7
Papaikou, 1634 L-9
Pauwela D-9
Pearl City, 30993 G-4
Pepeekeo, 1813 K-9
Poamoho F-3
Pohakupo G-6
Pohoiki M-10
Poipu, 975 C-3
Princeville, 1244 A-3
Puako, 397 K-7
Puhi, 1210 C-3
Pukalani, 5879 E-9
Pukoo C-7
Pulehu E-9
Punaluu, 672 N-8
Punaluu E-4
Pupukea, 4111 E-3
Puu Waawaa L-7
Puuanahulu K-7
Puuiki E-10
Sunset Beach D-3
Ualapue D-7
Ulupalakua E-8
Volcano, 1516 M-9
Wahiawa, 17386 F-3
Waiahole F-5
Waialee D-3
Waialua, 3943 E-2
Waialua C-7
Waianae, 8758 G-2
Waiehue D-8
Waihee D-8
Waikane, 717 F-5
Waikapu, 729 E-8
Waikoloa Vil., 2248 K-7
Wailua, 2018 B-4
Wailua E-9
Wailuku, 10688 D-8
Waimalu, 29967 G-4
Waimanalo, 3508 G-6
Waimanalo Beach, 4185 H-6
Waimea, 1840 E-3
Waimea C-2
Waimea (Kamuela), 5972 K-7
Waiohinu N-8
Waipahu, 31435 G-3
Waipio, 11812 K-8
Waipio Acres, 5304 F-3
Whitmore Vil., 3373 F-3
Wood Valley M-8

IDAHO
PG. 89

CAPITAL
Boise

NICKNAME
Gem State

POPULATION
1,189,251, rank 40

AREA
83,564 sq mi, rank 13

Counties
Ada, 205775 L-2
Adams, 3254 H-2
Bannock, 66026 M-7
Bear Lake, 6084 M-8
Benewah, 7937 D-2
Bingham, 37583 L-7
Blaine, 13552 L-5
Boise, 3509 J-3
Bonner, 26622 B-2
Bonneville, 72207 L-8
Boundary, 8332 A-2
Butte, 2918 K-6
Camas, 727 K-4
Canyon, 90076 K-2
Caribou, 6963 M-8
Cassia, 19532 M-5
Clark, 762 J-7
Clearwater, 8505 E-3

Custer, 4133 J-5
Elmore, 21205 L-3
Franklin, 9232 N-8
Fremont, 10937 J-8
Gem, 11844 J-2
Gooding, 11633 L-4
Idaho, 13783 F-3
Jefferson, 16543 K-7
Jerome, 15138 M-5
Kootenai, 69795 C-2
Latah, 30617 E-2
Lemhi, 6899 H-5
Lewis, 3516 E-2
Lincoln, 3308 L-5
Madison, 23674 K-8
Minidoka, 19361 M-5
Nez Perce, 33754 F-2
Oneida, 3492 M-7
Owyhee, 8392 M-2
Payette, 16434 J-2
Power, 7086 M-7
Shoshone, 13931 D-3
Teton, 3439 K-8
Twin Falls, 53580 M-4
Valley, 6109 H-3
Washington, 8550 J-1

Cities and Towns

Aberdeen, 1406 L-6
Acequia, 106 M-6
Ahsahka, 600 E-2
Albion, 305 M-6
Almo, 40 N-5
American Falls, 3757 M-6
Ammon, 5002 K-8
Arbon, 10 M-7
Arco, 1016 K-6
Arimo, 311 M-7
Ashton, 1114 J-8
Athol, 346 C-2
Atlanta, 20 K-4
Atomic City, 25 K-6
Avery, 10 D-3
Bancroft, 393 M-8
Banida, 100 N-8
Banks, 40 J-2
Basalt, 407 L-7
Bayview, 350 C-2
Bellevue, 1275 K-5
Bennington, 200 M-8
Big Cr. H-3
Blackfoot, 9646 L-7
Blanchard, 90 B-1
Bliss, 185 L-4
Bloomington, 197 N-8
Boise, 126685 K-2
Bone, 10 L-8
Bonners Ferry, 2193 A-2
Border N-9
Bovill, 256 D-2
Bowmont, 125 K-2
Bridge, 10 N-6
Bruneau, 10 L-3
Buhl, 3516 M-4
Burgdorf G-3
Burke, 90 C-3
Burley, 8702 M-5
Butte City, 59 K-6
Calder, 10 C-2
Caldwell, 18400 K-2
Camas, 80 J-7
Cambridge, 374 H-2
Carey, 427 L-5
Careywood, 10 B-2
Carmen, 40 G-5
Cascade, 877 J-3
Castleford, 179 M-4
Cataldo, 80 C-2
Centerville K-3
Challis, 1073 J-5
Chatcolet, 72 D-2
Chester, 175 J-8
Chesterfield, 40 L-8
Chilly, 20 J-5
Chubbuck, 7791 L-7
Clark Fork, 448 B-2
Clarkia, 20 D-2
Clayton, 26 J-4
Clifton, 228 N-8
Cobalt H-5
Cocolalla, 90 B-2
Coeur d'Alene, 24563 C-2
Colburn, 175 B-2
Conda, 20 M-8
Coolin, 100 B-2
Corral, 10 L-4
Cottonwood, 822 F-2
Council, 831 H-2
Craigmont, 542 F-2

MOUNT DALY, SNOWMASS VILLAGE, CO

ILLINOIS
PG. 90–93

ABC1234

CAPITAL
Springfield

NICKNAME
Land of Lincoln

POPULATION
11,846,544, rank 6

AREA
56,345 sq mi, rank 24

Counties

INDIANA
PG. 93–95

12 A1234

CAPITAL
Indianapolis

NICKNAME
Hoosier State

POPULATION
5,840,528, rank 14

AREA
36,185 sq mi, rank 38

Counties

CONNECTICUT RIVER, EAST HADDAM, CT

Monrovia, 673 L-7
Monterey, 230 D-7
Montezuma, 1134 K-4
Montgomery, 351 O-5
Monticello, 5237 F-6
Montmorenci G-5
Montpelier, 1880 G-11
Moorefield, 125 O-12
Mooreland, 465 I-11
Moores Hill, 649 N-12
Mooresville, 5541 K-8
Morgantown, 978 M-8
Morocco, 1044 E-4
Morris N-12
Morristown, 980 L-10
Morton K-6
Moscow M-10
Mt. Auburn, 125 M-9
Mt. Ayr, 151 E-4
Mt. Carmel, 108 M-13
Mt. Comfort K-9
Mt. Etna, 111 F-10
Mt. Pleasant I-7
Mt. Sterling O-12
Mt. Summit, 238 I-11
Mt. Vernon, 7217 S-1
Mt. Zion F-11
Mulberry, 1262 H-6
Muncie, 71035 H-11
Munster, 19949 B-4
Nabb, 200 P-10
Napoleon, 238 N-11
Nappanee, 5510 C-9
Nashville, 873 N-8
Nead F-8
Nebraska P-11
Needham M-9
Needmore N-8
New Albany, 36322 S-9
New Alsace N-12
New Amsterdam, 30 T-8
New Bellsville N-8
New Boston T-9
New Boston T-6
New Carlisle, 1446 A-7
New Castle, 17753 J-11
New Chicago, 2066 *M-12
New Corydon F-13
New Goshen K-4
New Harmony, 846 T-2
New Haven, 10659 D-12
New Lebanon P-4
New Lisbon, 355 K-11
New London G-8
New Market, 614 J-6
New Maysville K-6
New Middletown, 82 T-9
New Mt. Pleasant G-12
New Paris, 1007 B-9
New Pekin, 1095 R-9
New Philadelphia R-9
New Point, 296 N-11
New Providence, 270 R-9
New Richmond, 312 H-5
New Ross, 331 K-6
New Salem, 200 L-11
New Unionville, 500 N-7
New Washington R-10
New Waverly F-8
New Whiteland, 4097 L-8
New Winchester K-7
Newark N-6
Newbern N-10
Newberry, 207 P-5
Newburgh, 2880 U-4
Newport, 627 K-4
Newtonville U-5
Newtown, 243 I-5
Newville, 200 C-13
Nine Mile E-11
Nineveh M-8
Noblesville, 17655 J-9
Norman P-8
N. Grove F-9
N. Hayden C-4
N. Judson, 1582 D-6
N. Liberty, 1366 A-8
N. Manchester, 6383 E-10
N. Salem, 499 K-7
N. Terre Haute, 4331 M-4
N. Vernon, 5311 P-10
N. Webster, 881 C-10
Norway F-7
Nulltown L-12
Oak Forest M-12
Oakford G-8
Oakland City, 2810 S-4
Oaktown, 655 O-4
Oakville I-11
Ober C-7
Ockley G-7
Odell, 80 H-5
Odon, 1475 O-5
Ogden Dunes, 1499 B-5
Ogilville N-8
Oldenburg, 715 M-11
Omega H-9
Ontario A-11
Onward, 63 E-8
Oolitic, 1424 P-7
Orange L-11
Orestes, 458 H-10
Oriole T-7
Orland, 361 A-12
Orleans, 2083 Q-7
Osceola, 2099 B-8
Osgood, 1688 N-11
Ossian, 2428 E-12
Oswego C-10
Otisco, 350 R-10
Otterbein, 1291 G-5
Otwell S-4
Owasco G-7
Owensburg, 225 P-6
Owensville, 1053 S-3
Oxford, 1273 G-4
Packerton D-10
Palestine D-9
Palmer C-5
Palmyra, 621 S-8
Paoli, 3542 R-7
Paragon, 515 M-7
Paris Crossing, 200 O-10
Parker City, 1323 H-11
Parr, 150 D-5
Patoka, 704 S-3
Patricksburg, 250 M-5
Patriot, 190 Q-13
Patronville U-5
Paxton P-4
Peabody D-10
Pelzer U-4
Pence G-4
Pendleton, 2309 J-10
Pennville, 637 G-12
Peoria F-9
Perkinsville I-9
Perrysburg F-8
Perrysville, 443 I-4
Perth L-5
Peru, 12843 F-8
Petersburg, 2449 R-4
Philomath L-11
Pickard H-8
Pierceton, 1030 D-10
Pike, 150 J-7
Pimento, 300 N-4
Pine Vil., 134 K-5
Pittsboro, 815 K-7
Pittsburg F-7
Plainfield, 14953 L-7
Plainville, 444 O-5
Plato B-11
Pleasant D-12
Pleasant Lake, 750 B-12
Pleasant Mills, 175 F-13
Pleasant View, 850 L-9
Pleasantville N-5
Plum Tree F-11
Plymouth, 8303 C-8
Poe D-12
Pt. Isabel, 125 G-8
Poland M-5
Poneto, 236 F-11
Portage, 29060 B-5
Porter, 3118 B-5
Portersville R-5
Portland, 6483 G-12
Poseyville, 1089 T-2
Prairie Cr. N-4
Preble E-12
Prince's Lakes, 1055 M-8
Princeton, 8127 S-3
Pulaski, 175 E-6
Quercus Gr. O-13
Quincy, 250 M-6
Raccoon K-6
Radnor F-7
Raglesville O-5
Ragsdale O-4
Raleigh K-11
Raub F-4
Raymond, 50 N-13
Rays Crossing L-10
Redkey, 1383 G-12
Reiffsburg F-12
Remington, 1247 F-5
Rensselaer, 5045 E-5
Rexville, 175 P-11
Reynolds, 528 F-6
Richland City U-5
Richmond, 38705 K-13
Richvalley F-9
Ridgeport P-6
Ridgeville, 808 H-12
Rigdon H-10
Riley, 232 M-4
Rising Sun, 2311 P-13
Rivare E-13
Riverside H-5
Riverview N-3
Roachdale, 902 K-6
Roann, 447 E-9
Roanoke, 1018 E-11
Rob Roy H-4
Robinwood M-2
Rochester, 5969 D-8
Rockfield, 225 F-7
Rockford F-11
Rocklane L-8
Rockport, 2315 U-5
Rockville, 2706 K-5
Rocky Ripple, 751 *J-17
Roland R-6
Roll, 225 G-11
Rolling Prairie, 800 B-7
Rome U-7
Rome City, 1138 B-11
Romney H-6
Rosedale, 783 L-4
Roseland, 706 *B-19
Roselawn D-4
Ross *M-11
Rosston J-8
Rossville, 1175 G-7
Royal Ctr., 859 E-7
Royalton *H-15
Rugby N-10
Rushville, 5533 L-11
Russellville, 336 K-5
Russiaville, 988 G-8
St. Anthony S-6
St. Bernice L-4
St. Croix T-7
St. Henry S-6
St. Joe, 452 C-12
St. John, 4921 C-4
St. Joseph, 400 S-9
St. Leon, 493 N-12
St. Louis Crossing N-9
St. Meinrad, 700 T-6
St. Paul, 1032 M-10
St. Peter, 175 M-12
St. Wendel T-3
Salamonia, 138 G-13
Salem, 5619 R-8
Salem F-13
Saltillo, 117 R-8
Saluda R-11
San Jacinto P-11
San Pierre, 550 D-6
Sandborn, 455 P-5
Sandusky M-11
Santa Claus, 927 T-6
Santa Fe F-8
Saratoga, 266 H-12
Sardinia, 150 N-10
Schererville, 19926 B-4
Schneider, 310 D-4
Schnellville S-6
Scipio, 225 P-10
Scott City S-4
Scottsburg, 5334 Q-10
Sedalia, 175 G-7
Seelyville, 1090 M-4
Sellersburg, 5745 S-10
Selma, 800 H-11
Selvin, 200 S-5
Servia, 225 E-10
Sevastopol D-9
Sexton L-11
Seymour, 15605 P-9
Shadeland, 1674 G-6
Shamrock Lakes, 207 G-11
Shannondale I-6
Sharpsville, 769 G-8
Shelburn, 1147 N-4
Shelby, 450 D-4
Shelbyville, 15336 M-10
Sheridan, 2046 I-8
Shipshewana, 524 B-10
Shirley, 817 K-10
Shoals, 853 R-6
Silver Lake, 528 D-9
Silverville Q-6
Sitka F-6
Smithfield H-11
Smithville, 750 P-7
Solitude, 125 T-2
Solsberry P-6
Somerset F-9
Somerville, 223 S-4
S. Bend, 105511 B-8
S. Boston R-9
S. Ctr. B-7
S. Milford B-11
S. Whitley, 1482 D-10
Southport, 1969 L-8
Southwest B-9
Southwood N-1
Sparksville, 100 Q-8
Sparta N-12
Spartanburg I-13
Spearsville N-8
Speedway, 13092 K-8
Spelterville L-1
Thorntown, 1506 J-7
Tippecanoe D-8
Tipton, 4751 H-9
Tobinsport U-7
Tocsin, 300 E-12
Topeka, 912 B-10
Toto C-6
Town of Pines, 789 B-6
Trafalgar, 531 M-8
Trail Cr., 2463 A-6
Treaty F-9
Trevlac, 350 N-8
Tri-Lakes, 3299 C-11
Trinity Sprs. Q-6
Troy, 465 U-6
Tunker D-10
Tunnelton Q-8
Twelve Mile E-8
Twin Lakes C-8
Tyner, 300 C-7
Ulen, 50 J-7
Underwood, 450 R-10
Union R-4
Union City, 3612 I-13
Union Mills B-6
Uniondale, 289 E-11
Unionport J-12
Uniontown P-9
Universal, 392 L-4
Upland, 3295 G-10
Urbana, 300 E-10
Utica, 411 S-10
Valeene, 200 S-7
Valentine B-11
Valley City T-8
Vallonia O-8
Valparaiso, 24414 B-5
Van Buren, 934 F-10
Vandalia N-6
Veedersburg, 2192 J-4
Velpen S-5
Vera Cruz, 83 F-12
Vernon, 370 P-10
Versailles, 1791 P-11
Vevay, 1393 Q-12
Vicksburg P-5
Vienna R-10
Vigo N-3
Vincennes, 19859 Q-3
Wabash, 12127 E-9
Wadena F-4
Wadesville, 500 T-3
Wakarusa, 1667 B-9
Waldron, 1100 M-10
Walkerton, 2061 C-7
Wallace, 89 J-5
Wallen D-12
Walton, 1053 F-8
Wanatah, 852 C-6
Warren, 185 F-11
Warren Park, 1763 K-9
Warsaw, 10968 C-9
Washington, 10838 P-5
Waterford, 2200 B-6
Waterloo, 2040 C-12
Waveland, 474 K-5
Waverly L-8
Wawpecong G-9
Waymansville P-9
Waynesburg N-10
Waynetown, 911 J-5
Webster, 550 J-12
W. Baden Sprs., 675 R-7
W. College Corner, 686 L-13
W. Franklin U-3
W. Harrison, 318 N-13
W. Lafayette, 25907 G-6
W. Lebanon, 760 H-4
W. Terre Haute, 2330 M-4
Westfield, 3304 J-8
Westphalia Q-4
Westpoint, 450 H-6
Westport, 1478 N-10
Westville, 5255 B-6
Wheatfield, 821 D-5
Wheatland, 439 R-4
Wheeler *N-13
Wheeling G-11
Whiteland, 2446 L-8
Whitestown, 476 J-8
Whitesville J-6
Whitewater, 111 J-13
Whiting, 5155 B-4
Wilders C-6
Wilkinson, 446 K-10
Williams, 300 Q-6
Williams Cr., 425 *H-18
Williamsport, 1798 H-4
Willow Branch K-10
Wilmot C-10
Wilson M-10
Winamac, 2262 D-7
Winchester, 5095 H-12
Windfall, 779 H-9
Windsor H-11
Winfield, 645 C-5
Wingate, 263 I-5
Winona Lake, 4053 D-9
Winslow, 875 S-4

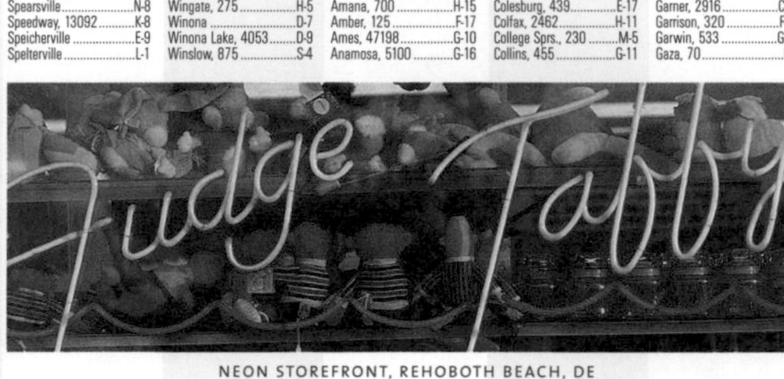

NEON STOREFRONT, REHOBOTH BEACH, DE

Spencer, 2609 N-6
Spencerville, 350 C-12
Spiceland, 757 K-11
Spraytown P-9
Sprs. Hills, 112 *K-17
Spr. Lake, 216 K-9
Springport, 194 J-11
Springville P-6
Spurgeon, 149 S-4
Stacer T-3
Stanford P-6
Star City, 450 E-7
State Line City, 182 H-4
Staunton, 592 M-5
Steam Corner J-5
Stendal S-5
Stevenson T-4
Stewartsville T-2
Stilesville, 298 L-7
Stillwell, 250 B-6
Stinesville, 204 N-7
Stockdale E-9
Stockwell, 400 H-6
Stone Bluff H-4
Stone Head N-8
Story P-8
Straughn, 318 K-11
Stroh, 700 B-11
Sullivan, 4663 P-4
Sulphur R-6
Sulphur Sprs., 257 J-11
Sumava Resorts D-4
Summitville, 1010 H-10
Sunman, 623 N-12
Swanington F-4
Swayzee, 1059 G-9
Sweetser, 924 F-9
Switz City, 293 O-5
Sycamore G-9
Sydney D-10
Sylvania J-4
Syracuse, 2729 C-10
Tab G-4
Talbot G-4
Talma D-8
Tampico Q-8
Tangier J-4
Taswell S-7
Taylorsville, 1044 N-9
Teegarden C-8
Tefft D-5
Tell City, 8088 U-6
Templeton G-5
Tennyson, 267 T-5
Terhune H-8
Terre Haute, 57475 M-4
Thomaston C-6
Thornhope E-7
Wirt O-11
Wolcott, 886 F-5
Wolcottville, 879 B-11
Wolflake, 350 C-10
Woodburn, 1445 D-13
Woodland B-8
Woodland Park S-13
Woodruff B-11
Worthington, 1473 N-5
Wyatt, 225 B-8
Wynnedale, 269 *K-17
Yankeetown, 400 U-4
Yeddo, 200 J-4
Yeoman, 131 F-8
Yorktown, 4106 H-10
Young America, 300 G-8
Youngstown M-4
Yountsville J-5
Zanesville, 673 E-11
Zenas N-10
Zionsville, 5385 J-8
Zulu D-12

IOWA
PG. 96–97

IOWA LBC 123 DUBUQUE

CAPITAL
Des Moines

NICKNAME
Hawkeye State

POPULATION
2,851,792, rank 30

AREA
56,275 sq mi, rank 25

Counties
Adair, 8409 K-7
Adams, 4866 L-6
Allamakee, 13855 B-16
Appanoose, 13743 M-12
Audubon, 6830 I-6
Benton, 22429 G-14
Black Hawk, 123798 E-14
Boone, 25186 G-8
Bremer, 22813 D-14
Buchanan, 20844 E-15
Buena Vista, 19965 D-5
Butler, 15731 D-12
Calhoun, 11508 E-7
Carroll, 21423 G-6
Cass, 15128 K-6
Cedar, 17381 H-17
Cerro Gordo, 46733 C-11
Cherokee, 14098 D-4
Chickasaw, 13295 C-13
Clarke, 8287 L-9
Clay, 17585 C-5
Clayton, 19054 D-16
Clinton, 51040 G-19
Crawford, 16775 G-5
Dallas, 29755 H-8
Davis, 8312 M-13
Decatur, 8338 M-9
Delaware, 18035 E-16
Des Moines, 42614 L-17
Dickinson, 14909 B-5
Dubuque, 86403 F-17
Emmet, 11569 B-6
Fayette, 21843 C-14
Floyd, 17058 C-12
Franklin, 11364 D-11
Fremont, 8226 L-4
Greene, 10045 G-7
Grundy, 12029 E-12
Guthrie, 10935 J-7
Hamilton, 16071 F-9
Hancock, 12638 C-9
Hardin, 19094 E-11
Harrison, 14730 H-3
Henry, 19226 L-16
Howard, 9809 B-14
Humboldt, 10756 D-8
Ida, 8365 F-4
Iowa, 14630 H-14
Jackson, 19950 F-18
Jasper, 34795 H-11
Jefferson, 16310 L-14
Johnson, 96119 H-15
Jones, 19444 F-17
Keokuk, 11624 J-13
Kossuth, 18591 C-8
Lee, 38687 N-16
Linn, 168767 F-15
Louisa, 11592 K-16
Lucas, 9070 L-10
Lyon, 11952 B-2
Madison, 12483 K-8
Mahaska, 21522 J-13
Marion, 30001 J-11
Marshall, 38276 G-11
Mills, 13202 L-4
Mitchell, 10928 B-12
Monona, 10034 F-2
Monroe, 8114 L-12
Montgomery, 12076 L-5
Muscatine, 39907 J-17
O'Brien, 15444 C-4
Osceola, 7267 B-4
Page, 16870 M-5
Palo Alto, 10669 C-7
Plymouth, 23388 D-2
Pocahontas, 9525 E-6
Polk, 327140 H-10
Pottawattamie, 82628 J-4
Poweshiek, 19033 H-13
Ringgold, 5420 M-8
Sac, 12324 E-5
Scott, 150979 H-19
Shelby, 13230 H-4
Sioux, 29903 C-3
Story, 74252 G-10
Tama, 17419 G-13
Taylor, 7114 M-6
Union, 12750 L-8
Van Buren, 7676 M-14
Wapello, 35687 L-13
Warren, 36033 J-10
Washington, 19612 J-15
Wayne, 7067 M-10
Webster, 40342 E-8
Winnebago, 12122 B-9
Winneshiek, 20847 B-15
Woodbury, 98276 E-3
Worth, 7991 B-11
Wright, 14269 D-9

Cities and Towns
Abingdon, 50 K-14
Ackley, 1696 E-11
Ackworth, 100 J-10
Adair, 894 J-7
Adel, 3304 H-8
Afton, 953 L-8
Agency, 616 L-13
Ainsworth, 506 K-16
Akron, 1450 D-1
Albert City, 779 E-6
Albia, 3727 L-12
Albion, 585 G-12
Alburnett, 456 F-15
Alden, 855 E-10
Alexander, 170 D-10
Algona, 6015 C-8
Alleman, 340 H-9
Allerton, 599 M-10
Allison, 1000 D-12
Alpha C-14
Alta, 1840 E-5
Alta Vista, 246 B-13
Alton, 1063 C-3
Altoona, 7191 H-10
Alvord, 200 B-2
Amana, 700 H-15
Amber, 125 F-17
Ames, 47198 G-10
Anamosa, 5100 G-16
Anderson, 80 M-4
Andover, 60 H-19
Andrew, 319 F-18
Angus, 50 H-8
Ankeny, 18482 H-10
Anthon, 638 F-3
Aplington, 1034 E-12
Arbor Hill, 10 J-6
Arcadia, 485 G-5
Archer, 131 C-4
Aredale, 88 D-12
Argyle, 200 M-16
Arion, 148 G-4
Arispe, 92 L-8
Arlington, 465 D-15
Armstrong, 955 B-7
Arnolds Park, 953 B-5
Arthur, 272 F-5
Asbury, 2013 F-18
Ashton, 482 B-4
Aspinwall, 52 G-5
Atalissa, 357 I-17
Athelstan, 31 M-7
Atkins, 637 G-15
Atlantic, 7432 J-6
Attica, 125 K-12
Auburn, 283 F-7
Audubon, 2524 H-6
Aurelia, 1034 D-5
Aurora, 196 E-15
Austinville E-11
Avery, 125 L-12
Avoca, 1497 J-4
Ayrshire, 195 C-6
Badger, 569 E-8
Bagley, 303 H-7
Baldwin, 137 G-18
Balltown, 64 E-17
Bancroft, 857 B-8
Bankston, 35 E-17
Barnes City, 221 J-13
Barnum, 174 E-7
Bartlett, 20 L-3
Bassett, 74 C-13
Batavia, 520 L-14
Battle Cr., 818 F-4
Baxter, 1052 H-11
Bayard, 511 H-7
Beacon, 509 J-12
Beaconsfield, 27 M-8
Beaman, 183 F-12
Beaver, 60 G-8
Bedford, 1528 M-6
Beebeetown J-4
Belknap, 70 M-13
Belle Plaine, 2834 G-14
Bellevue, 2239 F-19
Belmond, 2500 D-10
Beloit B-1
Bennett, 395 H-17
Benton, 39 M-7
Bentonsport, 30 M-15
Berkley, 39 G-8
Bernard, 123 F-18
Bertram, 201 G-16
Bettendorf, 28132 J-19
Bevington, 67 K-9
Big Rock H-18
Bingham, 60 M-5
Birmingham, 386 L-15
Blairsburg, 269 E-9
Blairstown, 672 G-14
Blakesburg, 333 L-13
Blanchard, 67 M-5
Blencoe, 250 G-3
Blockton, 213 M-7
Bloomfield, 2580 M-13
Blue Grass, 1214 J-18
Bluffton, 80 B-15
Bode, 335 G-8
Bonaparte, 465 M-15
Bondurant, 1584 H-10
Boone, 12392 G-9
Bouton, 149 H-8
Boxholm, 214 F-8
Boyden, 651 B-3
Boyer, 30 F-5
Braddyville, 219 M-5
Bradford, 150 E-11
Bradgate, 124 D-7
Brandon, 320 F-14
Brayton, 148 J-6
Breda, 467 F-6
Bremer, 90 D-13
Bridgewater, 209 K-7
Brighton, 684 K-15
Bristow, 197 D-12
Britt, 2133 C-9
Bronson, 209 E-2
Brooklyn, 1439 H-13
Brooks, 100 L-6
Brunsville, 137 D-2
Bryant F-1
Buck Gr., 20 G-5
Buckeye, 105 E-10
Buckingham, 70 F-13
Buffalo, 1260 J-18
Buffalo Ctr., 1081 B-9
Burchinal, 90 C-11
Burlington, 27208 M-17
Burr Oak, 175 A-15
Burt, 575 B-8
Bussey, 494 K-12
Calamus, 379 H-18
Callender, 384 F-8
Calmar, 1026 C-15
Calumet, 160 D-4
Cambria L-9
Cambridge, 714 G-10
Canton, 30 F-17
Cantril, 222 M-14
Carbon, 60 L-6
Carl, 30 K-7
Carlisle, 3241 J-10
Carpenter, 102 B-11
Carroll, 9579 G-6
Carson, 705 K-4
Carter Lake, 3200 K-3
Cascade, 1812 F-17
Casey, 441 J-7
Castalia, 177 C-15
Castana, 159 G-3
Cedar Falls, 34298 E-13
Cedar Rapids, 108751 G-15
Center Jct., 166 F-17
Center Pt., 1693 F-15
Centerville, 5936 M-12
Central City, 1063 F-16
Chapin, 175 D-11
Chariton, 4616 L-11
Charles City, 7878 C-12
Charleston, 50 M-16
Charlotte, 359 G-19
Charter Oak, 497 G-4
Chatsworth, 103 C-2
Chelsea, 336 G-13
Cherokee, 6026 D-4
Chester, 158 A-13
Chillicothe, 119 L-13
Churchtown B-16
Churdan, 423 F-7
Cincinnati, 363 M-12
Clare, 161 E-8
Clarence, 936 G-17
Clarinda, 5104 M-5
Clarion, 2703 D-9
Clarksville, 1382 D-12
Clayton, 41 D-17
Clear Lake, 8183 C-10
Clearfield, 417 M-7
Cleghorn, 275 D-4
Clermont, 523 C-15
Cleves, 50 E-11
Climbing Hill, 100 E-3
Clinton, 29201 G-19
Clio, 103 M-10
Clive, 7446 H-9
Clutier, 219 G-13
Coburg, 58 L-5
Coggon, 645 F-16
Coin, 278 M-5
Colesburg, 439 E-17
Colfax, 2462 H-11
College Sprs., 230 M-5
Collins, 455 G-11
Colo, 771 G-11
Columbia, 125 K-11
Columbus City, 328 K-16
Columbus Jct., 1616 K-16
Colwell, 94 C-13
Conesville, 334 J-16
Conrad, 964 F-12
Conroy, 175 H-14
Conway, 57 M-7
Coon Rapids, 1283 H-7
Cooper, 50 G-8
Coppock, 36 K-15
Coralville, 10347 H-16
Corley J-5
Cornelia, 150 D-9
Corning, 1806 L-6
Correctionville, 897 E-4
Corwith, 354 C-9
Corydon, 1675 M-10
Cotter, 50 J-16
Coulter, 252 D-10
Council Bluffs, 54315 K-3
Craig, 116 D-2
Crawfordsville, 265 K-16
Crescent, 513 J-3
Cresco, 3669 B-14
Creston, 7911 L-7
Cromwell, 120 L-7
Crystal Lake, 266 B-9
Cumberland, 295 K-6
Cumming, 132 J-9
Cushing, 220 E-4
Cylinder, 112 C-8
Dakota City, 1024 D-8
Dallas Ctr., 1454 H-8
Dana, 71 G-8
Danbury, 430 F-4
Danville, 926 L-16
Davenport, 95333 J-18
Davis City, 257 M-9
Dawson, 174 H-8
Dayton, 818 F-8
De Soto, 1033 J-8
De Witt, 4514 H-19
Decatur City, 177 M-9
Decorah, 8063 B-15
Dedham, 264 G-6
Deep River, 345 J-13
Defiance, 312 H-5
Delaware, 176 E-16
Delhi, 485 E-16
Delmar, 517 G-18
Deloit, 295 G-5
Delta, 409 K-13
Denison, 6604 G-5
Denmark, 400 M-16
Denver, 1600 D-13
Derby, 135 L-10
Des Moines, 193187 J-10
Dexter, 628 J-8
Diagonal, 298 M-8
Dickens, 214 C-6
Dike, 875 E-13
Dinsdale F-13
Dixon, 202 H-18
Dolliver, 103 A-7
Donahue, 316 H-18
Donnan, 7 D-15
Donnellson, 940 M-16
Doon, 476 B-2
Dorchester, 80 A-16
Douds, 250 L-14
Dougherty, 107 D-11
Dow City, 439 G-4
Downey, 125 H-16
Dows, 660 E-10
Drakesville, 172 M-13
Dubuque, 57546 E-18
Dumont, 705 D-12
Dunbar, 100 G-12
Duncan C-9
Duncombe, 488 F-9
Dundee, 174 E-16
Dunkerton, 746 E-14
Dunlap, 1251 H-4
Durango, 34 E-18
Durant, 1549 H-17
Dyersville, 3703 F-17
Dysart, 1230 G-13
Eagle Gr., 3671 D-9
Earlham, 1157 J-8
Earling, 466 H-5
Earlville, 822 E-16
Early, 649 F-5
E. Amana, 90 H-15
E. Peru, 132 K-9
Eddyville, 1010 K-13
Edgewood, 776 E-16
Edna, 30 B-3
Elberon, 203 G-13
Eldon, 1070 L-14
Eldora, 3038 F-11
Eldridge, 3378 H-18
Elgin, 637 C-15
Elk Horn, 672 J-5
Elk Run Hts., 1088 E-14
Elkader, 1510 D-16
Elkhart, 388 H-10
Elliott, 398 K-5
Ellston, 44 L-8
Ellsworth, 451 F-10
Elma, 653 B-13
Elvira G-19
Elwood G-18
Ely, 517 G-15
Emerson, 476 L-4
Emmetsburg, 3940 C-7
Epworth, 1297 E-17
Essex, 916 L-5
Estherville, 6720 B-6
Evansdale, 4638 E-14
Everly, 706 C-5
Exira, 955 J-6
Exline, 187 M-12
Fairbank, 1018 E-14
Fairfax, 780 G-15
Fairfield, 9955 L-15
Fairport, 175 J-17
Farley, 1354 F-17
Farmersburg, 291 C-16
Farmington, 655 M-15
Farnhamville, 414 F-7
Farragut, 498 M-4
Faulkner, 60 E-11
Fayette, 1317 D-15
Fenton, 346 C-8
Ferguson, 166 G-12
Fernald, 125 G-10
Fertile, 382 B-10
Festina C-15
Finchford, 125 E-13
Floris, 172 L-13
Floyd, 359 B-12
Fonda, 731 E-6
Fontanelle, 712 K-7
Forest City, 4430 B-10
Ft. Atkinson, 367 C-15
Ft. Dodge, 26057 E-8
Ft. Madison, 11618 M-16
Fostoria, 209 C-5
Franklin, 152 M-15
Frankville, 125 B-15
Fraser, 120 G-9
Fredericksburg, 1011 C-14
Fredonia, 281 K-16
Fremont, 701 K-13
Froelich C-16
Fruitland, 511 J-17
Fulton, 120 H-19
Galt, 43 D-10
Galva, 398 E-5
Garden City, 150 G-10
Garden Gr., 229 L-10
Garnavillo, 727 D-16
Garner, 2916 C-10
Garrison, 320 F-14
Garwin, 533 G-12
Gaza, 70 C-4
Geneva, 169 D-11
George, 1066 B-3
Georgetown L-11
Germantown, 100 D-4
Gibson, 63 K-13
Gifford, 70 F-11
Gilbert, 796 G-9
Gilbertville, 748 E-14
Gillett Gr., 67 C-6
Gilman, 586 G-12
Gilmore City, 560 D-7
Gladbrook, 881 F-12
Glasgow, 40 M-15
Glenwood, 4571 L-3
Glidden, 1099 G-6
Goldfield, 710 E-9
Goodell, 201 C-10
Goose Lake, 221 G-19
Gowrie, 1028 F-8
Graettinger, 813 B-6
Graf, 78 E-17
Grafton, 282 B-11
Grand Jct., 808 G-8
Grand Mound, 620 H-18
Grand River, 151 K-9
Grandview, 556 K-17
Granger, 793 H-9
Grant, 123 K-6
Granville, 298 C-3
Gravity, 218 M-6
Gray, 83 G-5
Greeley, 263 E-16
Green Island, 54 G-19
Green Mtn. F-12
Greene, 1142 D-13
Greenfield, 2074 K-7
Greenville, 84 C-5
Grimes, 2658 H-9
Grinnell, 9043 H-12
Griswold, 1049 K-5
Grundy Ctr., 2491 F-12
Guernsey, 70 H-13
Guthrie Ctr., 1614 H-7
Guttenberg, 2257 D-17
Halbur, 215 G-6
Hale, 60 G-17
Hamburg, 1248 M-4
Hamilton, 135 K-12
Hamlin, 70 J-6
Hampton, 4133 D-11
Hancock, 201 K-4
Hanlontown, 193 B-10
Harcourt, 306 F-8
Hardy, 47 D-9
Harlan, 5148 H-5
Harper, 147 J-14
Harpers Ferry, 284 B-17
Harris, 170 A-5
Hartford, 768 J-10
Hartley, 1632 C-4
Hartwick, 115 H-13
Harvey, 235 K-12
Hastings, 187 L-4
Havelock, 217 D-7
Haverhill, 144 G-12
Hawarden, 2439 C-2
Hawkeye, 460 C-14
Hayesville, 62 K-14
Hayfield, 60 C-9
Hazleton, 733 E-15
Hedrick, 810 K-14
Henderson, 206 K-4
Hepburn, 41 L-6
Hesper A-15
Hiawatha, 5354 G-15
Highland Ctr., 20 K-13
Highlandville, 30 A-15
Hills, 662 J-16
Hillsboro, 151 L-15
Hinton, 697 E-2
Hiteman, 60 L-12
Holland, 215 F-12
Holmes E-9
Holstein, 1449 E-4
Holy Cross, 304 E-17
Homestead H-15
Hopeville L-8
Hopkinton, 695 F-16
Hornick, 222 F-3
Hospers, 643 C-3
Houghton, 127 M-16
Hubbard, 814 F-11
Hudson, 2037 E-13
Hull, 1724 B-3
Humboldt, 4438 D-8
Humeston, 553 L-10
Huntington, 50 A-6
Hurstville, 100 G-18
Huxley, 2047 G-10
Iconium, 30 L-12
Ida Gr., 2357 F-4
Imogene, 88 L-4
Independence, 5972 E-15
Indianola, 11340 J-10
Inwood, 824 B-2
Ionia, 304 C-13
Iowa Ctr. G-10
Iowa City, 59738 H-16
Iowa Falls, 5424 E-11
Ira, 100 H-11
Ireton, 597 C-2
Irving G-14
Irvington, 40 C-8
Irwin, 394 H-5
Jackson Jct., 87 C-14
Jacksonville H-5
Jamaica, 232 H-8
Jamison, 30 K-9
Janesville, 822 E-13
Jefferson, 4292 G-7
Jerico, 10 C-14
Jesup, 2121 E-14
Jewell, 1106 F-9
Johnston, 4702 H-9
Joice, 245 B-10
Jolley, 68 E-7
Jordan, 60 G-9
Kalona, 1942 J-15
Kamrar, 203 F-9
Kanawha, 763 C-9
Kellerton, 314 M-8
Kelley, 246 G-9
Kellogg, 626 H-12
Kendallville B-14
Kensett, 298 B-11
Kent, 65 L-7
Keokuk, 12451 N-16
Keomah Vil., 99 K-13
Keosauqua, 1020 M-15
Keota, 1000 J-15
Kesley, 150 E-12
Keswick, 284 J-14
Key West E-18
Keystone, 568 G-14
Killduff, 150 J-12
Kimballton, 289 H-5
King, 450 E-18
Kingsley, 1129 E-3
Kinross, 89 J-14
Kirkman, 98 H-5
Kirkville, 177 K-13
Kiron, 301 F-5
Klemme, 587 C-10
Knierim, 71 E-7
Knoke, 60 E-6
Knoxville, 8232 K-11
Koszta, 70 H-14
La Motte, 219 F-18
La Porte City, 2128 F-14
Lacey, 70 J-13
Lacona, 357 K-10
Ladora, 308 H-14
Lake City, 1841 F-6
Lake Mills, 2143 B-10
Lake Park, 996 A-5
Lake View, 1303 F-6
Lakeside, 522 E-5
Lakota, 281 B-8
Lambs Gr., 212 H-11
Lamoille G-11
Lamoni, 2319 M-9
Lamont, 471 E-15
Lanesboro, 182 F-7
Langdon, 125 B-6
Langworthy, 90 F-17
Lansing, 1007 B-16
Lanyon, 100 F-8
Larchwood, 739 A-2
Larrabee, 175 D-4
Latimer, 430 D-10
Laurel, 271 G-12
Laurens, 1550 D-6
Lawler, 517 C-14
Lawton, 482 E-2
Le Claire, 2734 H-19
Le Grand, 854 G-12
Le Mars, 8454 D-2
Le Roy, 34 L-10
Ledyard, 164 B-8
Lehigh, 536 F-8
Leighton, 142 K-12
Leland, 311 B-10
Lenox, 1303 L-7
Leon, 2047 M-9
Lester, 257 A-2
Letts, 390 J-17
Lewis, 433 K-5
Liberty Ctr. K-10
Libertyville, 264 L-14
Lidderdale, 202 G-6
Lime Sprs., 438 A-14
Lincoln, 173 F-12
Linden, 201 H-8
Lineville, 289 M-10
Linn Gr., 194 D-5
Lisbon, 1452 G-16
Liscomb, 258 F-12
Little Rock, 493 A-3
Little Sioux, 205 H-3
Littleport, 88 D-16
Littleton E-14
Livermore, 436 D-8
Lockridge, 270 L-15
Logan, 1401 H-3
Lohrville, 453 F-7
Lone Rock, 185 B-8
Lone Tree, 979 J-16
Long Gr., 605 H-18
Lorimor, 377 K-8
Lost Nation, 467 G-18
Lourdes, 30 B-13
Lovilia, 551 K-12
Low Moor, 280 H-19
Lowden, 726 G-17
Lowell, 100 L-16
Lu Verne, 328 D-8
Luana, 190 C-16
Lucas, 224 L-10
Luther, 154 G-9
Luton, 10 F-2
Luxemburg, 257 E-17
Luzerne, 110 G-14
Lyman, 125 K-6
Lynnville, 393 J-12
Lytton, 320 E-6
Macedonia, 262 K-4
Macksburg, 110 K-8
Madrid, 2395 G-9
Magnolia, 204 H-3
Malcom, 447 H-13
Mallard, 360 C-7
Maloy, 36 M-7
Malvern, 1210 L-4
Manchester, 5137 E-16
Manilla, 898 G-5
Manly, 1349 B-11
Manning, 1484 G-6
Manson, 1844 E-7
Maple Hill B-7
Mapleton, 1294 F-3
Maquoketa, 6111 G-18
Marathon, 320 D-6
Marble Rock, 361 C-12
Marcus, 1171 D-4
Marengo, 2270 H-14
Marion, 20403 G-15
Mark, 60 M-13
Marne, 149 J-5
Marquette, 479 C-17
Marshalltown, 25178 G-12
Martelle, 290 G-16
Martensdale, 491 J-9
Martinsburg, 157 K-14
Marysville, 65 K-12
Mason City, 29040 C-11
Masonville, 129 E-15
Massena, 372 K-6
Massillon, 100 G-17
Matlock, 92 B-3
Maurice, 243 C-3
Maxwell, 788 G-10
May City, 100 B-4
Maynard, 513 D-15
Maysville, 170 H-18
McCallsburg, 292 F-10
McCausland, 308 H-19
McClelland, 139 K-4
McGregor, 797 C-17
McIntire, 147 B-13
Mechanicsville, 1012 G-16
Mediapolis, 1637 L-17
Melbourne, 669 G-11
Melcher-Dallas, 1302 K-11
Melrose, 150 L-11
Melvin, 250 B-4
Menlo, 356 J-7
Meriden, 193 D-4
Merrill, 729 D-2
Meservey, 292 D-10
Middletown, 386 L-17
Miles, 409 G-19
Milford, 2170 B-5
Miller, 80 C-10
Millersburg, 188 J-14
Millerton, 44 L-11
Millville, 20 D-17
Milo, 864 K-10
Milton, 506 M-14
Minburn, 346 H-8
Minden, 498 J-4
Mineola, 150 K-4
Mingo, 252 H-11
Missouri Valley, 2888 J-3
Mitchell, 170 B-12
Mitchellville, 1670 H-10
Modale, 289 H-3
Moingona, 175 G-9
Mona A-12
Mondamin, 403 H-3
Moneta, 29 C-5
Monmouth, 169 G-17
Monona, 1520 C-16
Monroe, 1739 J-11
Monteith, 70 H-7
Montezuma, 1651 J-13
Monticello, 3522 F-17
Montour, 312 G-12
Montrose, 957 N-16
Moorhead, 259 G-3
Moorland, 209 E-8
Moravia, 679 L-12
Morley, 85 G-16
Morning Sun, 841 K-17
Morrison, 113 F-12
Morse, 125 H-16
Morton Mills, 40 L-6
Moulton, 613 M-13
Mt. Auburn, 134 F-14
Mt. Ayr, 1796 M-8
Mt. Etna, 40 K-6
Mt. Hamill, 50 M-16
Mt. Pleasant, 8027 L-16
Mt. Sterling, 53 M-15
Mt. Union, 140 L-16
Mt. Vernon, 3657 G-16
Mt. Zion, 40 M-15
Moville, 1306 E-3
Murray, 731 L-9
Muscatine, 22881 J-17
Mystic, 545 M-12
Nashua, 1476 C-13
Nashville G-18
Nemaha, 112 E-5
Neola, 894 J-4
Nevada, 6009 G-10
Nevinville, 20 K-7
New Albin, 534 A-16
New Hampton, 3660 C-13
New Hartford, 683 E-13
New Haven, 100 B-12
New Liberty, 139 H-18
New London, 1922 L-16
New Market, 454 M-6
New Providence, 240 F-11
New Sharon, 1136 J-13
New Vienna, 376 E-17
New Virginia, 433 K-9
Newburg, 100 H-12
Newell, 1089 E-6
Newhall, 854 G-14
Newkirk C-3
Newton, 14789 H-11
Nichols, 366 J-16
Nodaway, 153 L-6
Nora Sprs., 1505 C-12
N. Buena Vista, 145 D-17
N. English, 944 J-14
N. Liberty, 2926 H-16
N. Washington, 107 C-13
Northboro, 78 M-5
Northwood, 1940 B-11
Norwalk, 5726 J-9
Norway, 583 G-15
Norwood, 20 K-10
Numa, 151 M-12
Oakland, 1496 K-5
Oakland Acres, 152 H-12
Oakville, 442 K-17
Ocheyedan, 539 B-4
Odebolt, 1158 F-5
Oelwein, 6691 D-15
Ogden, 1909 G-8
Okoboji, 775 B-5
Olds, 205 K-16
Olin, 663 G-17
Ollie, 207 K-14
Onawa, 2936 G-3
Oneida, 49 E-16
Onslow, 216 G-17
Oran D-14
Orange City, 4940 C-3
Orchard, 93 B-12
Orient, 376 K-7
Orleans, 560 A-6
Osage, 3439 B-12
Osceola, 4164 L-9
Oskaloosa, 10632 K-13
Ossian, 810 C-15
Osterdock, 49 D-17
Otho, 529 E-8
Otley, 150 J-11
Oto, 118 F-3
Otranto, 30 A-12
Otter Cr., 50 F-18
Ottosen, 72 D-7
Ottumwa, 24488 L-13
Owasa, 37 E-11
Oxford, 663 H-15
Oxford Jct., 581 G-17
Oyens, 113 D-3
Pacific Jct., 548 L-3
Packwood, 208 K-14
Palmer, 230 E-7
Palo, 514 G-15
Panama, 201 H-4
Panora, 1100 H-7
Paris, 80 F-16
Paris, 80 M-13
Park View, 2192 H-19
Parkersburg, 1804 E-12
Parnell, 209 J-14
Paton, 255 F-8
Patterson, 128 K-9
Paullina, 1134 C-4
Pekin K-14
Pella, 9270 J-12
Peoria J-12
Peosta, 128 E-18
Percival, 125 M-3
Perkins B-3
Perry, 6652 H-8
Pershing K-12
Persia, 312 J-4
Peterson, 390 C-5
Pierson, 341 E-3
Pilot Mound, 199 F-8
Pioneer, 46 E-7
Pisgah, 268 H-3
Plainfield, 455 D-13
Plano, 75 M-11
Pleasant Gr., 70 L-16
Pleasant Hill, 3671 J-10
Pleasant Plain, 128 K-15
Pleasanton, 58 M-9
Pleasantville, 1536 J-11
Plover, 101 D-7
Plymouth, 453 B-11
Pocahontas, 2085 D-7
Polk City, 1908 H-9
Pomeroy, 762 E-7
Popejoy, 92 E-10
Portsmouth, 209 H-4
Postville, 1472 C-15
Prairie City, 1360 J-11
Prairieburg, 213 F-16
Prescott, 287 L-7
Preston, 1025 G-19
Primghar, 950 C-4
Princeton, 806 H-19
Prole J-9
Promise City, 132 M-11
Protivin, 305 B-14
Pulaski, 221 M-14
Quasqueton, 579 E-15
Quimby, 334 E-4
Radcliffe, 574 F-10
Rake, 238 A-9
Ralston, 119 G-7
Randalia, 88 D-15
Randall, 161 F-10
Randolph, 243 L-4
Rathbun, 89 M-12
Readlyn, 773 D-14
Reasnor, 191 J-12
Red Oak, 6264 L-5
Redding, 119 M-7
Redfield, 883 J-8
Reinbeck, 1605 F-13
Rembrandt, 229 D-5
Remsen, 1513 D-3
Renwick, 287 D-9
Rhodes, 272 G-11
Riceville, 827 B-13
Richland, 522 K-14
Rickardsville, 171 E-17
Ricketts, 105 F-4
Ridgeway, 295 B-14
Rinard, 71 F-7
Ringsted, 481 B-7
Rippey, 275 G-8
River Sioux, 90 H-3
Riverside, 824 J-16
Riverton, 333 M-4
Robins, 875 G-15
Rock Falls, 130 B-11
Rock Rapids, 2601 A-3
Rock Valley, 2540 B-2
Rockford, 863 C-12
Rockwell, 1008 C-11
Rockwell City, 1981 F-7
Rodman, 56 C-7
Rodney, 65 F-3
Roland, 1035 F-10
Rolfe, 721 D-7
Rome, 124 L-15
Rose Hill, 171 K-13
Ross, 80 H-6
Rossie, 68 C-5
Rossville, 125 B-16
Rowan, 189 D-10
Rowley, 272 F-15
Royal, 466 C-5
Rubio, 50 K-15
Rudd, 429 C-12
Runnells, 306 J-10
Russell, 531 L-11
Ruthven, 707 C-6
Rutland, 149 D-8
Ryan, 382 F-16
Sabula, 710 G-19
Sac City, 2492 E-6
Sageville, 288 E-18
St. Ansgar, 1063 B-12
St. Anthony, 112 G-11
St. Charles, 537 K-9
St. Donatus, 145 F-18
St. Lucas, 174 C-14
St. Marys, 113 K-9
St. Olaf, 111 C-16
St. Paul, 120 M-16
Salem, 453 L-16
Salix, 367 F-2
Sanborn, 1345 B-4
Sand Sprs., 70 F-17
Sandyville, 59 J-10
Saratoga, 100 B-13
Saylorville, 2709 H-10
Scarville, 92 A-10
Schaller, 768 E-5
Schleswig, 851 F-4
Schley, 40 B-14
Scotch Gr. F-17
Scranton, 583 G-7
Searsboro, 164 J-12
Selma, 80 L-14
Seney, 100 D-3
Sergeant Bluff, 2772 E-2
Sewal, 60 M-11
Sexton C-8
Seymour, 869 M-11
Shambaugh, 190 M-5
Shannon City, 97 L-8
Sharpsburg, 116 M-7
Sheffield, 1174 D-11
Shelby, 637 J-4
Sheldahl, 315 H-9
Sheldon, 4937 B-3
Shell Rock, 1385 D-13
Shellsburg, 765 G-15
Shenandoah, 5572 M-5
Sherrill, 148 E-18
Shueyville, 223 H-15
Siam, 40 M-6
Sibley, 2815 B-4
Sidney, 1253 M-4
Sigourney, 2111 K-14
Silver City, 252 K-4
Sioux Ctr., 5074 C-3
Sioux City, 80505 E-2
Sioux Rapids, 761 D-5
Slater, 1268 H-9
Sloan, 938 F-2
Smithland, 235 F-3
Soldier, 205 G-3
Solon, 1050 H-16
Somers, 161 F-7
S. Amana H-14
S. English, 224 J-14
Spencer, 11066 C-5
Sperry L-17
Spillville, 387 B-14
Spirit Lake, 3871 B-6
Spragueville, 118 G-19
Spr. Hill, 86 J-9
Springbrook, 116 F-19
Springville, 1068 G-16
Stacyville, 481 B-12
Stanhope, 447 F-9
Stanley, 116 E-15
Stanton, 692 L-5
Stanwood, 646 G-17
State Ctr., 1248 G-11
Steamboat Rock, 335 F-11
Stennett, 40 K-5
Stockport, 260 L-15
Stockton, 187 H-18
Storm Lake, 8769 E-5
Story City, 2959 F-10
Stout, 192 E-12
Strahan, 40 L-4
Stratford, 715 F-9
Strawberry Pt., 1357 D-16
Struble, 67 D-2
Stuart, 1522 J-8
Sully, 841 J-12
Summitville, 125 N-16
Sumner, 2078 D-14
Sunbury, 100 H-17
Superior, 128 B-6
Sutherland, 714 C-4
Swaledale, 190 C-11
Swan, 76 J-11
Swea City, 634 B-8
Swedesburg, 150 K-16
Swisher, 645 H-15
Tabor, 957 L-4
Taintor J-12
Tama, 2697 G-13
Teeds Gr., 100 G-19
Templeton, 321 G-6
Tennant, 78 J-4
Terril, 383 B-6
Thayer, 79 L-8
Thompson, 498 B-9
Thor, 205 D-8
Thornburg, 91 J-13
Thornton, 431 C-10
Thurman, 239 L-4
Tiffin, 460 H-15
Tingley, 179 L-8
Tipton, 2998 H-17
Titonka, 612 B-8
Toddville, 450 G-15
Toeterville B-12
Toledo, 2380 G-13
Toolesboro K-17
Toronto, 132 G-18
Tracy, 300 K-12
Traer, 1552 F-13
Trenton, 125 L-15
Treynor, 897 K-4
Tripoli, 1188 D-14
Troy, 60 M-14
Truesdale, 132 D-5
Truro, 391 K-9
Turin, 95 G-3
Udell, 76 M-12
Ulmer F-6
Underwood, 515 J-4
Union, 448 F-11
Unionville, 133 M-12
University Park, 604 K-13
Urbana, 595 F-15
Urbandale, 23775 J-9
Ute, 395 G-4
Vail, 388 G-5
Valeria, 69 H-11
Van Horne, 695 G-14
Van Meter, 751 J-9
Van Wert, 249 L-9
Varina, 102 D-6
Ventura, 590 C-10
Vernon View M-20
Victor, 966 H-14
Villisca, 1332 L-6
Vincent, 185 E-8
Vining, 78 G-13
Vinton, 5103 F-14
Viola, 70 G-16
Volga, 306 D-16
Voorhies, 90 F-13
Wadena, 236 D-15
Wahpeton, 484 B-5
Walcott, 1356 H-18
Walford, 303 G-15
Walker, 673 F-15
Wall Lake, 875 F-5
Wallingford, 196 B-6
Walnut, 857 J-5
Wapello, 2013 K-17
Ware, 30 D-6
Washburn, 1000 E-14
Washington, 7074 K-15
Washta, 284 E-4
Waterloo, 66467 E-13
Waterville, 140 B-16
Waubeek F-16

WAIANAPANPA STATE PARK, HI

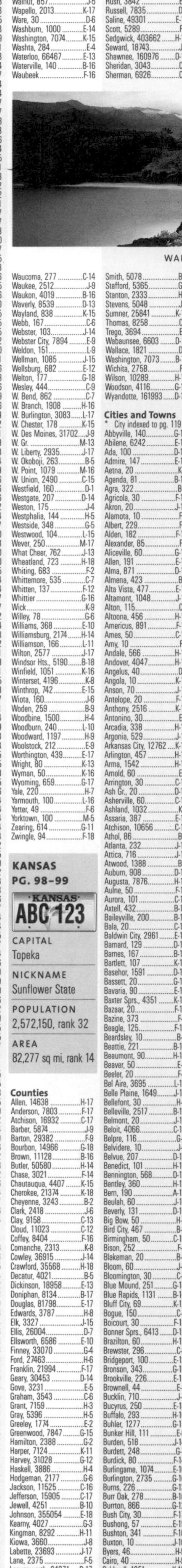

Waucoma, 277 C-14
Waukee, 2512 J-9
Waukon, 4019 B-16
Waverly, 8539 D-13
Wayland, 838 K-15
Webb, 167 C-6
Webster, 103 J-14
Webster City, 7894 E-9
Weldon, 151 L-9
Wellman, 1085 J-15
Wellsburg, 682 E-12
Welton, 177 G-18
Wesley, 444 C-9
W. Bend, 862 C-7
W. Branch, 1908 H-16
W. Burlington, 3083 L-17
W. Chester, 178 K-15
W. Des Moines, 31702 J-9
W. Gr. M-13
W. Liberty, 2935 J-17
W. Okoboji, 263 B-5
W. Point, 1079 M-16
W. Union, 2490 C-15
Westfield, 160 D-1
Westgate, 207 D-14
Weston, 175 J-4
Westphalia, 144 H-5
Westside, 348 G-5
Westwood, 104 L-15
Wever, 250 M-17
What Cheer, 762 J-13
Wheatland, 723 H-18
Whiting, 683 F-2
Whittemore, 535 C-7
Whitten, 137 F-12
Whittier G-16
Wick K-9
Willey, 78 G-6
Williams, 368 E-10
Williamsburg, 2174 H-14
Williamson, 166 L-11
Wilton, 2577 J-17
Windsor Hts., 5190 B-18
Winfield, 1051 K-16
Winterset, 4196 K-8
Winthrop, 742 E-15
Wiota, 160 J-6
Woden, 259 B-9
Woodbine, 1500 H-4
Woodburn, 240 L-10
Woodward, 1197 H-9
Woolstock, 212 E-9
Worthington, 439 E-17
Wright, 80 K-13
Wyman, 50 K-16
Wyoming, 659 G-17
Yale, 220 H-7
Yarmouth, 100 L-16
Yetter, 49 F-6
Yorktown, 100 M-5
Zearing, 614 G-11
Zwingle, 94 F-18

KANSAS
PG. 98–99

KANSAS ABC 123

CAPITAL
Topeka

NICKNAME
Sunflower State

POPULATION
2,572,150, rank 32

AREA
82,277 sq mi, rank 14

Counties
Allen, 14638 H-17
Anderson, 7803 F-17
Atchison, 16932 C-17
Barber, 5874 J-9
Barton, 29382 F-9
Bourbon, 14966 G-18
Brown, 11128 B-16
Butler, 50580 H-14
Chase, 3021 F-14
Chautauqua, 4407 K-15
Cherokee, 21374 K-18
Cheyenne, 3243 B-2
Clark, 2418 J-6
Clay, 9158 C-13
Cloud, 11023 C-12
Coffey, 8404 F-16
Comanche, 2313 K-8
Cowley, 36915 J-14
Crawford, 35568 H-18
Decatur, 4021 B-5
Dickinson, 18958 E-13
Doniphan, 8134 B-17
Douglas, 81798 E-17
Edwards, 3787 H-8
Elk, 3327 J-15
Ellis, 26004 D-7
Ellsworth, 6586 E-10
Finney, 33070 G-4
Ford, 27463 H-6
Franklin, 21994 F-17
Geary, 30453 D-14
Gove, 3231 E-5
Graham, 3543 C-6
Grant, 7159 H-3
Gray, 5396 H-5
Greeley, 1774 E-2
Greenwood, 7847 G-15
Hamilton, 2388 G-2
Harper, 7124 K-11
Harvey, 31028 G-12
Haskell, 3886 H-4
Hodgeman, 2177 G-6
Jackson, 11525 C-16
Jefferson, 15905 C-17
Jewell, 4251 B-10
Johnson, 355054 E-18
Kearny, 4027 G-3
Kingman, 8292 H-11
Kiowa, 3660 J-8
Labette, 23693 J-17
Lane, 2375 F-5
Leavenworth, 64371 D-17
Lincoln, 3653 D-10
Linn, 8254 F-18
Logan, 3081 E-3
Lyon, 34732 F-15
Marion, 12888 G-13
Marshall, 11705 B-14
McPherson, 27268 F-11
Meade, 4247 J-5
Miami, 23466 E-18
Mitchell, 7203 C-10
Montgomery, 38816 J-16
Morris, 6198 E-14
Morton, 3480 J-2
Nemaha, 10446 B-15
Neosho, 17035 H-17
Ness, 4033 F-7
Norton, 5947 B-7
Osage, 15248 F-16
Osborne, 4867 C-9
Ottawa, 5634 D-12
Pawnee, 7555 F-8
Phillips, 6590 B-8
Pottawatomie, 16128 C-15
Pratt, 9702 H-9
Rawlins, 3404 B-4
Reno, 62389 G-11
Republic, 6482 B-12
Rice, 10610 F-10
Riley, 67139 C-13
Rooks, 6039 C-8
Rush, 3842 E-8
Russell, 7835 D-9
Saline, 49301 E-11
Scott, 5289 F-4
Sedgwick, 403662 H-12
Seward, 18743 J-4
Shawnee, 160976 D-16
Sheridan, 3043 C-5
Sherman, 6926 C-2
Smith, 5078 B-9
Stafford, 5365 G-9
Stanton, 2333 H-2
Stevens, 5048 J-3
Sumner, 25841 K-12
Thomas, 8258 C-4
Trego, 3694 E-6
Wabaunsee, 6603 D-15
Wallace, 1821 D-2
Washington, 7073 B-12
Wichita, 2758 F-3
Wilson, 10289 H-16
Woodson, 4116 G-16
Wyandotte, 161993 D-18

Cities and Towns
* City indexed to pg. 119
Abbyville, 140 G-10
Abilene, 6242 E-13
Ada, 100 D-11
Admire, 147 E-15
Aetna, 20 K-8
Agenda, 81 B-12
Agra, 322 B-8
Agricola, 30 F-17
Akron, 20 J-13
Alamota, 10 F-5
Albert, 229 F-8
Alden, 182 F-10
Alexander, 85 F-7
Aliceville, 60 G-16
Allen, 191 E-15
Alma, 871 D-15
Almena, 423 B-7
Alta Vista, 477 E-14
Altamont, 1048 J-17
Alton, 115 C-9
Altoona, 456 H-16
Americus, 891 F-15
Ames, 50 C-12
Amy, 10 F-5
Andale, 566 H-12
Andover, 4047 H-13
Angelus, 40 D-5
Angola, 10 K-17
Anson, 70 J-12
Antelope, 20 F-13
Anthony, 2516 K-11
Antonino, 30 E-8
Arcadia, 338 H-19
Argonia, 529 J-11
Arkansas City, 12762 K-13
Arlington, 457 H-10
Arma, 1542 H-18
Arnold, 60 E-6
Arrington, 30 C-16
Ash Gr., 20 D-10
Asherville, 60 C-11
Ashland, 1032 K-7
Assaria, 387 E-12
Atchison, 10656 C-17
Athol, 86 B-9
Atlanta, 232 J-14
Attica, 716 J-10
Atwood, 1388 B-4
Auburn, 908 D-16
Augusta, 7876 H-13
Aulne, 50 F-13
Aurora, 101 C-12
Axtell, 432 B-15
Baileyville, 200 B-15
Bala, 20 C-13
Baldwin City, 2961 E-17
Barnard, 129 D-11
Barnes, 167 B-13
Bartlett, 107 K-17
Basehor, 1591 D-18
Bassett, 20 G-17
Bavaria, 90 E-11
Baxter Sprs., 4351 K-18
Bazaar, 20 F-14
Bazine, 373 F-7
Beagle, 125 F-18
Beardsley, 10 B-4
Beattie, 221 B-14
Beaumont, 90 H-14
Beaver, 50 E-9
Beeler, 20 F-6
Bel Aire, 3695 L-19
Belle Plaine, 1649 J-13
Bellefont, 30 H-7
Belleville, 2517 B-12
Belmont, 20 J-11
Beloit, 4066 C-11
Belpre, 116 G-8
Belvidere, 10 J-8
Belvue, 207 D-15
Benedict, 101 H-16
Bennington, 568 D-12
Bentley, 360 H-12
Bern, 190 A-15
Beulah, 60 J-18
Beverly, 131 D-11
Big Bow, 50 H-3
Bird City, 467 B-3
Birmingham, 50 C-16
Bison, 252 F-8
Blakeman, 20 B-4
Bloom, 60 J-6
Bloomington, 30 C-9
Blue Mound, 251 G-18
Blue Rapids, 1131 B-14
Bluff City, 69 K-11
Bogue, 150 C-7
Boicourt, 30 F-18
Bonner Sprs., 6413 D-18
Brazilton, 60 H-18
Brewster, 296 C-3
Bridgeport, 100 E-12
Bronson, 343 G-18
Brookville, 226 E-11
Brownell, 44 E-7
Bucklin, 710 J-7
Bucyrus, 250 E-18
Buffalo, 293 H-16
Buhler, 1277 G-11
Bunker Hill, 111 E-9
Burden, 518 J-14
Burdett, 248 G-7
Burdick, 80 F-14
Burlingame, 1074 E-16
Burlington, 2735 G-16
Burns, 226 G-13
Burr Oak, 278 B-10
Burrton, 866 G-12
Bush City, 30 F-17
Bushong, 57 E-15
Bushton, 341 F-10
Buxton, 10 J-16
Byers, 46 H-9
Cairo, 40 H-9
Caldwell, 1351 K-12
Calista, 10 H-10
Calvert, 40 B-7
Cambridge, 74 J-14
Caney, 2062 K-16
Canton, 794 F-12
Carbondale, 1526 E-16
Carlton, 39 E-13
Carlyle, 90 G-17
Carneiro, 20 E-11
Cassoday, 95 G-14
Castleton, 40 H-11
Catherine, 100 D-8
Cawker City, 588 C-10
Cedar, 25 B-9
Cedar Bluffs, 30 A-5
Cedar Pt., 39 F-14
Cedar Vale, 760 K-14
Centerville, 90 F-18
Centralia, 452 B-15
Centropolis, 90 E-17
Chanute, 9488 H-17
Chapman, 1264 D-13
Charleston, 20 H-5
Chase, 577 F-10
Chautauqua, 132 K-15
Cheney, 1560 H-11
Cherokee, 651 J-18
Cherryvale, 2464 J-17
Chetopa, 1357 K-18
Cimarron, 1626 H-5
Circleville, 153 C-16
Claflin, 678 F-9
Claudell, 20 B-8
Clay Ctr., 4613 C-13
Clayton, 91 B-6
Clearwater, 1875 J-12
Clements, 10 F-14
Cleveland, 20 H-10
Clifton, 561 C-13
Climax, 57 H-15
Clinton, 80 D-17
Clyde, 793 C-12
Coats, 127 J-9
Codell, 50 D-8
Coffeyville, 12917 K-16
Colby, 5396 C-4
Coldwater, 939 J-8
Collyer, 144 D-6
Colony, 447 G-17
Columbus, 3268 K-18
Colwich, 1091 H-12
Concordia, 6167 C-12
Conway Sprs., 1384 J-12
Coolidge, 90 G-2
Copeland, 290 J-5
Corbin, 60 K-12
Corning, 142 B-15
Corwin, 20 K-10
Cottonwood Falls, 889 F-14
Council Gr., 2228 E-14
Countryside, 312 *G-3
Courtland, 343 B-11
Covert, 10 C-9
Coyville, 78 H-16
Crestline, 150 K-19
Crystal Sprs., 50 J-11
Cuba, 242 B-12
Cullison, 120 H-9
Culver, 162 D-11
Cummings, 80 C-17
Cunningham, 535 H-10
Damar, 112 C-7
Danville, 56 J-11
De Soto, 2291 D-18
Dearing, 428 K-16
Deerfield, 677 G-4
Delavan, 40 E-14
Delia, 172 D-15
Delphos, 494 C-11
Denison, 225 C-16
Denmark, 30 D-10
Dennis, 150 J-17
Densmore, 10 B-7
Denton, 166 B-17
Derby, 14699 J-13
Devon, 80 G-18
Dexter, 320 K-14
Dighton, 1361 F-5
Dodge City, 21129 H-6
Doniphan, 50 B-17
Dorrance, 195 E-9
Douglass, 1722 J-13
Dover, 125 D-16
Downs, 1119 C-9
Dresden, 73 B-5
Duluth, 50 C-15
Dundee, 100 F-9
Dunlap, 65 E-15
Duquoin, 10 J-11
Durham, 119 F-13
Dwight, 365 E-14
Earlton, 69 H-17
Eastborough, 896 M-19
Easton, 405 C-17
Edgerton, 1244 E-18
Edmond, 37 B-7
Edna, 438 K-17
Edson, 50 C-3
Edwardsville, 3979 *F-1
Effingham, 540 C-17
El Dorado, 11504 H-14
Elbing, 184 G-13
Elgin, 118 K-15
Elk City, 334 J-16
Elk Falls, 122 J-15
Elkhart, 2318 K-2
Ellinwood, 2329 F-9
Ellis, 1814 D-7
Ellsworth, 2294 E-10
Elmdale, 83 F-14
Elmo, 50 E-13
Elmont, 450 D-16
Elsmore, 91 H-17
Elwood, 1079 B-18
Elyria, 90 F-12
Emmeram, 10 D-8
Emmett, 165 C-15
Emporia, 25512 F-15
Englevale, 50 H-18
Englewood, 96 K-6
Ensign, 192 H-6
Enterprise, 865 E-13
Erie, 1276 H-17
Esbon, 167 B-10
Eskridge, 518 E-15
Eudora, 3006 D-17
Eureka, 2974 H-15
Everest, 310 B-17
Fairmount, 250 D-18
Fairport, 10 D-8
Fairview, 306 B-16
Fairway, 4173 *G-3
Fall River, 113 H-15
Falun, 125 E-12
Fanning, 40 B-17
Farlington, 125 H-18
Faulkner, 40 K-18
Fellsburg, 20 H-8
Florence, 636 G-13
Fontana, 131 F-18
Ford, 247 H-7
Formoso, 128 B-11
Ft. Dodge, 550 H-6
Ft. Scott, 8362 H-18
Fostoria, 80 C-14
Fowler, 571 J-6
Frankfort, 927 B-14
Franklin, 450 H-18
Frederick, 18 F-10
Fredonia, 2599 J-16
Freeport, 8 K-11
Friend, 30 F-4
Frontenac, 2588 J-19
Fulton, 191 G-18
Furley, 80 H-13
Galatia, 47 E-9
Galena, 3308 K-19
Galesburg, 160 J-17
Galva, 651 F-12
Garden City, 24097 G-4
Garden Plain, 731 H-12
Gardner, 4277 E-18
Garfield, 236 G-8
Garland, 100 H-19
Garnett, 3210 F-17
Gas, 505 G-17
Gaylord, 173 B-9
Gem, 104 C-4
Geneseo, 382 F-10
Geuda Sprs., 219 K-13
Girard, 2794 H-18
Glade, 101 B-8
Glasco, 556 C-11
Glen Elder, 448 C-10
Glendale, 30 E-11
Goddard, 1804 H-12
Goessel, 506 F-12
Goff, 156 B-16
Goodland, 4983 C-2
Goodrich, 90 F-18
Gordon, 60 H-13
Gorham, 284 E-8
Gove, 103 D-5
Grainfield, 357 D-5
Grandview Plaza, 1233 D-14
Grantville, 250 D-16
Great Bend, 15427 F-9
Greeley, 339 F-17
Green, 150 C-13
Greenleaf, 353 B-13
Greensburg, 1792 H-8
Grenola, 256 J-15
Gretna, 10 B-8
Gridley, 356 G-16
Grigston, 20 F-5
Grinnell, 348 D-5
Grove, 10 D-16
Gypsum, 365 E-12
Hackney, 10 K-13
Haddam, 195 B-12
Halford, 20 C-4
Halls Summit, 10 F-16
Halstead, 2015 G-12
Hamilton, 301 G-15
Hamlin, 50 B-16
Hammond, 30 G-19
Hanover, 696 B-13
Hanston, 326 G-7
Hardtner, 198 K-9
Harlan, 20 C-9
Harper, 1735 J-11
Harris, 39 F-17
Hartford, 541 F-16
Harveyville, 267 E-16
Havana, 121 K-16
Haven, 1198 H-11
Havensville, 135 C-15
Haviland, 624 H-8
Hays, 18632 E-8
Haysville, 8364 H-12
Hazelton, 128 K-10
Healy, 250 E-5
Hedville, 100 E-11
Heizer, 80 F-9
Hepler, 150 H-18
Herington, 2685 E-13
Herkimer, 100 B-14
Herndon, 170 B-4
Hesston, 3012 G-12
Hewins, 30 K-15
Hiattville, 60 H-18
Hiawatha, 3603 B-16
Hickok, 50 H-3
Highland, 942 B-17
Hill City, 1835 C-7
Hillsboro, 2704 F-13
Hillsdale, 250 E-18
Hitschmann, 20 E-9
Hoisington, 3182 F-9
Holcomb, 1400 G-4
Hollenberg, 28 A-13
Holton, 3196 C-16
Holyrood, 492 E-10
Home, 175 B-14
Homewood, 100 F-17
Hope, 404 E-13
Hopewell, 30 H-8
Horace, 168 F-2
Horton, 1885 B-16
Howard, 815 J-15
Howell, 40 H-6
Hoxie, 1342 C-5
Hoyt, 489 C-16
Hudson, 159 G-9
Hugoton, 3179 J-3
Humboldt, 2178 H-17
Hunnewell, 87 K-12
Hunter, 116 D-10
Huron, 75 B-17
Hutchinson, 39308 G-11
Hymer, 10 F-14
Idana, 70 C-13
Independence, 9942 J-16
Industry, 40 D-13
Ingalls, 301 H-5
Inman, 1035 G-11
Iola, 6351 G-17
Ionia, 60 B-10
Iowa Pt., 40 A-17
Isabel, 104 J-9
Iuka, 190 H-9
Jamestown, 325 C-11
Jefferson, 70 K-16
Jennings, 188 B-6
Jetmore, 850 G-6
Jewell, 529 B-10
Johnson City, 1348 H-2
Jct. City, 20604 D-14
Kackley, 20 B-11
Kalvesta, 20 G-6
Kanona, 10 B-5
Kanopolis, 605 E-10
Kanorado, 276 C-2
Kansas City, 151521 D-18
Keats, 150 D-14
Kechi, 517 H-13
Kelly, 50 B-15
Kendall, 20 G-3
Kensington, 553 B-8
Kimball, 60 H-17
Kincaid, 170 G-17
Kingman, 3196 H-11
Kingsdown, 50 J-7
Kinsley, 1875 G-7
Kiowa, 1160 K-10
Kipp, 100 E-12
Kirwin, 269 B-8
Kismet, 421 K-5
La Crosse, 1427 F-8
La Cygne, 1066 F-18
La Harpe, 650 G-17
Labette, 74 J-17
Lafontaine, 90 J-16
Lake City, 20 J-9
Lake Quivira, 983 *F-1
Lakin, 2060 G-3
Lamont, 60 G-15
Lancaster, 299 C-17
Lane, 247 F-18
Langdon, 62 H-10
Langley, 20 F-11
Lansing, 7120 C-18
Larned, 4490 G-8
Latham, 160 J-14
Latimer, 20 E-14
Lawrence, 65608 D-17
Le Loup, 125 E-17
Le Roy, 568 G-16
Leavenworth, 38495 C-18
Leawood, 19693 *J-3
Lebanon, 364 B-9
Lebo, 835 F-16
Lecompton, 619 D-17
Lehigh, 180 F-13
Lenexa, 34034 D-18
Lenora, 329 C-6
Leon, 707 H-14
Leona, 39 B-17
Leonardville, 374 C-13
Leoti, 1738 F-3
Leoville, 50 C-5
Levant, 90 C-4
Lewis, 451 G-8
Liberal, 16573 K-4
Liberty, 140 K-16
Liebenthal, 112 E-8
Lincoln, 1381 D-10
Lincolnville, 197 F-13
Lindsborg, 3076 F-12
Linn, 472 B-13
Linwood, 409 D-18
Little River, 496 F-11
Logan, 633 B-7
Lone Elm, 32 G-17
Lone Star, 50 E-17
Long Island, 170 B-7
Longford, 68 D-12
Longton, 389 J-15
Loretta, 20 E-8
Lorraine, 147 F-10
Lost Sprs., 106 F-13
Louisburg, 1964 E-18
Louisville, 215 C-15
Lovewell, 10 B-11
Lowemont, 125 C-17
Lucas, 452 D-9
Ludell, 80 B-4
Luray, 261 D-9
Lydia, 20 F-3
Lyndon, 964 E-16
Lyons, 3688 F-10
Macksville, 488 G-8
Madison, 845 G-15
Mahaska, 98 A-12
Maize, 1520 H-12
Manchester, 80 D-12
Manhattan, 43081 D-14
Mankato, 1037 B-10
Manning, 30 F-5
Manter, 186 J-2
Maple City, 20 K-14
Maple Hill, 406 D-15
Mapleton, 96 G-18
Marienthal, 90 F-3
Marietta, 30 B-14
Marion, 1906 F-13
Marquette, 593 F-11
Marysville, 3359 B-14
Matfield Green, 33 G-14
Mayetta, 267 C-16
Mayfield, 110 J-12
McCracken, 231 E-7
McCune, 462 J-18
McDonald, 184 B-3
McFarland, 224 D-15
McLouth, 719 D-17
McPherson, 12422 F-12
Meade, 1526 J-5
Medicine Lodge, 2453 J-9
Medora, 350 G-11
Melrose, 60 K-18
Melvern, 423 F-16
Menlo, 50 C-5
Mentor, 100 E-12
Meriden, 622 D-16
Merriam, 11821 *G-3
Michigan Valley, 90 E-17
Milan, 109 J-12
Milberger, 30 E-9
Mildred, 46 G-17
Milford, 384 D-13
Miller, 50 E-15
Milton, 100 J-11
Miltonvale, 484 C-12
Mingo, 30 C-4
Minneapolis, 1983 D-12
Minneola, 705 J-6
Mission, 9504 *G-3
Mission Hills, 3446 *G-4
Mitchell, 20 F-11
Modoc, 20 F-4
Moline, 473 J-15
Mont Ida, 60 F-17
Montana, 80 J-18
Montezuma, 838 H-5
Montrose, 20 B-11
Monument, 80 D-4
Moran, 551 G-17
Morehead, 30 J-17
Morganville, 181 C-13
Morland, 234 C-6
Morrill, 299 A-16
Morrowville, 173 B-13
Moscow, 252 J-3
Mound City, 789 G-18
Mound Valley, 405 J-17
Moundridge, 1531 G-12
Mt. Hope, 805 H-12
Mulberry, 555 H-19
Mullinville, 289 H-7
Mulvane, 4674 J-13
Munden, 143 B-12
Munjor, 300 E-8
Murdock, 100 H-11
Muscotah, 194 C-16
Narka, 113 A-12
Nashville, 118 J-10
Natoma, 392 D-8
Navarre, 60 E-13
Neal, 70 H-15
Nekoma, 30 F-7
Neodesha, 2837 J-16
Neosho Falls, 157 G-17
Neosho Rapids, 235 F-15
Ness City, 1724 F-6
Netawaka, 167 B-16
New Albany, 60 H-16
New Almelo, 40 C-6
New Cambria, 152 E-12
New Lancaster, 30 F-18
New Strawn, 428 F-16
Newton, 16700 G-12
Nickerson, 1137 G-11
Nicodemus, 20 C-7
Niles, 90 D-12
Niotaze, 99 K-16
Norcatur, 198 B-6
N. Newton, 1262 G-12
Northbranch, 30 A-10
Norton, 3017 B-6
Nortonville, 643 C-17
Norway, 40 B-11
Norwich, 455 J-11
Oak Hill, 13 D-12
Oak Valley, 20 J-16
Oaklawn, 3200 N-19
Oakley, 2045 D-4
Oberlin, 2197 B-5
Odin, 100 F-9
Offerle, 228 H-7
Ogallah, 40 D-7
Ogden, 1494 D-14
Oketo, 116 A-14
Olathe, 63352 D-18
Olivet, 59 F-16
Olmitz, 130 F-9
Olpe, 431 F-15
Olsburg, 192 C-14
Onaga, 761 C-15
Oneida, 79 B-16
Osage City, 2689 E-16
Osawatomie, 4590 F-18
Osborne, 1778 C-9
Oskaloosa, 1074 D-17
Oswego, 1870 K-18
Otis, 385 F-8
Ottawa, 10667 E-17
Overbrook, 920 E-16
Overland Park, 111790 D-18
Oxford, 1143 J-13
Ozawkie, 403 D-17
Page City, 60 D-4
Palco, 295 D-7
Palmer, 121 B-13
Paola, 4698 E-18
Paradise, 66 D-9
Park, 150 D-5
Park City, 5081 H-13
Parker, 256 F-18
Parkerville, 28 E-14
Parsons, 11924 J-17
Partridge, 213 G-11
Patterson, 20 G-12
Pauline N-5
Pawnee Rock, 367 F-8
Paxico, 174 D-15
Peabody, 1349 G-13
Peck, 175 J-12
Penalosa, 21 H-10
Pendennis, 10 E-5
Penokee, 60 C-6
Perry, 881 D-17
Perth, 70 K-12
Peru, 206 K-15
Petrolia, 70 H-17
Pfeifer, 40 E-8
Phillipsburg, 2828 B-8
Piedmont, 50 H-15
Pierceville, 90 H-5
Piqua, 125 G-17
Pittsburg, 17775 J-18
Plains, 957 J-5
Plainville, 2173 D-8
Pleasant Gr., 300 E-17
Pleasanton, 1231 G-18
Plevna, 117 G-10
Plymell, 10 H-4
Plymouth, 90 F-15
Pomona, 835 E-17
Portis, 129 C-9
Potter, 90 C-17
Potwin, 448 G-13
Powhattan, 111 B-16
Prairie View, 111 B-7
Prairie Vil., 23186 *G-3
Pratt, 6687 H-9
Prescott, 301 G-18
Preston, 177 H-9
Pretty Prairie, 601 H-11
Princeton, 275 F-17
Protection, 625 K-7
Quenemo, 369 E-17
Quincy, 20 G-16
Quinter, 945 D-6
Radium, 47 G-9

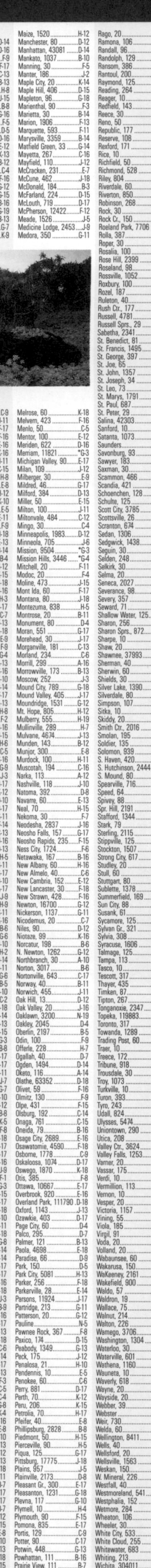

Rago, 20 J-11
Ramona, 106 E-13
Randall, 96 B-11
Randolph, 129 C-14
Ransom, 386 E-6
Rantoul, 200 E-17
Raymond, 125 F-10
Reading, 264 F-16
Reager, 10 B-6
Redfield, 143 H-18
Reece, 30 H-14
Reno, 50 D-17
Republic, 177 B-11
Reserve, 108 A-16
Rexford, 171 C-5
Rice, 10 C-12
Richfield, 50 J-2
Richmond, 528 F-17
Riley, 804 C-14
Riverdale, 60 J-12
Riverton, 850 K-18
Robinson, 268 B-17
Rock, 30 J-13
Rock Cr., 150 C-16
Roeland Park, 7706 *F-3
Rolla, 387 K-2
Roper, 30 H-16
Rosalia, 100 H-14
Rose Hill, 2399 H-13
Roseland, 98 J-18
Rossville, 1052 D-16
Roxbury, 100 F-12
Rozel, 187 G-7
Ruleton, 40 C-2
Rush Ctr., 177 F-8
Russell, 4781 E-9
Russell Sprs., 29 D-4
Sabetha, 2341 B-16
St. Benedict, 81 B-15
St. Francis, 1495 B-2
St. George, 397 D-14
St. Joe, 65 H-12
St. John, 1357 G-9
St. Joseph, 34 C-12
St. Leo, 73 J-10
St. Marys, 1791 D-15
St. Paul, 687 J-17
St. Peter, 29 D-6
Salina, 42303 E-12
Sanford, 10 G-8
Satanta, 1073 J-4
Saunders J-1
Savonburg, 93 H-17
Sawyer, 183 J-9
Saxman, 30 F-11
Scammon, 466 J-18
Scandia, 421 B-11
Schoenchen, 128 E-8
Schulte, 125 H-12
Scott City, 3785 F-4
Scottsville, 26 C-11
Scranton, 674 E-16
Sedan, 1306 K-15
Sedgwick, 1438 G-12
Seguin, 30 C-5
Selden, 248 C-5
Selkirk, 30 F-3
Selma, 20 G-17
Seneca, 2027 B-15
Severance, 98 B-17
Severy, 357 H-15
Seward, 71 G-9
Shallow Water, 125 F-4
Sharon, 256 J-10
Sharon Sprs., 872 D-2
Sharpe, 10 F-16
Shaw, 20 H-17
Shawnee, 37993 D-18
Sherman, 40 J-18
Sherwin, 60 J-18
Shields, 30 E-5
Silver Lake, 1390 D-16
Silverdale, 80 K-13
Simpson, 107 C-11
Sitka, 10 K-7
Skiddy, 20 E-14
Smith Ctr., 2016 B-9
Smolan, 195 E-12
Soldier, 135 C-15
Solomon, 939 E-12
S. Haven, 420 K-12
S. Hutchinson, 2444 G-11
S. Mound, 80 J-17
Spearville, 716 H-7
Speed, 64 B-7
Spivey, 88 J-10
Spr. Hill, 2191 E-18
Stafford, 1344 G-9
Stark, 79 H-17
Sterling, 2115 G-10
Stippville, 125 J-18
Stockton, 1507 C-8
Strong City, 617 F-14
Studley, 20 C-6
Stull, 60 D-17
Stuttgart, 80 B-7
Sublette, 1378 J-4
Summerfield, 169 A-15
Sun City, 88 J-9
Susank, 61 E-9
Sycamore, 125 J-16
Sylvan Gr., 321 D-10
Sylvia, 308 G-10
Syracuse, 1606 G-2
Talmage, 125 D-13
Tampa, 113 F-13
Tasco, 10 C-6
Tescott, 317 D-11
Thayer, 435 J-17
Timken, 87 F-8
Tipton, 267 C-10
Tonganoxie, 2347 D-17
Topeka, 119883 D-16
Toronto, 317 H-16
Towanda, 1289 H-13
Trading Post, 60 F-18
Traer, 10 B-5
Treece, 172 K-18
Tribune, 918 F-2
Trousdale, 30 H-8
Troy, 1073 B-17
Turkville, 10 D-8
Turon, 393 H-10
Tyro, 243 K-16
Udall, 824 J-13
Ulysses, 5474 H-3
Uniontown, 290 H-18
Utica, 208 E-6
Valley Ctr., 3624 H-12
Valley Falls, 1253 C-17
Varner, 20 H-11
Vassar, 175 E-16
Verdi, 10 D-12
Vermillion, 113 B-15
Vernon, 10 G-16
Vesper, 20 D-10
Victoria, 1157 E-8
Vining, 55 C-12
Viola, 185 J-12
Virgil, 91 G-15
Voda, 20 D-6
Volland, 20 D-15
Wabaunsee, 60 D-15
Wakarusa, 150 E-16
WaKeeney, 2161 D-6
Wakefield, 900 D-13
Waldo, 57 D-9
Waldron, 19 K-10
Wallace, 75 D-3
Walnut, 214 H-18
Walton, 226 G-13
Wamego, 3706 D-15
Washington, 1304 B-13
Waterloo, 30 H-11
Waterville, 601 B-14
Wathena, 1160 B-18
Wauneta, 10 K-15
Waverly, 618 F-16
Wayne, 20 B-12
Wayside, 20 K-16
Webber, 39 B-11
Webster C-7
Weir, 730 J-18
Welda, 60 G-17
Wellington, 8411 J-12
Wells, 40 D-12
Wellsford, 20 H-8
Wellsville, 1563 E-17
Weskan, 150 E-2
W. Mineral, 226 J-18
Westfall, 40 D-11
Westmoreland, 541 C-14
Westphalia, 152 G-17
Wetmore, 284 B-16
Wheaton, 106 C-15
Wheeler, 30 B-2
White City, 533 E-14
White Cloud, 255 A-17
Whitewater, 683 G-13
Whiting, 213 C-16
Wichita, 304011 H-12
Willard, 110 D-16
Williamsburg, 261 F-17
Willis, 86 B-16
Willowbrook, 95 G-11
Willowdale, 50 J-10
Wilmore, 78 J-8
Wilmot, 60 J-14
Wilsey, 149 E-14
Wilson, 834 E-10
Winchester, 613 C-17
Windhorst, 10 H-7

KENTUCKY
PG. 100–101

CAPITAL
Frankfort

NICKNAME
Bluegrass State

POPULATION
3,883,723, rank 24

AREA
40,409 sq mi, rank 37

Counties

Cities and Towns

COPELAND PRAIRIE, BIG CYPRESS NATIONAL PRESERVE, FL

LOUISIANA
PG. 102–103

CAPITAL
Baton Rouge

NICKNAME
Pelican State

POPULATION
4,350,579, rank 22

AREA
47,751 sq mi, rank 31

Parishes

Cities and Towns

MAINE
PG. 104–105

CAPITAL
Augusta

NICKNAME
Pine Tree State

POPULATION
1,243,316, rank 39

AREA
33,265 sq mi, rank 39

Counties

Cities and Towns

UNDERGROUND, ATLANTA, GA

Marlboro, 70 P-9
Mars Hill, 1400 E-10
Marshfield, 200 N-12
Marshville, 200 N-11
Martin, 125 R-6
Martinsville, 225 R-6
Masardis, 40 E-9
Matinicus, 60 R-7
Mattawamkeag, 400 J-9
Mayfield Corner L-5
Mcfarlands Corner, 70 P-6
Mechanic Falls, 2388 O-3
Meddybemps, 20 L-12
Medford K-7
Medford Ctr., 10 K-7
Medway, 650 J-8
Mercer, 70 N-4
Mexico, 2302 N-2
Meyers Mill E-10
Milbridge, 500 P-10
Milford, 2228 M-8
Millinocket, 6922 I-8
Millvale, 125 N-8
Milo, 2129 K-7
Milton, 40 P-2
Minot, 400 O-3
Minturn, 175 Q-9
Molunkus, 20 J-9
Monarda, 20 H-9
Monhegan, 50 S-6
Monmouth, 500 O-4
Monroe, 30 N-7
Monson, 100 K-6
Monticello, 300 F-10
Moody, 1000 U-2
Moody Pt., 800 U-2
Moose River, 175 J-3
Moosehead J-5
Moro, 10 F-9
Morrill, 175 P-7
Moscow, 350 L-4
Mt. Vernon, 175 P-4
Mountainville, 150 Q-8
Muscongus, 150 R-6
Myra M-9
Naples, 300 R-2
Naskeag, 80 Q-8
Nequasset, 450 R-5
New Gloucester, 500 R-3
New Harbor, 225 R-6
New Limerick, 40 G-10
New Portland, 125 M-4
New Sharon, 200 N-4
New Sweden, 200 C-10
New Vineyard, 150 M-4
Newagen, 80 S-5
Newburgh Ctr., 250 N-7
Newcastle, 1200 R-5
Newfield, 125 S-1
Newport, 1843 M-6
Newry, 20 P-2
Nobleboro, 400 Q-6
Norcross I-8
Norridgewock, 1496 N-5
N. Alfred, 225 T-2
N. Amity, 30 G-10
N. Anson, 400 M-5
N. Bancroft, 10 H-10
N. Berwick, 1568 U-2
N. Bethel, 50 P-2
N. Bradford, 125 L-7
N. Bridgton, 225 Q-2
N. Brooklin, 125 P-8
N. Brooksville, 80 P-8
N. Castine, 175 P-8
N. Chesterville, 100 N-4
N. Cutler, 20 N-12
N. Deer Isle, 200 Q-8
N. Dexter, 70 L-6
N. Dixmont, 150 N-6
N. E. Carry I-5
N. Edgecomb, 300 R-5
N. Fairfield, 300 N-5
N. Fryeburg, 125 Q-1
N. Guilford, 30 K-6
N. Haven, 300 Q-7
N. Jay, 350 N-3
N. Lebanon, 200 T-1
N. Leeds, 100 O-4
N. Lincoln, 350 K-9
N. Livermore, 100 P-3
N. Lovell, 40 Q-1
N. Lubec M-13
N. Manaville, 10 M-9
N. Monmouth, 600 O-4
N. New Portland, 200 M-4
N. Newburgh, 125 N-6
N. Newport, 60 M-6
N. Newry, 10 O-2
N. Norway, 150 Q-2
N. Palermo, 125 P-6
N. Paris, 150 P-2
N. Parsonsfield, 50 S-1
N. Penobscot, 60 P-8
N. Perry, 200 L-13
N. Pownal, 125 R-3
N. Scarborough, 650 S-3
N. Searsmont, 60 P-7
N. Sedgwick, 100 P-8
N. Shapleigh, 100 S-1
N. Turner, 400 O-3
N. Vassalboro, 750 N-5
N. Wade D-9
N. Waldoboro, 150 Q-6
N. Waterboro, 300 S-2
N. Waterford, 125 P-2
N. Whitefield, 100 Q-5
N. Windham, 4077 S-3
N. Woodstock, 125 P-2
Northeast Harbor, 500 Q-9
Northfield, 40 M-11
Northport, 150 P-7
Norway, 3023 Q-2
Notre Dame, 10 B-10
Number Four, 175 I-5
Oakfield, 500 G-9
Oakland, 3510 N-5
Ocean Park, 1000 T-3
Ocean Pt., 100 S-5
Ogunquit, 800 U-2
Olamon, 175 L-8
Old Orchard Beach, 7789 T-3
Old Town, 8317 M-8
Onawa K-6
Oquossoc, 50 M-2
Orient, 40 H-10
Orland, 500 N-8
Orono, 9789 M-8
Orrington, 350 N-8
Otis L-8
Otisfield, 60 R-2
Otter Crk., 250 Q-9
Ouellette, 30 B-9
Owls Head, 250 Q-7
Oxbow, 50 E-8
Oxford, 1284 Q-2
Palermo, 200 P-6
Palmyra, 200 M-6
Parent, 20 B-10
Paris, 400 Q-2
Parker Head, 150 S-5
Parkman, 60 L-6
Parsonsfield, 20 S-1
Passadumkeag, 100 L-8
Patten, 850 G-9
Pejepscot, 300 R-4
Pemaquid, 125 R-5
Pemaquid Pt., 70 R-5
Penobscot, 125 P-8
Perham, 80 D-9
Perry, 125 M-13
Peru, 125 P-3
Phair D-10
Phillips, 600 M-3
Phippsburg, 200 S-5
Pine Pt., 600 T-3
Pittsfield, 3222 M-6
Pittston, 350 Q-5
Pittston Farm I-4
Plaisted, 50 B-8
Pleasant Pt., 600 M-13
Pleasant Pond K-4
Plymouth, 20 M-6
Poland, 300 Q-3
Popham Beach, 50 S-5
Port Clyde, 300 R-6
Portage, 225 D-8
Porter, 150 S-1
Portland, 64157 S-3
Pownal Ctr., 175 R-3
Prairie, 10 K-7
Prentiss, 40 J-10
Presque Isle, 10550 D-10
Pretty Marsh T-10
Princeton, 125 K-11
Pripet, 70 P-7
Prospect, 150 N-7
Prospect Harbor, 200 P-10
Prouts Neck, 80 T-3
Pulpit Harbor Q-7
Quimby, 70 C-8
Quoddy M-13
Randolph, 1949 O-5
Rangeley, 450 M-2
Raymond, 350 R-3
Razorville, 100 Q-6
Readfield, 500 P-4
Red Beach, 30 L-12
Reed, 30 H-10
Richmond, 1775 Q-5
Richmond Corner, 175 Q-4
Richville, 250 S-2
Riley, 400 P-3
Ripley, 175 M-6
Riverside, 250 P-5
Robbinston, 125 L-13
Robinhood, 100 R-5
Robinsons, 125 E-10
Rockland, 7972 Q-7
Rockport, 900 Q-7
Rockville, 225 Q-7
Rockwood, 30 H-5
Rome, 125 N-4
Roque Bluffs, 10 N-12
Ross Corner, 125 S-2
Round Pond, 350 R-6
Roxbury, 40 N-2
Rumford, 5419 N-2
Rumford Pt., 50 P-2
Sabattus, 1200 O-4
Saco, 15181 T-3
St. Agatha B-9
St. Albans, 200 M-6
St. David, 125 A-9
St. Francis, 250 B-7
St. George, 350 R-6
St. John, 50 B-8
Salem, 90 M-3
Salsbury Cove, 300 P-9
Sandy Cr., 125 N-2
Sanford, 10296 T-2
Sangerville, 500 L-6
Sagonac, 10 L-9
Sargentville, 80 Q-8
Scarborough, 2586 T-3
Scotland, 650 U-2
Seal Cove, 70 U-10
Seal Harbor, 300 Q-9
Searsmont, 90 Q-6
Searsport, 1151 P-7
Seawall, 125 V-11
Sebago, 80 R-2
Sebago Lake, 550 S-2
Sebec, 100 K-7
Sebec Lake K-6
Seboeis, 10 K-8
Seboomook H-5
Sedgwick, 125 P-8
Selden, 10 H-10
Shaker Vil., 125 R-3
Shapleigh, 150 T-1
Sheridan, 250 D-9
Sherman, 200 H-9
Sherman Mills, 300 H-9
Sherman Sta., 150 H-9
Shin Pond, 60 G-8
Shirley Mills, 150 K-5
Sidney, 150 P-5
Silvers Mills, 200 L-6
Sinclair, 100 B-9
Skinner J-2
Skowhegan, 6990 N-5
Small Pt. Beach, 50 S-4
Smithfield, 80 N-5
Smyrna Mills, 200 G-9
Soldier Pond, 100 B-8
Solon, 400 M-4
Somerset, 60 M-4
Somerville, 90 P-6
Somesville, 250 P-9
Songo Lock, 500 R-2
Sorrento, 100 P-9
S. Acton, 50 T-1
S. Addison, 100 P-11
S. Andover, 30 N-2
S. Arm N-1
S. Bancroft H-10
S. Berwick, 2300 U-2
S. Bridgton, 150 R-2
S. Casco, 650 R-2
S. China, 300 P-5
S. Dover, 30 L-7
S. Eliot, 3112 U-1
S. Gardiner, 50 Q-5
S. Gouldsboro, 100 P-10
S. Gray, 400 R-3
S. Hancock, 400 P-9
S. Harpswell, 550 S-4
S. Hiram, 900 S-1
S. Lagrange, 100 L-8
S. Lebanon, 350 U-1
S. Levant, 125 M-7
S. Liberty, 70 P-6
S. Limington, 200 S-2
S. Lincoln, 150 K-8
S. Lubec, 100 M-13
S. Monmouth, 300 O-4
S. Orrington, 450 N-8
S. Paris, 2320 Q-2
S. Parsonsfield, 60 S-1
S. Penobscot, 125 P-8
S. Portland, 23163 S-3
S. Princeton, 30 K-11
S. Robbinston, 125 L-13
S. Sanford, 3929 T-2
S. Sebec, 10 L-7
S. Springfield, 10 K-10
S. Trescott, 40 M-13
S. Waldoboro, 225 R-6
S. Warren, 250 Q-6
S. Waterford, 50 Q-2
S. Windham, 1500 S-3
S. Windsor P-5
S. Woodstock, 125 P-2
S. Woodville J-8
Southwest Harbor, 950 Q-9
Spaulding, 20 L-9
Spragueville D-10
Springfield, 100 J-10
Springvale, 3542 T-2
Spruce Head, 300 R-7
Squa Pan, 20 F-9
Squaw Brook H-5
Stacyville, 50 H-8
Standish, 600 S-2
Starboard, 225 N-12
Starks, 30 N-4
State Road, 100 D-10
Steep Falls, 300 S-2
Stetson, 100 M-7
Steuben, 150 P-10
Stickney Corner, 150 Q-6
Stillwater, 1600 M-8
Stockholm, 100 C-9
Stockton Sprs., 550 P-7
Stonington, 850 Q-8
Stow, 80 Q-1
Stratton, 450 L-3
Stricklands, 70 M-8
Strong, 550 M-3
Sullivan, 175 P-9
Sumner, 100 P-3
Sunset, 300 Q-8
Sunshine, 150 Q-8
Surry, 150 P-8
Swans Island, 100 Q-9
Swanville, 250 P-7
Sweden, 20 Q-2
Tarratine L-5
Temple, 250 N-3
Tenants Harbor, 500 R-6
The Forks, 20 K-4
Thomaston, 2445 Q-6
Thompson Corners, 20 J-10
Thorndike, 200 N-6
Timoney, 80 G-10
Tomah J-11
Topsfield, 60 K-11
Topsham, 6147 R-4
Town Hill S-11
Trenton, 100 P-9
Trevett, 200 S-5
Troutdale K-5
Troy, 100 N-6
Tunk Lake, 40 N-10
Turner, 550 O-3
Turner Ctr., 150 O-3
Union, 450 Q-6
Unionville, 60 N-10
Unity, 600 N-6
Upper Abbot, 125 L-6
Upper Dresden Q-5
Upper Frenchville, 125 B-9
Upper Gloucester, 450 R-3
Upton, 30 N-1
Van Buren, 2759 B-10
Vanceboro, 60 J-11
Vassalboro, 350 P-5
Verona N-8
Vienna, 125 P-4
Vinalhaven, 750 R-8
Waite, 80 K-11
Waldo, 50 P-7
Waldoboro, 1420 Q-6
Wales Corner, 150 O-4
Wallagrass, 125 B-8
Waltham, 50 N-9
Wards Cove, 200 R-2
Warren, 900 Q-6
Washburn, 800 D-9
Washington, 175 Q-6
Waterboro, 900 T-2
Waterford, 50 Q-2
Waterville, 17173 N-5
Waukeag, 175 P-9
Wayne, 200 P-4
Webster Corner, 1000 O-4
Weeks Mills, 150 P-5
Welchville, 600 Q-3
Weld, 200 N-3
Weld Corner, 20 N-3
Wellington, 50 L-5
Wells, 1000 U-2
Wells Beach, 500 U-2
Wesley, 30 M-11
W. Athens, 60 M-5
W. Baldwin, 175 R-2
W. Bethel, 150 P-1
W. Bowdoin, 350 R-4
W. Buxton, 400 S-2
W. Charleston, 60 L-7
W. Corinth, 175 M-7
W. Enfield, 250 K-8
W. Falmouth, 950 S-3
W. Farmington, 3500 N-4
W. Forks, 20 K-4
W. Franklin, 250 N-9
W. Gorham, 500 S-2
W. Gray, 225 R-3
W. Harrington, 125 N-10
W. Lebanon, 350 T-1
W. Levant, 40 M-7
W. Lubec, 150 M-13
W. Mills, 80 N-4
W. Minot, 175 O-3
W. Mt. Vernon, 60 N-4
W. Newfield, 90 S-1
W. Old Town, 20 M-8
W. Paris, 550 P-2
W. Pembroke, 300 M-12
W. Penobscot, 40 P-8
W. Peru, 350 P-3
W. Point, 175 S-4
W. Poland, 350 R-3
W. Princeton, 70 L-11
W. Ripley, 20 M-6
W. Rockport, 450 Q-7
W. Seboeis, 10 J-7
W. Sidney, 400 P-5
W. Southport, 300 S-5
W. Sumner, 50 P-3
W. Trenton, 225 U-10
W. Tremont, 300 U-10
W. Washington, 125 Q-6
Westbrook, 16121 S-3
Westfield, 150 E-10
Westmanland C-9
Weston, 20 H-10
Wheelock, 10 B-8
Whitefield, 125 Q-5
Whiting, 100 M-12
Whitneyville, 150 N-11
Williamsport, 50 K-6
Wilsons Mills, 20 M-1
Wilton, 2453 N-3
Winn, 150 J-9
Winnecook, 90 N-6
Winslow, 5436 N-5
Winslows Mills, 90 Q-6
Winter Harbor, 250 P-10
Winterport, 1274 N-7
Winterville, 125 D-8
Winthrop, 2819 P-4
Wiscasset, 1233 R-5
Woodland, 1287 C-9
Woodland (Baileyville), 1287 L-12
Woolwich, 300 R-5
Wyman, 200 P-10
Wytopitlock, 40 I-10
Yarmouth, 3338 S-3
York Beach, 1700 U-2
York Harbor, 2555 U-2
York Vil., 2000 U-2

MARYLAND
PG. 106–108

Maryland ABC 123

CAPITAL
Annapolis

NICKNAME
Old Line State

POPULATION
5,071,604, rank 19

AREA
10,460 sq mi, rank 42

Counties
Allegany, 74946 B-5
Anne Arundel, 427239 F-13
Baltimore, 692134 C-13
Calvert, 51372 H-14
Caroline, 27035 G-17
Carroll, 123372 C-11
Cecil, 71347 C-16
Charles, 101154 J-12
Dorchester, 30236 J-16
Frederick, 150208 C-9
Garrett, 28138 C-2
Harford, 182132 C-15
Howard, 187328 E-12
Kent, 17842 E-16
Montgomery, 757027 E-11
Prince George's, 729268 G-13
Queen Anne's, 33953 E-17
St. Mary's, 75974 K-13
Somerset, 24440 L-17
Talbot, 30549 G-16
Washington, 121393 B-7
Wicomico, 76339 J-18
Worcester, 35028 K-19

Cities and Towns
* City indexed to pg. 108
\# Independent city population not included in county figures.

Aberdeen, 13087 C-15
Accident, 349 B-2
Accokeek, 4477 H-12
Accokeek Acres, 1500 H-12
Adamstown, 650 D-10
Adelphi, 13524 K-4
Aldino, 350 C-15
Allen, 200 H-18
Allens Fresh J-12
Andrews, 70 K-16
Annapolis, 33187 F-14
Annapolis Jct. H-7
Antietam, 300 Q-8
Aquasco, 250 H-13
Arbutus, 19750 F-4
Arden-on-the-Severn, 2427 K-6
Arnold, 20261 F-14
Arundel on the Bay, 1000 F-14
Arundel Vil., 8000 G-6
Ashton, 1800 C-2
Aspen Hill, 45494 F-12
Avenue, 500 K-13
Baden, 225 H-13
Baldwin, 850 C-14
Baltimore, 736014 D-13
Baltimore Highlands, 10400 F-5
Banks O'Dee K-16
Barclay, 170 E-17
Barnesville, 170 E-10
Barrellville B-4
Barstow, 150 G-6
Barton, 530 C-3
Bartonsville, 900 D-10
Bay Ridge, 2300 F-14
Bayberry K-8
Bayside Beach H-9
Bayview B-16
Beaver Crk., 200 B-9
Beacon Hill L-9
Beallsville, 150 E-10
Bel Air, 8860 C-15
Bel Alton, 400 J-12
Belcamp, 1900 C-15
Bellevue, 175 H-15
Bellhaven Beach J-8
Beltsville, 14476 F-12
Belvedere Hts., 7900 K-8
Benedict, 450 J-13
Benfield J-5
Bentley Sprs., 175 B-13
Berlin, 2616 K-20
Berwyn Hts., 2952 K-5
Bestgate J-6
Bethesda, 62936 F-11
Bethlehem, 600 G-16
Betterton, 360 C-16
Beulah, 125 H-17
Beverly Beach, 1600 G-14
Bishop, 200 J-20
Bishops Head K-16
Bishopville, 300 J-20
Bivalve K-17
Bladensburg, 8064 L-5
Bloomington C-3
Bond Mill Park, 3400 H-6
Boonsboro, 2445 C-9
Boring, 550 C-13
Bowie, 37589 F-13
Bowleys Quarters, 5595 D-14
Bowling Green, 2000 C-4
Boxhill North, 2900 C-15
Boxiron, 30 L-19
Bozman H-15
Braddock Hts., 4778 D-9
Bradshaw B-10
Brandywine, 1406 H-13
Brentwood, 3005 L-5
Breton Bay, 750 K-13
Bridgeport, 2702 B-9
Bridgeport, 100 F-17
Brightwood Acres K-10
Brinklow G-4
Brock Hall, 1200 H-13
Brookeville, 54 E-12
Brooklandville, 2200 B-5
Brooklyn Park E-5
Brooms Island, 400 J-14
Brownsville F-16
Brunswick, 5117 D-9
Bryans Road, 3809 H-12
Bryantown, 550 H-13
Buckeystown, 450 D-10
Bucklodge, 200 E-10
Bucktown J-16
Burkittsville, 194 D-9
Burnt Store J-13
Burrsville, 175 E-17
Burtonsville, 5853 E-12
Butler, 225 C-13
Buttertown, 350 C-16
Cabin Creek, 175 I-16
Cabin John, 4500 K-2
California, 7626 K-14
Calvert, 450 B-16
Calvert Beach, 1500 J-14
Calvert Manor, 650 H-12
Calverton, 12610 K-5
Cambridge, 11514 H-16
Camp Sprs., 16392 G-12
Cape St. Claire, 7878 F-14
Capitol Hts., 3633 M-5
Captains Hill, 600 K-20
Cardiff, 650 B-15
Carney, 25578 C-7
Carpenter Pt., 400 C-16
Carrollton C-12
Cascade, 1500 B-10
Catonsville, 35233 E-13
Cavetown, 1400 B-9
Cearfoss, 800 B-8
Cecilton, 489 D-17
Cedar Beach E-9
Cedar Gr., 950 E-11
Cedar Lawn, 900 B-8
Cedarton, 30 A-3
Cedarville, 250 H-13
Centreville, 2097 F-16
Ceresville L-10
Champ, 150 K-16
Chaneyville, 500 H-13
Chaptico, 175 K-13
Charlestown, 578 C-16
Charlotte Hall, 1992 J-13
Chase C-10
Chattolanee B-5
Chelsea Beach, 4400 J-7
Cheltenham, 650 H-13
Cherry Hill B-17
Chesaco Park D-8
Chesapeake Beach, 2403 H-14
Chesapeake City, 735 C-17
Chesapeake Ranch Estates, 5423 K-14
Chester, 1900 F-15
Chesterfield M-5
Chestertown, 4005 E-16
Chesterville D-16
Cheverly, 6023 F-12
Chevy Chase, 2675 K-3
Chickamuxen J-11
Childs B-17
Chillum, 31309 L-4
Choptank, 250 H-16
Church Cr., 113 J-16
Church Hill, 481 E-16
Churchton, 1800 G-14
Churchville, 1200 C-15
Claggettsville, 250 D-11
Claiborne, 225 G-15
Clarksburg, 600 E-11
Clarksville, 900 E-12
Clear Spr., 415 B-8
Clements, 150 K-13
Clinton, 19987 G-12
Cloverly H-4
Cobb Island, 750 K-13
Cockeysville, 19388 C-13
Cokesbury, 200 L-18
Coleman, 250 D-16
Colesville, 18819 F-12
College Park, 21927 K-5
Colonial Park K-10
Coltons Pt., 350 K-13
Columbia, 75883 E-12
Columbia Beach, 700 G-14
Comus E-10
Conowingo B-15
Contee K-1
Cooksville, 125 D-12
Copenhaver J-2
Coral Hills, 11032 M-5
Cordova, 400 G-16
Cornersville, 1100 J-16
Corriganville, 1000 B-4
Costen, 80 L-18
Cove Pt., 300 J-14
Craigtown, 550 C-16
Crapo, 70 K-16
Creagerstown C-10
Crellin D-1
Cresaptown, 2100 C-4
Crisfield, 2880 M-17
Crocheron K-16
Crofton, 12781 F-13
Crosby, 300 C-15
Crownsville, 1514 F-14
Crumpton, 500 E-16
Crystal Beach D-16
Cub Hill C-7
Cumberland, 23706 B-4
Damascus, 3817 D-11
Dames Quarter, 200 L-17
Daniel, 650 D-12
Dares Beach, 1400 H-14
Darlington, 350 B-15
Deale, 4151 G-14
Deer Park, 419 D-2
Delight A-2
Delmar, 1430 J-18
Denton, 2977 G-17
Derwood, 2000 E-11
Dickerson, 250 E-10
District Hts., 6704 M-5
Dominion, 600 E-15
Doncaster J-11
Dorrs Corner K-5
Dorsey, 1000 G-3
Doubs, 750 D-10
Dowell, 750 K-14
Drayden L-14
Drum Pt., 1700 K-14
Dublin, 650 B-15
Dufief H-1
Dundalk, 65800 E-14
Dunkirk, 750 G-13
Eagle Harbor, 38 H-13
Earleville, 125 D-16
E. New Market, 153 H-17
Easton, 9372 G-16
Eastview, 650 C-12
Eckhart Mines B-4
Eden, 600 K-18
Edesville, 250 E-15
Edgemere, 9226 E-14
Edgewater, 2900 N-7
Edgewood, 23378 C-15
Eldersburg, 9720 D-12
Eldorado, 49 H-17
Elioak F-1
Elk Mill B-17
Elk Neck C-16
Elkridge, 12953 E-13
Elkton, 9073 C-17
Ellerslie, 600 B-4
Ellicott City, 41396 E-13
Elliott, 10 K-16
Elvaton, 3500 J-6
Emmitsburg, 1688 B-10
Emmorton, 4000 C-15
Emory Gr. G-2
Epping Forest J-6
Essex, 40872 D-14
Etchison, 350 E-11
Evergreen Park F-8
Ewell, 300 M-16
Ewingville, 150 E-16
Fairland, 19828 F-12
Fairlee, 250 E-15
Fairmount L-17
Fairmount Hts., 1238 M-5
Fairview B-9
Fallston, 5730 C-14
Farmington, 350 B-16
Faulkner, 250 J-12
Feagaville, 600 D-10
Federal Hill B-14
Federalsburg, 2365 H-17
Ferndale, 16355 G-5
Fiddlesburg J-10
Fishing Cr., 300 K-15
Flintstone, 250 B-5
Flohrville, 950 D-12
Forest Hts., 2859 N-4
Forestville, 16731 N-6
Fork C-14
Ft. Howard E-14
Fountain Head, 1000 B-9
Fowblesburg, 600 C-13
Franklinville A-10
Frederick, 40148 D-10
Fredericktown C-16
Friendly, 9028 G-12
Friendship, 400 G-14
Friendsville, 577 B-1
Frostburg, 8075 B-3
Fruitland, 3511 K-18
Fullerton, 10100 C-8
Fulton, 850 E-12
Funkstown, 1136 C-8
Gaithersburg, 39542 E-11
Galena, 324 D-17
Galestown, 123 H-17
Galesville, 600 G-14
Gambrier, 1000 C-12
Gambrills K-5
Gapland, 100 D-9
Garrison, 5045 B-3
Georgetown D-17
Germantown, 41145 E-11
Gittings B-9
Gibson, 650 C-15
Gibson Island K-8
Girdletree, 300 L-19
Glen Arm, 500 C-14
Glen Burnie, 37305 E-13
Glen Echo, 234 K-2
Glen Echo Hts. K-2
Glen Hills F-1
Glenarden, 5025 F-12
Glencoe, 450 C-13
Glendale G-6
Glenn Dale, 9689 F-13
Glenwood, 650 D-12
Glyndon, 1200 C-13
Golden Beach, 2944 J-13
Goldsboro, 185 F-17
Golts D-17
Goodwill, 150 L-18
Gorman, 175 D-2
Gortner D-1
Goshen, 1300 E-11
Graceham, 450 C-10
Granite D-13
Grantsville, 505 B-2
Grasonville, 2439 F-15
Great Mills, 2600 K-14
Green Haven, 14416 E-14
Green Hill, 50 K-17
Greenbelt, 21096 F-12
Greensboro, 1632 F-17
Guilford, 5900 H-2
Hagerstown, 35445 B-9
Hack Pt., 400 D-16
Halethorpe, 150 F-4
Halfway, 8873 C-8
Hampstead, 2608 C-13
Hampton, 4926 B-6
Hancock, 1926 B-7
Hanover G-4
Harewood *C-10
Harewood Park, 3400 D-15
Harmans *H-4
Harmony G-17
Harney B-11
Harpers Choice *F-1
Harrisonville *C-2
Harrisville, 600 B-16
Harrisville, 450 D-11
Harundale *H-6
Harwood G-13
Harwood Park *G-3
Havre de Grace, 8952 C-16
Hebbville, 10900 *D-3
Hebron, 665 J-17
Helen, 500 J-13
Henderson, 66 F-17
Henrys Crossroads J-17
Herald Harbor, 1707 *K-6
Hereford, 550 C-13
Heritage Harbor *M-6
Hermanville, 1100 K-14
Hernwood *C-2
Hickory C-15
Hickory Ridge *G-1
High Ridge H-6
Highland, 800 E-12
Highland Beach, 102 F-14
Hillandale, 10318 J-4
Hillcrest Hts., 17136 G-12
Hillsboro, 164 F-16
Hillsmere Shores, 3321 *N-8
Hobbs, 150 G-17
Holbrook *C-2
Holly Beach *E-10
Hollywood, 650 K-14
Honga, 225 K-15
Hoopersville K-15
Hopewell, 550 M-17
Hudson, 250 H-15
Hughesville, 1319 J-13
Hunt Valley C-13
Huntingtown, 150 H-14
Hurlock, 1706 H-17
Hutton D-1
[illegible] B-8
Hyattstown, 60 D-10
Hyattsville, 13864 F-12
Ijamsville, 225 D-10
Ilchester *F-3
Indian Head, 3531 H-11
Indian Sprs. B-7
Indiantown, 60 K-19
Ingleside, 125 E-17
Ironshire, 225 K-19
Ironsides J-11
Issue K-12
Jacksonville, 900 C-14
Jacobsville *J-7
Jarrettsville, 2148 C-14
Jefferson D-9
Jessup, 6537 E-13
[illegible] K-17
Johnsville, 125 C-11
Jonestown, 500 H-17
Joppa *B-10
Joppatowne, 11084 D-15
Keedysville, 464 C-9
Kennedyville, 175 D-16
Kensington, 1713 J-3
Kentland L-6
Kenmore Park, 20 D-16
Kenwood, 1000 *D-8
Kenwood Beach, 600 J-14
Kettering, 9901 M-6
Keymar, 350 C-11
Keysers Ridge B-2
Keysville, 80 C-11
Kings Contrivance *H-1
Kings Park *C-2
Kingston, 175 L-17
Kingstown, 1660 E-16
Kingsville, 3550 *A-9
Kitzmiller, 275 D-2
Knollwood K-5
Knoxville D-9
La Plata, 5841 J-12
La Vale, 2600 B-4
Ladiesburg, 250 C-11
Lake Shore, 13269 E-14
Lakesville K-16
Landover, 5052 L-5
Landover Hills, 2074 L-5
Langley Park, 17474 K-4
Lanham, 7800 L-6
Lansdowne, 2500 *F-5
Largo, 9475 M-6
Laurel, 19438 F-13
Lawsonia, 1326 M-17
Layhill H-4
Laytonsville, 248 E-11
Le Gore, 350 C-10
Leitersburg, 900 B-9
Leonardtown, 1475 K-13
[illegible] D-11
Lewisdale K-4
Lewistown, 600 C-10
Lewistown, 175 G-16
Lexington Park, 9943 K-14
Libertytown, 250 C-11
[illegible] K-19
Lineboro B-13
Linkwood J-16
Linthicum, 7547 *G-5
Lions Corner *H-6
Lisbon, 250 D-12
Little Orleans B-6
Loch Lynn Hts., 461 D-2
Lochearn, 25240 D-13
Lonaconing, 1122 C-3
Londontown, 5700 F-14
Long Beach, 1000 J-14
Long Green, 1000 C-14
Long Reach *G-2
Longridge K-18
Loveville, 850 K-13
Longwoods, 250 G-16
Love Pt., 30 F-15
Lower Marlboro, 450 H-13
Luke, 184 C-3
Lusby, 450 J-14
Lutherville, 16442 D-14
Luxmanor J-3
Lynch, 200 D-16
Madison, 225 H-15
Madison, 70 K-16
Madonna C-14
Mago Vista Beach *K-8
Manchester, 2810 B-12
Manokin, 150 L-18
Marbury, 1244 H-11
Mardela Sprs., 360 J-17
Margate *H-6
Marion, 600 L-17
Marley, 11200 E-14
Marriottsville D-12
Marshall Hall H-11
Marydel, 143 E-17
Maryland City, 6813 *J-2
Maryland Line B-13
Marywood, 6000 C-15
Massey, 200 D-17
Mattawoman, 300 H-12
Matthews, 100 G-16
Mauganville, 2100 B-8
Mayo, 2537 G-14
McAlpine *A-5
McCoole *F-2
McDaniel, 400 C-3
McHenry, 200 G-15
McKay Beach, 600 C-2
Mechanicsville, 750 L-14
Melitota, 225 J-13
Melrose, 750 E-15
Melson, 225 B-12
Middle River, 24616 L-17
Middleborough D-14
Middleburg *E-9
Middletown, 1834 C-11
Midland D-9
Midland, 574 B-13
Midlothian C-3
Milford C-3
Millersville *D-4
Millington, 409 *K-5
Mitchellville E-17
Monie, 50 L-17
Monkton C-14
Monrovia D-11
Montebello *H-3
Montgomery Vil., 32315 E-11
Montpelier, 11800 J-6
Montrose, 4800 J-2
Morgantown, 300 K-12
Morganza, 500 K-13
Moscow C-3
Mt. Airy, 3730 C-9
Mt. Carmel D-11
Mt. Harmony, 300 *J-8
Mt. Pleasant, 550 *E-2
Mt. Rainier, 7954 C-12
Mt. Savage, 1200 L-5
Mt. Vernon, 300 B-4
Mt. Victoria K-17
Mt. Vista K-12
Mt. Wesley, 80 *A-9
Mtn. L-19
Mtn. *A-10
Mtn. Lake Park, 1938 D-2
Mountaindale, 300 C-10
Muirkirk J-6
Myersville, 464 C-9
Nanjemoy, 300 J-11
Nanticoke, 250 K-17
Neavitt, 250 H-15
New Carrollton, 12002 F-12
New Market, 328 D-11
New Midway C-11
New Windsor, 757 C-11
Newark, 175 K-19
Newburg, 300 K-12
Newcomb, 600 G-15
Newmarket J-13
Newport, 175 J-12
Newton, 250 G-16
Newtown, 80 D-15
Newtown J-12
Nikep, 650 C-3
Normans, 650 F-15
Norrisville, 300 B-14
N. Beach, 1173 H-14
N. East, 1913 C-16
N. Pt. Village *E-8
N. Shore *K-8
Nottingham *C-9
Oak Crest *K-1
Oakland, 2078 D-12
Oakland, 1741 C-1
Oakland Mills *G-2
Oakview K-4
Oakville, 50 K-18
Oakwood, 400 B-15
Ocean City, 5146 K-20
Ocean Pines, 4251 J-20
Odenton, 12833 F-13
Oldtown, 200 C-5
Olivet Hill, 250 D-17
Olney, 23019 E-12
Oraville J-13
Orchard Beach, 4400 *H-7
Orchard Hills J-9
Oriole, 200 L-17
Overlea, 12137 D-14
Owen Brown *G-2
Owings H-14
Owings Mills, 9474 C-13
Oxford, 699 F-15
Oxon Hill, 8900 G-12
Palmer Park, 7019 L-6
Paradise Beach *H-8
Paramount A-10
Park Hall, 800 L-14
Parkton B-13
Parkville, 31617 D-14
Parole, 10054 N-11
Parsonsburg, 600 J-19
Pasadena, 10012 *J-6
Patapsco C-12
Patuxent J-13
Patuxent *K-3
Pendennis Mt. M-13
Perry Hall, 22723 D-14
Perryman, 2160 C-15
Perryville, 2456 C-16
Petersburg, 175 H-17
Pfeiffer Corners *G-2
Phoenix, 500 C-13
Pikesville, 24815 D-13
Pine Orchard *E-1
Pinehurst *J-9
Piney Pt., 700 L-14
Pinto C-4
Piscataway, 150 H-12
Pisgah, 175 J-11
Pittsville, 602 J-19
Pleasant Hills, 2591 C-14
Plum Pt. H-14
Pocomoke City, 3922 L-18
Pt. of Rocks, 850 E-9
Pomfret H-12
Pomona, 150 E-16
Pomonkey, 750 H-12
Poolesville, 3796 E-10
Popes Cr., 125 J-12
Port Deposit, 685 C-16
Port Republic J-14
Port Tobacco, 36 J-12
Potomac, 45634 F-11
Potomac Hts., 1524 H-11
Potomac Park, 1900 C-4
Potomac View, 200 K-12
Powellville, 225 K-19
Preston, 437 H-17
Price, 100 E-16
Prince Frederick, 1885 J-14
Princess Anne, 1666 K-18
Providence *B-7
Public Landing, 90 L-19
Pumphrey, 5483 *G-5
Pumpkin Ctr. C-5
Putty Hll. *C-7
Pylesville, 350 B-14
Quantico, 300 J-17
Queen Anne, 250 F-16
Queenstown, 453 F-16
Quince Orchard, 18456 E-11
Randallstown, 26277 D-13
Randle Cliff Beach, 800 H-14
Randolph Hills, 14300 J-3
Rawlings, 750 C-4
Rayville B-13
Redland, 16145 E-11
Rehobeth, 50 L-18
Reids Gr., 80 J-17
Reisterstown, 19314 D-13
Reliance, 20 H-17
Rhodes Pt. M-16
Rhodesdale, 70 H-17
Riderwood *B-5
Ridge, 400 L-15
Ridgely, 1034 F-17
Ridgeway *J-4
Ringgold B-9
Rising Sun, 1263 B-16
Rison J-11
Ritchie M-6
Riva, 3438 *N-6
Riverdale, 5185 L-5
Riverside J-11
Riviera Beach, 11376 E-14
Robbins, 40 J-16
Roberts, 100 E-16
Rock Hall, 1584 E-15
Rock Pt., 750 K-13
Rockdale, 16100 D-13
Rockville, 44835 F-11
Rocky Ridge, 450 C-10
Rodgers Forge *C-6
Romancoke, 800 G-15
Rosaryville, 8976 G-13
Rose Haven, 1400 H-14
Rosedale, 18703 D-14
Rosedale Estates N-5
Rosemont, 256 D-9
Rossmoor Leisure World, 6182 H-3
Rossville *D-8
Royal Oak, 750 G-15
Rugby Hall *L-7
Rumbley L-17
Ruthsburg, 125 F-16
Ruxton *B-5
Sabillasville, 350 B-10
St. Charles, 28717 H-12
St. Clement Shores, 800 K-13
St. George Island, 250 L-14
St. Inigoes, 650 L-14
St. James C-9
St. Leonard, 250 J-14
St. Mary's City, 900 L-14
St. Michaels, 1301 G-15
Salem J-17
Salisbury, 20592 K-18
Sandgates, 550 J-14
Sandy Spr., 1100 G-4
Sandyville, 1000 C-12
Sassafras, 100 D-17
Savage, 6000 E-13
Scaggsville E-12
Scientists Cliffs, 500 J-14
Scotland, 300 L-15
Scotland Beach, 125 L-15
Seabrook, 9700 K-6
Seat Pleasant, 5359 M-5
Secretary, 528 H-16
Security J-10
Selby Beach G-14
Selbysport B-2
Seneca E-11
Severn, 24499 E-13
Severn Gr. M-11
Severna Park, 25879 F-14
Shady Side, 4107 G-14
Sharpsburg, 659 C-8
Sharptown, 609 J-17
Shawsville, 250 C-14
Shelltown, 40 M-18
Sherwood, 100 G-15
Sherwood Forest *L-7
Shiloh, 250 K-12
Shore Acres *K-8
Shoreham Beach, 1300 G-14
Showell, 225 J-20
Silesia G-12
Silver Hill, 16500 N-5
Silver Run B-12
Silver Spr., 76046 F-12
Simpsonville, 4400 E-12
Skidmore *L-9
Skipton, 200 G-16
Smallwood, 950 C-12
Smithsburg, 1221 B-9
Smithville, 150 G-17
Smithville, 30 J-15
Snow Hill, 2217 L-19
Solley *H-7
Solomons, 300 K-14
Somerset, 993 K-3
S. Gate, 27564 *H-6
Sparks, 1800 C-13
Sparrows Pt. *G-8
Spencerville, 2900 H-4
Spr. Gap C-4
Spr. Garden Estates, 2400 C-10
Stevenson *B-4
Stevensville, 1862 F-15
Still Pond, 350 D-16
Stockton, 350 L-19
Stronghold E-10
Sudlersville, 428 E-17
Suitland, 17300 G-12
Sunderland, 1400 H-14
Sunnybrook, 2300 C-14
Sunshine E-12
Swanton C-2
Sykesville, 2303 D-12
Takoma Park, 16700 K-4
Tall Timbers, 300 L-14
Tammany Manor L-8
Taneytown, 3695 B-11
Tantallon, 7900 H-12
Taylors Island, 100 J-15
Taylorsville, 900 C-12
Temple Hills, 6865 N-5
Templeville, 66 E-17
Texas *A-5
Thayerville C-2
Thompsontown, 90 H-17
Thurmont, 3398 C-10
Tilghman, 700 H-15
Tilghmanton, 500 C-8
Timonium D-13
Toddville, 150 K-16
Tolchester Beach, 175 E-15
Tompkinsville K-13
Tonytank, 3500 K-18
Town Pt., 550 C-17
Towson, 49445 D-14
Tracys Landing G-14
Trappe, 974 H-16
Tunis Mills, 225 G-15
Tuscarora E-10
Twin Harbors *K-7
Tyaskin, 250 K-17
Tylerton M-16
Union Bridge, 910 C-11
Union Mills, 300 B-12
Uniontown, 300 C-11
Unionville, 175 G-16
Unionville C-11
Upper Fairmount L-17
Upper Falls *B-9
Upper Hill, 175 L-17
Upper Marlboro, 745 G-13
Upperco C-13
Urbana, 400 D-10
Vale Summit C-4
Valley Lee, 400 L-14
Venice on the Bay *H-8
Ventnor *J-9
Vienna, 264 J-17
Waldorf, 15058 H-12
Walker Mill, 10920 M-5
Walkersville, 4145 C-10
Wango K-19
Wards Chapel *B-1
Warwick, 300 D-17
Waterbury *K-6
Waterloo, 900 E-13
Waterview, 100 K-17
Webster, 1200 C-15
Welcome, 175 J-11
Wellville J-14
Wenona, 500 L-16
Wesley, 80 K-16
W. Denton, 300 G-17
W. Friendship, 700 D-12
W. Liberty, 350 B-14
Westernport, 2454 C-3
Westminster, 13068 C-12
Westover, 100 L-17
Westphalia N-6
Westview *E-4
Wetipquin, 100 K-17
Whaleysville, 250 J-19
Wheaton, 53720 F-12
White Hall, 300 C-13
White Marsh, 8183 *C-9
White Oak, 18671 J-4
White Plains, 3560 H-12
White Pt. Beach, 200 K-14
Whiteburg L-18
Whiteford, 700 B-15
Whitehaven, 70 K-17
Whites Ferry E-9
Whiton, 30 K-19
Wilde Lake *F-1
Willards, 708 J-19
Williamsburg, 60 H-17
Williamsport, 2103 C-8
Williston, 450 G-17
Willows, 900 H-14
Windyhill H-16
Winfield D-12
Wittman, 300 G-15
Wolfsville C-9
Woodbine, 400 D-12
Woodfield, 2500 E-11
Woodland Pt., 125 K-12
Woodlawn, 32907 *D-4
Woodlawn, 1600 B-16
Woodmoor *D-4
Woodmore, 2874 L-7
Woodsboro, 513 C-10
Woodstock *D-1
Woodyard N-6
Woolford, 150 J-15
Worthington *F-2
Worthington *A-3
Worton, 225 D-16
Wye Mills, 300 F-16
Yellow Sprs., 1100 C-10
Zihlman B-4

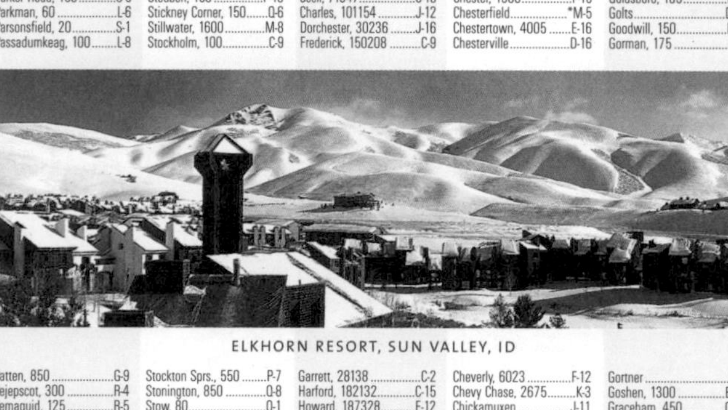
ELKHORN RESORT, SUN VALLEY, ID

MASSACHUSETTS
PG. 109–111

Massachusetts 123-ZBC The Spirit of America

CAPITAL
Boston

NICKNAME
Bay State

POPULATION
6,092,352, rank 13

AREA
8,284 sq mi, rank 45

Counties
Barnstable, 186605 K-17
Berkshire, 139352 D-2
Bristol, 506325 H-13
Dukes, 11639 M-17
Essex, 670080 B-14
Franklin, 70092 C-5
Hampden, 456310 F-7
Hampshire, 146568 E-4
Middlesex, 1398468 D-13
Nantucket, 6012 N-19
Norfolk, 616087 F-13
Plymouth, 435276 H-15
Suffolk, 663906 E-14
Worcester, 709705 D-9

Cities and Towns
* City indexed to pg. 109

Abington, 13817 G-15
Accord, 2300 F-15
Acoaxet, 175 L-14
Acton, 2700 D-12
Acushnet, 3170 K-15
Adams, 6356 C-3
Adamsville, 200 B-5
Agawam, 27323 G-6
Alford, 100 F-1
Allerton *G-9
Amesbury, 12109 A-15
Amherst, 17824 E-6
Andover, 8242 C-14
Arlington, 44630 D-14
Arlington Hts. *D-4
Ashburnham, 1000 C-9
Ashby, 550 B-10
Ashfield, 550 D-5
Ashland, 12066 F-12
Ashley Falls, 450 G-2
Assinippi, 2700 F-15
Assonet, 1200 J-14
Athol, 8732 C-8
Attleboro, 42068 H-13
Auburn, 15005 F-10
Avon E-14
Ayer, 2889 C-11
Baldwinville, 1795 C-8
Ballardvale, 3500 C-14
Bancroft, 125 E-3
Barnstable, 2790 K-18
Barre, 1094 D-8
Barre Plains, 1200 E-8
Becket, 350 E-3
Becket Ctr., 100 E-3
Bedford, 12996 D-13
Bedford Sprs. K-2
Belchertown, 2339 E-7
Bellingham, 4535 G-12
Belmont, 24720 E-13
Berkley, 850 J-14
Berkshire, 400 C-3
Berlin, 650 D-11
Bernardston, 1000 B-6
Beverly, 38195 C-15

THE MUSEUM OF SCIENCE AND INDUSTRY, CHICAGO, IL

Billerica, 37609 C-13
Blackstone, 2900 G-11
Blandford, 400 F-4
Bliss Corner, 4908 N-12
Blue Hills *J-5
Bolton, 400 D-11
Bondsville, 1992 F-7
Boston, 574283 E-14
Bourne, 1284 J-17
Bournedale J-17
Boxborough, 1400 D-12
Boxford, 2072 C-14
Boylston E-10
Bradford B-14
Braintree, 33836 F-14
Braintree Highlands *K-7
Braleys L-11
Bramanville N-6
Brant Rock, 2300 G-16
Brewster, 1818 J-19
Bridgewater, 7242 G-15
Briggsville, 750 B-3
Brimfield, 400 G-8
Brockton, 92788 G-14
Brookfield, 1200 F-8
Brookline, 54718 E-14
Bryantville, 2600 G-15
Buckland, 125 C-5
Burlington, 23302 D-13
Buzzards Bay, 3250 J-17
Byfield, 850 B-15
Cahoon Hollow, 10 H-20
Cambridge, 95802 E-14
Canton, 18530 F-14
Carlisle, 800 D-13
Carver, 900 H-16
Cedarville J-17
Centerville, 9190 K-18
Central Vil., 600 L-14
Chaffinville, 3100 E-10
Charlemont, 250 C-4
Charlton, 1100 F-9
Charlton City, 1400 F-9
Charlton Depot, 1200 F-9
Chartley, 1600 H-13
Chatham, 1916 K-20
Chelmsford, 32388 C-13
Chelsea, 28710 E-14
Cherry Valley M-5
Cheshire, 1200 C-3
Cheshire Harbor, 450 C-3
Chester, 800 E-4
Chesterfield, 250 E-4
Chicopee, 56632 F-6
Chilmark, 200 M-16
Clarksburg B-3
Clayton, 50 G-2
Cliftondale *C-7
Clinton, 7943 D-11
Cochituate, 6046 E-13
Cohasset, 3300 F-16
Cold Spr., 30 F-3
Cole Corner *J-9
Colrain, 200 C-5
Concord, 3500 D-13
Conway, 350 D-5
Cordaville, 1530 E-12
Cotuit, 2364 K-18
Coury Hts. L-12
Cummington, 300 D-4
Dalton, 4100 D-3
Danvers, 24174 C-15
Dedham, 23782 F-14
Deerfield, 450 C-6
Dennis, 2633 J-19
Dennis Port, 2775 K-19
Dighton, 1200 J-14
Dorothy Pond M-6
Douglas, 800 G-10
Dover, 2163 F-13
Dracut C-13
Drury, 100 C-3
Dudley, 1800 G-9
Dunstable, 650 B-12
Duxbury, 1637 G-16
Dwight, 550 E-6
E. Arlington *D-4
E. Blackstone, 1600 G-12
E. Braintree *J-8
E. Brewster, 850 J-20
E. Bridgewater, 4000 G-15
E. Brookfield, 1396 F-9
E. Dennis, 2584 J-19
E. Douglas, 1945 G-11
E. Falmouth, 5577 K-17
E. Freetown, 1200 J-15
E. Harwich, 3828 K-20
E. Leverett, 250 D-6
E. Lexington *D-3
E. Longmeadow, 13367 G-6
E. Marion, 550 J-16
E. Millbury M-7
E. Milton *H-6
E. Northfield, 150 B-6
E. Orleans, 1800 J-20
E. Otis, 200 F-3
E. Pepperell, 2296 C-11
E. Princeton, 300 D-10
E. Sandwich, 3171 J-17
E. Saugus *C-7
E. Wareham, 1700 J-16
E. Weymouth *J-9
E. Windsor, 80 D-4
Eastham, 1100 J-20
Easthampton, 15537 E-5
Edgartown, 1100 M-17
Edgemere M-7
Ellisville H-17
Erving, 250 C-7
Essex, 1507 C-16
Everett, 35701 *D-6
Fairhaven, 16132 K-15
Fall River, 92703 K-14
Falmouth, 4047 L-17
Farley, 200 C-6
Feeding Hills, 4400 G-5
Fiskdale, 2189 G-8
Fitchburg, 41194 C-10
Five Corners, 2100 G-14
Florida, 90 C-3
Forestdale, 2833 K-17
Forge Vil., 2300 C-12
Foxboro, 5706 G-13
Framingham, 64994 E-12
Franklin, 9965 G-12
Gardner, 20125 C-9
Gay Head, 175 M-16
Georgetown, 3000 B-14
Gilbertville, 1000 E-8
Gill C-6
Gleasondale D-12
Glen Mills, 750 B-15
Glendale, 250 E-2
Glenridge *J-1
Gloucester, 28716 C-16
Goshen, 250 D-5
Grafton, 2400 F-11
Granby, 1327 F-6
Granville, 350 G-4
Great Barrington, 2810 F-2
Green Harbor, 3000 G-16
Greenbush, 550 F-16
Greenfield, 14016 C-6
Greenwood *B-6
Griswoldville, 150 C-5
Groton, 1044 C-11
Groveland, 2800 B-14
Hadley, 1200 E-6
Halifax, 1000 G-15
Hamilton C-15
Hampden, 500 G-7
Hancock, 125 C-2
Hanover, 2200 G-15
Hanover Ctr. *M-10
Hanson, 2188 G-15
Hardwick, 150 E-8
Hartsville, 150 F-2
Harvard, 800 D-11
Harwich, 1668 K-19
Harwich Port, 1742 K-19
Hatfield, 1234 E-6
Haverhill, 58969 B-14
Hawley, 70 C-4
Haydenville, 700 E-5
Head of Westport K-14
Heath, 150 B-4
Hingham, 5454 F-15
Hingham Ctr. *J-10
Hinsdale, 750 D-3
Hixville, 500 K-14
Holbrook, 11041 F-14

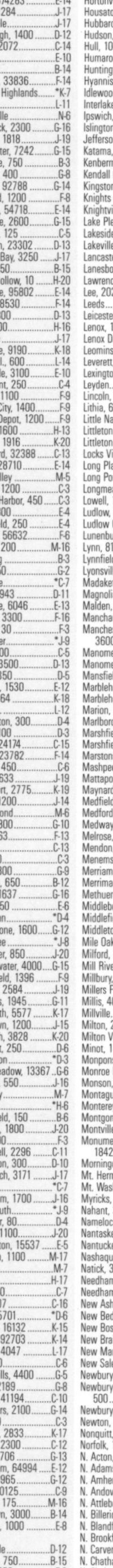

Holden, 4200 E-10
Holland, 1331 G-8
Holliston, 3400 F-12
Holyoke, 43704 F-6
Hoosac Tunnel B-3
Hopedale, 3961 F-12
Hopkinton, 2305 F-12
Hortonville, 850 J-13
Housatonic, 1184 E-1
Hubbardston, 400 D-9
Hudson, 14267 E-11
Hull, 10466 E-15
Humarock, 2000 F-16
Huntington, 950 E-4
Hyannis, 14120 K-18
Idlewood M-16
Interlaken, 225 E-2
Ipswich, 4132 B-15
Islington *J-3
Jefferson, 600 E-9
Katama, 125 M-17
Kenberma *H-10
Kendall Green *E-2
Kingston, 4774 G-16
Knights Corner, 50 E-7
Knightville E-4
Lake Pleasant, 350 C-6
Lakeside, 300 K-14
Lakeville, 2048 J-15
Lancaster, 1700 D-11
Lanesborough, 850 D-2
Lawrence, 72043 B-14
Lee, 2020 E-2
Leeds E-5
Leicester, 1800 E-9
Lenox, 1687 E-2
Lenox Dale, 1100 E-2
Leominster, 38145 D-10
Leverett, 500 D-6
Lexington, 28974 D-13
Leyden B-6
Lincoln, 650 *D-1
Lithia, 60 D-4
Little Nahant *B-8
Littleton, 2800 C-12
Littleton Common, 2867 C-12
Locks Vil., 225 D-7
Long Plain, 1500 K-15
Long Pond, 1200 J-16
Longmeadow, 15467 G-6
Lowell, 103439 C-13
Ludlow, 7400 F-6
Ludlow Ctr., 350 F-6
Lunenburg, 1600 C-10
Lynn, 87122 D-15
Lynnfield, 11542 C-14
Lyonsville C-5
Madaket, 125 N-19
Magnolia, 1100 C-16
Malden, 53884 D-14
Manchaug, 850 G-10
Manchester-by-the-Sea, 3600 C-16
Manomet, 2900 H-17
Manomet Beach H-17
Mansfield, 7170 G-13
Marblehead, 19971 D-15
Marblehead Neck *B-10
Marion, 1426 J-16
Marlborough, 36255 E-11
Marshfield, 4002 G-16
Marshfield Hills, 2201 G-16
Marstons Mills, 8017 K-18
Mashpee, 1700 K-17
Mattapoisett, 2949 K-16
Maynard, 10325 D-12
Medfield, 5985 F-13
Medford, 54407 D-14
Medway, 4000 F-12
Melrose, 28150 *C-6
Mendon, 1100 G-11
Menemsha, 100 M-16
Merrimac, 2900 A-14
Methuen, 43789 B-14
Middleborough, 6837 H-15
Middlefield, 80 E-4
Middleton, 1200 C-14
Mile Oak Ctr. J-16
Milford, 23339 F-11
Mill River, 225 F-2
Millbury, 4700 F-10
Millers Falls, 1084 C-6
Millis, 4081 F-12
Millville, 700 G-11
Milton, 25725 E-14
Milton Vil. *H-6
Minot, 100 F-16
Monponsett, 1700 G-15
Monroe Bridge, 60 B-4
Monson, 2101 G-7
Montague, 600 C-6
Monterey, 250 F-2
Montgomery, 150 F-5
Montville, 60 F-2
Monument Beach, 1842 J-17
Morningdale, 2500 E-10
Mt. Hermon, 300 B-6
Mt. Washington, 60 G-2
Myricks, 600 J-14
Nahant, 3828 D-15
Nantucket, 3069 N-19
Natick, 30510 E-13
Needham, 28911 E-13
Needham Hts. *G-3
New Ashford, 150 C-2
New Bedford, 93768 K-15
New Boston, 50 G-2
New Braintree, 250 E-8
New Marlborough, 40 G-2
New Salem, 70 D-7
Newbury B-15
Newburyport, 17189 B-15
Newton, 83829 E-13
Nonquitt, 350 L-15
Norfolk, 1900 F-13
N. Acton, 1000 D-12
N. Adams, 16797 B-3
N. Amherst, 6239 D-6
N. Andover, 22792 B-14
N. Attleboro, 16178 H-13
N. Billerica, 6200 C-13
N. Blandford F-4
N. Brookfield, 2635 E-8
N. Carver, 700 H-16
N. Chatham, 750 J-20
N. Chelmsford, 4900 C-12
N. Cohasset, 1600 F-15
N. Dartmouth, 2200 K-15
N. Dighton, 1300 H-13
N. Eastham, 1570 H-20
N. Easton, 3700 G-14
N. Egremont, 200 F-1
N. Falmouth, 2625 K-17
N. Grafton, 3600 F-10
N. Hanover *L-10
N. Hatfield, 550 D-6
N. Leverett, 250 D-6
N. Lexington *C-2
N. Middleboro, 850 H-15
N. New Salem, 300 C-7
N. Orange, 200 C-7
N. Otis, 40 F-3
N. Oxford, 1200 F-9
N. Pembroke, 2485 G-16
N. Reading, 2800 C-14
N. Plymouth, 3450 H-16
N. Plympton, 450 G-16
N. Randolph *K-6
N. Rehoboth H-13
N. Rutland D-9
N. Saugus *B-7
N. Scituate, 4891 F-16
N. Swansea, 1100 J-13
N. Tisbury, 200 M-16
N. Truro, 550 G-19
N. Uxbridge, 4200 G-11
N. Weymouth *J-8
Northampton, 29289 E-5
Northborough, 5761 E-11
Northbridge, 3000 F-11
Northfield, 1322 B-6
Northville, 2400 G-15
Norton, 1899 H-13
Norwell, 1300 F-16
Norwich, 350 E-4
Norwood, 28700 F-13
Nutting Lake, 5700 *A-2
Oak Bluffs, 1100 M-17
Oakdale E-10
Oakham, 300 E-9
Oakland Vale *C-6
Ocean Bluff, 2500 G-16
Ocean Gr., 3169 J-13
Old Furnace E-8
Onset, 1461 J-16
Orange, 3791 C-7
Orleans, 1699 J-20
Osterville, 2911 K-18
Otis, 200 F-3
Otter River, 850 C-8
Oxford, 5969 G-10
Palmer, 4069 F-7
Paxton, 1000 E-9
Peabody, 47039 D-15
Pelham, 150 E-7
Pemberton *G-8
Pembroke, 2800 G-16
Pepperell, 2350 B-11
Peru, 150 D-3
Petersham, 350 D-8
Phillipston, 175 C-8
Pigeon Cove C-16
Pinehurst, 6614 D-13
Pittsfield, 48622 D-2
Plainfield, 125 C-4
Plainville, 2500 G-13
Pleasant Lake, 800 J-19
Plymouth, 7258 H-16
Plympton, 250 H-15
Pocasset, 2756 K-17
Polpis, 90 M-20
Pondville N-5
Ponkapoag *K-5
Popponesset Beach, 500 K-17
Princeton, 225 D-9
Princeton Sta., 225 D-9
Provincetown, 3374 G-19
Quidnet, 10 M-20
Quincy, 84985 F-14
Randolph, 30963 F-14
Raynham, 1900 H-14
Raynham Ctr., 3709 H-14
Reading, 23708 C-14
Rehoboth, 700 J-13
Revere, 42786 D-14
Richmond, 450 E-1
Ringville, 250 D-4
Rio Vista *A-1
Risingdale, 225 F-2
Rochdale, 1400 F-9
Rochester, 800 J-15
Rock, 850 J-15
Rockland, 16123 F-15
Rockport, 5448 C-16
Rowe, 150 B-4
Rowley, 1144 B-15
Royalston, 800 B-8
Russell, 600 F-4
Rutland, 2145 E-9
Sagamore, 2589 J-17
Sagamore Beach, 1200 J-17
Salem, 38091 D-15
Salisbury, 3729 A-15
Salisbury Beach, 1300 A-15
Sand Hills, 2400 F-16
Sandisfield, 50 G-3
Sandwich, 2998 J-17
Santuit, 350 K-17
Saugus, 25549 D-14
Savoy, 125 C-3
Saxonville, 12000 E-12
Scituate, 5069 F-16
Seekonk J-13
Sharon, 5893 G-14
Shattuckville, 225 C-5
Sheffield, 750 G-2
Shelburne, 300 C-5
Shelburne Falls, 1996 C-5
Sheldonville, 500 G-12
Sherborn, 1200 F-12
Sherwood Forest *J-1
Shirley, 1559 C-11
Shrewsbury, 24146 E-10
Shutesbury, 125 D-7
Siasconset, 300 N-20
Silver Beach, 500 K-16
Silver Hill *F-1
Silver Lake, 1000 G-16
Sippewisset, 350 L-17
Somerset, 17655 J-14
Somerville, 77478 D-14
S. Acton, 2700 E-12
S. Amherst, 5053 E-6
S. Ashburnham, 1110 C-9
S. Ashfield C-5
S. Athol D-7
S. Berlin, 800 E-11
S. Carver, 400 H-16
S. Chatham, 800 K-20
S. Dartmouth, 1000 K-15
S. Deerfield, 1906 D-6
S. Dennis, 3559 K-19
S. Duxbury, 3017 G-16
S. Easton, 3600 G-14
S. Egremont, 450 F-1
S. Hadley, 17196 E-6
S. Hadley Falls, 4300 F-6
S. Hingham *K-9
S. Lancaster, 1772 D-11
S. Lee, 200 E-2
S. Lynnfield *C-6
S. Middleboro, 750 J-15
S. Natick E-13
S. Orleans, 1100 J-20
S. Royalston, 300 C-8
S. Sandisfield, 20 G-3
S. Sudbury E-12
S. Swansea J-13
S. Truro H-19
S. Walpole, 1900 G-13
S. Wareham, 1300 J-16
S. Wellfleet, 500 H-20
S. Westport, 600 L-14
S. Weymouth, 1100 F-15
S. Williamstown C-2
S. Worthington, 80 E-4
S. Yarmouth, 10358 K-19
Southampton, 500 E-5
Southborough, 1700 E-12
Southbridge, 13631 G-9
Southfield, 100 G-2
Southwick, 2000 G-5
Spencer, 6306 F-9
Springfield, 156983 G-6
Standish, 400 G-16
Sterling, 1300 D-10
Still River, 400 D-11
Stockbridge, 900 E-2
Stoneham, 22203 D-14
Stoneville N-5
Stoughton, 26777 F-14
Stow, 600 D-12
Sturbridge, 2093 G-8
Sudbury, 2300 E-12
Summit Gr. M-11
Sunderland, 850 D-6
Surfside, 175 N-19
Sutton, 650 F-10
Swampscott, 13650 D-15
Swansea J-13
Swift River D-4
Swifts Beach, 2700 J-16
Taunton, 49832 H-14
Teaticket, 1856 L-17
Templeton, 800 C-8
Tewksbury, 27266 C-13
Texas, 1300 F-8
Three Rivers, 3006 F-7
Tisbury L-16
Tolland G-3
Topsfield, 2711 C-15
Town Crest Vil. G-3
Townsend, 1164 C-11
Townsend Harbor, 1700 C-11
Truro, 400 G-20
Tully, 30 C-7
Turners Falls, 4731 C-6
Tyngsboro B-12
Tyringham, 80 F-2
Upton, 1800 F-11
Uxbridge, 3300 G-11
Vineyard Haven, 1762 L-17
Wakeby, 1600 K-17
Wakefield, 24825 D-14
Wales, 350 G-8
Walpole, 5495 F-13
Waltham, 57878 E-13
Waquoit Vil. L-17
Ware, 6533 F-8
Wareham, 2607 J-16
Warren, 1500 F-8
Warwick, 150 B-7
Washington, 250 E-3
Watertown, 33284 E-13
Waterville, 950 B-8
Watson, 60 C-4
Wauwinet, 10 M-20
Waverly *G-3
Wayland, 1300 E-13
Webster, 11649 G-10
Wellesley, 26615 E-13
Wellfleet, 1000 H-20
Wendell, 100 C-7
Wenham, 2300 C-15
W. Acton, 1900 D-12
W. Barnstable K-18
W. Becket, 100 E-3
W. Bedford *B-1
W. Boxford, 1200 C-14
W. Boylston, 3700 E-10
W. Bridgewater, 2400 G-14
W. Brimfield, 125 F-7
W. Brookfield, 1419 F-8
W. Chatham, 1400 J-20
W. Chesterfield, 100 D-4
W. Concord, 5761 D-12
W. Cummington, 125 D-4
W. Dennis, 2307 K-19
W. Falmouth, 1752 K-16
W. Granville, 20 G-4
W. Groton, 750 C-11
W. Hanover *M-9
W. Hawley, 50 C-4
W. Hingham *J-8
W. Otis, 125 F-3
W. Pelham, 1300 E-6
W. Royalston, 400 B-8
W. Springfield, 27537 G-5
W. Sterling, 450 D-10
W. Stockbridge, 750 E-1
W. Tisbury, 350 M-16
W. Townsend, 1300 B-10
W. Upton, 1900 F-11
W. Wareham, 2059 J-16
W. Warren, 1100 F-8
W. Whately, 450 D-5
Westborough, 3917 E-11
Westfield, 38372 G-5
Westford, 1200 C-12
Westhampton, 250 E-5
Westminster, 1300 D-9
Weston E-13
Westport Pt., 350 L-14
Westwood, 12557 F-13
Weymouth, 54063 F-15
Weymouth Hts. *J-8
Weymouth Landing *J-8
Whately, 450 D-5
Wheelwright, 400 E-8
White Horse Beach, 2300 H-17
White Island Shores, 1827 J-16
Whitinsville, 6539 G-11
Whitman, 13240 G-15
Williamsburg, 600 D-5
Williamstown, 4791 B-2
Wilmington C-13
Winchendon, 4316 B-9
Winchendon Sprs., 1100 B-9
Winchester, 20267 D-14
Winchester Highlands *C-5
Windsor, 125 C-3
Winthrop, 18127 E-15
Woburn, 35943 D-14
Woods Hole, 800 L-16
Woodville, 500 F-11
Worcester, 169759 F-10
Worthington Corners, 250 D-4
Wrentham, 2600 G-13
Yarmouth, 2400 K-18
Yarmouth Port, 4271 K-18
Zoar, 175 C-4

MICHIGAN
PG. 112–114

MICHIGAN ABC 123 GREAT LAKES

CAPITAL
Lansing

NICKNAME
Great Lakes State

POPULATION
9,594,350, rank 8

AREA
58,527 sq mi, rank 23

Counties
Alcona, 10145 K-10
Alger, 8972 E-5
Allegan, 105665 T-5
Alpena, 30605 J-10
Antrim, 18185 J-7
Arenac, 14931 M-10
Baraga, 8746 D-2
Barry, 50057 S-6
Bay, 111723 N-9
Benzie, 12200 K-5
Berrien, 161378 U-4
Branch, 41502 U-7
Calhoun, 135982 T-7
Cass, 49477 U-5
Charlevoix, 21468 H-7
Cheboygan, 21398 G-8
Chippewa, 34604 D-7
Clare, 24952 M-7
Clinton, 57883 R-8
Crawford, 12260 K-8
Delta, 37780 E-4
Dickinson, 26831 E-1
Eaton, 92879 S-7
Emmet, 25040 G-7
Genesee, 430459 Q-10
Gladwin, 21896 M-8
Gogebic, 18052 C-6
Grand Traverse, 64273 K-6
Gratiot, 38982 P-8
Hillsdale, 43431 U-8
Houghton, 35446 C-11
Huron, 34951 N-11
Ingham, 281912 S-8
Ionia, 57024 R-7
Iosco, 30209 L-10
Iron, 13175 C-11
Isabella, 54624 N-7
Jackson, 149756 T-8
Kalamazoo, 223411 T-6
Kalkaska, 13497 K-7
Kent, 600631 Q-6
Keweenaw, 1701 A-12
Lake, 8583 M-5
Lapeer, 74768 Q-11
Leelanau, 16527 J-5
Lenawee, 91476 U-9
Livingston, 115645 S-10
Luce, 5763 D-6
Mackinac, 10674 D-6
Macomb, 717400 R-12
Manistee, 21265 L-5
Marquette, 70887 D-1
Mason, 25537 M-4
Mecosta, 37308 P-6
Menominee, 24920 G-1
Midland, 75651 N-9
Missaukee, 12147 L-7
Monroe, 133600 U-11
Montcalm, 53059 P-6
Montmorency, 8936 J-9
Muskegon, 158983 Q-5
Newaygo, 38202 P-5
Oakland, 1083592 S-11
Oceana, 22454 N-4
Ogemaw, 18681 L-9
Ontonagon, 8854 C-10
Osceola, 19442 N-6
Otsego, 17957 H-8
Ottawa, 187768 R-5
Presque Isle, 13743 H-9
Roscommon, 19776 L-8
Saginaw, 211946 P-9
St. Clair, 145607 R-12
St. Joseph, 58913 U-6
Sanilac, 39928 P-12
Schoolcraft, 8302 E-4
Shiawassee, 69770 Q-9
Tuscola, 55498 P-10
Van Buren, 70060 T-5
Washtenaw, 282937 T-10
Wayne, 2111687 T-11
Wexford, 26360 L-6

Cities and Towns
* City indexed to pg. 114

Acme, 650 J-6
Ada *B-4
Adamsville U-5
Addison, 632 U-9
Adrian, 22097 U-10
Afton, 100 H-8
Agnew, 250 R-4
Ahmeek, 148 A-12
Akron, 421 P-11
Alabaster, 40 M-10
Alamo, 250 T-5
Alanson, 677 G-7
Alba, 300 J-7
Alberta, 150 C-12
Albion, 10066 T-8
Alden, 200 J-6
Alger M-9
Algonac, 4551 S-13
Allegan, 4547 S-5
Allen, 211 U-8
Allen Park, 31092 *L-6
Allendale, 6950 R-5
Allouez, 225 A-12
Alma, 9034 P-8
Almont, 2354 R-11
Aloha, 175 H-9
Alpena, 11354 J-11
Alpha, 219 C-12
Alto, 300 R-6
Alverno, 225 G-8
Amasa, 200 D-12
Ann Arbor, 109592 T-10
Applegate, 297 P-13
Arcadia, 350 K-4
Argentine, 1907 R-10
Argyle, 125 P-12
Armada, 1548 R-12
Arnheim B-12
Ashley, 518 Q-8
Ashton, 200 M-6
Assyria, 300 S-7
Athens, 990 T-6
Atlanta, 200 J-9
Attica, 700 Q-11
Atwood, 90 H-6
Au Gres, 838 M-10
Au Sable, 1542 L-11
Au Train, 225 D-3
Auburn, 1855 N-9
Auburn Hills, 17076 *C-7
Augusta, 927 T-6
Aura, 150 B-12
Avoca, 350 Q-13
Azalia, 80 U-10
Bach, 90 N-11
Bad Axe, 3484 N-12
Baldwin, 821 N-5
Bancroft, 599 R-9
Bangor, 1922 T-4
Baraga, 1231 B-12
Barbeau, 20 D-8
Bark River, 450 G-2
Baroda, 657 U-3
Barryton, 393 N-6
Barton City, 30 K-10
Bath, 1200 R-8
Battle Cr., 53540 T-7
Bay City, 36936 P-10
Bay Port, 500 N-11
Bay Shore, 550 H-7
Bear Lake, 339 L-4
Beaverton, 1150 N-8
Bedford, 600 T-6
Beecher, 14465 *D-2
Belding, 5966 Q-6
Bellaire, 1164 J-6
Belleville, 3997 T-11
Bellevue, 1365 S-7
Bentley, 175 N-9
Benton Harbor, 12818 T-4
Benzonia, 449 K-5
Bergland C-10
Berkley, 15960 *H-7
Berrien Sprs., 1927 U-4
Berville, 450 R-12
Bessemer, 2272 C-9
Bete Grise, 10 A-13
Beulah, 421 K-5
Beverly Hills, 10610 *G-6
Big Bay, 125 C-1
Big Rapids, 10849 P-6
Bingham Farms, 1001 *G-6
Birch Run, 992 Q-10
Birmingham, 19997 *G-7
Black River, 100 J-11
Blaine D-13
Blanchard, 350 P-7
Bliss, 70 F-7
Blissfield, 3172 U-10
Bloomfield Hills, 4288 *F-6
Bloomingdale, 503 T-5
Boon, 150 L-6
Boyne City, 3503 H-7
Boyne Falls, 369 H-7
Brampton, 80 F-2
Branch, 150 N-5
Bravo S-4
Breckenridge, 1301 P-8
Breedsville, 213 T-4
Brethren, 250 L-5
Brevort, 20 F-7
Bridgeport, 8569 P-10
Bridgman, 2140 U-3
Brighton, 5686 S-10
Brimley, 450 D-8
Bristol, 60 M-6
Brockway Q-12
Bronson, 2342 U-7
Brooklyn, 1027 T-9
Brown City, 1244 Q-12
Bruce Crossing, 225 C-11
Brutus, 175 E-8
Buchanan, 4992 U-4
Buckley, 402 K-6
Buena Vista, 8196 P-10
Burlington, 294 T-7
Burnips, 400 R-5
Burr Oak, 882 U-6
Burt, 1169 Q-10
Burt Lake, 160 H-8
Burton, 27617 R-10
Byron, 573 R-10
Caledonia, 885 R-6
California U-9
Calumet, 818 A-12
Camden, 482 V-8
Capac, 1583 Q-12
Carleton, 2770 U-11
Carney, 197 G-1
Caro, 4054 P-11
Carp Lake, 150 F-7
Carrollton, 6521 P-9
Carson City, 1158 Q-7
Carsonville, 583 P-12
Caseville, 857 M-11
Casnovia, 376 Q-5
Caspian, 1031 D-12
Cass City, 2276 P-11
Cassopolis, 1822 U-5
Cedar, 250 J-5
Cedar River, 30 G-2
Cedar Sprs., 2600 Q-6
Cedarville, 400 F-9
Cement City, 493 U-9
Center Line, 9026 *H-8
Central Lake, 954 H-6
Centreville, 1516 U-6
Champion, 250 C-13
Channing, 250 E-12
Charlevoix, 3116 H-6
Charlotte, 8389 S-8
Chatham, 268 D-3
Cheboygan, 4999 G-8
Chelsea, 4398 T-9
Chesaning, 2567 Q-9
Chippewa Lake, 125 N-6
Christmas, 250 D-3
Clare, 3021 N-8
Clarkston, 1005 *D-5
Clarksville, 394 S-6
Clawson, 12732 *G-7
Clayton, 338 U-9
Climax, 677 T-6
Clinton, 2475 U-10
Clio, 2629 Q-10
Coleman, 1232 N-8
Coloma, 1619 T-4
Columbiaville, 934 Q-11
Comins, 150 J-9
Concord, 944 T-8
Constantine, 2095 U-6
Conway, 300 G-7
Cooks, 100 F-3
Coopersville, 3421 Q-5
Copemish, 222 K-5
Copper City, 198 A-12
Copper Harbor, 50 A-13
Cornell, 90 F-2
Corunna, 3091 R-9
Covert, 650 T-4
Covington, 40 C-12
Crystal Falls, 1922 D-12
Crystal Valley, 175 N-4
Curtis, 250 E-5
Custer, 300 N-4
Dafter, 250 D-8
Daggett, 260 F-1
Dansville, 429 S-9
De Tour Vil., 407 F-9
De Witt, 4702 R-8
Dearborn, 97775 T-11
Dearborn Hts., 58264 *K-6
Decatur, 1838 T-5
Deckerville, 1015 P-13
Deer Park E-6
Deerfield, 1000 U-10
Deerton, 30 D-3
Delton, 872 S-6
Detroit, 951270 T-11
Dexter, 2338 T-10
Dimondale, 1342 S-8
Dollar Bay, 950 A-12
Dorr, 2800 S-5
Douglas, 1214 S-4
Dowagiac, 6409 U-4
Dowling, 150 S-6
Drayton Plains *E-5
Drenthe, 300 S-5
Dryden, 628 R-11
Dundee, 3522 U-10
Dunningville, 150 S-5
Durand, 4283 R-9
Eagle River, 20 A-12
E. Grand Rapids, 10507 *C-3
E. Jordan, 2240 H-7
E. Lansing, 46525 S-8
E. Leroy, 300 T-7
E. Tawas, 2887 L-10
Eastpointe, 34077 *H-9
Eastport, 200 H-6
Eaton Rapids, 5330 S-8
Eau Claire, 494 U-4
Eben Jct., 250 E-4
Eckerman E-7
Edmore, 1244 P-7
Edwardsburg, 1142 U-4
Elberta, 478 K-4
Elk Rapids, 1700 J-6
Elkton, 958 N-11
Ellsworth, 418 H-6
Elsie, 957 Q-8
Emmett, 251 R-12
Empire, 355 J-5
Engadine, 300 E-6
Ensign, 40 F-3
Escanaba, 13659 F-2
Essexville, 4088 P-10
Estey, 150 N-8
Estral Beach, 430 U-11
Evart, 1744 N-6
Evans, 225 Q-6
Ewen, 175 C-11
Fair Plain, 8051 U-3
Fairfield U-9
Fairgrove, 592 P-11
Fairport, 125 G-3
Fairview, 600 K-9
Faithorn, 20 F-1
Falmouth, 250 L-7
Farmington, 10132 *H-5
Farmington Hills, 74652 *G-5
Farwell, 851 N-7
Fayette, 10 G-3
Felch, 80 E-1
Fenton, 10582 R-10
Ferndale, 22105 *H-7
Ferry, 250 P-4
Ferrysburg, 3040 Q-4
Fife Lake, 394 K-6
Filion, 225 N-12
Findley U-6
Flat Rock, 8488 T-11
Flint, 124943 Q-10
Flushing, 8348 Q-10
Ford River, 150 G-2
Forest Lake, 20 D-3
Forestville, 153 N-13
Foster City, 60 F-1
Fostoria, 600 Q-11
Fountain, 175 M-4
Fowlerville, 2648 S-9
Frankenmuth, 4408 P-10
Frankfort, 1546 K-4
Franklin, 2937 *G-6
Fraser, 15297 *G-9
Frederic, 200 J-8
Freeland, 5147 P-9
Freeport, 458 S-6
Fremont, 4224 P-5
Fruitport, 1090 Q-4
Fulton, 200 T-6
Gaastra, 339 D-12
Gagetown, 337 N-11
Gaines, 366 R-10
Galesburg, 1988 T-6
Galien, 593 U-3
Garden, 268 F-3
Garden City, 30047 *K-5
Garnet, 40 E-6
Gay, 40 A-13
Gaylord, 3681 J-8
Genesee, 1800 Q-10
Germfask, 125 E-5
Gibraltar, 4264 U-11
Girard, 250 U-7
Gladstone, 5032 F-2
Gladwin, 3001 N-8
Glen Arbor, 200 J-5
Glendale, 300 T-5
Glendora, 350 U-3
Glennie, 90 K-10
Gobles, 769 T-5
Goetzville, 100 F-9
Good Hart, 50 G-7
Goodrich, 916 R-11
Gould City, 80 E-5
Grand Blanc, 7760 R-10
Grand Haven, 11168 R-4
Grand Jct., 350 T-4
Grand Ledge, 7813 S-8
Grand Marais, 300 D-5
Grand Rapids, 197800 R-6
Grandville, 16263 R-5
Grant, 764 P-5
Grass Lake, 903 T-9
Grawn, 1600 K-6
Grayling, 1944 K-8
Green, 80 B-10
Greenbush, 225 K-10
Greenland, 300 C-11
Greenville, 8101 Q-6
Grind Stone City, 100 M-12
Gros Cap, 90 F-8
Grosse Ile, 9781 *N-7
Grosse Pointe, 5670 *J-10
Grosse Pointe Farms, 9764 *J-10
Grosse Pointe Park, 12443 *J-10
Grosse Pointe Woods, 17080 *J-10
Gwinn, 2370 E-1
Hadley, 450 R-11
Hale, 600 L-10
Hamburg, 350 S-10
Hamilton, 1170 S-5
Hamtramck, 18372 *J-8
Hancock, 4323 A-12
Hanover, 481 T-8
Harbert, 450 U-3
Harbor Beach, 1837 N-13
Harbor Sprs., 1540 G-7
Harper Woods, 14254 *H-10
Harrietta, 169 L-6
Harrison, 1835 M-7
Harrisville, 514 K-11
Hart, 1942 N-4
Hartford, 2341 T-4
Hartland, 350 S-10
Haslett, 10230 R-9
Hastings, 7095 S-6
Hawks, 60 H-10
Hazel Park, 18963 *H-8
Hemlock, 1466 P-9
Hermansville, 750 F-1
Hersey, 354 N-6
Hessel, 200 F-8
Higgins Lake, 60 K-8
Highland Park, 16746 *J-8
Hillman, 701 J-10
Hillsdale, 8233 U-8
Holland, 35048 S-4
Holly, 6135 R-10
Holt, 11315 S-8
Holton, 600 P-4
Homer, 1851 T-8
Honor, 328 K-5
Hope, 200 N-8
Hopkins, 592 S-5
Houghton, 7010 A-12
Houghton Lake, 3749 L-8
Howard City, 1585 Q-6
Howell, 9232 S-10
Hubbard Lake, 300 J-10
Hubbardston, 400 Q-7
Hubbell, 1174 A-12
Hudson, 2499 U-9
Hudsonville, 7160 R-5
Hulbert, 80 E-7
Huntington Woods, 6151 *H-7
Huron Beach, 225 G-9
Hyde, 300 F-2
Idlewild, 350 N-5
Imlay City, 3869 Q-11
Indian River, 2008 H-8
Ingalls, 175 H-2
Inkster, 30115 *L-5
Interlochen, 600 K-5
Ionia, 10569 R-7
Iron Mtn., 8154 F-1
Iron River, 3386 E-12
Ironton, 200 H-7
Ironwood, 6293 C-9
Isabella, 40 G-3
Ishpeming, 6686 D-1
Ithaca, 3098 Q-8
Jackson, 36316 T-8
Jacobsville, 10 B-13
Jamestown, 750 S-5
Jasper, 400 U-10
Jenison, 17882 R-5
Johannesburg, 400 J-8
Jones, 450 U-5
Jonesville, 2337 U-8
Kalamazoo, 77145 T-6
Kaleva, 509 L-5
Kalkaska, 2226 K-7
Karlin, 100 K-5
Kawkawlin, 1600 N-9

Keego Harbor, 2932 *F-5
Keeler T-4
Kent City, 899 Q-5
Kenton, 20 C-11
Kentwood, 37826 R-5
Keweenaw Bay, 150 B-12
Kinde, 473 M-12
Kinderhook, 350 V-7
Kingsford, 5480 E-12
Kingsley, 738 K-6
Kingston, 439 P-11
Kinross, 175 E-8
Kipling, 300 F-2
Kiva, 50 E-2
Koss, 80 G-1
La Branche, 10 F-1
La Salle, 350 U-11
Lachine, 225 H-10
Lacota S-4
Laingsburg, 1148 R-9
Lake, 500 M-7
Lake Angelus, 328 *E-5
Lake Ann, 217 K-5
Lake City, 858 L-7
Lake George, 400 M-7
Lake Linden, 1203 A-12
Lake Michigan Beach, 1694 T-4
Lake Odessa, 2256 R-7
Lake Orion, 3057 R-11
Lakeport, 700 Q-13
Lakeview, 1108 P-6
Lakewood Club, 659 P-4
Lambertville, 7860 V-10
Langston, 300 Q-6
L'Anse, 2151 B-12
Lansing, 127321 R-8
Lapeer, 7759 Q-11
Lathrup Vil., 4329 *H-6
Laurium, 2268 A-12
Lawrence, 915 T-5
Lawton, 1685 T-5
Le Roy, 251 M-6
Leland, 350 J-5
Lennon, 534 R-10
Leonard, 357 R-11
Leonidas U-6
Leslie, 1872 S-8
Levering, 300 G-7
Lewiston, 900 J-9
Lexington, 779 Q-13
Lexington Hts., 1000 Q-13
Lilley N-5
Lincoln, 337 K-11
Lincoln Park, 41832 T-11
Linden, 2415 R-10
Linwood, 1200 N-9
Litchfield, 1317 U-8
Little Lake, 225 E-2
Livonia, 100850 S-11
Long Lake, 200 L-10
Long Rapids H-10
Loretto, 150 F-1
Lovells, 80 J-8
Lowell, 3983 R-6
Ludington, 8507 M-4
Lum, 500 Q-11
Luna Pier, 1507 U-11
Lupton, 350 L-9
Luther, 343 M-5
Luzerne, 250 K-9
Lyons, 824 R-7
Mackinac Island, 469 F-8
Mackinaw City, 875 F-8
Macomb *C-9
Madison Hts., 32196 *G-6
Mancelona, 1370 J-7
Manchester, 1753 T-9
Manistee, 6734 M-4
Manistique, 3456 F-4
Manitou Beach, 650 U-8
Manton, 1161 L-6
Maple City, 225 J-5
Maple Rapids, 680 Q-8
Maple Ridge M-10
Marcellus, 1193 U-5
Marenisco, 300 C-10
Marine City, 4556 R-13
Marion, 807 L-7
Marion Sprs., 200 Q-9
Marlette, 1924 P-12
Marne *A-1
Marquette, 21977 D-1
Marshall, 6891 T-7
Martin, 462 S-5
Marysville, 9515 R-13
Mason, 6768 S-8
Mass City, 300 B-11
Mattawan, 2456 T-5
Mayfield, 225 K-6
Maybee, 500 U-11
Mayville, 1010 P-11
McBain, 692 M-6
McBrides, 236 P-7
McFarland E-2
McLeods Corner, 20 E-6
McMillan, 100 D-5
Mears, 400 N-4
Mecosta, 393 N-6
Melstrand, 10 D-4
Melvin, 148 Q-12
Melvindale, 11216 *L-7
Memphis, 1221 R-12
Mendon, 920 U-6
Menominee, 9398 H-1
Meredith, 125 M-8
Merrill, 755 P-9
Merriman, 125 D-12
Merritt, 90 L-7
Merriweather, 125 C-10
Mesick, 406 L-5
Metamora, 447 R-11
Michiana, 164 V-3
Michigamme, 300 C-12
Michigan Ctr., 4863 T-9
Middleton, 450 Q-8
Middleville, 1966 S-6
Midland, 38053 P-9
Midland Park, 450 T-6
Mikado, 175 K-11
Milan, 4040 U-10
Milford, 5511 S-10
Millersburg, 250 H-9
Millington, 1114 Q-11
Minden City, 233 N-12
Mineral Hills, 200 D-12
Mio, 1886 K-9
Moddersville, 40 M-7
Mohawk, 750 A-12
Monroe, 22902 U-11
Montague, 2276 P-4
Montgomery, 388 V-8
Montrose, 1811 Q-10
Moore Park U-6
Moorestown, 90 L-7
Moran, 175 E-7
Morenci, 2342 V-9
Morley, 528 P-6
Morrice, 630 R-9
Moscow, 250 U-8
Mottville, 400 U-5
Mt. Clemens, 18405 S-12
Mt. Forest N-9
Mt. Morris, 3292 Q-10
Mt. Pleasant, 23285 P-7
Muir, 667 Q-7
Mullett Lake, 300 G-8
Mulliken, 590 R-7
Munger, 350 P-10
Munising, 2783 D-3
Muskegon, 40283 Q-4
Muskegon Hts., 13176 Q-4
Nadeau, 175 G-1
Nahma, 20 F-3
Napoleon, 1332 T-9
Nashville, 1654 S-7
Nathan, 20 G-1
National City L-10
National Mine, 400 D-1
Naubinway, 175 E-6
Negaunee, 4741 D-1
Nestoria, 10 C-12
New Baltimore, 5798 R-12
New Boston *M-5
New Buffalo, 2317 U-3
New Era, 520 P-4
New Greenleaf, 125 N-12
New Haven, 2331 R-12
New Lothrop, 596 Q-9
…waygo, 1336 P-5
…erry, 1873 D-6
…458 U-4
… B-11
…12 U-8
…23 Q-11
… H-5
…9 Q-4
… E-1
… H-5
… *H-4
…5 Q-4
… E-13
… S-11
… J-8
…1

Olivet, 1604 S-7
Omena, 150 H-5
Omer, 385 M-10
Onaway, 1039 H-9
Onekama, 515 L-4
Onondaga, 450 S-8
Onsted, 801 U-9
Ontonagon, 2040 B-11
Orchard Lake, 2286 *F-5
Orleans, 250 Q-7
Ortonville, 1252 R-11
Oscoda, 1061 L-11
Osseo, 550 U-8
Ossineke, 1091 J-11
Otisville, 724 Q-11
Otsego, 3937 S-5
Otsego Lake, 300 J-8
Otter Lake, 474 Q-11
Ovid, 1442 Q-9
Owendale, 285 N-11
Owosso, 16322 R-9
Oxbow *F-4
Oxford, 2929 R-11
Ozark E-7
Painesdale, 550 B-12
Palmer, 500 D-1
Paradise, 125 C-7
Parchment, 1958 *A-6
Paris, 450 N-6
Parkdale L-4
Parma, 809 T-8
Patterson Gardens, 3900 U-11
Paulding, 70 C-11
Paw Paw, 3169 T-5
Paw Paw Lake, 3782 T-4
Paynesville, 125 C-11
Pearl Beach, 3394 S-13
Peck, 558 Q-12
Pelkie, 40 B-12
Pellston, 583 G-7
Pentwater, 1050 N-4
Pequaming, 20 B-12

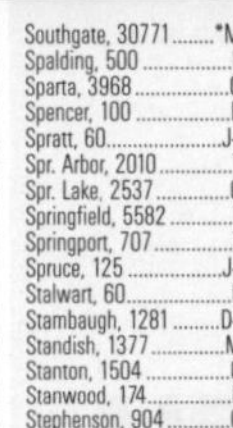

COVERED BRIDGE, MADISON COUNTY, IA

Perkins, 150 F-2
Perrinton, 393 Q-8
Perronville, 100 F-1
Perry, 2163 R-9
Peshawbestown, 200 J-6
Petersburg, 1201 U-10
Petoskey, 6056 G-7
Pewamo, 520 Q-7
Phoenix A-12
Pickford, 500 E-8
Pierport, 70 L-4
Pierson, 207 Q-6
Pigeon, 1207 N-11
Pinckney, 1603 S-10
Pinconning, 1291 N-9
Pinnebog, 60 M-11
Plainfield, 250 S-9
Plainwell, 4057 S-5
Pleasant Lake, 850 T-9
Pleasant Ridge, 2775 *H-7
Pleasant Valley, 80 P-8
Pleasant View, 40 G-7
Plymouth, 9560 S-11
Pointe Aux Pins, 10 F-8
Pontiac, 71166 S-11
Port Austin, 815 M-12
Port Hope, 313 M-12
Port Huron, 32694 Q-13
Port Sanilac, 656 P-13
Portage, 41042 T-6
Portland, 3889 R-7
Posen, 263 H-10
Potterville, 2225 S-8
Powers, 271 G-1
Prescott, 314 M-10
Presque Isle, 125 H-11
Princeton, 200 D-1
Prudenville, 1513 L-8
Pullman, 700 S-4
Quincy, 1680 U-7
Raco, 20 D-8
Ralph, 40 E-1
Ramsay, 750 C-9
Randville, 40 D-12
Rapid City, 550 J-6
Rapid River, 500 F-2
Ravenna, 919 Q-5
Reading, 1127 U-8
Red Oak, 40 K-9
Redford, 58387 *J-5
Reed City, 2379 N-6
Reese, 1414 P-10
Remus, 250 P-7
Republic, 300 E-1
Rexton, 70 E-6
Rhodes, 125 N-9
Richland, 465 T-6
Richmond, 4141 R-12
River Rouge, 11314 *L-7
Riverview, 13894 *M-7
Rives Jct., 650 T-8
Rochester, 7130 *E-8
Rochester Hills, 61766 R-11
Rock, 150 E-2
Rockford, 3750 Q-6
Rockland, 250 B-11
Rockwood, 3141 U-11
Rodney, 175 N-6
Rogers City, 3642 G-10
Romeo, 3520 R-12
Romulus, 22897 T-11
Roosevelt Park, 3885 Q-4
Roscommon, 858 K-8
Rose City, 686 L-9
Roseburg Q-12
Rosebush, 333 N-8
Rosedale, 50 D-9
Roseville, 51412 *G-9
Rothbury, 407 P-4
Rousseau, 10 B-11
Royal Oak, 65410 S-11
Rudyard, 500 E-8
Ruth, 250 N-12
Saginaw, 69512 P-9
Sagola, 50 D-12
St. Charles, 2144 Q-9
St. Clair, 5116 R-13
St. Clair Shores, 68107 S-12
St. Helen, 2390 L-8
St. Ignace, 2568 F-8
St. Jacques, 50 F-3
St. James, 200 F-6
St. Johns, 7284 Q-8
St. Joseph, 9214 T-3
St. Louis, 3828 P-8
Saline, 6660 T-10
Sand Lake, 456 Q-6
Sand River, 80 D-2
Sands, 100 D-1
Sandusky, 2403 P-12
Sanford, 889 N-8
Saranac, 1461 R-7
Saugatuck, 954 S-4
Sault Ste. Marie, 14689 D-8
Sawyer, 200 U-3
Schaffer, 250 F-2
Schoolcraft, 1517 U-5
Scottville, 1287 M-4
Sears, 100 N-6
Sebewaing, 1923 N-11
Selkirk, 90 L-9
Seney, 70 D-5
Shelby, 1871 P-4
Shepherd, 1413 P-8
Sheridan, 730 Q-7
Sherwood, 320 U-6
Shields, 6634 P-9
Shingleton, 500 D-4
Shoreham, 737 U-3
Sidnaw, 50 C-11
Silver City, 20 B-10
Sister Lakes, 1000 U-4
Six Lakes, 450 P-7
Skandia, 300 D-2
Skanee, 40 B-12
Skidway Lake, 2569 M-9
Smyrna, 300 Q-6
Snover, 250 P-12
S. Boardman, 500 K-6
S. Branch, 125 L-10
S. Haven, 5563 S-4
…n, 5857
…e 5266

Southgate, 30771 *M-7
Spalding, 500 F-1
Sparta, 3968 Q-5
Spencer, 100 K-7
Spratt, 60 J-10
Spr. Arbor, 2010 T-8
Spr. Lake, 2537 Q-4
Springfield, 5582 T-6
Springport, 707 T-8
Spruce, 125 J-11
Stalwart, 60 E-9
Stambaugh, 1281 D-12
Standish, 1377 M-9
Stanton, 1504 Q-7
Stanwood, 174 P-6
Stephenson, 904 G-1
Sterling, 520 M-9
Sterling Hts., 117810 S-12
Steuben, 10 E-4
Stevensville, 1230 U-3
Stockbridge, 1202 S-9
Stronach, 350 M-4
Sturgis, 10130 V-6
Sumner, 300 Q-7
Sunfield, 610 R-7
Sunrise Bay, 561 J-5
Swanson, 10 G-1
Swartz Cr., 4851 R-10
Sylvan Lake, 1884 *F-5
Tallmadge *B-1
Tallman M-4
Tapiola, 40 B-12
Tawas City, 2009 L-10
Taylor, 70811 T-11
Tecumseh, 7462 U-10
Tekonsha, 722 U-7
Temperance, 6542 V-11
Temple, 200 M-7
Thomaston, 90 C-10
Thompson, 30 F-4
Thompsonville, 416 K-5
Three Lakes, 10 C-12
Three Oaks, 1786 V-3
Three Rivers, 7413 U-5
Tipton, 300 U-9
Toivola, 20 B-11
Topinabee, 250 G-8
Torch Lake, 175 H-6
Tower, 350 H-9
Traunik, 20 E-3
Traverse City, 15155 K-5
Trenary, 125 E-3
Trenton, 19584 T-11
Trout Cr., 225 C-11
Trout Lake, 175 F-7
Trowbridge Park, 1831 D-1
Troy, 72884 S-11
Turner, 158 M-10
Tustin, 236 M-6
Twin Lake, 1328 P-4
Twin Lakes, 30 B-11
Twining, 169 M-10
Ubly, 921 N-12
Union, 500 V-5
Union City, 1767 U-7
Union Lake, 2500 *E-4
Unionville, 590 N-10
Utica, 5081 *F-8
Valley Ctr. Q-12
Vandalia, 357 V-5
Vanderbilt, 605 H-8
Vandercook Lake, 4642 T-9
Vassar, 2823 P-10
Vermontville, 776 S-7
Vernon, 913 R-9
Verona, 90 N-12
Vestaburg, 550 P-7
Vicksburg, 2216 T-6
Vogel Ctr., 175 M-7
Wakefield, 2318 C-9
Waldenburg *F-9
Waldron, 581 V-8
Walhalla, 250 N-4
Walker, 17279 R-5
Walkerville, 262 N-4
Walled Lake, 6278 *G-4
Walloon Lake, 400 H-7
Warren, 144864 S-12
Washington *D-8
Waterford, 66692 R-11
Waters, 225 K-8
Watersmeet, 450 C-11
Watervliet, 1867 T-4
Watrousville, 200 P-11
Watton, 30 C-12
Wauceda, 175 F-1
Wayland, 2751 S-5
Wayne, 19899 *L-5
Webberville, 1698 S-9
Weidman, 696 N-7
Wellston, 450 M-5
W. Acres *F-4
W. Branch, 1914 L-9
W. Olive R-4
Westland, 84724 T-11
Weston, 300 V-9
Westphalia, 780 R-7
Wetmore, 300 D-3
White Cloud, 1147 P-5
White Pigeon, 1458 V-5
White Pine, 700 B-10
Whitefish Pt. C-7
Whitehall, 3027 P-4
Whitmore Lake, 3251 S-10
Whittaker T-10
Whittemore, 463 M-10
Williamsburg, 350 K-6
Williamston, 2922 S-8
Wilmot P-11
Winegars, 50 M-8
Winn, 250 P-7
Winona, 30 B-11
Wisner, 200 N-10
Witch Lake, 60 C-13
Wixom, 8550 S-11
Wolf Lake, 4110 Q-4
Wolverine, 283 H-8
Woodbury, 175 R-7
Woodhaven, 11631 T-11
Woodland, 466 R-7
Woodland Beach, 2309 U-11
Woodland Park, 150 N-5
Wyandotte, 30938 T-11
Wyoming, 63891 R-5
Yale, 1977 Q-12
Yates *E-8
Ypsilanti, 24846 T-10
Zeeland, 5417 R-5
Zilwaukee, 1850 P-9

MINNESOTA PG. 115–117

CAPITAL
St. Paul

NICKNAME
Gopher State

POPULATION
4,657,758, rank 20

AREA
84,402 sq mi, rank 12

Counties

Aitkin, 12425 L-8
Anoka, 243641 Q-9
Becker, 27881 J-4
Beltrami, 34384 F-5
Benton, 30185 P-7
Big Stone, 6285 P-2
Blue Earth, 54044 U-7
Brown, 26984 T-5
Carlton, 29259 L-10
Carver, 47915 R-7
Cass, 21791 J-6
Chippewa, 13228 Q-4
Chisago, 30521 P-9
Clay, 50422 J-2
Clearwater, 8309 H-4
Cook, 3868 F-13
Cottonwood, 12694 U-4
Crow Wing, 44249 M-7
Dakota, 275227 S-9
Dodge, 15731 U-9
Douglas, 28674 N-4
Faribault, 16937 V-7
Fillmore, 20777 U-11
Freeborn, 33060 U-9
Goodhue, 40690 S-10
Grant, 6246 N-3
Hennepin, 1032431 Q-8
Houston, 18497 V-12
Hubbard, 14939 J-5
Isanti, 25921 P-8
Itasca, 40863 H-8
Jackson, 11677 V-4
Kanabec, 12802 M-9
Kandiyohi, 38761 Q-5
Kittson, 5767 D-1
Koochiching, 16299 E-8
Lac qui Parle, 8924 R-2
Lake, 10415 G-13
Lake of the Woods, 4076 E-5
Le Sueur, 23239 S-8
Lincoln, 6890 S-2
Lyon, 24789 S-3
Mahnomen, 5044 J-3
Marshall, 10993 E-2
Martin, 22914 U-6
McLeod, 32030 R-6
Meeker, 20846 Q-6
Mille Lacs, 18670 N-8
Morrison, 29604 M-7
Mower, 37385 V-10
Murray, 9660 T-3
Nicollet, 28076 S-6
Nobles, 20098 U-3
Norman, 7975 J-2
Olmsted, 106470 T-10
Otter Tail, 50714 L-3
Pennington, 13306 F-3
Pine, 21264 M-10
Pipestone, 10491 T-2
Polk, 32498 G-2
Pope, 10745 P-4
Ramsey, 485765 Q-9
Red Lake, 4525 G-3
Redwood, 17254 S-4
Renville, 17673 R-5
Rice, 49183 S-8
Rock, 9806 U-2
Roseau, 15026 D-3
St. Louis, 198213 G-10
Scott, 57846 R-8
Sherburne, 41945 P-7
Sibley, 14366 S-7
Stearns, 118791 P-6
Steele, 30729 T-8
Stevens, 10634 P-3
Swift, 10724 Q-3
Todd, 23363 M-5
Traverse, 4463 N-2
Wabasha, 19744 T-11
Wadena, 13154 L-5
Waseca, 18079 U-8
Washington, 145896 Q-9
Watonwan, 11682 U-5
Wilkin, 7516 L-2
Winona, 47828 U-11
Wright, 68710 Q-7
Yellow Medicine, 11684 R-3

Cities and Towns

* City indexed to pg. 115

Ada, 1708 H-2
Adams, 756 V-10
Adolph, 10 K-11
Adrian, 1141 U-3
Aitkin, 1698 L-8
Akeley, 393 K-5
Albany, 1548 P-6
Albert Lea, 18310 V-8
Alberta, 136 P-3
Albertville, 1251 Q-8
Alborn, 60 J-10
Alden, 623 U-8
Aldrich, 70 L-5
Alexandria, 7838 N-4
Alida, 30 H-5
Alma City T-8
Almelund, 100 P-10
Almora, 50 M-4
Alpha, 105 V-5
Altura, 349 T-11
Alvarado, 356 F-1
Alvwood, 10 G-7
Amboy, 517 U-7
Amiret, 70 T-3
Amor L-3
Andover, 15216 Q-8
Angle Inlet B-5
Angora, 30 G-10
Angus, 40 F-2
Annandale, 2054 Q-7
Anoka, 17192 Q-9
Apple Valley, 34598 R-9
Appleton, 1552 Q-3
Arco, 104 S-2
Arden Hills, 9199 *D-5
Argyle, 636 E-1
Arlington, 1886 S-7
Arnesen D-5
Arnold, 2891 K-11
Ash Cr. V-2
Ash Lake F-9
Ashby, 469 M-3
Askov, 343 M-10
Atkinson, 50 L-10
Atwater, 1053 Q-5
Audubon, 411 K-3
Aurora, 1965 H-11
Austin, 21907 V-9
Averill, 10 J-2
Avoca, 150 U-4
Avon, 970 P-6
Babbitt, 1562 G-11
Backus, 240 K-6
Badger, 381 D-3
Bagley, 1388 H-4
Baker, 80 K-2
Balaton, 737 T-3
Bald Eagle *C-8
Ball Bluff, 30 K-9
Ball Club, 80 H-7
Barnesville, 2066 K-2
Barnum, 482 L-10
Barrett, 350 N-3
Barrows, 80 M-7
Barry, 40 P-2
Bassett H-12
Basswood, 80 L-4
Battle Lake, 698 M-4
Baudette, 1146 D-6
Baxter, 3695 M-6
Bay Lake, 50 L-7
Bayport, 3200 Q-10
Bear River, 30 G-9
Beardsley, 297 P-1
Beaulieu, 30 H-3
Beaver Bay, 147 J-13
Beaver Cr., 249 V-2
Bechyn, 40 S-5
Becida, 50 H-5
Becker, 902 P-7
Bejou, 110 H-3
Belgrade, 700 P-5
Belle Plaine, 3149 S-8
Bellechester, 110 S-10
Bellingham, 247 Q-2
Beltrami, 137 H-2
Belview, 383 S-4
Bemidji, 11245 H-5
Bena, 147 H-7
Benedict, 150 J-6
Benson, 3235 Q-4
Bergen, 40 U-5
Bergville, 30 G-7
Berner, 20 G-4
Beroun, 125 N-9
Bertha, 507 M-5
Bethel, 394 P-8
Big Bend City, 100 Q-3
Big Falls, 341 F-7
Big Lake, 3113 Q-8
Big Woods, 50 E-1
Bigelow, 232 V-3
Bigfork, 384 G-8
Bingham Lake, 155 U-5
Birchdale, 50 E-7
Birchwood Vil., 1042 *D-8
Bird Island, 1326 R-5
Biscay, 113 R-6
Biwabik, 1097 H-10
Bixby, 60 U-9
Blackberry, 100 J-8
Blackduck, 718 G-6
Blaine, 38975 Q-9
Blakeley, 50 S-7
Blomkest, 183 R-5
Blooming Prairie, 2043 U-9
Bloomington, 86335 R-8
Blue Earth, 3745 V-7
Blue Grass, 50 L-5
Bluffton, 187 L-4
Bock, 115 N-8
Border, 40 D-7
Borup, 119 J-2
Bovey, 662 H-8
Bowlus, 260 N-6
Bowstring, 40 H-8
Boy River, 43 J-7
Boyd, 251 R-3
Bradford, 200 P-8
Braham, 1139 N-9
Brainerd, 12353 M-7
Branch P-9
Brandon, 441 N-4
Breckenridge, 3708 M-2
Breezy Pt., 432 L-7
Brennyville, 100 N-7
Brevik, 50 J-6
Brewster, 532 U-4
Bricelyn, 426 V-7
Brimson, 20 J-11
Britt, 125 G-10
Brook Park, 125 N-9
Brooklyn Ctr., 28887 *C-4
Brooklyn Park, 56381 *C-3
Brooks, 158 G-3
Brookston, 107 K-10
Brooten, 589 P-5
Browerville, 782 M-5
Browns Valley, 804 P-1
Brownsdale, 695 U-9
Brownsville, 415 U-13
Brownton, 781 R-6
Bruno, 89 M-10
Brunswick, 225 N-9
Brushvale, 20 L-2
Buckman, 201 N-7
Buffalo, 7302 Q-7
Buffalo Lake, 734 R-6
Buhl, 915 H-10
Burnett, 60 K-11
Burnsville, 51288 R-9
Burr, 30 P-2
Burtrum, 172 N-6
Butler, 10 K-4
Butterfield, 509 U-5
Buyck, 10 F-10
Byron, 2441 T-10
Caledonia, 2846 V-12
Callaway, 212 K-3
Calumet, 382 H-8
Cambridge, 5094 P-9
Campbell, 233 M-2
Canby, 1826 S-2
Cannon Falls, 3232 S-9
Canton, 362 V-11
Canyon, 30 J-10
Caribou C-2
Carlisle, 60 L-3
Carlos, 361 N-5
Carlton, 923 K-10
Carp, 10 D-6
Carver, 744 R-8
Cass Lake, 923 H-6
Castle Danger, 20 J-12
Castle Rock, 30 S-9
Cedar Mills, 80 R-6
Celina, 20 G-9
Center City, 451 P-10
Centerville, 1633 *B-7
Central, 20 L-5
Central Lakes J-10
Ceylon, 461 V-6
Champlin, 16849 *B-3
Chandler, 316 U-3
Chanhassen, 11736 R-8
Charlesville, 10 N-2
Chaska, 11339 R-8
Chatfield, 2226 U-11
Chickamaw Beach, 132 K-6
Chisago City, 2009 P-9
Chisholm, 5290 H-9
Chokio, 521 P-3
Circle Pines, 4704 *B-6
Clara City, 1307 R-4
Claremont, 530 T-9
Clarissa, 637 M-5
Clarkfield, 924 R-3
Clarks Gr., 675 U-8
Clear Lake, 315 P-7
Clearbrook, 560 G-4
Clearwater, 597 P-7
Clements, 191 S-5
Clementson, 40 D-6
Cleveland, 699 T-7
Climax, 264 G-1
Clinton, 574 P-2
Clinton Falls T-9
Clitherall, 109 M-4
Clontarf, 172 P-4
Cloquet, 10885 K-10
Clotho, 30 M-5
Cloverdale, 70 N-10
Cloverton, 10 M-11
Coates, 186 R-9
Cobden, 62 T-5
Cohasset, 1970 J-8
Cokato, 2180 Q-7
Cold Spr., 2459 P-6
Coleraine, 1041 J-8
Collegeville, 100 P-6
Collis, 30 P-2
Cologne, 563 R-8
Columbia Hts., 18910 *D-5
Comfrey, 433 T-5
Comstock, 123 K-1
Conger, 143 V-8
Cook, 680 G-10
Coon Rapids, 52978 *B-3
Corcoran, 5199 Q-8
Cormorant, 70 K-3
Corning U-9
Correll, 60 Q-3
Corvuso R-6
Cosmos, 610 R-6
Cottage Gr., 22935 R-9
Cotton, 70 J-10
Cottonwood, 982 S-4
Courtland, 412 T-6
Cove M-8
Craigville G-8
Crane Lake, 20 F-10
Croftville C-11
Cromwell, 221 K-9
Crookston, 8119 G-2
Crosby, 2073 L-7
Cross Lake, 1132 K-7
Crow River, 40 Q-6
Crown, 80 P-8
Crystal, 23788 *D-3
Culver, 40 K-10
Currie, 303 T-3
Cushing, 40 M-6
Cusson, 10 F-9
Cutler, 30 L-8
Cuyuna, 172 L-7
Cyrus, 328 P-3
Dakota, 360 U-13
Dalbo, 80 P-8
Dale, 50 K-3
Dalton, 234 M-3
Danube, 562 R-5
Danvers, 98 Q-3
Darfur, 128 T-5
Darwin, 252 Q-6
Dassel, 1082 Q-6
Dawson, 1626 R-3
Day, 30 N-8
Dayton, 4443 Q-8
De Graff, 149 Q-4
Debs, 20 G-5
Deephaven, 3653 *F-1
Deer Cr., 303 L-4
Deer River, 838 H-7
Deerwood, 524 L-7
Delano, 2709 Q-7
Delavan, 245 U-7
Delft, 90 U-5
Delhi, 69 S-4
Dellwood, 887 *C-8
Denham, 36 M-9
Dennison, 152 S-9
Dent, 177 L-4
Detroit Lakes, 7141 K-3
Dexter, 303 U-10
Dilworth, 3562 K-2
Dodge Ctr., 1954 T-9
Donaldson, 45 E-1
Donnelly, 221 N-3
Dora Lake G-7
Doran, 78 M-2
Dorothy, 20 G-2
Dorset, 100 J-5
Douglas, 175 T-10
Dover, 416 U-11
Dovray, 60 T-4
Downer, 20 K-2
Duelm, 100 P-7
Duluth, 85493 K-11
Dumont, 126 N-2
Dundas, 473 S-9
Dundee, 107 U-4
Dunnell, 187 V-5
Dunvilla, 50 K-3
Duquette, 60 L-10
Duxbury M-10
Eagan, 47409 *H-6
Eagle Bend, 524 M-5
Eagle Lake, 1703 T-7
E. Beaver Bay J-13
E. Bethel, 8050 P-9
E. Chain, 60 V-6
E. Grand Forks, 8658 F-1
E. Gull Lake, 687 L-6
E. Lake, 30 L-9
Easton, 229 U-7
Ebro, 60 H-4
Echo, 304 S-4
Eden Prairie, 39311 *H-1
Eden Valley, 732 Q-6
Edgerton, 1106 U-2
Edina, 46070 *H-2
Effie, 130 G-8
Eitzen, 221 V-13
Elba, 220 T-11
Elbow Lake, 1286 N-3
Eldred, 50 G-2
Elgin, 733 T-11
Elizabeth, 152 L-3
Elk River, 11143 Q-8
Elko, 223 S-8
Elkton, 142 V-10
Ellendale, 549 U-9
Ellsworth, 580 V-3
Elmdale, 130 N-6
Elmore, 709 V-7
Elrosa, 205 P-5
Ely, 3968 G-11
Elysian, 445 T-8
Embarrass, 70 G-11
Emily, 813 K-7
Emmons, 439 V-8
Empire, 300 S-9
Erdahl, 30 N-4
Erhard, 181 L-3
Ericsburg, 60 E-8
Erskine, 422 G-3
Esko, 1300 K-10
Estes Brook P-8
Etna, 40 V-10
Euclid, 70 F-2
Evansville, 566 N-4
Eveleth, 4064 H-10
Everdell, 20 K-3
Evergreen, 40 K-4
Eyota, 1448 U-11
Fairfax, 1276 S-5
Fairhaven, 80 Q-7
Fairmont, 11265 V-6
Faith, 50 K-3
Falcon Hts., 5380 *F-6
Faribault, 17085 T-8
Farming P-6
Farmington, 5940 S-9
Farwell, 74 N-4
Federal Dam, 118 J-7
Felton, 211 J-2
Fergus Falls, 12362 M-3
Fernando, 50 S-6
Fertile, 853 H-2
Fifty Lakes, 299 K-7
Fillmore U-11
Finland, 80 H-13
Finlayson, 242 M-9
Fisher, 413 G-1
Flensburg, 213 N-6
Flom, 60 J-3
Floodwood, 574 K-9
Florence, 53 T-3
Florenton, 125 H-10
Florian E-2
Foley, 1854 P-7
Forada, 171 N-4
Forbes, 50 H-10
Forest Ctr., 10 G-13
Forest City, 125 Q-6
Forest Lake, 5833 Q-9
Foreston, 354 N-8
Ft. Ripley, 92 M-6
Fosston, 1529 H-4
Fossum, 10 J-3
Fountain, 327 U-11
Fourtown, 10 F-4
Fox, 125 D-3
Foxhome, 160 M-2
Franklin, 441 S-5
Frazee, 1176 K-4
Freeborn, 301 U-8
Freedhem, 50 M-7
Freeport, 556 P-6
French River, 300 K-11
Fridley, 28335 Q-9
Frontenac, 350 S-11
Frost, 236 V-7
Fulda, 1212 U-4
Funkley, 15 G-6
Garden City, 250 T-7
Garfield, 203 N-4
Garrison, 138 M-7
Garvin, 149 T-3
Gary, 200 H-3
Gatzke E-4
Gaylord, 1935 S-7
Gem Lake, 439 *D-7
Gemmell, 30 F-7
Geneva, 444 U-9
Genola, 85 N-7
Gentilly, 100 G-2
Georgetown, 107 J-1
Georgeville P-5
Gheen, 30 F-10
Ghent, 316 S-3
Gibbon, 712 S-6
Gilbert, 1934 H-10
Gilman, 192 N-7
Glen, 50 L-8
Glencoe, 4648 R-7
Glendorado, 100 P-8
Glenville, 778 V-9
Glenwood, 2573 P-4
Gluek, 40 R-4
Glyndon, 862 K-2
Godahl T-6
Golden Valley, 20971 *E-2
Gonvick, 302 G-4
Good Thunder, 561 T-7
Goodhue, 533 S-10
Goodland, 60 J-9
Goodridge, 115 F-3
Goodview, 2878 T-12
Gordonsville, 125 V-9
Gowan, 30 K-9
Graceton, 30 D-5
Graceville, 671 P-2
Granada, 374 U-6
Grand Falls, 10 F-8
Grand Marais, 1171 C-11
Grand Meadow, 967 U-10
Grand Portage, 100 B-13
Grand Rapids, 7976 J-8
Grandy, 175 P-9
Granger, 50 V-11
Granite Falls, 3083 R-4
Grasston, 119 N-9
Greaney, 20 F-9
Green Isle, 239 S-7
Green Valley, 150 S-3
Greenbush, 800 D-3
Greenleaf, 40 R-6
Greenleafton, 125 V-11
Greenview P-8
Greenwald, 209 P-5
Grey Eagle, 353 N-6
Grove City, 547 Q-6
Grove Lake, 50 P-5
Grygla, 220 F-4
Gully, 128 G-4
Gutches Gr. N-5
Guthrie, 50 H-6
Hackensack, 245 K-6
Hader S-10
Hadley, 94 T-3
Hagan Q-3
Hallock, 1304 D-1
Halma, 73 D-2
Halstad, 611 H-1
Ham Lake, 8924 Q-9
Hamburg, 538 S-7
Hammond, 205 T-11
Hampton, 363 S-9
Hancock, 723 P-3
Hanley Falls, 246 R-4
Hanska, 443 T-6
Harding, 90 N-7
Hardwick, 234 U-2
Harmony, 1081 V-11
Harris, 843 P-9
Hartland, 270 U-8
Hassman, 40 L-8
Hastings, 15445 R-9
Hasty, 225 P-7
Hatfield, 66 U-2
Hawick, 125 Q-5
Hawley, 1655 K-2
Hay Cr., 30 S-10
Hayfield, 1283 U-10
Hayward, 246 V-9
Hazel Run, 81 R-3
Hector, 1166 R-6
Heidelberg, 73 S-8
Henderson, 746 S-7
Hendricks, 684 S-2
Hendrum, 309 J-1
Henning, 738 M-4
Henriette, 78 N-9
Herman, 485 N-3
Hermantown, 6761 K-11
Heron Lake, 730 U-4
Hewitt, 269 M-5
Hibbing, 18046 H-9
Hill City, 469 J-8
Hillman, 45 N-7
Hills, 607 V-2
Hilltop, 749 *D-4
Hinckley, 946 N-9
Hines, 50 G-6
Hitterdal, 242 K-2
Hoffman, 672 N-4
Hokah, 687 U-13
Holdingford, 561 N-6
Holland, 216 T-2
Hollandale, 289 U-9
Holloway, 123 Q-4
Holmes City, 100 N-4
Holt, 88 F-3
Holyoke, 100 L-10
Hope, 125 U-9
Hopkins, 16534 *G-2
Houston, 1020 U-13
Hovland, 20 B-12
Howard Lake, 1343 Q-7
Hoyt Lakes, 2348 H-11
Hubbard, 200 K-5
Hugo, 4417 Q-9
Humboldt, 74 D-1
Huntersville, 10 K-5
Huntley, 150 V-7
Hutchinson, 11523 R-6
Ihlen, 101 U-2
Illgen City, 30 H-13
Independence, 40 Q-8
Industrial, 10 E-1
Inger, 30 H-8
Inguadona, 30 J-7
International Falls, 8325 E-8
Inver Gr. Hts., 22477 *H-7
Iona, 158 U-3
Iron Jct., 133 H-10
Ironton, 553 L-7
Isabella, 100 H-12
Isanti, 1228 P-9
Island Lake, 40 G-5
Island View, 150 E-9
Isle, 566 M-8
Ivanhoe, 751 S-2
Jacobson, 60 J-9
Janesville, 1969 T-8
Jasper, 599 U-2
Jeffers, 443 T-4
Jenkins, 262 L-6
Johnsburg V-10
Johnson, 46 P-2
Jordan, 2909 S-8
Judson, 70 T-7
Kabekona, 40 J-5
Kabetogama, 40 E-9
Kanaranzi, 80 V-3
Kandiyohi, 506 Q-5
Karlstad, 881 E-2
Kasota, 655 T-7
Kasson, 3514 T-10
Keewatin, 1118 H-9
Kelliher, 348 G-6
Kellogg, 423 T-11
Kelly Lake, 20 H-9
Kelsey, 40 J-10
Kennedy, 337 D-1
Kenneth, 81 U-3
Kensington, 295 N-4
Kent, 131 L-2
Kenyon, 1552 T-9
Kerkhoven, 732 Q-4
Kerrick, 56 M-10
Kettle River, 190 L-9
Kiester, 606 V-8
Kilkenny, 167 T-8
Kimball, 690 Q-6
Kimberly, 20 L-8
Kinbrae, 18 U-4
Kingsdale M-11
Kingston, 131 Q-6
Kinney, 257 H-10
Klossner, 100 S-6
Knife River, 300 J-12
Kragnes, 40 J-1
La Crescent, 4311 U-13
La Prairie, 438 J-8
La Salle, 98 T-6
Lac qui Parle, 50 Q-3
Lafayette, 462 S-6
Lake Benton, 693 T-2
Lake Bronson, 272 D-2
Lake City, 4391 S-11
Lake Crystal, 2084 T-7
Lake Elmo, 5903 *E-9
Lake George, 150 J-5
Lake Henry, 90 P-5
Lake Hubert L-7
Lake Itasca, 20 J-5
Lake Lillian, 229 R-5
Lake Park, 638 K-3
Lake Shore, 693 L-6
Lake Wilson, 319 T-3
Lakefield, 1679 U-5
Lakeville, 24854 S-9
Lamberton, 972 T-4
LaMoille, 60 U-12
Lancaster, 342 D-2
Landfall, 685 *F-8
Lanesboro, 858 U-11
Lansing, 225 U-9
Laporte, 101 J-6
Larsmont, 100 J-12
Lastrup, 112 M-7
Lauderdale, 2700 *E-5
Lavinia, 100 H-5
Lawler, 30 L-9
Lawndale, 20 L-2
Lax Lake H-13
Le Ctr., 2006 S-8
Le Roy, 904 V-10
Le Sueur, 3714 S-7
Leader, 20 L-6
Leavenworth, 30 T-5
Leetonia, 40 H-9
Lengby, 112 H-4
Lenora V-12
Leonard, 26 G-5
Leonidas, 70 H-10
Leota, 250 U-3
Lester Prairie, 1180 R-7
Lewiston, 1298 U-12
Lewisville, 255 U-6
Lexington, 2279 *B-5
Libby, 10 K-8
Lilydale, 506 *G-6
Lime Cr., 50 U-4
Lincoln, 40 M-6
Linden Gr. G-9
Lindford, 10 E-8
Lindstrom, 2461 P-9
Lino Lakes, 8807 *A-6
Lismore, 248 U-3
Litchfield, 6041 Q-6
Little Canada, 8971 *E-6
Little Falls, 7232 N-6
Little Marais, 30 H-13
Little Rock, 50 N-7
Little Sauk, 125 N-5
Littlefork, 838 E-8
Lockhart, 30 H-2
Loman, 50 E-7
London, 90 V-9
Long Beach, 204 P-4
Long Prairie, 2786 N-5
Longville, 224 J-7
Lonsdale, 1252 S-8
Louisburg, 42 Q-3
Lowry, 233 N-4
Lucan, 235 S-4
Lude, 60 E-1
Lutsen, 100 C-11
Luverne, 4382 U-2
Lyle, 504 V-10
Lynd, 287 S-3
Mabel, 745 V-12
Madelia, 2237 T-6
Madison, 1951 Q-2
Madison Lake, 643 T-7
Magnolia, 155 V-3
Mahnomen, 1154 H-3
Mahtomedi, 5569 *C-8
Mahtowa, 80 L-10
Makinen, 60 H-10
Malmo, 69 M-8
Manannah, 100 Q-6
Manchester, 69 U-8
Manhattan Beach, 61 K-7
Mankato, 31459 T-7
Mantorville, 874 T-10
Maple Bay, 80 G-3
Maple Gr., 38736 Q-8
Maple Lake, 1394 Q-7
Mapleton, 1526 U-7
Mapleview, 206 U-9
Maplewood, 30954 *E-7
Marble, 618 H-8
Marcell, 60 H-8
Marcoux, 10 G-3
Marietta, 20 Q-3
Marine on St. Croix, 602 P-9
Markham, 60 H-11
Marshall, 12023 S-3
Marty P-6
Max, 40 H-7
Mayer, 471 R-7
Maynard, 419 R-4
Maywood P-5
Mazeppa, 722 T-10
McGrath, 62 M-9
McGregor, 376 K-9
McIntosh, 665 G-3
McKinley, 116 H-10
Meadowlands, 92 J-10
Medford, 1163 T-9
Medicine Lake, 385 *E-2
Meire Gr., 124 P-5
Melby, 80 M-3
Melrose, 2561 P-5
Melrude H-10
Menahga, 1076 K-5
Mendota, 164 *G-6
Mendota Hts., 9431 *G-6
Mentor, 94 G-3
Meriden T-8
Merrifield, 250 L-7
Middle River, 285 E-3
Midway, 30 K-10
Miesville, 135 S-10
Milaca, 2182 N-8
Milan, 350 Q-3
Millerville, 104 M-4
Millville, 163 T-10
Milroy, 297 T-4
Miltona, 281 M-5
Minneapolis, 368383 R-9
Minneiska, 127 T-12
Minneota, 1417 S-3
Minnesota City, 256 T-12
Minnesota Lake, 681 U-7
Minnetonka, 48370 *G-1
Minnetonka Beach *F-1
Mizpah, 64 F-7
Moland T-9
Money Cr., 70 U-12
Montevideo, 5499 R-3
Montgomery, 2399 S-8
Monticello, 4941 Q-8
Montrose, 1008 Q-7
Moorhead, 32295 K-1
Moose Lake, 1206 L-10
Mora, 2905 N-9
Morgan, 965 T-5
Morris, 5613 P-3
Morristown, 784 T-8
Morton, 448 S-5
Motley, 441 M-6
Mound, 9634 R-8
Mounds View, 12541 *C-5
Mtn. Iron, 3362 H-10
Mtn. Lake, 1906 U-5
Murdock, 282 Q-4
Murphy City, 20 H-12
Myrtle, 72 V-9
Nashua, 63 M-2
Nashwauk, 1026 H-9
Nassau, 83 Q-2
Naytahwaush, 378 J-4
Nebish, 90 G-5
Nelson, 177 N-4
Nerstrand, 210 S-9
Nett Lake, 50 F-9
Nevis, 375 J-5
New Auburn, 363 S-7
New Brighton, 22207 *D-5
New Germany, 353 R-7
New Hope, 21853 *D-2
New London, 971 Q-5
New Market, 227 S-8
New Munich, 314 P-5
New Prague, 3569 S-8
New Richland, 1237 U-8
New Ulm, 13132 T-6
New York Mills, 940 L-4
Newfolden, 345 E-2
Newport, 3720 *G-8
Nickerson, 40 L-10
Nicollet, 795 T-7
Nielsville, 100 H-1
Nimrod, 65 L-5
Nininger *J-9
Nisswa, 1391 L-7
Norcross, 86 N-3
Norseland, 70 S-7
N. Branch, 4267 P-9
N. Mankato, 10164 T-7
N. Oaks, 3386 *C-6
N. Redwood, 203 S-5
N. St. Paul, 12376 *D-8
Northcote, 10 D-1
Northfield, 14684 S-9
Northome, 283 G-7
Northrop, 276 U-6
Norwood, 1351 R-7
Noyes, 30 C-1
Oak Ctr. S-10
Oak Gr., 5488 Q-9
Oak Park, 125 N-7
Oak Park Hts., 3486 Q-10
Oakdale, 18374 *E-8
Oakland, 60 U-9
Odessa, 155 Q-2
Odin, 102 U-5
Ogema, 164 J-3
Ogilvie, 510 N-8
Okabena, 223 U-4
Oklee, 441 G-3
Olivia, 2623 R-5
Onamia, 676 M-8
Onigum J-6
Opole N-6
Orleans D-1
Ormsby, 159 U-6
Orono, 7285 R-8
Oronoco, 727 T-10
Orr, 265 F-9
Ortonville, 2205 Q-2
Osage, 150 K-5
Osakis, 1256 N-5
Oslo, 362 F-1
Osseo, 2704 *C-2
Ostrander, 276 V-10
Otisco, 60 U-8
Otsego, 5219 Q-8
Ottawa, 125 S-7
Ottertail, 313 L-4
Outing, 100 K-7
Owatonna, 19386 T-9
Oylen, 50 L-5
Padua P-5
Palisade, 144 K-8
Palmers, 80 K-12
Park Rapids, 2863 K-5
Parkers Prairie, 956 M-4
Payne J-10
Paynesville, 2275 P-6
Pease, 178 N-8
Pelican Rapids, 1886 L-3
Pemberton, 228 U-8
Pengilly, 350 H-9
Pennington, 30 H-6
Pennock, 476 Q-5
Pequot Lakes, 843 L-6
Perham, 2075 L-4
Perley, 132 J-1
Petersburg, 30 V-5
Peterson, 259 U-12
Phelps, 40 L-3
Philbrook, 30 M-6
Pierz, 1014 N-7
Pigeon River, 20 B-12
Pillager, 306 M-6
Pillsbury N-6
Pine Brook, 175 P-8
Pine Cr., 80 M-7
Pine City, 2613 N-9
Pine Island, 2125 T-10
Pine River, 871 K-6
Pine Sprs., 436 *D-8
Pinecreek, 50 C-3
Pinewood, 50 H-5
Pipestone, 4554 T-2
Pitt, 20 D-6
Plainview, 2768 T-11
Plato, 355 R-7
Plummer, 277 G-3
Plymouth, 50889 R-8
Ponemah, 704 F-6
Ponsford, 200 J-4
Porter, 210 S-2
Preston, 1530 U-11
Princeton, 3719 P-8
Prinsburg, 502 R-5
Prior Lake, 11482 R-8
Proctor, 2974 K-11
Prosit, 40 J-10
Puposky, 70 G-5
Quamba, 124 N-9
Racine, 288 U-10
Radium, 10 F-2
Ramey N-7
Ramsey, 12408 Q-8
Randall, 571 M-6
Randolph, 331 S-9
Ranier, 199 E-8
Rapidan T-7
Rauch G-9
Ray, 30 E-9
Raymond, 668 Q-4
Reading, 125 U-4
Reads Landing, 70 S-11
Red Lake, 1068 G-5
Red Lake Falls, 1481 G-3
Red Wing, 15134 S-10
Redby, 787 G-5
Redwood Falls, 4859 S-5
Regal, 51 P-5
Remer, 342 J-8
Renville, 1315 R-5
Revere, 117 T-4
Rice, 610 P-7
Richfield, 35710 *G-4
Richmond, 965 P-6
Richville, 125 L-4
Richwood, 100 K-3
Riverton, 122 L-7
Robbin, 40 F-1
Robbinsdale, 14396 *D-3
Robinson, 10 G-11
Rochert, 350 K-3
Rochester, 85806 T-10
Rock Cr., 1040 N-9
Rockford, 3484 Q-8
Rockville, 750 P-6
Rollingstone, 697 T-12
Rollins, 10 J-11
Ronneby, 58 P-8
Roosevelt, 180 D-5
Roscoe, 141 P-6
Rose Cr., 360 V-10
Roseau, 2756 D-3
Rosemount, 8622 *K-6
Rosen, 60 Q-2
Roseville, 33485 *E-5
Rosewood, 100 G-2
Ross, 20 D-4
Rossburg, 50 J-8
Rothsay, 443 L-2
Round Lake, 463 V-4
Round Prairie, 100 N-5
Royalton, 815 N-6
Rush City, 1497 P-9
Rushford, 1696 U-12
Rushford Vil., 705 U-12
Rushmore, 381 U-3
Russell, 394 S-3
Ruthton, 328 T-3
Rutledge, 152 M-9
Sabin, 495 K-2
Sacred Heart, 603 R-4
Saginaw, 150 K-10
St. Anthony, 7727 *D-5
St. Anthony, 81 N-6
St. Augusta, 650 P-7
St. Charles, 2642 U-11
St. Clair, 633 T-7
St. Cloud, 48812 P-7
St. Francis, 2538 P-8
St. George, 100 S-6
St. Hilaire, 298 F-3
St. James, 4364 U-6
St. Joseph, 3294 P-6
St. Leo, 111 R-3
St. Louis Park, 43787 *F-3
St. Martin, 274 P-6
St. Michael, 2506 Q-8
St. Nicholas, 125 P-6
St. Paul, 272235 R-9
St. Paul Park, 4965 *H-8
St. Peter, 9421 T-7
St. Rosa, 75 N-6
St. Stephen, 607 N-6
St. Vincent, 116 C-1
St. Wendell P-6
Salol, 100 D-4
Sanborn, 459 T-5
Sandstone, 2057 M-9
Santiago, 100 P-7
Sargeant, 78 U-10
Sartell, 5393 P-7
Sauk Centre, 3581 N-5
Sauk Rapids, 7825 P-7
Saum, 60 F-6
Savage, 9906 R-8
Sawyer, 175 K-10
Scanlon, 878 K-10
Schley, 10 H-6
Schroeder, 80 C-10
Seaforth, 87 S-4
Searles, 225 T-6
Sebeka, 662 L-5
Sedan, 63 P-4
Shafer, 368 P-10
Shakopee, 11739 R-8
Shaw J-10
Sheldon, 60 U-12
Shelly, 225 H-1
Sherack, 20 F-2
Sherburn, 1105 V-5
Sheshebee, 90 K-9
Shevlin, 157 H-5
Shieldsville S-8
Shooks, 30 G-6
Shoreview, 24587 *C-5
Shotley F-6
Shovel Lake K-8
Side Lake G-9
Silica J-9
Silver Bay, 1894 H-13
Silver Cr., 200 Q-7
Silver Lake, 764 R-7
Silverdale, 10 F-9
Simpson, 70 U-10
Sioux Valley, 50 V-4
Skibo, 10 H-11
Skime E-4
Skyline, 272 T-7
Slayton, 2147 T-3
Sleepy Eye, 3694 T-5
Sobieski, 199 N-6
Sogn S-9
Solway, 74 H-5
Soudan, 450 G-11
S. Haven, 193 Q-7
S. St. Paul, 20197 *G-7
Spicer, 1020 Q-5
Spr. Gr., 1153 V-12
Spr. Hill, 77 P-5
Spr. Lake, 30 G-7
Spr. Lake Park, 6532 *C-4
Spr. Valley, 2461 U-10
Springfield, 2173 T-5
Squaw Lake, 139 H-7
Stacy, 1081 P-9
Stanton, 100 S-9
Staples, 3104 M-5
Starbuck, 1143 P-4
Steen, 176 V-2
Stephen, 707 E-1
Stewart, 566 R-6
[illegible] J-12
Stewartville, 4520 U-10
Stillwater, 13882 Q-10
Stockholm Q-7
Stockton, 529 T-12
Storden, 283 T-4
[illegible] P-9
Strandquist, 98 E-2
Strathcona, 40 E-3
Sturgeon Lake, 230 L-9
Sunburg, 117 Q-4
Sunfish Lake, 413 *G-6
Sunrise, 175 P-9
Svea, 150 R-5
Swan River, 20 J-9
Swanville, 324 N-6
Swatara, 60 K-8
[illegible] D-5
Swift Falls, 100 P-4
Syre, 10 J-2
Tabor, 50 F-1
Taconite, 310 H-8
Taconite Harbor, 10 H-13
Talmoon, 50 H-8
Tamarack, 63 L-9
Taopi, 83 V-10
Taunton, 175 S-3
Taylors Falls, 694 P-10
Tenney, 4 M-2
Tenstrike, 184 G-6
Terrace, 40 P-4
Terrebonne, 40 G-3
Theilman, 50 T-11
Thief River Falls, 8010 F-3
Tintah, 74 M-2
Tobique, 10 J-7
Tofte, 150 C-10
Togo, 10 G-9
Toimi H-12
Toivola J-10
Tower, 502 G-11
Tracy, 2059 T-4
Trail, 67 G-4
[illegible] S-7
Trimont, 745 U-6
Trommald, 80 L-7
Trosky, 120 U-2
[illegible] U-11
Truman, 1292 U-6
Turtle River, 62 H-6
Twig, 350 K-10
Twin Lakes, 154 V-8
Twin Valley, 821 J-2
Two Harbors, 3651 J-12
[illegible] J-5
Tyler, 1257 T-2
Ulen, 547 J-2
Underwood, 284 M-3
Upsala, 371 N-6
Urbank, 73 M-4
[illegible] U-11
Vadnais Hts., 11041 *D-7
Vasa S-10
Verdi, 60 T-2
Vergas, 287 K-3
Vermillion, 510 S-9
Verndale, 560 L-5
Vernon Ctr., 339 U-7
Vesta, 302 S-4
Victoria, 2354 R-8
Viking, 103 F-2
Villard, 247 N-4
Vineland, 438 M-8
Vining, 84 M-4
Viola, 70 T-11
Virginia, 9432 H-10
Wabasha, 2384 S-11
Wabasso, 684 S-4
Waconia, 3498 R-7
Wadena, 4131 L-5
Wahkon, 197 M-8
Waite Park, 5020 P-7
Waldorf, 243 U-8
Walker, 950 J-6
Walnut Gr., 625 U-4
Walters, 86 V-8
Waltham, 170 U-10
Wanamingo, 847 T-10
Wanda, 103 T-4
Wannaska, 30 D-4
Warba, 137 J-9
Ward Sprs., 125 N-5
Warman, 70 M-9
Warren, 1813 F-2
Warroad, 1679 D-5
Warsaw, 550 T-8
Waseca, 8385 T-8
Waskish F-6
Watab, 450 P-7
Waterville, 1771 T-8
Watkins, 880 Q-6
Watson, 211 Q-3
Waubun, 330 J-3
Waverly, 600 Q-7
Wayzata, 3806 *E-1
Wealthwood L-8
Weaver, 70 T-11
Weber, 90 P-9
Wegdahl, 50 R-4
Welch S-10
Welcome, 790 V-6
Wells, 2465 U-8
Weme, 30 G-4
Wendell, 159 M-3
W. Concord, 871 T-9
W. St. Paul, 19248 *G-7
W. Union, 54 N-5
Westbrook, 853 T-4
Westbury, 30 K-3
Westport, 47 N-5
Whalan, 94 U-11
Wheaton, 1615 N-2
Whipholt, 60 J-6
White Bear Lake, 24704 *D-8
White Earth, 319 J-3
White Rock, 90 S-10
Whiteface J-10
Whyte H-12
Wilbert V-6
Wilder, 83 U-4
Wilkinson, 50 J-6
Willernie, 584 *D-8
Williams, 212 D-5
Willmar, 17531 Q-5

SHAKER VILLAGE, PLEASANT HILL, KY

Willow River, 284 M-9
Wilmont, 351 U-3
Wilno, 20 S-2
Wilson, 100 U-12
Wilton, 171 H-5
Windom, 4283 U-5
Winger, 167 H-3
Winnebago, 1565 U-7
Winona, 25399 T-12
Winsted, 1581 R-7
Winthrop, 1279 S-6
Winton, 169 G-12
Wirock U-3
Wirt, 30 G-7
Withrow *C-9
Witoka, 100 U-12
Wolf Lake, 35 K-4
Wolverton, 158 L-1
Wood Lake, 406 S-4
Woodbury, 20075 R-9
Woodland, 496 *F-1
Woodland, 10 M-9
Woodstock, 159 T-3
Worthington, 9977 V-4
Wrenshall, 296 L-10
Wright, 144 K-9
Wrightstown, 50 M-5
Wyattville, 50 U-12
Wykoff, 493 U-11
Wylie, 10 F-2
Wyoming, 2142 Q-9
Young America, 1354 R-7
Zemple, 63 H-8
Zerkel, 60 H-4
Zim, 90 H-10
Zimmerman, 1350 P-8
Zumbro Falls, 237 T-10
Zumbrota, 2312 T-10

MISSISSIPPI PG. 118

CAPITAL
Jackson

NICKNAME
Magnolia State

POPULATION
2,716,115, rank 31

AREA
47,689 sq mi, rank 32

Counties

Adams, 35356 K-4
Alcorn, 31722 A-9
Amite, 13328 K-4
Attala, 18481 E-7
Benton, 8046 A-8
Bolivar, 41875 D-4
Calhoun, 14908 C-8
Carroll, 9237 D-6
Chickasaw, 18085 D-8
Choctaw, 9071 E-7
Claiborne, 11370 H-4
Clarke, 17313 H-9
Clay, 21120 D-9
Coahoma, 31665 C-5
Copiah, 27592 J-5
Covington, 16527 J-7
De Soto, 67910 A-6
Forrest, 68314 L-8
Franklin, 8377 J-4
George, 16673 L-9
Greene, 10220 K-9
Grenada, 21555 D-7
Hancock, 31760 M-7
Harrison, 165365 M-8
Hinds, 254441 H-5
Holmes, 21604 E-6
Humphreys, 12134 F-5
Issaquena, 1909 G-4
Itawamba, 20017 C-9
Jackson, 115243 M-9
Jasper, 17114 H-8
Jefferson, 8653 J-4
Jefferson Davis, 14051 J-6
Jones, 62031 J-8
Kemper, 10356 G-9
Lafayette, 31826 B-7
Lamar, 30424 K-7
Lauderdale, 75555 H-9
Lawrence, 12458 K-6
Leake, 18436 F-7
Lee, 65581 B-9
Leflore, 37341 E-6
Lincoln, 30278 K-5
Lowndes, 59308 E-9
Madison, 53794 G-6
Marion, 25544 K-7
Marshall, 30361 B-7
Monroe, 36582 D-9
Montgomery, 12388 D-7
Neshoba, 24800 G-8
Newton, 20291 H-8
Noxubee, 12604 F-9
Oktibbeha, 38375 E-8
Panola, 29996 C-6
Pearl River, 38714 L-7
Perry, 10865 K-8
Pike, 36882 K-5
Pontotoc, 22237 C-8
Prentiss, 23278 B-9
Quitman, 10490 C-6
Rankin, 87161 H-6
Scott, 24137 G-7
Sharkey, 7066 F-5
Simpson, 23953 J-6
Smith, 14798 H-7
Stone, 10750 L-8
Sunflower, 32867 E-5
Tallahatchie, 15210 D-6
Tate, 21432 B-6
Tippah, 19523 A-8
Tishomingo, 17683 B-10
Tunica, 8164 B-5
Union, 22085 B-8
Walthall, 14352 L-6
Warren, 47880 G-5
Washington, 67935 F-4
Wayne, 19517 J-9
Webster, 10222 D-7
Wilkinson, 9678 L-3
Winston, 19433 F-8
Yalobusha, 12033 C-7
Yazoo, 25506 G-6

Cities and Towns

Abbeville, 399 B-7
Aberdeen, 6837 D-9
Ackerman, 1573 E-8
Agricola, 200 L-9
Albin, 40 D-6
Alcorn, 1200 J-4
Algoma, 420 C-8
Alligator, 187 C-5
Amory, 7093 C-9
Anding, 225 G-5
Anguilla, 883 F-5
Ansley, 70 N-7
Arcola, 564 E-5
Arm, 125 J-6
Arnold Line, 1800 E-1
Artesia, 484 E-9
Ashland, 490 A-8
Askew B-6
Auburn, 20 K-5
Avalon, 30 D-6
Avon E-4
Bailey, 450 G-9
Baird, 30 E-5
Baldwyn, 3204 B-9
Banks, 20 A-6
Banner, 90 C-7
Barnett, 125 H-9
Basic, 80 H-9
Bassfield, 249 K-7
Batesville, 6403 C-6
Battles, 175 J-9
Baxterville, 125 L-7
Bay St. Louis, 8063 M-8
Bay Sprs., 1729 H-8
Beatty, 10 E-7
Beaumont, 1054 K-8
Beauregard, 206 J-5
Becker, 225 D-9
Belen, 125 C-6
Bellefontaine, 80 D-8
Belmont, 1554 B-10
Belzoni, 2536 E-5
Benndale, 100 L-9
Benoit, 641 D-4
Benton, 300 F-6
Bentonia, 390 G-6
Beulah, 460 D-4
Big Cr., 123 D-7
Big Pt., 300 M-9
Bigbee Valley, 175 E-10
Biggersville, 175 A-9
Biloxi, 46319 M-9
Black Hawk, 70 E-6
Blaine, 100 D-5
Blue Mtn., 667 B-8
Blue Sprs., 140 B-8
Bobo, 200 C-5
Bogue Chitto, 689 F-8
Bogue Chitto, 383 K-5
Bolivar, 60 D-4
Bolton, 637 G-5
Bond, 350 L-8
Booneville, 7955 B-9
Bourbon, 40 E-5
Boyle, 651 D-5
Brandon, 11089 H-6
Braxton, 141 H-6
Brazil, 60 C-6
Brewer, 225 K-9
Brookhaven, 10243 J-5
Brooklyn, 350 L-8
Brooksville, 1098 E-9
Brownsville, 70 G-5
Bruce, 2127 C-8
Buckatunna, 300 J-9
Bude, 969 K-4
Burns, 70 H-7
Burnside, 20 F-8
Burnsville, 949 A-10
Byhalia, 955 A-7
Byram, 150 H-6
Caledonia, 821 D-10
Calhoun City, 1838 D-8
Camden, 20 F-7
Canaan, 30 A-8
Canton, 10062 G-6
Carlisle, 50 H-5
Carnes, 250 L-8
Carpenter, 30 H-5
Carriere, 600 M-7
Carrollton, 221 E-6
Carson J-7
Carter, 80 F-5
Carthage, 3819 G-7
Cary, 392 F-4
Cayuga, 60 H-5
Cedar Lake M-2
Centreville, 1771 L-4
Charleston, 2328 C-6
Chatawa, 150 L-5
Chatham, 40 F-4
Cheraw, 150 K-7
Chicora, 90 J-9
Chunky, 292 G-8
Church Hill, 20 J-4
Clara, 350 J-9
Clarksdale, 21180 C-5
Cleveland, 15384 D-5
Cliftonville E-9
Clinton, 21847 G-6
Coahoma, 254 C-5
Cockrum, 175 A-7
Coffeeville, 825 C-7
Coila, 30 E-6
Coldwater, 1502 B-6
Coles, 125 K-4
Collins, 2541 J-7
Collinsville, 1364 G-9
Columbia, 6815 K-7
Columbus, 23799 E-9
Como, 1387 B-6
Conehatta, 925 G-8
Corinth, 11820 A-9
Courtland, 329 C-6
Crandall, 30 H-9
Crawford, 668 E-9
Crenshaw, 978 B-6
Crosby, 465 K-4
Crossroads, 90 L-7
Crowder, 758 C-6
Cruger, 548 E-6
Crystal Sprs., 5643 H-6
Daleville, 175 G-9
Darbun, 80 K-6
Darling, 300 C-6
Darlove, 30 E-5
De Kalb, 1073 F-9
De Lisle, 800 M-8
De Soto, 250 H-9
Decatur, 1248 G-8
Dennis, 150 B-10
Derma, 1023 D-8
Dexter, 90 L-6
Diamondhead, 2661 M-8
D'Iberville, 6566 M-9
D'Lo, 421 H-6
Doddsville, 149 D-5
Dossville, 70 F-8
Drew, 2349 D-5
Dublin, 70 C-5
Duck Hill, 586 D-7
Duffee, 60 G-8
Dumas, 407 A-9
Duncan, 416 C-5
Dundee, 125 B-5
Durant, 2838 F-7
Eagle Bend, 80 G-4
Eastport, 10 A-10
Ebenezer, 80 F-6
Ecru, 696 B-8
Eddiceton, 80 K-5
Eden, 88 F-5
Edinburg, 100 G-7
Edwards, 1279 H-5
Egypt, 40 D-9
Electric Mills, 40 F-9
Elliott, 175 D-7
Ellisville, 3634 J-8
Enid, 225 C-6
Enterprise, 477 H-9
Escatawpa, 3902 M-9
Estill, 70 E-4
Ethel, 454 E-7
Etta, 50 B-8
Eupora, 2145 E-8
Evansville, 60 B-5
Fairview, 150 C-10
Falcon, 167 B-6
Falkner, 232 A-8
Farrell, 200 C-5
Fayette, 1853 J-4
Fernwood, 300 K-5
Fitler, 30 F-4
Flora, 1482 G-6
Florence, 1831 H-6
Flowood, 2860 C-2
Fontainebleau N-4
Forest, 5060 G-7
Forkville, 30 G-7
Ft. Adams, 10 K-3
Foxworth, 500 K-6
French Camp, 320 E-7
Friars Pt., 1334 C-5
Fruitland Park L-8
Fulton, 3387 C-9
Gallman, 300 H-5
Garden City, 80 K-4
Garlandville, 50 H-8
Gatesville, 70 H-6
Gattman, 120 D-10
Gautier, 10088 M-9
Geeville, 40 B-9
Georgetown, 332 J-6
Gholson, 20 F-9
Gillsburg, 20 L-5
Glancy, 30 J-5
Glen, 221 A-9
Glen Allan, 400 F-4
Glendale E-2
Glendora, 165 D-6
Gloster, 1323 K-4
Golden, 202 B-10
Goodman, 1256 F-6
Goss, 125 K-6
Grace, 125 F-4
Grand Gulf, 30 H-4
Greenville, 45226 E-4
Greenwood, 18906 E-6
Greenwood Sprs., 50 D-10
Grenada, 10864 D-7
Gulfport, 64145 M-8
Gunnison, 611 D-4
Guntown, 692 B-9
Hamburg, 90 J-4
Hamilton D-9
Harmontown, 60 B-7
Harperville, 250 G-7
Harriston, 60 J-4
Harrisville, 175 H-6
Hatley, 529 C-9
Hattiesburg, 45325 K-8
Hazlehurst, 4221 J-5
Heads, 20 E-5
Heidelberg, 981 J-8
Helena M-5
Hermanville, 125 H-5
Hernando, 3125 A-6
Hickory, 493 G-8
Hickory Flat, 535 B-8
Highpoint, 150 E-8
Hillhouse, 30 C-5
Hillsboro, 300 G-7
Hinchcliff, 40 C-6
Hiwannee, 90 J-9
Holcomb, 250 D-6
Hollandale, 3576 E-5
Holly Bluff, 200 F-5
Holly Sprs., 7261 B-7
Hollywood, 150 B-6
Hopewell, 150 H-6
Horn Lake, 9069 A-6
Hot Coffee, 150 J-7
Houston, 3903 D-8
Howard, 30 F-6
Howison, 100 M-8
Hudsonville, 70 A-7
Hurley, 500 M-9
Hushpuckena, 20 C-5
Independence, 300 B-7
Indianola, 11809 E-5
Ingomar, 400 B-8
Inverness, 1174 E-5
Isola, 732 E-5
Itta Bena, 2377 E-6
Iuka, 3122 A-10
Jackson, 202062 H-6
James, 90 E-4
Janice, 30 L-8
Jayess, 175 K-6
Johns, 175 H-7
Johnston, 125 K-5
Jonestown, 1467 C-5
Jumpertown, 438 B-9
Kilmichael, 826 E-7
Kiln, 1262 M-7
Kirby, 20 J-4
Kirkville, 40 B-9
Kokomo, 125 K-6
Kolola Sprs., 150 D-9
Kosciusko, 6986 F-7
Kossuth, 245 A-9
Lafayette Sprs., 100 C-8
Lake, 369 G-8
Lake Cormorant, 150 A-6
Lakeshore, 225 N-7
Lamar, 175 A-8
Lambert, 1131 C-6
Lamont, 250 E-4
Latimer, 3222 M-9
Lauderdale, 300 G-9
Laurel, 18827 J-8
Le Tourneau, 200 H-4
Leaf, 100 L-9
Leakesville, 1129 K-9
Learned, 111 H-5
Leedy, 175 A-10
Leflore, 50 D-6
Leland, 6366 E-4
Lena, 175 G-7
Lessley, 10 K-3
Lexie, 125 L-6
Lexington, 2227 F-6
Liberty, 624 K-5
Little Rock, 150 G-8
Long Beach, 15804 M-8
Longview, 350 E-8
Lorman, 50 J-4
Louin, 289 H-8
Louise, 343 F-5
Louisville, 7169 F-8
Lucedale, 2592 L-9
Ludlow, 250 G-7
Lula, 224 B-5
Lumberton, 2121 L-7
Lyman M-8
Lynchburg, 2071 A-6
Lyon, 446 C-5
Maben, 752 E-8
Macon, 2256 E-9
Madden, 30 G-8
Madison, 14692 G-6
Magee, 3607 J-6
Magnolia, 2245 K-5
Mantachie, 1107 C-9
Mantee, 134 E-8
Marietta, 287 B-9
Marion, 1359 G-9
Marks, 1758 C-6
Martinsville, 200 J-5
Mashulaville, 50 F-9
Matherville, 50 J-9
Mathiston, 818 E-8
Maxie, 20 L-8
Mayersville, 795 G-4
Maysville F-4
Mayhew, 40 E-9
McAdams, 200 F-7
McCall Cr., 125 K-5
McCallum, 40 K-8
McComb, 11591 K-5
McCondy D-9
McCool, 169 E-8
McDonald, 70 G-8
McHenry, 225 L-8
McLain, 536 K-9
McLaurin, 250 K-8
McNair, 50 J-4
McNeill, 450 M-7
McVille, 50 F-5
Meadville, 453 K-4
Memphis, 70 M-8
Mendenhall, 2463 H-6
Meridian, 41036 G-9
Merigold, 572 D-5
Merrill, 30 L-9
Mesa, 90 K-6
Metcalfe, 1092 E-4
Michigan City, 40 A-8
Midnight, 225 F-5
Midway, 80 F-6
Miller, 125 A-7
Minter City, 90 D-6
Mississippi State, 3500 E-9
Mize, 312 J-7
Money, 80 D-6
Monticello, 1755 J-6
Montpelier, 30 D-8
Montrose, 106 H-8
Moorhead, 2417 E-5
Morgan City, 139 E-6
Morgantown, 225 K-6
Morton, 3212 G-7
Moselle, 350 K-8
Moss J-8
Moss Pt., 17837 M-9
Mound Bayou, 2222 D-5
Mt. Carmel, 125 J-7
Mt. Olive, 914 J-7
Mt. Pleasant, 300 A-7
Myrick, 300 J-8
Myrtle, 358 B-8
Natchez, 19460 J-3
Necaise, 80 M-7
Neely, 10 K-9
Nesbit, 700 A-6
Neshoba, 60 G-8
Nettleton, 2462 C-9
New Albany, 6775 B-8
New Augusta, 668 K-8
New Hamilton D-9
New Hebron, 373 J-6
New Hope, 1663 E-10
New Houlka, 558 C-8
Newport, 35 A-6
Newton, 3701 G-8
Nicholson, 1400 M-7
Nitta Yuma, 70 F-5
N. Carrollton, 578 E-6
N. Tunica, 1314 B-5
Noxapater, 441 F-8
Oak Gr., 1400 K-7
Oak Vale, 150 K-6
Oakland, 553 C-6
Oakley, 250 H-5
Ocean Sprs., 15221 M-9
Ofahoma, 20 G-7
Okolona, 3267 C-9
Olive Branch, 3567 A-7
Oma, 40 J-6
Onward, 20 G-4
Osyka, 483 L-5
Ovett, 150 K-8
Oxford, 9984 C-7
Ozona, 400 M-7
Pace, 354 D-5
Pachuta, 268 H-9
Paden, 123 B-10
Paris, 175 C-7
Pascagoula, 25899 M-9
Pass Christian, 5557 M-8
Pattison, 175 J-4
Paulding, 200 H-8
Paulette, 10 F-9
Paynes, 150 D-6
Pearl, 19588 H-6
Pearlington, 1603 N-7
Pelahatchie, 1553 G-7
Penton, 40 A-6
Percy, 50 F-4
Perkinston, 700 L-8
Petal, 7883 K-8
Pheba, 175 D-8
Philadelphia, 6758 F-8
Philipp, 250 D-6
Phoenix, 60 G-5
Picayune, 10633 M-7
Pickens, 1285 F-6
Pinckneyville, 40 L-3
Piney Woods, 80 H-6
Pinola, 150 J-6
Pittsboro, 277 D-8
Plantersville, 1046 C-9
Pocahontas, 40 G-6
Polkville, 129 H-7
Pontotoc, 4570 C-8
Pope, 171 C-6
Poplar Cr., 60 E-7
Poplarville, 2561 L-7
Port Gibson, 1810 H-4
Porterville, 40 G-9
Potts Camp, 483 B-8
Prairie, 20 D-9
Prairie Pt., 30 E-9
Prentiss, 1487 J-7
Preston, 250 F-9
Pricedale, 125 K-6
Prichard, 30 B-6
Prismatic, 60 G-9
Puckett, 294 H-7
Pulaski, 90 H-7
Purvis, 2140 K-7
Quincy, 40 D-10
Quitman, 2736 H-9
Quito, 100 E-6
Raleigh, 1291 H-7
Randolph, 150 C-8
Raymond, 2275 H-5
Red Banks, 125 A-7
Red Lick, 100 J-4
Redwater, 289 F-7
Redwood, 125 G-5
Reform, 125 E-8
Renfroe, 90 F-7
Renova, 636 D-5
Rich, 60 B-5
Richland, 4014 H-6
Richton, 1034 K-8
Ridgeland, 11714 G-6
Rienzi, 339 B-9
Ripley, 5371 B-8
Roberts, 20 H-8
Robinsonville, 100 A-6
Rockport, 40 J-6
Rodney, 30 J-4
Rolling Fork, 2444 F-4
Rome, 90 D-5
Rose Hill, 90 H-8
Rosedale, 2595 D-4
Rosetta, 70 K-4
Roxie, 568 J-4
Ruleville, 3245 D-5
Runnelstown, 250 K-8
Ruth, 100 K-5
Sallis, 139 F-7
Saltillo, 1782 C-9
Sanatorium, 900 J-7
Sand Hill, 40 H-9
Sandersville, 853 J-8
Sandhill, 125 G-6
Sandy Hook, 50 L-7
Sanford, 300 K-7
Sarah, 20 B-6
Sardis, 2128 B-6
Sarepta, 60 C-8
Satartia, 59 G-5
Saucier, 900 M-8
Savage, 100 B-6
Schlater, 404 D-6
Scobey, 10 D-7
Scooba, 541 F-9
Scott, 150 D-4
Sebastopol, 281 G-8
Seminary, 231 J-7
Senatobia, 4772 B-6
Shannon, 1419 C-9
Sharon, 30 G-6
Shaw, 2349 D-5
Shelby, 2926 C-5
Sherard, 40 C-5
Sherman, 528 C-9
Shivers, 70 J-6
Shubuta, 577 J-9
Shuqualak, 570 F-9
Sidon, 596 E-6
Silver City, 348 F-5
Silver Cr., 190 J-6
Silver Run, 30 L-8
Skene, 200 D-5
Slate Spr., 118 D-8
Slayden, 60 A-7
Sledge, 577 C-5
Smithdale, 200 K-5
Smithville, 871 C-9
Sontag, 125 J-6
Soso, 366 J-8
Southaven, 17949 A-6
Springville, 90 C-8
Stafford Sprs., 175 J-8
Stallo, 125 F-8
Standing Pine, 346 G-7
Stanton, 300 J-4
Star, 400 H-6
Starkville, 18458 E-9
State Line, 395 K-9
Steens, 70 D-10
Stewart, 175 E-7
Stonewall, 1148 H-9
Stovall, 30 C-5
Stringer, 125 J-8
Sturgis, 198 E-8
Summerland, 30 J-8
Summit, 1566 K-5
Sumner, 368 C-6
Sumrall, 903 K-7
Sunflower, 729 E-5
Suqualena, 150 G-9
Swan Lake, 60 D-6
Swiftown, 80 E-5
Sylvarena, 110 H-7
Talowah, 100 L-7
Taylor, 288 C-7
Taylorsville, 1412 J-7
Tchula, 2186 E-6
Terry, 613 H-6
Thaxton, 431 C-8
Thomastown, 100 F-7
Thompson, 30 K-5
Thorn, 200 D-8
Thornton, 70 F-6
Tie Plant, 450 D-7
Tilden, 100 C-10
Tillatoba, 124 C-6
Tinsley, 50 G-5
Tiplersville, 100 A-8
Tippo D-6
Tishomingo, 332 B-10
Toccopola, 154 C-8
Tomnolen, 90 E-8
Toomsuba, 175 G-9
Trebloc, 40 D-9
Tremont, 342 C-10
Troy, 60 C-8
Tucker, 459 G-8
Tuckers Crossing, 350 J-8
Tula, 200 C-8
Tunica, 1175 B-5
Tupelo, 30685 C-9
Tuscola, 125 G-7
Tutwiler, 1391 C-5
Tylertown, 1938 K-6
Tyro, 20 B-7
Union, 1875 G-8
Union Church, 50 J-5
Utica, 1033 H-5
Vaiden, 789 E-7
Valley Park, 60 G-5
Vance, 80 C-6
Vancleave, 3214 M-9
Vardaman, 920 D-8
Vaughan, 60 F-6
Verona, 2893 C-9
Vicksburg, 26886 G-4
Vossburg, 80 H-8
Wade, 150 M-9
Walls, 200 A-6
Walnut, 523 A-8
Walnut Gr., 389 G-7
Walthall, 167 D-8
Wanilla, 90 J-6
Washington, 250 J-4
Water Valley, 3610 C-7
Waterford, 90 B-7
Waveland, 5369 M-8
Waynesboro, 5143 J-9
Wayside, 70 E-4
Webb, 605 D-6
Weir, 525 E-8
Wenasoga, 175 A-9
Wesson, 1510 J-5
West, 184 E-7
W. Point, 8489 D-9
Wheeler, 300 B-9
White Apple, 80 K-4
Whitfield D-3
Whitfield, 90 K-8
Wiggins, 3185 L-8
Wiggins, 100 G-7
Wilkinson, 125 K-4
Williamsburg, 90 J-7
Williamsville, 400 F-7
Winborn, 125 B-8
Winchester, 50 J-9
Winona, 5965 E-7
Winstonville, 277 D-5
Winterville, 175 E-4
Woodland, 182 D-8
Woodville, 1393 K-4
Wool Market, 1166 M-2
Wortham L-1
Wyatte, 10 B-7
Yazoo City, 12427 F-5
Zama, 40 F-8

MISSOURI PG. 119–121

CAPITAL
Jefferson City

NICKNAME
Show Me State

POPULATION
5,358,692, rank 16

AREA
69,697 sq mi, rank 19

Counties

Adair, 24577 B-7
Andrew, 14632 B-2
Atchison, 7457 A-1
Audrain, 23599 D-8
Barry, 27547 M-4
Barton, 11312 J-3
Bates, 15025 G-3
Benton, 13859 G-5
Bollinger, 10619 K-12
Boone, 112379 E-7
Buchanan, 83083 D-2
Butler, 38765 L-11
Caldwell, 8380 C-4
Callaway, 32809 F-8
Camden, 27495 H-6
Cape Girardeau, 61633 J-13
Carroll, 10748 D-5
Carter, 5515 L-11
Cass, 63808 G-3
Cedar, 12093 J-4
Chariton, 9202 D-6
Christian, 32644 L-6
Clark, 7547 A-9
Clay, 153411 D-3
Clinton, 16595 D-3
Cole, 63579 G-7
Cooper, 14835 F-6
Crawford, 19173 H-10
Dade, 7449 J-4
Dallas, 12646 J-6
Daviess, 7865 B-4
De Kalb, 9967 C-3
Dent, 13702 J-9
Douglas, 11876 L-7
Dunklin, 33112 N-13
Franklin, 80603 G-10
Gasconade, 14006 G-9
Gentry, 6848 B-3
Greene, 207949 K-5
Grundy, 10536 B-5
Harrison, 8469 B-4
Henry, 20044 G-4
Hickory, 7335 H-6
Holt, 6034 B-2
Howard, 9631 E-6
Howell, 31447 L-9
Iron, 10726 J-11
Jackson, 633232 E-3
Jasper, 90465 K-3
Jefferson, 171380 G-11
Johnson, 42514 F-4
Knox, 4482 B-8
Laclede, 27158 J-6
Lafayette, 31107 E-5
Lawrence, 30236 K-4
Lewis, 10233 B-8
Lincoln, 28892 E-10
Linn, 13885 C-6
Livingston, 14592 C-5
Macon, 15345 C-7
Madison, 11127 J-12
Maries, 7976 H-8
Marion, 27682 C-9
McDonald, 16938 L-3
Mercer, 3723 A-5
Miller, 20700 G-7
Mississippi, 14442 L-14
Moniteau, 12298 G-7
Monroe, 9104 D-8
Montgomery, 11355 E-9
Morgan, 15574 G-6
New Madrid, 20928 M-13
Newton, 44445 L-3
Nodaway, 21709 A-2
Oregon, 9470 L-10
Osage, 12018 G-9
Ozark, 8598 M-7
Pemiscot, 21921 N-13
Perry, 16648 J-13
Pettis, 35437 F-5
Phelps, 35248 H-8
Pike, 15969 D-10
Platte, 57867 D-2
Polk, 21826 J-5
Pulaski, 41307 J-8
Putnam, 5079 A-6
Ralls, 8476 D-9
Randolph, 24370 D-7
Ray, 21971 D-4
Reynolds, 6661 K-10
Ripley, 12303 L-11
St. Charles, 212907 F-11
St. Clair, 8457 H-5
St. Francois, 48904 J-12
St. Louis, 993529 F-11
Saline, 23523 E-6
Schuyler, 4236 B-7
Scotland, 4822 A-8
Scott, 39376 L-13
Shannon, 7613 K-9
Shelby, 6942 C-8
Ste. Genevieve, 16037 H-12
Stoddard, 28895 L-13
Stone, 19078 L-5
Sullivan, 6326 B-6
Taney, 25561 M-6
Texas, 21476 K-8
Vernon, 19041 H-3
Warren, 19534 F-10
Washington, 20380 H-11
Wayne, 11543 K-11
Webster, 23753 K-6
Worth, 2440 A-3
Wright, 16758 K-7

Cities and Towns

* City indexed to pg. 119
\# Independent city population not included in county figures.

Adrian, 1582 G-3
Advance, 1139 K-13
Affton, 21106 F-15
Agency, 642 C-3
Airport Drive, 818 *H-9

BIRCH POINT STATE PARK, ME

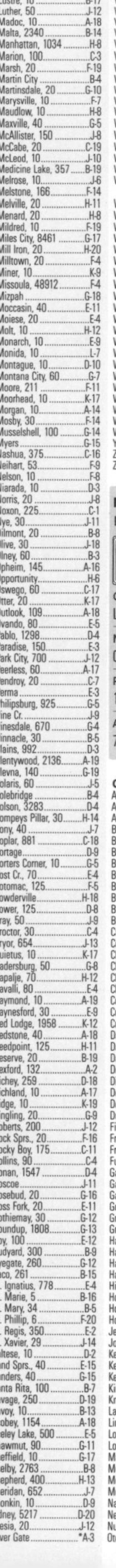

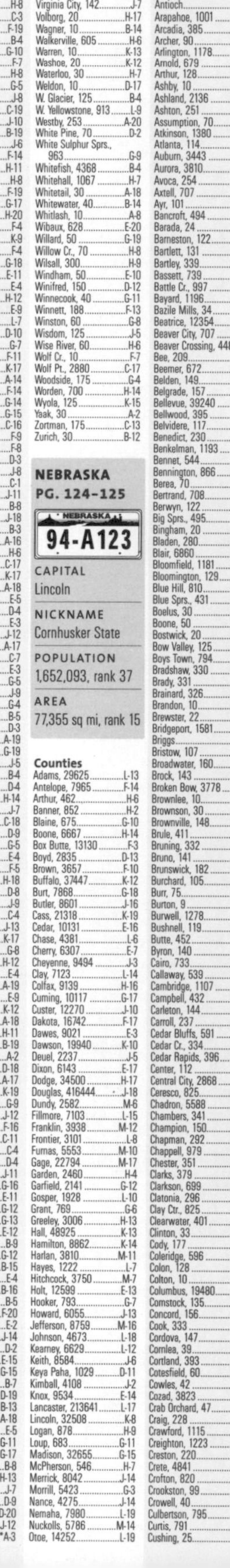

OAK ALLEY PLANTATION, VACHERIE, LA

MONTANA
PG. 122–123

5P-1234A

CAPITAL
Helena

NICKNAME
Treasure State

POPULATION
879,372, rank 44

AREA
147,046 sq mi, rank 4

Counties

Cities and Towns

NEBRASKA
PG. 124–125

94-A123

CAPITAL
Lincoln

NICKNAME
Cornhusker State

POPULATION
1,652,093, rank 37

AREA
77,355 sq mi, rank 15

Counties

Cities and Towns

NEVADA
PG. 126

123·HBC

CAPITAL
Carson City

NICKNAME
Silver State

POPULATION
1,603,163, rank 38

AREA
110,561 sq mi, rank 7

Counties

NEW HAMPSHIRE
PG. 127

ABC-123

CAPITAL
Concord

NICKNAME
Granite State

POPULATION
1,162,481, rank 42

AREA
9,279 sq mi, rank 44

Cities and Towns
Independent city population is not included in county figures

Counties

Cities and Towns

TILGHMAN ISLAND, MD

NEW JERSEY
PG. 128–129

CAPITAL
Trenton

NICKNAME
Garden State

POPULATION
7,987,933, rank 9

AREA
7,787 sq mi, rank 46

Counties

Cities and Towns

NEW MEXICO
PG. 130–131

CAPITAL
Santa Fe

NICKNAME
Land of Enchantment

POPULATION
1,713,407, rank 36

AREA
121,593 sq mi, rank 5

Counties

Cities and Towns

NEW YORK
PG. 132–137

CAPITAL
Albany

NICKNAME
Empire State

POPULATION
18,184,774, rank 3

AREA
49,108 sq mi, rank 30

Counties

BOSTON, MA

Cities and Towns

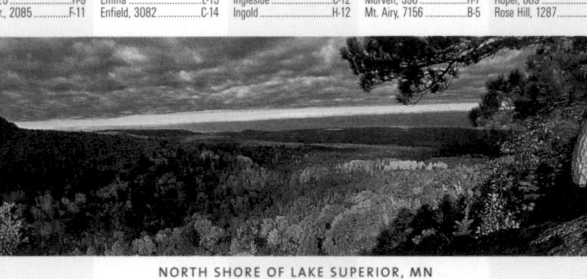

NORTH SHORE OF LAKE SUPERIOR, MN

CRANBERRY BOG, SOUTH CARVER, MA

NORTH CAROLINA

PG. 138–140

CAPITAL
Raleigh

NICKNAME
Tar Heel State

POPULATION
7,322,870, rank 11

AREA
52,669 sq mi, rank 28

Counties

Cities and Towns

* City indexed to pg. 140

NORTH DAKOTA

PG. 141

CAPITAL
Bismarck

NICKNAME
Flickertail State

POPULATION
643,539, rank 47

AREA
70,703 sq mi, rank 17

Counties

Cities and Towns

NEWFOUND LAKE, NH

OREGON
PG. 148–149

CAPITAL
Salem

NICKNAME
Beaver State

POPULATION
3,203,735, rank 29

AREA
97,073 sq mi, rank 10

Counties

Cities and Towns

PENNSYLVANIA
PG. 150–154

CAPITAL
Harrisburg

NICKNAME
Keystone State

POPULATION
12,056,112, rank 5

AREA
45,308 sq mi, rank 33

Counties

Cities and Towns
* City indexed to pg. 154

CHACO CANYON, NM

WHITEFACE MOUNTAIN, NY

RHODE ISLAND
PG. 155

CAPITAL
Providence

NICKNAME
Ocean State

POPULATION
990,225, rank 43

AREA
1,212 sq mi, rank 50

Counties

Cities and Towns

SOUTH CAROLINA
PG. 156

CAPITAL
Columbia

NICKNAME
Palmetto State

POPULATION
3,698,746, rank 26

AREA
31,113 sq mi, rank 40

Counties

Cities and Towns

SOUTH DAKOTA
PG. 157

CAPITAL
Pierre

NICKNAME
Mount Rushmore State

POPULATION
732,405, rank 45

AREA
77,116 sq mi, rank 16

Counties

Cities and Towns

Cities and Towns

LINN COVE VIADUCT, NC

TENNESSEE
PG. 158–159

CAPITAL
Nashville

NICKNAME
Volunteer State

POPULATION
5,319,654, rank 17

AREA
42,144 sq mi, rank 34

Counties

TEXAS
PG. 160–164

SBC 12A

CAPITAL
Austin

NICKNAME
Lone Star State

POPULATION
19,128,261, rank 2

AREA
266,807 sq mi, rank 2

Counties

Cities and Towns

* City indexed to pg. 164

TURTLE RIVER STATE PARK, ND

HOLY CITY, WICHITA MOUNTAINS WILDLIFE REFUGE, OK

CRATER LAKE NATIONAL PARK, OR

UTAH
PG. 165

CAPITAL
Salt Lake City

NICKNAME
Beehive State

POPULATION
2,000,494, rank 34

AREA
84,899 sq mi, rank 11

Counties

VERMONT
PG. 166

CAPITAL
Montpelier

NICKNAME
Green Mountain State

POPULATION
588,654, rank 49

AREA
9,614 sq mi, rank 43

Counties

VIRGINIA
PG. 167–169

CAPITAL
Richmond

NICKNAME
Old Dominion

POPULATION
6,675,451, rank 12

AREA
40,767, rank 36

Counties

Cities and Towns

* City indexed to pg. 167
# Independent city population not included in county figures

WASHINGTON
PG. 170–171

CAPITAL
Olympia

NICKNAME
Evergreen State

POPULATION
5,532,939, rank 15

AREA
68,138 sq mi, rank 20

Counties

Cities and Towns

ROGUE RIVER, CRATER LAKE NATIONAL PARK, OR

THE BREAKERS, NEWPORT, RI

WEST VIRGINIA
PG. 173

CAPITAL
Charleston

NICKNAME
Mountain State

POPULATION
1,825,754, rank 35

AREA
24,231 sq mi, rank 41

Counties

WISCONSIN
PG. 174–175

CAPITAL
Madison

NICKNAME
Badger State

POPULATION
5,159,795, rank 18

AREA
56,153 sq mi, rank 26

Counties

Cities and Towns

WYOMING
PG. 176

CAPITAL
Cheyenne

NICKNAME
Equality State

POPULATION
481,400, rank 50

AREA
97,809 sq mi, rank 9

Counties

Cities and Towns

SANTEE, SC

ALBERTA
PG. 179

ABC-123

CAPITAL
Edmonton

POPULATION
2,696,826, rank 4

AREA
255,286 sq mi, rank 5

Cities and Towns
* City indexed to pg. 177

BRITISH COLUMBIA
PG. 178–179

ABC 123

CAPITAL
Victoria

POPULATION
3,724,500, rank 3

AREA
365,946 sq mi, rank 4

Cities and Towns
* City indexed to pg. 177

BADLANDS NATIONAL PARK, SD

MANITOBA
PG. 181

123 ABC

CAPITAL
Winnipeg

POPULATION
1,113,898, rank 5

AREA
250,946 sq mi, rank 7

Cities and Towns
* City indexed to pg. 177

NEW BRUNSWICK
PG. 186–187

BAA - 123

CAPITAL
Fredericton

POPULATION
738,133, rank 8

AREA
28,355 sq mi, rank 10

Cities and Towns

NORTHWEST TERRITORIES
PG. 177

10635

CAPITAL
Yellowknife

POPULATION
64,402, rank 11

AREA
1,322,903 sq mi, rank 1

Cities and Towns

NOVA SCOTIA
PG. 186–187

CDE 123

CAPITAL
Halifax

POPULATION
909,282, rank 7

AREA
21,425 sq mi, rank 11

Cities and Towns

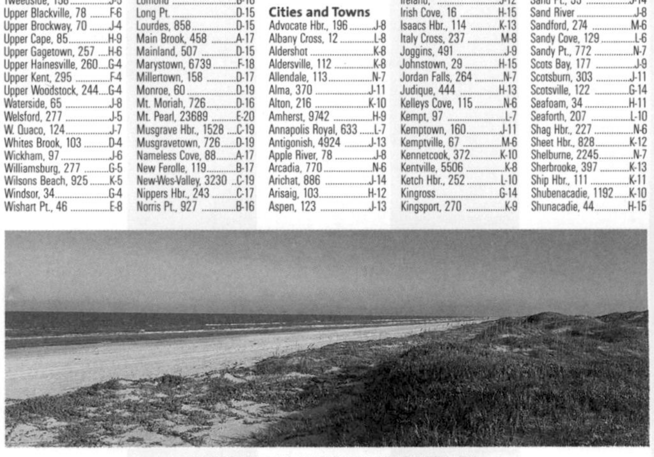

PADRE ISLAND NATIONAL SEASHORE, TX

NEWFOUNDLAND
PG. 187

ATA 123

CAPITAL
St. John's

POPULATION
551,792, rank 9

AREA
156,649 sq mi, rank 9

Cities and Towns
* City indexed to pg. 177

ONTARIO
PG. 181–183

123 ABC

CAPITAL
Toronto

POPULATION
10,753,573, rank 1

AREA
412,579 sq mi, rank 3

Cities and Towns
* City indexed to pg. 177
† City indexed to pg. 181

COURTHOUSE TOWERS, ARCHES NATIONAL PARK, UT

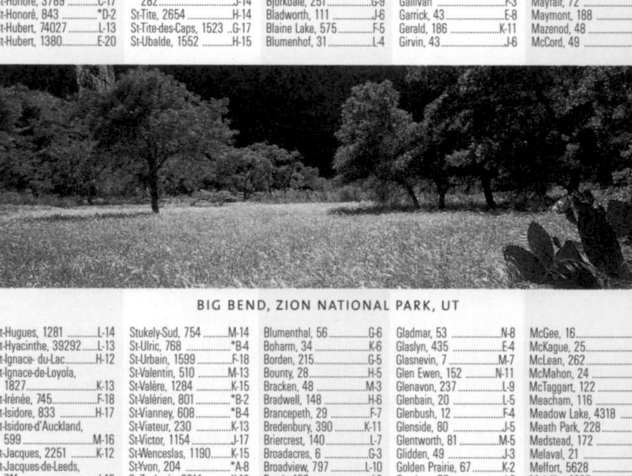

BIG BEND, ZION NATIONAL PARK, UT

QUÉBEC
PG. 184–186

CAPITAL
Québec

POPULATION
7,138,795, rank 2

AREA
594,857 sq mi, rank 2

Cities and Towns
* City indexed to pg. 177
† City indexed to pg. 186

PRINCE EDWARD ISLAND
PG. 186–187

CAPITAL
Charlottetown

POPULATION
134,557, rank 10

AREA
2,185 sq mi, rank 12

Cities and Towns

SASKATCHEWAN
PG. 180–181

CAPITAL
Regina

POPULATION
990,237, rank 6

AREA
251,866 sq mi, rank 6

Cities and Towns
* City indexed to pg. 177

YUKON TERRITORY
PG. 177

CAPITAL
Whitehorse
POPULATION
30,766, rank 12
AREA
186,660 sq mi, rank 8

Cities and Towns

Mexico

MEXICO
PG. 188–189
CAPITAL
Mexico City
POPULATION
95,772,462
AREA
756,066 sq mi

Cities and Towns

ROCHESTER, VT

Puerto Rico & Virgin Islands

PUERTO RICO
PG. 190
CAPITAL
San Juan
POPULATION
3,782,862
AREA
3,435 sq mi

Cities and Towns

U.S. VIRGIN ISLANDS
PG. 190
CAPITAL
Charlotte Amalie, St. Thomas
POPULATION
97,564
AREA
134 sq mi

Cities and Towns

Special Features

Includes National Park Service sites, recreation areas, museums, ·ical sites, and other select of interest on pg. 56–191.

B

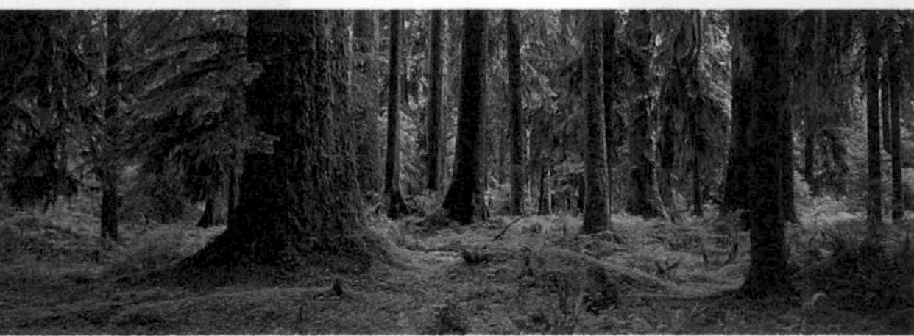
HALL OF MOSSES TRAIL, OLYMPIC NATIONAL PARK, WA

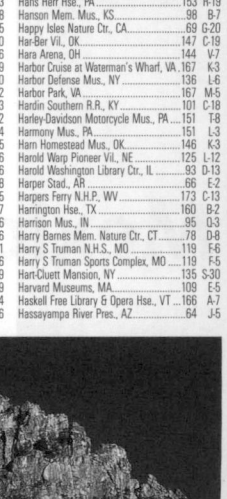

QUIDI VIDI HARBOR, NEWFOUNDLAND, CANADA

GRAND TETON NATIONAL PARK, WY

EL PALACIO, SAYIL, YUCATÁN, MEX

Q

R

S

T

CRUZ BAY, ST. JOHN, U.S. VIRGIN ISLANDS

U

V

W

Y

Z

Writers:
David Lansing, Kay and William G. Scheller

Regional Guides map reliefs:
Tibor G. Tóth/Tóth Graphix

Cover photography:
Jackson Hole, WY (t)-top; Cumberland Island, GA (m)-middle; Yosemite NP, CA (b)-bottom, Susan G. Drinker.

Foreword and Introduction photography:
Pg. 4: Admiral Nimitz and officers (t), courtesy U. S. Navy; Rendering of map (b), Volkmer Wentzel/National Geographic Society. **Pg. 5:** Mount Rainier NP, WA (t), Chuck Pefley/Tony Stone Images (TSI); Lincoln Highway motor caravan, 1913 (m), and (b), courtesy Detroit Public Library, National Automotive History Collection, MI.

Chapter introductions photography:
Pg. 2–3: Garrapata State Park, near Carmel, CA, Terry Donnelly. **Pg. 8–9:** Great Smoky NP, TN, Zandria Muench Beraldo. **Pg. 56–57:** Alaska Highway, AK, Paul Souders/TSI. **Pg. 192–193:** Glacier NP, MT, David Muench. **Pg. 214–215:** Wisconsin River Valley, WI, Mary Liz Austin.

Regional Guides photography:
Pg. 10–11, Alaska: (D) Carr Clifton; (G) Kim Heacox/TSI; (H) Art Wolfe/TSI; (I) Marcia Pennington/Unicorn Stock Photos; (K) Wolfgang Kaehler Photography; (M) Mark Kelley/TSI; (N) Greg Probst/TSI; (O) Larry Ulrich/TSI. Totem and ptarmigan, PhotoDisc; salmon, Gary Vestal/TSI. **Pg. 12–13, Pacific Northwest:** (B) Greg Vaughn/TSI; (C) Terry Donnelly; (F) Brett Baunton/TSI; (H) Greg Vaughn/TSI; (K) and (L) Peter Pearson/TSI; (M) courtesy Washington State Tourism Division; (N) Terry Donnelly. Rose, airplane, and beaver, PhotoDisc. **Pg. 14–15, Far West:** (D) Ed Pritchard/TSI; (E) Moldvay/TSI; (F) Greg Probst/TSI; (H) Traveler's Resource/TSI; (J) Roger M. Smith/Vision Impact Photography; (K) Drinker Durrance Group; (L) courtesy Nevada Commission on Tourism; (N) Phil Schermeister/TSI. Butterfly, PhotoDisc; dice, Osentoski & Zoda/Envision; mushroom cloud, Los Alamos National Lab/Peter Arnold, Inc. **Pg. 16–17, Southwest:** (B) David Hiser/TSI; (D) David Ball/TSI; (E) Roger M. Smith/Vision Impact Photography; (G) Carr Clifton; (L) John Elk III/TSI; (N) Rob Boudreau/TSI; (O) Lois Moultan/TSI. Pennies, chile, cactus, and hummingbird, PhotoDisc. **Pg. 18–19, Longhorn Country:** (C) and (D) Laurence Parent Photography; (H) James Randklev/TSI; (I), (L), and (M) John Elk III; (N) Jim Argo. Steer, oil drill, and Native American headdress, PhotoDisc. **Pg. 20–21, Southern Rockies:** (C) Ted Wood/TSI; (E) Susan G. Drinker; (F) Paul Grebliunas/TSI; (G) Chad Ehlers/TSI; (I) courtesy Purgatory Resort; (J) David Hiser/TSI; (K) Dick Durrance II; (N) Comstock. Peaches and marmot, PhotoDisc. **Pg. 22–23, Northern Rockies:** (B) Terry Donnelly; (C) Fred Lindholm/Sun Valley Chamber of Commerce; (D) Quicksilver Studios; (H) Chuck Haney; (I) Nicholas DeVore/TSI; (J) Mark Keller/Superstock; (M) Andre Jenny/Unicorn Stock Photos; (N) Terry Donnelly. Potatoes, elk, and rodeo rider, PhotoDisc. **Pg. 24–25, Northern Great Plains:** (B) Glen Allison/TSI; (C) Tom Dietrich/TSI; (E) Tom Bean; (F) Richard Day/Daybreak Imagery; (K) Larry Ulrich/TSI; (P) Cathlyn Melloah/TSI; (Q) Mary Liz Austin. Cow, PhotoDisc; wheat, Nick Gunderson/TSI; gold, Neal & Mary Mishler/TSI; pig, PhotoDisc. **Pg. 26–27, Southern Great Plains:** (B) Doris De Witt/TSI; (C) Charlie Reidel/courtesy Kansas Travel and Tourism Division; (D) courtesy NCAA; (F) Donovan Reese/TSI; (H) Doris De Witt/TSI; (J) Peter Pearson/TSI; (K) Michael Hubrich; (M) Buddy Mays/Travel Stock; (N) Bob Krist/TSI. Bat and beer, PhotoDisc; tornado, Peter Rauter/TSI. **Pg. 28–29, Great Lakes:** (A) GALA/Superstock; (E) Don Carney/Eastern National; (F) Ray Malace/FPG; (H) courtesy Henry Ford Museum; (I) David Muench; (J) Al Michaud/FPG; (K) courtesy Apostle Islands National Seashore; (N) James Blank/FPG; (O) courtesy Circus World Museum. Wolf, cherries, and cow, PhotoDisc. **Pg. 30–31, Heartland:** (A) Peter Pearson/TSI; (B) Terry Donnelly; (D) Mark Segal/TSI; (F) Steve Leonard/TSI; (H) Peter Pearson/TSI; (J) Jake Rajs/TSI; (K) David Muench/TSI; (N) Kevin R. Morris/TSI; (P) Piet van Lier Photography/courtesy Rock and Roll Hall of Fame and Museum; (Q) Tony Linck/Superstock. Guitar, PhotoDisc; Chicago Tribune Building, Randy Wells/TSI; tire, courtesy Goodyear Tire and Rubber Co. **Pg. 32–33, Appalachians:** (B) Hiroyuki Matsumoto/TSI; (C) Paul Harris/TSI; (F) John Elk III/TSI; (H) Michael Hubrich; (J) Adam Jones; (M) Steve Shaluta, Jr./courtesy West Virginia Division of Tourism; (N) Joseph Sohm/TSI; (P) Larry Ulrich/TSI. Cotton, PhotoDisc; horse, S. Cordier Photo/Megapress; coal, PhotoDisc. **Pg. 34–35, South:** (A) Courtesy Louisiana Office of Tourism; (D) Mark Segal/TSI; (E) John Elk III; (H) Larry Ulrich/TSI; (J) Peter Poulides/TSI; (K) James Randklev/TSI; (M) Scott Goldsmith/TSI; (N) H. Schmeiser/Unicorn Stock Photos; (Q) Roger M. Smith/Vision Impact Photography. Crawfish, courtesy Louisiana Office of Tourism; pinecone and eagle, PhotoDisc. **Pg. 36–37, Florida:** (A) Superstock; (C) courtesy DNPS of Spaceport, Inc.; (E) Laurence Parent Photography; (F) Uniphoto; (H) Ken Biggs/TSI; (I) Alan Smith/TSI; (J) David Muench/TSI; (K) Michael Townsend/TSI; (M) Darrell R. Jones. Oranges and golf bag, PhotoDisc; tarpon, Bill Meng/courtesy Wildlife Conservation Society/New York Zoological Society. **Pg. 38–39, Coastal South:** (A) Greg Probst/TSI; (D) James Randklev/TSI; (E) Chuck Pefley/TSI; (H) courtesy North Carolina Travel, Film and Sports Development; (J) David Muench/TSI; (K) courtesy Pinehurst Resorts & CC; (N) Michael Townsend/TSI; (O) David Muench/TSI; (R) James Randklev/TSI. Peanut, PhotoDisc; tobacco, J. Faircloth/Transparencies, Inc.; turtle, Courteau Photo/Megapress. **Pg. 40–41, Capitol Area:** (C) Marc Muench/TSI; (D) Peter Gridley/FPG; (E) Robert Shafer/TSI; (F) Randy Wells/TSI; (G) Jon Ortner/TSI; (I) Maxwell Mackenzie/TSI; (J) Tom Payne; (K) Kevin Fleming; (L) Connie Coleman/TSI; (M) Kent English/courtesy Maryland Office of Tourism; (O) Jerry Wachter Photography, Ltd. Smithsonian, PhotoDisc; crab, courtesy Maryland Office of Tourism; ham, Steve Needham/Envision. **Pg. 42–43, Middle Atlantic:** (D) David Muench/TSI; (E) courtesy Commonwealth Media Services; (F) Sylvain Grandadam/TSI; (G) courtesy Commonwealth Media Services; (I) Cosmo Condina/TSI; (K) Rich LaSalle/TSI; (N) Sylvain Grandadam/TSI; (O) Bob Krist/TSI; (P) R & D Aitkenhead/Positive Images; (R) David Muench/TSI. Binoculars and lures, PhotoDisc; clam, courtesy Wildlife Conservation Society. **Pg. 44–45, Southern New England:** (B) courtesy Litchfield Hills Travel Council, CT; (C) courtesy Mark Twain House, Hartford, CT; (F) Joe Sohm/Unicorn Stock Photos; (I) Kindra Clineff/courtesy Massachusetts Office of Travel and Tourism; (K) Doris De Witt/TSI; (L) Sara Gray/TSI; (N) Tom Till/TSI; (O) Jim McElholm/courtesy Providence and Warwick Convention and Visitors Bureau, RI; (Q) Dick Durrance II. U.S.S. *Nautilus*, courtesy Submarine Force Museum; cranberries, J. Pharand Photo/Megapress; rings, PhotoDisc. **Pg. 46–47, Northern New England:** (A) David Muench/TSI; (D) Jon Gilbert Fox Photo/courtesy Billings Farm and Museum; (E) Don and Pat Valenti/TSI; (F) Sara Gray/TSI; (G) Susan G. Drinker; (H) Joseph Sohm/TSI; (K) Tom Mackie/TSI; (M) William S. Helsel/TSI; (O) Steve Vidler/TSI; (P) James Randklev/TSI. Maple syrup, Steven Needham/Envision; lobster, PhotoDisc; moose, Superstock. **Pg. 48–49, Eastern Canada:** (A) Dick Durrance II; (C) Chris Thomaidis/TSI; (D) Stephen Krasemann/TSI; (E) courtesy New Brunswick Department of Tourism, Can; (F) Rob Boudreau/TSI; (H) Cosmo Condina/TSI; (I) George Hunter/TSI; (L) Winston Fraser; (N) D. E. Cox/TSI. Caribou, Art Wolfe/TSI; salmon, Schafer & Hill/Peter Arnold, Inc.; hare, Carolyn Chatterton. **Pg. 50–51, Western Canada:** (B) Joel Rogers/TSI; (C) Peter Timmermans/TSI; (D) Wolfgang Kaehler Photography; (F) James Randklev/TSI; (G) Maxine Cass; (J) courtesy Saskatchewan Environment and Resource Management; (L) Don Poulton; (N) Dave Reede. Orca, Fred Felleman/TSI; newspaper, PhotoDisc; silos, PhotoDisc. **Pg. 52–53, Mexico:** (C) Mark Lewis/TSI; (D) Phil Schermeister/TSI; (E) Alan Smith/TSI; (F) Raymond Gendreau/TSI; (I) DDB Stock Photo; (K) DDB Stock Photo; (L) Kevin Schafer/TSI; (M) David Hiser/TSI. Marlin, Darrell Jones/TSI; burro and flamingos, PhotoDisc. **Pg. 54, Hawaii:** (A) Richard A. Cooke III/TSI; (B) John Elk III; (E) John Callahan/TSI; (F) Douglas Peebles. Pineapple and orchid, PhotoDisc. **Pg. 55, Puerto Rico/Virgin Islands:** (D) Mark Lewis/TSI; (E) John Marshall/TSI; (F) Bob Krist; (H) Bob Krist. Coffee and mongooses, PhotoDisc.

National Parks photography:
Pg. 194: Acadia (both) and Arches, Susan G. Drinker; Badlands, David Muench. **Pg. 196:** Banff (t), David Muench; Banff (b), Panoramic Images; Big Bend, Stan Jorstad/PhotoMark; Bryce Canyon, Susan G. Drinker. **Pg. 198:** Death Valley, Susan G. Drinker; Denali (t), Stan Jorstad/PhotoMark; Denali (b), David Muench; Everglades, Dick Durrance II. **Pg. 200:** Glacier Bay, Stan Jorstad/PhotoMark; Grand Canyon (t), Susan G. Drinker; Grand Canyon (b), Dick Dietrich; Grand Tetons, Susan G. Drinker. **Pg. 202:** Great Smoky (t), Dick Durrance II; Great Smoky (b), David Muench; Hawaii Volcanoes, Susan G. Drinker; Hot Springs, David Muench. **Pg. 204:** Mammoth Cave and Mesa Verde, Stan Jorstad/PhotoMark; Olympic (t), Dick Durrance II; Olympic (b), Susan G. Drinker. **Pg. 206:** Prince Edward Island, Tom Till Photography; Redwood, Stan Jorstad/PhotoMark; Rocky Mountains, David Muench; Shenandoah, Stan Jorstad/PhotoMark. **Pg. 208:** Virgin Islands, Voyageurs, Waterton–Glacier, and Zion, Stan Jorstad/PhotoMark. **Pg. 210:** Yellowstone (t) and Yosemite (t), Susan G. Drinker; Yellowstone (b) and Yosemite (b), Stan Jorstad/PhotoMark.

Scenic Drives photography:
Pg. 216–217: Alaska, Carr Clifton; Washington, David Hiser/TSI; Oregon, Paul Souders/TSI; California (t), Charles A. Mauzy/TSI; California (b), David Muench; Arizona, Tom Till/TSI. **Pg. 218–219:** New Mexico, Laurence Parent Photography; Oklahoma, Jim Argo; Colorado, Carr Clifton; Utah, Raymond G. Barnes/TSI; Idaho, John Marshall/TSI; Wyoming, Larry Ulrich/TSI. **Pg. 220–221:** North Dakota, Carr Clifton; South Dakota, James P. Rowan/TSI; Missouri, Tom Till/TSI; Minnesota, Ryan-Beyer/TSI; Michigan and Wisconsin, Terry Donnelly. **Pg. 222–223:** Ohio, David M. Dennis; Kentucky, Glen Allison/TSI; Mississippi, James P. Rowan/TSI; Florida, Roger M. Smith/Vision Impact Photography; Georgia, Andre Jenny/Unicorn Stock Photos; Maryland, Michael Townsend/TSI. **Pg. 224–225:** New York (t), Larry Ulrich/TSI; New York (b), Walter Schmid/TSI; Connecticut, Ron Robinson/courtesy Connecticut River Valley and Shoreline; Massachusetts, Ken Biggs/TSI; New Hampshire, Ryan Beyer/TSI; Vermont, David Muench/TSI. **Pg. 226–227:** Nova Scotia, Michael Ventura/TSI; Quebec, Yves Marcoux/TSI; Alaska/Yukon Territory, Tom Bean; Mexico, Frances Schroeder/Superstock; Hawaii, James Randklev/TSI; Puerto Rico, Tom Bean.

Resources photography:
Pg. 228–229: Chugach Mountains, AK, Chris Noble/TSI; Garden of the Gods, CO, Dick Durrance II; Big Sur, CA, David Muench; Vermont, Superstock.

Index photography & illustrations:
Pg. 232–233: Alabama, courtesy Alabama Bureau of Tourism and Travel; Alaska, Ken Graham/TSI; Arizona, Susan G. Drinker; Arkansas, A. C. Haralson/courtesy Arkansas Department of Parks and Tourism. **Pg. 234–235:** California, Dick Durrance II; Colorado (both), Susan G. Drinker; Connecticut, Joseph Sohm/TSI. **Pg. 236–237:** Delaware, Kevin Fleming; Hawaii and Florida, Susan G. Drinker; Georgia, courtesy Georgia Department of Industry, Trade, and Tourism. **Pg. 238–239:** Idaho, Cliff Hollenbeck/TSI; Illinois, Peter Pearson/TSI; Iowa, Joseph Sohm/TSI; Kentucky, courtesy Shaker Village. **Pg. 240–241:** Louisiana, courtesy Louisiana Department of Tourism; Maine, Dick Durrance II; Maryland, Cindy Tunstall/courtesy Maryland Office of Tourism Development; Massachusetts, Jeremy Walker/TSI. **Pg. 242–243:** Massachusetts, courtesy Massachusetts Office of Travel and Tourism; Minnesota, courtesy Minnesota Office of Tourism; Montana, M. Van Donsel/courtesy Travel Montana; Nebraska, courtesy Nebraska Division of Travel and Tourism. **Pg. 244–245:** New Hampshire, Charles Sleicher/TSI; New Mexico, Dennis O'Clair/TSI; New York, Dennis O'Clair/TSI; North Carolina, Judi Scharms. **Pg. 246–247:** North Dakota, courtesy North Dakota Parks and Recreation Department; Oklahoma, Raymond G. Barnes, TSI; Oregon (l)-left and (r)-right, Paul Souders/TSI. **Pg. 248–249:** Rhode Island, Wayne Bartz/TSI; South Carolina, courtesy South Carolina Division of Tourism; South Dakota, Charles Williams/courtesy South Dakota Tourism; Texas, Robert E. Daemmrich/TSI. **Pg. 250–251:** Utah (l), Dick Durrance II; Utah (r), Susan G. Drinker; Vermont, Lois Moulton/TSI; Washington, Susan G. Drinker. **Pg. 252–253:** Washington, Stuart Westmorland/TSI; West Virginia, Steve Shaluta, Jr./courtesy West Virginia Division of Tourism; Wyoming, Liz Mymans/TSI; Newfoundland, Susan G. Drinker. **Pg. 254:** Mexico, Robert Frerck/TSI; Virgin Islands, Mark Lewis/TSI.

License plate illustrations courtesy of Interstate Directory Publishing Company, Inc.

Copyright information:
GeoSystems Global Corporation
3710 Hempland Road
Mountville, PA 17554

Printed in China

ISBN 1-57262-328-4
10 9 8 7 6 5 4 3 2 1

Comments or suggestions
should be directed to:
The American Road Atlas & Travel Planner
GeoSystems Global Corporation
P.O. Box 3261
Lancaster, PA 17604
e-mail at info@ngroads.com
888.647.6277

Sections of the Scenic Drives chapter previously appeared in an altered form in *National Geographic's Guide to Scenic Highways and Byways* and the *New England* and *Canada* volumes of National Geographic's *Driving Guides to America* series. This text appears courtesy of National Geographic's Book Division.

Road data for Pennsylvania and Ohio based upon data from Navigation Technologies Corporation.

**Published by
GeoSystems Global Corporation
in association with
National Geographic Maps
and Melcher Media, Inc.**

Produced by Melcher Media, Inc.

Design by 2x4

GeoSystems Global Corporation
Barry Glick, President
and Chief Executive Officer
James Thomas, Chief Operating Officer
and Chief Financial Officer
William Muenster, Senior Vice President,
Development and Production
Jim Hilliard, Vice President,
Mapping Products and Services
Dennis White, Director,
Lancaster Cartographic Operations
Eric Riback, Senior Marketing Manager
Ed Kladky, Marketing Coordinator
Kathy Kinney, Product Development Manager
Jay Sandberg, Assistant Product
Development Manager
Randy Sands, Manager,
Manufacturing and Distribution
Andy Green, Project Manager
Bob Harding, Managing Editor
Marley Amstutz and Dana Wolf, Editors
Andrew DeWitt, Brian Goudreau,
Andy Skinner, Doug Smith, Matt Tharp,
Bill Truninger, Paul Yatabe, Cartographers
John Fix, Dave Folk, Mark Leitzell,
Larry Meyers, Todd Stark, GIS

National Geographic Society
John M. Fahey, Jr., President
and Chief Executive Officer
Gilbert M. Grosvenor, Chairman of the Board

National Geographic Ventures
C. Richard Allen, President

National Geographic Maps
Allen Carroll, Managing Director
Kevin P. Allen, Director of Map Services
Steven D. Lownds, Director of
Finance and Strategic Planning
Daniel J. Ortiz, Director of Map Ventures
John F. Shupe, Director of Cartographic
and Geographic Standards
Eric Lindstrom, Linda Kriete, Gus Platis,
Dana Gantz, Maureen Flynn, Peter Jolicoeur,
Dierdre Bevington-Attardi, Map Editors
Ronald E. Williamson, Director of
Product Engineering

Melcher Media, Inc., New York City
Charles Melcher, President
Duncan Bock, Project Editor
Kate Giel and Gillian Sowell, Editors
Andrea Hirsh, Director of Production
Philomena Mariani, Ian Wilker,
William McRae, Chris Mitchell, Line Editors
Linda Ferrer and the Picture Editing Group,
Photography Researchers
Gretchen Vitamvas, Production Assistant
Avital Fryman, Abraham Safdie,
Editorial Assistants

2x4, New York City
Susan Sellers, Art Director
David Israel, Designer

Special thanks to:
Aaron Ackermann, Heather Caldwell,
Doris Cotterell, Isabel Cuervo,
Emily Donaldson, Kate Ferrer,
Cathe Giffuni, Maura Ginty, Kathy Iwasaki,
Chelsea Kain, Kevin Kwan, Katherine Lewis,
Joel Van Liew, Nanette Maxim,
Jennifer Moyse, Miranda Schwartz,
Elizabeth Sharp, Judith Smith, Laura Strauss,
Sheryl Swann, and Megan Worman
(at Melcher Media).
John Ericson, Chris Gruber, Fred Hofferth,
Ron Rittenhouse, Candace Ryan,
Martha Tyzenhouse, and Mike Weaver
(at GeoSystems).

National Geographic Maps is
a wholly-owned subsidiary of
the National Geographic Society.

Better Travels with National Geographic

On this page you'll find an array of other quality travel products from National Geographic. Venture to far-flung corners of the globe with **NATIONAL GEOGRAPHIC** magazine and spectacular National Geographic videos. Plan great vacations with the award-winning **NATIONAL GEOGRAPHIC TRAVELER** magazine and the Society's fact-filled, illustrated travel guides. In all the outstanding products below, you'll enjoy dazzling images, incomparable maps, and detailed travel information just like you find in **The American Road**.

Give new worlds to discover with NATIONAL GEOGRAPHIC.

Delight your friends – or yourself – with membership in the National Geographic Society. It's the perfect gift for any occasion!

Every month, readers circle the globe with **NATIONAL GEOGRAPHIC** magazine to enjoy breathtaking sights . . . meet fascinating people . . . unlock age-old mysteries . . . keep up with science and technology.

Members also receive as many as five full-color wall maps in selected issues of the magazine. And we'll send gift cards to you to sign and present or mail to your gift recipients.

$27*, 12 Issues

*U. S. rate. To Canada, US$31 (C$42). Elsewhere, US$45. Add 5% sales tax for memberships sent to MD. Canadian dues include 7% GST. While all dues support the Society's mission of expanding geographic knowledge, 80% is designated for the magazine subscription, and no portion should be considered a charitable contribution.

Call today for a world of adventures! 1.800.447.0647

TDD only: 1.888.822.8207, U. S. and Canada only

NGZDCM2

TRAVELER MAGAZINE

Rated "Best Travel Magazine" four years in a row!

Visit resorts, cities, museums, and little-known places in the U. S., Canada, and abroad. From weekend getaways to dream vacations, this award-winning bimonthly has everything you need to plan the perfect trip, plus the kind of lively articles and stunning photography that you expect from National Geographic.

#10004 $17.95*

*U. S. addresses. C$33.10 or US$24.35 (includes 7% GST) for Canada (to NB, NF, or NS: C$35.57 or US$26.17; includes 15% HST); US$25.50 for all other countries.

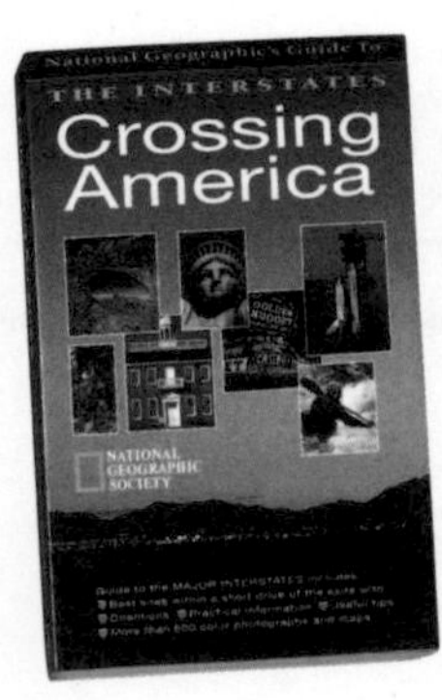

CROSSING AMERICA: NATIONAL GEOGRAPHIC'S GUIDE TO THE INTERSTATES

Grab this handy guidebook and take off!

Turn your next driving trip into a great adventure with this exciting guide to the major U. S. interstates. You'll discover hundreds of things to do and places to go within a short drive of the highway – historic sites and towns, state and national parks, scenic areas and recreational facilities, and more. 500 illustrations. 82 maps. $5\frac{1}{4}$" x $8\frac{1}{2}$". 352 pages. © 1995

#00984 SOFTCOVER $19.95 †
#00985 HARDCOVER $24.95 †

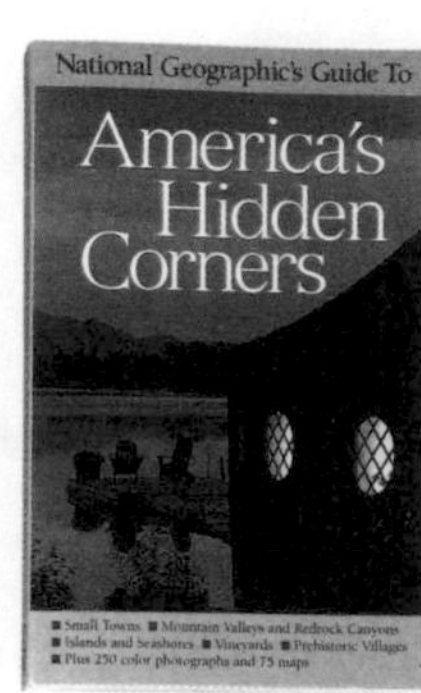

NATIONAL GEOGRAPHIC'S GUIDE TO AMERICA'S HIDDEN CORNERS

Take the road less traveled and discover unique getaways across America.

If you're a traveler who prefers exploring off-the-beaten-path destinations to taking prepackaged tours, you'll find plenty of travel ideas that suit your style in this superb guide. You'll journey to places well off the tourist routes. From historic small towns and quaint villages to quiet coastal regions and pristine deserts and mountain ranges.

Organized by region, this guide introduces you to more than 75 great escapes nationwide – featuring at least one in every state. More than 250 photographs. 76 detailed maps. $5\frac{3}{8}$" x $8\frac{11}{16}$". 384 pages. © 1997

#07211 $21.95 †

WORLD'S LAST GREAT PLACES VIDEO SET

Venture to some of the world's least-known lands!

These are truly exotic locales, memorably captured in exquisitely produced videos. From tropical forests to arid plains, fiery volcanoes to distant snowcapped mountains, you'll encounter the awesome wonders of unspoiled nature. Four-video set contains ARCTIC KINGDOM: *Life at the Edge*, VIRUNGA: *The Heart of Africa*, OKAVANGO: *Africa's Wild Oasis*, and YELLOWSTONE: *Realm of the Coyote.*

Each video approximately 60 minutes.

#50960 FOUR-VIDEO SET $59.95 †

† plus shipping and handling and applicable tax.